Social Work Fields of Practice

Social Work Fields of Practice

Historical Trends, Professional Issues, and Future Opportunities

Catherine N. Dulmus
Karen M. Sowers

WILEY

JOHN WILEY & SONS, INC.

Library of Congress Cataloging-in-Publication Data:
Social work fields of practice : historical trends, professional issues, and future opportunities / [edited by] Catherine N. Dulmus, Karen M. Sowers.
   p. cm.
   Includes bibliographical references and index.
ISBN 978-1-118-17692-4 (pbk.)
ISBN 978-1-118-26487-4 (ebk)
ISBN 978-1-118-24026-7 (ebk)
ISBN 978-1-118-22724-4 (ebk)
   1. Social servic—Practice—United States. 2. Social workers—United States. I. Dulmus, Catherine N. II. Sowers, Karen M. (Karen Marlaine)
   HV40.8.U6S63 2012
   361.3'20973—dc23   2011052824

Printed in the United States of America
10 9 8 7 6 5 4 3 2 1

We proudly and lovingly dedicate this book to each of our sons
Joshua Benjamin Dulmus
Son, brother, husband, father of precious Rachael, trusted friend, social worker,
avid Buffalo Bills and Yankees fan
Michael Wilken Hoag
Son, old soul and warm heart, martial artist and teacher extraordinaire, trusted
friend and personal champion

Contents

Preface

The profession of social work is more than 100 years old. As with any dynamic profession, the fields of social work practice have changed in scope and depth to reflect the changing demographics, social problems, and socioeconomic patterns. Despite the varied functions and methods of our profession, it has always been committed to social justice and the promotion of well-being for all. The profession has made great strides and is experiencing a resurgence of energy, commitment, and advancement as we shape our profession to address current and anticipated realities. This book is designed as a beginning introductory text on the fields of practice in social work for undergraduate and graduate students in social work programs. The text provides a broad overview of the traditional and emerging fields in the profession. This book addresses the Council on Social Work Education (CSWE) required competencies for accreditation. Specifically, the book addresses the following required accreditation competencies:

- Educational Policy 2.1.4: Engage diversity and difference in practice
- Educational Policy 2.1.5: Advance human rights and social and economic justice
- Educational Policy 2.1.7: Apply knowledge of human behavior and the social environment
- Educational Policy 2.1.9: Respond to the contexts that shape practice

The 13 chapters that comprise this edited text represent the core fields of practice in social work. Whether at the undergraduate or graduate level, the materials in this text provide students with a broad, yet comprehensive overview of the breadth of practice, highlighting the critical importance of specific practice areas while also introducing new and emerging fields of practice in social work such as military social work, veterinary social work, and international social work practice. Chapter offerings also include the growing fields of gerontology, substance abuse counseling, and mental health practice with additional chapters focusing on fields of practice that are deeply rooted in our profession, such as child welfare, school social work, and family-centered practice. Chapters on diversity and immigrant and indigenous populations recognize the commitment of our profession to working with culturally diverse people in effective, relevant, and meaningful ways.

This edited work is written by leading social work scholars in their own fields of practice. Each chapter provides an overarching question for reflection at the beginning of each chapter to spur students' critical thinking while reading the material. At the end of each chapter, a list of key terms, review/discussion questions, and relevant web resources are provided.

As our world has become ever more complex, so have our social problems. The social work profession has made great strides in developing new fields of practice and new knowledge and technologies to advance our efficacy in addressing the multilevel and complex social issues facing us today. Given our rapidly changing world, it seems imperative to provide a current perspective on the fields of practice in social work. The content in this book is contemporaneous and reflects our current state of practice as well as creative solutions to both old and emerging trends in practice.

As editors, we have endeavored to create a contemporary work grounded in the values, ethics, and ideals of our profession. We are particularly grateful to our esteemed chapter authors who contributed to this book. Their expertise and thoughtfulness have made this book a text that is substantial and relevant. Their excitement and commitment to our profession and to their specific fields of practice are evident in each of their chapters. As social workers, we invite you to consider the great breadth and versatility of this great profession. No matter what area of social work practice may intrigue you the most, you can be assured that your work will make a difference in profound ways!

Catherine N. Dulmus
Karen M. Sowers

About the Editors

Catherine N. Dulmus, PhD, is Associate Professor, Associate Dean for Research, and Director of the Buffalo Center for Social Research at the University at Buffalo, and Research Director at Hillside Family of Agencies in Rochester, NY. She received her baccalaureate degree in Social Work from Buffalo State College in 1989, her master's degree in Social Work from the University at Buffalo in 1991, and a doctoral degree in Social Welfare from the University at Buffalo in 1999. Dr. Dulmus is a researcher with interests that include community-based research, child and adolescent mental health, evidence-based practice, and university-community partnerships, and has made recent contributions that focus on fostering interdependent collaborations among practitioners, researchers, schools, and agencies critical in the advancement and dissemination of new and meaningful knowledge. She has authored or coauthored several journal articles and books and has presented her research nationally and internationally. Prior to being awarded a PhD, her social work practice background encompassed almost a decade of experience in the fields of mental health and school social work.

Karen M. Sowers, PhD, is Professor and Dean of the College of Social Work at the University of Tennessee, Knoxville. She is the University of Tennessee, Knoxville Beaman Professor for Outstanding Research and Service. Dr. Sowers received her baccalaureate degree in Sociology from the University of Central Florida, and her master's degree and PhD degree in social work from Florida State University. Dr. Sowers serves on several local, national, and international boards. Dr. Sowers is nationally known for her research and scholarship in the areas of international practice, juvenile justice, child welfare, cultural diversity, and culturally effective intervention strategies for social work practice, evidence-based social work practice, and social work education.

Contributors

Erin Allen, LMSW
Colorado State University
Argus Institute
Veterinary Teaching Hospital
Fort Collins, Colorado

Geneva Brown, PhD
Private Practice
Knoxville, TN

Sharon Warren Cook, PhD
Department of Sociology
   and Social Work
North Carolina Agricultural
   and Technical State University
Greensboro, North Carolina

Iris B. Carlton-LaNey, PhD
School of Social Work
University of North Carolina
Chapel Hill, North Carolina

Amy Chanmugam, MSSW, LCSW
School of Social Work
University of Texas—Austin
Austin, Texas

King Davis, PhD
Hogg Foundation for Mental Health
University of Texas—Austin
Austin, Texas

Elizabeth DePoy, PhD
Center for Community Inclusion
   and Disability Studies
University of Maine
Orono, Maine

Alberta J. Ellett, PhD
School of Social Work
University of Georgia
Athens, Georgia

Doreen Elliott, PhD
School of Social Work
University of Texas—Arlington
Arlington, Texas

Marilyn Flynn, PhD
School of Social Work
University of Southern California
Los Angeles, California

Cynthia Franklin, PhD, LCSW, LMFT
School of Social Work
University of Texas—Austin
Austin, Texas

Beth Gerlach, MSSW, LCSW
School of Social Work
University of Texas—Austin
Austin, Texas

Roberta R. Greene, PhD
School of Social Work
University of Texas—Austin
Austin, Texas

Stephen Gilson
School of Social Work
University of Maine
Orono, Maine

Anthony M. Hassan, EdD
University of Southern California
School of Social Work
Los Angeles, California

Hyejin Jung, MSW
School of Social Work
University of Texas
Austin, Texas

Sarina Lyall, LMSW
University of Tennessee
College of Veterinary Medicine
Department of Veterinary Social Work
Knoxville, Tennessee

Samuel A. MacMaster, PhD
College of Social Work
University of Tennessee—Knoxville
Nashville, Tennessee

Tina Maschi, PhD
Fordham University
School of Social Services
Lincoln Center Campus
New York, New York

Jon Matsuoka, PhD
Consuelo Foundation
Honolulu, Hawaii

Hamilton I. McCubbin, PhD
Kamehamena Schools
Honolulu, Hawai'i

Janelle Nimer, PhD
Animal Assisted Healing Center
Kaysville, Utah

Teresa Nolen-Pratt, LCSW
Cherokee Health Systems
Knoxville, Tennessee

Robin E. Perry, PhD
Department of Social Work
Florida A&M University
Tallahassee, Florida

Bethanie A. Poe
University of Tennessee
College of Veterinary Medicine
Department of Veterinary Social Work
Knoxville, Tennessee

Uma A. Segal, PhD
School of Social Work
University of Missouri—St. Louis
St. Louis, Missouri

David W. Springer
School of Social Work
Portland State University
Portland, Oregon

Lori K. Holleran Steiker, PhD
School of Social Work
University of Texas—Austin
Austin, Texas

Elizabeth Strand, PhD
University of Tennessee
College of Veterinary Medicine

Department of Veterinary Social Work
Knoxville, Tennessee

Barbara Thomlison, PhD
School of Social Work
College of Social Work, Justice,
and Public Affairs
Florida International University
Miami, Florida

Raymond J. Thomlison, PhD
School of Social Work
College of Social Work, Justice,
and Public Affairs

Florida International University
Miami, Florida

Katherine van Wormer, PhD
Department of Social Work
University of Northern Iowa
Cedar Falls, Iowa

Jan Yorke, PhD
School of Social Work
Laurentian University, Orillia Campus
Barrie, Ontario

Chapter 1
Child Welfare and Social Work Practice

Robin E. Perry and Alberta J. Ellett

> What are the many intervening events and variables that have led to the evolution of child welfare as it is today?

Child welfare, as it is generally recognized and discussed in this chapter, includes child protective services, foster care, adoption services for children and their families, and, increasingly, prevention of child maltreatment. As a specialization, child welfare has a long and rich history within the profession of social work. The work in child welfare is perhaps more complex than any social work practice area due to the risk of serious injury to children in multiproblem families, federal mandates, public scrutiny, court and multiple oversight mechanisms, underfunding, and high employee turnover. This important work needs the attention of professional social workers with the knowledge, skills, abilities, and values to work with clients affected by parental conditions such as substance abuse, mental illness, limitations, and involvement with the legal system. Unlike in most areas of social work, child welfare workers regularly make home visits to work with their clients and to transport children and parents (typically using their own vehicles). They are expected to make expert decisions about child safety, and spend considerable time in court with their cases. In addition, child welfare work is situated within a complex external sociopolitical environment that influences the size, minimum qualifications, and direction of the workforce, funding for employees and services to clients, continuously changing legal mandates and attendant practice issues, and ongoing public scrutiny. Thus, recruiting and retaining professional social workers to do this important work while remaining committed to child welfare is an ongoing challenge.

Pecora, Whitaker, Maluccio, Bart, and Plotnick (2000) cite the American Humane Association when reporting an estimated increase in reports of maltreatment from 669,000 in 1976 to 2,178,000 in 1987. By the 1990s, the rate of maltreatment in the United States was being referred to as an epidemic (U.S. Advisory Board on Child Abuse and Neglect, 1990). Four National Incidence Studies provide the best incidence data on maltreatment to date. Although there have been some modifications in procedures used, debate regarding the significance and meaning of findings and recommended modifications to future studies (Children's Bureau, 2000; King, Trocmé, & Thatte, 2003; Rogers, Gray, & Aitken, 1992; Sedlak, 2001), the National Incidence Studies conducted in 1979 to 1980 (NIS-1), 1986 to 1987 (NIS-2), and 1993 to 1995 (NIS-3) suggest an increase in the rate of maltreatment incidence (as a rate per 1,000) from 9.8 to 23.1 or from 625,000 to 1,553,800 incidents (Sedlak, 1988, 1991; Sedlak & Broadhurst, 1996). Reports of maltreatment by state officials may not capture the true incidence rates of maltreatment.

In 1995, data collected via the National Child Abuse and Neglect Data System (NCANDS) reported that approximately 1.1 million children were victims of abuse and neglect (a figure significantly less than NIS-3 estimates in 1993 to 1995) and a victimization rate of approximately 15 children per 1,000 (U.S. Department of Health and Human Services, 1997). This rate of victimization resulted from nearly two million reports of maltreatment related to three million estimated children. These same reports suggest a decrease in the victimization rate between 2001 and 2009 (U.S. Department of Health and Human Services, 2003, 2004, 2005, 2006, 2010) from 12.5 children per 1,000 to 10.1 children per 1,000. Regardless, the estimated 762,940 victims that came to the attention of child welfare agencies in 2009 is a significant number. The observed decrease in victimization rate, however, is not realized in the rate of report of maltreatment. Between 2001 and 2009, the rate (and number) investigated from maltreatment has increased from 43.2 children per thousand children (3,136,000 children) to 48.1 children per thousand (3,635,686 children). The most recent NIS-4 study (on data collected between 2005–2006) corroborates some of these observed trends, reporting a decrease in the child maltreatment rate between 1993 and 2005–2006 from 23.1 children per thousand to 17.1 children per thousand. There was also a slight decrease in the national incidence of endangerment standard from 41.9 to 39.5 children per thousand across the two studies (Sedlak et al., 2010). Although noteworthy gains have been made in reducing the rate of maltreatment in the United States over the past decade, child maltreatment is still an issue of concern for society.

The purpose of this chapter is to provide information and timely discussion of historical trends, current issues, and future projections in child welfare as they relate to the development and continued professionalization of child welfare within the larger social work profession. The focus and scope begins with historical trends in child welfare and their interface with social work education and practice. Included in this chapter are: (a) an analysis of historical workforce trends and professional issues, (b) a discussion of the current professional status of child welfare, (c) child welfare research, and (d) future projections and recommendations about the continued professionalization of child welfare. Questions the readers may wish to ponder as they read this chapter include the following: What are the major influences that social work has had on child welfare policy, practice, and research over the past 100 years? What leadership role does the profession currently have (or should it have) in child welfare within the United States? What impact does/would the reprofessionalization of child welfare have upon the quality of practice and child welfare outcomes?

History of Social Work and the Child Welfare Partnership

Child Welfare Workforce and Professional Social Workers

Concern for the welfare of children within the U.S. social work community likely began with children being placed in orphanages rather than in almshouses. This practice was subsequently followed by the enlightened practice of placing more than 200,000 children with Midwestern farming families via the orphan trains begun by Charles Loring Brice of the Children's Aide Society of New York, beginning in 1852 and ending in 1929. When youth who were placed on farms ran away and reported their mistreatment, Brice sent *agents* to do home studies to assess families before the orphan train arrived. Early efforts to meet the needs of dependent children were run by religious and private charity and aide societies until additional assistance was needed, resulting in the public/private mix of child welfare services that continues to the present. Thus, the early evolution of child welfare is rooted in social work and the need for professionals to intervene in the lives of troubled children and their families.

Throughout most of the 20th century, there was debate (that ebbed and flowed at different times) regarding the defining features of social work and whether social work deserved professional status. In 1915, Abraham Flexner spoke at the Conference on Charities and Corrections to address the question of social work as a profession. He concluded that it was not, preferring to title it a semiprofession due to its lack of an educationally or intellectually transmissible skill or technique, and a knowledge base founded on scientific literature (Flexner, 1915). Flexner's speech was profound and had a mobilizing effect on social work at the time (Austin, 1978; Deardorff, 1930; Hodson, 1925). Indeed, the formation of the Association of Training Schools of Professional Social Work in 1919 (renamed the American Association of Schools of Social Work in 1933, hereafter referred to as AASSW) and the American Association of Social Workers (hereafter referred to as AASW) in 1921 represented structured efforts toward training and monitoring practice and providing a representative association for all social workers.

One of the main tasks of the AASSW and the AASW was to distinguish professional social work from the practice of the well intended (early charity work) and to convince society (and more particularly government authorities) that social workers were educated in "proven methods of service." These tasks, however, proved formidable in Flexner's opinion, given the inability to pinpoint the time when charitable acts became professional activities (Flexner, 1915).

By the time the AASW was formed in 1921 (West, 1933), social work practice had diversified beyond providing relief to the poor into the fields of mental hygiene (Lee & Kenworthy, 1929; Lowrey, 1926; Macdonald, 1920), medicine (Bartlett, 1957; Cannon, 1913), education (Culbert, 1933; Meredith, 1933), child and family services (Pumphrey & Pumphrey, 1961; Walker, 1928) and criminal justice (Brown, 1920; Williamson, 1935). Consequently, there were a variety of associations and organizations already formed (or in the process of forming) that social workers (professionally trained or not) could, and did, belong to. These included the Family Welfare Association of America (formed in 1911); the American Association of Hospital Social Workers (formed in 1918) (Deardorff, 1930); the Child Welfare League of America (CWLA in 1920); the American Association of Psychiatric Social Workers (formed in 1922 as a section of AAHSW, from which it separated in 1926); the National Association of School Social Workers (formed in 1919); the International Migration Service; the National Association of Traveler's Aid Societies; the National Committee on Visiting Teachers; and the National Probation Association. The diversity of settings in which self-ascribed social workers could be found led Walker (1928) to conclude: "It was suggested that social work was 'not so much a definite field, as an aspect of work in many fields,' and that social work has grown up to supply the shortcomings of the professions, whose development may not yet be completed" (pp. 88–89). These findings were reinforced by Conrad (1930) and Abbott (1933). Conrad notes that in a program review of 24 of the 29 accredited schools in 1928, 13 were graduate programs, of which nine would admit students who did not possess any undergraduate degree. Further, there were 42 different courses of study. Abbott described most school curricula in the 1930s as having a "frequently inadequate organization" (p. 145).

The first schools of social work (and year formed) included: the New York School of Philanthropy (1898), the Chicago School of Civics and Philanthropy (1901),[1] the Boston School of Social Work (1904), the Philadelphia Training School for Social Work (1908), and the Missouri School of Social Economy (1908). Interestingly, none of these early schools had a primary focus on child welfare issues or training, despite the import child welfare issues had for early leaders in social work and identified links between child welfare and social work practice at that time.

These early schools were considered private institutions structured to: (a) train individuals to meet the service/administrative needs of Charity Organization Society (Richmond, 1897), (b) further the academic study (pragmatic study) of the effects of poverty and attempted solutions/charitable relief acts (Conrad, 1930), and (c) teach skills specific to the distribution of relief and personal and family rehabilitation (Devine, 1915). These curricula priorities were in response to the demands of agencies in the communities in which schools were formed, not necessarily to address the demands of all populations served by social workers throughout the United States. As a result, each school varied in form and focus. The philosophy guiding the structure of each school reflected the diversity of opinions regarding the role and mission of this newly developing profession. Hence the emphasis on medical social work in Boston, economics and rural poverty in Missouri, social reform and public aspects of social work and social research in Chicago, and the "intensive study of personality factors entering into problems of social maladjustment" (Abbott, 1933, p. 146) in the New York and Pennsylvania schools. This would change over time. By 1928, there were 29 accredited schools of social work in the United States of which 17 (58%) had courses (not necessarily a specialization) in child welfare (Conrad, 1930).

In its infancy, social work was closely aligned with child welfare issues and children's services (protection, placement, care, etc.). The influence and advocacy of Jane Addams, who was elected president of the National Conference of Charities and Corrections in 1909 and the only social worker to receive a Nobel Peace Prize (in 1931), along with Lillian Wald, who was originally a nurse by trade, led to the first White House Conference on the Care of Dependent Children in 1909 and the subsequent formation of the U.S. Children's Bureau in 1912. The influence of Florence Kelley (another prominent social work leader) cannot be understated. She was also influential in creating the Children's Bureau, advocating the passage of early federal child welfare legislation (e.g., the 1921 Sheppard-Tower Act to reduce infant mortality), promoting child labor reform, and improving maternal and child health services throughout the United States (Goldmark, 1953; Sklar, 1995). Another prominent social work pioneer, Julia Lathrop, was appointed the first chief of the Children's Bureau in 1912, only to be succeeded by Edith and Grace Abbott, other social work leaders.

Despite the documented influence and early leadership of social workers in advocating for, organizing, and structuring a foundation for child welfare services in the United States, little is known about the number of social workers or social work graduates (from professional schools) that assumed positions within child welfare settings. It seems fair to conjecture that the early schools of social work were not necessarily responsive to demands for social workers within an ever-increasing market (public and private) of child welfare services. Indeed, in their study of the curricula of the 38 member schools, the AASSW observed a "marked difference in educational philosophy" (p. 39) along with course subjects and the manner in which they were taught between and among schools (AASSW, 1942). Attempts to find data that reported or projected a census of social workers stratified by field of practice (including child welfare) or employment settings prior to 1950 were futile, some information is available regarding the number of social work graduates, AASW membership information, and the size of social work workforce using Census Bureau Data (AASW, 1936, 1938, 1945, 1946; Bureau of the Census, 1914, 1915, 1921, 1923, 1930, 1940, 1950; Culbert, 1933).

It is clear from a review of these data that the majority of self-identified "social workers" (from Census data) and members of the AASW were not necessarily graduates from accredited schools of social work. Many individuals who enrolled in social work programs in the 1930s and 1940s dropped out of studies to assume positions in an expanding public sector, where jobs were more plentiful than in other service sectors during the Great Depression. Further, membership criteria of the AASW did not demand the possession of a degree or diploma in social work from an accredited school (as comparisons between the number of graduates and increases in AASW membership statistics for any given year will reveal). The estimates of social workers determined by the Census Bureau are based on self-reported data. Further, the Census Bureau has changed the definition or occupational titles of those classified as social workers across census years. These changes appear to have reflected general changes in titles or occupations recognized during each period. For example, in 1910 there was no occupational listing for "social worker" or "social welfare worker." The 15,970 individuals commonly thought of as early social workers in 1910 were referred to as "Religious and Charity Workers" (Bureau of the Census, 1914). This occupational classification was considered "semiprofessional." In 1920, the Census Bureau revised the occupation title of "Religious and Charity Workers" to "Religious, Charity and Welfare Workers." The specific job titles that were contained in this occupational category included those considered in the 1910 census, with the notable addition of "social worker (any)," "welfare worker," and "welfare supervisor" (Bureau of the Census, 1921). These occupations were classified as semiprofessional pursuits by the Census Bureau (Bureau of the Census, 1923, p. 494). Partly in response to lobbying efforts of the AASW, the Census Bureau revised its classification system in 1930 to include as a "professional" occupation "social and welfare worker." The occupational title of "social and welfare worker" would apply for the 1930 through 1960 Census. Beginning in 1970, the occupational title was changed from "social and welfare worker" to simply "social worker." Unfortunately, there was no distinction or classification of social workers as child welfare workers. Information regarding the number of child welfare workers and those with social work education and training backgrounds would have to come from limited agency and Children's Bureau reports and select labor studies.

By 1939, 709 individuals were reportedly working in public child welfare units (Children's Bureau, 1940). However, the 1930s witnessed an expansion of public child welfare services. By 1938, the Children's Bureau had approved 44 states' child welfare programs (Children's Bureau, 1940.) In addition, the Children's Bureau perceived a social work degree as an important foundation for early child welfare practice. The Children's Bureau recommended at least one year of MSW education for direct service workers and the MSW degree for child welfare supervisors. The Children's Bureau funded educational leave to states to send their child welfare employees to graduate schools of social work and proudly reported that by 1939, 35 states and Hawaii had sent 256 individuals to work on their MSW degrees.

The formation of the Council on Social Work Education (CSWE) in 1952 and the National Association of Social Workers in 1955 brought about an intensification of efforts aimed at seeking professional recognition and social sanction for social work. NASW embraced the diversity of activities that represented social work practice, including child welfare practice. Although there is some reference to child welfare practice as a focus of interest within social work curricula in period publications, little was known about the numbers of social workers that practiced in public and private child welfare agencies (or within any other field of practice, for that matter). Toward this end, two studies by the U.S. Bureau of Labor Statistics attempted to answer who social workers were, where they worked, and what they did. These findings provide a baseline for analyzing practice trends among social work graduates and for understanding the relative significance of child welfare settings as a labor market for social workers.

The 1950 and 1960 U.S. Bureau of Labor Statistics Studies

The U.S. Bureau of Labor Statistics (BLS), in conjunction with the Federal Security Agency (in 1950) and the U.S. Department of Health, Education, and Welfare (in 1960), engaged in the most comprehensive national study of salaries and working conditions in social work to date. The 1950 study was published in 1952 by the AASW and was partially sponsored by the National Social Welfare Assembly. It combined survey data solicited separately by the BLS and the Federal Security Agency in 1950. Both studies utilized representative (stratified random) sampling methods to survey social workers in state, county, and municipal agencies that administered child welfare and public assistance services in the United States. Weights were assigned to each case in accordance with its probability of selection (BLS, 1952, pp. 23–26; BLS, 1962, pp. 109–115). Subsequent population estimates were generated and tabulated as results of the study.[2]

Findings from these studies demonstrate that the public sector was the overwhelming employer of social workers in both 1950 and 1960. The ratio of the proportionate distribution of social workers in the public (at or about 65%) to the private sector (at or about 35%) remained relatively constant despite the increase in public sector services throughout the 1950s. The overall majority of social workers in the public sector were employed in public assistance. However, child welfare agencies were the second largest employer of social workers in the United States. In total, 17% of all public sector social workers ($N = 48,149$) worked in public child welfare agencies in 1950. This percentage represents approximately 8,185 social workers and seems in conflict with later estimates (by the Children's Bureau) in 1956 of 5,628 public child welfare workers (Low, 1958, as cited in Lindsey, 2004) employed in the United States. These contradictions highlight concern about select estimation procedures used or cited in publications of the time. The BLS study, however, attempted to maximize the external validity of their findings using more rigorous sampling and estimation procedures. Given such, the share of social workers employed in public settings represented by child welfare workers increased to 25.2%

by 1960 (of 66,806). When public and private settings are considered, in total, 17% and 22.7% of all social workers in the United States were employed in child welfare (public and private) agencies in 1950 and 1960, respectively.

When level of graduate education experience is considered, in 1950, 54.3% of social workers employed in public child welfare, compared to 66% of those in private child welfare agencies, had graduate social work experience. When the proportion of workers with MSWs is considered, the rate increases slightly, from 23.8% in 1950 to 24.3% in 1960. Further, when the distribution of all MSWs in the workforce (both sectors combined) is considered, the child welfare agencies employed more MSWs than any other field, increasing from 25.5% in 1950 to 29.0% in 1960. Child welfare services had become a dominant market for MSW graduates throughout the United States by 1960, when employment in child welfare was a respected and prestigious area of social work practice.

Terpstra (1996) aptly reports a close, collaborative working relationship between schools of social work and child welfare agencies. Child welfare content was included in schools of social work curricula and agencies readily hired social work graduates between 1935 and the early 1970s. Information in the 1950 and 1960 BLS studies (when contrasted against CSWE statistics) suggests an imbalanced or disproportionate focus of interest in child welfare within accredited MSW programs. For example, psychiatric services employed 12.6% of all MSWs in 1950, compared to 18.6% of all MSWs in 1960. When the distribution of MSW students by field placement setting in 1960 is observed from CSWE documents (CSWE, 1960, 1962a), 25.6% of all students (assigned to field instruction) were placed in "psychiatric services," followed by 14.7% in family service agencies and 13.8% in child welfare settings. Given this information, it appears schools were disproportionately training more students for psychiatric services than the market could absorb. Although 29% of all employed MSWs were employed in child welfare services in 1960, only 13.8% of all graduate students were receiving field training in this area.[3] There would be no marked increase in the proportion of MSW students receiving field placements or training in child welfare within accredited MSW programs throughout the 1960s (CSWE, 1960, 1962a, 1962b, 1963, 1964; Dea, 1966; DeVera, 1966; Loewenberg, 1967, 1968, 1970) despite forecasted increased demand for more graduate educated child welfare workers (U.S. Department of Health, Education, and Welfare, 1965).

Deprofessionalization of Child Welfare

Child welfare is often described as a professional area within social work practice. This perspective assumes that child welfare exhibits core characteristics that define a profession. As with medicine, law, and other professions, the extent to which child welfare conforms to these characteristics determines the extent to which child welfare can be considered a professional area within social work.

What are some of the more visible and accepted characteristics of a profession? Most would agree that the primary elements that are shared by and define professions in our society include:

- A knowledge base (protracted preparation program usually in a professional school within a college or university)
- A set of professional skills
- Public sanction and recognition (such as professional license, organization membership)
- A code of ethics, set of values
- Accountability within profession itself (rewards and sanctions)
- An essential social function performed
- Reasonable autonomy in one's practice/work
- Continuous professional development, generally through annual continuing education

Social work seems to meet these criteria for defining a profession, and child welfare is considered a professional practice area in social work.

Social work is the only profession to claim child welfare as its own and to prepare graduates for this important and complex work. Disciplines other than social work (e.g., psychology and medicine) conduct research on child maltreatment and/or provide treatment services. However, social work has from its inception addressed child welfare from a much larger perspective that includes concern for (a) professional education/preparation for child welfare work; (b) strength-based, family-centered practice; (c) advocacy for children and families; (d) access and allocation of resources; and (e) safety, permanency, and well-being of children and families. The argument is made that child welfare as a practice area in social work has historically gone through a period of deprofessionalization and needs to regain its professional status.

There are a number of factors that historically contributed to the deprofessionalization of public child welfare services in the United States. Influences include (but are not limited to) amendments to the Social Security Act in the 1960s, failure on the part of schools of social work to meet the assessed need for social workers (particularly MSWs) in child welfare in the 1960s and 1970s, the exponential growth of demands placed on child welfare systems following passage in 1974 of the Child Abuse Prevention and Treatment Act, and philosophical and practice priorities that redefined professional social work practice and a migration of social workers from public sector employment.

The Social Security Act (SSA) of 1935 included child welfare services under the Children's Bureau that emphasized professionalism with the goal of hiring trained social workers to address the "protection and care of homeless, dependent, neglected and children in danger of becoming delinquent" (Children's Bureau, 1940). Aid to Dependent Children (ADC) was established to enable *deserving women* who were widowed or abandoned by their husbands to raise their children rather than become wards of the state with the ADC program administered by the Board of Public Assistance (A. J. Ellett & Leighninger, 2007). In 1962, amendments to the SSA changed the ADC program to Aid to Families with Dependent Children (AFDC), changing the purpose from preserving families to an antipoverty program. Social workers and activists recruited families for the AFDC program that grew beyond the program's capacity. In response to the 1967 amendments to the SSA, child welfare programs were subsumed under the larger AFDC organization to provide their professional services to poor families. In so doing, child welfare caseworkers whose caseloads were growing even faster than the AFDC's lost their social work leadership and expertise as well as their identity with, and connections to, social work education (A. J. Ellett & Leighninger, 2007; Terpstra, 1996). Regardless, prior to the 1967 SSA amendments, the assessed need for social workers (especially MSWs) for public child welfare practice was particularly high.

A few studies attempted to gauge where demand for social workers was greatest. Some studies (Social Security Bulletin, 1961, as cited in Barker & Briggs, 1968; U.S. Department of Health, Education, and Welfare, 1965; Witte, 1960) were more comprehensive and rigorous in design than others (American Public Welfare Association, 1958; Board of Social Work Examiners, 1950, 1958; Bureau of Research and Statistics, 1956; French, 1947; French & Rosen, 1958). In 1965, the U.S. Department of Health, Education, and Welfare conducted a manpower study concluding that, "for programs in which agencies in the Department of Health, Education, and Welfare are directly concerned, the gap between the available number of social workers with graduate social work education and those estimated as needed by 1970 approaches 100,000 persons" (p. 79). Among these 100,000 needed workers, 21,000 MSWs (21% of the forecasted need for all MSWs) were needed in public child welfare by 1970. The U.S. Department of Health, Education, and Welfare report (1965) served as a primary impetus for the expansion of social work programs, intensification of recruitment efforts (beginning in high school) and revisions of school curricula as a means of meeting the current and anticipated demand for social workers in an ever-expanding public social service market (Kendall, 1964; Pins, 1965; Wittman, 1965).

As the role of the public service sector increased during the 1950s and 1960s,[4] concern was expressed about the extent to which schools of social work could meet the market demands for professional social workers (Board of Social Work Examiners, 1958; Cohen, 1970; Pins, 1965; Ross & Lictenberg, 1963; U.S. Department of Health, Education, and Welfare, 1965). It appears schools were unable to meet the demand for those seeking training in social work. In a CSWE (1964) report, 48 of 59 schools demonstrated that 962 qualified applicants were turned away from member schools because they could not be accommodated by existing resources. Although U.S. Department of Health, Education, and Welfare estimated a need for 100,000 new MSWs between 1965 and 1970, CSWE statistics list the enrollment of MSWs (in two-year programs) ranging from a low of 8,186 in 1965 to a high of 13,008 in 1970 (Dea, 1966; DeVera, 1966; Eldredge, 1971; Loewenberg, 1967, 1968, 1970; Loewenberg & Shey, 1969) for which as little as 10% (in 1970) to as high as 14.1% (in 1965 and 1966) of students' primary field of practice was child welfare. Figures suggest a duplicate count of 64,105 MSW students enrolled in MSW programs in the United States between 1965 and 1970. Given that students may be counted twice in this aggregate sum, the number of graduates during this time would be significantly less (almost half) and tragically unresponsive to the identified need in the public sector for 100,000 MSWs (21,000 for public child welfare) during this same period of time. Thus, although there was an expansion of public sector jobs and of the number of schools of social work (and their associated curricula), it was not a proportionate, measured response to the demand for social workers across various fields of practice, especially child welfare.

These demands prompted a reevaluation of the importance of the BSW as a professional degree by CSWE and other leaders in social work (Chernin & Taylor, 1966; Western Interstate Commission for Higher Education, 1965; Winston, 1965; Witte, 1966). This occurred despite the fact that the U.S. Department of Education did not consider a bachelor degree a "first professional degree" during this time period (Ross & Lichtenberg, 1963). The generalist practice model would rise in prominence and direct the structure of many social work curriculums in the expansion of schools offering Bachelor of Social Work degrees (Western Interstate Commission for Higher Education, 1965). It was thought that the versatility of a generalist degree best suited an expanding and dynamic social service sector. These events led, in part, to a proportional deemphasis and focus on child welfare practice in U.S. MSW programs throughout the 1970s, 1980s, and 1990s (Eldredge, 1971; Hidalgo & Spaulding, 1987; Lennon, 1992, 1993, 1994, 1995, 1996; Purvine, 1972; Ripple, 1974, 1975; Rubin, 1981, 1982, 1983, 1984, 1985; Rubin & Whitcomb, 1978, 1979; Sheehan, 1976; Shyne & Whitcomb, 1977; Spaulding, 1988, 1990, 1991), despite the fact that public child welfare agencies have long been perceived as key training and employment settings for professional social workers in the United States (Bureau of Labor Statistics, 1952, 1962, 2006; CSWE, 1952, 1960, 1963; Lennon, 1992, 1995, 1996; Loewenberg, 1970; Rubin, 1981, 1983, 1984, 1985; Sheehan, 1976; Spaulding, 1988, 1990). Regardless, following 1970 and throughout much of the 1990s, fewer than 10% of MSW students chose primary fields of practice or social problem concentrations in the study of child welfare (although slightly higher percentages were placed in child welfare field settings between 1985 and 1995). Thus, the unresponsiveness of MSW programs and the minimization of the importance of the MSW as a preferred professional degree for public child welfare, in combination with other policy and practice events, helped contribute to the deprofessionalization of public child welfare in the United States. These events would have a compounded effect as the service demands placed on child welfare agencies/systems dramatically increased in the 1970s and 1980s.

Following the regular use of X-rays, radiologists drew the public's attention to nonaccidental injuries of children and the occurrence of child abuse and neglect. In the 1960s, every state in the country passed child abuse and neglect reporting laws, and federal legislation was subsequently enacted in 1974 with the Child Abuse Prevention and Treatment Act, which required the states to set up a registry and response system to such reports. From 1976 to 1986, the number of reports tripled and continued to increase into the mid-1990s, while funding for states to provide child protective services did not (CWLA, 1993; U.S. Department of Health and Human Services, 1996). More reporting led to more than 500,000 children in foster care by 1980. High caseloads spurred turnover and lost expertise of experienced child welfare professionals. In order to hire enough caseworkers, administrators dropped the minimum qualification for BSW and MSW degrees for child welfare employees, and schools of social work dropped child welfare content in their curricula (Karger, 1982).

As these events unfolded, some writers perceived the movement of graduate educated social workers away from public sector employment (including child welfare) as an outgrowth of a view of professionalism that reinforced a preoccupation of social workers that wanted to work with economically affluent and highly motivated clients (Falck, 1984; Katz, 1982; O'Conner, Dalgleish, & Khan, 1984; Reeser & Epstein, 1990; Reisch & Wenocur, 1986; Rubin & Johnson, 1984; Specht & Courtney, 1994). The steady increase of NASW members engaged in private practice in the 1980s and 1990s (Gibelman & Schervish, 1993, 1997; Kelley & Alexander, 1985; NASW, 1983; Wallace, 1982), coupled with the prominence of psychotherapy/clinical methods as preferred modes of intervention taught in many graduate schools throughout the United States, helped fuel this debate. Irrespective of its origins, it is clear that over a 30-year period, legitimate concern was expressed regarding the perceived deprofessionalization of many public social service jobs, making a large portion of social work positions engaged in income support and public child welfare unappealing to the professionally educated (Aaron, 1978; Beck, 1969; Dobelstein, 1985; Dressel, Waters, Sweat, Clayton, & Chandler-Clayton, 1988; A. J. Ellett & Leighnigner, 2007; Frabricant, 1985; Getzel, 1983; Ginsberg, Shiffman, & Rogers, 1971; Groulx, 1983).

In addition to these influences, the change in purpose of public assistance and the trend of increased work/caseloads, there were other concomitant circumstances that perpetuated deprofessionalization of child welfare. These included a focus on investigation over services to improve family functioning, rationing services, specialization within child welfare, class action lawsuits, and increasing oversight of the child welfare system beyond the courts by court-appointed special advocates, citizen review panels, and governor's child advocates, none of whom require social work education or child welfare experience. The press for accountability further requires increased time spent on written documentation, preparation for state and federal audits, and media investigations, resulting in reduced time available to work with clients. Deprofessionalization of child welfare has also resulted in hiring untrained, nonsocial workers, increased worker turnover, loss of degreed social workers, reduced public confidence in child welfare staff, and lost professional status (A. J. Ellett & Leighninger, 2007).

Current Status of Child Welfare: Issues, Practice, and Controversies

As described at the beginning of this chapter, child welfare work plays out in a taxing, complex environment embedded in a larger, and often times problematic, external environment. Most would agree that child welfare work is difficult and requires advanced social work knowledge and skills (elements of a profession) to be successful with clients. Though the work is difficult, and the history of child welfare documents considerable deprofessionalization, there are a number of ongoing efforts that can move child welfare toward greater professionalization in the years ahead. Those considered most important from our perspectives are described in the sections that follow.

Accountability

During the past three decades, child welfare practice has been characterized by increased attention to accountability issues and concerns. It is possible to assert that increased accountability in child welfare may be the result of historical deprofessionalization (e.g., a diminution in required credentials). Accountability in child welfare, as in all professions, is a necessary but insufficient condition for professional practice. In child welfare, however, the unwritten standards and expectations set by the general public and policymakers seem to reflect perfect casework practice with little margin for error. Child welfare agencies and staff are expected to make error-free assessments and decisions, unlike professionals in other fields (e.g., medicine and law). In child welfare, there is public outrage in child fatality and serious injury cases, and the assumption of error and subsequent blame for faulty practice typically follows. There is general acceptance that doctors sometimes make mistakes and cannot save the lives of all patients, so errors in their practice are overlooked and/or forgiven. Similarly, law enforcement officers cannot prevent the murder of an intimate partner violence victim after an investigation and are held blameless in these situations. The high standards for professional practice in child welfare, combined with historical deprofessionalization, have resulted in multiple accountability systems not seen in other professions. These systems are briefly described in the following sections.

The Courts

To assure that parents' rights are protected from unlawful government intrusion into the sanctity of the family, the courts have heard cases since the Mary Ellen case in 1874. The first juvenile court was established in Cook County (Chicago) in 1899 and courts have had jurisdiction over the removal from and return of children to their parent(s) or custodian(s). Courts also have jurisdiction over adoption surrenders and termination of parental rights. The court's oversight of these judicial hearings assures parents' due process in these life-altering matters with regard to their children. Over the past three decades, federal legislation has increased the courts' scrutiny and oversight of child welfare systems. Federal legislation now delineates specific limitations on and outcome expectations in child welfare cases (A. J. Ellett & Leighninger, 2007; A. J. Ellett & Steib, 2005).

Guardian Ad Litem and Court Appointed Special Advocate

The Child Abuse Prevention and Treatment Act of 1974 (CAPTA) requires that a *guardian ad litem* (GAL) be appointed by the court to act in the best interest of children in child abuse and neglect judicial proceedings (Blome & Steib, 2007). CAPTA was the first federal child maltreatment reporting law to protect what were considered a few children. Public child welfare agencies were quickly overwhelmed with the numbers of families reported, as were GAL attorneys to represent children in court. CAPTA provided limited funding to states that was insufficient to meet the far greater need.

The first Court Appointed Special Advocate (CASA) program was developed in Seattle, Washington, in 1977 out of the realization that overwhelmed caseworkers and GALs could not provide the details they believed necessary to rule in child abuse and neglect cases (Weisz & Thai, 2003). These volunteers have access to child records, children, caseworkers, and attorneys and can participate in meetings to understand both the case and the needs of the child to the degree necessary to make recommendations to the court (Welte, 2005). The federal Victims of Child Abuse Act of 1990 states that a "court appointed special advocate shall be available to every victim of child abuse or neglect in the United States that needs such an advocate" (Youngclarke, Ramos, & Granger-Merkle, 2004, p. 110). There are now more than 900 CASA programs (Weisz & Thai, 2003). Research on the effectiveness of CASA programs is inconclusive, due in part to less stringent methodologies, and studies have not generally compared child outcomes of CASA volunteers to outcomes of child welfare employees (Blome & Steib, 2007).

Foster Care Reviews

Since an increasing number of children who are placed in foster care (over 500,000) often remained in care for years, the Adoption Assistance and Child Welfare Act of 1980 was passed to bring additional oversight and accountability. This Act requires a case plan for every child in foster care, in addition to a court, administrative, or citizen review every six months with at least one of these reviews held in court annually. The purpose of these reviews is to provide parental due process and reasonable efforts to prevent foster care and reunification services, as well as to assess:

- The continued need for and appropriateness of the placement
- Level of compliance with the case plan
- Extent of progress made to alleviate the problems that necessitated placement in foster care
- The projected date the child can be returned home or placed for adoption or legal guardianship (National Association of Foster Care Reviewers, n.d.)

Parents and children are invited to attend these reviews along with the caseworker and others involved with the family. In administrative or citizen reviews, the administrator or citizen has no line authority for management of the case. Citizen reviewers are volunteers who are provided varied training to explain the child welfare system, the review process, and types of required decisions. Recommendations from administrative and citizen reviews are sent to the court for judicial approval. It is incumbent on the agency and worker to adhere to administrative review recommendations even if resources for clients are not available (Blome & Steib, 2007).

Citizen Review Panels

The CAPTA legislation was amended in 1996 to require states to have Citizen Review Panels in their child protective service programs for the purpose of additional oversight at both the case and system level. These panels are to "examine existing information management system reports, conduct case record reviews, and interview workers, families and mandated reporters" (Blome & Steib, 2007) and then to make recommendations that are advisory to the agency. This legislation, which encourages that panel composition consist of members from other review processes, seems redundant. To date, a comprehensive evaluation of Citizen Review Panel processes and outcomes has not been completed.

Court Approval of Case Plans

Since reasonable efforts lacked a definition, some children reunified with parents were subsequently maltreated, while others lingered in foster care for years to provide parents opportunities to regain custody of their children. The Adoption and Safe Families Act of 1997 (ASFA) amended PL 96–272 of 1980 to better the balance parents' rights with children's safety and to reduce time in foster care. The goals as delineated in the ASFA for child welfare cases are for safety, permanence, and child and family well-being. Increased court oversight of child welfare now includes court approval of case plans that were previously the role and responsibility of child welfare professionals (A. J. Ellett & Steib, 2005). Many concerns have subsequently been raised by child welfare workers, attorneys, judges, and others about this legislation, including the possible creation of legal orphans since the law requires "termination of parental rights for children in foster care 15 of the last 22 months," when it is unlikely that the parents can fulfill their parental duties (Adoption and Safe Families Act of 1997).

The Press and Child Advocates

The press has the duty to accurately report and inform citizens of issues of concern in child welfare. When children are victims of preventable death and injuries, the community wants to know what happened and to hold parents and/or child welfare employees responsible. What is often missing in these tragic stories are the federal and state mandates that child welfare systems support families in caring for their children and protect parents' rights to due process in child abuse and neglect cases. Unfortunately, sensationalized stories rather than success stories tend to capture the public's attention. More investigative reporting that goes beyond the tragedy to expose parental conditions leading to maltreatment; shortage of foster and adoptive homes for children with special needs; underfunded child welfare agencies; and on-call, overworked, and underpaid employees is needed. Professional organizations assume the role of advocates for abused and neglected children. Child Advocates look for solutions they believe will resolve problems and organize to promote legislation, investigation, funding, class action lawsuits, and so on. Class action lawsuits against child welfare state, county, and local systems have been filed in about half of the states with nearly all entering into consent decrees. These actions often move governors and legislatures to better fund and staff child welfare agencies; however, they also result in federal court oversight.

Child and Family Service Reviews

The Children's Bureau is the federal oversight agency for state child welfare systems and it makes decisions about the receipt of federal funding. Beginning in 2000, all states have now completed at least two Child and Family Service Reviews (CFSRs) from the Children's Bureau, and all states had deficiencies. The CFSR reviews have found that positive client outcomes are tied to frequent worker contact with parents and children (Blome & Steib, 2007).

Child welfare agency and employee accountability are essential to improve child welfare outcomes for children and families. Most agencies have internal reviews or quality assurance in place. Legislative committees and governors' task forces are still other means of child welfare system oversight and accountability. Child welfare employees report being overwhelmed trying to provide competent child welfare services, while at the same time, multiple oversight groups require information from these employees to point out what they have not been able to accomplish (A. J. Ellett, Ellett, & Rugutt, 2003). As previously described, multiple levels of oversight may have resulted from deprofessionalization in child welfare, and such oversight is not characteristic of other professions, such as medicine and law. Has accountability reached a level in child welfare of diminishing returns for children, families, agencies, employees, and society as a whole (Blome & Steib, 2007)? With limited child welfare funding, would clients, employees, and systems benefit if funding for redundant oversight was instead used to better fund and staff child welfare systems and courts to improve services and raise salaries to attract and retain social work professionals and attorneys in the juvenile court system (Blome & Steib, 2007)?

Concomitant with the development and implementation of multiple child welfare accountability and oversight systems, there is much discussion about factors and conditions that can serve to enhance the professionalization of child welfare. Some of the more prominent of these are discussed in the sections that follow.

Privatization

While child welfare service provision evolved from religious and private societies, following passage of the Social Security Act in 1935, until 1990 the majority of child welfare services were delivered by the public sector. With growing numbers of children in state custody and increased cost for their care, during the 1990s, states began making a decided philosophical shift to move many child welfare services to the private sector, presuming that they would deliver better child welfare services at a substantial savings through managed care focused on outcomes. Effectiveness evaluation research of privatized versus public child welfare services has been elusive, inconclusive, and lacking in rigor (Collins-Camargo et al., 2007). The U.S. Children's Bureau funded the Quality Improvement Center on Privatization of Child Welfare Services (QICPCWS) 2006–2011 to "conduct a knowledge gaps analysis, fund and conduct cross-site evaluation of research and demonstration projects, promote the expansion of the evidence base, and facilitate ongoing dialogue among child welfare administrators, policy makers, researchers, and practitioners regarding public/private partnership in service provision" (Collin-Camargo, Ensign, & Flaherty, 2008, p. 72). The QICPWS studied contract payment systems, contract management, and ongoing oversight of privatized services in 12 states and found there is great variation that changed over time (Flaherty, Collins-Camargo, & Lee, 2008a). In another study, the QICPWS learned that stakeholders need to develop trust, shared vision, and leadership to sustain efforts, and establish performance standards and communication among partners for successful privatization implementation (Flaherty, Collins-Camargo, & Lee, 2008b) Selected results from the QICPCWS national survey (QICPCWS, 2006) of private child welfare agencies ($N = 446$) find that most private agency leaders are experienced, have graduate degrees, head large agencies operating on an average of 63 years with large budgets (of which 69% are government funded), provide a variety of services, and are autonomous, networked, and accredited (McBeath, Collins-Camargo & Chuang, 2011).

Toward Reprofessionalization in Child Welfare: Recruitment, Retention, and Agency/University Title IV-E Partnerships

Public child welfare services are sanctioned to provide important protective, preventative, and preservative services for children and families with complex needs and across a myriad of contexts. These children and families deserve the highest level of professional expertise and competence.

In the 1990s, there was an intensified effort to reprofessionalize public child welfare. The social work profession has taken the lead in this effort, which involved advocating for better working conditions for child welfare workers, for more resources for the training of child welfare workers, and for the development and maintenance of unique university-agency partnerships (using Title IV-E funds) to prepare social workers for careers in public child welfare settings (Briar-Lawson & Wiesen, 1999; E. J. Clark, 2003; Hopkins, Mudrick, & Rudolph, 1999; McDonald & McCarthy, 1999; NASW, 2004a, 2004b; Pecora, Briar, & Zlotnik, 1989; Risley-Curtiss, 2003; U.S. General Accounting Office [GAO], 2003; Zlotnik, 2002; 2003; Zlotnik, Strand, & Anderson, 2009). It is the intensification and outgrowth (since the 1990s) of formal partnerships between schools of social work and state agencies overseeing the provision of child protection services that has received the most attention as an agent of reprofessionalization (Briar, Hansen, & Harris, 1992; Briar-Lawson & Wiesen, 1999; Hopkins et al., 1999; McDonald & McCarthy, 1999; Risley-Curtiss, 2003; Zlotnik, 1993, 2003) although the measured impact—at a national level—is not entirely known. Zlotnik (2006) cites several sources (American Public Human Services Association, 2005; Cheung & Taylor, 2005; Zlotnik, DePanfilis, Daining, & Lane, 2005) when reporting that more than 40 states have some form of Title IV-E educational program with BSW and MSW programs.

Title IV-E funded educational and financial incentives were initially developed with the goal of increasing the numbers of MSWs seeking employment in public child welfare (Grossman, Laughlin, & Specht, 1992). Federal Title IV-E money was used for the provision of stipend and training support for social work students who dedicate one year of service to a public child welfare agency for each year of support received. These incentives may have stimulated new interest in public child welfare among social work students, although it is unclear to what degree this may have occurred. It is clear (at least in California) that there was a noteworthy amount of MSW students interested in child welfare practice, prior to and following the implementation of the Title IV-E stipend programs (Perry, 2001, 2004), and that several years of program operation contributed to the majority of child welfare workers and supervisors possessing a master's degree in California (Clark & Fulcher, 2005).

Perry (2001) found that the percentage of all entering MSW students throughout California (between 1992 and 1996) that had a distinct interest in public child welfare ranged from a low of 10.2% to a high of 15.6%. It appears the interest in child welfare practice remains strong, but the longevity of interest may wane once individuals are employed and work environments fail to reinforce career ambitions. In this regard, the Title IV-E incentives may have served less as a recruitment tool than a source of support or additional reinforcement to prepare for a job or career in public child welfare among those already interested in the field. Perry (2004) found the most notable influences on MSW students' interest in public child welfare included the impact of past practice and practice training experiences. Findings from this study suggest that governments or schools of social work interested in reprofessionalizing public child welfare services might best focus their time, energy, and money on those currently working in or those with past work experience in public child welfare.

In this context, reprofessionalization can begin with those already employed in child welfare who are committed to work with children and families in need, yet lack a professional degree/education. Those with past experience in public child welfare, and those exposed to and training within public child welfare agencies within graduate programs (regardless of whether they participate in Title IV-E training programs) consider public child welfare as a viable and important sector for career MSWs. Regardless, as A. J. Ellett (2006) notes, most students of Title IV-E partnership programs (throughout the United States) generally take specific child welfare courses, fulfill their social work degree internships in public child welfare agencies and have a work obligation within a public child welfare agency on graduation. These experiences, it is assumed and some findings suggest, increase the likelihood that Title IV-E graduates are more likely to enter child welfare positions with the requisite knowledge, skills, and dispositions and a clear understanding of what child welfare work entails than are non–Title IV-E graduates (Barbee et al., 2009; Gansle & Ellett, 2002). These graduates report a stronger professional commitment to child welfare than those without BSW or MSW degrees (A. J. Ellett et al., 2003).

The initial focus of many of these collaborative programs was on MSW programs (Grossman et al., 1992) and represented a refocus on the historical precedent and practice (pre-1965) that perceived the MSW as a desired/preferential professional degree for child welfare practice. However, their impact and influence quickly extended into BSW programs as well. The Title IV-E partnerships have received tremendous support from educational institutions (S. Clark, 2003; Grossman et al., 1992; Perry, 2004), the National Association of Social Workers (E. J. Clark, 2003; NASW, 2004a, 2004b), child welfare associations (CWLA, 1991; National Association of Public Child Welfare Administrators, 1987) as well as Federal and State agencies that have asserted social workers are better skilled and apt for engaging in competent practice within the child welfare field (GAO, 2003; Zlotnik, 2003). There are isolated findings that assert that MSW students attain better outcomes with clients than those with bachelor degrees, Title IV-E stipend recipients are more knowledgeable and skilled in child welfare practice than others, and that social work–educated workers remain in public child welfare longer than others (Barbee et al., 2009; Booz-Allen & Hamilton, Inc., 1987; Dhooper, Royse, & Wolfe, 1990; A. J. Ellett, 2000; A. J. Ellett et al., 2003; Fox, Miller, & Barbee, 2003; Gansle & Ellett, 2002; Hopkins et al., 1999; Jones & Okamura, 2000; Lewandowski, 1998; Lieberman, Hornby, & Russell, 1988; Olsen & Holmes, 1982; Rosenthal & Waters, 2004; Russell & Hornby, 1987; Scannapieco & Connell-Carrick, 2003; University of Southern Maine, 1987). Alternatively, there are isolated findings that suggest that participation in a Title IV-E program has no measurable impact on retention rates

(Rosenthal, McDowell, & White, 1998) and that the performance of child welfare workers (primarily with undergraduate degrees) is not dependent on the educational background of workers (Perry, 2006a). All of these studies have varied methodological rigor and limited external validity. More importantly, there are few studies that link or contrast the impact of reprofessionalization efforts and the educational background and training of child welfare workers to child welfare outcomes while controlling for the varied contexts in which workers practice. Despite an increase of social work graduates in public child welfare settings (brought about by these partnerships), concern still exists regarding the rate of turnover and job satisfaction among all child welfare workers, factors impacting on the poor retention rates of qualified staff, organization climates, the increase in complexity and seriousness of the types of cases that confront workers, and the administrative demands placed on workers that subsequently limit contact time and the attainment of desired outcomes with children and families (Cahalane & Sites, 2004; Cyphers, 2001; Dickinson & Perry, 2002; A. J. Ellett et al., 2003; Glisson & Durick, 1988; Henry, 1990; McNeely, 1989; NASW, 2004a, 2004c; Oktay, 1992; GAO, 2003; Weiner, 1991). As Perry (2006a) notes: "Even the most competent worker's ability to maximize client outcomes will be strained at best, and eliminated at worst, when they have a high caseload of multiproblem families, little supervisory support, burdensome paperwork demands that limit client contact time, limited reinforcements (including poor pay), and work within a dysfunctional organizational climate" (p. 444). A more critical examination of the impact of professional training and workforce conditions on client outcomes in child welfare settings is needed in order to improve the efficiency and efficacy of service delivery in the public and private sector settings. More importantly, more detailed and rigorous studies are needed to determine whether Title IV-E partnerships have a longitudinal effect on maximizing the likelihood of worker competence, obtaining desired outcomes for child welfare populations, increasing the quality of service, and improving retention rates of quality workers. There is general support within the literature for these initiatives (Dickinson, 2006; A. J. Ellett, 2006; Hughes & Baird, 2006; McCarthy, 2006; Perry, 2006a).

Supervision and Mentorship

Accountability has become a dominant issue framing current child welfare practice. As a result, agencies have typically responded by requiring supervisors to focus more directly on task supervision, rather than the more traditional focus on mentoring and professional development to strengthen practice skills. Task supervision is primarily motivated by issues such as compliance, record keeping, and a cult of efficiency and accountability. For example, supervisors use information system reports to determine whether workers are making first client contacts within the prescribed time frame, monthly contacts with parents and children, court reports submitted timely, and so on (Collins-Camargo, 2006).

Although advances in the use of automated systems, dynamic data bases, personal digital devices, voice dictation and other technologies have documented benefits for child welfare practice (Anderson, 2004; Barton Child Law and Policy Clinic, 2002; Computer Associates, 2004; Compuware Corporation, 2005; Kershaw, 2002; Microsoft, 2004a, 2004b; Miller, 2001; National Resource Center for Information Technology in Child Welfare, 2002, 2003; NPower New York, 2002), these benefits exist only if they enable the streamlining and minimization of burdensome administrative, bureaucratic functions that take away from client contact time, real case-work (i.e., really working with cases) and professional practice aimed at the development of working relationships and goal attainment with client systems (Cyphers, 2001; A. J. Ellett et al., 2003; GAO, 2003; Malm, Bess, Leos-Urbel, Green, & Markowitz, 2001; NASW, 2004a; Samantrai, 1992; Vinokur-Kaplan & Hartman, 1986). Child and family services reviews conducted between 2001 through 2004 found that the frequency of contact and visits between caseworkers and children and parents is consistently associated with the attainment of desired outcomes associated with child safety, permanency, and child well-being (Administration for Children and Families, 2004). Professional child welfare workers need the time with clients to practice their trade and, perhaps more importantly, they need quality supervision, mentorship, and a learning environment to advance their knowledge and applied skill set.

Child welfare practice is multifaceted, demanding and requires a foundation of knowledge in (but not limited to) social policy, state laws and protocols, child development, family dynamics, conflict/crisis management and resolution, case management, critical thinking, substance abuse, mental health issues and organizational functioning (Horejsi, Bertsche, Francetich, Collins, & Francetich, 1987; Rittner & Wodarski, 1999; Rothman, 1991). The pressures placed on child welfare workers and individuals and entities for which they are accountable to are enormous, well-documented and include (but are not limited to): maltreated children, children of clients, families, foster care providers, abusive parents/caregivers, the court system, agency administrators, the community and media, and so on (Crosson-Tower, 2002).

Salas (2004) and others (Beggs, 1996; GAO, 1995, 2003; NASW, 2004c; Perry & Houlious, 2006; Rycus & Hughes, 1994) have listed the multitude of performance expectations and responsibilities child welfare workers (protective investigators and service workers) are required to meet. The above functions (if competently completed) require a foundation in knowledge and practice experience. These functions, however, may involve an additional series of interrelated tasks and an expanded skill set. Perry, Graham, Kerce, and Babcock (2004) found that child protective investigators in Florida are required, as part of their work requirements, to be competent in 141 separate essential tasks as a means of fulfilling performance expectations established by state laws and service protocols. In a similar task analysis of child and family service (not protective investigators) workers in central Florida, Perry and Houlious (2006) itemized a total of 115 separate essential tasks that workers may be called on each day in order to fulfill job expectations.

Findings From Pertinent Research Studies

The workload demands brought about by heavily mandated services and the associated stress with providing protective, preservative, and prevention-based interventions with multiproblem families can have an aversive impact on the retention of quality social workers beginning their professional career. Within these contexts, quality/competent supervision and worker–supervisor relationships are paramount for the recruitment and retention of child welfare workers (Child Welfare Training Institute, 1997; Cyphers, 2001; Dickinson & Perry, 2002; Fleischer, 1985; McCarthy, 2004; Mor Barak, Nissly, & Levin, 2001; Smith, 2004). Workers require supervisors who have experience and competency-based knowledge and are perceived as being supportive of workers' efforts to gain knowledge and experience and increase their competency. These are important consider-ations in evaluating the performance of supervisors (Drake & Washeck, 1998; Kadushin, 1992; McCarthy, 2004; Ruston & Nathan, 1996). Here, the quality of the supervisor–worker relationship is frequently cited as an important consideration in the professional development and/or learning of workers, the minimization of worker stress and burnout, and with the max-imization of worker retention in a field beset with high turnover (Dickinson & Perry, 2002; A. J. Ellett et al., 2003; Gleeson, 1992; McCarthy, 2004).

An abundance of literature highlights the skills and knowledge con-sidered representative of quality supervision or management in the human service fields, including child welfare (Bunker & Wijnberg, 1988; Kadushin, 1985; Menefee, 1998; Menefee & Thompson, 1994; Middleman & Rhodes, 1985; Morton & Salas, 1994; Preston, 2004; Salas, 2004; Tropman, Faller, & Feldt, 2004). Social work educators and researchers typically endorse the MSW degree as preferred for those assuming supervisor and/or manage-ment positions in child welfare and social service agencies (CWLA, 1984; Edwards, 1987; Rittner & Wodarski, 1999). These endorsements seemed to be based on the historical role of social work in educating and training professionals to assume supervisory and administrative roles in social ser-vice agencies. Historically, the MSW degree has been the preferred degree for child welfare supervisors and is still endorsed as such by the NASW (2005), CWLA (1984), and the Council on Accreditation for Children and Family Services (2001). The endorsement of MSWs typically results from critical reviews of curricula in graduate schools of social work and the applicability and relevance of these curricula to on-the-job demands and competencies required of child welfare supervisors. Although it is clear social work (as a profession) and schools of social work have been lead-ers in developing specialized curricula and programs to prepare social workers for supervisory roles in child welfare, there is some disagree-ment as to the extent to which a social work degree enhances the skills of those who assume supervisor positions in contrast to those without a social work degree (Perry, 2006b; Thyer, Williams, Love, & Sowers-Hoag, 1989). Regardless, select studies and writings have highlighted the need for child welfare supervision to become less of a regulatory exercise in favor of an opportunity for a quality, reflective, practice-oriented, and supportive exchange between worker and mentor (Collins-Camargo, Sullivan, Washeck, Adams & Sundet, 2009).

Several large-scale research studies completed recently provide support for the importance of quality supervision in child welfare. Most of these studies have been completed using measures specifically developed for child welfare of personal (self-efficacy and human caring) and organizational (organizational culture, morale, evidence-based practice and quality supervision) variables related to organizational outcomes (intent to remain employed; A. J. Ellett, Collins-Camargo, & Ellett, 2006). C. D. Ellett (1995) found that the highest levels of satisfaction among a group of long-term employees in child welfare was quality supervision. In a two-state study (Louisiana $n = 562$ and Arkansas $n = 357$), A. J. Ellett (2000) reported a statistically significant correlation (.27; $p < .0001$) between professional sharing and support (an element of quality supervision) and intent to remain employed. Using structural equation modeling ($n = 990$) of organizational/occupational commitment with intention to remain, Landsman (2001) found a positive relationship between supervisory support and job satisfaction ($r = .30$), which was positively linked to occupational and organizational commitment and intent to remain employed in child welfare. Renner, Porter, & Preister (2009) found that child welfare retention improved in Missouri following implementation of the supervisory plan, as did supervisor and team effectiveness in addition to satisfaction with their jobs. From a sample of 767 child welfare workers, Chenot, Benton, and Hansung, (2009) determined that supervisor support was crucial in employee retention not only in an agency, but also in the field of child welfare, while "passive defensive organizational culture has a negative effect on early career workers, but not on mid or late career workers" (p. 129). In a study of 305 IV-E child welfare program graduates, Cahalane and Sites (2009) found job satisfaction, emotional exhaustion, and personal accomplishment predictive of those who remained employed in child welfare beyond their legal work commitment and recommend organizations develop positive work climates to retain highly skilled and educated employees. A. J. Ellett and colleagues (2003) completed a large statewide study of retention and turnover in child welfare ($n = 1423$, survey; $n = 385$, 60 focus groups). This study documented a rather strong, positive correlation ($r = .63$; $p < .0001$) between intentions to remain employed in child welfare and *professional commitment* (a dimension of human caring). Workers' perceptions of professional support and the quality of supervision and administration were positively related to a measure of intention to remain employed in child welfare ($r = .36$, $r = .33$). Focus group participants identified supervisors' professional support and guidance as important to strengthening work-related self-efficacy beliefs and intentions to remain employed in child welfare (A. J. Ellett, Ellis, Westbrook, &

Dews, 2007). Westbrook (2006) completed a statewide study in Georgia of 1,033 child welfare staff perceptions of multiple dimensions of organizational culture and relationships between these perceptions and their intentions to remain employed in child welfare. Her results showed a rather strong relationship between intent to remain employed in child welfare and supervisory support ($r = .45$) and administrative support ($r = .43$). Strolin-Golzman and colleagues (2009) used design teams as an intervention to achieve organizational change to increase employee retention. Using university-agency teams in six western sites, Potter, Comstock, Brittain. & Hanna (2009) conducted needs assessments in 2004 to develop intervention strategies, with positive results in 2006 of employees' perceptions significantly improved around community support, client family resources, and job satisfaction. Further, employee stress and emotional exhaustion were lower. Collins-Camargo (2005) completed a study of linkages between supervision, organizational culture promoting evidence-based practice, self-efficacy, and public child welfare outcomes with 876 child welfare workers and supervisors in a Midwestern state. She found that 53% of the culture variance promoting evidence-based practice was explained by the effectiveness of supervision measure. In addition, she found a significant difference in the level of self-efficacy expectations (the extent to which workers believed that work tasks were likely to result in desired outcomes such as the ability to effect positive change in clients) and the perceived effectiveness of supervision for workers regardless of years of service.

An interesting and quite timely finding from the Collins-Camargo (2005) study was that effective supervision and professional organizational culture were predictors of case outcome indicators at a level similar to the predictive strength of larger community indicators, such as poverty. Findings from her study highlight the need for a quality supervisor–worker relationship built on a strong knowledge base and commitment to competency-based practice. Considered collectively, findings from the research studies described above, as well as many others, show that quality supervision in child welfare makes important contributions to: (a) creating an organizational culture focused on achieving positive outcomes; (b) maintaining a sense of hope within staff that their efforts can make a difference in client outcomes; (c) strengthening the professional commitment of staff and subsequent employee retention; and (d) enhancing worker knowledge, critical thinking, and self-reflective learning.

Evidence-Based Practices, Social Work Research, and Child Welfare

As circumstances and events (since the mid-1960s) accelerated the deprofessionalization of child welfare practice, research in child welfare (most notably since the 1980s) thrived. There appeared to be an inverse relationship between the decrease in professional social workers entering and remaining in public child welfare settings and the exponential growth of child welfare knowledge brought about by social work leadership in research and the establishment of evidence-based practice standards. Social work and social work researchers made significant strides toward advancing child welfare knowledge on a number of fronts (Barth, Berrick, & Gilbert, 1994; Berrick, Barth, & Gilbert, 1996). This is not to suggest that social workers did not make significant contributions to social work knowledge prior to the 1980s, as they did (for select examples, see Fanshel, 1962; Fanshel & Maas, 1962; Fanshel & Shinn, 1978; Kadushin, 1965, 1970; Kadushin & Seidl, 1971; Maas & Engler, 1959; Norris & Wallace, 1965; Stein, Gambrill, & Wiltse, 1978). However, the past 25 years has been a particularly active period where social work leadership in child welfare research has been dominant and has made contributions of particular import to advancing knowledge, policy, and providing a foundation for evidence-based practice.

As a profession, social work has clearly established a standing of prominence within child welfare research. It would be difficult to highlight all of the accomplishments and significant outcomes generated from this active period of discovery. Several volumes would be needed to highlight, discuss, and debate the significance of research conducted during the past quarter century. Regardless, notable contributions by social workers can be found across a myriad of fields of interest/study in child welfare including (for example) child protection and maltreatment (Daro & Mitchel, 1990), foster care (Lindsey, 1991a, 1991b; Webster, Barth, & Needell, 2000; Whitaker & Maluccio, 2002; Wulczyn, Harden, & George, 1998), foster care youth and independent living programs (Cook, 1992; Courtney & Barth, 1996), kinship care (Berrick, Barth, & Needell, 1994; Courtney & Needell, 1997; Hegar & Scannapieco, 1999), ethnic/racial disproportionality (Barth, 2005; Courtney & Skyles, 2003; Derezotes, Testa, & Poertner, 2005; Needell, Brookhart, & Lee, 2003), prevention (Daro & Donnelly, 2003; Daro & McCurdy, 2006); family preservation (Lindsey, Martin, & Doh, 2002; Pecora, Fraser, & Haapala, 1991); and permanency planning (Barth & Berry, 1987, 1994; Barth, Courtney, Berrick, & Albert, 1994; Maluccio, Fein, & Olmstead, 1986). Particular note is made of the contributions of select research institutes/organizations, their leaders, and their associates (current and former), including but not limited to the Child Welfare Research Group affiliated with the Center for Social Services Research at the University of California at Berkeley, Chapin Hall at the University of Chicago, the Urban Institute, and Casey Family Programs.

The emphasis on accountability corresponded with an expansion of research initiatives and an interest in the development of evidence-based practice standards. Although the CWLA has been a leader in the establishment and refinement of practice standards for child welfare practice (CWLA, 1984, 1995, 1998, 1999a, 1999b, 2000), other initiatives have resulted in the establishment of training, knowledge, and curriculum standards for child welfare workers (Berrick, Needell, Shlonsky, Simmel, & Pedrucci, 1998; California Social Work Education Center, 2006; S. Clark, 2003; NASW, 2005; Rycus & Hughes, 1994, 1998; Stein & Gambrill, 1976; Stein & Rzepnicki, 1984). These standards have been generated, in some cases, from prevailing logic or opinion regarding the skills and knowledge needed to perform well as a frontline worker, consensus among experts or key stakeholders in academia and state agencies, and/or practice knowledge garnered from existing evaluation or cross-sectional research studies. These standards are an important foundation from which to build practice and knowledge. However, within the last decade, attention has focused on the need to critically appraise the validity of practice assumptions and findings generated from studies with noteworthy limitations (Dingwall, 1989; Lindsey et al., 2002; Perry, 2006a; Rossi, 1994; Shlonsky & Gambrill, 2001) to move toward more evidence-based practice models, to emphasize critical thinking, and to focus on more advanced longitudinal outcome studies that rigorously test the success or failure of different practice interventions and policy initiatives (Barth, Crea, John, Thoburn, & Quinton, 2005; California Social Work Education Center, 2006; Chaffin & Friedrich, 2004; Courtney, 2000; Dawson & Berry, 2002; Gambrill, 2003; Gibbs, 2003; Gibbs & Gambrill, 1999; National Association of Public Child Welfare Administrators, 2005; Roberts & Yaeger, 2006; Shlonsky & Gibbs, 2004; Shlonsky & Wagner, 2005; Thomlison 2003, 2005; Usher & Wildfire, 2003; Wulczyn, Barth, Yuan, Harden, & Landsverk, 2005).

Research on specific interventions with maltreated children and their families with demonstrated efficacy evidence has been rapidly building. The California Evidence-Based Clearinghouse for Child Welfare (www.cebc4cw.org) includes program descriptions and empirical support, and rates each accordingly. In *Clinician's Guide to Evidence-Based Practice Programs and Interventions for Maltreated Children and Families at Risk,* Alan Rubin (2011) has devoted a chapter to each of 20 such programs. The intervention with the strongest evidence for effectiveness with traumatized children and nonoffending parents is Trauma-Focus Cognitive Behavioral Therapy (Rubin, 2011); Parent-Child Interaction Therapy uses live, immediate coaching of parents while they interact with their children (Niec, Eyberg, & Chase 2011); and Multisystemic Therapy for Child Abuse and Neglect is a team approach in which the therapist fully shares responsibility for the child's safety with the CPS caseworker (Swenson & Schaeffer, 2011) to name a few. These recent events/trends reflect an evolution in perspective and spirit that, when manifested, will build on knowledge already garnered from an active period of investigation and further advance knowledge about the efficacy of interventions meant to solve real problems encountered by children and families.

Professionalizing and Improving Child Welfare

Perhaps the most important alterable variable related to the future professionalization and improvement of child welfare is the quality of the workforce. A continued, integrated focus on workforce development that includes concern for personal, organizational, and work context variables is needed to move toward a professional model of child welfare practice.

The sections that follow briefly describe important elements of the child welfare workforce and attendant concepts, issues, and concerns that need to be addressed if child welfare is to continue on the path of greater professionalization and improvement of services to children and families in need.

An Increased Societal Need for Child Welfare Services

It is apparent that the provision of social services for children and families in need will be necessary as the size and complexity of the general population continues to increase. Given the multiple and serious problems that abusing and neglecting families face, the work within child welfare will remain complex and challenging. Substance abuse, mental illness, cognitive deficits, teen parenthood, and incarceration do not lend themselves to quick resolutions. Children in families with one or more of these problems often have developmental delays, behavioral and/or emotional disorders, and/or lack adequate problem-solving and social skills. In one of the largest studies ($N = 17,000$) conducted from 1995–1997 to assess connections between child abuse and neglect and outcomes later in life, the Centers for Disease Control and Prevention (1997) in collaboration with Kaiser Permanente found that experiencing multiple types of adverse childhood events (ACEs) has negative consequences for future health and social problems. These families typically need multiple social services. Therefore, accurate assessments and the ability to communicate with and actively engage family members in planning and implementing evidence-based interventions will remain critical elements of child welfare practice.

An Increased Need to Prepare Child Welfare Professionals

The U.S. Department of Labor and NASW projections identify an increasing future demand for social workers in a variety of practice areas, especially in child welfare (Bureau of Labor Statistics, U.S. Department of Labor, 2006; Center for Health Workforce Studies and Center for Workforce Studies, 2006). Thus, it will be important in the years ahead for those preparing social workers (colleges and universities) and for professional associations (e.g., CSWE, SSWR, NASW) to continue to support child welfare as an important identity in the social work profession. Colleges and universities preparing social workers will need to continue to develop and implement curricula that respond to the projected increase in the national need for child welfare workers. Currently, many students enter MSW programs with the belief that they desire careers as private, clinical practitioners. The changing market and work context factors (e.g., managed care, growth in medical field) have diminished the likelihood that there will be a sufficient need for all social work graduates who desire full time jobs in private practice. Thus, colleges and universities that prepare social workers for the future will need to be keenly aware of societal changes and the increased need for child welfare workers, and adjust their social work curricula accordingly.

Social Work Education Partnerships Between University and Child Welfare

The Title IV-E child welfare education and training collaborations between universities and agencies have been wise investments and have been important to enhance professionalization of child welfare. These partnerships exist in nearly all states and have increased the number of child welfare workers with BSW and MSW degrees. The national Title IV-E effort includes:

- Preservice and continuing education for child welfare employees, as well as for foster and adoptive parents
- Stipends for employees and potential employees working to obtain BSW and MSW degrees
- Support for expanding child welfare content in college/university curricula
- Support for internships in child welfare agencies
- Formal education and on-the-job experiences that engage students and/or child welfare employees in social work theory, research, and practice

Multiple benefits have accrued to child welfare and social work education through these partnerships. Among these are (a) strengthening advocacy and developing a stronger voice for child welfare; (b) improving child welfare practice; (c) developing greater leadership capacity; and (d) increasing the number of child welfare employees obtaining doctoral degrees (many of whom take positions in higher education, which increases the number of knowledgeable and experienced child welfare faculty). Some social work educators also participate in the development of agency IV-B Plans and Program Improvement Plans in response to Child and Family Service Reviews. It is thought that all of these activities and others emanating from Title IV-E partnerships have contributed to and strengthened professionalization of the child welfare workforce in ways that better meet the needs of children and their families.

Employee Recruitment, Selection, and Retention

The Title IV-E social work education partnerships have, by design, included recruitment of BSW and MSW students (including child welfare employees) for the purpose of educating and preparing graduates for a career in child welfare. While degreed social workers have professional knowledge and some practice skills, many are not suited for the taxing work of child welfare, and some self-select out. As these partnerships have evolved, more attention is being given to selecting students and employing workers who possess the personal characteristics identified through recent research that enhance employee retention and strengthen the child welfare workforce.

Selection of Title IV-E students is a key component of the Title IV-E partnership in Georgia for example, where applicants are jointly interviewed and selected by an experienced panel of child welfare agency professionals and university faculty.

Currently, too little attention is being paid to the importance of employee selection as an important means of strengthening the child welfare workforce and improving the quality of services to children and families. Many applicants for child welfare positions are hired without regard to the requisite knowledge and skills needed to survive and to be successful in child welfare, and many do not remain in child welfare practice very long. While there has been recent discussion and debate about the value of the social work degree for successful and competent practice in child welfare (see Dickinson, 2006; A. J. Ellett, 2006; Hughes & Baird, 2006; Lieberman & Levy, 2006; McCarthy, 2006; Perry, 2006a, 2006b; Zlotnik, 2006), there are emerging lines of inquiry designed to improve employee selection with the goal of strengthening employee retention and reducing employee turnover.

In Georgia, for example, high turnover among newly hired child welfare workers is a major concern (28% within the first 90 days before being assigned cases). To address this concern, the University of Georgia, in partnership with the Georgia Division of Family and Children Services developed a comprehensive Employee Selection Protocol (ESP) (A. J. Ellett, Ellett, Ellis, & Lerner, 2009; A. J. Ellett, Ellett, Westbrook, & Lerner, 2006). The ESP is standardized across applicants and includes three major components: (1) web-based text, realistic job preview video, and self-assessment for likely job fit; (2) written application materials that include cover letter, resume, writing sample, and references; and (3) onsite completion of an in-basket assessment exercise and a semistructured interview by a panel of three experienced child welfare professionals. The ESP was piloted during the spring and summer of 2007 and is required of participating universities in the selection process for selecting students for child welfare stipends. One important element of the ESP is the web-based self-assessment. The assessment is completed after reading the web text and viewing the realistic job preview. It is framed around assessment indicators known to be positively related to child welfare workers' intentions to remain employed in child welfare (A. J. Ellett et al., 2003; Ellis, Ellett, & DeWeaver, 2007). It is expected that the results of the self-assessment task will encourage some applicants to discontinue the application process and self-select out of child welfare. Many applicants for child welfare stipends and positions in Georgia (and in other states as well), particularly those without a social work degree, have little understanding of the complexities and expectations of the work, and after considerable investments of time and money in 12 weeks of on-the-job training/certification programs, they leave child welfare for other employment. The ESP has been successfully implemented in Georgia to select stipend students, better informing them about the nature of child welfare work, and has led to the selection of better qualified candidates, the saving of human and financial investments made in students who become new workers, and the reduction of existing high employee turnover rates.

Credentialing, Career Concerns, and a Vision for the Future of Child Welfare

Credentialing is an important component of any profession. Credentials communicate a level of professional competence, expertise, and account-ability to the larger society. Credentialed professions also typically reap greater monetary investments and rewards and generate greater public confidence, respect, and prestige than noncredentialed occupations. Though not guaranteeing competence and expertise, credentials have strong symbolic value. One only needs to consider the strong symbolic value of credentials in high-paying professions such as medicine and law to understand their value, and the prestige and trust placed in highly credentialed doctors and lawyers. According to A. J. Ellett (2006):

> As with academic credentials in any profession, the social work degree has considerable symbolic value and it serves to signal the public that child welfare is a profession worthy of considerably increased, and hopefully continued investment. (p. 410)

As previously described in this chapter, the MSW was once considered the appropriate entering level credential for child welfare work. However, and perhaps largely because of increased demands for more workers to cover ever-increasing caseloads, most states do not require a BSW as an entry level credential, though most require at least a bachelor degree in a related discipline (e.g., psychology, sociology, counseling, education; CWLA, 1999b; Lieberman et al., 1988; Perry, 2006a).

As mentioned, there is ongoing debate and discussion about the value of the social work degree to competent practice. However, the lack of a professional degree requirement as an initial credential (BSW) in child welfare is problematic from several perspectives. First, the message is sent to the public that anyone with a bachelor degree can do this complex work. Second, the lack of a BSW requirement suggests that there is no body of specialized knowledge that is important to include in college/university curricula. Third, and perhaps most importantly, a signal is sent to the general public and to policymakers that child welfare work is not professional work (anyone can do it) and is not worthy of increased monetary investments. Thus, those employed in child welfare are viewed as workers, not as professionals. These same issues apply and same arguments can be made about the lack of MSW degree requirement for child welfare supervisors.

Child welfare workers have few options for professional advancement within a child welfare organization. Lack of such options has been shown to contribute to child welfare employee turnover (A. J. Ellett et al., 2003; Westbrook, Ellis, & Ellett, 2006). Within the child welfare organization, a job assignment might change (e.g., child protective services, foster care, adoptions); however, there are few opportunities for career advancement to higher-level positions. Therefore, the predominant model for increased compensation is a lateral model in which length of employment, sometimes indexed by education level (e.g., BA, BSW, MSW), rather than the nature of the work, is the predominant factor that determines salary increases. For most child welfare staff, there are few career choices beyond moving from front-line worker to supervisor. What seems needed to further professionalize child welfare is rethinking and redesigning child welfare in a way that:

- Is sensitive to career options and choices
- Accommodates individual differences in employees' interests, knowledge, and skills
- Provides differentiated pay for differentiated work
- Includes opportunities for competency/performance-based rewards through merit-based and bonus-based pay
- Values, encourages, and rewards the attainment of appropriate advanced degrees (e.g., MSW rather than BSW)
- Designates clear qualification and designates different levels of renewable licensing and professional certification for work in each child welfare position
- Provides mentoring and close supervision and support for new employees
- Is sensitive to reasonable case/workloads balanced with other job responsibilities
- Implements a valid and reliable job performance evaluation system

Each of these redesign elements would be included in a new plan for child welfare that targets better education, practice, credentialing, professional development, supervision, compensation, retention, and ultimately, improved services and outcomes for children and families.

As indicated by attempts to redesign other professions (e.g., teaching, nursing), realizing this vision for child welfare will not be an easy task and it will require considerable resources and support from policymakers, the general public, and perhaps strategic champions who will advocate for the professionalization of child welfare as the means to achieve outcomes for children and families.

Conclusion

This chapter addresses the history of child welfare as a distinct practice area of social work, its early development as a profession, and its subsequent deprofessionalization. As a result of deprofessionalization, child welfare has become highly regulated with multiple levels of oversight not found in other professions. A discussion of the contributions of Title IV-E university/agency partnerships to the preparation of child welfare staff, the documented need for quality supervision and administration, and social work research identifying evidence-based practice to professionalize child welfare, is included. The final section describes the increasing societal need for child welfare services, social work education's important role in the preparation of child welfare staff and the need for continued higher education and child welfare agency partnerships and collaboration. A vision for employee selection, retention, and credentialing is discussed as the means to professionalize child welfare and to ultimately improve services and outcomes for children and their families.

NOTES

1. Conrad (1930) suggests this school was formed in 1903, not 1901 (as AASSW documents suggest), as the Institute of Social Science. This school was formed as a result of the efforts of Graham Taylor of Chicago Commons and Julia Lathrop of Hull House. In 1907, its name would be changed to the Chicago School of Civics and Philanthropy. The Philadelphia Training School for Social Work became the Pennsylvania School for Social Service in 1916.

2. In this study, a *social worker* was considered anyone employed in a "social work" position or capacity within a multitude of agencies recognized (initially) by the National Advisory Committee of Social Workers as actual and potential employers of social workers. Thus, the BLS definition of a social worker conforms to Census Bureau definitions, unlike that of a "professional" social worker as defined by representative professional associations. Regardless, information regarding whether individuals participated in and achieved a graduate degree in social work was obtained. The 1950 study was replicated in 1960 by the BLS and the National Social Welfare Assembly. Utilizing the same sample plan and weighting procedures, population estimates for a universe of 115,799 social workers in the United States were obtained from 28,290 completed survey instruments. Like the 1950 study, this study utilized information solicited independently from three agencies within the Department of Health, Education, and Welfare via a survey of all (42,137) social workers employed by state and local governments. Approximately 20% (8,358) of these were combined with 19,932 (of a possible 24,218) social workers who responded to the BLS survey to make up the study sample.

3. These types of discrepancies between where MSW students receive their field placement versus where they are likely to be employed cast doubt on the usefulness of relying on field placement statistics as a means of monitoring market trends for social work services. It is conjectured that the demand for, and receptiveness to, providing field training in any service sector or agency is shaped by influences separate from the market demands for these students once they graduate. Should this conjecture defy refutation, implications for social work education abound. Additional study is needed to

determine whether training received in graduate school adequately prepares students for employment in varied service sectors that express differential demands for social workers. Further, it would be interesting to ascertain whether graduate students have a more or less accurate understanding of the demand for their services once they graduate than schools of social work.

4. There were 78 additions to existing legislation, amendments, or new legislation that expanded resources (public services) for social work manpower between 1956 and 1965 (U.S. Department of Health, Education, and Welfare, 1965). Aaron (1978) demonstrated how direct expenditures on human resources (social services) and in-kind benefits by the U.S. federal government as a percentage of full employment GNP increased from 6.3% in 1961 to 8.7% in 1969 to 13.4% in 1976. The reader should refer to the following resources for descriptions of the social welfare state in the United States and its growth and expanding functions through the 1960s (Aaron, 1978; Barr, 1987; Dobelstein, 1985; Ginsburg, 1979; Pigou, 1952; Wolf & Lebeaux, 1968). The direct effect of the expansion of the welfare state on social work manpower can be examined by the 42% increase in "social welfare" manpower between 1950 and 1960 (Bureau of Labor Statistics, 1962). Further, educational training support for various "social work" positions was provided for by the Vocational Education Act of 1963, the Manpower Development and Training Act of 1963, and the Economic Opportunity Act of 1964.

5. Because supervision is such an important element of child welfare employee retention and professional development, considerable text is devoted to the discussion of supervision and to findings from pertinent research studies that identify the quality of supervision as an important element of child welfare practice.

Key Terms

Child welfare	Evidence-based practice	Social work education

Review Questions for Critical Thinking

1. What are the major historical factors that led to the deprofessionalization of child welfare systems through the 1980s?

2. Is child welfare practice complex? If so, what are the defining features of its complexity?

3. Why are social workers the best-qualified professionals to work within the child welfare field? What should the entry-level qualifications be for a child welfare worker?

4. What role should research and evidence-based practice have in child welfare? Are most child welfare practices evidence-based?

5. How responsive is social work education to the market demand for child welfare workers with a particular knowledge and skill set? What knowledge and skill set is imperative for competent child welfare practice?

Online Resources

American Humane Association: Children www.americanhumane.org/children

The American Humane Association has been advocating for the protection of children since 1877. The organization is engaged in research, professional training and development, information dissemination, and advocacy on a variety of child welfare issues.

Child Welfare Information Gateway www.childwelfare.gov

The U.S. Children's Bureau clearinghouse gathers vast amounts of information and reports on topical areas in child welfare.

My Child Welfare Librarian http://naic.acf.hhs.gov/admin/subscribe.cfm

This website, offered by the National Clearinghouses on Child Abuse and Neglect Information and the National Adoption Information Clearinghouse, allows users to register without cost to receive monthly lists of library materials in specific categories chosen by the user, such as safety, permanency, well-being, prevention, workforce, and more.

Children's Bureau Express http://cbexpress.acf.hhs.gov

Children's Bureau Express is an electronic newsletter designed to provide child welfare professionals with brief, concise information on current issues, research, and promising practices.

California Clearinghouse for Evidence-Based Practice in Child Welfare www.chadwickcenter.org

The California Clearinghouse, at San Diego Children's Hospital's Chadwick Center for Children and Families, gathers and reviews information on evidence-based practices and provides links to other evidence-based practice sites.

Casey Life Skills www.casey.org

Casey Family Programs provide information about youth development and preparation for life skills. The site also offers a link to the free Ansell-Casey Life Skills Assessment tool which youth and their caregivers can take online to a get a free, confidential assessment.

Center for the Study of Social Policy www.cssp.org

The Center for the Study of Social Policy is a policy research and resource center that partners with federal, state, and local public agencies and with private sector organizations, foundations, and community members to promote public policies and practices that (in part) prevent child abuse, promote child development, address child and family poverty, and promote racial/ethnic equality within systems of care.

Chapin Hall www.chapinhall.org

Chapin Hall is a leading policy research institute at the University of Chicago that focuses on a multitude of child welfare topics, including (but not limited to) child welfare and foster care systems, economic supports for families, home visitation and maltreatment prevention, and workforce development.

Child Trends www.childtrends.org/index.cfm

Child Trends is a nonprofit research and policy center that focuses on a variety of child development and child and family welfare topics including (but not limited to): child poverty, child welfare, early childhood development, fatherhood and parenting, evaluation, and indicators of child well-being.

Child Welfare League of America www.cwla.org

The Child Welfare League of America represents a coalition of public and private child welfare agencies throughout the United States and Canada. They are advocates for children and families (through policy and practice initiatives) and are a leading influence (via research, publications, and training) in the establishment of practice standards for child welfare.

National Child Welfare Workforce institute www.ncwwi.org

The National Child Welfare Workforce Institute provides resources, information, training, and networking opportunities for practitioners, supervisors, and administrators in the effort to improve outcomes for children and families through workforce development.

National Indian Child Welfare Association www.nicwa.org

The National Indian Child Welfare Association (NICWA) provides assistance to tribes and other service providers to ensure services are provided from a community and strengths-based perspective and in compliance with the Indian Child Welfare Act of 1978 (ICWA). The organization is engaged in advocacy, community development, technical assistance, training, and research.

FRIENDS National Resource Center for Community-Based Child Abuse Prevention http://friendsnrc.org

Family Resource Information, Education, and Network Development Services (FRIENDS) created this Web site to help provide technical assistance and training to Community-Based Child Abuse Prevention (CBCAP) state lead agencies in their ability to maximize their ability to meet CBCAP program requirements dealing with (although not limited to) outcome accountability, parent leadership, evidence-based and evidence-informed practices, and system change.

References

Aaron, H. J. (1978). *Politics and the professors: The great society in perspective.* Washington, DC: Brookings Institute Press.

Abbott, E. (1933). Education for social work. In F. S. Hall (Ed.), *Social work yearbook: 1933.* New York, NY: Sage.

Administration for Children and Families. (2004). General findings from the federal child and family services review. Retrieved March 17, 2005, from www.acf.dhhs.gov/programs/cb/cwrp/results.htm

American Association of Schools of Social Work. (1942). *Education for the public social services*. Chapel Hill, NC: University of North Carolina Press.

American Association of Social Workers. (1936). We stand up to be counted. *Compass*, *17*(7), 1.

American Association of Social Workers. (1938). Report of special committee on structure and participation. *Compass*, *19*(9), 15–24.

American Association of Social Workers. (1945). School enrollment increases. *Compass*, *26*(2), 8–12.

American Association of Social Workers. (1946). Students in schools of social work. *Compass*, *27*(3), 25–28.

American Public Human Services Association. (2005). *Report from the 2004 child welfare workforce survey: State agency findings*. Washington, DC: Author.

American Public Welfare Association. (1958). *Planning, costs and procedures in public welfare administration*. Chicago, IL: Author.

Anderson, R. (2004, January/February). The child welfare workforce gets wired. *Children's Voice*, 32–33.

Austin, D. M. (1978). Research and social work: Educational paradoxes and possibilities. *Journal of Social Service Research*, *2*(2), 159–176.

Barbee, A. P., Antle, B., Sullivan, D. J., Huebner, R., Fox, S., & Hall, J. C. (2009). Recruiting and retaining child welfare workers: Is preparing social work students enough for sustained commitment to the field? *Child Welfare*, *88*(5), 69–86.

Barker, R. L., & Briggs, T. L. (1968). *Differential use of social work manpower: An analysis and demonstration study*. New York, NY: National Association of Social Workers Press.

Barr, N. (1987). *The economics of the welfare state*. Stanford, CA: Stanford University Press.

Barth, R. P. (2005). Child welfare and race: Models of disproportionality. In D. Derezotes, J. Poertner, & M. Testa (Eds.), *Race matters in child welfare: The overrepresentation of African American children in the system* (pp. 25–46). Washington, DC: Child Welfare League of America.

Barth, R. P., Berrick, J. D., & Gilbert, N. (Eds.). (1994). *Child welfare research review* (Vol. I). New York, NY: Columbia University Press.

Barth, R. P., & Berry, M. (1987). Outcomes of child welfare services under permanency planning. *Social Service Review*, *61*, 71–90.

Barth, R. P., & Berry, M. (1994). Implications of research on the welfare of children under permanency planning. In R. P. Barth, J. D. Berrick, & N. Gilbert (Eds.), *Child welfare research review* (pp. 323–368). New York, NY: Columbia University Press.

Barth, R. P., Courtney, M., Berrick, J. D., & Albert, V. (1994). *Pathways through child welfare services: From child abuse to permanency planning*. New York, NY: Aldine de Gruyter.

Barth, R. P., Crea, T. M., John, K., Thoburn, J., & Quinton, D. (2005). Beyond attachment theory and therapy: Towards sensitive and evidence-based interventions with foster and adoptive families in distress. *Child and Family Social Work*, *10*, 257–268.

Bartlett, H. M. (1957). *50 years of social work in the medical setting: Past significance/future outlook*. New York, NY: National Association of Social Workers Press.

Barton Child Law and Policy Clinic. (2002). *Workplace supports to improve Georgia's Child Protective Services*. Atlanta, GA: Emory University.

Beck, B. M. (1969). Nonprofessional social work personnel. In C. Grosser, W. E. Henry, & J. G. Kelley (Eds.), *Nonprofessionals in the human services* (pp. 66–77). San Francisco, CA: Jossey-Bass.

Beggs, M. (1996). *In a day's work: Four child welfare workers in California*. San Francisco, CA: San Francisco Study Center.

Berrick, J., Barth, R. P., & Gilbert, N. (Eds.). (1996). *Child welfare research review* (Vol. 2). New York, NY: Columbia University Press.

Berrick, J., Barth, R. P., & Needell, B. (1994). A comparison of kinship foster homes and foster family homes. *Children and Youth Service Review, 16*(1/2), 33–63.

Berrick, J., Needell, B., Shlonsky, A., Simmel, C., & Pedrucci, C. (1998). *Assessment, support, and training for kinship care and foster care: An empirically based curriculum*. Berkeley, CA: University of California, Berkeley Child Welfare Research Center.

Blome, W. W., & Steib, S. (2007). An examination of oversight and review in the child welfare system: The many watch the few serve the many. *Journal of Public Child Welfare, 1*(3), 3–26.

Board of Social Work Examiners. (1950). *Report of survey of social workers registered in California*. San Francisco, CA: Author.

Board of Social Work Examiners. (1958). *Sixth biennial report to the governor*. Sacramento, CA: Author.

Booz-Allen & Hamilton, Inc. (1987). *The Maryland social work services job analysis and personnel qualifications study*. Baltimore, MD: Maryland Department of Human Resources.

Briar, K., Hansen, V., & Harris, N. (Eds.). (1992). *New partnerships: Proceedings from the national public child welfare symposium*. Miami, FL: Florida International University.

Briar-Lawson, K., & Wiesen, M. (1999). Effective partnership models between state agencies, the university, and community service providers. In *Child welfare training symposium: Changing paradigms of child welfare practice: Responding to opportunities and challenges* (pp. 73–86). Washington, DC: U.S. Children's Bureau.

Brown, C. L. (1920). Coordinating the work of public and private agencies in probation service. In *Proceedings of the national conference of social work at the forty-seventh annual session*. Chicago, IL: University of Chicago Press.

Bunker, D., & Wijnberg, M. (1988). *Supervision and performance: Managing professional work in human service organizations*. San Francisco, CA: Jossey-Bass.

Bureau of the Census. (1914). *Population 1910: Occupation statistics*. Washington, DC: U.S. Government Printing Office.

Bureau of the Census. (1915). *Index to occupations: Alphabetical and classified*. Washington, DC: U.S. Government Printing Office.

Bureau of the Census. (1921). *Classified index to occupations*. Washington, DC: U.S. Government Printing Office.

Bureau of the Census. (1923). *Abstract of the fourteenth census of the United States: 1920*. Washington, DC: U.S. Government Printing Office.

Bureau of the Census. (1930). *Alphabetical index of occupations: Fifteenth census of the United States*. Washington, DC: U.S. Government Printing Office.

Bureau of the Census. (1940). *Alphabetical index of occupations and industries: Sixteenth census of the United States*. Washington, DC: U.S. Government Printing Office.

Bureau of the Census. (1950). *1950 census of population: Alphabetical index of occupations and industries*. Washington, DC: U.S. Government Printing Office.

Bureau of Labor Statistics. (1952). *Social workers in 1950*. New York, NY: American Association of Social Workers.

Bureau of Labor Statistics. (1962). *Salaries and working conditions of social welfare manpower in 1960*. New York, NY: National Social Welfare Assembly.

Bureau of Labor Statistics. (2006). Occupational outlook handbook, 2006–2007 edition. Social workers. Retrieved March 21, 2006, from www.bls.gov/oco/ocos060.htm

Bureau of Research and Statistics. (1956). *Survey of interest in professional social work training*. Sacramento, CA: State of California Department of Social Welfare.

Cahalane, H., & Sites, E. W. (2004). *Is it hot or cold? The climate of child welfare employee retention*. Unpublished manuscript, University of Pittsburgh.

Cahalane, H. & Sites, E. W. (2009). "The climate of child welfare employee retention." *Child Welfare, 87*(1), 91–114.

California Social Work Education Center. (2006). *Critical thinking in child welfare assessment: Safety, risk and protective capacity: Trainer's guide*. Berkeley, CA: Author. Retrieved March 2, 2007, from http://calswec.berkeley.edu/CalSWEC/Assess_Trainer_Binder_v1_1.pdf.

Cannon, I. M. (1913). *Social work in hospitals: A contribution to progressive medicine*. New York, NY: Sage.

Center for Health Workforce Studies & Center for Workforce Studies. (2006). *Licensed social workers in the U.S., 2004*. Washington, DC: National Association of Social Workers Press.

Centers for Disease Control and Prevention (1997). Adverse childhood experiences study. Retrieved from www.cdc.gov/ace/index.htm

Chaffin, M., & Friedrich, W. (2004). Evidence-based treatments in child abuse and neglect. *Children and Youth Services Review, 26*, 1097–1103.

Chenot, D., Benton, A. D. & Hansung, K. (2009). The influence of supervisor support, peer support, and organizational culture among early career social workers in child welfare services. *Child Welfare, 88*(5), 129–147.

Chernin, M., & Taylor, H. B. (1966). Principles of organization of undergraduate social service education programs: Content and supporting courses. In *Observations on undergraduate social welfare education*. New York, NY: Council on Social Work Education.

Cheung, M., & Taylor, T. (2005). National survey of IV-E stipends and paybacks. Retrieved October 29, 2005, from www.uh.edu/ocp/CWEP/State%20Stipend%203—05.pdf

Child Welfare League of America. (1984). *CWLA standards for organization and administration for all child welfare services*. Washington, DC: Author.

Child Welfare League of America. (1991). *A blueprint for fostering infants, children, and youths in the 1990s*. Washington, DC: Author.

Child Welfare League of America. (1993). *The child welfare state book*. Washington, DC: Author.

Child Welfare League of America. (1995). *CWLA standards of excellence for family foster care services*. Washington, DC: Author.

Child Welfare League of America. (1998). *CWLA standards of excellence for services for abused or neglected children and their families*. Washington, DC: Author.

Child Welfare League of America. (1999a). *CWLA standards of excellence for kinship care services*. Washington, DC: Author.

Child Welfare League of America. (1999b). *Minimum education required by state child welfare agencies, percent, by degree type, state child welfare agency survey.* Washington, DC: Author.

Child Welfare League of America. (2000). *CWLA standards of excellence for adoption services.* Washington, DC: Author.

Child Welfare Training Institute. (1997). *Retention of child welfare caseworkers.* Portland, ME: Muskie School of Southern Maine and Bureau of Child and Family Services, Department of Human Services.

Children's Bureau. (1940). *Child welfare services under the Social Security Act, Appendix: Text of the sections of the Social Security Act relating to grants to states for child welfare services* (Publication #257). Washington, DC: U.S. Department of Labor.

Children's Bureau. (2000). *Symposium on the third national incidence study of child abuse and neglect: A summary report on proceedings, February 24–25, 1997.* Washington, DC: U.S. Department of Health and Human Services.

Clark, E. J. (2003). Written testimony of Elizabeth J. Clark, executive director national association of social workers for the human resources subcommittee U.S. committee on ways and means. Retrieved January 5, 2005, from www.socialworkers.org/advocacy/issues/child_welfare.asp

Clark, S. (2003). The California collaboration: A competency-based child welfare curriculum project for master's social workers. *Journal of Human Behavior in the Social Environment,* 7(1/2), 135–157.

Clark, S., & Fulcher, G. (2005). *The 2004 California public child welfare workforce study.* Berkeley, CA: University of California, California Social Work Education Center, Berkeley School of Social Welfare.

Cohen, N. (1970). The schools of social work within the university system. In C. W. McCann (Ed.), *Exploring the interfaces of social work education* (pp. 19–42). Boulder, CO: Western Interstate Commission for Higher Education.

Collins-Camargo, C. (2005). *A study of the relationship among effective supervision, organizational culture promoting evidence-based practice, worker self-efficacy, and outcomes in public child welfare.* Unpublished doctoral dissertation, University of Kentucky, Lexington.

Collins-Camargo, C. (2006). Clinical supervision in public child welfare themes from findings of a multistate study. Professional development. *International Journal of Continuing Social Work Education,* 9(2/3), 100–110.

Collins-Camargo, C., Ensign, L. & Flaherty, C. (2008). The National Quality Improvement Center on the Privatization of Child Welfare Services. *Research on Social Work Practice,* 18(1), 72–81.

Collins-Camargo, C., Hall, J., Flaherty, C., Ensign, K, Garstka, T., Yoder, B., & Metz, A. (2007). Knowledge development and transfer on public/private partnerships in child welfare service provision: Using multisite research to expand the evidence base. *Professional Development: The International Journal of Continuing Social Work Education,* 10(3), 14–31.

Collins-Camargo, C., Sullivan, D. J., Washeck, B., Adams, J. & Sundet, P. (2009) One state's effort to improve recruitment, retention, and practice through multifaceted clinical supervision interventions. *Child Welfare,* 88(5), 87–107.

Computer Associates. (2004). CA child welfare solutions: Technology to help improve lives. Retrieved February 10, 2005, from www.ca.com/Files/Brochures/child_welfare_solutions.pdf

Compuware Corporation. (2005). Child welfare agency steps up service through automation with Compuware. Retrieved February 10, 2005, from www.compuware.com/pressroom/customers/2249_eng_html.htm

Conrad, I. F. (1930). Education for social work. In F. S. Hall (Ed.), *Social work yearbook: 1929* (pp. 148–154). New York, NY: Sage.

Cook, R. (1992). *A national evaluation of Title IV-E foster care independent living programs for youth: Phase 2 final report*. Rockville, MD: Westat.

Council on Accreditation for Children and Family Services. (2001). *COA standards and self-study manual, private organizations* (7th ed.). New York, NY: Author.

Council on Social Work Education. (Ed.). (1960). *Statistics on social work education: November 1, 1960, and academic year 1959–1960*. New York, NY: Author.

Council on Social Work Education. (Ed.). (1962a). *Statistics on social work education: November 1, 1961, and academic year 1961–1962*. New York, NY: Author.

Council on Social Work Education. (Ed.). (1962b). *Statistics on social work education: November 1, 1962, and academic year 1962–1963*. New York, NY: Author.

Council on Social Work Education. (Ed.). (1963). *Statistics on social work education: November 1, 1963, and academic year 1962–1963*. New York, NY: Author.

Council on Social Work Education. (Ed.). (1964). *Statistics on social work education: November 1, 1964, and academic year 1963–1964*. New York, NY: Author.

Courtney, M. E. (2000). Research needed to improve the prospects for children in out-of-home placement. *Children and Youth Services Review, 22*(9–10), 743–761.

Courtney, M. E., & Barth, R. P. (1996). Pathways of older adolescents out of foster care: Implications for independent living services. *Social Work, 41*(1), 75–83.

Courtney, M. E., & Needell, B. (1997). Outcomes of kinship foster care: Lessons from California. In R. P. Barth, J. D. Berrick, & N. Gilbert (Eds.), *Child welfare research review* (Vol. 2, pp. 130–149). New York, NY: Columbia University Press.

Courtney, M. E., & Skyles, A. (2003). Racial disproportionality in the child welfare system. *Children and Youth Services Review, 25*, 355–358.

Crosson-Tower, C. (2002). *Understanding child abuse and neglect* (5th ed.). Boston, MA: Allyn & Bacon.

Culbert, J. F. (1933). Visiting teachers. In F. S. Hall (Ed.), *Social work year book: 1933*. New York, NY: Sage.

Cyphers, G. (2001). *Report from the child welfare workforce study: State and county data and findings*. Washington, DC: American Public Human Services Association.

Daro, D., & Donnelly, A. C. (2003). Child abuse prevention: Accomplishments and challenges. Retrieved March 10, 2007, from www.endabuse.org/programs/children/files/prevention/ChildAbusePrevention.pdf

Daro, D., & McCurdy, K. (2006). Interventions to prevent child maltreatment. In L. S. Doll, S. E. Bonzo, J. A. Mercy, D. A. Sleet, & E. N. Haas (Eds.), *The handbook of injury and violence prevention*. New York, NY: Springer.

Daro, D., & Mitchel, L. (1990). *Current trends in child abuse reporting and fatalities: The results of the 1989 annual 50 states survey*. Washington, DC: National Commission for the Prevention of Child Abuse.

Dawson, K., & Berry, M. (2002). Engaging families in child welfare services: An evidence-based approach to best practice. *Child Welfare, 81*, 293–317.

Dea, K. L. (Ed.). (1966). *Statistics on social work education: November 1, 1965, and academic year 1964–1965*. New York, NY: Council on Social Work Education.

Deardorff, N. R. (1930). Social work as a profession. In F. S. Hall (Ed.), *Social work year book: 1929*. New York, NY: Sage.

Derezotes, D., Testa, M. F., & Poertner, J. (Eds.). (2005). *Race matters in child welfare: The overrepresentation of African American children in the system*. Washington, DC: Child Welfare League of America.

DeVera, R. (Ed.). (1966). *Statistics on social work education: November 1, 1966, and academic year 1965–1966*. New York, NY: Council on Social Work Education.

Devine, E. T. (1915). Education for social work. In *National conference of charities and correction*. Baltimore, MD: Hildemann.

Dhooper, S. S., Royse, D. D., & Wolfe, L. C. (1990). Does social work education make a difference? *Social Work, 35*(1), 57–61.

Dickinson, N. (2006). Commentary on "Do social workers make better child welfare workers than nonsocial workers?" by Robin Perry [Special issue]. *Research on Social Work Practice, 16*, 431–433.

Dickinson, N., & Perry, R. (2002). Factors influencing the retention of specially educated public child welfare workers. *Journal of Health and Social Policy, 15*(3/4), 89–103.

Dingwall, R. (1989). Some problems about predicting child abuse and neglect. In O. Stevenson (Ed.), *Child abuse: Professional practice and public policy* (pp. 28–53). London, UK: Harvester Wheatsheaf.

Dobelstein, A. W. (1985). The bifurcation of social work and social welfare: The political development of social services. *Urban and Social Change Review, 18*(2), 9–12.

Drake, B., & Washeck, J. (1998). A competency-based method for providing worker feedback to CPS supervisors. *Administration in Social Work, 22*(3), 55–74.

Dressel, P., Waters, M., Sweat, M., Clayton, O., & Chandler-Clayton, A. (1988). Deprofessionalization, proletarianization, and social welfare work. *Journal of Sociology and Social Welfare, 15*(2), 113–131.

Edwards, R. L. (1987). The competing values approach as an integrating framework for the management curriculum. *Administration in Social Work, 11*(1), 1–13.

Eldredge, J. F. (Ed.). (1971). *Statistics on social work education: November 1, 1971, and academic year 1970–1971*. New York, NY: Council on Social Work Education.

Ellett, A. J. (2000). *Human caring, self-efficacy beliefs, and professional organizational culture correlates of employee retention in child welfare*. Unpublished doctoral dissertation, Louisiana State University, Baton Rouge.

Ellett, A. J. (2006). Broad study but narrow question: A friendly critique of Perry's article. *Research on Social Work Practice, 16*, 406–411.

Ellett, A. J. (2007). Linking self-efficacy beliefs to employee retention in child welfare: Implications for theory, research, and practice. *Journal of Evidence-Based Social Work, 4*(3/4), 39–68.

Ellett, A. J., Collins-Camargo, C., & Ellett, C. D. (2006). Personal and organizational correlates of outcomes in child welfare: Implications for supervision and continuing professional development. *Professional Development: International Journal of Continuing Social Work Education, 9*(2/3), 44–53.

Ellett, A. J., Ellett, C. D., Ellis, J. I., & Lerner, C. B. (2009). A research-based child welfare employee selection protocol: Strengthening retention of the workforce. *Child Welfare, 88*, 49–68.

Ellett, A. J., Ellett, C. D., & Rugutt, J. K. (2003). *A study of personal and organizational factors contributing to employee retention and turnover in child welfare in Georgia.* Athens, GA: University of Georgia, School of Social Work.

Ellett, A. J., Ellett, C. D., Westbrook, T. M., & Lerner, B. (2006). Toward the development of a research-based employee selection protocol: Implications for child welfare supervision, administration, and professional development. *Professional Development: International Journal of Continuing Social Work Education, 9*(2/3), 111–120.

Ellett, A. J., Ellis, J., Westbrook, T., & Dews, D. G. (2007). A qualitative study of 369 child welfare professionals' perspectives about factors contributing to employee retention and turnover. *Children and Youth Services Review, 29*, 264–281.

Ellett, A. J., & Leighninger, L. (2007). What happened? An historical analysis of the deprofessionalization of child welfare with implications for policy and practice. *Journal of Public Child Welfare, 1*(1), 3–33.

Ellett, A. J., & Steib, S. D. (2005). Child welfare and the courts: A statewide study with implications for professional development, practice and change. *Research on Social Work Practice, 15*(5), 339–352.

Ellett, C. D. (1995). *A study of professional personnel needs* (Vol. 1). Baton Rouge, LA: Louisiana State University, Office of Research and Economic Development.

Ellis, J. I., Ellett, A. J., & DeWeaver, K. (2007). Human caring in the social work context: Continued development and validation of a complex measure. *Research on Social Work Practice, 17*, 66–76.

Falck, H. S. (1984). A loud and shrill protest. *Journal of Education for Social Work, 20*(2), 3–4.

Fanshel, D. (1962). Research in child welfare: A critical analysis. *Child Welfare, 41*(10), 484–507.

Fanshel, D., & Maas, H. (1962). Factorial dimensions of the characteristics of children in placement and their families. *Child Development, 33*, 123–144.

Fanshel, D., & Shinn, E. (1978). *Children in foster care: A longitudinal investigation.* New York, NY: Columbia University Press.

Flaherty, C., Collins-Camargo, C., & Lee, E. (2008a). Privatization of child welfare services: Lessons learned from experienced states. *Professional Development: The International Journal of Continuing Social Work Education, 11*(1), 6–18.

Flaherty, C., Collins-Camargo, C., & Lee, E. (2008b). Privatization of child welfare services: Lessons learned from experienced states regarding site readiness assessment and planning. *Children and Youth Services Review, 30*(7), 809–820.

Fleischer, B. J. (1985). Identification and strategies to reduce turnover among child welfare case workers. *Child Care Quarterly, 14*(2), 130–139.

Flexner, A. (1915). Is social work a profession? In *National Conference of Charities and Corrections.* Baltimore, MD: Hildemann.

Fox, S., Miller, V., & Barbee, A. P. (2003). Finding and keeping child welfare workers: Effective use of training and professional development. *Journal of Human Behavior in the Social Environment, 7*(1/2), 67–81.

Frabricant, M. (1985). The industrialization of social work practice. *Social Work, 30*(5), 389–395.

French, D. (1947). The schools report: Statistics on social work education. *Compass, 28*(3), 15–20.

French, D., & Rosen, A. (1958). Personnel entering social work employment from schools of social work, 1957. In *Recruitment for social work education and social work practice*. New York, NY: Council on Social Work Education.

Gambrill, E. (2003). Evidence-based practice: Implications for knowledge development and use in social work. In A. Rosen & E. K. Proctor (Eds.), *Developing practice guidelines for social work intervention: Issues, methods, and research agenda* (pp. 37–58). New York, NY: Columbia University Press.

Gansle, K., & Ellett, A. (2002). Child welfare knowledge transmission, practitioner retention, and university-community impact: A study of Title IV-E child welfare training. *Journal of Health and Social Policy, 15*(3/4), 69–88.

Getzel, G. S. (1983). Speculations on the crisis in social work recruitment: Some modest proposals. *Social Work, 28*(3), 235–237.

Gibbs, L. (2003). *Evidence-based practice for the helping professions: A practical guide with integrated media*. Monterey, CA: Brooks/Cole.

Gibbs, L., & Gambrill, E. (1999). *Critical thinking for social workers: Exercises for the helping professions* (2nd ed.). Thousand Oaks, CA: Pine Forge Press.

Gibelman, M., & Schervish, P. H. (1993). *Who we are: The social work labor force as reflected in the NASW membership*. Washington, DC: National Association of Social Workers Press.

Gibelman, M., & Schervish, P. H. (1997). *Who we are: A second look*. Washington, DC: National Association of Social Workers Press.

Ginsberg, M. I., Shiffman, B. M., & Rogers, M. (1971). Nonprofessionals in social work. In C. Grosser, W. E. Henry, & J. G. Kelley (Eds.), *Nonprofessionals in the human services* (pp. 193–202). San Francisco, CA: Jossey-Bass.

Ginsburg, N. (1979). *Class, capital and social policy*. London: Macmillan.

Gleeson, J. P. (1992, Fall). How do child welfare caseworkers learn? *Adult Education Quarterly, 43*, 15–29.

Glisson, C., & Durick, M. (1988). Predictors of job satisfaction and organizational commitment in human service organizations. *Administrative Science Quarterly, 33*(1), 61–81.

Goldmark, J. (1953). *Impatient crusader*. Urbana, IL: University of Illinois Press.

Grossman, B., Laughlin, S., & Specht, H. (1992). Building the commitment of social work education to publicly sponsored social services: The California model. In K. Briar, V. Hansen, & N. Harris (Eds.), *New partnerships: Proceedings from the National Public Welfare Training Symposium, 1991* (pp. 55–72). Miami, FL: Florida International University.

Groulx, L. (1983). Deprofessionalization of social services: Demands of democracy or pretensions to a new power? *International Social Work, 26*(3), 38–44.

Hegar, R. L., & Scannapieco, M. (Eds.). (1999). *Kinship foster care: Practice, policy, and research*. New York, NY: Oxford University Press.

Henry, S. (1990). Nonsalary retention incentives for social workers in public mental health. *Administration in Social Work, 14*(3), 1–15.

Hidalgo, J., & Spaulding, E. C. (1987). *Statistics on social work education in the United States: 1986*. Washington, DC: Council on Social Work Education.

Hodson, W. (1925). Is social work professional? A reexamination of the question. In *Proceedings of the National Conference of Social Work at the Fifty-Second Annual Session*. Chicago, IL: University of Chicago Press.

Hopkins, K. M., Mudrick, N. R., & Rudolph, C. S. (1999). Impact of university–agency partnerships in child welfare on organizations, workers, and work activities. *Child Welfare, 78*(6), 749–773.

Horejsi, C., Bertsche, J., Francetich, S., Collins, B., & Francetich, R. (1987). Protocols in child welfare: An example. *Child Welfare, 65*, 423–431.

Hughes, R. C., & Baird, C. (2006). B.A.s are B.S. in child welfare: Did anybody learn anything? *Research on Social Work Practice, 16*, 434–437.

Jones, L. P., & Okamura, A. (2000). Reprofessionalizing child welfare services: An evaluation of a Title IV-E training program. *Research on Social Work Practice, 10*, 607–621.

Kadushin, A. (1965). Introductions of new orientations in child welfare research. In M. Norris & B. Wallace (Eds.), *The known and unknown in child welfare research: An appraisal* (pp. 28–39). New York, NY: Child Welfare League of America.

Kadushin, A. (1970). *Adopting older children.* New York, NY: Columbia University Press.

Kadushin, A. (1985). *Supervision in social work* (2nd ed.). New York, NY: Columbia University Press.

Kadushin, A. (1992). *Supervision in social work* (3rd ed.). New York, NY: Columbia University Press.

Kadushin, A., & Seidl, F. W. (1971). Adoption failure: A social work postmortem. *Social Work, 16*, 32–38.

Karger, H. J. (1982). Reclassification: Is there a future in public welfare for the trained social worker? *Social Work, 28*(6), 427–433.

Katz, A. J. (1982). Social work education: The near future. *Administration in Social Work, 6*(2/3), 147–157.

Kelley, P., & Alexander, P. (1985). Part-time private practice: Practical and ethical considerations. *Social Work, 30*(3), 254–258.

Kendall, K. (1964). Expansion and improved quality. *Social Work Education, 12*(6), 1, 27–31.

Kershaw, S. (2002, September 3). Digital photos give the police a new edge in abuse cases [electronic version]. *New York Times*, p. A1.

King, G., Trocmé, N., & Thatte, N. (2003). Substantiation as a multitier process: The results of a NIS-3 analysis. *Child Maltreatment, 8*, 173–182.

Landsman, M. J. (2001). Commitment in public child welfare. *Social Services Review, 75*, 386–419.

Lee, P., & Kenworthy, M. (1929). *Mental hygiene and social work.* New York, NY: Commonwealth Fund.

Lennon, T. M. (1992). *Statistics on social work education in the United States: 1991.* Alexandria, VA: Council on Social Work Education.

Lennon, T. M. (1993). *Statistics on social work education in the United States: 1992.* Alexandria, VA: Council on Social Work Education.

Lennon, T. M. (1994). *Statistics on social work education in the United States: 1993.* Alexandria, VA: Council on Social Work Education.

Lennon, T. M. (1995). *Statistics on social work education in the United States: 1994.* Alexandria, VA: Council on Social Work Education.

Lennon, T. M. (1996). *Statistics on social work education in the United States: 1995.* Alexandria, VA: Council on Social Work Education.

Lewandowski, C. A. (1998). Retention outcomes of a public child welfare long-term training program. *Professional Development: International Journal of Continuing Social Work Education, 1*, 38–46.

Lieberman, A., Hornby, H., & Russell, M. (1988). Analyzing the educational backgrounds and work experiences of child welfare personnel: A national study. *Social Work, 33*, 485–489.

Lieberman, A., & Levy, M. M. (2006). The (mis)measurement of job performance in child welfare using (non)experimental design. *Research on Social Work Practice, 16*, 417–418.

Lindsey, D. (1991a). Factors affecting the foster care placement decision: An analysis of national survey data. *American Journal of Orthopsychiatry, 61,* 272–281.

Lindsey, D. (1991b). Reliability of the foster care placement decision: A review. *Research in Social Work Practice, 2,* 65–80.

Lindsey, D. (2004). *The welfare of children.* New York, NY: Oxford University Press.

Lindsey, D., Martin, S., & Doh, J. (2002). The failure of intensive casework services to reduce foster care placements: An examination of family preservation studies. *Children and Youth Services Review, 24,* 743–775.

Loewenberg, F. M. (Ed.). (1967). *Statistics on social work education: November 1, 1967, and academic year 1966–1967.* New York, NY: Council on Social Work Education.

Loewenberg, F. M. (1968). *Statistics on social work education: November 1, 1968, and academic year 1967–1968.* New York, NY: Council on Social Work Education.

Loewenberg, F. M. (Ed.). (1970). *Statistics on social work education: November 1, 1970, and academic year 1969–1970.* New York, NY: Council on Social Work Education.

Loewenberg, F. M., & Shey, T. H. (Ed.). (1969). *Statistics on social work education: November 1, 1969, and academic year 1968–1969.* New York, NY: Council on Social Work Education.

Lowrey, L. G. (1926). Some trends in the development of relationships between psychiatry and general social case work. *Mental Hygiene, 10*(2), 277–284.

Maas, H., & Engler, R. (1959). *Children in need of parents.* New York, NY: Columbia University Press.

Macdonald, V. M. (1920). *Social work and the national committee for mental hygiene.* In *Proceedings of the national conference of social work at the forty-seventh annual session.* Chicago, IL: University of Chicago Press.

Malm, K., Bess, R., Leos-Urbel, J., Green, R., & Markowitz, T. (2001). *Running to keep in place: The continuing evolution of our nation's child welfare system* (Occasional Paper No. 54). Washington, DC: Urban Institute.

Maluccio, A., Fein, E., & Olmstead, K. (1986). *Permanency planning for children: Concepts and methods.* New York, NY: Tavistock.

McBeath, B., Collins-Camargo, C., & Chuang, E. (2011). *Portrait of private agencies in the child welfare system: Principal results from the national survey of private child and family serving agencies.* Quality Improvement Center on the Privatization of Child Welfare Services: Publisher.

McCarthy, M. L. (2004). The relationship between supervision and casework retention in county based child welfare systems. *Dissertation Abstracts International: A. Humanities and Social Sciences, 65*(3), 1119A.

McCarthy, M. L. (2006). The context and process for performance evaluations: Necessary preconditions for the use of performance evaluations as a measure of performance–A critique of Perry. *Research on Social Work Practice, 16,* 419–423.

McDonald, J., & McCarthy, B. (1999). Effective partnership models between the state agencies, community, the university, and community service providers. In *Child Welfare Training Symposium: Changing Paradigms of Child Welfare Practice: Responding to Opportunities and Challenges* (pp. 43–72). Washington, DC: U.S. Children's Bureau.

McNeely, R. L. (1989). Gender, job satisfaction, earning, and other characteristics of human service workers during and after midlife. *Administration in Social Work, 13*(2), 99–116.

Menefee, D. (1998). Identifying and comparing competencies for social work management: II. A replication study. *Administration in Social Work, 22*(4), 53–61.

Menefee, D., & Thompson, J. (1994). Identifying and comparing competencies for social work management: A practice driven approach. *Administration in Social Work, 18*(3), 1–25.

Meredith, L. A. (1933). Education and social work. In F. S. Hall (Ed.), *Social work year book: 1933* (pp. 137–142). New York, NY: Sage.

Microsoft. (2004a). Child care and welfare systems from Microsoft partners. Retrieved February 10, 2005, from www.microsoft.com/Resources/Government/welfare.aspx?pf=true

Microsoft. (2004b). Florida child welfare agency improves care for kids and use of resources. Retrieved March 28, 2005, from www.microsoft.com/resources/casestudies/CaseStudy.asp?CaseStudyID=15543

Middleman, R. R., & Rhodes, G. B. (1985). *Competent supervision.* Englewood Cliffs, NJ: Prentice-Hall.

Miller, J. (2001). PDAs cut social workers' paper. Government Computer News, 7(12). Retrieved February 10, 2005, from www.gcn.com/state/7_12/tech-report/16783–1.html

Mor Barak, M., Nissly, J., & Levin, A. (2001). Antecedents to retention and turnover among child welfare, social work, and other human service employees: What can we learn from past research? A review and meta-analysis. *Social Service Review, 75*, 625–661.

Morton, T. D., & Salas, M. K. (1994). *Supervising child protective services caseworkers.* Washington, DC: U.S. Department of Health and Human Services, Administration for Children and Families.

National Association of Foster Care Reviewers. (n.d.). Foster care review: Past and present. Retrieved March 2, 2006, from www.nafcr.org/docs/foster_cae_review

National Association of Public Child Welfare Administrators. (1987). *Guidelines for a model system of protective services for abused and neglected children and their families.* Washington, DC: American Public Welfare Association.

National Association of Public Child Welfare Administrators. (2005). *Guide for child welfare administrators on evidence-based practice.* Washington, DC: American Public Human Services Association. Available from www.aphsa.org/home/doc/Guide-for-Evidence-Based-Practice.pdf

National Association of Social Workers. (1983). Membership survey shows practice shifts. *NASW News, 28*, 6–7.

National Association of Social Workers. (2004a). The case for retaining the Title IV-E child welfare training program. Retrieved March 1, 2005, from www.socialworkers.org/advocacy/updates/2003/081204b.asp

National Association of Social Workers. (2004b). Fact sheet: Title IV-E child welfare training program. Retrieved January 20, 2005, from www.socialworkers.org/advocacy/updates/2003/081204a.asp

National Association of Social Workers. (2004c). *If you're right for the job, it's the best job in the world.* Washington, DC: Author.

National Association of Social Workers. (2005). *NASW standards for social work practice in child welfare.* Washington, DC: Author.

National Center for Child Abuse and Neglect. (1988). *Study findings: Study of national incidence and prevalence of child abuse and neglect*. Washington, DC: U.S. Department of Health and Human Services.

National Resource Center for Information Technology in Child Welfare. (2002). Handheld devices and social work practice. NRC-ITCW Tips, Tools, and Trends, 3. Retrieved March 24, 2005, from www.nrccwdt.org/docs/ttt_handheld.pdf

National Resource Center for Information Technology in Child Welfare. (2003). Document imaging promising practice. *NRC-ITCW Tips, Tools and Trends*, 7. Retrieved March 24, 2005, from www.nrccwdt.org/docs/ttt_docimg.pdf

Needell, B., Brookhart, A., & Lee, S. (2003). Black children and foster care placement in California. *Children and Youth Services Review, 25*(5/6), 393–408.

Niec, L., Eyberg, S., & Chase, R. (2011). Parent-child interaction therapy: Implementing and sustaining a treatment program for families of young children with disruptive behavior disorders. In A. Rubin (Ed.), *Programs and interventions for maltreated children and families at risk*. Hoboken, NJ: John Wiley & Sons.

Norris, M., & Wallace, B. (Eds.). (1965). *The known and unknown in child welfare research: An appraisal*. New York, NY: Child Welfare League of America.

NPower New York. (2002). Mobile technology in the nonprofit world. Retrieved February 10, 2005, from www.npowerny.org/tools/mobilereport1.pdf

O'Conner, I., Dalgleish, L., & Khan, J. (1984). A reflection of the rising spectre of conservatism: Motivational accounts of social work students. *British Journal of Social Work, 14*(3), 227–240.

Oktay, J. S. (1992). Burnout in hospital social workers who work with AIDS patients. *Social Work, 37*(5), 432–439.

Olsen, L., & Holmes, W. (1982). Educating child welfare workers: The effects of professional training on service delivery. *Journal of Education for Social Work, 18*(1), 94–102.

Quality Improvement Center on Privatization in Child Welfare. (2006). *Literature review on the privatization of child welfare services. Planning and learning*. Lexington, KY: University of Kentucky, & Technologies.

Panel on Research on Child Abuse and Neglect, Commission. (1993). *Understanding child abuse and neglect (Report of the Commission on Behavioral and Social Sciences and Education of the National Research Council)*. Washington, DC: National Academy Press.

Pecora, P., Briar, K., & Zlotnik, J. (1989). *Addressing the program and personnel crisis in child welfare: A social work response*. Silver Springs, MD: National Association of Social Workers Press.

Pecora, P., Fraser, M., & Haapala, D. (1991). Client outcomes and issues for program design. In K. Wells & D. Biegel (Eds.), *Family preservation services: Research and evaluation* (pp. 3–32). Newbury Park, CA: Sage.

Pecora, P., Whitaker, J., Maluccio, A., Barth, R., & Plotnick, R. (2000). *The child welfare challenge: Policy, practice, and research*. New York, NY: Aldine de Gruyter.

Perry, R. (2001). The classification, intercorrelation, and dynamic nature of MSW student practice preferences. *Journal of Social Work Education, 37*, 523–542.

Perry, R. (2004). Factors influencing MSW students' interest in public child welfare. *Journal of Human Behavior in the Social Environment, 10*(2), 1–31.

Perry, R. (2006a). Do social workers make better child welfare workers than nonsocial workers? *Research on Social Work Practice, 16*, 392–405.

Perry, R. (2006b). Education and child welfare supervisor performance: Does a social work degree matter? *Research on Social Work Practice*, *16*, 591–604.

Perry, R., Graham, J., Kerce, K., & Babcock, P. (2004, August). *Determining workload standards for child protective services: Overview of an interactive web-based data collection instrument*. Paper presented at the 44th annual workshop of the national association for welfare research and statistics. Oklahoma City, Oklahoma.

Perry, R., & Houlious, C. (2006). *The partnership for strong families task analysis study*. Tallahassee, FL: Institute for Child and Family Services Research.

Pigou, A. C. (1952). *The economics of welfare* (4th ed.). London, UK: Macmillan.

Pins, A. M. (1965). Development of social work recruitment: A historical review. *Social Service Review*, *39*(1), 53–62.

Potter, C. C., Comstock, A., Brittain, C., & Hanna, M. (2009). Intervening in multiple states: Findings from the Western Regional Recruitment Project. *Child Welfare* *88*(5), 169–185.

Preston, M. S. (2004). Mandatory management training for newly hired child welfare supervisors: A divergence between management research and training practice? *Administration in Social Work*, *28*(2), 81–97.

Pumphrey, R. E., & Pumphrey, M. W. (1961). *The heritage of American social work: Readings in its philosophical and institutional development*. New York, NY: Columbia University Press.

Purvine, M. (Ed.). (1972). *Statistics on graduate social work education in the United States: 1972*. New York, NY: Council on Social Work Education.

Reeser, L. C., & Epstein, I. (1990). *Professionalization and activism in social work: The sixties, the eighties, and the future*. New York, NY: Columbia University Press.

Reisch, M., & Wenocur, S. (1986). The future of community organization in social work: Social activism and the politics of profession building. *Social Service Review*, *60*(1), 70–93.

Renner, L. M., Porter, R. L., & Preister S., (2009). Improving the retention of child welfare workers by strengthening skills and increasing support for supervisors. *Child Welfare* *88*(5), 109.

Richmond, M. (1897). The need of a training school in applied philanthropy. In I. C. Barrows (Ed.), *Proceedings of the National Conference of Charities and Correction* (pp. 181–186). Toronto, Ontario, Canada: George H. Ellis.

Ripple, L. (Ed.). (1974). *Statistics on graduate social work education in the United States: 1973*. New York, NY: Council on Social Work Education.

Ripple, L. (Ed.). (1975). *Statistics on social work education in the United States: 1974*. New York, NY: Council on Social Work Education.

Risley-Curtiss, C. (2003). Current challenges and future directions for collaborative child welfare educational programs. *Journal of Human Behavior in the Social Environment*, *7*(1/2), 207–226.

Rittner, B., & Wodarski, J. S. (1999). Differential uses for BSW and MSW educated social workers in child welfare services. *Children and Youth Services Review*, *21*, 217–238.

Roberts, A., & Yaeger, K. (Eds.). (2006). *Foundations of evidence-based social work practice*. New York, NY: Oxford University Press.

Rogers, C. M., Gray, E., & Aitken, S. (1992). *Final report: Summary proceedings and recommendations of the National Incidence Study Expert Conference*. Washington, DC: Consulting Services and Research.

Rosenthal, J. A., McDowell, E. C., & White, T. L. (1998). *Retention of child welfare workers in Oklahoma.* Norman, OK: University of Oklahoma, School of Social Work.

Rosenthal, J. A., & Waters, E. (2004, July). *Retention and performance in public child welfare in Oklahoma: Focus on the child welfare professional enhancement program graduates.* Paper presented at the Weaving Resources for Better Child Welfare Outcomes Conference, Santa Fe, NM.

Ross, B., & Lichtenberg, P. (1963). *Enrollment in schools of social work.* New York, NY: Council on Social Work Education.

Rossi, P. H. (1994). Review of *Families in crisis. Children and Youth Services Review, 16,* 461–465.

Rothman, J. (1991). A model of case management: Toward empirically based practice. *Social Work, 36,* 520–528.

Rubin, A. (Ed.). (1981). *Statistics on social work education in the United States: 1980.* New York, NY: Council on Social Work Education.

Rubin, A. (1982). *Statistics on social work education in the United States: 1981.* New York, NY: Council on Social Work Education.

Rubin, A. (1983). *Statistics on social work education in the United States: 1982.* New York, NY: Council on Social Work Education.

Rubin, A. (1984). *Statistics on social work education in the United States: 1983.* New York, NY: Council on Social Work Education.

Rubin, A. (1985). *Statistics on social work education in the United States: 1984.* Washington, DC: Council on Social Work Education.

Rubin, A. (2011). Clinician's guide to evidence-based practice: Programs and interventions for maltreated children and families at risk. Hoboken, NJ: John Wiley & Sons.

Rubin, A., & Johnson, P. J. (1984). Direct practice interests of entering MSW students. *Journal of Education for Social Work, 20*(2), 5–16.

Rubin, A., & Whitcomb, G. R. (Eds.). (1978). *Statistics on social work education in the United States: 1977.* New York, NY: Council on Social Work Education.

Rubin, A., & Whitcomb, G. R. (Eds.). (1979). *Statistics on social work education in the United States: 1978.* New York, NY: Council on Social Work Education.

Russell, M., & Hornby, H. (1987). 1987 *National Study of Public Child Welfare Job Requirements.* Portland, ME: University of Southern Maine, National Child Welfare Resource Center for Management and Administration.

Ruston, A., & Nathan, J. (1996). The supervision of child protection work. *British Journal of Social Work, 26,* 357–374.

Rycus, J., & Hughes, R. (1994). *Child welfare competencies: Promoting family-centered, culturally relevant, and interdisciplinary child welfare practice and training.* Columbus, OH: Institute for Human Services.

Rycus, J., & Hughes, R. (1998). *Field guide to child welfare* (Vols. 1–4). Washington, DC: Child Welfare League of America.

Salas, M. (2004). *Supervising child protective services caseworkers.* Washington, DC: U.S. Department of Health and Human Services, Administration for Children and Families.

Samantrai, K. (1992). Factors in the decision to leave: Retaining social workers with MSWs in public child welfare. *Social Work, 37*(5), 454–458.

Scannapieco, M., & Connell-Carrick, K. (2003). Do collaborations with schools of social work make a difference for the field of child welfare? Practice, retention, and curriculum. *Journal of Human Behavior in the Social Environment, 7*(1/2), 35–51.

Sedlak, A. (1988). *Study of national incidence and prevalence of child abuse and neglect: Final report*. Washington, DC: U.S. Department of Health and Human Services.

Sedlak, A. (1991). *National incidence and prevalence of child abuse and neglect: 1988*. Rockville, MD: Westat.

Sedlak, A. (2001). *A history of the national incidence study of child abuse and neglect*. Rockville, MD: Westat.

Sedlak, A., & Broadhurst, D. D. (1996). *The third national incidence study of child abuse and neglect (NIS-3): Final report*. Washington, DC: U.S. Department of Health and Human Services, National Center on Child Abuse and Neglect.

Sedlak, A. J., Mettenburg, J., Basena, M., Petta, I., McPherson, K., Greene, A., & Li, S. (2010). *Fourth National Incidence Study of Child Abuse and Neglect (NIS–4): Report to Congress*. Washington, DC: U.S. Department of Health and Human Services, Administration for Children and Families.

Sheehan, J. C. (Ed.). (1976). *Statistics on social work education in the United States: 1975*. New York, NY: Council on Social Work Education.

Shlonsky, A., & Gambrill, E. (2001). The need for comprehensive risk management systems in child welfare. *Children and Youth Services Review, 23*, 79–107.

Shlonsky, A., & Gibbs, L. (2004). Will the real evidence-based practice please stand up? Teaching the process of evidence-based practice to the helping professions. *Brief Treatment and Crisis Intervention, 4*, 137–152.

Shlonsky, A., & Wagner, D. (2005). The next step: Integrating actuarial risk assessment and clinical judgment into an evidence-based practice framework in CPS case management. *Children and Youth Services Review, 27*, 409–427.

Shyne, A. W., & Whitcomb, G. R. (Eds.). (1977). *Statistics on social work education in the United States: 1976*. New York, NY: Council on Social Work Education.

Sklar, K. K. (1995). *Florence Kelley and the nation's work*. New Haven, CT: Yale University Press.

Smith, B. D. (2004). Job retention in child welfare: Effects of perceived organizational support, supervisor support, and intrinsic job value. *Children and Youth Services Review, 27*, 153–169.

Spaulding, E. C. (1988). *Statistics on social work education in the United States: 1987*. Washington, DC: Council on Social Work Education.

Spaulding, E. C. (1990). *Statistics on social work education in the United States: 1989*. Alexandria, VA: Council on Social Work Education.

Spaulding, E. C. (1991). *Statistics on social work education in the United States: 1990*. Alexandria, VA: Council on Social Work Education.

Specht, H., & Courtney, M. E. (1994). *Unfaithful angels: How social work has abandoned its mission*. New York, NY: Free Press.

Stein, T., & Gambrill, E. (1976). *Decision making in foster care: A training manual*. Berkeley, CA: University Extension Publications.

Stein, T., Gambrill, E., & Wiltse, K. T. (1978). *Children in foster homes: Achieving continuity of care*. New York, NY: Praegar Press.

Stein, T., & Rzepnicki, T. (1984). *Decision-making in child welfare services: Intake and planning*. Hingham, MA: Kluwer-Nijoff/Kluwer Academic.

Strolin-Goltzman, J., Lawrence, C., Auerback, C., Caringi, J., Claiborne, N., Lawson, H., McCarthy, M., McGowan, B., Sherman, R., & Shim, M. (2009). Design teams: A promising organizational intervention for improving turnover rates in the child welfare workforce. *Child Welfare, 88*(5), 149–168.

Swenson, C. C., & Schaeffer, C. M. (2011). Multisystemic therapy for child abuse and neglect. In A. Rubin (Ed.), *Clinician's guide to evidence-based practice: Programs and interventions for maltreated children and families at risk* (pp. 31–41). Hoboken, NJ: John Wiley & Sons.

Terpstra, J. (1996). *Child welfare, from there to where?* Unpublished manuscript, U.S. Children's Bureau, Washington, DC.

Thomlison, B. (2003). Characteristics of evidence-based child maltreatment interventions. *Child Welfare, 82*, 541–569.

Thomlison, B. (2005, September). Using evidence-based knowledge to improve policies and practices in child welfare: Current thinking and continuing challenges. *Research on Social Work Practice, 15*(5), 321–322.

Thyer, B. A., Williams, M., Love, J. P., & Sowers-Hoag, K. (1989). The MSW supervisory requirement in field instruction: Does it make a difference? *Clinical Supervisor, 6*, 249–256.

Tropman, J., Faller, K., & Feldt, S. (2004). *Essentials of supervisory skills for child welfare managers.* Ann Arbor, MI: University of Michigan, School of Social Work. Retrieved July 12, 2005, from www.umich.edu/tpcws/articles/EntireEditedManual_91404CE.pdf#search='child20welfare%20supervisors'

University of Southern Maine. (1987). *Professional social work practice in public child welfare: An agenda for action.* National Child Welfare Resource Center for Management Administration, Portland, ME: Author.

U.S. Advisory Board on Child Abuse and Neglect. (1990). *Child abuse and neglect: Critical first steps in response to a national emergency.* Washington, DC: U.S. Department of Health and Human Services.

U.S. Department of Health, Education, and Welfare. (1965). *Closing the gap in social work manpower: Report of the departmental task force on social work education and manpower.* Washington, DC: U.S. Government Printing Office.

U.S. Department of Health and Human Services. (1996). *National child abuse and neglect report.* Washington, DC: Author.

U.S. Department of Health and Human Services, Administration on Children, Youth, and Families. (1997). *Child maltreatment, 1995.* Washington, DC: U.S. Government Printing Office.

U.S. Department of Health and Human Services, Administration on Children, Youth, and Families. (2001). *Child maltreatment, 1999.* Washington, DC: U.S. Government Printing Office.

U.S. Department of Health and Human Services, Administration on Children, Youth, and Families. (2003). *Child maltreatment, 2001.* Washington, DC: U.S. Government Printing Office.

U.S. Department of Health and Human Services, Administration on Children, Youth, and Families. (2004). *Child maltreatment, 2002.* Washington, DC: U.S. Government Printing Office.

U.S. Department of Health and Human Services, Administration on Children, Youth, and Families. (2005). *Child maltreatment, 2003.* Washington, DC: U.S. Government Printing Office.

U.S. Department of Health and Human Services, Administration on Children, Youth, and Families. (2006). *Child maltreatment, 2004.* Washington, DC: U.S. Government Printing Office.

U.S. Department of Health and Human Services, Administration on Children, Youth, and Families. (2010). *Child maltreatment, 2009.* Washington, DC: U.S. Government Printing Office.

U.S. General Accounting Office. (1995). *Child welfare: Complex needs strain capacity to provide services.* Washington, DC: Author.

U.S. General Accounting Office. (2003). *Child welfare: HHS could play a greater role in helping child welfare agencies recruit and retain staff*. Washington, DC: Author.

Usher, C. L., & Wildfire, J. B. (2003). Evidence-based practice in community-based child welfare systems. *Child Welfare, 82*, 597–614.

Vinokur-Kaplan, D., & Hartman, A. (1986). A national profile of child welfare workers and supervisors. *Child Welfare, 65*(4), 323–335.

Walker, S. H. (1928). *Social work and the training of social workers*. Chapel Hill, NC: University of North Carolina Press.

Wallace, M. E. (1982). Private practice: A nationwide study. *Social Work, 27*, 262–267.

Webster, D., Barth, R. P., & Needell, B. (2000). Placement stability for children in out-of-home care: A longitudinal analysis. *Child Welfare, 79*, 614–632.

Weiner, M. E. (1991). Motivating employees to achieve. In R. E. Edwards & J. A. Yankey (Eds.), *Skills for effective human services management* (pp. 302–316). Silver Spring, MD: National Association of Social Workers Press.

Weisz, V., & Thai, N. (2003). The court-appointed special advocate (CASA) program: Bringing information to child abuse and neglect cases. *Child Maltreatment, 9*, 204–210.

Welte, M. (2005). *Major federal child welfare laws*. Retrieved July 2, 2006, from www.casanet.org/reference/major-child-welfare-laws.htm

West, W. M. (1933). Social work as a profession. In F. S. Hall (Ed.), *Social work year book: 1933* (pp. 492–496). New York, NY: Sage.

Westbrook, T. M. (2006). *Initial development and validation of the Child Welfare Organizational Culture Inventory*. Unpublished doctoral dissertation, University of Georgia, Athens.

Westbrook, T. M., Ellis, J., & Ellett, A. J. (2006). Improving retention among public child welfare staff: What can we learn from the insight and experiences of committed survivors? *Administration in Social Work, 30*(4), 37–62.

Western Interstate Commission for Higher Education. (1965). *Report of the conferences on undergraduate education for the social services: An examination of the role of undergraduate education in the preparation of personnel for corrections and social welfare*. Inglewood, CA: California State Colleges.

Whitaker, J., & Maluccio, A. (2002). Rethinking "child placement": A reflective essay. *Social Service Review, 76*, 108–134.

Williamson, M. (1935). *The social worker in the prevention and treatment of delinquency*. New York, NY: Columbia University Press.

Winston, E. (1965). New dimensions in public welfare: Implications for social work education. In *Council on social work education social work. Education and social welfare manpower: Present realities and future imperatives*. New York, NY: Council on Social Work Education.

Witte, E. F. (1960). Developing professional leadership for social programs. *The Annals of the American Academy of Political and Social Sciences, 329*(1), 123–136.

Witte, E. F. (1966). Articulation between graduate and undergraduate education for the social services. In *Observations on undergraduate social welfare education* (pp. 27–34). New York, NY: Council on Social Work Education.

Wittman, M. (1965). Information on personnel needs and social work students: Implications for manpower planning and research and for programs of recruitment and education. In *Social work education and social welfare manpower: Present realities and future imperatives* (pp. 15–25). New York, NY: Council on Social Work Education.

Wolf, E. P., & Lebeaux, C. N. (1968). Class and race in the changing city: Searching for new approaches to old problems. In L. F. Schmore (Ed.), *Social science and the city: A survey of urban research* (pp. 99–129). New York, NY: Praeger.

Wulczyn, F. H., Barth, R. P., Yuan, Y. T., Harden, B. J., & Landsverk, J. (2005). *Beyond common sense: Child welfare, child well-being and the evidence for policy reform.* New Brunswick, NJ: Aldine.

Wulczyn, F. H., Harden, A. W., & George, R. M. (1998). *Foster care dynamics, 1983–1997: An update from the multistate foster care data archive.* Chicago, IL: University of Chicago, Chapin Hall Center for Children.

Youngclarke, D., Ramos, K., & Granger-Merkle, L. (2004). A systematic review of the impact of court appointed special advocates. *Journal of the Center for Families, Children, and the Courts,* 109–126.

Zlotnik, K. (1993). *Social work education and public human services: Developing partnerships.* Alexandria, VA: Council on Social Work Education.

Zlotnik, J. (2002). Preparing social workers for child welfare practice: Lessons from an historical review of the literature. *Journal of Health and Social Policy, 15,* 5–21.

Zlotnik, J. (2003). The use of Title IV-E training funds for social work education: An historical perspective. *Journal of Human Behavior in the Social Environment, 7,* 5–20.

Zlotnik, J. (2006). No simple answers to a complex question: A response to Perry. *Research on Social Work Practice, 16,* 414–416.

Zlotnik, J., DePanfilis, D., Daining, C., & Lane, M. M. (2005). *Factors influencing retention of child welfare staff: A systematic review of research.* Washington, DC: Institute for the Advancement of Social Work Research.

Zlotnik, J. L., Strand, V. C., & Anderson, G. R. (2009). Introduction: Achieving positive outcomes for children and families: Recruiting and retaining a competent child welfare workforce. *Child Welfare, 88*(5), 7–21.

Chapter 2
Family-Centered Practice

A System-Based Approach to Strengthening Families

Barbara Thomlison and Raymond J. Thomlison

> What challenges are present in family-centered practice in various fields of service? Child welfare? Child mental health? School based social work? Substance abuse?

Family relationships are sources of the most intense emotions in people's lives; they are both the source of joy and happiness under positive circumstances (Baumeister & Leary, 1995; Scherer, Wallbott, & Summerfield, 1986) and great distress and sorrow when things go badly (Bowlby, 1982; Mira, 2007). Therefore, since family and family relationships are important to who we become as individuals, it is critical to think of approaching child and youth problem behaviors with a family-centered approach. Many different types of family-centered interventions exist that are as diverse as the families they serve. These interventions have been applied to numerous disorders among children, adolescents, and adults, and have demonstrated efficacy with each target population (Liddle & Rowe, 2006). Family-centered interventions generally demonstrate superior effects to no-treatment groups or alternative treatments (Shadish, Ragsdale, Glaser, & Montgomery, 1995). Engagement and retention rates of children, youth, and their families are enhanced even with the most difficult problems. Family-centered interventions appear to be most effective with child behavior problems, substance use disorders, and marital and relationship stress (Dishion & Kavanagh, 2003; Kumpfer & Alvarado, 1998; Shadish et al., 1995; Szapocznik & Williams, 2000).

Strong families are the key to raising competent and healthy children and preventing child and youth problems. Consistent with a system-based approach to strengthening families, family-centered practice uses an ecological or contextual conceptual framework to engage the family system in helping them improve their ability to parent their children. As a framework, family-centered practice requires an individualized array of formal and informal services and supports to meet the family's needs. Research suggests that when families are strong and parents are competent, there are significant decreases in the risk of child and youth problem behaviors, mental health problems, delinquency, criminal behavior, and other interrelated problems as the factors that mediate these risks (Fraser, Kirby, & Smokowksi, 2004; Kazdin & Weisz, 2003).

Family-centered interventions are comprehensive in nature, and they conceptually employ an ecological–developmental approach within a family system perspective to understand family processes and continuity of problem behavior over time. This framework captures the ongoing interactions among aspects of contexts and persons. Problem behaviors are viewed as having multiple determinants, and there are multiple pathways to a specific problem behavior (Ferrer-Wreder, Stattin, Cass Lorente, Tubman, & Adamson, 2004), including the assumption that family-of-origin experiences impact, in a significant manner, children's relationships and developmental outcomes (Widom, 1989). Child and youth behavior problems serve a function within the family system and are initiated and maintained by maladaptive interpersonal processes (Liddle & Rowe, 2006). Interventions therefore target multiple risk factors to change destructive interactional patterns and enhance protective factors to reinforce positive ways of responding to establish more adaptive outcomes.

This chapter provides a summary of family-centered interventions for social workers, educators, and those practitioners interested in an effective intervention approach to selected child and youth problem behaviors. The chapter has two goals. First, it provides background information on the theoretical context for family-centered practice. A summary of the ecological–developmental perspective is provided to aid in understanding the influences from transactions of multiple contexts on family behavior. Given that a number of risk and protective factors have been linked to different adjustment patterns among children and adolescents, a brief overview of risk and resiliency factors linked to outcomes is presented. This assists in understanding what is needed to overcome problems and which protective factors to focus on as the critical supports and opportunities for children and families.

Second, the chapter identifies exemplary family-centered interventions as preventing problems in childhood and promoting the advancement of positive youth development. Based on the number of effective family-focused strategies for targeted family needs and family types, only parenting and family strengthening programs are included here (Kumpfer & Alvarado, 1998). These evidence-informed programs are classified within a framework developed by the Institute of Medicine into three categories: universal, selective, and indicated preventive interventions. Each of the interventions included here are based on published findings from studies that employed either a representative community sample or a clinical sample with an appropriate control group, clearly defined the problem targeted by the intervention, and described the intervention in adequate detail to permit replication. In some cases, a treatment manual is available (Thomlison & Craig, 2005). To the extent possible, the programs are organized by the guidelines proposed by the Institute of Medicine (Mrazek & Haggerty, 1994). The first category attempts to prevent problems and the second and third categories provide services to those at risk for or identified as having a problem:

- *Universal preventive interventions* target the general public or an entire population of interest, such as schools or a group of classrooms, without attempting to identify which particular children are at risk (e.g., childhood immunizations; media-based parenting information campaign).

- *Selective preventive interventions* target subgroups of the general population who are at higher risk for developing a problem than other members of the broader population (e.g., folic acid for women of childbearing age; information and advice for specific parenting or child behavior or development concerns).

- *Indicated preventive interventions* target individuals who have detectable signs or symptoms of difficulty but not long-standing serious problems or full-blown clinical disorders (e.g., parent education and skills training for children with multiple behavior problems or aggressive behavior or learning delays).

Family-Centered Practice

Prior to family-centered practice, practitioners approached problem solving by focusing on individual maladaptive behaviors, believing the solution was within the individual and attempting to deal with intrapsychic aspects of the personality. The influence of family-centered practice first appeared in the 1950s as researchers such as Scherz, Bateson, Jackson, Haley, and Satir (as cited in Janzen, Harris, Jordan, & Franklin, 2006) observed that the only way to understand or help the individual was within the interaction of family members and the various contextual influences with which the family interacts. The assumption is that the individual can be understood only within the context of the family and that family dynamics contribute to the individual's functioning. In this regard, the child or adolescent is part of the family and therefore cannot be understood or helped apart from the family if changes in behavior are to be maintained. By seeing members of the family, the practitioner then has information about family interaction, family difficulties, and family supports. Then the role of each member in the family structure and process is apparent. Attending to the family as a transactional system requires the practitioner to think in terms of two or more people interacting and influencing each other (Thomlison, 2007). Thus, a different perspective of problem formulation and problem solution is required because the family as a unit, and not the individual, requires the intervention. In particular, evidence-based or empirically supported family-centered interventions that are ecologically sound need to be used when making a clinical decision to offer service (Gambrill, 2006). Although outcomes of research differ by type of family intervention, overall, family-centered interventions tend to have more immediate and direct impact on improving family difficulties (Kumpfer & Alvarado, 1998) and family functioning (Liddle & Rowe, 2006).

Family-centered practice is not one method or model of practice but a way of thinking about practice or intervention. It is an ideology in which families are a central and lasting element in children's lives (Dishion & Kavanagh, 2003). When children experience problems, services often place the child in the center as the main focus for change. However, if the family is not involved, then there are low expectations for the family to change and the family can continue to blame the child for difficulties (Dishion & Kavanagh, 2003; Szapocznik & Williams, 2000). More importantly, it is essential that families understand their role in their child's development and behavior difficulties. In this way, family-centered intervention provides the information and skills, called *psychoeducation*, necessary to raise healthy children and promote learning opportunities. The environment in which the child and family develop informs us about their strengths, supports, emerging competencies, stresses, and needs (Thomlison, 2007, p. 14). This view of family-centered practice underscores the value of maintaining and enhancing family relationships.

Eight Core Principles Organize Family-Centered Practice

Principles underpinning family-centered practice are supported by the empirical research in family interventions. By working with child, youth, family, and extrafamilial system levels and targeting change in these systems and at these system interactions, family-centered practice aims to move the family toward a more functional developmental pathway. The frameworks provided for family-centered practice emerged from tested principles and concepts in evaluated practice programs. The principles were designed to target risk factors and enhance protective factors associated with problem behaviors. The eight principles of effective interventions are:

1. *The focus is the entire family.* Families are unique systems of influence on each individual and work with both the child and the family system.

2. *The family is viewed as the expert and therefore the best source for solutions to their difficulties.* Families need to be involved as full partners in the change process. Family functioning is the key to creating opportunities for new, developmentally healthy behaviors. Therefore, it is a family-directed intervention.

3. *Place emphasis on family strengths, assets, and their aspirations because this promotes resilience.* Reframe the problem as strength because this leads to finding more strength.

4. *Be sensitive, nonjudgmental, and, above all, do not blame.*

5. *Interventions need to have multicomponents that address critical domains and influence the development and perpetuation of the behaviors to be prevented.* The context of interventions considers

individual, biological, social, cognitive, interpersonal, familial, developmental, and social environmental factors, personal beliefs, and cultural values as influences that contribute to the development and continuation of problem behavior.

6. *Environmental influences play a critical role in impacting various individual and family behaviors.* Interventions need to fit the community and cultural norms of the family.

7. *Consider each family's personal beliefs and preferences.* This affirms that the family's own solutions to problems are the ones that are most effective and long-lasting. Families are engaged in ways that are relevant to their situation and sensitive to the values of their culture (Kumpfer & Alvarado, 1998)

8. *The goal is to instill hope in the family, provide realistic possibilities, build positive experiences for family members, and to look forward* (Thomlison, 2007). The practitioner's attitude to change is important, creating a working agenda and clinical focus, prompting behavior change, and revising interventions as necessary (Liddle, 2010).

Theoretical Framework for Family-Centered Practice

Although intervention programs vary among the developers, all programs are alike in that they begin with knowledge about risk and protective factors emerging from multiple systems and domains of individual and family functioning to guide intervention (Liddle, 2010). Treatment outcomes and clinically relevant conclusions from process studies of family change mechanisms inform the theory and conceptual framework for practice. With respect to theory, this approach draws on both the structural (Minuchin, 1974) and strategic family systems theories (Haley, 1976; Szapocznik & Williams, 2000) and other empirically derived findings from developmental psychopathology prevention studies. This section summarizes the major conceptual elements to family-centered practice, including ecological-transaction model, family structural framework, social development model, and social learning systems, as well as the family risk and resiliency factors as the unifying descriptive and predictive framework for strengthening families. The emphasis on the family in these perspectives is consistent with application to most minority culturally defined values on the developmental trajectories of children and family interventions (Kumpfer, Alvarado, Smith, & Bellamy, 2002; Szapocznik & Williams, 2000).

Ecological–Transactional Overview

An ecological perspective focuses both on the individual and the context. Children and youth, and their families, are viewed as operating or influenced by interdependent parts or systems ranging from peers to schools, neighborhood, and community contexts (Fraser, 2004). In social work, some individuals refer to this as the person-in-environment perspective first described by Tharp and Wetzel in 1969 (Gambrill, 1997, p. 212). This perspective captures the ongoing interactions in different contexts and domains of family functioning, the multiple environments they experience, and their prior developmental history. All of these systems interact in an ongoing manner and they constantly influence each other. Development is influenced then by the social ecological transactions throughout childhood and beyond (Bronfenbrenner, 1986).

The family is a unique system, with particular responsibilities and functions. It is a special environment for socializing children and youth. A family interacts and is interdependent with parts of itself and with other systems from the environment outside the family. Families and the multiple systems interacting with them mutually influence each other's behavior. Any and all change affects the family members. The family needs to be able to create a balance between change and stability—adaptation or maladaptation. Understanding families and their social environments helps to locate the place for these system interventions. This model provides a rationale for intervention efforts that target multiple risk factors for a specific problem behavior outcome and enhance protective factors predictive of more adaptive outcomes (Ferrer-Wreder et al., 2004). It does not tell us which interventions to use, but evidence-supported practice assists with that decision (Roberts & Yeager, 2004; Thomlison, 2007).

Within the systems influencing the family, the idea is to identify risk factors, or those influences leading to harm, and the strengths or protective factors and influences that will lead to resilience. By approaching a complicated family situation from the ecological perspective, the practitioner can be somewhat more objective about the family issues. Practitioners who see the family context as interactions of multiple systems—the family and its social environments—will be better able to build on strengths in families and promote family self-change, a notion critical to practice. The goal of many intervention programs is to change the family's attitudes, motivations, skills, knowledge, and behaviors. Families then can be linked to resources they need to be successful. When children and youth have supportive connections between and across their social contexts, family, school, neighborhood, and community, then prosocial outcomes and positive development occur. Interventions may also be designed to address the child, youth, and family within a particular environment or in multiple contexts.

Family Structure

As a system-based approach, family-centered practice emphasizes the importance of family structure, family subsystems, boundaries, and the patterns of interactions as integral to understanding family functioning. Interactions between families and their environments determine how parents and children adapt to the stresses in their environments. Family interactions that elicit satisfactory responses in the family structure (patterns of interactions) meet individual and family demands and needs, and families flourish; where there is difficulty responding effectively, disorganization and dysfunction results (Nichols & Schwartz, 2004; Thomlison, 2007). Maladaptive family interactions are understood to be an important contributor to ongoing problem behaviors and to the maintenance of problem behaviors (Szapocznik & Williams, 2000). Lack of personal and familial skills and resources are the primary reasons families have difficulty responding positively to stress and demands in their environments. Other factors include family experiences and the lack of opportunity for building resilient factors (Rothery & Enns, 2001).

Family structure refers to the boundaries or "invisible demarcations or dividers between family members or among parts of the system, such as between parents and children (the parent-child subsystem), or between the family and the community" (Thomlison, 2007, p. 38). Families function through these boundary interactions and functions often define boundaries. The major subsystems defining boundaries that develop in the family structure over time include the couple subsystem, the parental subsystem, the sibling subsystem, and the parent-child subsystem (Janzen et al., 2006). Parental roles may be filled by other caregivers such as grandparents, aunts, or nonrelated individuals.

Structure develops around belief systems, ideas, or roles. Interactions then regulate contact between the individuals, children, and parents and therefore determine the amount of contact with others outside of the family (Nichols & Schwartz, 2004). This interaction can be characterized as satisfactory or unsatisfactory responses from other family members. It organizes the ways in which family members interact and supports autonomy and differentiation of its members. Repeated transactions result in interactional patterns between the family, its members, and the community and establish healthy functioning or dysfunction. The greater the clarity and distinction of interactional patterns, the more effective the family functions. Boundaries and interaction patterns change across the life span. Healthy boundaries allow members to shift and change as needed (Thomlison, 2007). Healthy development emerges.

In addition, family interactions emerge from family rules that are overt (articulated) or covert (implicit). Rules, either implicit or explicit, prescribe the agreed-on relational patterns that organize and provide family management. Both rules and roles describe the characteristics and functioning of the family system. For example, the power hierarchy is influenced by the rules indicating the differential levels of authority between the parents and the children. Interventions should aim at changing family patterns of interaction between parents and children to help them achieve an improved style of communication and thereby change family relations that in turn changes family problems. Family structures are improved, and healthy family functioning through improved parenting occurs.

Social Development Model

The primary social contexts for child and youth development are the family, school, peer, and neighborhood, and these are interrelated system influences. The social development model (SDM) developed by Catalano, Haggerty, Oesterle, Fleming, and Hawkins (2004) attempts to build attachment and commitment of individuals to these socializing units. It is through their impact on family members that interactions with these systems have an impact on children and youth (Hawkins et al., 1992). They may enrich or impoverish the individual's development (Szapocznik & Williams, 2000). They may support or undermine the individual's development. Cultural patterns and acculturation and institutionalized policies also contribute in both positive and damaging ways to influence the child's and youth's development. "The stronger and more complementary the linkages within and between systems, the more powerful their influence on a child's development" (Perrino et al., as cited in Szapocznik & Williams, 2000, p. 127). Children directly participate and learn patterns of behavior, whether prosocial or antisocial, from these environments through four processes:

1. Opportunities for involvement in activities and interactions with others
2. Actual involvement
3. Skill for involvement and interaction with others
4. Perceived rewards from involvement and interaction

Involvement is seen as part of the socialization process that leads to bonding, and the values and beliefs of the social unit acts as a mediator of the effect of bonding on behavior outcomes. Prosocial or antisocial behavior is impacted by social interactions. Children will form social bonds to significant others if the following conditions are met:

- The child thinks there is a viable change for a social interaction to take place.
- The child has to actually engage in a social encounter.
- Children and their partners must have adequate skills to successfully interact.
- The child expects that the social exchange will be a rewarding experience (Ferrer-Wreder et al., 2004, p. 160).

Through this additive and cyclical social learning process children are able to develop lasting positive attachments.

Social Skills Training

A social skills approach describes the mechanisms by which individuals learn to behave in social contexts and influences both prosocial and antisocial patterns of behavior. It is based on the notion of competence, which suggests that behavior problems are the result of deficits in the child's or youth's or parent's response to a situation. Interactional patterns are the basis for change in behavior. Teaching prosocial interactional skills and competencies enhances relationships and improves day-to-day functioning between children, their families, and others in their environment. These techniques attempt to change the stimuli and cues that reinforce negative behavior. A social skills training approach is effective in teaching parents more appropriate discipline methods, which is helpful in strengthening families. For children and youth, effective techniques include: withholding attention, natural and logical consequences, time-out, assigning extra work, and taking away privileges (Janzen et al., 2006). Intervention components attempt to improve the parent-child relationship and then focus on family communication, parental monitoring, and discipline (Kumpfer & Alvarado, 1998). The programs are distinguished from parent education because they include a structured set of behavioral skills in parenting. Other skills-training techniques include behavioral rehearsal to teach role performance and build confidence and contracting for changes in behavior. Learning new skills involves a four-step process:

1. The practitioner models or demonstrates the skill.
2. The child and parent role-play and practice the skill in front of the practitioner.
3. The parent and child are assigned to practice the skill in daily life.
4. The practitioner provides feedback to the child and parent regarding the success in learning the new skill (Janzen et al., 2006, p. 161; Thomlison, 2007).

Teaching parents to increase monitoring and supervision of children and youth is a strong mediator of peer influence (Dishion, French, & Patterson, 1995; Kumpfer & Alvarado, 1998). Parenting skills training programs are effective in reducing coercive family interactions (Dishion & Kavanagh, 2003; Webster-Stratton, Kolpacoff, & Hollingsworth, 1988) and improving parental monitoring (Dishion & Kavanagh, 2003).

Risk Factors

Risk factors include characteristics or conditions such as biological, psychological, behavioral, social, and environment factors that, if present for a given child or youth, make it more likely that this child or youth, rather than another child or youth selected from the general population, will experience a specific problem (Fraser, 2004; Thomlison & Craig, 2005). Risk factors are present in every system with which the child interacts. Risk factors often occur together or cluster to produce heightened susceptibility for a problem. As the number of risk factors increases, the cumulation exerts an increasingly strong influence on parent and child (Dishion & Kavanagh, 2003; Fraser, Kirby, & Smokowski, 2004). Examples of common risk factors at the neighborhood and community system level include too few opportunities for education and employment, racial discrimination, injustice, and poverty. Risk factors at the family level include child maltreatment, family history of behavioral problems, family conflict and marital discord, poor parent mental health, poor parent–child relationship, poor supervision of the child, and harsh parenting (Fraser, 2004; Thomlison, 2004).

The more risk factors a child or youth experiences in interactions with various systems, the more likely that he or she will experience problems such as substance abuse, delinquency, school dropout, and other related problems (Dishion & Kavanagh, 2003). Not all risk factors are susceptible to change, such as gender, race, or genetic susceptibility to substance use (National Institute for Drug Abuse, 2003). Research has found, however, that specific risks can be reduced, for example, by treating mental disorders, improving parent and family management skills, and family interactions (Dishion & Kavanagh, 2003; Janzen et al., 2006). Hawkins and colleagues (1992), Kumpfer and Alvarado (1998), and other researchers repeatedly identify the following 10 factors that increase vulnerability in children and youth:

1. Lack of bonding to family, school, or community
2. Frequent, early antisocial behavior
3. Family history of high-risk behaviors
4. Poor family management
5. High family conflict
6. Social and economic deprivation
7. Failure in school
8. Low commitment to education
9. Associating with delinquent peers
10. Disorganization of community

Risky Parenting Practices

Many childhood and adolescent behavior disorders are strongly and consistently linked to a number of poor or ineffective parenting practices that maintain antisocial behavior into and through adolescence (Liddle & Rowe, 2006). Two factors are related to these outcomes. First, antisocial behavior is learned at an early age in the home through negative reinforcement of coercive patterns, which then generalizes to school and peer group environments. When there is both coercive parenting and poor parental monitoring at age 4 or 5, there is the emergence of conduct problems among socioeconomically disadvantaged minority children by age 6 (Liddle & Rowe, 2006, p. 97). Second, family conditions such as child maltreatment, family violence, conflict between parents, and harsh or abusive parenting and child-rearing practices increase the risk factors for child and adolescent problem behaviors. In addition, parental conditions such as substance abuse and mental disorders are strongly related to family risk factors for behavior problems. Again, children who do not have positive parent–child interactions are twice as likely to have persistent behavioral problems as those who have positive interactions (Bry, Catalano, Kumpfer, Lochman, & Szapocznik, 1998; Dishion & Kavanagh, 2003; Liddle & Rowe, 2006). For example, poor parenting practices, such as inadequate supervision of children, inconsistent responses to children's behavior, and constant nagging, may increase the risk that a child will be noncompliant at home, school, and in other settings. Frequently, families are experiencing several of these risk factors simultaneously, thereby compounding the developmental issues facing the child.

> Research on parenting clarifies that it is what parents do, and not their history, that has the most influence on children's protection and risk. Parents who have insight about their own past, and who have acquired parenting skills to respond competently, are less likely to perpetuate pathology across generations. (Dishion & Kavanagh, 2003, p. 13)

Research identifies the following ineffective parenting practices:

- *Child maltreatment and family violence:* Children and adolescents exposed to parental maltreatment and family violence tend to develop aggressive and violent coping styles in their interpersonal relationships and in their school and peer environments. This behavior places them at risk for delinquency, criminal behavior, and school dropout. Women who are exposed to intimate partner violence are less able to care for their children (Kumpfer, Molgaard, & Spoth, 1996; Thomlison, 2004).
- *Conflict between parents:* The presence of spousal discord, threats of separation, and conflict in the social support network are associated with distress and ability to parent (Dishion & Kavanagh, 2003; Webster-Stratton & Taylor, 2001). Children also learn aggression through observing aggression in their family (Hawkins et al., 1992).
- *Harsh discipline practices:* Parents who are low on warmth and nurturing qualities and high on criticism are likely to use harsh or excessive physical punishment in their problem-solving responses to child discipline situations (Kumpfer & Alvarado, 1998). Coercive parent-child interactions may emerge when children display aggressive and noncompliant behaviors toward a parent with distorted child-rearing knowledge (Dishion & Kavanagh, 2003). Webster-Stratton and Taylor (2001) found that children who are more impulsive and quick to anger tend to overwhelm parents and raise the risk of negative parental responses such as those characterized by high arousal, anger, and harsh discipline—all risk factors for ineffective parenting. For a more thorough review of risk factors for conduct disorders, see Dishion and Kavanagh (2003), Webster-Stratton and Taylor (2001), and Hawkins and colleagues (1992).
- *Poor family management:* Parents who lack involvement with, or spend little time with their child, and who are unavailable to provide

support in times of stress have poor family management skills. This includes low levels of supervision and poor monitoring of child and adolescent behavior, and ineffective skills to manage child and youth behaviors (Hawkins et al., 1992; Olds, 2002). Children who experience nonnurturing relationships show impairment in their ability to develop positive and reciprocal interpersonal relationships with others and are described by their parents as noncompliant compared with children who have strong bonds of attachment, who develop a deep sense of belonging and security (Dishion & Kavanagh, 2003). A predictable, stable, and consistent parenting environment is central for attachments to develop.

Family Protective and Resilience Factors

At the heart of any given intervention is the aim of enhancing specific protective factors to permit functioning under adversity. Resilience allows the child or family to maintain a normative or high level of functioning when confronted with a time-limited stressor or a developmental challenge. Protective factors mediate or moderate the effect of the risk factors and result in reducing the risk that the problem will occur. Protective factors such as strong family bonds and success in school help safeguard children from many problems. Personal attributes and positive school, peer, and community conditions lower the chances of poor developmental outcomes in the presence of risk (Fraser, 2004; Pollard, Hawkins, & Arthur, 1999; Thomlison, 2004). Protective factors appear to buffer or balance the negative impact of risk factors. An example of a protective factor linked to positive adolescent development is a family's positive and promotive daily interactions (Kumpfer & Alvarado, 1998). Caring and support, positive experiences, and ongoing opportunities for participation in families and communities are powerful protective factors (Ferrer-Wreder et al., 2004).

One consistent finding in the resilience research is that positive parent–child interaction is the most influential factor in shaping child and youth behavior (Fraser, Kirby, & Smokowski, 2004; Kumpfer & Alvarado, 1998). So, how do these relationships develop? Positive parent–child interactions and relationships develop among parents with high self-esteem and self-efficacy and who function within normal boundaries of socially accepted behavior and social competence (Kinard, 1999; Rutter, 1987, 2000). Protective parent–child interactions include:

- Use of nonviolent methods of teaching and discipline
- High levels of warmth and acceptance and low levels of criticism
- Low levels of stress and aggression in the family
- High levels of monitoring and supervision of children
- A positive and supportive parent–child relationship
- The presence of a supportive spouse or partner

- Socioeconomic stability, success at work and school
- Sufficient social supports and positive adult role models in their lives (Dishion & Kavanagh, 2003; Thomlison, 2004)

Research consistently emphasizes parenting skill and competence as one of the strongest protective factors, regardless of child characteristics such as easygoing temperament or other personal attributes (Guterman & Embry, 2004; Olds & Kitzman, 1993; Osofsky & Thompson, 2000; Veltman & Browne, 2001).

When problem behaviors emerge within the context of family risk factors, they are likely to continue in other settings or systems and through adolescence (Bernard, 2002; Dishion & Kavanagh, 2003). Researchers and prevention specialists (Kumpfer, Alexander, McDonald, & Olds, 1998) suggest that the major strength of a family-centered approach to many child and adolescent problems is improving the ways that parents care for and socialize their children, so that family relationships improve. These interventions teach skills that are effective for improving family communication and discipline and establishing firm and consistent rule-making in parents of young children (Kumpfer et al., 1996, 1998; Spoth, Kavanagh, & Dishion, 2002; Webster-Stratton, 1998; Webster-Stratton & Taylor, 2001).

Bry, Catalano, Kumpfer, Lochman, and Szapocznik (1998) and other researchers identify the following five major types of family protective factors in promoting resilience to child and youth problems:

1. Supportive parent–child relationships
2. Positive discipline methods
3. Monitoring and supervision
4. Families who advocate for their children
5. Parents who seek information and support

Kumpfer and Alvarado (1998) and Dunst and Trivett (1994) found characteristics of strong, resilient African American families to be a strong economic base, a strong achievement orientation, adaptability of family roles, spirituality, strong kinship bonds, racial pride, display of respect and acceptance, resourcefulness, community involvement, and family unity characteristics. A strong family is the basis of positive family socialization processes; therefore, when strong family management functions are present in family systems, these processes act as a protective factor (Dishion & Kavanagh, 2003).

Positive parental attachment, relational competence, and parent–child interaction in particular afford children the opportunity to develop skills for positive social interaction and behavior (Bernard, 2006; Liddle & Rowe, 2006). Although many succeed regardless of their families, it is the effect of parenting that acts as a protective factor in the more extreme situations, such as in violent and unsafe homes (Blum et al., 2000; Masten et al., 1999).

Family-Centered Programs

Family-centered practice approaches are being implemented across program areas and service systems. This chapter does not intend to cover all those programs (see online resources at the end of the chapter). Selecting effective family-centered interventions must be done carefully with the target population in mind and knowledge of the developmental stage of the child and youth, as well as the types of risk factors in the family served. Be sure the interventions are of sufficient intensity and duration to address the large number of risk factors and inadequate number of protective factors that affect everyone (Ferrer-Wreder et al., 2004; Fraser, 2004). Many programs are too narrow in focus and do not attend to the full range of child and youth outcomes, such as the cognitive, behavioral, emotional, physical, and social needs of the child, nor do they attend to the child's and youth's needs in all environments. Program termination occurs when positive developmental changes are demonstrated to have a long-term impact (Kumpfer & Alvarado, 1998). Family-centered programs effective in reducing risk factors and increasing protective factors are parent training, family therapy, and family skills training (also referred to as behavioral family therapy).

Parent Training Programs

Behavioral parenting training programs are the most extensively evaluated programs available. Many research studies have demonstrated their effectiveness in reducing disruptive child behaviors and coercive child parent interactions and in improving parental monitoring (Kumpfer & Alvarado, 1998; Patterson, Reid, & Dishion, 1992). Younger children are the population of focus. Essentially, parent management programs aim to develop and increase parental skills while correcting parental behaviors that contribute to negative behavior problems (Liddle & Rowe, 2006). Behavioral parent training consists of four components: (1) initial assessment of parenting issues, (2) teaching parents new skills, (3) application of the new skills by the parent with their children (homework or out-of-session practice), and (4) feedback by the facilitator or trainer (Taylor & Biglan, 1998). A minimum of 45 hours of training is necessary to modify risk factors for child and adolescent behavior problems (Kumpfer & Alvarado, 1998). Programs follow a treatment or intervention manual for session topics addressing information, skills, and strategies for managing child behaviors. Many of the parent training programs evolved from the model developed by Gerald Patterson of the Oregon Social Learning Center (Patterson, Reid, & Dishion, 1992). Examples of exemplary and comprehensive parent training programs are *Incredible Years: Parents, Teachers and Children Training Series* (Webster-Stratton, Hollinsworth, & Kolpacoff, 1989 [BASIC]; Webster-Stratton, Kolpacoff, & Hollinsworth, 1988 [BASIC]), and *Treatment Foster Care* (Chamberlain, 1994; Chamberlain & Reid, 1991). For a summary of effective parent training programs, see the Online Resources at the end of the chapter.

Family Therapy Programs

Family therapy programs are well suited to families of preteens and adolescents who are experiencing problems. The aim is to determine the function that children's behavior problems serve within the family system and target change in the maladaptive interactional patterns to establish more effective problem-solving approaches in the family. Family communication improves, and family control and management improve as well as family relationships. These programs are classified as comprehensive in nature and target indicated populations. This approach has demonstrated reductions in delinquency, antisocial behaviors, and drug use in youth. Four well-researched and exemplary programs are structural family therapy (brief strategic family therapy; Szapocznik, Scopetta, & King, 1978), functional family therapy (Alexander & Parsons, 1982; Alexander, Robbins, & Sexton, 2000), multidimensional family therapy (Liddle, 1999; Liddle, 2010), and multisystemic therapy (Henggeler & Borduin, 1990; Henggeler, Schoenwald, Borduin, Rowland, & Cunningham, 1998).

Family Skills Training Programs

Family skills training programs provide children and families with several skill components combining family systems therapy and behavioral skill training targeted to selective populations. The goal is to improve family and parental functioning by improving parenting skills. These comprehensive interventions include parent skill training, social skills training for children, and behavioral family therapy (parent-child activities, also called behavioral parent training or family skills training). These programs combine practical, social, and instrumental supports and at the same time use a high dose of role-playing with ample coaching included (Kumpfer & Alvarado, 1998). Kumpfer and Alvarado (1998) note that "family skills training affects the largest number of measured family and youth risk and protective factors" (p. 7). Through structured activities, the aim is to improve family cohesion, unity, and attachment; reduce conflict; and improve communication so that parent-child bonding and attachment are attained. The objectives are realized through activities such as coaching in therapeutic play, observation and videotape feedback, coaching and interactive practice of parent–child positive play. Exemplars of effective family skills training programs include the Nurturing Parenting Program (Bavolek, 1987; Bavolek, McLaughlin, & Comstock, 1983); Families and Schools Together (FAST; Conduct Problems Prevention Research Group, 2000; McDonald, Coe-Braddish, Billingham, Dibble, & Rice, 1991); and Strengthening Families Program (SFP; 14-session program; Kumpfer, DeMarsh, & Child, 1989) and Strengthening Families Program (SFP; 7-session program; Kumpfer et al., 1996; Molgaard & Kumpfer, 1994); and Family Effectiveness Training (FET for Hispanic adolescents; Szapocznik, Santisteban, Rio, Perez-Vidal, & Kurtines, 1989).

See Table 2.1 for examples of family-centered programs.

Table 2.1 Family-Centered Programs.

Program Title	Developmental Period	Levels of Intervention	Cultural Relevance/Outcome Evaluations	Theoretical Basis	Implemented by
Parent Training Programs					
Incredible Years: Parents, Teachers, and Children Training Series	Childhood	Universal	Canada, United States, Great Britain, and Norway	Cognitive Social Learning Theory (Patterson's Social Learning Model)	Trained therapists and interventionists, parents, and teachers
Treatment Foster Care	11 to 18 years old	Selected Indicated (comprehensive) Indicated	United States and Canada	Behavioral skills training, social skills training, cognitive social learning theory	Trained therapists and interventionists, parents, teachers, and trained professional foster parents
Family Therapy Programs					
Functional Family Therapy	Late childhood or adolescence (11 to 18 years old)	Selected Indicated	United States and Sweden	Information processing, social cognitive, ecological–transactional, behavioral, and social learning theories	Trained therapists and social workers
Multisystemic Family Therapy	Adolescence (11 to 18 years old)	Selected Indicated (comprehensive)	United States, Canada, and Norway	Social ecology (Bronfenbrenner)	Master's level therapists, PhDs, and clinical supervisors
Brief Strategic Family Therapy Structural Family Therapy	Late childhood or adolescence (11 to 18 years old)	Indicated	United States—bicultural and Hispanic populations	Information processing, social cognitive, ecological–transactional, behavioral, and social learning theories	Trained therapists and social workers

Family Skills Training Programs

Program	Developmental period	Type of prevention	Countries	Theory	Staff
Strengthening Families Program	Preschool Childhood	Universal Selective	United States, Canada, Australia, Costa Rica, Spain, and Sweden	Resiliency model; social ecology of substance use	Trained staff
Nurse–Family Partnership	Adolescence Prenatal Infancy	Indicated Selective	United States—urban and rural	Social ecology (Bronfenbrenner), social learning, attachment theories	Nurses, trained nonprofessional home visitors
Incredible Years: Parents, Teachers, and Children Training Series	Early Childhood Childhood	Universal Selected Indicated (comprehensive)	Canada, United States, Great Britain, Norway	Cognitive Social Learning Theory (Patterson's Social Learning Model)	Trained therapists and interventionists, parents, and teachers
Families and Schools Together (FAST)	Childhood	Universal Indicated (comprehensive)	United States	Ecological–transactional, developmental theory based on risk and protective factors, cognitive social learning theory (Patterson's Social Learning Model)	Teachers, parents, low-risk classmates, paraprofessionals in education settings, and counselors
Nurturing Parent Program	0 to 18 years old	Selective	United States	Cognitive behavioral, social skills learning, attachment theory	Trained therapists and interventionists, and parents
Family Effectiveness Training	Adolescents	Selective	United States—(Miami), Hispanic youth	Information processing, social cognitive, ecological–transactional, behavioral and social learning theories	Trained therapists and interventionists, parents, and teachers
		Indicated			

Note: Based on *The Strengthening Families Exemplary Parenting and Family Strategies*, by K. L. Kumpfer, Washington, DC: U.S. Department of Justice, Office of Justice Programs, Office of Juvenile Justice and Delinquency Prevention; and *Successful Prevention and Youth Development Programs across Borders*, by L. Ferrer-Wreder, H. Statin, C. Cass Lorente, J. G. Tubman, and L. Adamson, 2004, New York, NY: Krueger Academic/Plenum Press.

See the other effective family-centered programs for a more extensive description of these programs (Kumpfer, 1999). We have presented some programs that are currently being disseminated. However, a final point needs to be made regarding the cost of delivering an effective family-centered intervention. According to the literature review of exemplary intervention programs, the following information about parenting programs emerged:

> Parent-training and family therapy intervention programs, particularly with young children who have shown aggressive behavior in school, were found to be relatively cost-effective over the long run at a cost of approximately $6,500 per serious felony prevented. However, the effects of this type of intervention usually does not show any significant consequences for at least 10 years because participating youths are usually in the 7- to 10-year age range. Delinquent supervision programs cost nearly $14,000 per serious crime prevented. (p. 33)

Parent support is another approach to complement these interventions.

Conclusions

In conclusion, it is important to remember that there is no "one size fits all," and selecting the family-centered approach will depend on the program area and the service system. Child welfare service systems will likely choose different programs than mental health service systems. Family-centered approaches are individualized, target family interactional changes, and work with the social context for changing the system. Although research is strong in this area, the adoption of family-centered programs in service systems has been slow. Tailored approaches are important, and implementation of programs requires that the agency increase its ownership of the program it intends to implement. Use of a family-centered perspective is a conceptual shift in the way practitioners think about what is helpful for children and youth. It is not only a specific set of strategies to use with families—for example, Incredible Years, or family group conferencing for child welfare (see Burford, Pennell, & Edwards, 2011)—a framework based on the way to protect children and youth, and strengthen and support their families. Participatory involvement in program selection increases the likelihood that family-centered programs will be adapted and implemented in the services organization.

Parents need to feel included and essential to aspects of treatment; therefore, the family is viewed as the client rather than focusing only on the child. Children of effective parents experience family cohesion, warmth, harmony, and the absence of neglect in their families (Kazdin & Weisz, 2003). The following characteristics guide family-centered approaches:

- Use of comprehensive (targeting family, peers, and community systems) resources. It is important to modify a broader range of risk or protective factors and processes in children and youth for longer-term positive outcomes.

- Family-centered strategies are more effective than child-focused-only or parent-focused-only approaches.

- Parenting and family interventions must be tailored to the developmental stage of the child or youth and the specific risk factors in the family served.

- Programs need to provide sufficient amounts and intensity of interventions to produce the desired effects and provide follow-up to maintain effects.

- Tailor the parent or family intervention to the cultural traditions of the families involved to improve recruitment, retention, and outcome effectiveness (Martinez & Eddy, 2005).

Excellent programs are identified to improve practices and child, youth, and family functioning. Nevertheless, to continue to go forward, researchers and practitioners need to move away from treating problems and move toward preventing problems. To address problem behaviors, more attention needs to be paid to the lack of support in the environments of children and youth—specifically, the lack of support in families, schools, and communities, and in the sociopolitical context. Policies need to be directed to improve the environments of children and youth rather than focused on changing individual characteristics or behaviors. In this way, research can inform policy, and the involvement of parents, policy makers, and politicians can demonstrate how essential it is to have a rationale for multiple problem prevention programs because children and youth are at risk for multiple negative outcomes because of their dysfunctional and stressed environments. There is now sufficient knowledge about the characteristics of effective family-centered programs for researchers and practitioners to support policies that encourage multicomponent, coordinated preventive interventions.

Key Terms

Ecological developmental framework	Family-centered framework	Family systems practice
Evidence-based practice	Family-centered practice	

Review Questions for Critical Thinking

1. What are the advantages of using a family-centered practice approach for children, youth, or families as part of your ongoing practice?

2. Give an example of how a family-centered practice framework is used to develop the intervention plan for services?

3. Identify specific child or youth problems that are potentially exacerbated or improved by family-centered practice?

4. Go to the Internet to find a specific family-centered program that may be appropriate for the populations with whom you are involved and discuss how it may be adapted in your setting.

Online Resources

Family-Centered Models: www.caseyfamilyservices.org/userfiles/pdf/teaming-comparing-approaches-2009.pdf
- Family Group Decision Making/Family Group Conferences
- Family Team Conferencing
- Permanency Teaming Process
- Team Decision Making

Compares each of four family-centered models used for involving families and sharing responsibility for getting children safely out of the child welfare system and home again. The unique elements of the practice approach for meeting the needs of children and families at different points in case management are compared.

Family-Centered Assessment: www.hunter.cuny.edu/socwork/nrcfcpp/downloads/newsletter/BPNPSummer00.pdf

Compares family-centered child welfare services with conventional child welfare services on engagement, assessment, safely planning, out-of-home placement approaches, implementation of service plan, permanency planning, and reevaluation of service plans.

Slides Reviewing Principles of Family-Centered Approaches: www.ssw.umich.edu/public/currentProjects/tpcws/permanencyPlanning/PhilosophyAndGoals.html

Provides slides, with Dr. W. Meezan narrating the key principles and philosophy of family-centered practice.

Guidelines for Assessment in Child Welfare Family-Centered Approaches: www.acf.hhs.gov/programs/cb/pubs/family_assessment/family_assessment.pdf

Describes comprehensive family assessment guidelines for child welfare using a family involved approach. Such assessment goes beyond the investigation to permit the identification and provision of services that are specifically targeted to address the family's needs and problems and ensure the child's safety, well-being, and permanency.

References

Alexander, J. F., & Parsons, B. V. (1982). *Functional family therapy: Principles and procedures*. Carmel, CA: Brooks/Cole.

Alexander, J. F., Robbins, M., & Sexton, T. (2000). Family-based interventions with older, at-risk youth: From promise to proof to practice. *Journal of Primary Prevention, 21*(2), 185–205.

Baumeister, R. F., & Leary, M. R. (1995). The need to belong: Desire for interpersonal attachment as a fundamental human motivation. *Psychological Bulletin, 117*, 497–529.

Bavolek, S. J. (1987, Winter). Validation of the nurturing program for parents and adolescents: Building nurturing interactions in families experiencing parent-adolescent conflict. Research report. Retrieved March 15, 2007, from www.nurturingparenting.com/research_validation/a9_np_validation_studies.pdf

Bavolek, S. J., McLaughlin, J. A., & Comstock, C. M. (1983). *The nurturing parenting programs: A validated approach for reducing dysfunctional family interactions*. Final report 1R01MH34862. Rockville, MD: National Institute of Mental Health.

Bernard, B. (2002). Turnaround people and places: Moving from risk to resilience. In D. Saleebey (Ed.), *The strengths perspective in social work practice* (3rd ed., pp. 213–227). Boston, MA: Allyn & Bacon.

Bernard, B. (2006). Using strengths-based practice to tap the resilience of families. In D. Saleebey (Ed.), *The strengths perspective in social work practice* (4th ed., pp. 197–220). Boston, MA: Allyn & Bacon.

Blum, R., Beuhring, T., Shew, M., Bearinger, L., Sieving, R., & Resnick, M. (2000). The effects of race/ethnicity, income, and family structure on adolescent risk behaviors. *American Journal of Public Health, 90*, 1879–1884.

Bowlby, J. (1982). *Attachment and loss. Vol. 1: Attachment*. New York, NY: Basic Books.

Bronfenbrenner, U. (1986). Ecology of the family as a context for human development: Research perspectives. *Developmental Psychology, 22*(6), 723–742.

Bry, B. H., Catalano, R. F., Kumpfer, K. L., Lochman, J. E., & Szapocznik, J. (1998). Scientific findings from family prevention intervention research. In R. Ashery & K. L., Kumpfer (Eds.), *Family-focused preventions of drug abuse: Research and interventions* (pp. 103–129). NIDA Research Monograph. Washington, DC: Superintendent of Documents U.S. Government Printing Office. Retrieved March 14, 2007, from www.hawaii.edu/hivandaids/Scientific%20Findings%20From%20Family%20Prevention%20Intervention%20Research.pdf

Burford, G., Pennell, J., & Edwards, M. (2011). Family team meetings as principled advocacy. *Journal of Public Child Welfare, 5*, 318–344.

Catalano, R. F., Haggerty, K. P., Oesterle, S., Fleming, C. B., & Hawkins, J. D. (2004). The importance of bonding to school for healthy development: Findings from the social development research group. *Journal of School Health, 74*, 252–262.

Chamberlain, P. (1994). *Family connections*. Eugene, OR: Castalia.

Chamberlain, P., & Reid, J. B. (1991). Using a specialized foster care community treatment model for children and adolescents leaving a state mental hospital. *Journal of Community Psychology, 19*, 266–276.

Conduct Problems Prevention Research Group. (2000). Merging universal and indicated prevention programs: The fast-track model. *Addictive Behaviors, 25*(6), 913–927.

Dishion, T. J., French, D. C., & Patterson, G. R. (1995). The development and ecology of antisocial behavior. In D. Cicchetti & D. J. Cohen (Eds.), *Developmental psychopathology. Vol. 2: Risk, disorder, and adaptation* (pp. 421–471). New York, NY: John Wiley & Sons.

Dishion, T. J., & Kavanagh, K. (2003). *Intervening in adolescent problem behavior: A family-centered approach.* New York, NY: Guilford Press.

Dunst, C. J., & Trivett, C. M. (1994). Methodological considerations and strategies for studying the long-term follow-up of early intervention. In S. Friedman & H. C. Haywood (Eds.), *Developmental follow-up: Concepts, domains, and methods* (pp. 277–313). San Diego, CA: Academic Press.

Ferrer-Wreder, L., Stattin, H., Cass Lorente, C., Tubman, J. G., & Adamson, L. (2004). *Successful prevention and youth development programs across borders.* New York, NY: Kluwer Academic/Plenum Press.

Fraser, M. W. (Ed.). (2004). *Risk and resilience in childhood: An ecological perspective* (2nd ed.). Washington, DC: National Association of Social Workers Press.

Fraser, M. W., Kirby, L., & Smokowski, P. R. (2004). Risk and resilience in childhood. In M. W. Fraser (Ed.), *Risk and resilience in childhood. An ecological perspective* (2nd ed., pp. 13–67). Washington, DC: National Association of Social Workers Press.

Gambrill, E. (1997). *Social work practice. A critical thinker's guide.* New York, NY: Oxford University Press.

Gambrill, E. (2006). Evidence-based practice and policy: Choices ahead. *Research on Social Work Practice, 16*(3), 338–357.

Guterman, N. B., & Embry, R. A. (2004). Prevention and treatment strategies targeting physical child abuse and neglect. In P. Allen-Meares & M. W. Fraser (Eds.), *Intervention with children and adolescents. An interdisciplinary perspective* (pp. 130–158). Boston, MA: Allyn & Bacon.

Haley, J. (1976). *Problem solving therapy.* San Francisco, CA: Jossey-Bass.

Hawkins, J. D., Catalano, R. F., Morrison, D. M., O'Donnell, J., Abbott, R. D., & Day, L. E. (1992). The Seattle social development project: Effects of the first four years on protective factors and problem behaviors. In J. McCord & R. Tremblay (Eds.), *Preventing antisocial behavior* (pp. 139–161). New York, NY: Guilford Press.

Henggeler, S. W., & Borduin, C. M. (1990). *Family therapy and beyond: A multisystemic approach to treating the behavior problems of children and adolescents.* Pacific Grove, CA: Brooks/Cole.

Henggeler, S. W., Schoenwald, S. K., Borduin, C. M., Rowland, M. D., & Cunningham, P. B. (1998). *Multisystemic treatment of antisocial behavior in children and adolescents.* New York, NY: Guilford Press.

Janzen, C., Harris, O., Jordan, C., & Franklin, C. (2006). *Family treatment: Evidence-based practice with populations at risk.* Belmont, CA: Brooks/Cole.

Kazdin, A. E., & Weisz, J. R. (2003). *Evidence-based psychotherapies for children and adolescents.* New York, NY: Guilford Press.

Kinard, E. M. (1999). Psychosocial resources and academic performance in abused children. *Children and Youth Services, 21*, 351–376.

Kumpfer, K. L. (1999). Strengthening America's families: Promising parent and family strategies for delinquency prevention. (User's guide prepared for the

U.S. Department of Justice under Grant No. 95-JN-FX-K010). Washington, DC: U.S. Department of Justice, Office of Justice Programs, Office of Juvenile Justice and Delinquency Prevention.

Kumpfer, K. L., Alexander, J. F., McDonald, L., & Olds, D. L. (1998). Family-focused substance abuse prevention: What has been learned from other fields. In R. Ashery, E. B. Robertson, & K. L. Kumpfer (Eds.), *Drug abuse prevention through family interventions (NIDA Research Monograph)*, *17*, 78–102. Retrieved February 25, 2007, from www.drugabuse.gov/pdf/monographs/Monograph177/078—102_Kumpfer.pdf

Kumpfer, K. L., & Alvarado, R. (1998, November). Effective family strengthening interventions. *OJJDP Juvenile Justice Bulletin* [NCJ 171121]. Washington, DC: U.S. Department of Justice, Office of Justice Programs, Office of Juvenile Justice and Delinquency Prevention.

Kumpfer, K. L., Alvarado, R., Smith, P., & Bellamy, N. (2002). Cultural sensitivity and adaptation in family-based prevention interventions. *Prevention Science*, *3*, 241–246.

Kumpfer, K. L., DeMarsh, J. P., & Child, W. (1989). *The Strengthening Families program: Parent training manual*. Salt Lake City, UT: University of Utah, Department of Health Education, and Alta Institute.

Kumpfer, K. L., Molgaard, V., & Spoth, R. (1996). The Strengthening Families program for the prevention of delinquency and drug use. In R. D. Peters & R. J. McMahon (Eds.), *Preventing childhood disorders, substance abuse, and delinquency* (pp. 241–267). Thousand Oaks, CA: Sage.

Liddle, H. A. (1999). Theory development in a family-based therapy for adolescent drug abuse. *Journal of Clinical Child Psychology*, *28*, 521–532.

Liddle, H. A. (2010). Multidimensional family therapy: A science-based treatment system. *The Australian and New Zealand Journal of Family Therapy*, *31*, 133–148

Liddle, H. A., & Rowe, C. L. (2006). Advances in family therapy research. In M. P. Nichols, R. C. Schwartz, & S. Minuchin (Eds.), *Family therapy: Concepts and methods* (6th ed., pp. 395–436). Needham Heights, MA: Allyn & Bacon.

Martinez, C. R., Jr., & Eddy, J. M. (2005). Effects of culturally adapted parent management training on Latino youth behavioral health outcomes. *Journal of Consulting and Clinical Psychology*, *73*(5), 841–851.

Masten, A. S., Hubbard, J. J., Gest, S. D., Tellegen, A., Garmezy, N., & Ramirez, M. (1999). Competence in the context of adversity: Pathways to resilience and maladaptation from childhood to late adolescence. *Development and Psychopathology*, *11*(1), 143–169.

McDonald, L., Coe-Braddish, D., Billingham, S., Dibble, N., & Rice, C. (1991). Families and schools together: An innovative substance abuse prevention program. *Social Work in Education*, *12*(2), 118–128.

Minuchin, S. (1974). *Families and family therapy*. Cambridge, MA: Harvard University Press.

Mira, S. (2007). *Maternal and paternal nurturance and involvement in intact and divorced families as a predictor of adult children's romantic relationship satisfaction*. Unpublished manuscript. Miami, FL: Florida International University.

Molgaard, V., & Kumpfer, K. L. (1994). *Strengthening Families program 2*. Ames, IA: Iowa State University, Social and Behavioral Research Center for Rural Health.

Mrazek, P. J., & Haggerty, R. J. (Eds.). (1994). *Reducing risks for mental disorders: Frontiers for preventive intervention research*. Washington, DC: National Academy Press.

National Institute for Drug Abuse. (2003). Evidence-based prevention practices. Retrieved January 8, 2007, from http://captus.samhsa.gov/southwest/documents/AppendixIEvidence-BasedPreventionPrac_000.doc

Nichols, M. P., & Schwartz, R. C. (2004). *Family therapy: Concepts and methods* (6th ed.). Needham Heights, MA: Allyn & Bacon.

Olds, D. L. (2002). Prenatal and infancy home visiting by nurses: From randomized trials to community replication. *Prevention Science, 31*(3), 153–172.

Olds, D., & Kitzman, H. (1993). Review of research on home visits for pregnant women and parents of young children. *Future of Children, 3*(3), 53–92.

Osofsky, J. D., & Thompson, M. D. (2000). Adaptive and maladaptive parenting: Perspectives on risk and protective factors. In J. P. Shonkoff & S. J. Meisels (Eds.), *Handbook of early childhood intervention* (2nd ed., pp. 54–76). New York, NY: Cambridge University Press.

Patterson, G. R., Reid, J. B., & Dishion, T. J. (1992). *Antisocial boys.* Eugene, OR: Castalia.

Pollard, J. A., Hawkins, J. D., & Arthur, M. W. (1999). Risk and protection: Are both necessary to understand diverse behavioral outcomes in adolescence? *Social Work Research, 23*(3), 145–158.

Roberts, A. R., & Yeager, K. R. (Eds.). (2004). *Evidence-based social work practice.* New York, NY: Oxford University Press.

Rothery, M., & Enns, G. (2001). *Clinical practice with families. Supporting creativity and competence.* New York, NY: Haworth Press.

Rutter, M. (1987). Psychosocial resilience and protective mechanism. *American Journal of Orthopsychiatry, 57*, 316–330.

Rutter, M. (2000). Resilience reconsidered: Conceptual considerations, empirical findings, and policy implications. In J. P. Shonkoff & S. J. Meisels (Eds.), *Handbook of early childhood intervention* (2nd ed., pp. 651–683). New York, NY: Cambridge University Press.

Scherer, K. R., Wallbott, H. G., & Summerfield, A. B. (1986). *Experiencing emotion: A cross-cultural study.* Cambridge, UK: Cambridge University Press.

Shadish, W. R., Ragsdale, K., Glaser, R. R., & Montgomery, L. M. (1995). The efficacy and effectiveness of marital and family therapy: A perspective from meta-analysis. *Journal of Marital and Family Therapy, 21*, 345–360.

Spoth, R. L., Kavanagh, K. A., & Dishion, T. J. (2002). Family-centered preventive intervention science: Toward benefits to larger populations of children, youth, and families. *Prevention Science, 3*(3), 145–152.

Szapocznik, J., Santisteban, D., Rio, A., Perez-Vidal, A., & Kurtines, W. M. (1989). Family effectiveness training: An intervention to prevent drug abuse and problem behavior in Hispanic adolescents. *Hispanic Journal of Behavioral Sciences, 11*, 3–27.

Szapocznik, J., Scopetta, M. A., & King, O. E. (1978). Theory and practice in matching treatment to the special characteristics and problems of Cuban immigrants. *Journal of Community Psychology, 6*, 112–122.

Szapocznik, J., & Williams, R. A. (2000). Brief strategic family therapy: Twenty-five years of interplay among theory, research, and practice in adolescent behavior problems and drug abuse. *Clinical Child and Family Psychology Review, 3*, 117–134.

Taylor, T., & Biglan, A. (1998). Behavioral family interventions for improving child-rearing: A review of the literature for clinicians and policy makers. *Clinical Child and Family Psychology Review, 1*(1), 41–60.

Thomlison, B. (2004). Child maltreatment: A risk and protective factor perspective. In M. W. Fraser (Ed.), *Risk and resilience in childhood: An ecological perspective* (2nd ed., pp. 89–133). Washington, DC: National Association of Social Workers Press.

Thomlison, B. (2007). *Family assessment handbook: An introduction and practical guide to family assessment and intervention* (2nd ed.). Belmont, CA: Brooks/Cole Wadsworth.

Thomlison, B., & Craig, S. (2005). Ineffective parenting. In C. Dulmus & L. Rapp-Paglicci (Eds.), *Handbook of preventive interventions for adults* (pp. 327–359). Hoboken, NJ: John Wiley & Sons.

Veltman, M. W., & Browne, K. D. (2001). Three decades of child maltreatment research: Implications for the school years. *Trauma, Violence, and Abuse: A Review Journal, 2*, 215–240.

Webster-Stratton, C. (1998). Preventing conduct problems in Head Start children. Strengthening parenting competencies. *Journal of Consulting and Clinical Psychology, 66*, 715–730.

Webster-Stratton, C., Hollinsworth, T., & Kolpacoff, M. (1989). The long-term effectiveness and clinical significance of three cost-effective training programs for families with conduct-problem children. *Journal of Consulting and Clinical Psychology, 57*(4), 550–553.

Webster-Stratton, C., Kolpacoff, M., & Hollinsworth, T. (1988). Self-administered videotape therapy for families with conduct-problem children: Comparison with two cost-effective treatments and a control group. *Journal of Consulting and Clinical Psychology, 56*(4), 558–566.

Webster-Stratton, C., & Taylor, T. (2001). Nipping risk factors in the bud: Preventing substance abuse, delinquency, and violence in adolescence through interventions targeted at young children (0–8 years). *Prevention Science, 2*(3), 165–192.

Widom, C. S. (1989). Does violence beget violence? A critical examination of the literature. *Psychological Bulletin, 106*, 3–28.

Chapter 3
School Social Work

Cynthia Franklin, Beth Gerlach, and
Amy Chanmugam

How do school social workers enhance the schools' academic programs?

School social work is a specific branch of the social work profession that works to support student learning and social and emotional adjustment through direct service, service coordination, and advocacy in an academic setting. Social workers have been providing school-based social services to children and families in the United States for more than 100 years and have evolved into a unique profession within the United States. School social work is also an international profession practiced in many other countries. School social workers support the right of every child to receive an education and successfully complete school (Allen-Meares, Franklin, & Hopson, 2010). School social workers believe that emotional and physical needs must be addressed for children to be able to fully benefit from the instruction provided at school. To enable the school to best meet its academic mission of educating students, school social workers provide a comprehensive approach to support the strengths of children and families.

This chapter defines the practice of school social work and provides an overview of the profession of school social work, including its history and important contributions to school programs. It highlights the growth of school social workers as a unique profession and identifies the organizations and professional associations that support U.S. school social workers. It also highlights the role of social workers in providing school-based social and mental health services and describes current models of school social services delivery. It further discusses the adaptations that school social workers have made in the past to meet changing demands and offer suggestions for continuing to serve the complex needs of children in the schools. Finally, this chapter recognizes the invaluable role of school social workers in addressing the needs of children and families, and the expertise and skills of the school social worker in building programs that help remove obstacles to learning.

Importance of School Social Work Practice

The politics and societal issues that surround educational systems have greatly impacted and shaped school social work practices (M. Kelly, 2009). The complexities of society, for example, are an integral part of the educational process in present day schools. School social workers are often asked to attend to a wide range of physical health, mental health, and psychosocial concerns, including crisis intervention, family and school violence, attendance issues, school dropouts, disability, military deployment and relocation stress, abuse, substance use, relationship difficulties, delinquency, poverty, teen pregnancy, and homelessness.

It is estimated that 12% to 22% of all children under the age of 18 are at some time in need of support for mental, emotional, or behavioral problems. In low-income schools affected by poverty, it is estimated that up to 50% of students have learning and emotional problems that are challenging their success in school and in life. In addition, based on the widespread challenges to children and families, it is inevitable that schools become the de facto mental health agency that offers services to children and adolescents. A 2005–2006 national survey by the Substance Abuse and Mental Health Services Administration (SAMHSA), for example, reported that 3.0 million youths (12.0%) received interventions for emotional or behavioral problems in schools, compared to 3.3 million youths aged 12 to 17 (13.3%) who received services for emotional or behavioral problems in a specialty mental health setting and around 752,000 (3.0%) who received such services in a general medical setting (SAMHSA, 2008 cited in Adelman & Taylor, 2010).

Definition of School Social Work Practice

As school social workers have evolved into a specialized profession with an important role in the schools, differing definitions and job descriptions have been provided for the important contributions of school social workers. Typical of these definitions has been a description of the role of the school social worker as a facilitator between school, home, and community relationships. The School Social Work Association of America (SSWAA), the largest U.S. school social work professional organization currently defines school social work in this way:

> School Social Work is a specialized area of practice within the broad field of the social work profession. School social workers bring unique knowledge and skills to the school system and the student services team. School Social Workers are instrumental in furthering the purpose of the schools: To provide a setting for teaching, learning, and for the attainment of competence and confidence. School social workers are hired by school districts to enhance the district's ability to meet its academic mission, especially where home, school and community collaboration is the key to achieving that mission. (www.sswaa.org)

History of School Social Work

School social work practice emerged because schools were required to educate an increasing population of diverse children and needed to link with community services to be able to do so. The origins of school social work can be traced to New York City; Boston, Massachusetts; and New Haven, Connecticut, in 1906. Social workers were already working in these areas with a community social welfare perspective, and the schools became the next natural extension for their professional attention. During the early 1900s, schools were struggling to meet the multifaceted needs of their students. At that time, compulsory education laws introduced more children into public schools, while growing immigration and urbanization increased the diversity. Social workers were called on to help facilitate understanding between the public schools and the families of the children enrolled.

The first school social workers brought their knowledge of the varied effects of poverty into the schools to help school staff meet the new challenges in public education. In addition, the school social workers were able to connect families who had little experience with public education to important resources in the community and help them to participate more meaningfully in their children's education. School social workers' prominence grew throughout the first part of the 1900s and played a key role in helping schools and families through difficult times, like the Great Depression.

As the mid-century approached, the psychoanalytic movement in the mental health field was also growing. School social workers responded to the changing trends in mental health services and began to focus more on therapeutic interventions and clinical social work. At this time, public schools were also shifting toward a system that was more bureaucratic and isolated. Models of comprehensive schooling that embraced health and social services gave way to a more individualized view of education and mental health (Franklin & Streeter, 1995). In turn, school social workers enhanced their focus on a more clinical approach to social casework.

However, with the influence of the social changes like school desegregation and civil rights occurring in the 1960s, school social workers and education reformers incorporated more of the ideas from comprehensive schooling models from their past. Throughout the 1960s and 1970s, they combined their clinical skills with their systems perspective and reenergized the field's focus on the need for interventions that include attention to individuals, families, schools, and communities. In addition, debates and legislation about student rights, discipline, educational opportunity, civil rights, and gender equality sparked a renewed commitment to educational policy and social change.

During the last quarter of the 20th century, there was an increased recognition that schools were often failing to meet the educational needs of their children. During this time, attention was focused on improving services and educational opportunities for children with learning and behavior problems, as well as children in poverty. School social workers were often included in the discussion of solutions for addressing the social and emotional problems that were adversely affecting learning. They have also been instrumental in the emphasis to prevent and intervene with the social issues that have permeated the public schools, such as substance abuse, teen parenting, and violence.

As we have entered the 21st century, school social workers have continued to be responsive to the needs of the school's most "at-risk" populations, supporting school reforms, such as School-Wide Behavior Supports and Response to Intervention, which emphasized prevention models leading to better outcomes for all students. The past 10 years have also ushered in many changes in education, such as revisions to the controversial educational policy, No Child Left Behind, that emphasizes performance improvements and greater accountability (Berzin et al., 2011; Frey, 2011). School social workers have continued to assist schools in their mission to educate students by applying both clinical and community practices and also have increased their involvement with teachers in the delivery of the best evidence-based approaches. These time-proven approaches of school social workers are especially relevant to today's schools because social workers seek solutions that make sense for the individual student in the context of the environment by using the guiding principles of the ecological approach. They work to achieve educational opportunities and achievement for all students by removing barriers to educational success and supporting changes at the individual, home, school, and community levels.

Professional Organizations, Credentials, and Standards for School Social Workers

In 1916, just 10 years after social workers began to formally work in schools, the National Conference of Visiting Teachers and Home and School Visitors was planned to support the work of school-based social services providers. Through the work of the conference, the National Association of Visiting Teachers was formed in 1919, later evolving into the National Association of School Social Workers (NASSW). In 1955, the National Association of Social Workers (NASW) was formed through the merging of seven different social work professional organizations, including the NASSW. NASW is currently more than 150,000 members strong and continues to dedicate specific attention to school social work.

In 1990, the International Network for School Social Work (INSSW) was formed to share information and provide resources to school social workers worldwide. The first international school social work conference was held in 1999 in Chicago and welcomed school social work professionals and educators from 20 different countries. Since then, the international school social community has exchanged information between 43 countries on six continents and has organized additional conferences in Sweden (2003), Korea (2006), New Zealand (2009), and Ghana (2012).

School social work practitioners and educators are also supported by their own professional organization, the School Social Work Association of America (SSWAA). The mission of the SSWAA "is dedicated to promoting the profession of School Social Work and the professional development of School Social Workers in order to enhance the educational experience of students and their families" (www.sswaa.org). SSWAA also publishes a wide variety of resources and brochures to be used in the field and holds an annual national conference dedicated to school social work practice, education, research, and policy.

In addition, many states and regions have professional organizations for school social workers. Some of these organizations also hold annual conferences for school social workers. For example, the Midwest School Social Work Association was formed in 1968 and represents 11 Midwestern states and their professional school social work organizations. Additionally, they organize an annual Midwest School Social Work Conference every fall and created a leadership council to address important issues in the field (www.midwest-ssw.org/history.html). As a statewide example, Texas also holds an annual school social work conference each spring with close to 500 attendees (Nowicki, as cited in Franklin, 2006).

School social work practitioners and educators can access support and resources and share research in a number of excellent social work journals. Two journals in particular provide information specific to the field of school social work. *Children and Schools* is published quarterly by NASW and provides original articles pertaining to research, practice, and policy in the school social work profession. The *School Social Work Journal* is sponsored by the Illinois Association of School Social Workers and is published twice a year. It also provides articles specific to social work practice in schools for social workers placed in schools, social work educators, and school social work policymakers.

Current Statistics About Numbers of School Social Workers

The diverse roles, complex funding streams, and varied employment titles make it difficult to accurately estimate the number of school social workers in the United States. The School Social Workers Association of America (SSWAA) estimates that there are approximately 18,000 social workers employed in U.S. schools. They estimate that prior to the economic downturn of 2008, there were as many as 20,000 to 22,000. Although many state school social work associations have reported staffing reductions, some areas or districts have continued to report increased hiring of school social workers (Frederick Streeck, personal communication, September 2011). While educational funding streams have become more limited in recent years at district, state, and federal levels, increased recognition of how issues like bullying, school climate, and social and emotional concerns affect student academics suggest that there may be increased investment in school mental health staff, including social workers, when economic conditions improve. Two bills introduced in the U.S. Congress in late 2011 include measures to increase hiring of school social workers.

Professional Standards

School social workers must have adequate training and maintain specific professional standards. NASW first developed a set of formal practice standards for school social work services in 1978. The standards are intended to serve as guidelines for best professional practice in the field of school social work. The standards were revised and updated in 1992 and in 2002 in order to reflect the current issues in the field and changes in educational policy. The school social work standards first require adherence to the NASW Code of Ethics for social work practice. They further include expectations about filling multiple responsibilities, cultural competency, proper assessment techniques, interdisciplinary collaboration, and policy awareness, to name a few. Currently, NASW supports 42 specific standards for professional practice for school social work services that can be accessed through the NASW website at www.socialworkers.org/practice/standards/NASW_SSWS.pdf.

Licensing and Credentials

Every school that employs a school social worker has expectations that he or she has been adequately trained and will function at a high professional standard. NASW has created a program for a Certified School Social Work Specialist that establishes a professional as meeting their explicit standards of school social work practice (Allen-Meares, 2004). However, each state, and even district, might have a different understanding about the necessary licensing and credentials for a school social worker. In fact, each state has its own educational jurisdiction that regulates the educational training, licensing, and credentials required to provide mental health services in a school. Some states are moving toward credentialing and certification of school social work professionals as a way to ensure a more uniform quality of personnel.

As of early 2009, ten states did not have specific standards for certification of school social workers (Mumm & Bye, 2011). Other states vary in educational requirements, ranging from requiring MSWs with specific school-related coursework to a bachelor's from any discipline. Ten states require that school social workers hold the BSW degree for certification, and 20 require the MSW (Altshuler & Webb, 2009). Beyond the type of educational degree, certification standards might include specific coursework requirements, a school-based internship, and passing an exam. For example, Illinois requires school social workers to have an MSW degree, have completed coursework in disabilities and school law, have completed a 600-hour practicum, and pass the Praxis II certification test, demonstrating competence in both social work and basic academic skills. Altshuler and Webb argue that social work organizations should further develop more consistently defined competencies for school social work practice.

Research on Tasks and Roles of School Social Workers

A substantial amount of research has examined the job responsibilities and tasks performed by school social workers in the past 40 years (Allen-Meares, 1977, 1994; Costin, 1969). In general, researchers have found a large number and wide range of tasks that school social workers are called on to perform, including case management, agency referrals, advocacy, therapy, crisis intervention, and home visits. Although certainly not surprising to busy school social workers, in a survey in the early 1990s, Allen-Meares (1994) found 104 tasks performed by school social workers, 100 of which were deemed at least "very important."

In a landmark study in 1969, Costin conducted a national survey of masters-level school social workers to determine how they viewed their roles in the schools. She established that school social workers felt their key task was clinical casework that focused on individual emotion and personality. She also found that school social workers ranked leadership and policy advocacy last in their service delivery and often struggled to entrust tasks to other school professionals. Through a historical lens, these findings fit with the trends in education during this time. In 1994, Allen-Meares replicated the Costin study and found that school social workers continued to be expected to fill multiple tasks and a wide range of roles. However, she found a trend away from the role of a primary clinical caseworker to the role of a home–school–community liaison. Again, the evolving role of school social workers seems to correspond with the progressive education reform of the time, the educational mandates that are in vogue, and how their jobs are funded. As public schools continue to change and evolve to meet the needs of students, school social work will likely respond in kind. However, the field will be challenged to balance the many expectations and to determine the roles and responsibilities best suited for school social work intervention.

The mass changes in education and the complexity in roles and tasks in the school social work field in the past 10 years inspired another national survey to update the understanding of the current state of the profession. The National School Social Work survey, administered in 2008, collected information from a national sample of school social workers ($n = 1,639$). The findings from the most recent survey suggest that despite the significant changes in education, school social practice has largely remained unchanged in professional demographics, practice settings, and service approach. For the most part, school social workers still practice within a clinical casework orientation and struggle with large caseloads and extensive administrative tasks. Most referrals are for students who are already facing emotional and behavioral problems affecting their academic achievement. The survey revealed that the student populations served continue to experience multiple barriers to learning and have few resources for support, leaving the school social worker as the primary source of mental health intervention. Due to the complex nature of student problems, combined with the emphasis in education on Response to Intervention

(RTI) and Positive Behavioral Supports (PBS), the authors echo the recommendations from earlier surveys for school social workers to increase their emphasis on multisystem change and prevention (M. Kelly, Berzin, Frey, Alvarez, Shaffer, & O'Brien, 2010).

It is also instructive to look at the individual states that have replicated the national survey to look at recent roles and tasks of school social workers. For example, M. S. Kelly (2007) conducted a cross-sectional survey of school social workers presently employed in Illinois. This survey was delivered to a sample of 821 school social workers in Illinois contacted via e-mail to participate in an online survey. Data obtained from this study ($n = 821$) found that an overwhelming majority of Illinois school social workers rate their job satisfaction as high, and their practice choices are largely unaffected by the mass school reforms that have taken place or the school climate issues around them. The majority of school social workers in Illinois report spending most of their time immersed in serving the demands of the special education/individualized education plan (IEP) process, and fewer report having time to do prevention work or deliver school social work services to a significant number of students in regular education. According to the findings in Kelly's survey, school social workers in Illinois appear to be specialized on the "core technology" of special education IEP mandates and individual and small group counseling, rather than participating in any of the recent practice innovations and community-based trends of the past two decades.

School-Based Practices and Program Innovations Impacting School Social Work

As was indicated earlier, social workers first entered schools to help with the demands of educating diverse student populations, and their roles continue to be shaped in relation to the changing demands on school systems. The primary mission of schools to educate students has been challenged by the ravaging effects of poverty, immigration, military deployments, emotional stress, increasing developmental disabilities such as autism spectrum disorders, substance abuse, and mental illnesses (Anderson-Butcher & Ashton, 2004; Franklin, Harris, & Allen-Meares, in press). The recent public sentiment is that the U.S. public education system is falling behind on important benchmarks such as academic achievement in math, science, and reading. In addition, the high school dropout rate often soars beyond 50% for schools in urban areas, leaving parents and policy makers gravely concerned about the abilities of our schools to educate a technologically advanced and democratically prepared citizenry. In response to these trends, federal mandates and policies were passed with the goal of improving the schools, and these policies have greatly influenced school social work practice. The most recent influential policies have been the No Child Left Behind Act (2002) and the reauthorization of Individuals with Disabilities Act (IDEA, 2004). In particular, IDEA created what has been called a "paradigm shift" in the way schools were to deliver their instruction, including the use of evidence-based practices, collaborative work in problem-solving teams, flexible roles, individualized assessment of students, and data-based decision-making (Franklin, Kim, Ryan, Kelly & Montgomery, 2011). Importantly, IDEA also mandated the use of Response to Intervention (RTI), a public health framework that promotes the use of three tiers of intervention corresponding to primary, secondary, and tertiary prevention. RTI is aimed at providing school-wide strategies that will help all children achieve positive academic and behavioral outcomes. RTI has been expanded to include school-wide positive behavioral supports aimed at improving the school climate, and evidence-based mental health practices within schools, and in particular has focused on classroom management abilities of teachers.

RTI frameworks have been influenced by school prevention and intervention research, and these programs are changing how student support services are being delivered in schools. Kelly, Raines, Stone, and Frey (2010) describe five of the current trends in contemporary school programs, including RTI-based programs.

1. Most resources aimed at school-wide, primary prevention
2. Focus on early screening and identifying students that need extra assistance through careful monitoring of student outcomes
3. School-wide supports and comprehensive interventions being delivered that address multiple risk factors such as school, home, and community
4. Emphasis on multitiered approaches that may become more intense for students who need greater assistance.
5. The use of evidence-based practices and data-based decision-making in designing programs (Kelly et al., 2010, pp. 6–9).

School social workers also frequently work in special education, and RTI has also changed the way special education functions, causing the roles of general education and special education programs to overlap more and increasing the work of general education teachers in helping children with serious challenges. In a typical RTI framework, for example, the school first implements universal prevention strategies in every classroom, followed by Tier 2 selective interventions, usually consisting of small group instruction for children that are shown through continuous progress monitoring in data-based assessments to need extra help beyond the universal level. Approximately 20% may require Tier 2. Approximately 5% of students who need help beyond the small group instruction (Tier 2) may be referred into Tier 3 (indicative) interventions that involve more intensive individualized instruction and/or therapeutic approaches. In such a framework, the school social worker takes on many roles, including collaborator and consultant to classroom teachers at Tier 1, as well as interventionist for Tier 2 and 3 students who need extra help to succeed academically.

Other contemporary educational trends that are impacting the present-day practice of school social work include the move toward greater parent- and community-based collaborations. As educators battled with the many social and emotional problems that students brought to the classroom each day, school social workers (and other mental health professionals) and education reformers emphasized the need for schools and communities to collaborate with each other in order to enhance student learning. In many ways, it is a natural partnership, since schools, families, and communities share a common goal of positive academic and social outcomes for children. Moreover, schools recognize the benefit of social services to address barriers to learning for students, and community agencies benefit from the access to vulnerable children and families (Taylor & Adelman, 2006). This can present a win-win situation for schools and community agencies when they successfully collaborate, and ultimately provide better services for children and families. School social workers may serve as the key facilitators of school-community collaborations, and sometimes are *the* link between the school and community. The trend, for community-based collaboration, however, has met some controversy within some states and has even been resisted by some school social workers, because school districts have sought to replace school social workers with community-based mental health workers in an attempt to save money in serving at-risk students (Franklin & Gerlach, 2006). The UCLA Mental Health project has considerable data and information on the school and community-based services and how to practice effectively in these types of school-based services programs (http://smhp.psych.ucla.edu). The long-term sustainment of collaboration and the appropriate policies and infrastructure for practice appear to be significant for all successful community collaborations with schools.

Multiple Responsibilities and Professional Ethics in School Social Work Practice

School social workers not only juggle numerous tasks and complex problems, they are also accountable to multiple stakeholders. School social workers must navigate multifaceted obligations that are sometimes competing or even in conflict (Kopels & Lindsey, 2006). It is imperative for school social workers to understand the NASW Code of Ethics, as well as legal mandates at the local, state, and federal level (e.g., FERPA, HIPAA). In addition, school social workers must be aware of the policies of their local school board and specific school. They must also have the self-knowledge to discern their own personal values from professional values (Raines, 2006). Often all of these responsibilities and expectations are compatible, but in situations with competing or conflicting obligations, school social workers must make difficult, carefully reasoned decisions in the best interest of their clients that uphold ethical values and standards such as client self-determination, privacy, and confidentiality. Examples of client issues that might trigger the need for risk management and ethical decision-making are substance abuse, child abuse and neglect, suicidal ideation, mental health assessments and diagnoses, sexually transmitted diseases, pregnancy, birth-control practices, parental rights, LGBT student rights, and conflicts between students who are both clients of the social worker (e.g., bullying, dating violence, breach of group confidentiality) (Chanmugam, 2009; Dibble, 2008; D. Kelly, 2005; Polowy & Morgan, 2011). Examples of school policies that could intersect with client issues and similarly require careful risk management and ethical approaches include disciplinary procedures, search and seizure practices, and mandatory drug testing policies (Polowy & Morgan, 2011). For school social workers to appropriately handle ethical dilemmas, they must have full knowledge of ethical standards and laws, as well as strong critical thinking, interpersonal, and communication skills. School social workers also use clinical supervision and professional consultation to help them resolve ethical questions, including legal consultation in some cases (Dibble, 2008; Raines, 2006).

An additional element adding to the complexity of school social work practice is the large, diverse group of community stakeholders interested in public school activities. Anything occurring in public schools falls under public scrutiny. Parents, politicians, school board members, religious leaders, social activists, taxpayers, and the media examine and discuss their perceptions of public schools' strengths and challenges. Again, school social workers must be aware of the larger context within which their practice occurs and skillfully determine when to become involved as consensus-builders or advocates.

In addition to the NASW Code of Ethics, consultation, and supervision, schools social workers can obtain assistance on ethical issues from position statements from school social work professional organizations, like the SSWAA and the Illinois Association of School Social Workers (Kopels & Lindsey, 2006). The SSWAA publishes an Ethical Guidelines series (www.sswaa.org/index.asp?page=90) to help school social workers with specific aspects of the job that contribute to its ethical complexity. For example, one set of guidelines focuses on the privacy rights of minors receiving services (Dibble, 2008), while another explores common situations and recommendations related to social work situated in a host setting (Frey & Lankster, 2008). The precise definition of "client" may at times be ambiguous in a school setting, where a social worker is in contact with hundreds of students, as well as parents, teachers, administrators, and community members. While it is clear in many cases who is a "client," it is possible that others benefit from interactions with the school social worker, for example in large-scale prevention efforts, without perceiving themselves as a client or granting formal voluntary informed consent or assent (Frey & Lankster, 2008; D. Kelly, 2005).

Confidentiality is one of the most pressing ethical concerns for school social workers. Although it is an unequivocal tenet of social work practice, a school can be one of the most difficult settings to interpret the rules of confidentiality for several reasons (Kopels & Lindsey, 2006). School social workers must follow the guidelines for confidentially in the NASW Code of Ethics, which requires client information to remain confidential unless there is a compelling reason to disclose it, as in cases of protection from harm. However, teachers, parents, and administrators all share a concern for student and school well-being and can have expectations that school social workers will disclose important information. School administrators and teachers may be keenly aware of functioning under the *in loco parentis* doctrine, carrying responsibility for the well-being of students entrusted to their supervision during school hours (Frey & Lankster, 2008). Furthermore, the interdisciplinary nature of the school setting teams social workers with other professionals who may be adhering to the ethical codes of their own disciplines (e.g., counselors, school psychologists), and with teachers who may not be familiar with the confidentiality ethos at all (Frey & Lankster, 2008; Kelly, 2005). School social workers may struggle with knowing when it is ethical to disclose client information while maintaining the trust of the child and family, and sustaining working relationships within the school. Ultimately, at the heart of the decision to keep client information confidential or to disclose information to concerned parties is the best interest of the client. However, the school social worker must be well informed of legal and ethical responsibilities, be clear on who their "client" is, and handle the situation with great sensitivity toward the child, family, and school personnel. It is best to use a standard ethical decision-making model that the school social worker has previously reviewed and rehearsed before it is actually needed, because of the inevitability of regular ethical dilemmas in the school setting (Dibble, 2008; Raines, 2006). School social workers also must be alert for unintentional breaches of client privacy or confidentiality in the school setting with highly trafficked teacher break rooms and work rooms, open doors, and limited private meeting spaces (Chanmugam, 2009).

In summary, numerous resources and practices are recommended to assist school social workers in managing inevitable ethical dilemmas. A preventative approach will increase the likelihood that ethical issues are handled appropriately and efficiently. A review of contents of school social work courses in accredited U.S. MSW programs found that confidentiality and ethics were covered in 93% of the courses, suggesting strong preparation to handle ethical decision-making in the school environment (Berzin & O'Connor, 2010). Unintentional breaches of privacy and confidentiality can be prevented with adoption of the NASW (2002) standard calling for school social workers to have an adequate private office. School social workers may use a preventative strategy of working within their districts to shape policies that are compatible with efforts of helping professionals, in addition to staying current on policies from all levels governing daily practice and adopting a standard ethical decision-making model (Dibble, 2008). D. C. Kelly (2005) suggests that school social workers conduct an ethics audit of their setting and use an educator role as a preventative method to handle ethical concerns. Social workers could educate colleagues from other disciplines in the school on their position's role, expertise, and boundaries and answer relevant questions such as how social work documentation requirements differ from school recordkeeping practices.

Current Social Work Settings in Public Schools

The work settings and employment configurations of school social workers vary. Most school social workers are either employed by a school district and work as part of the pupil services team or are employed by a community organization with a school-district contract (Franklin, 2006). In some cases, school social workers may be public sector employees (Lewis, 1998). For example, school-based services are provided by social workers with Community Youth Services in Houston, which is part of Harris County Children's Protective Services.

Regardless of the particular employment and practice configuration, all school social workers serve as members of interprofessional teams. Meeting the needs of students requires working with professionals and paraprofessionals serving in a variety of roles (Harris, Franklin, & Lagana-Riordan, 2010). Interprofessional teams are inevitable in the school setting and offer the opportunity of a collective voice advocating for the needs of children and youth. Team members, including the school social worker, can work together to address individual student needs as well as work toward the common goals of the school. Serving together on a team enables members to learn the perspectives of the other professions involved in the school community. Close collaboration with school staff on behalf of students requires a trusting relationship. School social workers must be aware of the priorities of the other personnel in the school as well as the goals they share in common. When serving in a consultant role with teachers or administrators, school social workers are directly assisting in the resolution of a current concern and indirectly developing the skills of the consultee to manage similar needs as they arise in the future, thus providing a cost-effective service (Albers & Kratochwill, 2006).

Administrative and Funding Configurations of School Social Work Service Delivery

In recent years, a variety of new organizational configurations and collaborations providing school-based services have emerged (Allen-Meares, 2006a). "At a time when a significant number of children are considered to be at risk for academic, behavioral, and social-emotional difficulties, schools are viewed as a location to address these issues through the provision of comprehensive intervention services" (Albers & Kratochwill, 2006, p. 971). Various school models have emerged in response to increased recognition that, because schools are central in the lives of children, they may serve as a primary conduit for delivery of services needed by the child or family. These models include School-Based Health Centers, Expanded School Mental Health Centers, and Community Schools (Franklin & Gerlach, 2006). All these models provide different ways for schools to link health, mental health, and social services into the school setting and make these services more accessible to students who need them. These approaches can be differentiated from the more traditional approach of hiring a school social worker to work for a school district, and they serve as alternative ways to connect social work services to school campuses. Many social workers work within these various community-based, school-linked programs providing social work services to students.

The community schools movement in particular creates school programs similar to those envisioned by early school social work leaders and those who were in the settlement house movements in Chicago, such as Jane Addams at Hull House. Community-based schools act as central market locations for an array of integrated health, mental health, social, and recreational services, usually brought into schools by community-based agencies and financed through multiple funding channels. The school building is open before and after school, evenings, weekends, and summers and becomes a central gathering place for community life. Parents are provided with opportunities to participate in school projects, to attend educational classes, and to build skills to help their children with homework. Family resource centers are organized by parent volunteers and provide space for counseling, meetings, family dinners, and socializing. For a community school to be effective, each community defines its own needs, identifies its own assets, creates its own vision of a community school, and decides what is needed to help children in school. All kinds of services might be provided, from nutrition services and transportation to health and social services, depending on the needs of the students and families (Dryfoos, 2002). The community school might also become active in resolving larger community issues, such as drug abuse, crime, and neighborhood violence, that affect children and their schooling. The school offers a hub for family support, advocacy, and problem solving.

Current Practice Models and Interventions in Use

According to Constable, Kuzmickaite, Harrison, and Volkmann (1999), even though the school social worker has many tasks and roles in job functioning, there are four common factors or tasks that are common to most school social work jobs:

1. Assessment as applied to both direct services and program development

2. Consultations with people across the school system (e.g., teacher and administrators) and as a member of a transdiscipinary team

3. Direct services to individuals, groups, and families

4. Program development activities that assist the school in developing and sustaining programs

School social workers perform these tasks using the ecological systems perspective as a framework and intervene with multiple systems at the different levels that impact the lives of children and adolescents. Services may target individual students, groups, parents, and families, or an entire classroom, school, district, neighborhood, or community (Allen-Meares, 2004; Dupper, 2003; Franklin, 2006). Teachers and administrators may also be seen as the focus for intervention and change (Broussard, 2003; Frey & Dupper, 2005; Dulmus & Sowers, 2004). Local needs and funding structures may determine the general focus of a school social worker's intervention (Harris et al., 2010).

Individuals

Most children in the United States attend public schools; thus the range of experiences and problems that are present in our society occur in the lives of the students whom school social workers know. Many students live in poverty. Students, or someone in their family, may have a mental illness, may have been abused or neglected, or might be involved with the criminal justice system. Many students have learning needs that require an advocate for special education services. Some may be dealing with issues of grief, or loss or separation from loved ones. Families may have relocated often or experienced homelessness. Some students, or a family member, may be abusing alcohol or drugs. School social workers may be called on to intervene because of these concerns at all levels, from individual crisis intervention to community or school-wide prevention or education initiatives.

When practice is focused at the individual student level, the school social worker uses assessment and counseling skills, consults with others as needed, and works to link the student with other resources and service systems to address concerns. With intervention at the individual level, the school social worker is often directly providing the service, or the school social worker may be collaborating with a community agency to bring the needed service into the school, or may be linking the client with services outside the school.

Effective and ethical practice requires knowledge and application of interventions that have been empirically supported or have a significant known track record as clinical best practices. A substantial number of school-based intervention methods for individual students meet these standards (Molina, Bowie, Dulmus, & Sowers, 2004). Franklin, Harris, and Allen-Meares (2006) have compiled detailed information on effective interventions into a comprehensive sourcebook for school social workers. Intervention information is included for most mental health diagnoses and developmental disabilities, as well as for a wide range of other specific student issues—for example, adolescent parents; sexual assault survivors; students who are experiencing grief and loss; and students who are gay, lesbian, bisexual, or transgender. A school social worker seeking information on effective practice to address a specific concern may turn to the sourcebook for an overview of empirically supported interventions. In the case of self-mutilating students, for example, information is provided on cognitive and behavioral intervention (Shepard, DeHay, & Hersh, 2006) as well as integrative, brief solution-oriented treatment (Selekman, 2006).

Online resources are also available to help school social workers access current information on empirically supported practices. The What Works Clearinghouse, for example, is provided by the U.S. Department of Education with the goal of disseminating evidenced-based reviews of practices in education (www.w-w-c.org). Having the knowledge of what type of intervention works for whom is a critical first step to providing ethical and effective services to individuals.

Parents and Families

School social workers may intervene with parents and families to address concerns related to an individual student, or they may target parents themselves for intervention. For a student who is often truant, for example, the social worker may visit the student's home to assess reasons for nonattendance and engage the parent in problem solving. The social worker may also encourage the parent's participation in school activities, such as teacher conferences and PTA meetings. Parents are the experts on their children, and schools and parents are interdependent in their efforts to attend to the child's learning needs (Franklin et al., 2010). A problem in the lives of the parents or family may be stressing the individual child. A strong research base supports the importance and benefits of parental involvement in their children's education (Chavkin, 2006).

Immigrant families and their school-age children may be experiencing additional stressors related to adjustment, cultural, and language issues (Franklin et al., 2010). The school social worker assists through skilled assessment of the family's needs, as well as recognition of barriers in the school that may be limiting their involvement and efforts to eliminate or diminish these barriers. School social workers can work to empower parents in their interactions with the school, including at the policy and decision-making level (Frey & Dupper, 2005).

In general, parents and schools can be encouraged and assisted to strengthen their partnership to the benefit of the children. Many avenues are open for the school social worker to contribute to the ongoing development of parent-school partnerships (Broussard, 2003; Chavkin, 2006; Dulmus & Sowers, 2004; Dupper, 2003; Franklin et al., 2010; Ward, Anderson-Butcher, & Kwiatkowski, 2006). A variety of specific strategies and successful practice examples are available for school social workers to draw on. Franklin et al. (2010) identify the objectives that guide school social work practice in addressing parent–school partnerships:

- Educating school personnel toward understanding the psychosocial strengths and needs of families and supporting school staff relationships with vulnerable families

- Offering relevant program interventions for parents and families based on an ongoing and current needs assessment
- Helping the interprofessional team, the PTA, and school staff develop avenues for parent involvement in the operations and programs of the school (p. 288)

Groups and Classrooms

School social workers often provide group services to children and adolescents. Empirical support exists for a considerable number of individual and group interventions, as discussed in the following section. In addition to the well-known clinical benefits, such as the reduction of isolation and improvement of socialization skills, groups may be considered an efficient way for school social workers to provide services (Franklin et al., 2010). Entire classrooms may also be the focus for school social work services. For example, a school social worker may collaborate with an elementary school teacher to assist with the development of rules for social behavior with peers in the classroom.

Interventions With the School

School-wide practice might include services such as prevention initiatives, teacher training, and initiatives to improve the overall school climate (Broussard, 2003; Hopson & Lawson, 2011). School-wide interventions may be used as a means to target individual student behavior or to change the school environment itself (Dupper, 2003; Frey & Dupper, 2005). The most successful prevention programs attempt to do both (Dupper, 2003). A large number of effective prevention programs are available for school social workers to learn about and replicate at their schools, including programs targeting violence, substance abuse, truancy, adolescent pregnancy, and transmission of sexually transmitted diseases. There are many ways school social workers can assist in making the school environment one that nurtures the development of children. Broussard (2003) describes several strategies that school social workers can use, for example, to address elements of the school culture that may be creating an environment that is unwelcoming of families of diverse cultures.

Frey and Dupper (2005) have developed a conceptual tool, the *clinical quadrant*, to assist school social workers with envisioning and planning a broad, ecological, and empowerment-based orientation to their overall practice. They note the complexity of school social work services, especially given recent legislation and education reform efforts, and encourage initiation of multilevel interventions. The clinical quadrant provides a clear graphic illustration of potential intervention targets and levels of service delivery. The authors recommend that school social workers develop skills in providing services that go beyond micro level interventions focusing on student change, and they emphasize that school social workers must be flexible in their ability to adapt services to the needs of their particular school, and at the multiple levels of service as needed.

Current Assessment Models

School social workers must assess the effectiveness of the services they provide, whether it is an intervention with an individual student or a school-wide prevention program. They need to assess which interventions are effective for ethical reasons, for their own planning purposes, and because they are accountable for their services to others and may need to report outcomes to multiple stakeholders. A variety of designs, methods, and measurement tools are available to assist school social workers in the evaluation of their practice at all levels (Cobb & Jordan, 2006; Dupper, 2003; Jayaratne, 2004; Lindsey & White, 2007; Powers, Bowen, & Rose, 2005).

Like school social workers, public schools must increasingly demonstrate that they are meeting outcome goals. Since enactment of the Goals 2000: Educate America Act, funding for individual schools is linked to their attainment of eight educational goals outlined in the legislation (Franke & Lynch, 2006). The No Child Left Behind Act of 2002 has further increased pressure on schools to demonstrate their effectiveness, primarily measured with the standardized testing results of their students. The outcome priorities of social work practice and the goals of the educational system may seem different on the surface, but areas of mutual concern underlie both sets of goals (Harris, Franklin, & Lagana-Riordan, 2010). For example, while school personnel may be concerned with student substance abuse primarily as an obstacle influencing academic outcomes such as grades and test scores, the school social worker may define substance abuse as a problem in multiple areas of the student's life, such as in the development of healthy peer relationships and individual identity. Professionals in the educational system and in social work are in agreement that substance abuse is a concern, and addressing the problem will further the outcome priorities of both groups. The recognition that there is substantial overlap in what must be done to meet the goals of the educational system and the goals of social work practice will assist the school social worker with defining, measuring, and reporting information about social work services in a way that links them with the priorities of the educational system. School social workers can then share the outcomes of their services with school administrators so they can better understand the contribution of school social work services on their campus (Bye, Shepard, Partridge, & Alvarez, 2009).The quality and effectiveness of school social work services may be evaluated in a variety of ways. Dupper (2003) notes that research designs familiar to social work practitioners, such as single-system and comparison group designs, are often appropriate for assessing the effectiveness of student-focused interventions in school settings. Measurement methods include the use of objective reports, test data, direct observations, standardized scales, and self-reports (Jayaratne, 2004). Cobb and Jordan

(2006) recommend using different types of assessment measures together to evaluate services. School records, such as attendance reports, may be helpful objective reports. Numerous standardized rapid assessment instruments addressing a wide spectrum of issues are available for use with children and families. Two in particular have a long record of use in school settings, with extensive data available on their psychometric properties: Achenbach's Child Behavior Checklist (1991, as cited in Cobb & Jordan, 2006) and the Conners Scales (1997, as cited in Cobb & Jordan, 2006). Several assessment instruments are available with software that can do the scoring for the measure (Lindsey & White, 2007).

The School Success Profile provides an ideal standardized and validated measurement instrument for planning and assessing school social work services informed by an ecological perspective, with attention to both risk and resilience factors. It captures information at the level of the individual student and across the contexts of the school, neighborhood, and community (Powers et al., 2005). The developers continue to refine the instrument and to provide Web-based resources for school social workers to use as a guide in their selection of appropriate empirically supported interventions.

School social work interventions at the level of systems, such as an entire school or neighborhood, must also be evaluated. While the unit of analysis is different, some of the basic designs and types of measurement tools are similar to those used in the evaluation of direct services to students (Dupper, 2003). For example, standardized instruments are available to assess classrooms and neighborhoods. School and district level data is collected on numerous variables that may be targets of social-work intervention, such as free/reduced-cost lunch program participation and dropout and truancy rates. Examples of indicators that may be studied to evaluate service effectiveness might include community utilization rates or teacher perceptions and attitudes. One area in particular where schools can be assessed and therefore targeted for change is school climate. A number of measures are available to assess the dimensions of school climate at various grade levels and from multiple perspectives. The Comprehensive School Climate Inventory (CSCI) is one example of an empirically validated measure designed to reflect the perceptions of the school environment from all members of the school community (National School Climate Center, n.d.)

Because of the variety and number of demands on a school social worker's time and the potential need to report program information to multiple stakeholders, efficient management of student and program data is critical. Computerized data management may save time while providing an excellent accountability tool, especially for school social workers with varied and dynamic caseloads and program responsibilities (Jonson-Reid, 2006). In addition, accessing and utilizing the school's database may save time for the social worker, and provide valuable information needed for evaluating student progress, such as attendance records, grades, and dropout data (Patterson, 2006). The use of spreadsheets provides an efficient means of organizing service-related information. Patterson describes the simple sequence needed to use spreadsheets to graphically display student or group change with single-system designs. These may serve as an easily produced and interpreted accountability tool.

Trends and Issues in Practice

As school systems embrace changes in public policies, management, and teaching practices, school social work must also restructure itself to best help schools. While there are always numerous school issues and reforms at both the local and national levels that may impact school social work, some of the most prevalent trends of our times include accountability issues, the push toward evidence-based practices, an increase in societal stress, emotional and behavioral disorders among student populations, and the increase in the use of technologies.

Accountability

Political trends at local and federal levels influence schools. The No Child Left Behind Act, as described earlier, has increased the need for public schools to be accountable for the educational outcomes of students. The stakes are high, with school funding tied to the school's ability to demonstrate student achievement. Standardized tests serve as a primary measure of student achievement, and are thus increasingly a focus of the educational system. The increasing emphasis on testing has been controversial, and the debate between both members of the public and professionals in the educational system is a prominent issue for school social workers and educators (Franklin, 2006). Front-line social workers are dealing with some of the fallout of the discussion, with increased stress on students, families, and educators, as they adapt to the focus on testing. Issues included in the discussion are the nature of school responses to the legislation, the stress of the high-stakes testing for children, the inappropriateness of the focus on standardized tests as the accountability measure for schools, and concerns related to measurement issues with ethnic-minority students, students with learning disabilities, and students learning English as a second language. Overall, the climate for professionals working in public schools today is performance and outcome-driven. This is coupled with increasing economic tensions that often leads to a reduction in funding and greater disparities between schools in affluent and non-affluent communities.

The growing accountability emphasis for schools also contributes to the need for social workers to be more accountable for the services they provide and to be able to demonstrate how their services support the educational mission of the school. As a result, school social workers must have (a) skills to evaluate their own services, (b) knowledge of measurement and evaluation tools, (c) the ability to link the interventions they provide to the outcomes that are important to the school, and (d) the means and skills to communicate or publicize their contribution to the welfare of students and the school to stakeholders (Franklin, 2006; M. Kelly, 2009).

Evidence-Based Practice

School social workers, like health professionals, educators, and social workers in other practice settings, are increasingly encouraged to select and provide interventions that have been supported with empirical research (Dupper, 2007; Franklin & Kelly, 2009). This practice trend calls for school social workers to use the best available research evidence to guide their practice with clients. In the absence of empirical evidence, best practices derived from research, and meeting certain standards, are encouraged in evidence-based practice. Franklin and Kelly (2009) illustrate steps school social workers can take to provide evidence-based services, including information on how to identify appropriate interventions and how to analyze effectiveness literature.

Service Trends

Children and youth considered to be at risk are increasingly receiving services through public schools (Franklin, 2006). This includes children with mental health needs, and especially impoverished and ethnic minority students with mental health needs. Research has suggested that one in five children may have an emotional and behavioral disorder and schools often serve as the primary site for both referral and services of these children (Stormont, Reinke, & Herman, 2011). It is likely that many children will not receive needed services unless they are provided through schools. Some groups are especially likely to encounter obstacles to receiving quality mental health services. African American and Latino children in particular may have difficulty accessing mental health services. These two groups show the highest rates of need for mental health services, yet are the least likely to receive quality services when they are not provided by public schools (RAND Health Research Highlights, 2001). African American children are also overrepresented in special education services (Frey & Dupper, 2005). Other groups who are likely to receive needed services through schools are homeless children, immigrants, and adolescent parents.

The directors of the SAMHSA-funded National Child Traumatic Stress Network have recommended that policy makers direct efforts toward assisting parents and teachers who have been traumatized, as a means of providing better support to children (Pynoos & Fairbank, 2003). They also note that some of the effective treatments for trauma that have been identified involve schools. With high rates of childhood exposure to traumatic events, wide media coverage of school violence around the country, and citizens of all ages living with continuing terrorist threats in the aftermath of 9/11, trauma-related mental health services continue to be needed.

In addition to the growing number of children needing mental health services, the number of children and youth coming to school with significant barriers to their learning is also increasing (Frey & Dupper, 2005). The number of students who are living in poverty is growing, as well as the number of students who have severe behavior problems. These trends indicate a continuing and growing need for school social work services.

School experiences and students' feelings and attitudes about school also come into play in school social work practice. Students may have safety concerns about school, and may actually have been victimized on the school campus (Dulmus & Sowers, 2004; Franklin, 2006). School social workers may intervene to address school-related concerns—for example, by providing crisis intervention services in response to a distressing event or experience on campus. Gay, lesbian, bisexual, and transgender (GLBT) youth may be at special risk for victimization at school (Elze, 2006; Frey & Dupper, 2005). School social workers may be proactive in taking specific steps to develop a climate in the school that is safe, nonstigmatizing, and affirming for GLBT youth (Elze, 2006).

Technology

Technology is a large part of the daily lives of children and adolescents, and plays a growing role in the provision of school social work services (Lindsey & White, 2007). It is essential for school social workers to be cognizant of technological resources and advances, because technology can assist with administrative duties and professional communications, be part of an intervention, or be encountered as a student or school issue of concern. Computer software programs can be valuable tools for collecting and reporting program information, as described previously. There are also interactive software programs available that have been created as part of interventions for children.

School social workers must stay current on how students are using technology, both at school and at home. For example, it is important to be aware of the growing use of Instant Messaging as a means for students to instantly communicate and socialize with peers (Lindsey & White, 2007). Facebook and other social media outlets are increasingly important to students, and devices such as smartphones and iPads may be used in the teaching process while also enabling students to be perpetually in contact with one another. One example of how technology use might arise as a student issue of concern is if something were communicated rapidly among students that had repercussions during the school day. Another technology-related student issue that might be brought to the attention of the school social worker is Internet sexual solicitation of children and youth, or unwanted exposure to sexual material online, which was reported by 25% of youth (ages 10 to 17) in a nationwide survey (Mitchell, Finkelhor, & Wolak, 2003).

Future Issues

The drive for schools and school social workers to be accountable for the services they provide by demonstrating measurable results is becoming standard practice. In addition, it will be increasingly important for school social workers to be able to clearly show how their services contribute to the school's educational mission by being able to participate with other school professionals including teachers, in improving test scores and overall academic achievement. The mental health of students is increasingly being forecast not only as being a major domain also mental health professionals like school social workers but that the responsibilities of all school personnel are to promote children's well-being (Frey & Alvarez, 2011). This means that the roles of school social workers as team leaders, consultants, supervisors, and trainers may be increasing as they are asked to equip teachers and other school personnel in the best evidence-based practices, and to help teachers by being essential links to family and community work. Furthermore, the practice trend calling for school social workers to be able to use data-based decision making and to work within multitiered response to intervention frameworks is likely to continue to increase as key legislation such as the Elementary and Secondary Education Act revisions come into law (Frey & Alvarez, 2011).

It is expected that children and youth will continue to need and receive mental health services through public schools in increasing numbers, especially impoverished and ethnic minority children (Franklin, Harris, & Allen-Meares, in press). School mental health services may be offered as a continuum of services ranging from mental health promotion, prevention, treatment, and maintenance (Frey & Alvarez, 2011). The way services are conceptualized and delivered may impact the roles of school social workers as they are asked to work more in teams with teachers in the delivery of school mental health services (Franklin, Kim, Ryan, Kelly & Montgomery, 2011). The increased focus on schools as a logical place to provide mental health services for children and youth may lead to increasing development of collaborations between schools and community service providers (Allen-Meares, 2006b). The coming decades may bring "unusual and innovative" partnerships and collaborations (Allen-Meares, 2006b, p. 1191). School social workers may well play a lead role in the development of these new partnerships, given their skills and expertise (Franklin & Gerlach, 2006).

School social workers can expect to work with increasingly complex issues and an increasingly diverse student population. Culturally competent practice skills, interventions, and assessment methods are essential for school social workers and other school personnel as the U.S. population becomes more culturally diverse (Broussard, 2003; Dupper, 2007; Franklin, 2006). Swick, Head-Reeves, and Barbarin (2006) describe the necessity of developing effective strategies for meeting the needs of these children and their families as "one of the most important challenges facing school personnel in the twenty-first century" (p. 793). As Dupper (2007) notes, "There is a growing mismatch between linguistically, culturally, economically and racially diverse children entering monolingual, white, Anglo, middle-class schools. Consequently, it is imperative that school social workers become sensitive to cultural differences and learn specific competencies that will increase the likelihood of interacting effectively with diverse children and their families" (p. 217). Clearly, school social workers will play a key role in this area.

Technology may bring both opportunities and challenges for school social workers in the future. Increased use of electronic technologies to communicate with others may require school social workers to be even more vigilant about client confidentiality (Franklin, 2006; Lindsey & White, 2007). Efforts to maintain confidentiality may need to be reviewed frequently as more communication takes place electronically, especially in the context of interprofessional collaboration in schools.

More rapid communication with other professionals involved with a child or family, however, provides obvious advantages for the ability of team members to work together to address issues. By facilitating the dissemination of information, electronic communication may also facilitate prevention. For example, one of the chapter authors was serving as a school social worker in September 2001. In the days after the 9/11 terrorist attacks, she was one of 30 or more school social workers to receive e-mail from a school social worker in a neighboring school district informing them of incidents of harassment and threats toward Muslim students on that campus. The social worker receiving the e-mail was able to instantly share the information with her principal. Together they developed a preventative strategy for their campus, which also entailed quick dissemination of information to teachers via e-mail. Presumably, many of the 30 social workers receiving the original message took similar steps, and may also have forwarded the information to further school social workers not on the original mailing list.

Increased use of technology is linked with other issues that will continue to be prominent in the future, such as the need to use data-based decision making and to demonstrate outcomes in students who are targeted for change. Various strategies were described earlier to utilize software in school social work services, including the overall management of programs, recordkeeping, tracking of student progress, administration of rapid assessment instruments, reporting of results to stakeholders, and even the administration of some innovative interventions. School social workers who have Internet access can readily obtain information on empirically supported interventions through websites such as the Campbell Collaboration Library (www.campbellcollaboration.org/index .asp) and the National Child Traumatic Stress Network (NCTSN, www .nctsnet.org/nccts/nav.do?pid=ctr_rsch_biblio_works/). NCTSN provides a "What Works?" bibliography for practitioners working with children and youth who have experienced trauma, with summaries of research articles that they may not be able to obtain as quickly through other means. The Campbell Collaboration Library provides a large, searchable, frequently updated website describing systematic reviews of the effectiveness of various interventions for a wide range of concerns.

The evidence-based practice movement is expected to continue in the future. In fact, Allen-Meares (in press) describes how the concept of evidence-based practice is growing, with an increased emphasis on being able to successfully transport and sustain research-based practices in real world settings. School social workers have also been encouraged to learn and apply an evidence-based practice framework that was first used in medicine to make sure they are selecting and using the best practice interventions with their clients (M. Kelly et al., 2010). It is increasingly important for school social workers to show a body of research on the effectiveness of their practices. Franklin, Kim, and Tripodi (2009) recently published the first systematic review of school social work research studies demonstrating that over the past 20 years, school social work research has continued to make modest progress. Kim and Franklin (2009) further published a systematic review showing that solution-focused brief therapy, a school-based intervention frequently used by social workers, is a promising practice for changing emotional and behavioral problems in youths and increasing their academic achievement. More systematic reviews showing the significance of school social work services are definitely indicated. In addition, there is a need to enhance the conceptual frameworks used by school social workers and to strengthen the theoretical connections between theory and practice interventions (Zammitt & Alvarez, 2011). In the future, more rigorous studies of school social work theories and practices will be required, making it possible for school social workers to demonstrate their critical importance to schools in increasingly tight budgetary situations. School social workers must therefore work to enhance their research data and their use of data, and build infrastructure to communicate their effective uses of data and outcomes to other school professionals and policy makers (Bye et al., 2009)

The roles of specialized instructional support personnel in schools are being expanded to focus more on school climate, teacher support services, increasing parental involvement, and family and community interventions. Frey and Dupper (2005) have highlighted the need for school social workers to move beyond providing services to individual students and families in order to increase system-focused interventions targeting the school ecology itself. School social workers must be skilled at providing services at the different possible levels of intervention and should not restrict their services to focus only on individuals. These types of ecologically minded interventions are consistent with the training of school social workers, and every indication is that school social workers may continue to be extremely important to school progress as schools take on needed reforms in the student services dimensions of their educational services.

Conclusion

This chapter defined the practice of school social work and provided an overview of the profession of school social work, including its history and important contributions within school programs. School social workers have grown as a unique profession among social workers and currently have their own professional associations, credentials, and practice standards. This chapter highlighted the role of school social workers in mental health services and described some contemporary issues for school social services delivery. It further discussed the adaptations that school social workers have made to meet changing demands and offered suggestions for what types of skills might be needed to continue to serve the complex needs of children in the schools.

Educating children in the 21st century is clearly quite complex, and the demands on schools to successfully educate increasingly challenging and diverse populations are making it more important for school social workers to be well-versed with varied areas of knowledge and skills. Franklin and colleagues (2011) recommend that those who are considering a career in school social work thoroughly assess themselves in terms of their general professional competency, cultural competency, professional values, ethics, and issues of transference and countertransference. Strong assessment skills are needed for all aspects of school social work, from determining student needs at an individual level, to evaluating the sociopolitical issues at play in the school or community. As described, skills are also needed in the areas of intervention, evaluation, communication, managing interprofessional groups and community partnerships, marketing, and connecting social work activities to the overall goals of the school (Franklin, 2006). In addition to these skills and areas of knowledge, personal flexibility and willingness to work with ambiguity clearly valuable assets that allow school social workers to manage the wide-ranging and complex areas they navigate on a daily basis.

Throughout their careers, school social workers use their personal assets and professional expertise to address student needs in the context of their environments of school, home, and community. Although there are many tasks that school social workers perform, four core tasks are assessments; system wide consultations; direct intervention with individuals, families, and groups; and program development. School social work practice has adjusted to trends in the field and in education reform; however, the basic charge to help all students successfully receive an education and to help remove learning barriers for vulnerable students has largely remained the same. School social workers meet this charge though dedication, advocacy, flexibility, and creativity, and will surely continue to do so as their role continues to evolve.

Key Terms

Accountability	Response to	School social work
Evidence-based	intervention	
practice	School climate	

Review Questions for Critical Thinking

1. What clinical skills and knowledge do school social workers need to address diverse student needs?

2. With whom do school social workers need to collaborate in order to provide the best services to students?

3. Why must school social workers be aware of trends in education?

4. What changes might school social workers advocate for at the school district or state level to help remove barriers to learning?

5. How have accountability and evidence-based practice affected school social work services?

Online Resources

NASW Standards for School Social Work Services: www.naswdc.org/practice/standards/NASW_SSWS.pdf

School Social Work Association of America: www.sswaa.org/

Center for Mental Health in Schools: http://smhp.psych.ucla.edu

References

Adelman, H. S., & Taylor, L. (2006). Want to work with schools? What is involved with successful linkages. In C. Franklin, M. B. Harris, & P. Allen-Meares (Eds.), *The school services sourcebook: A guide for school-based professionals* (pp. 955–970). New York, NY: Oxford University Press.

Adelman, H. S. & Taylor, L. (2010). *Mental health in schools: Engaging learners, preventing problems, & improving schools*. Thousand Oaks, CA: Corwin.

Albers, C. A., & Kratochwill, T. R. (2006). Teacher and principal consultations: Best practices. In C. Franklin, M. Harris, & P. Allen-Meares (Eds.), *The school services sourcebook: A guide for school-based professionals* (pp. 971–976). New York, NY: Oxford University Press.

Allen-Meares, P. (1977). Analysis of tasks in school social work. *Social Work, 22*, 196–201.

Allen-Meares, P. (1994). Social work services in schools: A national study of entry-level tasks. *Social Work, 39*(5), 560–565.

Allen-Meares, P. (2004). *Social work services in schools* (4th ed.). Boston, MA: Allyn & Bacon.

Allen-Meares, P. (2006a, Summer). One hundred years: A historical analysis of social work services in schools. *School Social Work Journal* [Special issue].

Allen-Meares, P. (2006b). Where do we go from here? Mental health workers and the implementation of an evidence-based practice. In C. Franklin, M. Harris, & P. Allen-Meares (Eds.), *The school services sourcebook: A guide for school-based professionals* (pp. 1189–1194). New York, NY: Oxford University Press.

Allen-Meares, P. (2010). *Social work services in schools* (4th ed.). Boston, MA: Allyn & Bacon.

Allen-Meares, P. (in press). Where do we go from here? Mental health workers and the implementation of an evidence-based practice. In C. Franklin, M. Harris, & P. Allen-Meares (Eds.), *The school services sourcebook: A guide for school-based professionals* (2nd ed). New York, NY: Oxford University Press.

Allen-Meares, P. A., Franklin, C., & Hopson, L. (2010). School social work. In E. Mullen (Eds.), *Oxford bibliographies on-line*. New York, NY: Oxford University Press.

Altshuler, S. J., & Webb, J. R. (2009). School social work: Increasing the legitimacy of the profession. *Children and Schools, 31*(4), 207–218.

Anderson-Butcher, D., & Ashton, D. (2004). Innovative models of collaboration to serve children, youths, families, and communities. *Children and Schools, 26*(1), 39–53.

Berzin, S. C., O'Brien, K. H. M., Frey, A., Kelly, M. S., Alvarez, M. E., & Shaffer, G. L. (2011). Meeting the social and behavioral health needs of students: Rethinking the relationship between teachers and school social workers. *The Journal of School Health, 81*, 493–501.

Berzin, S., & O'Connor, S. (2010). Educating today's school social workers: Are school social work courses responding to the changing context? *Children & Schools, 32*(4), 237–249.

Broussard, C. A. (2003). Facilitating home-school partnerships for multiethnic families: School social workers collaborating for success. *Children and Schools, 25*(4), 211–222.

Bye, L., Shepard, M., Partridge, J., & Alvarez, M. (2009). School social work outcomes: Perspectives of school social workers and school administrators. *Children & Schools, 31*(2), 97–108.

Center for Health and Health Care in Schools. (2001). Children's mental health needs, disparities and school-based services: A fact sheet. Retrieved March 10, 2005, from www.healthinschools.org/cfk/mentfact.asp

Center for Mental Health in Schools at UCLA. (2005). *Youngsters' mental health and psychosocial problems: What are the data?* Los Angeles, CA: Author.

Chavkin, N. F. (2006). Effective strategies for promoting parental involvement: An overview. In C. Franklin, M. Harris, & P. Allen-Meares (Eds.), *The school services sourcebook: A guide for school-based professionals* (pp. 629–640). New York, NY: Oxford University Press.

Chanmugam, A. (2009). A qualitative study of school social workers' clinical and professional relationships when reporting child maltreatment. *Children & Schools, 31*(3), 145–161.

Cobb, N. H., & Jordan, C. (2006). Identifying and using effective outcome measures. In C. Franklin, M. Harris, & P. Allen-Meares (Eds.), *The school services sourcebook: A guide for school-based professionals* (pp. 1043–1051). New York, NY: Oxford University Press.

Constable, R., Kuzmickaite, D., Harrison, W. D., & Volkmann, L. (1999). The emergent role of the school social worker in Indiana. *School Social Work Journal, 24*(1), 1–14.

Costin, L. B. (1969). An analysis of the tasks in school social work. *Social Service Review, 43*, 274–285.

Dibble, N. (2008). *School social work and the privacy of minors.* Columbia, SC: School Social Work Association of America. Retrieved from www.sswaa .org/userfiles/file/SSWServicesPrivacyofMinors.pdf

Dryfoos, J. G. (2002). Full-service community schools. *Phi Delta Kappan, 83*(5), 393–400.

Dulmus, C. N., & Sowers, K. M. (2004). *Kids and violence: The invisible school experience.* New York, NY: Haworth Press.

Dupper, D. R. (2003). *School social work: Skills and interventions for effective practice.* Hoboken, NJ: John Wiley & Sons.

Dupper, D. R. (2007). Incorporating best practices. In L. Bye & M. Alvarez (Eds.), *School social work: Theory to practice* (pp. 212–222). Belmont, CA: Brooks/Cole.

Elze, D. E. (2006). Working with gay, lesbian, bisexual, and transgender students. In C. Franklin, M. Harris, & P. Allen-Meares (Eds.), *The school services sourcebook: A guide for school-based professionals* (pp. 861–872). New York, NY: Oxford University Press.

Franke, T., & Lynch, S. (2006). Linking school social work interventions to educational outcomes for schools. In C. Franklin, M. Harris, & P. Allen-Meares (Eds.), *The school services sourcebook: A guide for school-based professionals* (pp. 1021–1030). New York, NY: Oxford University Press.

Franklin, C. (2006). The future of school social work practice: Current trends and opportunities. *Advances in Social Work, 6*(1), 167–181.

Franklin, C. (2010). The delivery of school social work services. In P. Allen-Meares (Ed.), *Social work services in schools* (6th ed., pp. 278–321). Boston, MA: Allyn & Bacon.

Franklin, C., & Gerlach, B. (2006, Summer). One hundred years of linking schools with communities: Current models and opportunities. *School Social Work Journal* [Special Issue].

Franklin, C., Harris, M., & Allen-Meares, P. (2006). *The school services sourcebook: A guide for school-based professionals.* New York, NY: Oxford University Press.

Franklin, C., Harris, M., & Allen-Meares, P. (in press). *The school services sourcebook: A guide for school-based professionals.* (2nd ed.) New York, NY: Oxford University Press.

Franklin, C., & Kelly, M. S. (2009). Becoming evidenced-informed in the real world of school social work practice. *Children & Schools, 31,* 46–58.

Franklin, C., Kim, J. S., Ryan, T., Kelly, M., & Montgomery, K. (2011). *Teacher implementation of school mental health services: Changing roles and effectiveness.* Manuscript under preparation.

Franklin, C., Kim, J. S., & Tripodi, S. (2009). A meta-analysis of published school social work practice studies from 1980–2007. *Research on Social Work Practice, 19,* 667–677.

Franklin, C., & Streeter, C. (1995). School reform: Linking public schools with human services. *Social Work, 40*(6), 773–782.

Frey, A., & Alvarez, M.E. (2011). Social work practitioners and researchers realize the promise. *Children & Schools, 33*(3), 131–135.

Frey, A. J., & Dupper, D. R. (2005). A broader conceptual approach to clinical practice for the 21st century. *Children and Schools, 27*(1), 33–44.

Frey, A., Lingo, A., & Nelson, C. M. (2011). Positive behavior support and response to intervention in elementary schools. In H. Walker & M. K. Shinn (Eds.), *Interventions for achievement and behavior problems: Preventive and remedial approaches* (pp. 397–433). Washington, DC: National Association for School Psychologists.

Frey, A. J., & Lankster, F. (2008). *School social work in host settings.* Columbia, SC: School Social Work Association of America. Retrieved September 10, 2011 from www.sswaa.org/userfiles/file/SSWservicesPrivacyofMinors.pdf

Harris, M., & Franklin, C., & Lagana-Riordan, K. (2010). The design of social work services. In P. Allen-Meares (Ed.), *Social work services in schools* (6th ed., pp. 278–321). Boston, MA: Allyn & Bacon.

Hopson, L. M., & Lawson, H. (2011). Social workers' leadership for positive school climates via data-informed planning and decision-making. *Children & Schools, 33*(2), 106–118.

Individuals with Disabilities Education Improvement Act of 2004, United States Department of Education. Retrieved September 15, 2011, www2.ed.gov/policy/speced/guid/idea/idea2004.html

Jayaratne, S. D. (2004). Evaluating practice and programs. In P. Allen-Meares (Ed.), *Social work services in schools* (4th ed., pp. 327–358). Boston, MA: Allyn & Bacon.

Jonson-Reid, M. (2006). Constructing data management systems for tracking accountability. In C. Franklin, M. Harris, & P. Allen-Meares (Eds.), *The school services sourcebook: A guide for school-based professionals* (pp. 1031–1042). New York, NY: Oxford University Press.

Kelly, D. C. (2005). Beyond problem solving: The social worker as risk manager and educator in educational-host settings. *School Social Work Journal, 29*(2), 40–52.

Kelly, M. S. (2007). *Illinois school social workers' use of practice interventions: Results from a statewide survey.* Unpublished doctoral dissertation. Chicago, IL: University of Chicago.

Kelly, M. (2009). *The domains and demands of school social work practice.* New York, NY: Oxford University Press.

Kelly, M., Berzin, S., Frey, A., Alvarez, M., Shaffer, G., & O'Brien, K. (2010). The state of school social work: Findings from the National School Social Work Survey. *School Mental Health, 2*(3), 132–141.

Kelly, M., Raines, J. C., Stone, S., & Frey, A. (2010). *School social work: An evidence-informed framework.* New York, NY: Oxford University Press.

Kim, J., & Franklin, C. (2009). Solution-focused, brief therapy in schools: A review of the outcome literature. *Children and Youth Services Review, 31*, 464–470.

Kopels, S., & Lindsey, B. C. (2006, Summer). The complexity of confidentiality in schools today: The school social worker context. *School Social Work Journal* (Special Issue).

Lewis, M. R. (1998). The many faces of school social work practice: Results from a research partnership. *Social Work in Education, 20*(3), 177–190.

Lindsey, B. C., & White, M. K. (2007). Technology and school social work. In L. Bye & M. Alvarez (Eds.), *School social work: Theory to practice* (pp. 288–296). Belmont, CA: Brooks/Cole.

National School Climate Center (n.d.). Measuring school climate (CSCI). Retrieved from: http://www.schoolclimate.org/programs/csci.php

Mitchell, K. J., Finkelhor, D., & Wolak, J. (2003). The exposure of youth to unwanted sexual material on the internet: A national survey of risk, impact, and prevention. *Youth and Society, 34*(3), 330–358.

Molina, I., Bowie, S. L., Dulmus, C. N., & Sowers, K. M. (2004). School-based violence prevention programs: A review of selected programs with empirical evidence. In C. N. Dulmus & K. M. Sowers (Eds.), *Kids and violence: The invisible school experience* (pp. 175–190). New York, NY: Haworth Press.

Mumm, A. M., & Bye, L. (2011). Certification of school social workers and curriculum content of programs offering training in school social work. *Children and Schools, 33*(1), 17–23.

National Association of Social Workers (2002). NASW Standards for School Social Work Services. Retrieved from www.socialworkers.org/practice/standards/NASW_SSW.pdf

Patterson, D. A. (2006). Using the school's database system to construct accountability tools. In C. Franklin, M. Harris, & P. Allen-Meares (Eds.), *The school services sourcebook: A guide for school-based professionals* (pp. 1053–1060). New York, NY: Oxford University Press.

Polowy, C.I. & Morgan, S. (2011). *NASW law notes: The legal rights of students*. Washington, DC: NASW Press.

Powers, J., Bowen, G., & Rose, R. (2005). Using social environment assets to identify intervention strategies for promoting school success. *Children and Schools, 27*(3), 177–187.

Pynoos, R., & Fairbank, J. (2003). The state of trauma in America, two years out. *Brown University Child and Adolescent Behavior Letter, 19*(10), 1–6.

RAND Health Research Highlights. (2001). Mental health case for youth. Retrieved March 10, 2005, from www.rand.org/publications/RB/RB4541

Raines, J. C. (2006). Confidentiality in school social work: To share or not to share. In R. Constable, C. R. Massat, S. McDonald, & J. P. Flynn (Eds.), *School social work: Practice, policy, and research* (6th ed., pp. 100–116). Chicago, IL: Lyceum Books.

Selekman, M. D. (2006). Integrative, solution-oriented approaches with self-harming adolescents. In C. Franklin, M. Harris, & P. Allen-Meares (Eds.), *The school services sourcebook: A guide for school-based professionals* (pp. 321–328). New York, NY: Oxford University Press.

Shepard, K., DeHay, T., & Hersh, B. (2006). Effective cognitive-behavioral interventions for self-mutilation. In C. Franklin, M. Harris, & P. Allen-Meares (Eds.), *The school services sourcebook: A guide for school-based professionals* (pp. 305–320). New York, NY: Oxford University Press.

Stormont, M., Reinke, W., & Herman, K. (2011). Teachers' knowledge of evidence-based interventions and available school resources for children with emotional and behavioral problems. *Journal of Behavioral Education, 20*(2), 138–147. doi: 10.1007/s10864-011-9122-0

Streeck, F. (2011). Personal communication, September, 2011, School Social Workers Association of America (SSWAA).

Streeter, C. L., & Franklin, C. (2002). Standards for school social work in the 21st century. In A. Roberts & G. Green (Eds.), *Social workers desk reference.* New York, NY: Oxford University Press.

Swick, D. C., Head-Reeves, D. M., & Barbarin, O. A. (2006). Building relationships between diverse families and school personnel. In C. Franklin, M. Harris, & P. Allen-Meares (Eds.), *The school services sourcebook: A guide for school-based professionals* (pp. 793–802). New York, NY: Oxford University Press.

Taylor, L., & Adelman, H. S. (2006). Want to work with schools? What is involved in successful linkages. In C. Franklin, M. B. Harris, & P. Allen-Meares (Eds.), *School services sourcebook: A guide for school-based professionals.* New York, NY: Oxford University Press.

Ward, H., Anderson-Butcher, D., & Kwiatkowski, A. (2006). Effective strategies for involving parents in schools. In C. Franklin, M. Harris, & P. Allen-Meares (Eds.), *The school services sourcebook: A guide for school-based professionals* (pp. 641–650). New York, NY: Oxford University Press.

Zammitt, K. A., & Alvarez, M. E. (2011). The need for conceptual framework of change. *Children & Schools, 33*(3), 1894–1898.

Chapter 4
Substance Abuse

Lori K. Holleran Steiker and
Samuel A. MacMaster

How can substance abuse be framed in a strength's perspective?

Social workers have empathically worked with and for addicts and alcoholics since the beginning of the profession's history (Straussner, 2001). Long before Alcoholics Anonymous (AA) was founded, social worker Mary Richmond (1917/1944) stated that "inebriety is a disease." Several decades later, the rest of the world caught up. In 1951, the World Health Organization came to the same conclusion, finally acknowledging alcoholism as a serious medical problem. In 1956, the American Medical Association declared alcoholism as a treatable illness, and in 1965 the American Psychiatric Association began to use the term *disease* to describe alcoholism. Richmond not only recognized alcoholism as a disease, she created an instrument to assess drinking patterns, family history of drinking, drug problems, concurrent mental illness, social contextual factors, and even an attention to gender differences with regard to alcohol use patterns. Richmond was not alone in this awareness and incorporation of addiction into practice, however; a significant number of social workers were vital members of the Yale Plan Clinics, the first outpatient facilities for the treatment of alcoholism (Straussner, 2001).

From the current head of the Substance Abuse and Mental Health Services Administration (SAMHSA), Charles Currie, to the first social worker to head the Association for Medical Educators and Researchers in Substance Abuse (AMERSA), Mary Ann Amodeo, social workers are being recognized for their leadership roles in the field of substance abuse. Some social workers have made groundbreaking contributions to the field of substance abuse scholarship and research. Diana DiNitto and Aaron McNeece have written quintessential books on substance abuse dynamics and policies with a systems base. Flavio Marsiglia has developed nationally acclaimed culturally grounded substance abuse prevention interventions and theoretical frameworks. Other social work researchers are on the cutting edge of a variety of substance abuse–related issues, including the following: Robert Schilling (HIV), Nabilia El Bassel (female condom), Carl

Leukefeld (criminal justice interventions), Roger A. Roffman (marijuana treatment), James Hall (rural case management), and E. Michael Gorman (the methamphetamine epidemic). A national effort between NIAAA and social work educators has developed a focused curriculum on treating addiction, *Social Work Education for the Prevention and Treatment of Alcohol Use Disorders,* to meet the continued training and education needs of practitioners who treat addicted individuals (NIAAA, 2005). As noted by the founder and editor of *Social Work Practice in the Addictions,* Shulamith Lala Ashenberg Straussner (2004, p. 8), "It is time that the important role of social workers in addictions, both past and present, is more widely recognized and that social workers be encouraged to further contribute to this field in the future."

Despite the significance of these trailblazers, not all social workers have involved themselves in, or understood the importance of, the field of addictions. Some studies examining alcohol dependence and adolescent treatment outcome have found social work's contribution lacking (Jenson, Howard, & Vaughn, 2004; Vaughn, Howard, & Jenson, 2004). For example, in the past decade, the highest percentage of substance abuse–related studies of the total articles published in 13 core social work journals was 5.9% in 1994 (Vaughn et al., 2004, p. 44).

Regardless of the paucity of the social work presence in the realm of alcohol, tobacco, and other drug (ATOD) research, the mark of social workers is growing and strengthening. Social workers are an ideal match for the field of substance abuse because the skills, knowledge, and value bases are harmonic. The following sections illustrate this point.

Holistic View

Social work emphasizes a holistic view of the person in the context of his or her environment. The biopsychosocial view of human behavior emerges with the goal of understanding the contributions of biological, psychological, and socioenvironmental factors and their interactions with a person's behavior (Saleebey, 1992; Simon, McNeil, Franklin, & Cooperman, 1991). More recently, social work has augmented this model to include "spirituality," so as to include all aspects in the dynamic nature of human functioning (C. Leukefeld & Leukefeld, 1999). Recent research has also shown the importance that neurophysiology plays in the process (Volkow, 2010). The biopsychosociospiritual model is an excellent guide for social work conceptualizations, but key substance-abuse experts note that too often, social workers neglect to address the biological aspects of the model (Flanzer, Gorman, & Spence, 2001). The biological aspects of an addict must not be overlooked, especially because this is an area of science that is definitive and can dispel the myths related to alcoholism as "moral weakness" or "lack of willpower." As noted by the National Institute on Drug Abuse (NIDA) official and social worker, Jerry Flanzer, "What is so exciting is that our — Mary Richmond's, Grace Coyle's, Bertha Reynolds's — understanding of the dynamic, reciprocal, influential effect of the environment, of personal relationships, psychological/ego processes and biology/'brain wiring' on the social human being is being substantiated by science daily" (Flanzer et al., 2001, p. 104). This holistic approach to defining addiction was further buttressed by the American Society of Addiction Medicine (2011), who redefined addiction to focus on the neurophysiology of the process. The definition below moves an understanding of addiction from being based on behaviors, to one based on neuroprocessing.

> *Addiction is a primary, chronic disease of brain reward, motivation, memory and related circuitry. Dysfunction in these circuits leads to characteristic biological, psychological, social and spiritual manifestations. This is reflected in an individual pathologically pursuing reward and/or relief by substance use and other behaviors. Addiction is characterized by inability to consistently abstain, impairment in behavioral control, and craving, diminished recognition of significant problems with one's behaviors and interpersonal relationships, and a dysfunctional emotional response. Like other chronic diseases, addiction often involves cycles of relapse and remission. Without treatment or engagement in recovery activities, addiction is progressive and can result in disability or premature death. (American Society of Addiction Medicine, 2011)*

According to the social work profession, individual strengths are as important as personal concerns (i.e., that which hinders optimal functioning). Strengths, such as coping skills, talents, positive self-concept, ethnic identity, and spiritual belief may assist the client in resolving existing difficulties. Resilience is a concept that epitomizes and can help operationalize the strengths perspective (Saleebey, 1997). Resiliency theory (Werner & Smith, 1992; S. Wolin & Wolin, 1993) is part of the social work backbone, supporting most practitioners' interventions. Regarding drug users, resilience has been defined as "the ability to tolerate, to adapt to, or to overcome life crises" (Beauvais & Oetting, 1999, p. 103).

Social workers, with the strengths-based perspective, have long advocated person in environment, resilience models, and infusion of hope in helping relationships. Starting at the beginning of the millennium, a major shift in the substance abuse realm began. As noted by William White in the *Journal of Substance Abuse Treatment*, "There is growing evidence that the alcohol and other drug (AOD) problems arena is on the brink of shifting from longstanding pathology and intervention paradigms to a solution focused recovery paradigm" (White, 2007, p. 229). Due to the number of recovering individuals leading productive lives and the longevity of many recovering people's abstinence and sobriety, the Recovery Movement came into existence and has received more and more attention. "The values and beliefs of the consumer–survivor recovery movement are closely aligned with those of the (social work) profession, and...the movement offers social workers a more promising perspective from which to practice" (Carpenter, 2002, p. 86). Some would go as far as saying, "The vision of recovery is reshaping the fields of mental health and addiction services" (Gagne, White, & Anthony, 2007).

Social workers, holding roles in micro, meso, and macro helping positions, are uniquely poised to have powerful perspective, resources, relationships, and skills with disadvantaged individuals, groups, and communities. The profession exists where the proverbial "rubber hits the road" in what Singer, Pollio, and Stiffman (in press) call *real-world* settings.

While the social worker examines aspects of the individual's functioning, he or she is trained to keep the complex interplay between the various personal issues in mind. For example, a client's culture and ethnicity have profound implications throughout all aspects of the client's life experience. In general, social workers recognize that (a) there is normally an extensive history of life experiences that impact the client's presentation, (b) coping mechanisms are more solidified and complex, and often less mutable, and (c) there are numerous areas of inquiry based on individual, family, and community functioning and interactions.

In an article that outlines the findings of the Addictions Service Task Force, Singer, Pollio, and Stiffman (in press, p. 4) highlight that the profession of social work emphasizes the complex interactions of person and context; "The recognition of this complexity is especially important in research in the addictions and HIV to address such coexisting issues as poverty, addiction, health disparities, and polymorbidity, and how these issues are manifested intrapersonally, interpersonally, and environmentally."

Two major conceptual perspectives set the stage for social work in the substance abuse arena: the ecological and the health disparities. The ecological perspective emphasizes person-in-environment and the ensuing dynamic interactions between biological, psychological, social, and cultural elements, rather than utilizing a focus on either individual or environmental factors alone (Germain & Bloom, 2000). This is contrary to other disciplines, such as medicine and psychology, which tend to view phenomena as primarily an internal process occurring on an individual basis.

The Social Work Addictions Task Force (Singer & Pollio, in press) also notes that the field of social work is unique in that it has customarily focused on underprivileged populations. In fact, the goal of the National Association of Social Worker's Code of Ethics is to "help meet the basic human needs of all people, with particular attention to the needs and empowerment of people who are vulnerable, oppressed, and living in poverty" (National Association of Social Workers [NASW], 1999, p. 1).

Thus, another fundamental perspective that illuminates the natural marriage between the social work and substance abuse fields is a focus on the health disparities perspective. Health disparities occur within a larger context of historical and contemporary inequalities with respect to social and economic realities, and provide a more focused framework from which the ecological perspective is developed. The Institute of Medicine (Smedley, Stith, & Nelson, 2003) has developed a provider-level model describing the complex interactions between clients, healthcare providers, and system-level factors that lead to these disparities. These factors include social, economic, and cultural influences; stereotyping and prejudice by clinicians; and the interactions between clinicians and service recipients (which may be subject to ambiguity and misunderstanding). From this perspective, these factors lead to racially inequitable clinical decisions and resulting outcomes.

These perspectives provide the foundation for a comprehensive approach that seeks to integrate two more specific models of treatment engagement and access that focus specifically on the interaction of the individual and the service system. It is the underlying assumption in holistic social work intervention that these are dynamic interactions that exist between service users and service providers, and that the perspective of the client can be better understood by the service provider; and this understanding will lead to the development and provision of more culturally congruent services.

Evidencing the recognition of the importance of social work perspective, the Department of Health and Human Services has recently developed the first National Institute of Health (NIH) "Road Map" Plan for Social Work Research (2003), which encourages each institute and center to include social workers in grants and provides supplements to pay for these individuals to become involved in individual research projects. The NIH Road Map initiative (2003) acknowledges the intricacy of health-related issues. Professional social workers strive to develop paradigms that capture the complexities of substance use/abuse–related services. Further evidencing the growing interest and presence of social workers in the addictions field during the past decade or so is the formation and rapid growth of the Alcohol, Tobacco, and Other Drugs specialty section of the NASW.

According to the NASW Practice Research Network (2001), about 1% of practicing social workers designate their primary area as addictions. While this may seem small, the number is growing. In addition, social workers in mental health, employee assistance programs (EAPs), hospitals, schools, and other community settings are enhancing their awareness, knowledge, skills, and interventions for substance use/abuse–related cases out of necessity (i.e., so many cases include substance-related factors). In fact, many professionals feel that they would be remiss if they did not become competent in the area of drug and alcohol abuse due to the prominence of these problems.

Historically, many social service practitioners have had ambivalence about substance-abusing clients, as evidenced by failures to assess, minimization, poor data acquisition/retention and a tendency to pass substance-abusing clients on to other agencies (Amodeo & Fassler, 2001; Lightfoot & Orford, 1986). One hopeful finding is that while a study in the mid-1980s illuminated that agencies were more of a hindrance than a help to social workers with regard to working with substance-abusing clients (Lightfoot & Orford, 1986), a more recent study found that a majority of social workers noted that their agencies were indeed helpful, especially in the areas of supervision, administration, substance abuse–specific training, flexibility regarding client assignment to workers, and opportunities to educate and supervise others on substance abuse–related issues (Amodeo & Fassler,

2001). In addition, social work researchers have fortunately found that the following three pivotal experiences lead to positive therapeutic attitudes and behaviors of clinicians toward substance-abusing clients: (1) specific clinical training in substance abuse, (2) opportunities to work with these clients, and (3) supervisory and staff support (Cartwright & Gorman, 1993).

Clearly, social work clients in virtually all settings present drug- and alcohol-related issues; therefore, assessment of these problems is critical (Kaplan, 2005). In fact, according to NASW (2001), 43% of the Practice Research Network members surveyed reported that they screened clients for substance use disorders. However, while the presence of bachelor's level social workers in the addictions field is growing, research has also found a fairly low involvement of master's level social workers in this area (Sun, 2001).

Social workers tend to receive scant training in substance use and abuse (Amodeo & Fassler, 2001; Hall, Amodeo, Shaffer, & Vanderbilt, 2000; McVinney, 2004). Despite attempts to highlight the need for all social workers to be educated in drug and alcohol problems, most graduate schools still offer a smattering of electives and little mandatory education on the subject (McVinney, 2004; O'Neill, 2001; Straussner, 2004). For this reason, the next section provides a basic outline of substance abuse diagnostic and intervention related concerns.

Overview of Substance Abuse Problems

Due to the fact that most social work education programs do not have mandatory substance abuse courses, it is the authors' contention that this chapter would be remiss if it did not contain an overview of fundamental, basic information concerning work with substance–abusing clients. When assessing any individual, it is important for social workers to consider the possibility of substance-related disorders, which consist of substance use, abuse, and/or dependence. The *Diagnostic and Statistical Manual of Mental Disorders* (4th ed., text revision, *DSM-IV-TR;* American Psychiatric Association [APA], 2000) offers a detailed way to diagnose various drug dependencies, alcoholism, and polysubstance (at least three of the 11 classes of substances in a 12-month period) dependencies.

Fundamental features of substance-related disorders include (a) the taking of a drug, medication, drink, or substance in order to experience an altered state; and (b) a cluster of cognitive, behavioral, and physiological symptoms when the substance use is continued, despite problems associated with its use. Substance-related disorders are divided into two primary groupings: substance use disorders (primarily dependence and abuse) and substance-induced disorders (i.e., intoxication, withdrawal, and mental health consequences of abuse).

There are 11 classes of substances: alcohol, amphetamines, caffeine, cannabinoids, cocaine, hallucinogens, inhalants, nicotine, opioids, phencyclidine, sedatives/hypnotics/anxiolytics, polysubstance use (use of three or more of the above noted). In addition, there are *other* (substances not included in the 11 classes), and *unknown* (when substance is not known, including medication overdose or reactions and toxins) designations. The *DSM-IV-TR* provides the criteria for the diagnoses associated with each of the 11 classes of substances.

Substance dependence includes a maladaptive pattern of substance use leading to clinically significant impairment or distress, as manifested by three (or more) of the following, occurring at any time in the same 12-month period (APA, 2000):

Tolerance, as defined by either of the following: (a) a need for markedly increased amounts of the substance to achieve intoxication or desired effect or (b) markedly diminished effect with continued use of the same amount of the substance.

Withdrawal, as manifested by either of the following: (a) the characteristic withdrawal syndrome for the substance or (b) the same (or a closely related) substance is taken to relieve or avoid withdrawal symptoms.

The substance is taken in larger amounts or over a longer period than was intended.

A persistent desire or unsuccessful efforts to cut down or control substance use.

A great deal of time is spent in activities necessary to obtain the substance (e.g., visiting multiple doctors or driving long distances), use the substance (e.g., chain-smoking) or recover from its effects.

Important social, occupational, or recreational activities are given up or reduced because of substance use.

The substance use is continued despite knowledge of having a persistent or recurrent physical or psychological problem that is likely to have been caused or exacerbated by the substance (e.g., current cocaine use despite recognition of cocaine-induced depression, or continued drinking despite recognition that an ulcer was made worse by alcohol consumption).

The primary distinguishing characteristics between a person who uses substances and one who is dependent on the substance are as follows: (a) the phenomena of craving, which is a psychological and biological drive, experienced by addicts, to use more substances regardless of consequences; (b) the need for more and/or stronger substances for the same effect; (c) progression, or increasing problems and consequences of use over time; and (d) the eventual fatality of the illness if untreated. These aspects are the grounds for the characterization of substance abuse and dependence as a disease.

One of the most prominent substance-related disorders that social work clinicians encounter is alcohol abuse or dependence. As described by the *DSM-IV-TR* (APA, 2000), 90% of American adults have tried alcohol at some time in their lives, and approximately two-thirds of men and one-third of women have had adverse experiences related to alcohol. Alcoholism has been recognized for many years by professional medical organizations as a distinct, primary, chronic, progressive, and often fatal disease. More than 60% of adults drank alcohol in the past year, and 32% of current drinkers had five or more drinks on at least one day in the past year (Centers for Disease Control and Prevention, 2006). Currently, nearly 14 million Americans—1 in every 13 adults— abuse alcohol or are alcoholics, with 53% of men and women in the United States reporting that one or more of their close relatives have a drinking problem (NIAAA, 2004). Eleven percent of 8th graders, 22% of 10th graders, and 29% of 12th graders had engaged in heavy episodic, or binge drinking within the past two weeks (Johnston, O'Malley, Bachman, & Schulenberg, 2006). Of 3.1 million Americans, approximately 1.4% of the population ages 12 and older received treatment for alcoholism and alcohol-related problems in 1997; treatment peaked among people between the ages 26 to 34 (SAMHSA, 2000).

The *DSM-IV-TR* (APA, 2000) has two broad categories for alcohol-related disorders: alcohol-use disorders and alcohol-induced disorders. Alcohol-use disorders include alcohol dependence and alcohol abuse. There are 13 different diagnoses under alcohol-induced disorders, including alcohol intoxication, alcohol withdrawal, alcohol-induced mood disorder, and alcohol-induced persisting dementia (APA, 2000, p. 212).

Once alcoholism is suspected, a social worker must assess a client for physical withdrawal symptoms that can be life threatening. Many social workers are surprised to learn that alcohol withdrawal is one of the most potentially fatal detoxifications, while cocaine and even heroin withdrawal, although very uncomfortable, are generally physically harmless.

Diagnosing substance-related disorders is complicated because (a) it is hard to differentiate chemically induced symptoms from symptoms of mental illness, (b) many clients have dual diagnoses, and (c) a major presenting issue of substance abuse is denial (i.e., a mechanism for minimizing and avoiding an issue). The symptoms of substance use and abuse often mimic symptoms of other mental illnesses, and vice versa. For example, almost all addicts have mood swings between periods of elation and apparent depression (e.g., restlessness, irritability, and discontentment); however, only some addicts may actually be diagnosed as bipolar disordered.

Many adults with diagnoses other than addiction use substances as a mechanism of self-medication. Still others can be diagnosed with concurrent illnesses. Such comorbidity, historically referred to as "dual diagnosis," is also referred to as coexisting psychological and substance disorder (COPSD), or, in 12-step recovery realms, "double trouble." COPSD individuals have complicated, multiproblem presentations in treatment, and inpatient and longer-term services may need to be provided to such individuals.

The other major complicating factor in diagnosing substance problems is the tendency for the user to minimize and deny the problems. Chemically dependent individuals are often aware that their use and subsequent behaviors are socially unacceptable. Therefore, they often become adept at hiding their use and manipulating and lying to cover up their actions. They also may try to minimize consequences and find ways to deceive others, especially the people who care about them, who, in turn, enable or perpetuate the problem through caretaking.

Substance abuse is a pattern of substance use that results in recurrent and significant adverse consequences associated with the frequent use of substances. This pattern can significantly impair all aspects of functioning. Substance dependence refers to a cluster of cognitive, behavioral, and physiological symptoms indicating the person continues to use the substance despite substantial substance-related problems (Munson, 2000). A repeated pattern of self-administration usually results in tolerance, withdrawal, and compulsive drug use. The criterion for abuse differs from dependence, which requires the client to meet three criteria in a 12-month period.

Substance abuse causes a wide variety of medical and psychiatric symptoms and diseases. Therefore, all patients presenting to the healthcare system should be considered for the diagnosis. However, certain organ systems and problems have such a high prevalence of underlying substance abuse that they must be viewed with an even higher index of suspicion. Common medical symptoms of substance abuse include vitamin deficiency, malnutrition, dyspepsia, upper gastrointestinal problems, peptic ulcer, hepatitis, pancreatitis, hypertension, new onset arrhythmia, cardiomyopathy, seizures, peripheral neuropathy, and AIDS. Trauma of any kind should arouse suspicion during an interview, especially accidents at work, single car crashes, and domestic violence. Substance abuse also manifests in the following behavioral, emotional, and cognitive problems: stress, insomnia, anxiety, depression, suicidal ideation or attempt, acute psychotic states, impaired cognition, and violent behavior. Perhaps the most subtle aspects of substance abuse are the associated social problems. Substance abusers are at high risk for marital and family problems, legal difficulties, loss of employment, and financial deterioration. Special consideration should be given to patients who are homeless, who are involved in prostitution, or who are in the criminal justice system.

Substance abusers are at particularly high risk for HIV/AIDS. During the course of an assessment, social workers must be alert to symptoms that may be related to HIV infection (Fisher & Harrison, 2000). According to Barthwell and Gilbert (1993), these signs and symptoms may include complaints of swollen lymph nodes, severe abdominal pain, diarrhea, visual changes, and severe dermatological conditions or rashes. In addition, a mental status exam may reveal AIDS-related cognitive impairments.

In addition, a number of substance-abuse clients present to social workers with some noteworthy trauma. For example, a recent study found significant association between past-month substance use and increased self and partner negative relationship behaviors (Najavits, Sonn, Walsh, & Weiss, 2004). Social workers engaged in direct practice are at risk for secondary exposure to traumatic events through their work with traumatized clients. In fact, according to social worker Brian Bride, many social workers are likely to experience at least some symptoms of STS, and a significant minority may meet the diagnostic criteria for PTSD (Bride,

2007). Thus, social workers working with at-risk clients should both be able to assess for trauma as well as recognize compassion fatigue, secondary trauma, and PTSD (Adams, Boscarino & Figley, 2006; Bride, 2007).

Assessment Instruments

The most common evaluative tool for physical withdrawal symptoms is the Clinical Institute Withdrawal Assessment (CIWA). The CIWA for Alcohol/Drugs Based on *DSM-IV-R* (CIWA-AD) is an 8-item scale for clinical quantification of the severity of the alcohol withdrawal syndrome. It originates from the 15-item CIWA-A and the more recent, revised 10-item CIWA-AR (Sullivan, Sykora, Schneiderman, Naranjo, & Sellers, 1989). It is a reliable, brief, uncomplicated, and clinically useful scale that can also be used to monitor response to treatment. This scale offers an increase in efficiency over the original CIWA-A scale while retaining clinical usefulness, validity, and reliability. It can be incorporated into the usual clinical care of patients undergoing alcohol withdrawal and into clinical drug trials of alcohol withdrawal.

There are a variety of assessment instruments that can be used to determine the presence, nature, and treatment directions with regard to clients with potential substance abuse problems. The most commonly utilized and widely accepted assessment tools are discussed briefly next.

CAGE

This screening test was developed by Dr. John Ewing, founding director of the Bowles Center for Alcohol Studies, University of North Carolina at Chapel Hill. CAGE (Mayfield, McLeod, & Hall, 1994) is an internationally used assessment instrument for identifying alcoholics and other substance abusers. It is particularly popular with primary caregivers. CAGE has been translated into several languages. The patient is asked four questions:

1. Have you ever felt you ought to *Cut* down your drinking (or drug use)?
2. Have people *Annoyed* you by criticizing your drinking (or drug use)?
3. Have you ever felt bad or *Guilty* about your drinking (or drug use)?
4. Have you had a drink (or used drugs) upon wakening (*Eye opener*) to steady your nerves, get you going, or get rid of a hangover?

Affirmative answers to two or more questions are a positive screen and should prompt further history.

Michigan Alcohol Screening Test

The Michigan Alcohol Screening Test (MAST; Selzer, 1971) is a written, 25-item screening test that may be given to a patient initially or in follow-up to another screening test, such as the CAGE. Its brevity makes it useful as an outpatient screening tool. Cut-off scores correlate well with more extensive diagnostic tests for alcohol disorders. The MAST has been modified for drug abuse (i.e., DAST).

Problem Oriented Screening Instrument for Teenagers

The Problem Oriented Screening Instrument for Teenagers (POSIT) is one of the most widely used instruments for adolescent substance use/abuse. It was developed by National Institute on Drug Abuse (NIDA) to identify potential problems and service needs of adolescents ages 12 to 19 years (Latimer, Winters, & Stinchfield, 1997). It is composed of 139 Yes/No questions under the following 10 subscales: Substance Use and Abuse; Physical Health Status; Mental Health Status; Family Relations; Peer Relations; Educational Status; Vocational Status; Social Skills; Leisure and Recreation; and Aggressive Behavior and Delinquency. It is a paper-and-pencil test, but a CD-Rom version is available. Social workers can administer this without training or additional qualifications.

Substance Abuse Subtle Screening Inventory

The Substance Abuse Subtle Screening Inventory (SASSI) is a single-page, paper-and-pencil questionnaire that takes approximately 15 minutes to complete. The test can be administered in individual or group settings and has an adult and adolescent version. In addition, it has a Spanish version.

The SASSI was developed 25 years ago and since has been empirically validated by numerous research studies attesting to its effectiveness as an assessment instrument to diagnose substance abuse disorders. The SASSI reportedly is accurate in its assessment of substance-dependent people in approximately 93% of all cases. The subscales of the SASSI inform the clinician about the client's attitude, defensiveness, emotional pain, insight into problems, and risk of unlawful behavior (The SASSI Institute, 2001).

Addiction Severity Index

The Addiction Severity Index (ASI), developed in 1980 by the Treatment Research Institute (TRI) (see www.tresearch.org/asi.htm or contact TRI, 600 Public Ledger Building, Philadelphia, PA 19106, (215) 399–0980) and collaborators from the University of Pennsylvania's Center for the Studies of Addiction, is an assessment for patients who present for substance abuse treatment. The semistructured interview takes approximately an hour to administer. It is an ecologically based measure providing information about the following domains: medical, employment/support, drug and alcohol use, legal, family history, family/social relationships, and psychiatric problems. Using a Likert scale (10 intervals), interviewer severity ratings indicate the degree of patient problems in each of the seven domains. While some of the scales collect historical accounts, the ASI's composite scores are based entirely on current information, therefore indicating the present status of the client. These scores are particularly valuable in treatment outcome studies because successive composite scores can be used to demonstrate the changes in patient status over time.

ASAM PPC-2R

In April 2001, the American Society of Addiction Medicine (ASAM) published the Second Edition—Revised of Its Patient Placement Criteria (ASAM PPC-2R), the most widely used and comprehensive national guideline for placement, continued stay, and discharge of patients with alcohol and other drug problems. This instrument was designed for better assessment of the needs of patients with co-occurring mental and substance-related disorders (dual diagnosis), for revised adolescent criteria, and for clarification of the residential levels of care.

The ASAM PPC-2R provides one set of guidelines for adults and one for adolescents, and five broad levels of care for each group (i.e., Early Intervention, Outpatient Treatment, Intensive Outpatient/Partial Hospitalization, Residential/Inpatient Treatment, and Medically Managed Intensive Inpatient Treatment). The diagnostic terminology used in the ASAM PPC-2R is consistent with the most recent language of the APA's *DSM-IV*. A strength of the measurement is that the type and intensity of treatment recommended are based on the patient's needs and not on limitations imposed by the treatment setting.

The ASAM PPC-2R is an excellent tool for use in treatment planning, as well as in navigating and coordinating with managed care organizations and public and private treatment providers.

Intervention: The Transtheoretical Model and Motivational Interviewing

Through research and practice experiences, it has become clear that effective work with substance users/abusers is best accomplished using the motivational interviewing technique, which grew from the stages of change (or transtheoretical) model created by Prochaska and DiClemente (1982). The transtheoretical model helps explain how both self-initiated and professionally assisted changes occur in addictive behavior. Prochaska and DiClemente put forth a five-stage theory based on empirical research. The basic premise of their work is that stages of change are temporal dimensions that say when particular shifts in attitudes, intentions, and behaviors occur. Table 4.1 outlines the model's stages. In general, each stage represents a period of time as well as a set of tasks needed for movement to the next stage. Although the time an individual spends in each stage may vary, the tasks to be accomplished are assumed to be uniform.

With regard to treatment implications, it is important to note that while the vast majority of addicted people are not in the action stage, most programs are action oriented. Studies indicate that only 10% to 15%

Table 4.1 The Transtheoretical Model.

1. Precontemplation stage

No intention to change in the foreseeable future.
Unaware or under aware that there is even a problem.
Present to treatment because of outside influences.
May even demonstrate change while pressure is on.
Resistance to recognizing or modifying a problem is the hallmark, for example, "I don't have any problems."

2. Contemplation stage

Aware problem exists—seriously thinking about overcoming it, but have not yet made a commitment to take action.
May be stuck here for a long time, for example, smokers—2 years.
"Knowing where you want to go, but not quite ready yet."
Weigh pros and cons of problem and solution—struggle with positive evaluations of their addiction and the amount of energy, effort, and loss it will cost to overcome the problem.

3. Preparation stage

Combines intention and behavioral criteria, for example, individuals in this stage are intending to take action in the next month and have unsuccessfully taken action in the past year.
Typically will report some action such as a decrease in the addictive behavior—but have not yet reached a criterion for effective action such as abstinence.
They are, however, intending to take such action in the future.

4. Action stage

Individuals modify their behavior, experiences, or environment to overcome their problems.
Involves the most overt behavioral changes and requires considerable commitment of time and energy.
Modifications here tend to be the most visible and receive greatest external recognition.
Don't confuse this stage with change, which often happens when the requisite work is overlooked that prepares changers for action and important efforts necessary to maintain the changes following action.
They have successfully altered the addictive behavior for a period of 1 day to 6 months, e.g., reached a certain criterion—does not necessarily satisfy the field's criterion for recovery.
Modification of the target behavior to an acceptable criterion and significant overt efforts to change are the hallmarks of action.

5. Maintenance

People work to prevent relapse and consolidate the gains attained during action.
Maintenance is not static and is viewed as a continuation of change. In addiction, it extends from about 6 months to indeterminate period past the initial action. For some, it's a lifetime of change.
Being able to remain free of the addiction behavior and being able to consistently engage in new, incompatible behavior for more than 6 months are the criteria for this stage.
Stabilizing behavior change and avoiding relapse are the hallmarks of maintenance.
Since relapse is the rule rather than exception with addictions, this model cannot be conceptionalized as a linear model with people neatly going from one stage to another; rather, the authors present it as a spiral pattern.
In relapse, some return to the stage before relapse. Others begin again somewhere in the middle, for example, 15% of smokers who relapsed regressed back to precontemplation stage. The majority recycle back to later stages, that is, they potentially learn from their mistakes.
In a cohort of individuals, the number of successes continues to increase gradually over time, but a large number stay in the pre- and contemplation stages.

Note: Adapted from "Transtheoretical Therapy: Toward a More Integrative Model of Change." by J. O. Prochaska and C. C. DiClemente, 1982 *Psychotherapy: Theory, Research and Practice, 19*(3), pp. 276–288.

are prepared for action; 30% to 40% in the contemplation stages, and 50% to 60% are in the precontemplation stages (Prochaska, DiClemente, & Norcross, 1992). Therefore, most programs will under serve, mis-serve, or not serve the majority of their target populations. The amount of progress clients make following intervention tends to be a function of their pretreatment stage of change. If clients progress from one stage to the next in the first month of treatment, they can double their chances of taking actions during the initial six months of the program. In summary, it is important for social workers to remember that action-oriented treatment may work with people who are in the preparation or action stages, but could be totally ineffective with individuals in the pre- or contemplation stages.

In precontemplative states, people process less information about their problems, devote less time and energy to reevaluating themselves, and experience fewer emotional reactions to the negative aspects of their problems. These clients tend to be less open with others about their problems, and do little to shift their attention or their environment in the direction of overcoming problems—they are the most resistant and least active patients. In contemplation stages, they are most open to consciousness-raising techniques—confrontations, educational processes, and so on. They reevaluate themselves more and struggle with questions such as "how do I think and feel about living in a deteriorating environment that places my families or friends at increasing risk for disease, poverty, or imprisonment?" In preparation stages, people begin to take small steps toward action—this is where it is appropriate to use counterconditioning and stimulus control techniques to begin reducing their use and to help them control situations in which they rely on substances.

During the action stage, they endorse higher levels of self-liberation, believe they have the autonomy to change their lives, and rely increasingly on support and understanding from helping relationships. In the maintenance stage, clients rely on all the processes that came before it. This stage entails an assessment of the conditions under which a person is likely to relapse and develops alternative responses for coping with such conditions. These findings clearly suggest the need to assess the stage of a client's readiness for change and to tailor interventions accordingly. Ultimately, efficient self-change depends on doing the right things (processes) at the right time (stages).

The concept of motivational interviewing evolved from experience in the treatment of problem drinkers (Miller & Rollnick, 1991). Miller and Rollnick (1991) define motivational interviewing as a directive, client-centered counseling style for eliciting behavior change by helping clients to explore and resolve ambivalence. Compared with nondirective counseling, it is more focused and goal-oriented. The examination and resolution of ambivalence is its central purpose, and the counselor is intentionally directive in pursuit of this goal. Rollnick and Miller (1995) describe the "spirit" of motivational interviewing as follows:

- Motivation to change is elicited from the client, and not imposed from without.

- It is the client's task, not the counselor's, to articulate and resolve his or her ambivalence.
- Direct persuasion is not an effective method for resolving ambivalence.
- The counseling style is generally a quiet and eliciting one.
- The counselor is directive in helping the client to examine and resolve ambivalence.
- Readiness to change is not a client trait, but a fluctuating product of interpersonal interaction.
- The therapeutic relationship is more like a partnership or companionship than expert/recipient roles.

This work is based in the collaboration between client and facilitator and is shaped by an understanding of what it takes for individuals to change a behavior that is not working for them.

The following are the motivational interviewing strategies (Miller, 1998) for social workers (which can be learned and practiced). The order is a general progression, but clinicians should follow the client's lead and utilize the most natural skill possible to allow for increasing trust and openness on the part of the client. Warmth, empathy, and reflective listening should be utilized in conjunction with each of these skills:

- Seek to understand the person's frame of reference, particularly via reflective, empathic listening.
- Express acceptance and affirmation.
- Question purposefully about client's feelings, ideas, concerns, and plans, affirming the client's freedom of choice and self-direction.
- Provide structured feedback to client, preferably tangible reports with screening scores, and so on.
- Elicit and selectively reinforce the client's own self-motivational statements, expressions of problem recognition, concern, desire and intention to change, and ability to change.
- Monitor the client's degree of readiness to change, and ensure that the client sets this pace, not the clinician.
- For work with adolescents, remember that it is best if the youth argues for change and elaborates about his or her ambivalence than if the therapist does this.
- Monitor and ''roll with'' resistance and try to keep it minimized; in essence, avoid argumentation.
- Summarize and reframe perceptions in a new light and reorganized forms. Motivate the client to acknowledge problems, consequences, and changes whenever possible.
- Shift, when ready, from reasons to change to a plan for change. Consider a change plan worksheet with such sections as: the changes I want to make; the most important reasons to make these changes;

the steps I plan to take in changing; the ways others can help me; I will know the plan is working if...; and some things that could interfere with my plans.

According to Miller (1998), the term *addiction* implies some reduction in volitional control of a behavior. Besides diminished volitional control, what qualifies a behavior as addicting is that it persists despite harmful consequences. The goal of the collaboration between client and clinician is to find motivations that outweigh the motivations of the problematic behavior. The competing motivations may be multiple, and suffering associated with an addictive behavior tends to increase over time, shifting the weight of payoffs and downsides. The subsequent transformation is described as follows:

> For a brief time in motivational interviewing, we lend clients another perspective, a mirror, a chance to step safely outside of their own frame of reference and to see themselves with new eyes. This is not done by saying, "Listen to me. Here is how I see you," which places the person in the role of a passive listener. It is done by a temporary kind of merging. From the perspective of the therapist we call it empathy, seeking to see the world through the eyes of the client. In a metaphoric sense, we temporarily step inside the client, or better—become one with the client. Naturally, this improves the therapist's understanding of the client, but I think that it also changes the client's perspective. It is as if the client, too, can step into this empathic frame of reference and look back upon himself or herself. From the merged perspective of empathy, the person sees that something is possible, and the seeing begins to make it possible. It was Fritz Perls' definition of teaching: to show a person that something is possible. We refer to it as supporting self-efficacy, but I think it's more than telling a client, "you can do it." It is somehow helping the client see that he or she can do it. (Miller, 1998)

Social Support Systems

Social workers use several methods to solidify the intervention and change process. Particularly salient is the use of family intervention and an emphasis on the development of social skills.

Family Intervention

An intervention is a deliberate process by which change is introduced into peoples' thoughts, feelings, and behaviors. A formal intervention usually involves several people (usually family members, employers/coworkers, clergy, friends, etc.) preparing themselves, approaching a person involved in some self-destructive behavior, and talking to the person in a clear and respectful way about the behavior in question with the immediate objectives being for the person to listen and to accept help. The overall objective of an intervention is to begin to relieve the suffering caused by self-destructive behavior—the suffering of the person engaged in it, as well as the suffering of family and friends.

To prepare for an intervention, family members and friends gather to discuss the details with an interventionist. They jointly decide what form the intervention will take (i.e., choosing locale, taking turns listing factual evidence of the person's addiction, sharing the consequence of noncompliance with intervention), identify who should be included in the intervention, develop education and treatment plans, develop an intervention plan and schedule and then execute the plans. Family and friends often enter this process with apprehension and frequently with a high level of frustration and anger. They often feel betrayed, confused, guilty, and defensive. They sometimes blame each other, as well as themselves and the addicted person, for their difficulties. It is for these reasons that social workers are ideal for this role. They are often trained in group work and consider the needs of participants as important to the process as the needs of the identified problem substance user. Often, the intervention consists of the family and friends listing the factual events and incidents that illustrate the person's problem with substances, and it is often helpful to have them presented without excessive emotional expression. This hones the focus on the substance abuser's consequences and undeniable behaviors rather than digressing into power struggles, pleas, and angry outbursts. Such intervention meetings have the power to transform the support system in ways necessary for lasting change to occur. When this cohesive group approaches the substance abuser, they offer something much better than an individual confrontation by a clinician.

Time for Social Skill Building

The most salient predictor of clients' positive changes in substance abuse treatment is retention (Singer, Pollio, & Stiffman, in press). By keeping clients engaged in treatment, substance abuse and other risky behaviors are also reduced. In addition, prosocial attitudes and behaviors can be cultivated and negative patterns addressed. Anecdotally, substance abuse counselors have noted that substance-abusing clients tend to have social intimacy challenges, perhaps due to the lack of healthy social skills and coping mechanisms (often delayed, restricted, or replaced by addictive behaviors). Thus, it takes time and skill building for clients to learn to utilize helping networks, peers, support groups, and therapeutic settings.

Social workers can help enhance clients' social skills in order to maximize their time and connections in treatment, but another important way to engage and retain clients is to culturally ground interventions. Clients stay when they feel a sense of belonging and resonate with the culture of the treatment.

Social Workers as Preventionists

Prevention of substance abuse is a complicated task. While much progress has been made in slowing the increase of youth substance abuse, few school-based prevention approaches have proven effective in reducing substance use among adolescents and even fewer have been tested with youth of minority cultures (Forgey, Schinke, & Cole, 1997). Social work researchers have championed the need for prevention programs that are grounded with respect to the culture of the targeted students. Culture has been redefined to include aspects beyond ethnicity, such as language, clothing, body language, music, and so on.

Historically, social workers provided information and education with the assumption that adolescent *awareness* of the health hazards of substances would lead to antidrug attitudes and subsequently the choice not to use. Research that questions the effectiveness of "information only" prevention programs (Botvin, 1995; Bukowski, 1985; Tobler, 1986) finds that not only does this form of intervention fail to produce reduction in drug use, but some programs led to a subsequent increase in the use of substances afterward (Falck & Craig, 1988). The best example is Drug Abuse Resistance Education (DARE), the most widespread drug prevention program in the United States with well over 3 million participants. Not only was DARE ineffective initially, but some researchers found an increase in students' substance use after receiving this intervention (Clayton, 1991; Harmon, 1993).

More recently, models consider the interplay of individual, social, and environmental factors (Falck & Craig, 1988). These models consider the complex, multilevel interaction of children with their environment and social systems. For example, the ecological model stresses the concept of multiple levels of influence on child development and the complex interaction of child and environment (Lorion, 1987; Tolan, Guerra, & Kendall, 1995). The focus is on social skills and general functioning rather than on substances alone.

Many social workers hold positions in schools. Thus far, the majority of school-based programs espousing the most successful social skills and ecological models have been implemented with majority culture youth (Wilson, Rodrigue, & Taylor, 1997). Though some programs have focused on minority youth, few have been designed to address culturally specific factors. Research efforts have focused superficially on cultural nuances (Forgey et al., 1997) and there is a need for cultural grounding and mechanisms to accurately ascertain such factors. Current research suggests that culturally grounded interventions are critically needed (Botvin, 1995; Gordon, 1994). Programs designed to serve the needs of minority youth have more impact when they reflect sensitivity to the unique cultural characteristics of the students (Botvin, 1995; Lee & Richardson, 1991).

In line with social work values and perspectives, Price and Lorion's (1989) important contribution to the field of prevention is the identification that successful prevention program designs do not necessarily lead to effective implementation. They make the crucial point that the intervention involves complex transactions among individuals, and the context adds further complexity by virtue of a "variety of dynamic organizational and cultural forces that can act either to protect and strengthen the innovation or to undermine and distort it" (p. 102). Program success depends on the sites taking ownership of the intervention. Also, the program must resonate with the culture, language, and mores of the participants (Holleran Steiker, in press).

There are several modes of intervention that affect the cultural grounding of a program. First, the program design can be population-specific; for example, the culturally tailored intervention (CTI) specifically targeted substance abuse among inner-city African American and Hispanic youth (Forgey et al., 1997). Second, the implementers can adapt an external program to the specific population at hand. An example of this is the life skills training model (Botvin, 1995), which only makes modifications to the generalized program, where warranted, to maximize cultural sensitivity, relevance and acceptability to varied populations. Third, programs can be modified, maintaining the core of the curricula, to include aspects of the recipients' culture. For example, Holleran Steiker and Hopson (2007) are studying the impact of adaptation of the Drug Resistance Strategies (DRS; NIDA, R01 DA05629) curriculum (see Hecht et al., 2003), by having youth rewrite scenarios in the workbooks and remake the videos demonstrating the drug resistance strategies. Social workers recognize and can implement programs in which the adolescent perspective allows for access to accurate vernacular, customs, and styles of the target population. Language usage in particular changes over short time spans and provides unique opportunities to connect with and understand the ideas and values of each specific group of adolescents (Shapiro, 1985).

Regardless of the technique, the accuracy of the cultural aspects of a prevention program is crucial for program effectiveness. Many prevention models have been devised based on conjectures and intuitions and even stereotypes (Kim, Coletti, Williams, & Hepler, 1995). Cultural groundedness can only be achieved with input from the target population. While there is scant attention to the role of adolescents in planning, designing, and implementing substance abuse prevention programs, Wodarski and Feit (1995) state, "there is a need for youth to provide input regarding what they feel are their greatest stresses and programs needed to directly address these issues" (p. 9). To use adolescent input to adapt prevention programs to the culture of the target population, there must be an openness to change, a willingness to allow the adolescents to be the "experts," and a commitment to listening to their contributions.

Cultural Considerations: Ethnicity

Ethnicity is a poignant factor with regard to drug experimentation, alcohol use and abuse, and substance-related behaviors. While a significant body of research exists noting the varied levels of drug involvement by ethnic group, the literature is flawed in that it often fails to consider contextual variables such as poverty, gender, and acculturation. The stressors of poverty, joblessness, homelessness, and mental illness often contribute to substance abuse disorders despite ethnic identity.

Research shows that youth of varied ethnic groups maintain a spectrum of attitudes and behaviors with regard to drugs and alcohol (Hecht, Trost, Bator, & MacKinnon, 1997; Korzenny, McClure, & Rzyttki, 1990; Marsiglia, Kulis, & Hecht, 2001; Moon, Hecht, Jackson, & Spellers, 1999). In addition, choices of substance vary by ethnic group (Bachman et al., 1991; Dryfoos, 1998; Kumpfer & Turner, 1991; Newcomb & Bentler, 1986; Pentz, Trebow, & Hansen, 1990).

Native Americans

Native Americans have twice the arrest rate than any other ethnic group for alcohol-related offenses, while drug rates were lower than other groups (Greenfeld & Smith, 1999). While many erroneously blame "the victims," the oppression related to colonialization is more recently being examined as a precipitant in Native American substance abuse (Yellowbird, 2001). Promising effective treatments are being developed that are culturally sensitive and built on the Native American traditions, values, and beliefs (Napoli, Marsiglia, & Kulis, 2003).

Latinos

As noted earlier, ethnic differences in drug use are not well understood by researchers. Few studies have effectively evaluated issues directly impacting Latinos/as regarding drug and alcohol use and abuse. Over the past 15 years or so, however, there has been a strong push toward comprehending the emergent problem of substance abuse among Latinos/as in the United States (De la Rosa, Holleran, & Ashenberg-Straussner, 2005).

When studies have utilized checklist models without more specific cultural determinants, findings have been misleading at best and damagingly stereotypical at worst. The assumption of homogeneity has pervaded the literature, obscuring important differences between Mexicans, Cubans, Puerto Ricans, Central Americans, South Americans, Spanish people, and others who have been lumped into the generic "Hispanic" label (Felix-Ortiz & Newcomb, 1995; McNeece & DiNitto, 2003). Latinos/as are diverse in areas of education, living environment, family composition, language, religion, traditions, and socioeconomic status.

Attitudes have been shown to inform behaviors. Alcohol and drug use among Hispanics are often seen as moral weaknesses caused by "bad spirits" to be removed only by God or divine intervention (Comas-Diaz, 1986). Though some believe Hispanics have a particularly strong resistance to services, others feel that this is a myth (Gonzalez-Ramos, 1990; McNeece & DiNitto, 2003).

Though *la familia* (the family) is of central importance to Latinos, and *confianza* (independence and trust) is a crucial value, systems-oriented prevention and interventions are important (McNeece & DiNitto, 2003). Latino/a cultural norms dictate a focus on concern with relational solidarity and family and the immediate circle of close friends (Collier, Ribeau, &

Hecht, 1986). However, familial patterns differ from culture to culture. For example, among Mexicans and Cubans, mother–son relationships are particularly close; maternal and sibling relationships are key in Puerto Rican families; and Peruvians and Bolivians feel a stronger commitment to family of origin than to their spouses and siblings (Comas-Diaz, 1986; Melus, 1980). The *verguenza* (shame) experienced by drug and alcohol users (particularly women) may isolate Latinos/as from their families.

La comunidad (the community) is a central force in Latino life. Despite the fact that ritual celebrations, or fiestas, typically involve the use of alcohol, attachment to the community should be explored as a potential mediator against drug use among Latino adolescents. Other cultural practices, such as the use of *curanderos/as,* folk healers, herbal medicine, and spirits to address alcohol and drug problems, have received little attention by researchers.

Regarding overall incidence, the large-scale 1984 National Alcohol Study, with a probability sample of close to 1,500 Hispanic Americans, found that the rate of frequent heavy drinking by Latino males is approximately 17% for 29-year-olds, 26% for 39-year-olds, 11% for 49-year-olds, 12% for 59-year-olds, and 3% for people 60 years old and over. When the heaviest drinking categories were composite, 44% of Mexican American men fell into the category, compared to 24% Puerto Ricans and 6% Cuban Americans. In general, single, college-educated Latino males making more than $30,000 were found to drink more (Caetano, 1989). Caetano also reported that Mexican American men and women fall most frequently into categories of heavy drinkers and abstainers when compared to Puerto Rican and Cuban Americans. Data from the Hispanic Health and Nutrition Examination Survey obtained on nearly 5,000 Hispanic people is consistent with other studies in that 44% were lifetime abstainers or light drinkers, more males were drinkers than females, and drinking was most highly correlated with higher levels of education and income (Christian, Zobeck, Malin, & Hitchcock, 1989).

In a study by Hecht et al. (1997), Latinos/as reported receiving drug offers at a significantly higher rate than either European Americans or African Americans. Latinas (females), in particular, were significantly more likely to be offered drugs than other females. These findings are consistent with studies that indicate more drug use among Latino/a adolescents, in general: among inner city 12-year-olds, use rates are equal or higher for Latinos and African Americans, and use begins earlier (Caetano, 1989).

With regard to gender, male drinking may be an acceptable practice among Latino males, and even justified as part of *machismo,* with the family provider having a "right to drink without criticism" (Caetano & Mora, 1988, p. 343). In contrast, there is a lack of empirical support for the belief that Hispanic drinking is more macho and aggressive than among other ethnic groups (Neff, Prihoda, & Hoppe, 1991). Latinas have considerably higher proportions of abstainers and fewer alcohol problems than American women in general (Caetano, 1989). However, drug offers were found to be more frequent to Latinas than any other group (Hecht et al., 1997). A large percentage of women who drank heavily were in the 50- to 59-year-old group, perhaps because they are U.S. born and acculturated (Caetano, 1989).

Acculturation is a primary area of concern regarding risk for drug and alcohol use. Research supports that recent immigrants differ in drug use patterns from members of ethnic groups who have settled into U.S. culture (Felix-Ortiz & Newcomb, 1995). Evidence also suggests that with acculturation, more people, particularly women of Hispanic origin, may become drinkers (Caetano, 1989; Gilbert & Alcocer, 1988). Felix-Ortiz and Newcomb (1995) report that Latino adolescents who report stronger cultural identification are less likely to use drugs. The stress of acculturation has been linked to problem behaviors, including delinquency, mental illness, and drug abuse (Oetting & Beauvais, 1990; Pabon, 1998; Rogler, Cortez, & Malgady, 1991; Szapocznik & Williams, 2000).

Some serious methodological problems exist in the study of Latino/a drug and alcohol use. First, research problems stem from lack of documentation, replicability, and experimental testing when studying minority youth and lack of specific studies of minority youth. Second, most studies of youth rely on school samples, and Hispanic Americans and other minority groups have higher dropout rates than European Americans (Gilbert & Alcocer, 1988). Third, report levels can be affected by how drinking and drugging categories and problems are defined (Caetano, 1989). Fourth, and perhaps most importantly, "A unidimensional measure of cultural identity distilled into a single score cannot capture the complexity of these relationships (i.e., domains of cultural identity)" (Felix-Ortiz & Newcomb, 1995, p. 161).

Several studies have been specifically designed to consider the complexity of cultural identity factors among Latinos/as. Schinke and colleagues (1992), in a study comparing Hispanic and non-Hispanic adolescents from the southwest, reported that mothers' high school dropout status and students' low grades were better predictors of substance use than ethnicity, and they concluded that social factors must be emphasized, as opposed to factors associated with ethnic racial group membership. A promising study at the Hispanic Research Center used folktales to improve children's self-esteem and prevent problem behaviors (Costantino, Malgady, & Rogler, 1985) and used a similar model for adolescents with Puerto Rican folk heroes and heroines as role models (Costantino, Malgady, & Rogler, 1986). A group of researchers have developed a program revolving around bicultural effectiveness training, which targets intergenerational and intercultural family adolescent conflicts and encourages development of better family relationships by appreciating Hispanic cultural values and behaviors and those adopted from mainstream American culture (Szapocznik & Williams, 2000).

Felix-Ortiz and Newcomb's (1995) study measures cultural identity multidimensionally and across domains (i.e., language, values, behavior, types/patterns of use) and entailed cultural identity scales that used factors including "defensive Latino activism" (i.e., activism, affiliation, and perceived discrimination) and "traditional family role expectations" (*respeto* and feminism). They found the following:

a. No significant effects for gender.

b. Those who reported greater familiarity with Latino culture reported significantly less marijuana use during past 6 months than those unfamiliar with the culture.

c. Marginal students (unfamiliar with either culture) used significantly more alcohol and more frequently, followed by biculturals.

d. No significant effect for English language proficiency, but significant main effect for Spanish language proficiency on all eight drug use scales; most at risk were those with limited English and Spanish language skills. In this study, good Spanish language skills were protective. Language variables were more powerful/consistent for girls.

e. Components of cultural identity associated with higher levels of drug use were: defensive Latino activism, external sociopolitical influences (i.e., perceived discrimination).

f. Components of cultural identity were associated with lower drug use: for Latinas, traditional family role expectations.

g. Feminism is associated with increased drug use among Latinas, perhaps due to conflict with family and community values and pressure to conform to traditional sex roles, and a need for rebellion (Felix-Ortiz & Newcomb, 1995).

Thus, they conclude that cultural identity affects drug use depending on the type of use, gender, and specific aspects of the individual's cultural identity.

African Americans and Substances

Racial disparities exist with regard to substance abuse and African Americans. African Americans experience substance dependence and abuse at rates slightly higher, but generally comparable to Caucasians: 9.5% versus 9.3%, respectively (National Survey on Drug Use and Health, 2004). Despite these comparable rates, African Americans enter treatment at disproportionately higher rates: African Americans account for 12% of the population, but 24% of treatment admissions (Treatment Data Episode Set, 2004). However, the rates for substance abuse treatment admissions for African Americans steadily declined between 1994 and 1999, while rates for admissions for the total population increased (Drug and Alcohol Service Information System [DASIS], 2002). This issue is skewed by higher rates of involvement in the criminal justice system, as criminal justice referrals were the most frequent referral source for African Americans, accounting for 37% of all admissions (DASIS, 2002). Therefore, disparities in treatment access are primarily among African Americans not involved in the criminal justice system.

Interventions, particularly prevention interventions, for African American youth and families should include "racial socialization" as a component in effective programs (Coard, Wallace, Stevenson, & Brotman, 2004). *Racial socialization* is defined as "the developmental processes by which children acquire the behaviors, perceptions, values, and attitudes of an ethnic group, and come to see themselves and others as members of the group" (Rotherham & Phinney, 1987, p. 11, as cited in Coard et al., 2004).

Broader Cultural Considerations

Ethnicity is only one component of cultural implications in a client's life. Culture can also be defined to include region, socioeconomic status, rural versus urban settings, agency milieus, and other factors. Culture consists of the distinguishing patterns of behavior and thinking that people living in social groups learn, create, and share (Bodley, 1994). Culture includes such aspects of living as beliefs, rules of behavior, language, and rituals. Groups of people who share a common culture and, in particular, common rules of behavior and a basic form of social organization, constitute a society. Thus, the terms *culture* and *society* are somewhat transposable. The people of a society collectively create and maintain culture. Culture has several distinguishing characteristics: (a) it is based on symbols and the ability to communicate using language, (b) people in the same society share common behaviors and ideology through culture, (c) it is learned or socially inherited, and (d) people use culture to quickly and flexibly adapt to changes in the world around them.

The "recovery" community (especially Alcoholics Anonymous and other 12-step programs) is a distinctive cultural community (Holleran & MacMaster, 2005; Matto, 2004). In light of the characteristics noted, 12-step programs demonstrate the construction of a shared reality through language, narrative, principals, actions, and values.

New arenas for social work assistance and intervention are emerging as our society grows in awareness and need for substance abuse changes. Social workers are also leading the field in looking to promote, create, and sustain communities where recovery is a norm, where recovering clients can live sober, clean lives and thrive. One such setting is CSRs (Centers for Students in Recovery) where students on university campuses can come for support, fellowship, meetings, and recreation (Holleran Steiker & Grahovic, 2011).

Cultural identity scales require more development and testing, as does measurement of distinct ethnic values, attitudes, and behaviors. It is clear that reliable and valid measures of ethnic identity are sorely needed (Trimble, 1995). Also, risk and protective factors may affect cultural identity factors (Felix-Ortiz & Newcomb, 1995).

Connections within the community might mediate drug use among minority populations. Reactive and defensive activism places the youth at risk and alienates them, as does perceived discrimination. Respect for others may counteract this alienation, offering a sense of attachment to the conventional order (Felix-Ortiz & Newcomb, 1995).

Misconceptions about minority drug and alcohol use and abuse are pervasive, primarily due to a lack of consideration of cultural and identity variables in past studies. Castro, Barrera, & Martinez (2004) emphasize the need for rigorous studies of culturally adapted versions of curricula. He suggests the importance of such studies, recommending controlled research trials in which cultural adaptations of model prevention programs are tested against their original versions.

One study that pursues the adaptation question was conducted by Holleran Steiker and Hopson (2007), who researched the value of culturally adapted versions of the Keepin' It REAL drug resistance curriculum (Hecht et al., 2003). Their findings suggested that having youth involved in the process of culturally adapting a program may be advantageous with regard to their own perceptions of drug dangers, possibly leading to positive changes in their own drug use behaviors.

Since treatment realms have had limited success with adolescents, it is critical that social workers champion prevention efforts to intervene before full-blown addiction or dependence occurs. It is critical that social workers not reinvent the wheel (i.e., they must utilize evidence-based programs). However, they must work toward building bridges between prevention interventions and the diverse cultures being served.

Conclusions

It is clear that social workers need to have a strong foundation of understanding with regard to drug and alcohol use, abuse, and implications in order to serve their clients effectively. Social workers in both the substance abuse and general practice fields can apply their uniquely holistic, ecological techniques based on empirically supported research to provide the best care for clients they serve.

In a study of the national substance abuse treatment infrastructures, alarming findings include: high levels of staff turnover, predominance of counselors at the exclusion of other disciplines, and extreme instability of the workforce at all levels within the national treatment system. Apart from counselors, there were very few other professional disciplines represented in most of these programs. For example, "only 54% of the programs had even a part-time physician on staff. Outside of methadone programs, less than 15% of programs employed a nurse. *Social workers* and psychologists were rarely mentioned (emphasis our own)" (McLellan, Carise & Kleber, 2003, p. 119). The authors suggest a need to provide meaningful financial incentives to physicians, nurses, social workers, psychologists, and counselors to make clinical careers within the addictions treatment system economically viable. Educational loan forgiveness programs contingent upon working a number of years in addiction treatment exist and may help to attract and retain clinically valuable personnel (McLellan, Carise, & Kleber, 2003).

Also, much more social work research is needed in the area of substance abuse. As powerfully noted by the Addictions Services Task Force:

> The social work profession is the largest allied health care profession in the United States. As such, social workers function in "real world" settings and provide care to individuals, groups, families and communities dealing with drug abuse and related problems. Social workers work in these settings in collaboration with members of numerous other disciplines. The breadth and depth of service provision and rich interdisciplinary collaborations afford social worker researchers the opportunity to design studies in an array of intervention sites and to maximize external validity through the use of "real-world" settings. (Singer & Pollio, in press, p. 4)

Mary Richmond started the social workers' quest to serve substance users and abusers and to retain their dignity, grace, and worth. This challenging work requires sensitivity, tenacity, and empathy. It is imperative that social workers continue to learn about, study, and open hearts to clients with substance abuse problems. This complex work starts with listening carefully to the experiences of those who struggle with these difficult issues. There is no profession better suited for this work.

Key Terms

Addiction	Intervention	Social skill building
Cultural groundedness, racial disparities	Motivational interviewing	Stage of change
	Recovery	Substance abuse
Dependency	Relapse	Substance abuse prevention
Dual-diagnosis	Resilience	Transtheoretical model
Harm reduction and non-abstinence-based models	Retention	
	Screening/assessment	

Review Questions for Critical Thinking

1. How can one differentiate between the terms substance use/abuse, dependency, and addiction? How are these terms useful or problematic in the field of social work with substance abusers?

2. What is the Transtheoretical Model and Stages of Change? How are these concepts applied to interventions with substance abusers?

3. How does culture impact substance abuse clients, and how should these factors influence social work interventions?

4. Looking at persona in environment, what aspects of clients' lives should be considered when working with someone who is a substance abuser?

5. Why is the shift in focus from addiction to recovery important, and how can this shift be actualized both on a micro/meso level with clients and on a macro level in society?

Online Resources

National Institute on Drug Abuse www.nida.nih.gov/nidahome.html and http://drugabuse.gov/scienceofaddiction

The National Institute on Drug Abuse's website, with the most extensive timely information and resources regarding drug abuse and intervention as well as a detailed monograph on addiction as a brain, body, and spiritual malady.

American Society of Addiction Medicine: www.asam.org

American Society of Addiction Medicine site, with the standing definition of addiction and other pertinent information about the science and treatment of addiction.

National Institute of Alcohol Abuse and Alcoholism: www.niaaa.hih .gov

Research, highlights, events, and links from the National Institute of Alcohol Abuse and Alcoholism.

National Substance Abuse and Mental Health Services Administration: www.samhsa.gov or http://store.samhsa.gov/home

The National Substance Abuse and Mental Health Services Administration sites, with extensive information and a clearinghouse of materials (many free) about such relevant topics as prevention, health, treatment, justice issues, research data, publications, public awareness, and addiction recovery.

Addiction Science Research and Education Center: www.utexas.edu/ research/asrec

Website of the latest findings in Addiction Science, written in terms that are easy to understand. This site has an outstanding list of myths about substances to discern truth from fiction about drugs.

References

Adams, R. E., Boscarino, J. A., & Figley, C. R. (2006). Compassion fatigue and psychological distress among social workers: A validation study. *American Journal of Orthopsychiatry, 76*(1), 103–108.

American Psychiatric Association. (2000). *Diagnostic and statistical manual of mental disorders* (4th ed., text rev.). Washington, DC: Author.

American Society of Addiction Medicine. (2011). *Public policy statement: Definition of addiction.* Washington, DC: Author.

Amodeo, M., & Fassler, I. (2001). Agency practices affecting social workers who treat substance-abusing clients. *Journal of Social Work Practice in the Addictions, 1*(2), 3–19.

Bachman, J. G., Wallace, J. M., O'Malley, P., Johnston, L., Kurth, C. L., & Neighbors, H. W. (1991). Racial/ethnic differences in smoking, drinking, and illicit drug use among American high school seniors, 1976–89. *American Journal of Public Health, 81,* 372–377.

Barthwell, A. G., & Gilbert, C. L. (1993). Screening for infectious diseases among substance abusers. *Treatment Improvement Protocol (TIP) Series, No. 6.* Rockville, MD: U.S. Department of Health and Human Services.

Beauvais, F., & Oetting, E. R. (1999). Drug use, resilience, and the myth of the golden child. In M. D. Glanz & J. L. Johnson (Eds.), *Resilience and development: Positive life adaptations* (pp. 101–106). New York, NY: Kluwer Academic/Plenum Press.

Bodley, J. H. (1994). *Cultural anthropology: Tribes, states, and the global system.* Mountain View, CA: Mayfield.

Botvin, G. J. (1995). Drug abuse prevention in school settings. In G. J. Botvin, S. Schinke, & M. A. Orlandi (Eds.), *Drug abuse prevention with multiethnic youth* (pp. 169–192). Newbury Park, CA: Sage.

Bride, B. E. (2007). Prevalence of secondary traumatic stress among social workers. *Social Work, 52*(1), 63–70.

Bukowski, W. J. (1985). School-based substance abuse prevention: A review of program research. *Journal of Children in Contemporary Society, 18*(1/2), 95–115.

Caetano, R. (1989). Differences in alcohol use between Mexican Americans in Texas and California. *Hispanic Journal of Behavioral Sciences, 11,* 58–69.

Caetano, R., & Mora, M. E. (1988). Acculturation and drinking among people of Mexican descent in Mexico and the United States. *Journal of Studies on Alcohol, 49*(5), 462–471.

Carpenter, J. (2002). Mental health recovery paradigm: Implications for social work. *Health and Social Work, 27*(2), 86–94.

Cartwright, A. K. J., & Gorman, D. M. (1993). Processes involved in changing the therapeutic attitudes of clinicians toward working with drinking clients. *Psychotherapy Research, 3,* 95–104.

Castro, F. G., Barrera, M., & Martinez, C. R. (2004). The cultural adaptation of prevention interventions: Resolving tensions between fidelity and fit. *Prevention Science, 5*(1), 41–45.

Centers for Disease Control and Prevention. (2006). *Health, United States, 2006: With chartbook of trends in the health of Americans.* Washington, DC: U.S. Department of Health and Human Services.

Christian, C., Zobeck, T., Malin, H., & Hitchcock, D. (1989). Hispanic alcohol use: General description, methodological issues, and preliminary findings (NIAAA Research Monograph No. 18, DHHS Pub. No. [ADM] 87–1435). In D. Spiegler, D. Tate, S. Aitken, & C. Christian (Eds.), *Alcohol use among U.S. ethnic minorities.* Washington, DC: U.S. Government Printing Office.

Clayton, S. (1991). Gender differences in psychosocial determinants of adolescent smoking. *Journal of School Health, 61,* 115–120.

Coard, S. I., Wallace, S. A., Stevenson, Jr., H. C., & Brotman, L. M. (2004). Towards culturally relevant preventive interventions: The consideration of racial socialization in parent training with African American families. *Journal of Child and Family Studies, 13*(3), 277–293.

Collier, M. J., Ribeau, S., & Hecht, M. L. (1986). Intercultural communication rules and outcomes within three domestic cultural groups. *International Journal of Intercultural Relations, 10*, 439–457.

Comas-Diaz, L. (1986). Puerto Rican alcoholic women: Treatment considerations. *Alcoholism Treatment Quarterly, 3*(11), 47–58.

Costantino, G., Malgady, R. G., & Rogler, L. H. (1985). *Cuento therapy, folktales as a culturally sensitive psychotherapy for Puerto Rican children.* Maplewood, NJ: Waterfront Press.

Costantino, G., Malgady, R. G., & Rogler, L. H. (1986). Cuento therapy: A culturally sensitive modality for Puerto Rican children. *Journal of Consulting and Clinical Psychology, 54*, 639–645.

De la Rosa, M., Holleran, L. K., & Ashenberg-Straussner, S. L. (2005). *Substance abusing Latinos: Current research on epidemiology, prevention, and treatment.* New York, NY: Haworth Press.

Drug and Alcohol Service Information System (DASIS) Report. (2002). *Black admissions to substance abuse treatment: 1999.* Washington, DC: U.S. Department of Health and Human Services.

Dryfoos, J. G. (1998). *Safe passage: Making it through adolescence in a risky society.* New York, NY: Oxford University Press.

Falck, R., & Craig, R. (1988). Classroom oriented, primary prevention programming for drug abuse. *Journal of Psychoactive Drugs, 20*(4), 403–408.

Felix-Ortiz, M., & Newcomb, M. D. (1995). Cultural identity and drug use among Latino and Latina adolescents. In G. J. Botvin, S. Schinke, & M. A. Orlandi (Eds.), *Drug abuse prevention with multiethnic youth* (pp. 147–165). Thousand Oaks, CA: Sage.

Fisher, G. L., & Harrison, T. C. (2000). *Substance abuse: Information for school counselors, social workers, therapists, and counselors.* Needham Heights, MA: Allyn & Bacon.

Flanzer, J., Gorman, E. M., & Spence, R. T. (2001). Fear of neuroscience: A dialogue about social work practice in the addictions. *Journal of Social Work Practice in the Addictions, 1*(3), 103–112.

Forgey, M. A., Schinke, S., & Cole, K. (1997). School-based interventions to prevent substance use among inner-city minority adolescents. In D. K. Wilson, J. R. Rodrigue, & W. C. Taylor (Eds.), *Health-promoting and health-compromising behaviors among minority adolescents.* Washington, DC: American Psychological Association.

Gagne, C., White, W., & Anthony, W. A. (2007). Recovery: A common vision for the fields of mental health and addictions. *Psychiatric Rehabilitation Journal, 31* (1), 32–37.

Germain, C., & Bloom, M. (2000). *Human behavior in the social environment: An ecological view.* New York, NY: Columbia University Press.

Gilbert, M. J., & Alcocer, A. M. (1988). Alcohol use and Hispanic youth: An overview. *Journal of Drug Issues, 18*(1), 33.

Gonzalez-Ramos, G. (1990). Examining the myth of Hispanic families' resistance to treatment: Using the school as a site for services. *Social Work in Education, 12*(4), 261–274.

Gordon, J. U. (1994). *Managing multiculturalism in substance abuse services.* Thousand Oaks, CA: Sage.

Greenfeld, L. A., & Smith, S. K. (1999). *American Indians and crime.* Washington, DC: U.S. Department of Justice, Office of Justice Programs, Bureau of Justice Statistics, NCJ 173386.

Hall, M. N., Amodeo, M., Shaffer, H. J., & Vanderbilt, J. (2000). Social workers employed in substance abuse treatment agencies: A training needs assessment. *Social Work, 45*(2), 141–154.

Harmon, M. A. (1993). Reducing the risk of drug involvement among early adolescents: An evaluation of Drug Abuse Resistance Education (DARE). *Evaluation Review, 17,* 221–239.

Hecht, M., Marsiglia, F. F., Elek-Fisk, E., Wagstaff, D. A., Kulis, S., Dustman, P., et al. (2003). Culturally-grounded substance use prevention: An evaluation of the Keeping it REAL curriculum. *Prevention Science, 4,* 233–248.

Hecht, M., Trost, M., Bator, R., & MacKinnon, D. (1997). Ethnicity and gender similarities and differences in drug resistance. *Journal of Applied Communication Research, 25,* 1–23.

Holleran, L. K., & MacMaster, S. A. (2005). Applying a cultural competency framework to twelve step programs. *Alcoholism Treatment Quarterly, 23*(4), 107–120.

Holleran Steiker, L. K. (in press). Making drug and alcohol prevention relevant: Adapting evidence-based curricula to unique adolescent cultures. *Family and Community Health.*

Holleran Steiker, L. K., & Grahovic, I. (2011). Special topics dialogue: University centers for students in recovery. *Journal of Social Work Practice in the Addictions, 11*(3), 290–294.

Holleran Steiker, L. K., & Hopson, L. M. (2007, February). Evaluation of culturally adapted, evidence-based substance abuse prevention programs for older adolescents in diverse community settings. Paper presented at the Advancing Adolescent Health Conference, University of Texas, Center for Health Promotion Research, Austin.

Jenson, J. M., Howard, M. O., & Vaughn, M. G. (2004). Assessing social work's contribution to controlled studies of adolescent substance abuse treatment. *Journal of Social Work Practice in the Addictions, 4*(4), 51–65.

Johnston, L. D., O'Malley, p. M., Bachman, J. G., & Schulenberg, J. E. (2006). Teen drug use continues down in 2006, particularly among older teens; but use of prescription-type drugs remains high. Ann Arbor, MI: University of Michigan, News and Information Services. Retrieved October 22, 2007, from www.monitoringthefuture.org.

Kaplan, L. E. (2005). Dual relationships: The challenges for social workers in recovery. *Journal of Social Work Practice in the Addictions, 5*(3), 73–90.

Kim, S., Coletti, S. D., Williams, C., & Hepler, N. A. (1995). Substance abuse prevention involving Asian/Pacific Islander American communities. In G. J. Botvin, S. Schinke, & M. A. Orlandi (Eds.), *Drug abuse prevention with multiethnic youth* (pp. 295–326). Newbury Park, CA: Sage.

Korzenny, F., McClure, J. & Rzyttki, B. (1990). Ethnicity, communication, and drugs. *Journal of Drug Issues, 20,* 87–98.

Kumpfer, K. L., & Turner, C. W. (1991) The social ecology model of adolescent substance abuse: Implications for prevention. *International Journal of the Addictions, 25*(4A), 435–563.

Latimer, W. W., Winters, K. C., & Stinchfield, R. D. (1997). Screening for drug abuse among adolescents in clinical and correctional settings using the problem-oriented screening instrument for teenagers. *American Journal of Drug and Alcohol Abuse, 23*(1), 79–98.

Lee, C. C., & Richardson, B. L. (Eds.). (1991). *Multicultural issues in counseling: New approaches to diversity.* Alexandria, VA: American Association for Counseling and Development.

Leukefeld, C. G., & Leukefeld, S. (1999). Primary socialization theory and a bio/psycho/social/spiritual practice model for substance use. *Substance Use and Misuse, 34*(7), 983–991.

Lightfoot, P. J. C., & Orford, J. (1986) Helping agents' attitudes towards alcohol related problems: Situations vacant? A test and elaboration of a model. *British Journal of Addiction, 81,* 749–756.

Lorion, R. (1987). Methodological challenges in prevention research. In J. A. Steinberg & M. M. Silverman (Eds.), *Preventing mental disorders: A research perspective* (DHHS Pub. No. [ADM] 87–1492). Washington, DC: U.S. Government Printing Office.

Marsiglia, F. F., Kulis, S., & Hecht, M. L. (2001). Ethnic labels and ethnic identity as predictors of drug use. *Journal of Research on Adolescence, 11*(1), 21–48.

Matto, H. C. (2004). Applying an ecological framework to understanding drug addiction and recovery. *Journal of Social Work Practice in the Addictions, 4*(3), pp. 5–22.

Mayfield, D., McLeod, G., & Hall, P. (1994). The CAGE questionnaire: Validation of a new measure. *American Journal of Psychiatry, 131,* 1121–1123.

McNeece, C. A., & DiNitto, D. M. (2003). *Chemical dependency: A systems approach* (3rd ed.). Needham Heights, MA: Allyn & Bacon.

McLellan, A. T., Carise, D., & Kleber, H. D. (2003). Can the national addiction treatment infrastructure support the public's demand for quality care? *Journal of Substance Abuse Treatment 25* 117–121.

McVinney, L. D. (2004). Epistemology of the bottle: The social construction of alcoholism and alcoholics in social work literature in the United States between 1950 and 1959. *Journal of Social Work Practice in the Addictions, 4*(4), 3–35.

Melus, A. (1980). Culture and language in the treatment of alcoholism: The Hispanic perspective. *Alcohol and Health Research World, 4*(4), 19–20.

Miller, W. (1998). Toward a motivational definition and understanding of addiction. *Motivational Interviewing Newsletter for Trainers, 5*(3), 2–6. Available from www.motivationalinterview.org/clinical/motmodel.html

Miller, W. R., & Rollnick, S. (1991). *Motivational interviewing: Preparing people to change addictive behavior.* New York, NY: Guilford Press.

Moon, D. G., Hecht, M. L., Jackson, K. M., & Spellers, R. E. (1999). Ethnic and gender differences and similarities in adolescent drug use and refusals of drug offers. *Substance Use and Misuse, 34*(8), 1059–1083.

Munson, C. E. (2000). *The mental health diagnostic desk reference.* Binghamton, NY: Haworth Press.

Najavits, L. M., Sonn, J., Walsh, M., & Weiss, R. D. (2004). Domestic violence in women with PTSD and substance abuse. *Addictive Behaviors, 29*(4), 707–715.

Napoli, M., Marsiglia, F. F., & Kulis, S. (2003). Sense of belonging in school as a protective factor against drug abuse among Native American urban adolescents in the Southwest. *Journal of Social Work Practice in the Addictions, 3*(2), 25–41.

National Association of Social Workers. (1999). Code of ethics. Retrieved October 22, 2007, from www.socialworkers.org/pubs/code/code.asp

National Association of Social Workers Practice Research Network. (2001). Substance abuse treatment activities. *PRN Datagram, 1*(4). Available from www.socialworkers.org/naswprn/surveyOne/substance.pdf

National Institute on Alcohol Abuse and Alcoholism. (2004). Alcohol abuse increases, dependence declines across decade: Young adult minorities emerge as high-risk subgroups. Retrieved October 22, 2007, from www.niaaa.nih.gov/NewsEvents/NewsReleases/NESARCNews.htm

National Institute on Alcohol Abuse and Alcoholism. (2005). *Social work curriculum on alcohol use disorders.* Bethesda, MD: Author.

National Institutes of Health. (2003). NIH plan for social work research [Report]. Washington, DC: Department of Health and Human Services. Retrieved October 22, 2007, from http://obssr.od.nih.gov/Documents/Publications/SWR_Report.pdf

National Survey on Drug Use and Health. (2004). *2002: Latest national survey on drug use and health.* Washington, DC: U.S. Department of Health and Human Services.

Neff, J. A., Prihoda, T. J., & Hoppe, S. K. (1991). "Machismo," self-esteem, education and high maximum drinking among Anglo, Black, and Mexican-American male drinkers. *Journal of Studies on Alcohol, 52*(5), 458–463.

Newcomb, M. D., & Bentler, P. M. (1986). Substance use and ethnicity: Differential impact of peer and adult models. *Journal of Psychology, 120*(1), 83–95.

Oetting, E. R., & Beauvais, F. (1990–1991). Orthogonal cultural identification theory: The cultural acculturation status on delinquency for Mexican-American adolescents. *American Journal of Community Psychology, 27*(2), 189–211.

O'Neill, J. V. (2001). Expertise in addictions said crucial. *NASW News, 46*(1), 10.

Pabon, E. (1998). Hispanic adolescent delinquency and the family: A discussion of sociocultural influences. *Adolescence, 33.*

Pentz, M. A., Trebow, E. A., & Hansen, W. B. (1990). Effects of program implementation on adolescent drug use behavior: The Midwestern Prevention Program (MPP). *Evaluation Review, 14*(3), 264–389.

Price, R. H., & Lorion, R. P. (1989). Prevention programming as organizational reinvention: From research to implementation. In D. Shaffer, I. Philips, & N. B. Enzer (Eds.), *Prevention of mental health disorders, alcohol and other drug use in children and adolescents. OSAP Prevention Monograph-2.* (DHHS Pub. No. [ADM] 90–1646). Washington, DC: U.S. Government Printing Office.

Prochaska, J. O., & DiClemente, C. C. (1982). Transtheoretical therapy: Toward a more integrative model of change. *Psychotherapy: Theory, Research, and Practice, 19*(3), 276–288.

Prochaska, J. O., DiClemente, C. C., & Norcross, J. C. (1992). In search of how people change: Applications to addictive behaviors. *American Psychologist, 47*(9), 1102–1114.

Richmond, M. E. (1944). *Social diagnosis.* New York, NY: Free Press. (Original work published 1917)

Rogler, L. H., Cortes, D. E., & Malgady, R. G. (1991). Acculturation and mental health status among Hispanics: Convergence and new directions for research. *American Psychologist, 46*, 585–597.

Rollnick, S., & Miller, W. R. (1995). What is motivational interviewing? *Behavioural and Cognitive Psychotherapy, 23*, 325–334.

Saleebey, D. (1992). *The strengths perspective in social work practice* (2nd ed.). New York, NY: Longman.

Schinke, S., Orlandi, M., Vaccaro, D., Espinoza, R., McAlister, A., & Botvin, G. (1992). Substance use among Hispanic and non-Hispanic adolescents. *Addictive Behaviors, 17,* 117–124.

Selzer, M. L. (1971). The Michigan Alcoholism Screening Test: The quest for a new diagnostic instrument. *American Journal of Psychiatry, 127,* 89–94.

Shapiro, T. (1985). Adolescent language: Its use for diagnosis, group identity, values, and treatment. *Adolescent Psychiatry, 12,* 297–311.

Simon, C., McNeil, J., Franklin, C., & Cooperman, A. (1991). Letters and comments: Authors respond. *Families in Society: Journal of Contemporary Human Services, 71*(9), 436–438.

Singer, M. I., Pollio, D. E., & Stiffman, A. (in press). Addictions services task force. *Journal of Social Service Research* [Special issue].

Smedley, B. D., Stith, A. Y., & Nelson, A. R. (Eds.). (2003). *Unequal treatment: Confronting racial and ethnic disparities in health care.* Washington, DC: National Academies Press, Institute of Medicine, Board on Health Sciences Policy.

Straussner, S. L. (2001). The role of social workers in the treatment of addictions: A brief history. *Journal of Social Work Practice in the Addictions, 1*(1), 3–9. Retrieved January 27, 2006, from http://alcoholstudies.rutgers .edu/history.html

Straussner, S. L. (2004). Social work in addictions: A historical perspective. *Currents of the New York City Chapter, NASW, 6,* 12.

Substance Abuse and Mental Health Services Administration. (2000, March). National Household Survey on Drug Abuse: Main findings, 1998. Available from www.samhsa.gov/OAS/OASftp.html

Substance Abuse Subtle Screening Inventory Institute. (2001). Substance Abuse Subtle Screening Inventory general information. Available from www.sassi .com/5–29–01/

Sullivan, J. T., Sykora, K., Schneiderman, J., Naranjo, C. A., & Sellers, E. M. (1989). Assessment of alcohol withdrawal: The revised Clinical Institute Withdrawal Assessment for Alcohol Scale (CIWA-AR). *British Journal of Addiction, 84,* 1353–1357.

Sun, A. (2001). Systematic barriers to the employment of social workers in alcohol and other drug agencies: A statewide survey. *Journal of Social Work Practice in the Addictions, 1*(1), 11–24.

Szapocznik, J., & Williams, R. A. (2000). Brief strategic family therapy: Twenty-five years of interplay among theory, research and practice in adolescent behavior problems and drug abuse. *Clinical Child and Family Psychology Review, 3*(2), 117–134.

Tobler, N. S. (1986). Meta-analysis of 143 adolescent drug prevention programs: Quantitative outcome results of program participants compared to a control comparison group. *Journal of Drug Issues, 4,* 537–567.

Tolan, P. H., Guerra, N. G., & Kendall, P. C. (1995). A developmental ecological perspective on antisocial behavior in children and adolescents: Toward a unified risk and intervention framework. *Journal of Consulting and Clinical Psychology, 63,* 579–584.

Treatment Data Episode Set (TEDS). (2004). *Treatment Data Episode Set (TEDS) 1992–2001.* Washington, DC: DHHS.

Trimble, J. E. (1995). Toward an understanding of ethnicity and ethnic identity, and their relationship with drug use research. In G. J. Botvin, S. Schinke, & M. A. Orlandi (Eds.), *Drug abuse prevention with multiethnic youth* (pp. 28–45). Thousand Oaks, CA: Sage.

Vaughn, M. G., Howard, M. O., & Jenson, J. M. (2004). Assessing social work's contribution to controlled outcome studies in the alcohol dependence treatment literature. *Journal of Social Work Practice in the Addictions, 4*(4), 37–49.

Volkow, N. (2010). *The science of addiction: Drugs, brains, and behavior.* Washington, DC: National Institute on Drug Abuse.

Werner, E., & Smith, R. (1992). *Overcoming the odds: High risk children from birth to adulthood.* New York, NY: Cornell University Press.

White, W. L. (2007). Addiction recovery: Its definition and conceptual boundaries. *Journal of Substance Abuse Treatment, 33:* 229–241.

Wilson, D. K., Rodrigue, J. R., & Taylor, W. C. (Eds.). (1997). *Health-promoting and health-compromising behaviors among minority adolescents.* Washington, DC: American Psychological Association.

Wodarski, J. S., & Feit, M. D. (1995). *Adolescent substance abuse: An empirical-based group preventive health paradigm.* New York, NY & London, UK: Haworth Press.

Wolin, S., & Wolin, S. (1993). *The resilient self: How survivors of troubled families rise above adversity.* New York, NY: Villard.

Yellowbird, M. (2001). Critical values and First Nations people. In R. A. Fong & S. Furoto (Eds.), *Culturally competent practice: Skills, interventions, and evaluations* (pp. 61–74). Needham Heights, MA: Allyn & Bacon.

Chapter 5

The Mental Health Field of Practice

King Davis and Hyejin Jung

> How can social workers influence policy change or advocate for amendments to existing legislation effecting mental health services?

Social workers often hear tragic stories in the media that involve/describe people with severe mental disorders. The story may portray a Texas mother with an extensive history of severe mental illness who kills her children, or an untreated mentally ill person who shoots a congresswoman and several of her supporters in Arizona. Subsequently, the general public may conclude that mental disorders are unique conditions that only a person with peculiar characteristics would experience/develop. Sensationalist news may also influence members of the public to believe that persons with serious mental disorders are more violent than the general public, or that treatment is ineffective. However, several recent national and international studies provide a different set of conclusions about the distribution of mental illness in the population, the effectiveness of treatment, and the role of public policies that govern care of the mentally ill. The World Health Report 2001 indicated that one in four people in the world develop a mental disorder, and that mental disorders are prevalent in all populations and countries regardless of age, gender, race/ethnicity, and economic status (Murthy, 2001). Services research completed in the United States also supports the ubiquity of mental disorders. Replicating the National Co-Morbidity Study, Kessler and colleagues (2005) reported that over a 6-month time span, close to 25% of the adult population, and 21% of children in the United States experience a *Diagnostic and Statistical Manual IV* mental disorder. Over a lifetime, however, Kessler and colleagues (2005) estimate that the prevalence of mental disorders in the adult population in the United States approaches 50%, excluding prevalence rates for severe mental illnesses such as schizophrenia. The rates of this mental disorder appear to remain stable at 0.5–3.0% of the population (Kessler et al., 2005).

Between 1990 to 2001, utilization of mental health services of all kinds increased by 65%, and the proportion of the population using services increased from 12% to 20% (Wang et al., 2006). These increases in utilization, however, were not distributed evenly across all potential service providers. As early as the 1990s, 43% of mental health episodes were treated in general medical settings, 40% were treated in the mental health specialty field, and close to 20% by "human services" professions (Wang et al., 2006). For some ethnic minorities, mental health services are provided almost exclusively by their religious leaders (Neighbors, Musick, & Williams, 1998). Between 1990 and 2001, the general medical setting showed the greatest increase (179%), with a corresponding increase for psychiatry of 117% and other mental health specialty a 59% increase (Wang et al., 2006). Treatment of mental disorders, mild and severe, now occurs more frequently in general medicine than in other sectors (Unutzer, Schoenbaum, & Druss, 2006; Wang et al., 2006). Treatment for mild to moderate mental health problems using integrated evidence-based approaches has shown excellent results (Nathan & Gorman, 2002; Unutzer, Schoenbaum, & Druss, 2006).

The prevalence of mental disorders in adults and children in the United States establishes a clear epidemiological base for mental health care as a major area of professional services and as a source of direct financial costs to the individual and the economy as a whole. For social workers, mental health treatment has been a traditional source of interest, identity, status, and career opportunities (Gibelman, 1999). Considering the preponderance of mental illness, its chronic nature, and its impact on a person's quality of life, increased demand for clinical social workers is inevitable. The *Mental Health Atlas 2005* reported that an average of 11.58 social workers per 100,000 population is employed in mental health settings, second only to psychiatric nurses among mental health professionals (World Health Organization, 2005). In the United States in 2008, behavioral health social workers occupied about 21% (137,000) of the 642,000 social work positions. The overall growth rate (approximately 20%) of social workers in mental health and substance abuse is anticipated to be faster than the average for all occupations by 2018 (U.S. Department of Labor, 2010).

Historically, a significant proportion (39.8%) of social workers found careers in public and private psychiatric hospitals, community mental health centers, general hospitals, outpatient clinics and private mental health practice (Gibelman, 2000; Gibelman & Schervish, 1993; Mander-scheid & Henderson, 2001). The extensive involvement of social workers in these clinical service areas has elevated the reputation of the profession. However, clinical social workers are often less involved in public mental health policy and legislative advocacy as these interface with mental health care (U.S. Department of Labor, 2010; Cohen, Bonnie, & Monahan, 2008). The long-term emphasis on clinical practice within social work may result in a false dichotomy between clinical practice and policy practice. The reality is that these two practice areas are highly interdependent but may lack a clear conceptual framework that demonstrates where and how they overlap. Effective clinical practice, grounded on the core values of social work, relies on a complex of public policies or legal requirements. These policies determine not only who can be served, but includes what services [EBPs] will be reimbursed, the standard of care, licensure requirements, commitment procedures, and how the rights of patients must be protected. Effective public policy in mental health should reflect knowledge, information, outcomes, and experiences translated from clinical care. The ability of clinicians to help translate their practice experiences into policy-ready positions is important in increasing services and funding while promoting the well-being of people with mental disorders and their families. Of importance is the fact that the majority of clinical services in mental health take place in agencies designed to create and maintain quality practice standards. Almost all of these agencies are subject to some form of governmental (federal, state, or local) policies designed to protect the public health and prevent excess costs. Knowledge of how these agencies are organized, managed, funded, and influenced by legislative policy is germane to clinical and policy practice. Most importantly, practicing within the parameters of prevailing public policy or law also protects the social worker from liability, unethical conduct, and potential loss of licensure.

The following narrative illustrates some of the linkages between clinical and policy practice and the value of a clear conceptual framework for defining policy generally and integrating specific mental health policies in clinical practice.

Narrative

Nhing Chu is a 32-year-old Chinese immigrant who has been in the United States for close to three years. Eighteen months ago, he had a confrontation with a neighbor over a parking space, and the incident escalated into a physical fight requiring the police. The police were unable to subdue Mr. Chu, and they were unable to understand his side of the incident because of his limited English. They relied on the neighbor's accusation that Chu had attacked him without provocation. Chu was charged with assault and jailed for several days. Because of his continued agitation with others while in the cell, the judge referred Chu for a mental health exam. The local mental health clinic physician conducted a brief mental status exam in English without an interpreter and concluded that Mr. Chu had schizophrenia with paranoid features and was a clear danger to others. Chu was involuntarily admitted to the state hospital some 45 miles from his city, and his employer and parents were notified. Since his admission to the hospital over a year ago, Chu has been confined to an isolated room and occasionally held in four-point restraints. According to the hospital's records, the ward nurses see Chu as violent, dangerous, extremely hostile, and threatening. He seems constantly agitated but is unable to participate in any clinical work, because he either does not understand English or refuses to speak with the hospital staff members. Because of these observations, Chu is unable to leave his room and is fed through an opening in the door. He is rarely allowed outside of his room for any length of time.

Mr. Chu's parents contacted the hospital director and requested that their son be released to them. The parents indicated that he was not a danger to himself or others and could be safely released. They also offered to have him leave the country if he were released, because his charges violated his visa status. When the hospital refused to release Chu, the parents hired a local attorney. Initially the attorney met with the hospital director and the medical director, but they refused to release Chu citing the statute that permits involuntary admission where there is a danger to others. Attorney Lee then brought the case before the local human rights commission. This commission administered by the state mental health authority was established a decade ago and reviews complicated cases where human rights violations may have occurred. If an issue cannot be resolved at the local level, the local group can petition for a hearing by the state body. After the local human rights group heard Chu's case, they concluded that he may have been misdiagnosed because of his limited understanding of English and because the hospital had not made any effort to include either a Chinese language clinician or an interpreter. The local group requested that the hospital follow through on its recommendations. The hospital director indicated that there were no local clinicians or interpreters who met the qualifications. Mr. Chu was not released and continued to remain in confinement.

The attorney for Mr. Chu asked the local human rights group to refer the case to the state human rights organization, and they complied. In addition, he sought the involvement of a local consumer advocacy organization and the NAMI chapter at the state level. Attorney Lee learned that there had been several cases of foreign nationals who had been involuntarily committed to this state hospital. Each of them had been placed in isolation without the benefit of services in their language. Because these cases appeared to represent a pattern of constitutional violations, Attorney Lee contacted the United State Justice Department to determine whether Chu's constitutional rights had been violated.

Linking Social Welfare/Public Policy to Clinical Practice

The narrative raises a number of complex questions about the definition, role, or utility of public policy to be considered as the chapter is read: What are the critical policy and practice issues within the narrative?

One reason for the ambiguity of policy definitions or meaning is the presence of hundreds of competing and contradictory definitions of social welfare policy, public policy, and related policies (e.g. economic, education, defense, and transportation) in social work literature (Popple & Leighninger, 2000). The number and range of competing definitions that are available tend to confuse the meaning of policy generally and lessen its ease of application and practice value to clinical work. For example, Dye (1981) defines public policy as whatever government decides to do or not to do. Popple and Leighninger (2000) define social welfare policy as principles and activities aimed at resolving dependency. When such definitions are broadened to include specific macro level policies, such as economics or civil rights, the application to clinical practice may wane further. Rarely is there a separate definition of mental health policy that could be useful to clinicians. However, Gil's (1973) macro level definition of social welfare policy modified for application in mental health is helpful for providing a context for the narrative and for linkages to clinical practice concerns:

> *Mental health policies are the principles and courses of action, adopted, financed, supported, and pursued by government, and designed to regulate services, structures, programs, providers, and resources in the mental health system as well as the roles, statuses, quality of life, constitutional and human rights, and relationships between the mentally disabled, other individuals, the mental health system, and society in general. (Davis, 1998, p. 12)*

This definition of policy pertains directly to the case narrative used here, in which a number of broad service and legal questions were involved and directly affected the delivery of clinical care. The overt policy and clinical practice issues include attention to immigration status, police involvement in psychiatric emergencies, cultural and linguistic competency (Salas-Lopez, Holmes, Mouson, & Soto-Greene, 2007), use of jails for persons with mental health diagnoses, forensic evaluation standards, involuntary commitment laws, use of restraints, and the right to treatment (Supreme Court of the United States, 2006). Throughout the narrative, it appears that the civil rights of the putative patient were limited or ignored. There was no evidence that attention was paid to language barriers in the diagnostic assessment and the judicial decision to involuntarily commit him to a state institution. The excessive use of restraints and isolation, which is described as occurring disproportionately with minority consumers, raises additional civil rights questions. More subtle policy and clinical concerns are the influence of ethnicity on diagnosis and commitment (Davis, Lewis, Zhang, & Thompkins, 2011; Lawson, Heplar, Holladay, & Cuffel, 1994), maintenance of accreditation standards, licensure, right to counsel, forced medication, and federal court decisions that require states to ensure effective treatment, discharge planning, and protection of constitutional rights. In this case narrative, the consequences of the clinical practice detached from policies can result in severe psychological trauma for Chu and his family. Additionally, there could be legal and ethical charges brought against the hospital and the staff that would threaten licensure and accreditation.

The information in Table 5.1 presents an overview of practice issues and specific policies and public laws that are pertinent to clinical practice by social work providers, consumers, families, inpatient treatment facilities, and to state mental health systems. The list is not exhaustive but only illustrative of the policy linkages in select clinical practice areas.

Of the various public policies listed in Table 5.1, the Civil Rights of Institutionalized Persons Act (42 U.S. C.), seems particularly important

Table 5.1 **Social Welfare Policy Regulations in Mental Health by Provider, Consumer, Facilities, and Systems.**

Social Welfare Practice Issues	Social Work Providers	Consumers of Service	Treatment Facilities	State Mental Health Systems
Clinical Practice	State Licensure Continuing Educ. EBPS Ethical Practice Cultural Competence Liability Insurance Health Reform Act	Peer Services Insurance Health Reform Act	State Licensure Required Health Code Liability Ins. Health Reform Act **CRIPA**	Parity Law **CRIPA** Health Reform Act McKinney Act Commitment Standards
Accreditation	CSWE		JCAHO NCCBHA	Optional NASMHPD
Reimbursement	State Licensure Use of EBPs Managed Care Guidelines Medicaid Medicare SCHIP TANF Customary Fees	Medicaid Medicare Social Security SSDI TANF	State Licensure Federal Qualification Private Insurance	Medicaid Medicare SCHIP
Constitutional and Human Rights	Code of Ethics Insanity Defense Competency	**CRIPA** Consumer Rights ADA Right to Treatment	**CRIPA**	**CRIPA**
Judicial Cases	*Wyatt v. Stickney* *Olmstead v. L.C.*	*Wyatt v. Stickney* *Olmstead v. L.C.*	*Wyatt v. Stickney* *Olmstead v. L.C.*	*Wyatt v. Stickney* *Olmstead v. L.C.*

in linking policy and clinical practice obligations to many of the multiple concerns raised in this narrative (Barczyk & Davis, 2010; National Council on Disability, 2005).

The Civil Rights of Institutionalized Persons Act of 1980 (CRIPA)

Historically, persons with varying degrees of mental illness have been admitted to large mental institutions operated by state and county governments (Grob, 1994; Rothman, 1970). Until passage of the Community Mental Health Centers Construction Act in 1963, most of these individuals spent decades living within the institutions, with limited possibility of returning to their communities (Joint Commission on Mental Illness and Health, 1961). By 1955, close to 600,000 people were housed in state and county mental hospitals. However, inside many of these institutions, studies point out the extent to which patients often were abused, neglected, and treated poorly;

languished without effective treatment or discharge plans; and sometimes were killed (Deutsch, 1948; Joint Commission on Mental Illness and Health, 1961). In response to the reported abuse of psychiatric patients, legal scholars made efforts to protect their constitutional rights through lawsuits against the states and the passage of new consumer rights laws and provisions (*Wyatt v. Aderholt*, 1974; Ennis, 1972; Ennis & Siegel, 1973). Efforts to obtain federal legislation that would allow the U.S. Department of Justice to investigate and remedy allegations of abuse, neglect, and violations of civil rights were not initially successful despite numerous findings of widespread abuse and civil rights violations in both prisons and state mental institutions (Geller, 2000; Holt, 1998; Powers, Mooney, & Nunno, 1990).

CRIPA (42 U.S.C. 1997) passed into law in 1980 after Congress reached a compromise and inserted a requirement that states shall be apprised that an investigation was pending. The law was designed to offer federal protection from abuse and loss of civil rights to groups (residents, patients, prisoners, consumers) who reside in public institutions. Amendments to the act have expanded its legal jurisdiction to private institutions. The institutions covered now under the law include state mental hospitals, facilities for the intellectually disabled, prisons, jails, private nursing homes, boarding homes, juvenile facilities, and hospitals. The Civil Rights Division of the United States Department of Justice (DOJ) is authorized to intervene in situations where there is a pattern of denying groups access to treatment, competent health care, discharge planning, safety, or freedom from abuse and unnecessary confinement. The Department of Justice cannot intervene on behalf of a single individual or in response to a single incident but does have the authority to intervene where there is a persistent pattern of infractions that threaten the entire population or large numbers of individuals in the institution. When a complaint is received, the Department of Justice is required to investigate the complaint but no time parameters are required. If a pattern of infractions is identified the DOJ alerts the state government and requests that the conditions be remedied. Failure to remedy the conditions in a set time frame subjects the state to a federal lawsuit, substantial fines, and federal intervention. By 2006, DOJ investigations of civil rights violations in state institutions had taken place in 34 states, with 433 suits filed and won (Barczyk & Davis, 2010).

This case narrative illustrates a number of clinical, policy, and legal dilemmas that impinge on the quality of care; however, few are more pertinent than the prospective violation of the patient's constitutional rights. These rights include the right to timely and effective treatment that is aimed at functional improvement, recovery, and planned return to the community. These rights were the basis of the *Wyatt v. Stickney* decision in Alabama (*Wyatt v. Stickney*, 1974, 2010) where the court found the state was violating constitutional rights by not providing a modicum of care that would result in improvements and eventual return to the community. The *Wyatt v. Stickney* (1974, 2010) case raised these seminal civil rights issues to a level that helped to establish new federal law. Where it can be proven that there is a pattern of violations of these or related constitutional rights of persons within an institution, legal remedies are available under the Civil Rights of Institutionalized Persons Act of 1980 (Barczyk & Davis, 2010; National Council on Disability, 2005). Violations within an institution can take the form of physical or sexual abuse, a lack of clinical treatment, failure to provide discharge planning, hazardous conditions, or failure to protect patients from excessive use of restraints, overutilization of medication, high-risk medical experiments, or practice by unlicensed individuals.

Conclusion

There is a close relationship between clinical and policy practice, as suggested in the narrative and the discussion. However, actualization of this relationship is hampered in part by the absence of a singular definition of policy and the long-standing separation of these two areas of practice within social work education. Practice requires skills and knowledge in both areas. However, it is a commonplace that clinical providers have limited knowledge of the range of social welfare policies that are available in their area of practice. In a recent pilot survey, second-year social work students were asked to self-rate their knowledge of 60 major social welfare policies. Almost all of the students self-rated their knowledge of all social welfare policies at the lowest level (Davis & Jung, 2011).

The chapter identified a number of important policy and clinical practice questions:

1. What is the definition of mental health policy and how does it apply in this case?
2. How did the hospital violate CRIPA?
3. Could knowledge of linguistic cultural competence care and of CRIPA regulations help prevent these violations?
4. Would a social worker have been able to assist the hospital in this case by assessing the needs of Mr. Chu and working with his family at admission?

Numerous features of clinical practice are dependent on a complex of macro-level policy requirements including licensure, clinical standards, liability insurance, entitlement programs, reimbursements, involuntary admissions, use of restraints, eliminating racial, ethnic, and gender disparities, and the protection of constitutional and human rights (Barnes, 2008; Davis et al., 2011). The intent of these governmental regulations is to create and maintain quality practice standards, ensure equitable access to services, protect the public health, lessen the financial burden on taxpayers, and ultimately promote the well-being of people served by social workers. Social workers can influence policy change or advocate for amendments to existing legislation. If they are aware of gaps in policy, social workers can raise their concerns through their professional associations. Social justice requires that social workers in the mental health field remain knowledge-able of how public policies and judicial decisions interface with and guide clinical practice.

Key Terms

Law and mental
   health

Mental health

Mental health
   policy

Review Questions for Critical Thinking

1. Discuss the distribution of mental illness in the United States.
2. Discuss the effectiveness of mental health treatment.
3. Discuss the role of public policies that govern the care of the mentally ill.
4. Review and discuss the civil rights of institutionalized persons.

Online Resources

International Association for Women's Mental Health: www .womenmentalhealth.com

International Society for Mental Health Online: www.ismho.org

International Society of Psychiatric-Mental Health Nurses: www.ispn-psych.org

The Clifford Beers Foundation: The International Centre for Mental Health Promotion: www.cliffordbeersfoundation.co.uk

World Association for Infant Mental Health: www.waimh.org

World Federation for Mental Health: www.wfmh.org

World Psychiatric Association: www.wpanet.org

References

Barczyk, A. N., & Davis, K. (2010). Analysis of the Civil Rights of Institutionalized Persons Act (CRIPA) of 1980. *Journal of Policy Practice, 8*(3), 188–203.

Barnes, A. (2008). Race and hospital diagnoses of schizophrenia and mood disorders. *Social Work, 53*(1), 77–83.

Civil Rights of Institutionalized Persons Act (1980). 42 U.S.C. 1997.

Cohen, B. J., Bonnie, R. J., & Monahan, J. (2008). *Understanding and applying Virginia's new statutory civil commitment criteria,* unpublished manuscript.

Davis, K. (1998). Race, health status, and managed health care. In F. L. Brisbane (Ed.), *Special collaborative edition CSAP cultural competence series* (pp. 145–163). CSAP Cultural Competence Series. Rockville, MD: Bureau of Primary Care, Center for Substance Abuse Prevention.

Davis, K., & Jung, H. (2011). *Application of a self-rating scale to assess student knowledge of social welfare policies.* Unpublished.

Davis, K., Lewis, A., Zhang, J., & Thompkins, A. (2011). Involuntary commitment policy: Disparities in admissions of African American men to state mental hospitals. In J. H. Schiele (Ed.), *Social welfare policy: Regulation and resistance among people of color* (pp. 63–91). New York, NY: Sage.

Deutsch, A. (1948). *The shame of the states.* New York, NY: Harcourt Brace.

Dye, T. R. (1981). *Understanding public policy* (4th ed.). Englewood Cliffs, NJ: Prentice-Hall.

Ennis, B. J. (1972). *Prisoners of psychiatry: Mental patients, psychiatrists, and the law.* New York, NY: Harcourt Brace Jovanovich.

Ennis, B. J., & Siegel, L. (1973). *The rights of mental patients.* New York, NY: Baron.

Geller, J. L. (2000). The last half-century of psychiatric services as refected in *Psychiatric Services. Psychiatric Services, 51,* 41–67.

Gibelman, M. (1999). The search for identify: Defining social work—Past, present, future. *Social Work, 44*(4), 298–310.

Gibelman, M. (2000). Say it ain't so, Norm! Reflections on who we are. *Social Work, 45*(5), 463–466.

Gibelman, M., & Schervish, P. H. (1993). *The social work labor force as reflected in the NASW membership.* Washington DC: National Association of Social Workers.

Gil, D. (1973). *Unraveling social policy.* Cambridge, MA: Schenkman.

Grob, G. N. (1994). *The mad among us: A history of the care of America's mentally ill.* Cambridge, MA: Harvard University Press.

Holt, K. E. (1998). *When officials clash: Implementation of the Civil Rights of Institutionalized Persons Act.* New York, NY: Praeger/Greenwood.

Joint Commission on Mental Illness and Health. (1961). *Action for mental health.* New York, NY: Science Editions.

Kessler, R. C., Berglund, P., Demler, O., Jin, R., Merikangas, L. R., & Walters, E. E. (2005). Lifetime prevalence and age-of-onset distributions of DSM IV disorders in the National Comorbidity Survey Replication. *Archives of General Psychiatry, 62,* 593–602.

Lawson, W. B., Heplar, H., Holladay, J., & Cuffel, B. (1994). Race as a factor in inpatient and outpatient admissions and diagnosis. *Hospital and community psychiatry, 45*(1), 72–74.

Manderscheid, R. W., & Henderson, M. J. (2001). *Mental health, United States, 2000.* Washington, DC: Center for Mental Health Services.

Murthy, R. S. (2001). *World health report 2001: Mental health new understanding new hope* Geneva, Switzerland: WHO.

Nathan, P. E., & Gorman, J. M. (2002). *A guide to treatments that work* (2nd ed.). New York, NY: Oxford University Press.

National Council on Disability. (2005). *The Civil Rights of Institutionalized Persons Act: Has it fulfilled its promise?* Washington, DC: National Council on Disability.

Neighbors, H. W., Musick, M. A., & Williams, D. R. (1998). The African American minister as a source of help for serious personal crises: Bridge or barrier to mental health. *Health Education and Behavior, 25,* 759–777.

Popple, P. R., & Leighninger, L. (2000). *The policy-based profession: An introduction to social welfare policy analysis for social workers* (2nd ed.). Boston, MA: Allyn and Bacon.

Powers, J. L., Mooney, A., & Nunno, M. (1990). Institutional abuse: A review of the literature. *Journal of Child and Youth Care, 4*(6), 81–95.

Rothman, D. (1970). *The discovery of the asylum.* Boston, MA: Little, Brown.

Salas-Lopez, D., Holmes, L., Mouson, D. M., & Soto-Greene, M. (2007). Cultural competence in New Jersey: Evolution from planning to law. *Journal of Health Care for the Poor and the Underserved, 18*(1), 35–43.

Supreme Court of the United States. (2006). *Olmstead, Commissioner, Georgia Department of Human Resources, et al. v. L. C., by Zimring, Guardian.* Cornell University Law School. Retrieved from http://supct.law.cornell.edu/supct/html/98-536.ZS.html

U.S. Department of Labor. (2010). *Occupational outlook handbook 2010–11. Bureau of Labor Statistics.* Retrieved from www.bls.gov/oco/ocos060.htm

Unutzer, J., Schoenbaum, M., & Druss, B. (2006a). Transforming mental health care at the interface with general medicine: Report for the President's New Freedom Commission for Mental Health. *Psychiatric Services, 57,* 37–47.

Wang, P. S., Demler, O., Olfson, M., Pincus, H. A., Wells, K. B., & Kessler, R. C. (2006). Changing profiles of service sectors used for mental health care in the United States. *American Journal of Psychiatry, 163*(7), 1187–1198.

World Health Organization. (2005). *Mental health atlas 2005.* Retrieved from www.who.int/mental_health/evidence/atlas/global_results.pdf

Wyatt v. Aderholt (1974). 503F 2d 1305 5th Cir.

Wyatt v. Stickney (2010). 344F. Supp. 373 (AL. 1974).

Chapter 6
Social Work Disability Practice

Elizabeth DePoy and Stephen Gilson

> How does explanatory legitimacy theory reshape thinking and action in social work disability and diversity practice?

Throughout much of the 20th century, disability in developed and some developing countries has been conceptualized primarily as an embodied deficit, creating and perpetuating disability as the object of professional intervention and in many cases discrimination, exclusion, and segregation. This view, while still a dominant explanatory theme for disability, is limiting to social workers who seek to advance the commitment of the profession to celebrate diversity and promote social justice for all people. Fortunately, rich theory and research developments in disability studies, humanities, natural and social sciences, and interdisciplinary fields have been instrumental in simultaneously broadening and deepening descriptive, explanatory, contextual, and axiological analyses of disability necessary to guide responsive and relevant social work in the 21st century. The aim of this chapter is to foster thought, discussion, and innovative, contemporary social work response by analyzing disability as an important and omnipotent element of contemporary human diversity, rights, and a platform for improving body-context fit. This analysis is framed through two contemporary theoretical lenses, Explanatory Legitimacy Theory (DePoy & Gilson, 2004), which unpacks and foregrounds the value and contextual dimensions of human assignment to categories, and Disjuncture Theory (DePoy & Gilson, 2011), which provides pluralistic explanatory guidance for informed social action relevant to disability in this global, technology-rich era.

To set the contextual stage for understanding and responding to disability as a profound element of human diversity, we enter the terrain with a discussion of the conceptual and chronological perimeters of human classification and an analysis of the emergence of current conceptualizations of the diversity lexicon. The two nested contemporary theories that guide thinking and analysis in this work, Explanatory Legitimacy Theory and Disjuncture Theory, then are presented. Explanatory Legitimacy Theory is a contemporary theoretical framework that analyzes category membership through three intersecting dimensions: description, explanation, and legitimacy. Disjuncture Theory is located within the explanatory dimension of Explanatory Legitimacy and provides an interactive and dynamic rationale for human action and participation within context. In the last section, the synthesis of these foundational parts is applied to disability practice in social work. This chapter concludes with principles and exemplars to guide social workers to advance social justice, to rethink diversity so that it includes but also extends beyond "bodies and backgrounds" variables, and to aim our action agendas at promoting complex solutions that are necessary for profound and meaningful social change.

In this chapter, the term *body* refers not only to a person's organic anatomy and physiology, but rather to the range of human phenomena that derive from bodies in action, interaction, thought, belief, and experience (DePoy & Gilson, 2011; Howson, 2004). This definition is potent in integrating the multiple elements of human experience and thus in conceptualizing diversity beyond observed characteristics, histories, or locations of the organic body. Thus, the body and its function include, but are not limited to, physiology and anatomy, and are comprised of the sensory body, the emotional body, the communicative and performing body, the spiritual body, the technological body, the economic body, the productive body, the body of ideas and meanings, and the body in multiple garb and spaces.

Intersection of Human Categorization and Diversity

In the United States and other economically developed countries, the term diversity in the late 20th and early 21st centuries generally has become a moniker to describe nondominant groups (Healy, 2009). Thus, within this narrow approach, diversity is ascribed to and owned, voluntarily or involuntarily, only by members of these population segments (Anderson & Middleton, 2011; DePoy & Gilson, 2011). How diversity arrived at this point has been examined from numerous disciplinary perspectives including, but not limited to rhetorical and cultural inquiry (Fishman & Garcia, 2010); population research (Kertzer & Arel, 2002); historical analyses of slavery, war, internment, holocaust and genocide (Rose, 2003); early 20th-century immigration patterns (Basson, 2004; 2008); exploitation (Shiao, 2004)); important intellectual and expressive shifts from monism to pluralism (Dallmayr, 2010); the political-economic context in which the concepts of diversity were developed in large part by the advancement of images, symbols, and interactivity (DePoy & Gilson, 2004); technology (Haidt, 2010), and media (Looker, 2010; Klien, 2003).Exemplifying the contemporary postmodern focus on symbol and meaning, Fishman and García (2010) suggest that social worth and political response are ascribed to bodies through language and representation. How these meanings emerge, in what contexts, and how symbols are interpreted are determined by the cultures, ethnicities, and linguistic contexts with which bodies interact, consume, and contribute.

Within this larger rubric of meaning, one critically important approach to explaining the evolution of the assignment of the term and concept of diversity to specific subpopulation categories holds the position of the interaction of population segments as explanatory of human difference. Both Parillo (2009) and Healy (2009) identified the foundation of current conceptualizations of diversity as power differentials, contentious and negative intergroup relations, and marginalization of immigrant, enslaved, interred, exploited, and conquered populations. They assert that unfortunate historical trends set the symbolic stage for equating negative implications of being marginalized and oppressed with the concept of diversity.

Looking to census data as explanatory of diversity meanings, Kertzer and Arel (2002) suggest that the continued practices in the United States of defining inclusion criteria and then counting the numbers of subpopulation groups members who posses these characteristics both construct nomothetic (group) diversity categories as well as tautologically reify and perpetuate them. Tautology refers to the circular reasoning, in this case of using different verbiage to say the same thing, such as defining minority status by population numbers and then using numbers to assert minority status. Looking at a similar data source, epidemiological data, Armstrong (2002) indicted the concept and measurement of the "normal body" over the past several centuries and suggested that large-scale screening and surveillance of the body resulted in identifying the most commonly occurring characteristics that were then gifted with the meaning of "desirability." Building on this concept, medicalizing bodies through surveillance of frequency, and then substantiating norms through tautological counting further serves to validate and ensconce meanings of "reality" within the concepts of normalcy and deviation (DePoy & Gilson, 2007; Rosenfeld & Faircloth, 2006).

Most recently, analysis of the human genome has contributed much debate and uncertainty to the diversity dialog. While genetics were held as biological evidence for racial difference and embodied diversity in early and mid 20th century history, the failure to empirically verify these ascriptions has upended biological diversity claims (Haidt, 2010; Painter, 2010), paving the way for more substantive and fluid analyses of and justice responses to racial and other forms of diversity.

A second school of thought that has been influential in delimiting diversity to "others" is classical developmental theory, a seminal body of work that often forms the substance of the Human Behavior in the Social Environment curriculum in social work education (DePoy & Gilson, 2012). A critical review of theorists such as Freud, Piaget, Erikson, and their contemporaries reveals these theories are primarily concerned with longitudinal progress of humans and the establishment of age-related norms and thus "not norms." The classical theorists did not differentiate among groups on the basis of the ethnic, racial, and cultural diversity characteristics that are common parlance in today's theoretical diversity world. Social scientists who sought to verify and build on these classical theories used nomothetic methods of inquiry that fell within the positivist tradition of research, following the Enlightenment path to identify within group commonalities and between group differences. It is curious that diversity theorizing and research aimed to find commonality rather than fundamental difference. Lurking within the well-intended goal of elucidating uniqueness and predicting difference, methodological, political, and social contexts therefore have left the diversity dialog victimized by the essentialism that it ostensibly opposes (DePoy & Gilson, 2012; DePoy & Gitlin, 2011).

Epistemologically, positivism leaves little conceptual room for interrogating and characterizing human diversity from an idiographic perspective (DePoy & Gitlin, 2011). Thus, through developmental lenses and their positivist epistemic support, those whose physical, social, communicative, psychological, emotional, spiritual, and behavioral bodies do not fit within two standard deviations from the mean on the normal curve are therefore located outside of normal, in groups of the abnormal, marginal, and to a large extent, undesirable (DePoy & Gilson, 2011). (See Figure 6.1.)

But with the important shifts in the social, political, and intellectual trends in the 21st century, "theoretical marginalia" is no longer useful in explaining the full range of contemporary, heterogeneous human experience in a global, multicultural, technologically advanced context, and thus postpositive and ultimately post-postmodern interdisciplinary thinking is gaining hegemony and acceptance (DePoy & Gilson, 2011). With post-positivism and post-postmodernism as intellectual and epistemic tools to frame thinking about human diversity, groups who in traditional positivist theories were considered marginal, or outside of the monistic norm, could be characterized as multifaceted, pluralistic, and worthy of theoretical attention, rather than simply portrayed as "different and unlike the desirables."

Thomas (2001) illuminated the importance of these current ontological and epistemological trends in explaining critical influences on meanings of diversity. He suggested that postpositivist ideas that moved beyond the acceptance of a single, discoverable truth eschewed not only monism but, to a greater or lesser degree, the construct of reality. The postmodernist emphasis on symbols (primarily language) as the mediators

Figure 6.1

Normal curve.

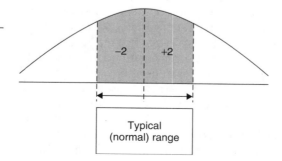

Typical
(normal) range

and even the creators of experience and interaction challenged a single "truth" as correct, prescriptive, and desirable, but left a substantive void for those seeking a reliable body of knowledge. Postmodern decomposition of traditional knowledge structures and content created somewhat of an intellectual vacuum begging for substance. Filling in this fortuitous vacancy left by the postmodernists, post-postmodern thinking has married disciplines previously thought to be disparate, unfriendly, and noncomplimentary (e.g., business and social justice), initiating the creation of compounds of knowledge matter that recompose solid ground to guide the complexity of the 21st-century global, technological thinking, and action landscapes (DePoy & Gilson, 2012). Thus the theoretical opportunity for equality of acknowledgment of all people as dynamic members of groups as well as diverse individuals has been born and is germinating innovative and fertile scholarship and praxis.

Gazing back in time through etymology is always robust in illuminating the terrain from which contemporary words have materialized and then shifted in assignment of meaning. Visiting the 1913 edition of Webster's Dictionary, diversity was defined as: dissimilitude; multiplicity of differences; variety. In contrast, some prevailing and representative examples of contemporary definitions of diversity are: "the condition of being diverse: variety; *especially*: the inclusion of diverse people (as people of different races or cultures) in a group or organization (Merriam-Webster, Incorporated, 2010), biological difference (Wilson, 1999), racial difference (Shiao, 2004), noticeable heterogeneity (Hyperdictionary.com, 2000–2009), and minority group membership (Basson, 2004, 2008; Healy, 2009). Thus, different from the turn of the 20th century meaning, thinking within a century later has contained a difference to the patina, or surface quality, that describes and identifies predefined groups and explains appearance, behavior, and experience of group members on the basis of static membership in a group that has already been defined as diverse.

Moreover, in much of contemporary social work literature, policy, and practice discourse, the term diversity has been further slenderized as a characteristic that belongs to groups perceived as nondominant and non-privileged, such as ethnic and racial minorities, women, nonheterosexual groups (Anderson & Middleton, 2011; Healy, 2009) and more recently, disabled groups (DePoy & Gilson, 2004). The tautology that defines diversity as minority, difference, and discrimination and then ascribes minority, difference, and discrimination to diversity is complete.

While the numerous influential factors discussed here have been posited for the important shift in the meanings attributed to the concept of diversity (DePoy & Gilson, 2007; Healy, 2009; Parillo, 2009), multiculturalism and the failure of multicultural thought to reach the goals of equivalence and symmetry among population groups has been impugned. An understanding of the evolution of multicultural thinking (Shiao, 2004) is therefore key in explaining how diversity came to be equated with "otherness" and to suggest purpose and guidance for uncoupling the two (Roberts, 2007). This next section contains an analysis of this evolution.

Multiculturalism, Category Identity, and Diversity

According to Goldberg (2009), multicultural thought moved from an assimilationist to an integrationist and then to an incorporationist approach. Table 6.1 presents the distinction among the three perspectives. Both assimilationist and integrationist schools of thought begin with the axiom that there is a dominant and desirable group that marginal groups clamor to join. The difference between assimilationist and integrationist thinking lies in the degree to which the marginal group, the "others" (Platt, 2011; Roberts, 2007), must acquire characteristics of the dominant group. However, both assimilationists and integrationists locate power within the dominant group that sits in judgment to determine the boundaries beyond which groups are marginal and, of those who are, which are acceptable for membership; how the "other" must act; and the extent to which the "other" will be allowed to participate in and share resources of the dominant culture.

The incorporationist approach differs significantly from its predecessors, in that it asserts symmetry among groups as the basis for cultural change. That is to say, all groups are seen as equivalent in value and in their capacity to collaboratively transform multicultural societies for the betterment of all. Within this approach, "otherness" becomes reframed as valued, leading to the reduction of bias (Roberts, 2007)

Consider a simple example of this model. Disabled individuals have typically been excluded from sports activities such as skiing. More recently, specialized volunteer programs have been developed for those who qualify as legitimate members of certain disability categories. In these groups, volunteers, many with limited skiing ability, who ski with typical equipment and methods, teach "disabled" individuals how to ski. Thus, the disabled skier is segregated, identifiable on the basis of his or her "special equipment" and often restricted to these specialized programs for instruction. Yet, what might be learned by everyone from atypical skiers? For the typical beginner or even the advanced skier, some of the equipment that is often prescribed only for mobility impaired skiers (such as additional skis, seated skiing devices, and ski-tip retention devices) might advance

Table 6.1 Comparison of Multicultural Perspectives.

Multicultural School of Thought	Viewpoints
Assimilationist	You can join us.
	You should join us.
	To join us, you need to be like us.
Integrationist	We can all live together in our world.
	Come and join us—We will help you ("others") come into the mainstream, but you do not have to be like us.
Incorporationist	We will transform each other for the betterment of all.

the sport of skiing for all. Theoretically, the principles of incorporation and group symmetry adhere in the practices of inclusive schooling, in which disabled students are physically located in regular education classrooms. That is to say, disabled and nondisabled students are expected to benefit and learn from one another (Ryan, 2005).

Despite the theoretical and rhetorical support for group symmetry (Kukathas, 2007), multicultural efforts in theory, research, education, and practice seem to be stalled primarily at the integrationist level of practice (DePoy & Gilson, 2011; Goldberg, 2009; Roberts, 2007; Shiao, 2004), and thus, diversity theory and application in large part have reflected approaches to the promotion of civil rights for predefined population groups that have been labeled as "diverse" on the basis of what has been referred to as *diversity patina*, or difference specific to "bodies and backgrounds" (DePoy & Gilson, 2004). While there have been benefits to this approach, restricting diversity theory and related specialized responses to those who have experienced discrimination remains incomplete and insufficient in itself as a method for promoting a more profound and substantive framework of human diversity and a platform on which to advance equity and justice.

Moreover, while it is well recognized that equating diversity with oppression and marginalization has been, and to some extent continues to be, an important intellectual trend, numerous scholars and theorists assert that this theory and its translation to action is now in need of rethinking and redoing. Continuing the restricted assignment of diversity to marginalized and oppressed categorical conceptualizations has long-term limiting consequences that are now timely to address (Badinter, 2006; Dallmayr, 2010; Roberts, 2007). First, viewing diversity as a characteristic of "otherness" orchestrates and continues the performance of separation and assignment of marked groups to specialized and thus segregated rights policies and programs, containing them within visible boundaries despite the inclusion rhetoric that dresses these methods (Titchkovsky, 2007).

Second, as paradoxically and eloquently revealed by Roberts (2007) in her examination of narratives of alterity, population-specific conceptualizations of diversity often maintain stereotyping (Moller-Okin, 1999; Rodriguez, 2002; Schneider, 2004; Steele, 2010) ghettoizing (DePoy & Gilson, 2011), and dualist conceptions of "us and them" by positing homogeneity within the very groups that are defined as diverse. Assuming group homogeneity on the basis of a single diversity patina characteristic such as disability or ethnicity has the potential to promote essentialist thinking and identity politics and to restrict theory application and community responses to assumed nomothetic need. Warnke (2008) reminds us that just as membership in a group is not exhaustive and constant throughout a life, needs are dynamic and changing as well.

There are two final points to note about equating diversity with that which is comparatively infrequent. First, doing so only ascribes diversity to those who lie at the extremes of the bell curve. As discussed later in this chapter, we suggest that attaining the ideal of "flattening the curve" is a participatory and socially just response (DePoy & Gilson, 2007) with the power to expand the theoretical paradigm of diversity to include and extend beyond minority group membership. Flattening the curve serves to enlarge the limits of acceptable and decrease members at the margins, ascribing uniqueness to increasingly more individuals, and thus providing opportunities not only to preserve gains from civil rights concepts and movements, affirmative action, and other population-specific responses, but also to advance equal opportunity and justice through two important mechanisms, group symmetry (Kukathas, 2007) and integral pluralism (Dallmayr, 2010).

Second, and even more critical, is that the essentialist diversity characteristic is considered causative rather than associative. What we mean here is that undesirables such as poverty, unemployment, and disproportionately low access to resources are often seen as a direct result of membership in a group rather than a correlate. From that reasoning, group-specific responses such as affirmative action are proposed to remediate the "caused agent" without taking on issues such as poverty directly. As such, the status quo of inequality is maintained without systemic change, pressure to act more profoundly is released, and ineffectual strategies continue to flood the political scene (Gelman, 2011).

Principles for Change

Three principles are proposed to guide meaningful change: group symmetry, integral pluralism, and logical response.

Group symmetry does not naïvely posit that all groups have equal capability (Nussbaum, 2007), opportunity, or access to resources. Rather, it is an ideal that refers to the equal value and contribution of disparate groups, and their subsequent reciprocal positive potential to transform multicultural environments (Goldberg, 2009; Kukathas, 2007). Since group symmetry has yet to be broadly actualized in theory and its application, group-specific affirmative thinking and strategies remain the dominant and comfortable response to inequity (Bonilla-Silva, 2003; Jacobs, 2004). However, group symmetry, if adopted as a social work ideal, has the potential to move social work thinking and action beyond group-specific conceptualizations to full participation.

Integral pluralism refers to the enlargement of diversity beyond patina category membership to the domain of both "oneness and manyness" in which varied beliefs, ideas, and experiences, as well as affinities, are negotiated through dialogue. Once again, this principle is not naïve, in that tension and conflict are inherent in difference (Dallmayr, 2010). Dialogue, however, confronts disagreement and thus can reposition diversity as the individuated and collective foundations for tolerance (Kukathas, 2007), transformation, and incorporation. Recognizing group membership as dynamic can collocate individuality and group identity as equals in the diversity dialogue.

Finally, logical response incorporates correct interpretation of data followed up with responsive action. Refraining from engaging in the error of interpreting association as causation in itself can provide a sound grounding from which to launch strategies for change that are directly aimed at outcome. As example, targeting policy change at poverty and limited access rather than its correlates directly pierces its hold, rather than eviscerating actions and then attempting to discover why they do not produce the outcome that they are rhetorically designed to achieve.

Explanatory Legitimacy

Explanatory Legitimacy is embedded within and builds on the genre of legitimacy theories, which have a long, interdisciplinary history that we believe is highly relevant and useful for social workers. According to Zeldich (2001), legitimacy theories can be traced as far back as the writings of Thucydides in 423 BCE, in which questions were posed and answered about the moral correctness of power and the way in which it was captured and retained. Although legitimacy theory was birthed by political theory, questions of legitimation have reared up in numerous domains, including but not limited to social norms and rules, distributive justice, and now in our conceptualization about who is a "legtimate client or client group" to capture social work attention and what social work responses should be legitimated as sound professional practice. Thus, consistent with legitimacy approaches, Explanatory Legitimacy Theory helps clarify the basis on which a phenomenon is seen as genuine, authentic, and worthy of social work response. As proposed, Explantory Legitimacy suggests that all theories are value-based, regardless of their content, because inherent in each is an explication of desired human experience and how social work can help facilitate it.

Moreover, drawing on the work of Shilling (2008), Explanatory Legitimacy synthesizes pragmatism within its foundation in legitimacy, providing the analytic framework for clarifying theoretical purpose. Capitalizing on the clarity of seminal legitimacy thinkers such as Habermas (Finlayson, 2004) and Parsons (1951), the Explanatory Legimacy framework clarifies theory types so that each can be compared to those similar in structure and subject. Explanatory Legitimacy lays bare the axiological (value) context for each theory, critically and abductively evaluting each for use on its own or in concert with others. Through Explanatory Legitimacy, three purposive elements of theory are therefore proposed: description, explanation, and legitimacy determination. Description, "the what," encompasses the full range of human activity (what people do and do not do and how they do what they do), appearance, and experience. Explanation, "the why," proposes multiple reasons for the occurrence of description. Legitimacy, "who is a bona fide member and how should each be treated," is the value-based driver of social work action in that it identifies "legitimate clients" and guides credible social work responses to those members. Legitimacy decisions are made on the fit of explanations with valued criteria for membership and response within the group of social work recipients as well as other groups such as disability.

Disability Within Explanatory Legitimacy

Within the Explanatory Legitimacy framework, disability is defined as a contextually embedded, dynamic grand category of human diversity. Who belongs, and what social work responses are afforded to category members, are based on differential, changing, and sometimes conflicting judgments about the value of explanations for diverse human phenomena (DePoy & Gilson, 2004, 2011).

Beginning with description and of particular importance to disability is the statistical concept of the *norm*, briefly discussed earlier and illustrated in Figure 6.1. Developed by Quetelet in the late 1800s, "the normal man," was both *physically and morally normal.* Quetelet's statistical creation resulted in the application of numbers to bodies (Davis, 1997) and further served to reify the binary concepts of normal and abnormal despite their operationalization as the most and least frequently occurring phenomena, respectively (Davis, 1997; DePoy & Gilson, 2004). Observation, measurement, and high frequency therefore turned to prescription, and anyone exhibiting infrequently observed activity, appearance, and/or experience was considered abnormal (DePoy & Gilson, 2004).

Since *normal* is a value statement, use of terms such as *normal* and *abnormal* does not provide the conceptual clarity sufficient for distinguishing description from axiology. Thus, in applying Explanatory Legitimacy to category membership, the terms *typical* and *atypical* are used along one axis as descriptive. They refer to magnitude rather than desirables (DePoy & Gilson, 2004).

A second axis within description is the observable–reportable continuum. *Observable* phenomena are activities and appearances that fall under the rubric of those that can be sensed and agreed upon. *Reportable* phenomena are experiences that can be known through inference only. This distinction is important to disability legitimacy in that descriptors that are observable provide more clarity and less room for disagreement than those that are inferred (reportable). For example, mobility is observable but intelligence is not. Intelligence must be inferred by indicators such as performance on an IQ test, verbal interchange, and so forth. Applied to disability, description is situated on the atypical end, but this location by itself is not sufficient for disability status (DePoy & Gilson, 2004, 2011). Consider the example of two individuals who approach a physician to provide documentation for a disability parking placard because distances are challenging for them to walk. A decision of who is eligible is not made on description.

Moving to explanation, multiple reasons could be posited for the descriptive request for parking in order to navigate less distance. Person A requests the placard due to instability from a stroke, while person B requests it because, being overweight, he prefers not to walk. The determination of disability status is still not clear at the explanatory level, since both, neither, or only one of our exemplars may be considered as disabled. Only at the point of legitimacy is category membership assigned, and it may be differentially assigned based on who is in the determination throne. For example, it may be that both individuals consider themselves disabled, but that the physician, valuing a diagnostic circumstance that is considered beyond the control of the owner, only considers disability assignment and thus eligibility for the placard for person A. Even from this simple example, the complexity of the value foundation of legitimate disability is obvious. If the physician sees obesity as voluntary and preventable, it is not likely that she will award the parking placard to Person B.

Now consider the exponentially expanded complexity of federal policy such as the Americans with Disabilities Act of 1990 and the Amendments Act of 2008. Who is legitimately covered and what responses should be proffered are multifaceted decisions based on values informed by a long and convoluted history of disability that we only touch on in the next section.

History in Brief

Looking backward in time, before *disability* was used to describe a group of people with long-term or permanent medical-diagnostic classifications that affected their daily activity in atypical ways, words such as *cripple*, *blind*, *deaf*, *handicapped*, and so forth were often used. These terms differentiated the atypical from the typical individual on the basis of a physical, sensory, cognitive, or mental difference, most frequently an absence or diminished capacity to perform a function compared with the typical.

An investigation of historical text directly or indirectly focusing on disability reveals the following four commonalities among geographic and time contexts:

1. What is atypical differs according to context.
2. In each era there has been more than a single potential assumed and accepted explanation for an atypical human characteristic.
3. These explanations form the basis on which axiological decisions are made regarding the legitimate categorization and subsequent response to category members.
4. The responses proffered provide an analytic window on the beliefs, values, politics, economics, intellectual trends, and level of technological development of the times, as well as a reflective platform

on how current definitions of disability influence how we interpret history. (Rose, 2003)

From early civilizations through contemporary times, attention to the atypical as a curiosity or undesirable to be eliminated has been thematic. As stated in the commonalities across chronological eras, however, the nature of the atypical and responses to it vary with context. Many explanations for the atypical floated outside of the organic body into the ethereal world of spirit, with divine punishment as the most common explanation for unacceptable difference. It is therefore not surprising that in general, what would be considered today as disability was met with disdain through exclusion and even consignment to premature death in some contexts.

In the Middle Ages, atypical bodies remained devalued, but moral purpose was added to the explanatory litany. The belief emerged that people with atypical bodies were placed on Earth purposively by a divine being as the object of charity to test the moral decency of typical counterparts. This moral imperative for "typicals" still inheres in charitable responses to disability today, illustrating the potency of history for analyzing current thinking and action.

As enlightenment thinking replaced its predecessor in the Western world, scientific explanations for corporeal function and appearance were sought, shifting reasons for the atypical from religious or divine to embodied pathology. That is not to say that religion or moral explanations for disability membership ever disappeared, as reflected in such frequently articulated statements such as "I was injured because I sinned" or "I must deserve this fate."

Scientism, technology, and professionalism of the 20th century have been instrumental in assigning and restraining disability within the corpus and as object of professional scrutiny, treatment, and cure (DePoy & Gilson, 2011). However, while the prevailing public view of disability remains medical, scholars within disability studies and increasingly within other disciplines have proposed human rights and diversity alternative views.

So now, returning to the present, two grand perspectives that battle with one another for hegemony are discussed, critically analyzed, and then synthesized into a dynamic explanatory framework to guide social work action.

Embodied and Constructed Explanations

Numerous contextual factors, including economic productivity, medical knowledge, technology, professional authority, globalism, immigration, and juxtaposition of diverse appearances, activities, and beliefs, and post-modern and post-postmodern intellectual thought have coalesced in the late 20th and early 21st century to produce two overarching and hotly debated explanations for the atypical: embodied and constructed (Gilson & DePoy, 2004).

Embodied definitions locate disability within humans and define it as an anomalous medical condition of long-term or permanent duration. Thus, within this conceptualization, the domains of disability definition, explanation, and response remain the property of the professional community. Terms such as cognitive, physical, and psychiatric disability reflect disability as located within the corpus and thus explained as organic pathology.

In opposition, however, to what was perceived as a deficit and undesirable and thus in need of cure or revision, the *constructed* explanatory school of disability emerged in the late 1980s and early 1990s. Within this broad theoretical category, disability was defined and explained as a set of limitations imposed on individuals (with or even without diagnosed embodied conditions) from external factors such as social, cultural, and other contextual influences.

Constructed explanations impute a range of political social, economic, and other factors that portray disability as exclusion, discrimination, truncation of rights, and devaluation (Nussbaum, 2007; Scully, 2008; Stein, 2006). Negative social attitudes, limited or nonexistent physical and communication access, and the denial of rights and privileges are examples of just some of the social practices that explain disability as conceptualized within these perspectives (Albrecht, 2005). Thus, within the constructed approaches there are many different emphases, each posited as an explanatory model of disability in itself. For example, looking at the political construction of disability, the barrier creating the disabling condition is disempowerment due to unequal earning opportunity for individuals with undesirable conditions (Davis, 2006). Also within the constructed school of thought but located on a different intellectual vector, the cultural approach suggests that all individuals who define themselves as disabled belong to a unique group and share a common cultural disability identity (Siebers, 2008). Membership in the culture is not attributed to a diagnostic condition, since diagnosis is irrelevant in this approach to determining who is disabled. Those individuals who perceive their conditions to be treated unfairly and constructed as undesirable by dominant social institutions are members of the culture of disability in that they share disadvantage and curtailment of civil rights (Stein, 2006; Siebers, 2008). While proponents of the constructed approach eschew embodied models of disability because these frameworks devalue, medicalize, and pathologize those who are legitimate members of the disability category, theorists such as Miceli (2010) and DePoy and Gilson (2011) suggest that bypassing the body does not do any theoretical work to guide responses to disability, since the atypical corpus, if not explicitly named as disabled, is part of the picture. Recently, in the game of lexical musical chairs, the term *impairment* has unseated disability as the identifier for an embodied condition, and disability has been reseated to denote the discrimination and negative treatment afforded to those with impairments (DePoy & Gilson, 2011; Henderson, 2006).

Given the continuing debate, confusion, and wordplay, we have proposed a synthetic explanation for disability using new terminology for clarity, Disjuncture Theory. In this thinking, bodies and contexts are both included as critical elements.

Disjuncture

Our initial thinking about disjuncture emerged from a conversation in a disability studies class in which we asked students to reflect on the rationale for the current "disability" standards for built and virtual environments. The students indicated that they just took these environmental features for granted and had not thought about why doorways, chair heights, computer access, and so forth could not be reconceptualized differently. After this conversation, we set out to learn more about built environmental design history and the rationale for disability standards that comply with the Americans with Disabilities Act (1990) and the Amendments Act of 2008. Two bodies of knowledge coalesced to inform our thinking. First, inquiry into the rationale for and derivation of architectural standards for door sizes, counter heights, and so forth, revealed the continued hegemony of DaVinci's Vitruvian man as both the foundational ideal and basis for estimating average adult body sizes to which mass-produced and standardized building and product design practices are fitted. Concurrently, assumptions about typical bodies, such as the ability to use both hands for manipulation, to walk with a typical gait, to hear, to see, and so forth, provide the prevailing data on which design is anchored. Bodies that do not conform to prescriptive averages therefore are challenged to participate in standardized built environments in which they do not fit.

The second repository of content emerged from human factors theory (Salvendy, 2006). This multidisciplinary field applies a characterization of human capacity to design of spaces, technology, and products.

Building on these works and the work of other theorists who explain disability as interactive, we have posited Disjuncture as one of many explanations that could form a solid axiological as well as praxis foundation for disability category membership and subsequent responses. Through this lens, disability is not a static or constant embodied phenomenon, nor is it exclusive to the contexts in which humans operate. Rather we recognize the body and its surroundings as equal entryways into and exits from disability and suggest that a potent explanation of disability is not simply an interaction but rather a poor fit between the two. Figure 6.2 depicts a visual of Disjuncture explanations and the continuum to their opposites, full juncture.

As represented in the image, both moderate or compliance juncture for us is still explanatory of disability, since an area of poor fit remains between embodied and surrounding contexts. As example, a poor fit could be explained as pathology, an environmental barrier, or even dissatisfaction with one's goal attainment. Explaining disability in this manner allows for multiple entry points, locations, and thus responses. Moreover, the embodied–constructed binary is transcended without neglecting either explanatory scheme.

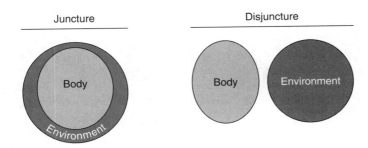

Figure 6.2

Disjuncture theory.

Viewing disability as disjuncture does not devalue individuals with atypical descriptions, nor hold designers of products, built environments, and services as fully responsible for creating juncture. Moreover, eliminating disjuncture does not provoke the constructed argument about the devaluation of "disabled bodies." Rather, reduction and elimination of disability from this approach refers to eschewing the ill fit, not the person who is considered disabled.

The disjunctures between atypical bodies and their contexts in and of themselves, however, are not the explanatory locus of disability. Rather, the intersection of bodies and diverse environments (including but not limited to built, natural, virtual, social, and expressive contexts) explains what ability is and is not. Note that disability still has not been determined at the explanatory stage. Legitimate determination and responses occur in the next stage, legitimacy. Before leaving the explanatory field and moving to disability legitimacy, a final point about this element of the Explanatory Legitimacy Framework is critical in guiding legitimate social work response. The reasons that are accepted as viable and accurate in explicating why the atypical is occurring or has occurred not only are the bedrock of value determination, but are fundamental and essential in shaping and framing a legitimate social work disability response.

As noted above, legitimacy, the third and most important definitional element of explanatory legitimacy, is comprised of two subelements: judgment and response. Judgment refers to value assessments of diverse groups and/or individuals about whether what a person does throughout life (and thus what a person does not do), how a person looks, and the degree to which a person's experiences fit within what is typical and have valid and acceptable explanations that are consistent with an all-too-often unspoken value set that locates people within or outside of a category. Responses are the actions (both negative and positive) that are deemed appropriate by those rendering the value judgments.

Applied to social work practice with disability, *legitimacy* refers to the primacy of judgment about acceptability and worth in shaping differential definitions of disability and in determining legitimate social work responses at the individual, community, social group, and policy levels to those who fit within diverse disability classifications. As a point of major emphasis,

Table 6.2 Comparative Legitimacy.

| Description | Explanation | Legitimacy | |
		Legitimate Disability Status	Response Examples
Unable to read social work textbook	Embodied: Medical diagnosis—blindness	Yes	Special services for blind students
Unable to read social work textbook	Constructed: Print format is not accessible	Yes	Make textbook available in CD and electronic formats
Unable to read social work textbook	Disjuncture: Information acquisition style does not fit with format presented	Yes	Create and deliver materials in multiple formats that can be translated into multiple languages for all qualified social work students

while values shape the boundaries of typical and atypical and how these descriptors are both identified and verified, legitimacy determination and response are made on the worth of the explanation. Thus, two individuals may possess identical atypical descriptions, but on the basis of different explanations, one may qualify as legitimately disabled and the other may not. See Table 6.2 to illustrate.

Social Work Practice: Healing the Disjuncture Between Bodies and Environments

To further illustrate the application of Explanatory Legitimacy to social work action specific to disability, two scenarios are introduced.

Scenario 1

On the first day of their Human Behavior in the Social Environment class, Bill and Crystal both bring audio recorders for note taking (description). Dr. Joseph asks Bill and Crystal to turn off the recorders, letting them both know that she does not allow students to record her lectures. After class, Bill talks with Dr. Joseph, indicating that he uses the recorder as an assistive device for a learning disability, as recommended by disabled student services (explanation 1). Crystal, however, records the lectures because she lives over an hour from the university and has a new infant who distracts her from reading at home. By listening to the recorded lectures, she is able to study in the car (explanation 2). In both cases, the observable atypical activity is audio recording a lecture when all other students are taking notes, either written or by using an electronic device. Bill has a medical-diagnostic explanation of learning disability, affirmed by disabled student services personnel on campus and Crystal has a constructed explanation for the atypical activity. For Dr. Joseph, only

Bill's explanation legitimates him as a disability category member worthy of special response. Thus, despite equivalent descriptive need, Bill can use the recording device and Crystal cannot.

Scenario 2

Two women present in the emergency room with broken noses and bruises (description). Because Sue was injured in a fall after tripping on her husband's shoes left on the floor (explanation), she is not considered to be a victim (illegitimacy as a victim). Heidi, who was injured directly by her partner (explanation), qualifies for legitimate victim status and is afforded the services and supports of the domestic violence system (legitimacy response). Knowing that Sue has very poor balance due to a brain injury (explanation), her husband left the shoes on the floor with intent to harm. On the basis of disability membership (disability legitimacy determination), Sue is tacitly and perhaps unintentionally denied credibility as a victim (victim illegitimacy determination), and thus is not met with access responses to social work services that may prevent further injury or even death (illegitimacy response).

Both examples highlight the link between the Explanatory Legitimacy Theory, participation, exclusion, and the disjuncture between individual and context. However, the alternative explanatory set for each scenario, despite identical descriptive need, creates differential platforms on which to render value judgments about category legitimacy and subsequently to guide a social work response. Consider Scenario 1. Both students had compelling descriptive need. However, because Bill was legitimately considered by Dr. Joseph as a member of the "disabled students group" on the basis of a diagnostic circumstance legitimated by a professional and thus sanctioned as worthy of specialized response, he qualified for an accommodation, whereas Crystal did not. Inherent in Dr. Joseph's decision to allow Bill to audio record the lecture are assumptions and beliefs about the diagnostic efficacy and embodied limitations of people who are classified as learning disabled. The operative explanatory comparisons made by Dr. Joseph and institutionalized in university policy privilege Bill over Crystal at least in this situation. Furthermore, to heal the disjuncture between Bill's learning context and his assumed bodily limitations, special accommodation was afforded to him that no other student, unless also a legitimate member of the disability group, would be able to use.

If responses to both students had been considered in terms of descriptive need rather than disability category membership, one possible option to equalize social work learning opportunity would be the extension of audio-recorded note taking to all students, unless course objectives are antithetical to this approach. The elements of the typical (as in Crystal's motherhood role), the atypical (incapacity to learn as others do), and the degree of assumed ability to control one's limitation, in this context, are important tacit scripts in ascribing both institutional policy and social work responses, and thus they establish a binary in which Bill's embodied status, not the learning context, is the locus of change. This approach to participation, referred to as reasonable accommodation, is condition specific and thus fails when atypical individuals and groups without legitimate disability category assignment experience a poor fit in a standardized situation. Within Scenario 1, eligibility for response relies on the legitimation of a "valued" explanation for atypical experience and thus is only available to those who display *a priori* professionally documented, embodied, acceptable excuses for incapacity.

Implicit in the response is the notion that without it, the student's deficits would impede his progress and successful completion of the course. Thus, he is treated as impaired, with his success dependent on the approval, willingness, and generosity of the institution and social work faculty. But this status does not come without cost, as it segregates and devalues.

Similarly, the descriptive needs for both Heidi and Sue are identical, because both were harmed and in need of medical intervention. However, in this case, the explanation of brain injury, Sue's legitimate disability status, met with exclusion from another important category, victim status. On the basis of potentially essentialist assumptions and attitudes about the illegitimacy of disabled women as intimate partners and thus potential victims of domestic violence, the domestic violence social work service, criminal justice, and social work support responses that are afforded to those whose harm is explained in typical ways were not available to Sue.

Applied to social work's concern with the larger arena of diversity, in which disability is only one element, Explanatory Legitimacy expands diversity conceptualizations and responses in several ways. First, building on contemporary theory, the following three-part definition of diversity that includes but moves beyond "bodies and backgrounds" approaches to categorical diversity is proposed:

1. Varied viewpoints, ideas, and experiences
2. The multiple "whats" and "whys" about humans
3. Body-context juncture

The first element of the definition places "bodies and backgrounds" categorical definitions of diversity, including disability, into a larger context of the full range of human activity, appearance, and experience. By expanding the focus to the realm of thoughts, beliefs, and experiences, population-specific and embodied phenomena are included but not the sole domain of diversity.

Second, specific to disability, the binary debate of disability as embodied or constructed should be expanded and broadened to multiple "whats" and "whys." And third, viewing diversity as an interactive rather than singular phenomenon enlarges the scope and nature of diversity and thus the potential social work responses to it.

Applied to diversity, disability is a complex element of human diversity that should be viewed by social workers through pluralistic rather than essentialist lenses. Disjuncture explanations serve this end. If disability is viewed as an ill fit between embodied phenomena and the contexts in which one acts, the opportunities for social workers to expand the range of legitimacy as well as their professional responses increase exponentially. Consider Bill and Crystal as examples. Both students had a descriptive need to have access to Dr. Joseph's lecture repeatedly after its initial delivery. From the lens of Disjuncture Theory, both students, had they been met at the level of descriptive need rather than value judgment levied at unacceptable explanations, might benefit. If the category necessary for a positive response to student need were reconceptualized away from population category to social work student enrollees, all students in the class would be included in equal learning opportunity responses, and none would be the object of doubt regarding capacity without the charitable response.

Given that Disjuncture Theory guides responses to move beyond singularly targeting bodies or contexts, the interaction of the two becomes the analytic unit as well as the broadened opportunity for responsive change. As suggested by Scenario 1, in the absence of purposive course objectives that require immediate verbatim recall of lecture materials, the social work education environment would have been an important locus for change such that all enrolled social work students with a full range of diverse learning styles and needs would be fully considered and afforded the equivalent opportunity for mastering the material and entering the social work profession.

The danger of asserting special treatment or advantage as the only reason for Bill's success would be eliminated if Dr. Joseph had used Disjuncture principles to reframe the problem and her response. This point can be illustrated in Scenario 2 as well. Equality of social work responses to descriptive harm and reported cause would provide equivalent social work resources to both Sue and Heidi.

Reconceptualizing disability and all diversity categories as continual rather than binary constructs has great potential to flatten the curve (Figure 6.3). What is meant by flattening the curve is the widening and ultimate elimination of the binary dimensions of the normal curve discussed above.

Informed by current "bodies and backgrounds" categorical diversity theory, an individual belongs either to the normal or not-normal category. Those lying beyond + or −2 standard deviations away from the mean, would not fit within contexts designed for assumed averages and thus would not legitimately qualify for social work responses that are built

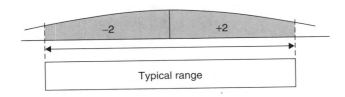

Figure 6.3

Flattened curve.

for and afforded to the typical social work service recipient. Flattening the curve would expand the range of acceptable human difference and variation and move standardized contexts to respond to a wider range of acceptable diversity that is characteristic of and necessary for integral pluralism and group symmetry in the contemporary global context.

Flattening the curve fits centrally within the social work mission. The metaphor does not refer to homogenization but rather acceptance and equality of response to expanded conceptualizations and operationalizations of diversity. Flattening the curve calls not only for rethinking diversity definitions but for retooling our thinking and action strategies about the essence, recognition, documentation, and responses to diversity.

Conclusion

This chapter concludes with an example that comparatively applies and analyzes the implementation of Explanatory Legitimacy and Disjuncture Theory in social work disability practice.

Consider Felicia, a 32-year-old woman who has sought clinical social work help for depression. Felicia uses a wheelchair for mobility, and although she would like to get married and have a family, she currently lives with her sister, brother-in-law, and two school-age nieces in a one-story wheelchair accessible house. Felicia is currently employed as a full-time clerk at a bookstore in a northeastern U.S. city. Recently, her work environment has become contentious because a new management team has created a merit system that engenders competition among the employees. Table 6.3 presents two social work responses on the basis of embodied and constructed explanations. Note that a new group for membership, legitimacy as a social work client, has been chosen.

Table 6.3 Social Work Responses.

Description	Explanation	Social Work Legitimacy	
		Eligibility for Clinical Social Work Response	Legitimate Social Work Response
Reportable depression Wheelchair user	Embodied: Diagnosed clinical depression due to disability	Yes	Referral to rehabilitation social worker; Referral for antidepressant medication
Reportable depression Wheelchair user	Constructed: Exclusion from typical social activity and intimacy; Competition in the workplace	Yes	Assists client to find disability social support group and provides problem-solving guidance for work-related issues

As depicted in Table 6.3, using explanatory legitimacy, we can analyze how each explanation guides the social worker's direction. The social worker who proceeds from an embodied explanation of depression focuses his effort on "healing" the body. Note that considering wheeled mobility as a medical disability provokes a referral to rehabilitation, not an uncommon response for professionals who do not "specialize" in working with the "disabled" population (MacDuffie, 2010). The desired outcome of this social work intervention would be alleviation of the depression.

The constructed explanation draws attention away from embodied phenomena to the assumed exclusion and truncation of participation in desired and necessary contexts. Proceeding on the explanation that Felicia is socially isolated, the social worker seeks and finds a social support group comprised of those who have similar circumstances. It is curious to note here that although the legitimate response addresses factors external to the material body, the corpus remains the locus of difference and thus disability. In this scenario, the desired outcome would be alleviation of the depression because of new social contacts and support.

Now consider a third approach in which the social worker proceeds from a Disjuncture explanation. From this explanatory perspective, both the embodied and contextual elements would be considered. The fit between Felicia and her home, social, and work environments would be the holistic focus. Possible social work responses would seek to flatten the curve by working to advance environments in which a full range of individuals could fit and be welcome. For example, if competition on the basis of merit was not a comfortable working environment for Felicia, the social worker might assist her in finding alternative work or in returning to higher education where she could also engage in a new social milieu. Or the social worker might work with Felicia's family to improve the home environment. If that goal could not be achieved, the social worker might assist Felicia in identifying and seeking alternative living options.

While working with Felicia individually, the social worker proceeding through the lens of Disjuncture Theory would be obliged to engage in professional activity at the contextual and policy levels of practice as well. For example, the social worker might work in the community to expand the range of housing options for individuals who use all types of mobility as well as for other elements of diversity, might attend to the promotion of educational programs for displaced and transitional workers, might advocate for policy changes related to improving poor work climates for all employees regardless of bodies and backgrounds category membership, or might work on efforts to organize fully participatory recreation and social opportunity for all community members. In this scenario, Felicia's wheeled mobility is an important element of her experience and is not eschewed, but considered as only one among many factors that have contributed to the body–context disjuncture. Healing the disjuncture requires rethinking assessments, strategies, and expected outcomes not only for Felicia, but for the communities in which she works, loves, and lives.

Key Terms

Disability   Explanatory Legitimacy Theory
Disjuncture Theory

Review Questions for Critical Thinking

1. Through Explanatory Legitimacy, what process for social work service eligibility is enacted?
2. How does Disjuncture Theory conceptualize disability and social work response?
3. What is meant by disability as diversity?

Online Resources

Society for Disability Studies: www.disstudies.org

Astos: www.astos.org

A resource to support collaboration, systematic thinking, and actions that contribute to social and economic justice.

Disability Studies Quarterly: www.dsq-sds.org

Review of Disability Studies: www.rds.hawaii.edu

Disability Research and Design Foundation: www.drdfonline.org

References

Albrecht, G. L. (Ed.). (2005). *Encyclopedia of disability.* Thousand Oaks, CA: Sage.

Anderson, S., & Middleton, V. (2011). *Explorations in diversity: Examining privilege and oppression in a multicultural society* (2nd ed.). Belmont, CA: Wadsworth.

Armstrong, D. (2002). *A new history of identity: A sociology of medical knowledge.* Basingstoke, UK: Palgrave Macmillan.

Badinter, E. (2006). *Dead-end feminism* (J. Borossa, Trans.). Cambridge, UK: Polity Press.

Basson, L. (2004). Blurring the boundaries of diversity: Racial mixture, ethnic ambiguity and indigenous citizenship in settler states. *International Journal of Diversity in Organisations, Communities, and Nations, 4.*

Basson, L. (2008). *White enough to be American? Race mixing, indigenous people, and the boundaries of state and nation.* Chapel Hill, NC: University of North Carolina Press.

Baudrillard, J. (1995). *Simulacra and simulation: The body in theory: History of cultural materialism* (S. Glaser, Trans.). Ann Arbor, MI: University of Michigan Press.

Bonilla-Silva, E. (2003). *Racism without racists: Color-blind racism and the persistence of racial inequality in the United States.* Lanham, MD: Rowman & Littlefield.

Dallmayr, F. (2010). *Integral pluralism: Beyond culture wars*. Lexington, KY: University Press of Kentucky.

Davis, L. (1997). *Enforcing normalcy*. London, UK: Verso.

Davis, L. J. (2006). *Disability studies reader* (Rev. 2nd ed.). New York, NY: Routledge.

DePoy, E., & Gilson, S. (2004). *Rethinking disability*. Belmont, CA: Brooks Cole.

DePoy, E., & Gilson, S. (2007). The bell-shaped curve: Alive, well, and living in diversity rhetoric. *The International Journal of Diversity in Organisations, Communities and Nations, 7*(3), 253–260.

DePoy, E., & Gilson, S. (2011). *Studying disability*. Thousand Oaks, CA: Sage.

DePoy, E., & Gilson, S. (2012). *Human behavior theory and applications*. Thousand Oaks, CA: Sage.

DePoy, E., & Gitlin, L. (2011). *Introduction to research*. St Louis, MO: Elsevier.

Dictionary.com LLC. (2010). *Dictionary.com*. Retrieved Oct. 5, 2010 from http://dictionary.reference.com/browse/class?&qsrc=

Finlayson, J. (2004). *Habermas: A very short introduction, 2004*. New York, NY: Oxford University Press.

Fishman, J. A., & García, O. (2010). *Handbook of language & ethnic identity: Disciplinary & regional perspectives*. New York, NY: Oxford Universisty Press.

Gelman, A. (2011, July 17). *Recently in Causal Inference Category*. Statistical Modeling, Causal Inference, and Social Science. Retrieved July 17, 2011 from www.stat.columbia.edu/~cook/movabletype/archives/causal-inference

Goldberg, D. T. (2009). *Multiculturalism: A critical reader*. Cambridge, MA: Blackwell.

Hyperdictionary.com (2000–2009). Retrieved October 5, 2011 from www.hyperdic.net

Haidt, J. (2010). Fast evolution. *Chronicle of Higher Education*, p. B10. Retrieved September 3, 2010 from www.chronicle.com

Healy, J. S. (2009). *Diversity in society*. Thousand Oaks, CA: Pine Forge Press.

Henderson, B. (2006). Impairment. In G. Albrecht (Ed.), *Encyclopedia of disability* (Vol. 2, pp. 920–922). Thousand Oaks, CA: Sage.

Howson, A. (2004). *The body in society*. Hoboken, NJ: John Wiley & Sons.

Jacobs, W. R. (2004). Learning and living difference that makes a difference: Postmodern theory and multicultural education. In F. Schultz (Ed.), *Annual editions: Multicultural education* (pp. 69–80). Guilford, CT: McGraw-Hill.

Kertzer, D., & Arel, D. (2002). *Census and identity*. Cambridge, UK: Cambridge University Press.

Klien, N. (2003). *No logo: Taking aim at the brand bullies*. New York, NY: HarperCollins.

Kukathas, C. (2007). *The liberal archipelago*. New York, NY: Oxford University Press.

Looker, E. D. (2010). *Digital diversity*. Waterloo, Ontario: Wilfred Laurier Press.

MacDuffie, H. (2010). *The effects of client disabled appearance on therapist alliance ratings*. Dissertation, University of Maine, Disability Studies and Social Work.

Merriam-Webster, Incorporated. (2010). *Diversity*. Retrieved September 18, 2010 from www.merriam-webster.com/dictionary/diversity

Miceli, M. (2010) The disavowal of the body as a source of inquiry in critical disability studies: The return of impairment? *Critical Disability Discourse*, 2: www.citeulike.org/user/lilwatchergirl/article/7973231

Moller-Okin, S. (1999). *Is multiculturalism bad for women?* Princeton, NJ: Princeton University Press.

Nussbaum, M. C. (2007). *Frontiers of justice: Disability, nationality, species membership.* Cambridge, MA: Belknap.

Painter, N. I. (2010). *The history of white people.* New York, NY: Norton.

Parillo, V. N. (2009). *Diversity in America* (3rd ed.). Thousand Oaks, CA: Pine Forge Press.

Parsons, T. (1951). *Toward a general theory of action.* Cambridge, MA: Harvard University Press.

Platt, L. (2011). *Understanding inequalities: Stratification and difference.* Malden, MA: Polity.

Roberts, K. G. (2007). *Alterity and narrative.* Albany, NY: SUNY Series.

Rodriguez, R. (2002). *Brown: The last discovery of America.* New York, NY: Viking Press.

Rose, M. (2003). *The staff of Oedipus.* Ann Arbor, MI: University of Michigan Press.

Rosenfeld, D., &. Faircloth, C. A. (2006). *Medicalized masculinities: The missing link?* Philadelphia, PA: Temple University Press.

Ryan, J. (2005). *Inclusive leadership.* Hoboken, NJ: Jossey-Bass.

Salvendy, G. (2006). *Handbook of human factors and ergonomics.* Hoboken, NJ: John Wiley & Sons.

Schneider, D. J. (2004). *The psychology of stereotyping.* New York, NY: Guilford Press.

Scully, J. L. (2008). *Disability bioethics.* Lanham, MD: Rowman & Littlefield.

Shiao, J. L. (2004). *Identifying talent, institutionalizing diversity: Race and philanthropy in post-civil rights America.* Durham, NC: Duke University Press.

Shilling, C. (2008). *Changing bodies: Habit, crisis, and creativity.* Thousand Oaks, CA: Sage.

Siebers, T. (2008). *Disability theory.* Ann Arbor, MI: University of Michigan Press.

Steele, C. (2010). *Whistling Vivaldi and other clues to how stereotype affects us.* New York, NY: W. W. Norton.

Stein, M. D. (2006). *Distributive justice and disability: Utilitarianism against egalitarianism.* New Haven, CT: Yale University Press.

Thomas, M. (2001). *Recent theories of human development.* Thousand Oaks, CA: Sage.

Titchkovsky, T. (2007). *Reading and writing disability differently: The textured life of embodiment.* Toronto, Ontario, Canada: University of Toronto Press.

Warnke, G. (2008). *After identity: Rethinking race, sex, and gender.* New York, NY: Cambridge University Press.

Wilson, E. O. (1999). *The diversity of life.* New York, NY: Norton.

World Health Organization. (2010). *International classification of functioning, disability, and health (ICF).* Retrieved October 9, 2010 from www.who.int/classifications/icf/en

Zeldich, M. (2001). Theories of legitimacy. In J. Jost & B. Major, *The psychology of legitimacy: Emerging perspectives on ideology, justice, and intergroup relations* (pp. 33–55). New York, NY: Cambridge University Press.

Chapter 7
Geriatric Social Work

A Field of Practice

Roberta R. Greene

Explain why the needs of older adults are complex and diverse

Geriatric social work practice is client-centered, focusing on clients' biopsychosocial and spiritual functioning. Practitioners engage in activities designed to obtain resources, such as housing, or help clients negotiate the sometimes complex health, mental health, community, and family systems (Gonyea, Hudson, & Curley, 2004). Geriatric social work practice encompasses a broad spectrum of roles and functions and addresses a variety of client needs ranging from acute health care to supportive social care (Gonyea et al., 2004). Social workers may act in a variety of roles: They may serve as part of healthcare teams, provide private care managers, or act as legislative aides. Social workers who specialize in assisting older adults and their families are employed in an array of settings, including senior centers, nursing homes, mental health and home healthcare agencies, and hospitals. Geriatric social workers may also be found in government agencies, corporations, and research and advocacy organizations.

This chapter focuses on geriatric social workers who engage in direct service, assessing clients and intervening to provide services; in program planning and evaluation, identifying needs and designing programs; in education and training, creating professional curricula and training for paraprofessionals; and in program interventions (Hooyman & Kiyak, 2005). Chronic health conditions, frailty, and cognitive decline can lead to a decrease in an older adult's functional capacity, making him or her unable to live in the community. In these instances, social workers attend to the individual's psychosocial care or a constellation of social, mental health, and emotional needs (Vourlekis, Zlotnik, Simons, & Toni, 2005).

Gonyea et al. (2004) have argued that although the broad scope of the social work mission in the field of aging is daunting, "this practice breadth affords social work the ability to make manifold contributions to the well-being of older people" (p. 2). This chapter provides an overview of that clinical practice spectrum. Given the wide range of settings in which geriatric social work is conducted, practice is understood within the broader attitudinal, political, social, economic, and demographic context in which it occurs. Practice trends are also inseparable from and closely linked to the sources of funding and modes of delivery of public services (Rose, 1992). Therefore, policy implications and the demographics of care delivery are relevant to clinical practice.

Practice Challenges

Social workers have been specializing in practice with older adults and their families for more than a century. However, during the past few decades, there have been dramatic changes in how social work services to the elderly have been defined and delivered. To understand the current nature of social work practice in the field of aging, it is important to take into account the major attitudinal, economic, and social forces that have been shaping it (Greene, 2005b). Among these are changes in family form and structure, modifications in help-seeking behaviors, and transformations in social services and healthcare delivery systems. Furthermore, recent research on how people age "has drastically altered the very foundations of existing paradigms regarding the elderly" (Scharlach & Kaye, 1997, p. xii). This challenge to existing paradigms is the result of decades of research examining the likelihood that people will experience a healthy and engaged old age (Holstein & Minkler, 2003). These forces have been so far-reaching that Berkman, Gardner, Zodikoff, and Harootyan (2005) have called for changes in social work practice that entail "engagement with intersecting biological, psychological, socioenvironmental, cultural, political, and economic contexts that are intertwined with aging in U.S. society" (p. 329).

Demographic Imperative

A comprehensive picture of geriatric social work practice must include the fact that advances in health care and technology have contributed to a "longevity revolution." Life expectancy at birth in the United States is now 75.2 years for men and 80.4 years for women (National Center for Health Statistics, 2004), and life expectancy for both men and women is expected to continue to increase. This creates a demographic imperative to attend to the very old, who may be frail and or suffer from chronic health and cognitive impairments. In 2011, the Baby Boomers (those born between 1946 and 1964) began to cross the age 65 threshold, and both the number and proportion of elderly people in the U.S. population will grow rapidly. By 2030, the older population is projected to be twice as large as in 2000, growing from 35 million to 71.5 million and representing nearly 20% of the total U.S. population (U.S. Decennial Census and Projections, 2000; see Figure 7.1).

The elderly population is also becoming increasingly ethnically diverse, which adds to the complexity of service needs (Takamura, 2001;

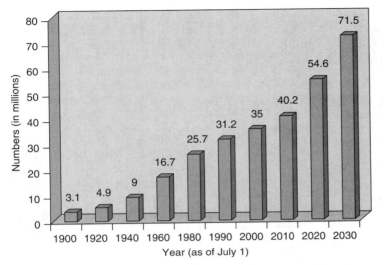

Figure 7.1

The growth of the U.S. population 65 years of age and older, 1900–2030.

Notes: Increments in years are uneven. Projections of the population by age are from the January 2004 Census Internet Release. Historical data are from "65+ in the United States," Current Population Reports, Special Studies, P23–P190; data for 2000 are from the 2000 Census; and 2003 data are from the Census estimates for 2003.

Torres-Gil & Moga, 2001). By the year 2050, the Caucasian population 65 years of age and older will have grown by 116.7%; African Americans by 262.1%; Asians by 720.3%; and Hispanics by 553.4% (Min, 2005; U.S. Department of Health and Human Services [DHHS], 1999). That is, the non-Hispanic Caucasian population 65 years of age and older, which accounted for 83% of the total U.S. population in 2003, is projected to account for 61% by 2050 (U.S. Census Bureau, 2004).

Most analysts agree that the dramatic growth in the numbers and proportion of older adults in the U.S. population portends an increased need for health and social services (Johnson, Tooley, & Wiener, 2007). These dramatic demographic changes have prompted a dispute among policymakers about the economic and social implications of the aging of U.S. society. Much of the debate centers on whether U.S. taxpayers can afford to continue to pay for escalating healthcare costs and the present range of aging programs and entitlements. Policymakers increasingly express concerns about how those who need health and social services will be served (Greene, 2005a). There is also a debate about the viability of formal caregiving systems and the proportion of the elderly population that will have a healthy aging experience. These emerging trends suggest the challenges and opportunities ahead for geriatric social work.

The future patterns of the use of health, social services, and long-term care are still unclear. The Baby Boomer generation may be more aggressive and educated consumers, considering themselves directors of their own care (Silverstone, 1996), whereas racial and ethnic minorities might underutilize services because of barriers such as language, lack of economic resources, and cultural preferences (Min, 2005). Nonetheless, it is clear that major shifts in the financing and delivery of health and human services are likely to strongly influence the lives of older adults and their families and, in turn, social work practice.

Social Workers for the Geriatic Community

Social workers perform multiple functions for older adults and their families at multiple system levels. However, one of the most serious challenges the profession has been facing is the shortage of social workers who are willing to be trained to work effectively in the field of gerontological social work. A comparison of National Association of Social Workers (NASW) data from 1988, 1991, 1995, and 2000 reveals that the percentage of members who identify aging as their primary practice area has remained below 5% throughout the 12-year period. In addition, the *NASW News* reported that only 25% of the NASW membership has caseloads in which 50% of patients are older than 50 years of age (Gonyea et al., 2004).

The National Institute on Aging and the Bureau of Labor Statistics have consistently indicated that more social workers will be needed to serve the increase in older adults (Lennon, 2004). Social work educators have also reiterated the need to educate social workers for an aging society (Greene, 1989; Scharlach, Damron Rodriguez, Robinson, & Feldman, 2000). The relative lack of emphasis on old age in social work curricula and the lack of enriched gerontological field practicum sites may have contributed to the shortage of gerontological social workers. Moreover, social workers who chose the aging field have tended to leave it because the marketplace does not provide sufficient incentives to stay ("Much of Social Work Workforce Also Aging...," 2005).

Without significant investment in workforce development, a serious shortage of social workers who can work with and for the growing aging population is inevitable. The NASW, the Council on Social Work Education, and other social work organizations are making a concerted effort to develop a trained and skilled geriatric social work workforce. The funding of training and research grants by the John Hartford Foundation beginning in 1998 has been an important impetus for the development of such a workforce.

Gerontology: A Biopsychosocial Discipline

Gerontology, the scientific and systematic study of aging, is a multidisciplinary field that addresses the biopsychosocial functioning of older adults (Greene, 1986, 2000b; Hooyman & Kiyak, 2005). The intellectual roots of gerontology can be traced to the historical traditions of its constitutive disciplines. Professionals in many fields in addition to social work, including nursing, medicine, dentistry, occupational and physical therapy, and architecture, specialize in gerontology, applying biopsychosocial princi-ples as appropriate to their mission. Clinical social workers in the field of aging usually conduct assessments of older adults' *functional age*, which involves an understanding of the biopsychosocial-spiritual behaviors that affect a person's ability or competence to perform tasks that are central to everyday life. *Biological factors* related to functional capacity include health, physical capacity, or vital life-limiting organ systems; *psychologi-cal factors* encompass an individual's affect state or mood, cognitive or mental status, and behavioral dimensions; *sociocultural aspects* involve the cultural, political, and economic aspects of life events (Greene, 2000b). *Spiritual factors* may include a person's relationship with his or her faith or religious community and/or that person's inner system of beliefs.

Definitions of Aging

Aging can be considered in three dimensions beyond chronological age: bio-logical, psychological, and social. *Chronological age* marks the passage of time or the number of years that have passed since an individual's birth and is the most commonly used definition of aging. Early in the 20th century, however, researchers became increasingly interested in using scientific methods to explain the aging process, particularly differences in individual longevity (Birren & Schroots, 1995; Sprott & Austad, 1995). Birren (1969), a pioneer in gerontological research, distinguished normal from pathological aspects of aging in three spheres: (1) biological age, encompassing the study of changes in various bodily systems and how these changes affect the phys-ical, psychological, and social functioning of older adults; (2) psychological age, involving a person's ability to adapt to and modify familiar and unfa-miliar environments, including his or her sensory and mental capacities as well as adaptive capacity and personality; and (3) social age, involving a person's position or role in a given social structure (where roles assigned based on age specify an individual's rights and responsibilities) as well as his or her ability to relate to and connect with others, which accounts for his or her functionality in a social context. Birren's popular conceptualiza-tion has been translated into social work practice models (Greene, 1986, 2000b; see below) and continues to guide the structure of geriatric social work (Hooyman & Kiyak, 2005; McInnis-Dittrich, 2002).

Contemporary Challenges

During the next three or four decades, there will be a very significant increase in the number of some very vulnerable groups of the elderly, including the oldest-old (those older than 85 years of age), those living alone (especially unmarried or widowed women and racial/ethnic minori-ties, and those who have neither living children nor siblings), and very low-income older persons. The oldest-old, especially those living alone and the poor, are expected to have the greatest service needs (Siegel, 1999).

Living Alone

As people age and their spouses die, the percentage of the population that lives alone increases. In 2003, half of women 75 years of age and older lived alone (U.S. Census Bureau, 2003). About 12% of the elderly residing alone had neither living children nor siblings (National Center for Health Statistics, 1998).

Poverty

The income situation among the elderly, on average, is relatively favorable, and the extent of poverty is lower than for the U.S. population as a whole (U.S. Census Bureau, 2004). There is, however, a wide disparity in the distribution of income and assets in the elderly population that is more dramatic among subgroups: The incomes of many elders fall below the poverty level or below 200% of the poverty level. Women, African Americans, Hispanics, people living alone, those living in rural areas, and especially individuals with a combination of these characteristics live in poverty to a disproportionate degree. In brief, a disproportionate number of racial/ethnic minority older persons are expected to enter old age with few assets and low incomes (Torres-Gil & Moga, 2001).

Access to Care and Economic Inequalities

There are persistent disparities by race/ethnicity, gender, and income in access to health care, in family caregiving patterns, and in the use of long-term supportive services. Future generations of minority elders will consist of two groups: (1) the current cohort of older people, those 65 years of age and older; and (2) the present middle-aged population that will be entering the 65 and older age bracket. Min (2005) predicted that because of differences in acculturation and life experiences, including educational attainment, career paths, and retirement plans, these two groups "will be very divergent, distinct, and complex, presenting enormous challenges to social work and testing our ability to respond to their needs" (p. 351). However, he concluded that because social workers have a longstanding commitment to helping those who are oppressed or marginalized, they are well positioned to assist minority elders.

The Changing Family

Geriatric social workers need to understand the consequences of demographic change on intergenerational family relationships (Bengtson, Giarrusso, Silverstein, & Wang, 2000). Major modifications in family structure and form have been underway and will continue to occur. Multigenerational families are becoming increasingly common, and family pyramids are becoming taller and narrower. Families used to have an elderly grandparent at the top and a broad base of children and grandchildren, but now the pyramid is likely to be taller, with great-grandparents still living, but with a narrower base because families have fewer children, grandchildren, and great-grandchildren. Families are also changing along the following lines and in some racially/ethnically specific ways:

- Divorces are resulting in an intricate set of intergenerational relationships, including biological children and grandchildren, stepchildren, and step-grandchildren.
- Grandparents are more frequently raising grandchildren.
- The population of older adults is more heterogeneous in terms of race/ethnicity and gender.
- The larger and modified extended families of African American and Hispanic families exhibit cultural differences in family reciprocity or mutual care (Greene, 2005a).

For centuries, the informal support of the family was critical in the care of older adults (Brody, 1985). Although they filled a crucial need, formal social services played a lesser role. With the longevity revolution and changes in the structure and form of the family, gerontologists are concerned about what the future holds for the family of later years—whether there will be continued strong solidarity and intergenerational support among family members and whether the family will continue to be the main source of support for its older members.

Current and Future Directions

Wellness philosophy is an umbrella term embracing positive approaches to individual well-being that is gaining broader acceptance among gerontologists (Greene, 2000a, 2000b, 2005a, 2005b). This involves a shift in practice paradigms to a "new gerontology." This shift suggests that practitioners should develop more positive programs that promote health and psychosocial well-being and use assertive rehabilitation strategies. There are a number of such positive approaches to aging; for example, Antonovsky's (1998) *salutogenesis orientation* refers to the study of how people naturally use their inner resources to strive for health. Similarly, Atchley (1999) proposed the positive idea of *life continuity*, in which older adults strive to maintain their thinking patterns, activities, living arrangements, and social relationships despite changes in health. *Successful aging*, according to Rowe and Kahn (1998), consists of three major factors: (1) avoiding disease by adopting a prevention orientation, (2) engaging in life by continuing social involvement, and (3) maintaining high cognitive and physical functioning through ongoing activity.

Some theorists have questioned how realistic this new gerontology or successful aging paradigm will be in addressing the health needs of older adults (Strawbridge, Wallhagen, & Cohen, 2002). They have argued that a focus on well-being and participation does not take into account the large numbers of individuals who do not have the power to achieve this "normative vision" (Holstein & Minkler, 2003, p. 787). They believe that the successful aging model may actually do harm to older people who are already marginalized, such as the poor and people of color.

However, Greene (2005a) has pointed out that social workers in the field of aging have often been tardy in adopting new theoretical concepts and practice strategies, lagging behind those in other fields of practice. Although there is a need for health promotion and disease prevention, she has suggested that practitioners should assess where an older adult falls on the continuum of functional capacity (from the most ability to the least capacity), assessing a client's capacity against the full continuum of services and care. She stated that this practice approach challenges clients to use their inner resources, continue their social involvement, and maintain their physical functioning (Vourlekis & Greene, 1992; see Table 7.1). An example of such practice includes resilience-enhancing models (Greene, 2007).

Problems and Major Issues Facing Older Adults

With the extraordinary growth of the population 65 years of age and older, it is critical for geriatric social workers to be more aware of those most

Table 7.1 Five Continua for the Elderly.

1. Continuum of Need

Independent (little or no need)	Moderately dependent	Dependent (multiple needs)

2. Continuum of Services

Health promotion/ disease prevention	Screening and early detection	Diagnosis and pretreatment	Treatment rehabilitation: Evaluation services	Continuing care skilled nursing and hospice

3. Continuum of Service Settings

Own home, apartment, etc.	Friend or relative's home, apartment, etc.	Congregate living situation	Subacute care facility (e.g., day hospital)	Acute-care facility (hospital)	Skilled facility (e.g., long-term and hospice care facility)	Continuing care (e.g., nursing home)

4. Continuum of Service Providers

Nonservice	Self-care	Family friends	Paraprofessionals (support network)	Professionals

5. Continuum of Professional Collaboration

Single discipline	Multidisciplinary	Interdisciplinary

Source: "The Role of Gerontological Social Work in Interdisciplinary Care" by N. Hooyman, G. Hooyman, and A. Kethley, 1981, March, Paper presented at the annual program meeting of the Council on Social Work Education, Louisville, KY. Reprinted with permission.

in need of care. For example, three sets of concerns should guide policy practice:

1. *Race:* Rates of disability are higher for African Americans older than 65 than for Caucasians. Moreover, a much higher proportion of African Americans with severe disabilities are likely to live with adults other than their spouses.
2. *Gender:* Rates of disability are higher among women in all age groups 65 and older, and disability rates are decreasing more for men than for women. Women 65 and older are more likely than men to live with adults other than a spouse and are much more likely to be residents of nursing homes.
3. *Income:* Persons 65 and older in the lowest income quartile are three times more likely to experience disability than those in the highest income quartile.

Assessment and Intervention

Geriatric social work practice has adopted traditional human behavior concepts and social work methods while adapting techniques to form its own practice and knowledge base. For example, social work's dual concern for the person and the environment is central to practice. History taking, or understanding a client's critical past events, is another frequently used technique in working with older adults, and the three core conditions of interviewing—empathy, warmth, and genuineness—are essential. This section discusses the major methodological differences that distinguish geriatric social work from general practice.

Special Assessment Issues

Geriatric assessment is differentiated by its particular attention to the nature of the aging population. Lichtenberg (2000) outlined four assessment principles for evaluating an older adult. The first is that age measured in years and age measured in functioning are not linearly related. Chronological age alone does not provide an appreciation of functional age or of a person's capacity to live effectively in his or her environment. An older adult's ability to live competently in his or her environment is central to the geriatric assessment process (Greene, 1986, 2000a). This person–environment perspective allows for a dynamic picture of the older adult's functioning as he or she continually adjusts to surrounding conditions (Hooyman & Kiyak, 2005). It offers information about how the individual responds to social and physical demands in the areas of health, social behavior, and cognition that influence his or her functioning (Lawton, 1989; Lawton & Nahemow, 1973; Parmelee & Lawton, 1990).

Lichtenberg's (2000) second principle is that clinical gerontologists should emphasize brief assessment instruments; in fact, he pointed to research that demonstrates the reliability and validity of many of them. Specialized assessment instruments, such as depression scales or mental status exams, can reduce the time it takes to evaluate older adults.

The third principle is that assessment must result in a delineation of strengths and weaknesses. Knowledge of a client's unique characteristics and capacities can inform the care-planning process as well as treatment recommendations.

Finally, his fourth principle is that clinicians should use multiple assessment methods to improve the quality of information. Because assessment instruments have rarely been validated with minority populations, social workers may want to use caution when adopting such instruments (Tran, Ngo, & Conway, 2003).

Geriatric Interdisciplinary Teams

Not all elderly clients need a geriatric assessment team. However, when an assessment involves a very frail older adult with multiple, complex needs, it is ideally conducted by an interdisciplinary team. Team members from various disciplines such as medicine, nursing, occupational therapy, nutritional counseling, and social work collectively set goals and share responsibilities and resources (Merck, 2005). The client and caregivers should also be part of the team and be included in team meetings. Meetings to evaluate outcomes should also involve the client.

Functional Assessment

The process of assessing older adults has a similar function and purpose to that of assessing other populations—to gain an understanding of the client's problems, needs, and strengths to develop an intervention plan (Naleppa & Reid, 2003) and to determine the resources needed to improve interpersonal functioning (Greene, 1989). Unfortunately, scientists and physicians have historically been concerned with determining what has gone wrong with older adults rather than with instituting preventive programs to promote health and well-being (Butler, Lewis, & Sunderland, 1998). Similarly, social changes that occur in later years that can bring about a sense of loss or isolation may go unnoticed.

It is not surprising, therefore, that most clients come to the attention of social workers when there is a problematic change in mental or physical status. Nonetheless, regardless of the service setting or the client's difficulty, geriatric social work practice is generally based on a philosophy of providing psychosocial care to support optimal functioning (Greene & Sullivan, 2004). It is as important for the social worker to learn the extent to which the person is able to live independently (should he or she so desire) as it is to learn whether he or she can benefit from health promotion and disease prevention programs. Being able to live at home is of extraordinary importance to many older people (Butler et al., 1998). To determine whether this is feasible, social workers conduct a functional assessment of a client's everyday competence, or his or her ability to care for himself or herself, manage his or her affairs, and live an independent, quality life in the community (Willis, 1991).

Social work assessments involve getting to know the whole person, including his or her motivations, interests, and capacity to change. Through this process, the social worker is better able to help an older client (and his or her family) plan for the future and make decisions about the kind of care that may be needed. Assessment then goes beyond diagnosis "to a broader appraisal of the interrelationships between the physiological, emotional, and sociocultural factors and the external environmental conditions that influence well-being" (Northen, 1995, p. 12).

Cross-Cultural Assessment

As discussed, aging is not an equal process for people in poverty or those who are members of minority groups. The consequences of diversity, such as a person's cultural, ethnic, or gender differences, can be barriers to clients of any age accessing and receiving services (Green, 2002; Pinderhughes, 1989). It is therefore important for social workers to become culturally self-aware. Practitioners who are more self-aware are less likely to impose their values and beliefs on a client (Poulin, 2005). The process of identifying practitioner biases may also allow for power differentials in the helping process to be addressed. A collaborative approach that promotes the client's participation in telling his or her own story is often best. In addition, clients who seek professional help may wish to define and resolve their own situations based on their experiences and perceptions (see Table 7.2).

Disabilities and Health Status

In a reference group of Medicare enrollees, the proportion of older Americans with chronic disabilities seemed to be declining, but the absolute number has increased (6.2 million to 6.8 million) because of the rapid increase in the overall elderly population. Disability is often measured by assessing limitations in an older adult's activities of daily living (ADLs; or basic self-care tasks) and instrumental activities of daily living (IADLs; or household and independent-living tasks). Practitioners often use six measures to assess a person's ADLs: whether the person is able to (1) feed himself or herself, (2) use the toilet by himself or herself, (3) take a bath or shower without assistance, (4) get dressed, (5) get in and out of a bed or chair, and (6) get around inside the home. Older women generally report more problems with physical functioning than older men. In 2002, 31% of women older than 65 years of age reported that they were unable to perform at least one of these six activities, compared to 18% of men. By 85 years of age, the proportions were 58% for women and 35% for men. IADLs are often assessed according to a person's ability to do the following six tasks: (1) use the telephone, (2) take medications, (3) manage money,

Table 7.2 Ethnic-Sensitive Inventory.

In working with ethnic minority clients, I:

Realize that my own ethnic and class background may influence my effectiveness.

Make an effort to ensure privacy and/or anonymity.

Am aware of the systematic sources (racism, poverty, and prejudice) of their problems.

Assist them to understand whether the problem is of an individual or a collective nature.

Consider it an obligation to familiarize myself with their culture, history, and other ethnically related responses to problems.

Am able to understand and "tune in" to the meaning of their ethnic dispositions, behaviors, and experiences.

Can identify the links between systematic problems and individual concerns.

Am sensitive to their fears of racism or prejudiced orientations.

Consider the implications of what is being suggested in relation to each client's ethnic reality (unique dispositions, behaviors, and experiences).

Clearly delineate agency functions and respectfully inform clients of my professional expectations of them.

Am able to understand that the worker–client relationship may last a long time.

Am able to explain clearly the nature of the interview.

Am respectful of their definition of the problem to be solved.

Am able to specify the problem in practical, concrete terms.

Am sensitive to treatment goals consonant to their culture.

Am able to mobilize social and extended family networks.

Adapted from "Use of Ethnic-Sensitive Inventory (ESI) to Enhance Practitioner Skills with Minority Clients," by Ho, 1991, *Journal of Multicultural Social Work, 1*(1), pp. 60–61.

(4) do light housework, (5) prepare meals, and (6) shop for groceries (Kaiser Family Foundation, 2002).

Respondent-Assessed Health Status

Practitioners will gain a somewhat different picture of an older adult's functional capacity if clients are asked to rate their own physical, emotional, and social health and well-being. Self-ratings of poor, fair, good, very good, and excellent are sound indications of well-being, because research has found that these self-ratings of health correlate with lower risks of mortality. From 2000 to 2002, 73% of people aged 65 and older rated their health as good or better. Regardless of age, older non-Hispanic Caucasian men and women were more likely to report good health than their non-Hispanic African American and Hispanic counterparts (National Center for Health Statistics, 2004).

Mental Health and Psychosocial Problems

Practitioners need to be alert for the most common mental health problems that can arise in old age. According to the U.S. Surgeon General's report on mental health, 1 of every 5 persons aged 55 and older experiences mental health concerns that are not part of the normal aging process (DHHS, 1999). In addition, the suicide rate for persons aged 65 years of age and older is higher than for any age group (Gonyea et al., 2004). Therefore, practitioners should screen for mental health issues. At the core of the assessment is a person's psychosocial functioning—the capacity to make reasonable decisions and carry them out, as well as the functional ability to live in his or her environment (Greene, 1986, 2000b).

Depression

The most common mental health problem in later life is depression (Greene, 2007). However, depression is frequently underdiagnosed and undertreated despite the fact that it is easily treatable by a combination of psychotherapy and medication. Because depression can be debilitating and often leads to other health problems, even suicide, geriatric social workers should become familiar with its everyday symptoms, including prolonged sadness, tiredness, loss of energy, eating and sleeping problems, weight gain or weight loss, difficulties in focusing, and thoughts of death and suicide (American Psychiatric Association, 1994; Lebowitz et al., 1997). If an older person makes suicidal statements, the practitioner should make a risk assessment that probes for the elderly client's intent. This includes the following questions: Have you really thought of hurting yourself? Have you thought of killing yourself? Have you planned how you would do it? Do you have the means, such as pills? (Philadelphia Corporation for Aging, 1995).

Dementia

Alzheimer's disease (AD) is the most common cause of dementia in older people. An estimated four million Americans currently suffer from AD or related forms of cognitive impairment. AD is characterized by cognitive and physical decline and may last over a period of 20 years. As the disease progresses, a person initially may not remember simple things like the names of objects. The late stages are characterized by a complete inability to feed or care for oneself. Individuals with AD live an average of 8 years after their initial diagnosis. Although psychosocial techniques provide some symptomatic relief, at present no therapy can reverse the progressive cognitive decline (Small et al., 1997).

Until they are in the final stage of the disease, most AD patients live at home and are cared for by a family member (most often a spouse). The burden of caring for an AD patient until the advanced stage of the disease can be a tremendous strain on family caregivers, who often experience fatigue, anxiety, irritability, anger, depression, social withdrawal, or various health problems. Social workers assisting clients with AD may need to assist the caregivers in dealing with their feelings of fatigue, frustration, and inadequacy and help them find additional caregiver resources and support (American Association for Geriatric Psychiatry, 2005).

Elder Abuse

Unfortunately, caregiving sometimes results in elder abuse. Abuse may take several forms. Neglect, the most common form of abuse, involves failure to provide essential physical or mental care for an older person. This may be unintentional or intentional (withholding food, medication, or water). Physical neglect includes withholding food or water, failing to provide proper hygiene, or failing to offer physical aids or safety precautions. Physical violence involves inflicting pain, injury, or impairment. These acts may be pushing, striking, slapping, pinching, force-feeding, or improperly using physical restraints or medications. Psychological abuse is any action by the caregiver that causes fear, isolation, confusion, or disorientation. These acts are intended to harm and may include verbal aggression that humiliates and infantilizes. Financial exploitation is the misuse of an older person's income or resources for the personal gain of another. Violation of rights is an abuse that involves depriving the older adult of legal rights and personal liberty. Another distinction is *domestic abuse*, which refers to several forms of maltreatment of an older person by someone who has a special relationship (often the caregiver) with the elder in the home; and *self-neglect*, which involves cognitively impaired older adults being unable to care for themselves (Sijuwade, 1995). Social workers should not hesitate to ask the elderly client about care difficulties, safety issues, and his or her general satisfaction with care (Lachs, Williams, O'Brien, Pillemer, & Charlson, 1998).

Anxiety Disorders

Anxiety disorders can range from simple nervousness before an important event to panic attacks. One of the most common behaviors is avoidance of what is perceived as a difficult situation. For example, older adults may avoid various activities because they are afraid of falling. However, practitioners can help an older adult clarify the source of this tension (Butler et al., 1998).

Addiction

Practitioners should ask direct questions about drug and alcohol use (Poulin, 2005). Although the extent of alcohol and drug abuse among people 65 years of age and older is difficult to measure, estimates range from 5% to 10% of the population (Pennsylvania Care Management Institute, 1990). Addiction may involve alcohol, prescription drugs, or nonprescription drugs. When working in combination, these addictions may have deadly consequences.

Intervention

Social workers employ several treatment approaches when working with older adults. Modalities may include both individual treatment as well as family treatment. Assessment of the client system guides the social worker's selection of the most appropriate and efficacious treatment approaches.

Individual

Research has documented that older adults may benefit from advances in (treatment) interventions, including crisis intervention, cognitive-behavioral therapy, and grief counseling (Butler et al., 1998; Greene, 2000b; McInnis-Dittrich, 2002). At the same time, many in the current cohort of older adults are reluctant to seek help from health and human services professionals because of perceived stigmas. Therapy interventions for clients suffering from dementia include the following:

- Allowing the client to ignore reality and retreat to a "safe" place.
- Accepting behavior as the person's attempt to communicate a need.
- Accommodating the person's feelings, however difficult this may be.
- Maintaining communication through various means. (Feil, 1993)

Family

Geriatric social workers base their family interventions on a number of conceptual frameworks. Family-centered practice models are based on an understanding of systems theory, the family life cycle, and issues of interdependence versus dependence.

Auxiliary Function Model

One of the earliest family-centered practice models was the auxiliary function model (Silverstone & Burack-Weiss, 1983). The clinicians who authored this model proposed that the major problems facing frail, impaired older adults were not disease or old age per se but rather the effects these conditions might have on their mental or physical functioning. The proponents of this model contend that therapy should be based on a supportive relationship and should be designed to counter the factors associated with depletion or loss. Therefore, the social worker's major goal in intervention should be to combat the family's feelings of helplessness in the face of its multiple losses—that is, to convey a sense of hope.

Functional-Age Model of Intergenerational Family Treatment

Greene (2000b) provided another resource for assessing and intervening with older adults and their families in caregiving situations. This model suggests that the social worker understand the "family as a mutually dependent unit with interdependent pasts and futures" (p. 38). In family crisis situations, the practitioner takes into account the developmental issues and the changing biopsychosocial needs of family members. To make an assessment, the social worker explores the functional capacity of the person needing care. The family is assessed as (1) a *social system*, or how the family group interact with and influence one another; (2) a set of reciprocal roles, involving the behavioral expectations members have for one another; and (3) a developmental unit, encompassing how the family faces life transitions.

Family-focused practice involves the following:

- Engaging the client system in treatment, which involves connecting with significant members of the client system.

- Making an assessment, which encompasses an evaluation of the functional capacity of the person receiving care and his or her family system.

- Working with other professionals to assess medical conditions, including medical and mental health diagnoses and factors associated with illness or disease.

- Reframing, or learning together how illness may affect all family members.

- Formulating a mutually developed intervention plan, which encompasses setting goals, establishing family responsibilities, and accessing resources.

- Implementing the plan, including mobilizing and reducing stress in the family system.

- Terminating or encompassing the evaluation of treatment and the sustainability of [client] hope. (Greene, 2000b, p. 53)

Family or Informal Case Management

The vast majority of older adults who need assistance are cared for by a family member (AARP, 2005). Tasks may involve direct personal care, such as bathing or grooming, or indirect care, such as cooking, cleaning, or running errands. Providing care for an older adult has become so widespread that Brody (1985) called this phase of the life course a "normative family stress" (p. 25). Therefore, social workers ought to consider the family the focus of case management services (see Table 7.3).

When an older adult has an acute or chronic illness, caregiving tasks may become so time-consuming that this affects the caregiver's ability to balance his or her own work and family obligations. In fact, an increasing percentage of the workforce is actively involved in caring for a relative or friend older than 50 years of age (elder care). According to a survey by the National Alliance for Caregiving and AARP, nearly one quarter of U.S. households—22.4 million—include a family caregiver for someone older than age 50. Nearly half of the U.S. workforce has elder care and/or child care responsibilities, and many struggle with the competing demands of work and family responsibilities. According to a MetLife 1999 report, 62% of caregivers surveyed reported asking someone at work—supervisors, coworkers, or management—for support or help in coping with their caregiving responsibilities.

Task-Centered Model

Naleppa and Reid's (2003) task-centered approach consists of three phases: (1) the initial phase, in which the social worker conducts intake and

Table 7.3   **Key Features of Family-Focused Social Work Case Management.**

Family-focused social work requires that the case manager:

Identify the family as the unit of attention.
Assess the frail or impaired person's biopsychosocial and spiritual functioning within a culturally sound family context.
Create a mutually agreed-on family care plan.
Refer client systems to services and entitlements not available within the natural support system.
Implement and coordinate the work that is done with the family.
Determine the services that need to be coordinated on behalf of the family.
Intervene clinically to ameliorate family emotional problems and stress accompanying illness or loss of functioning.
Identify resilience factors that contribute to family success.
Determine how the impaired person and family will interact with formal care providers.
Integrate formal and informal services provided by the family and other primary groups.
Offer or advocate for particular services that the informal support network is not able to offer.
Contact client networks and service providers to determine the quality of service provision.
Mediate conflicts between family and service providers to empower the family when it is not successful.
Collect information and data to augment the advocacy and evaluation efforts to ensure quality of care.

Adapted from *Social Work Case Management* (p. 12), by B. Vourlekis and R. R. Greene, 1992 Hawthorne, NY: Aldine de Gruyter.

assessment, selects the problems that require attention, and sets intervention goals; (2) the middle phase, in which the practitioner emphasizes the development of tasks that address the client's problems and sees that tasks are put forth, carried out, and reviewed; and (3) the final stage, which involves the end of the intervention process, including termination, reinforcing of accomplishments, and making of future plans.

The task-centered model stresses empirically tested methods and theories, is grounded in case data, and underscores client-defined problems. Time limits are built into the intervention plans — usually 4 to 12 sessions — and completed tasks are viewed as vehicles for change. This is intended to encourage client motivation and the successful completion of service activities and attainment of goals.

Group

Although social group work with the aged has a common philosophy and therefore may use similar techniques to those used with other age groups, one of the major purposes of group work with older adults is to provide connections to others in their own age group (Lowry, 1992). Social group work with older adults may be recreational or psychoeducational.

Table 7.4 Summary of Forums for Educating and Training Caregivers.

Forum	Summary
Community workshops and forums	Provide information about community services, may be single sessions lasting an hour to a day; can be sponsored by health and human services organizations.
Lecture series and discussion	Lectures are given by clinical experts on topics of interest to specific groups of caregivers.
Support groups	Offer mutual sharing of information, are usually unstructured, and encourage reciprocal and self-help among group members.
Psychoeducational and skills-building groups	Educate members, usually in short-term, structured groups; teach specific problem-solving and coping skills and share information about caregiving resources.
Individual counseling and training	Focuses on the individual caregivers' needs; helps caregivers with the emotional and coping skills needed to be effective in their role and to handle stress and identify rewards.
Family counseling	Helps the family system deal with issues related to caregiving; supports and sustains the care recipient and maintains family balance and cohesiveness; connects the family with other resources in the community.
Care coordination and management	Educates caregivers on how to perform caregiving roles more effectively and how to connect with formal caregivers.
Technology-based interventions	Use telephone-mediated groups, computer-mediated groups, and videoconferencing to educate and train caregivers.

Adapted from *Supporting Caregivers Through Education and Training* (pp. 10–12), by R. Toseland and T. Smith, prepared for the U.S. Administration on Aging, National Family Caregiver Support Program (NFCSP): Selected Issue Briefs, Washington, DC: U.S. Department of Health and Human Services.

Practitioners may also provide group members with an opportunity to reminisce (Greene, 1982, 2000b). Group methods are also used to educate, train, and support caregivers. Educational groups provide information about community services and resources. Psychoeducational and training groups offer short-term structured groups that teach specific problem-solving and coping skills, whereas support groups focus on a mutual sharing of information, encouraging reciprocal exchanges, and self-help (Toseland & Smith, 2001; see Table 7.4).

Formal Case Management: Community-Based Care

Case management is a traditional, integral part of social work practice. Because the care an individual may need often involves multiple sources, effective coordination and monitoring of care are essential. The case management process is designed to assist individuals and families with multiple service needs. It is used in various fields of practice, including mental health, HIV/AIDS treatment, as well as services for older adults.

The focus of a long-term care system is the person (and his or her family) whose decreased functional capacity places him or her in a position to need assistance with IADLs such as housekeeping, finances, transportation, meal preparation, and/or administering medication. The case manager is the person who facilitates the client's movement through the service delivery system and, according to Intagliata (1992), is the human service provider who is solely responsible for ensuring that the client's needs are met.

Case management is also conducted at a social systems macro level, with geriatric social workers serving as planners and administrators. Weil and Karls (1985) have outlined eight major case management functions:

1. Client identification and outreach, determining the target population and eligibility.
2. Client assessment and diagnosis, evaluating a client's level of functioning and service needs.
3. Service planning and resource identification with clients and members of service networks, describing the steps and issues in service delivery, monitoring, and evaluation.
4. Linking clients to needed services, connecting or securing client services.
5. Service implementation and coordination, service assessment and troubleshooting, getting the work done, or putting all the plan's pieces in place.
6. Monitoring of service delivery, overseeing and supervising client services.
7. Advocacy for and with the client in the service network, pressing for the client's needs.
8. Evaluation of service delivery and case management, determining the progress of the service plan, which may result in continued service with the same or a revised service plan, termination, or basic follow-up.

Finally, social workers can play an important role in encouraging and assisting older adults to continue to be productive members of their communities and society at large. Because older people have a lifetime of knowledge and skills and a willingness to share their experience, they should be thought of as assets, not burdens, to society. Their continuing engagement in meaningful and productive activities, such as volunteering, can provide significant economic benefits. In addition, engaging in productive activities in later life should result in positive physical, functional, and psychological outcomes for the older adults themselves (Harlow & Cantor, 1996; Herzog, Franks, Markus, & Holmberg, 1998; Lum & Lightfoot, 2005; Musick, Herzog, & House, 1999; Van Willigen, 2000; Wheeler, Gorey, & Greenblatt, 1998).

Key Terms

Continuum of care	Diversity	Family and social support
Demographic imperative	Functional capacity	

Review Questions for Critical Thinking

1. Distinguish chronological age from functional age.
2. Explain why assessment of older adults includes biopsychosocial and spiritual factors.
3. How can families be involved in the case management process for older adults?
4. Outline disparities faced by minority elders.

Online Resources

AARP: www.aarphealthcare.com

Administration on Aging: www.aoa.gov/prof/addiv/addiv.asp

Family Caregiving Alliance: www.caregiver.org

Retirement Research Foundation: www.rrf.org

The Gerontological Society of America: www.geron.org/careers

References

AARP. (2005). *Reimagining America: AARP's blueprint for the future.* Washington, DC: Author.

American Association for Geriatric Psychiatry. (2005). Patients and caregivers: Alzheimer's and related dementias fact sheet. Retrieved October 1, 2005, from www.aagponline.org/p_c/dementia.asp

American Psychiatric Association. (1994). *Diagnostic and statistical manual of mental disorders* (4th ed.). Washington, DC: Author.

Antonovsky, A. (1998). The sense of coherence: An historical and future perspective. In H. I. McCubbin, E. A. Thompson, A. I. Thompson, & J. E. Fromer (Eds.), *Stress, coping, and health in families* (pp. 3–20). Boston, MA: Allyn & Bacon.

Atchley, R. C. (1999). *Continuity and adaptation in aging.* Baltimore, MD: Johns Hopkins University Press.

Bengtson, V. L., Giarrusso, R., Silverstein, M., & Wang, H. (2000). Families and intergenerational relationships in aging societies. *Hallym International Journal of Aging, 2*(1), 3–10.

Berkman, B. J., Gardner, D. S., Zodikoff, B. D., & Harootyan, L. K. (2005). Social work in health care with older adults: Future challenges. *Families in Society, 86*, 329–337.

Birren, J. E. (1969). Principles of research on aging. In J. E. Birren (Ed.), *The handbook of aging and the individual* (pp. 161–172). Chicago, IL: University of Chicago Press.

Birren, J. E., & Schroots, J.J.F. (1995). History, concepts, and theory in the psychology of aging. In J. E. Birren & K. W. Schaie (Eds.), *Handbook of the psychology of aging* (pp. 3–23). San Diego, CA: Academic Press.

Brody, E. (1985). Parent care as normative family stress. *The Gerontologist, 25,* 19–29.

Butler, R. N., Lewis, M. I., & Sunderland, T. (1998). *Aging and mental health.* Boston, MA: Allyn & Bacon.

Feil, N. (1993). *The validation breakthrough.* Baltimore, MD: Health Professions Press.

Gonyea, J. G., Hudson, R. B., & Curley, A. (2004, Spring). The geriatric social work labor force: Challenges and opportunities in responding to an aging society. In *Institute for geriatric social work issue brief* (pp. 1–7). Boston, MA: Boston University, School of Social Work.

Green, J. (2002). *Cultural awareness in the human services.* Englewood Cliffs, NJ: Prentice-Hall.

Greene, R. R. (1982). Life review: A technique for clarifying family roles in adulthood. *Clinical Gerontologist, 2,* 59–67.

Greene, R. R. (1986). *Social work with the aged and their families.* Hawthorne, NY: Aldine de Gruyter.

Greene, R. R. (1989). The growing need for social work services for the aged in 2020. In B. S. Vourlekis & C. G. Leukefeld (Eds.), *Making our case* (pp. 11–20). Silver Spring, MD: National Association of Social Workers Press.

Greene, R. R. (2000a). Serving the aged and their families in the 21st century: Using a revised practice model. *Journal of Gerontological Social Work, 34*(1), 41–62.

Greene, R. R. (2000b). *Social work with the aged and their families* (2nd ed.). Hawthorne, NY: Aldine de Gruyter.

Greene, R. R. (2005a). The changing family of later years and social work practice. In L. Kaye (Ed.), *Productive aging* (pp. 107–122). Washington, DC: National Association of Social Workers Press.

Greene, R. R. (2005b). Redefining social work for the new millennium: Setting a context. *Journal of Human Behavior and the Social Environment, 10*(4), 37–54.

Greene, R. R. (2007). *Social work practice: A risk and resilience perspective.* Monterey, CA: Brooks/Cole.

Greene, R. R., & Sullivan, W. P. (2004). Putting social work values into action: Use of the ecological perspective with older adults in the managed care arena. *Journal of Gerontological Social Work, 42*(3/4), 131–150.

Harlow, R. E., & Cantor, N. (1996). Still participating after all these years: A study of life task participation in later life. *Journal of Personality and Social Psychology, 71,* 1235–1249.

Herzog, A. R., Franks, M. M., Markus, H. R., & Holmberg, D. (1998). Activities and well-being in older age: Effects of self-concept and educational attainment. *Psychology and Aging, 13,* 179–185.

Holstein, M. B., & Minkler, M. (2003). Self, society, and the "new" gerontology. *The Gerontologist, 43,* 787–796.

Hooyman, N., & Kiyak, H. (2005). *Social gerontology.* Boston, MA: Allyn & Bacon.

Intagliata, J. (1992). Improving the quality of community care for the chronically mentally disabled: The role of the case manager. In S. M. Rose (Ed.), *Case management and social work practice* (pp. 25–55). New York, NY: Longman.

Johnson, R. W., Tooley, D., & Wiener, J. (2007). *Meeting the long-term needs of the baby boomers: How changing families will affect paid helpers and institutions* (Discussion Paper No. 07-04). Washington, DC: Urban Institute. Available from www.urban.org/publications/311451.html

Kaiser Family Foundation. (2002, June). Key findings from a national survey: Long-term care from the caregiver's perspective. Retrieved December 15, 2005, from www.kff.org/kcmu.

Lachs, M. S., Williams, C. S., O'Brien, S., Pillemer, K., & Charlson, M. E. (1998). The mortality of elder mistreatment. *Journal of the American Medical Association, 208*, 428–432.

Lawton, M. P. (1989). Behavior relevant ecological factors. In K. W. Schaie & C. Scholar (Eds.), *Social structure and aging: Psychological processes* (pp. 57–78). Hillsdale, NJ: Lawrence Erlbaum.

Lawton, M. P., & Nahemow, L. (1973). Ecology and the aging process. In C. Eisdorfer & M. P. Lawton (Eds.), *Psychology of adult development and aging* (pp. 619–674). Washington, DC: American Psychological Association.

Lebowitz, B. D., Pearson, J. L., Schneider, L. S., Reynolds, C. F., Alexopoulos, G. S., Bruce, M. L., & Parmelee, P. (1997). Diagnosis and treatment of depression in late life: Consensus statement update. *Journal of the American Medical Association, 278*, 1186–1190.

Lennon, T. (2004). *Statistics on social work education in the United States: 2002.* Alexandria, VA: Council on Social Work Education.

Lichtenberg, P. A. (Ed.). (2000). *Handbook of assessment in clinical gerontology.* New York, NY: John Wiley & Sons.

Lowry, L. (1992). Social group work with the elderly: Linkages and intergenerational relationships. *Social Work with Groups, 15*(2/3), 109–127.

Lum, T. Y., & Lightfoot, E. (2005). The effects of volunteering on the physical and mental health of older people. *Research on Aging, 27*, 31–55.

McInnis-Dittrich, K. (2002). *Social work with elders: A biopsychosocial approach to assessment and intervention.* Boston, MA: Allyn & Bacon.

Merck. (2005). *Manual of geriatrics.* Retrieved October 1, 2005, from www.merck.com/mrkshared/mmg/sec1/ch7/ch7a.jsp/

Metlife (1999). *Juggling act study.* Bethesda, MD: National Alliance of Caregivers

Min, J. W. (2005). Cultural competency: A key to effective future social work with racially and ethnically diverse elders. *Families in Society, 86*, 347–357.

Much of social work workforce also aging, retiring: Challenge of aging population nearing. (2005, November). *NASW News*, p. 4.

Musick, M. A., Herzog, A. R., & House, J. S. (1999). Volunteering and mortality among older adults: Findings from a national sample. *Journal of Gerontology: Social Sciences, 54B*, S173–S180.

Naleppa, M., & Reid, W. J. (2003). *Gerontological social work: A task-centered approach.* New York, NY: Columbia University Press.

National Center for Health Statistics. (1998). *The National Health Interview Survey, 1994: Second supplement on aging.* Hyattsville, MD: Author.

National Center for Health Statistics. (2004). *Chart book on trends in the health of America.* Hyattsville, MD: Author.

Northen, H. (1995). *Clinical social work knowledge and skills.* New York, NY: Columbia University Press.

Parmelee, P. A., & Lawton, M. P. (1990). The design of special environments for the aged. In J. E. Birren & K. W. Schaie (Eds.), *Handbook of the psychology of aging* (pp. 464–488). San Diego, CA: Academic Press.

Pennsylvania Care Management Institute. (1990). *Care management orientation manual.* Philadelphia, PA: Author.

Philadelphia Corporation for Aging. (1995). *Clinical protocol series for care managers in community based long-term care* (Grant No. 90-AM-0688). Washington, DC: Administration on Aging.

Pinderhughes, E. B. (1989). *Understanding race, ethnicity, and power: The key to efficacy in clinical practice.* New York, NY: Free Press.

Poulin, J. (2005). *Strengths-based generalist practice.* Belmont, CA: Brooks/Cole.

Rose, S. (1992). *Case management and social work practice.* New York, NY: Longman.

Rowe, J. W., & Kahn, R. L. (1998). *Successful aging.* New York, NY: Pantheon.

Scharlach, A. E., Damron Rodriguez, J., Robinson, B., & Feldman, R. (2000). Educating social workers for an aging society: A vision for the 21st century. *Journal of Social Work Education, 36,* 521–538.

Scharlach, A. E., & Kaye, L. W. (Eds.). (1997). *Controversial issues in aging.* Boston, MA: Allyn & Bacon.

Siegel, J. S. (1999). Demographic introduction to racial/ethnic elderly populations. In T. P. Miles (Ed.), *Full color aging: Facts, goals, and recommendations for America's diverse elders* (pp. 1–19). Washington, DC: The Gerontological Society of America.

Sijuwade, P. O. (1995). Cross-cultural perspectives on elder abuse as a family dilemma. *Social Behavior and Personality, 23*(3), 247–251.

Silverstone, B. (1996). Older people of tomorrow: A psychosocial profile. *The Gerontologist, 36,* 27–32.

Silverstone, B., & Burack-Weiss, A. (1983). *Social work practice with the frail elderly and their families.* Springfield, IL: Charles C Thomas.

Small, G. W., Ravins, P. V., Barry, P. P., Buchholtz, N. S., Dekosky, S. T., Ferris, S. H., & Tune, L. E. (1997). Diagnosis and treatment of Alzheimer's disease and related disorders. *Journal of the American Medical Association, 278,* 1363–1371.

Sprott, R. L., & Austad, S. N. (1995). Animal models for aging research. In E. L. Schneider & J. W. Rowe (Eds.), *Handbook of the biology of aging* (pp. 3–20). San Diego, CA: Academic Press.

Strawbridge, W. J., Wallhagen, M. I., & Cohen, R. D. (2002). Successful aging and well being: Self rated compared with Rowe and Kahn. *The Gerontologist, 42,* 727–733.

Takamura, J. C. (2001). Towards a new era in aging and social work. *Journal of Gerontological Social Work, 36,* 1–11.

Torres-Gil, F., & Moga, K. B. (2001). Multiculturalism, social policy, and the new aging. *Journal of Gerontological Social Work, 36,* 13–22.

Toseland, R., & Smith, T. (2001). *Supporting caregivers through education and training* [Monograph]. Washington, DC: U.S. Department of Health and Human Services.

Tran, T. V., Ngo, D., & Conway, K. (2003). A cross-cultural measure of depressive symptoms among Vietnamese Americans. *Social Work Research, 27,* 56–64.

U.S. Census Bureau. (2003). Current population survey: Annual social and economic supplement. Available from www.census.gov/hhes/www/poverty/poverty04/pov04hi.html

U.S. Census Bureau. (2004). Population estimates and projections. Available from www.census.gov/ipc/wwwusinterimproj

U.S. Decennial Census and Projections. (2000). U.S Government Printing Office. Washington, DC: Author.

U.S. Department of Health and Human Services. (1999). Mental health: A report of the Surgeon General. Rockville, MD: Author.

Van Willigen, M. (2000). Differential benefits of volunteering across the life course. Journal of Gerontology: Social Sciences, 55B, S308–S318.

Vourlekis, B., & Greene, R. R. (1992). Social work case management. Hawthorne, NY: Aldine de Gruyter.

Vourlekis, B., Zlotnik, J., Simons, K., & Toni, R. (2005). Blueprint for measuring social work's contribution to psychosocial care in nursing homes: Results from a national conference. In Institute for geriatric social work issue brief (pp. 1–4). Boston, MA: Boston University, School of Social Work.

Weil, M., & Karls, J. (1985). Case management in human service practice. San Francisco, CA: Jossey-Bass.

Wheeler, J. A., Gorey, K. M., & Greenblatt, B. (1998). The beneficial effects of volunteering for older volunteers and the people they serve: A meta-analysis. International Journal of Aging and Human Development, 47, 69–79.

Willis, S. L. (1991). Cognition and everyday competence. In K. W. Schaie (Ed.), Annual review of gerontology and geriatrics (Vol. 11, pp. 80–109). New York, NY: Springer.

Chapter 8
Forensic Social Work

Current and Emerging Developments

Katherine van Wormer, David W. Springer, and Tina Maschi

> What is forensic social work? What are some of the reasons that the social work profession historically moved away from this field, and why today are they beginning to move back to reclaim the territory?

Social work assessment and treatment with crime victims, juvenile offenders, and convicted felons have been viewed by some as the weakest link of social work practice but by others as an area of boundless possibility, as the field of criminal justice expands into new directions, many of them compatible with the values of social work (Barsky, 2010; Roberts, Springer, & Brownell, 2007). Moreover, consistent with the social work focus on social justice and the mission to provide services to the most vulnerable and socially neglected (even despised) members of the community, the profession can be expected to provide leadership here. While social workers have worked in corrections since the earliest days of the profession, recent innovations in the criminal justice arena have opened up new opportunities for social workers in drug and mental health court systems, in helping prisoners who lack personal resources make a successful re-entry into the community, and in prevention work connected to victim assistance programming.

These opportunities are widely known by social work graduates who learn of field placements and job openings in the field of corrections, whose interpersonal skills and knowledge of mental health diagnosis and substance abuse treatment are in considerable demand for work with juvenile offenders, persons on probation and parole, and with methamphetamine (meth) addicts charged with criminal offenses and also brought before juvenile court for child neglect or abuse. Many specialty courts have developed innovative programs in recent years that provide ideal opportunities for employment of social workers. Some police departments use social workers to provide services to victims (Orzech, 2006). The social work profession is today beginning to take notice and return to its roots in this area, and slowly but surely, social work educators are beginning to offer the courses relevant to forensic social work.

Forensic social work is defined in the *Dictionary of Social Work* (Barker, 2003) as:

> *The practice specialty in social work that focuses on the law, legal issues, and litigation, both criminal and civil, including issues in child welfare, custody of children, divorce, juvenile delinquency, nonsupport, relatives' responsibilities, welfare rights, mandated treatment, and legal competency. Forensic social work helps social workers in expert witness preparation. It also seeks to educate law professionals about social welfare issues and social workers about the law. Many social workers in this field belong to the National Organization of Forensic Social Workers. Its Web site address is www.nofsw.org. (p. 166)*

This definition reveals how the practice of social work is integrated within courtroom and correctional settings, in situations of family violence, child neglect, and adult crime. This definition is at the intersection of social work and the law. Building on this definition, we operationally define forensic social work as policies, practices, legal issues and remedies, and social work roles with juvenile and adult offenders as well as victims of crimes. This definition describes the content of this chapter as well.

As students of social work find their way, often inadvertently, into jobs working with offenders and former offenders, working with persons who are court-ordered into treatment, social work education is beginning to take notice. Let the students lead, we might say, and the educators will follow.

Consider the following examples of typical forensic work roles:

- Ann works for the Lincoln (Nebraska) Area Agency on Aging, which is notified by the Corrections Department when an elderly inmate faces release and needs help in getting housing and other assistance.
- Laura, who is employed by the Crime Prevention Institute, helps organize a program of prison visits between mothers and daughters.
- Ted, as a victim assistance worker, helps crime victims secure the aid and protection they need and conducts victim offender conferencing at the victim's request.
- Mary did crisis intervention in immigrant families in which droves of Mexican workers were arrested for their immigration status and use of forged documents in a raid at a meatpacking plant; foster families had to quickly be found for some of the children.
- Ron is a substance abuse counselor who connects with probation services and drug court to provide court-ordered treatment; he also gets referrals from drug court.
- Joe works in supported housing in Seattle; his organization provides apartments for homeless people with serious mental and substance disorders, thereby removing them from the streets and from encounters with the police and courts.

- Gina is a clinical social worker in a domestic violence shelter with a large service population of immigrants and refugees; she works mainly in the program for women and children who were sexual trafficking victims.

As these real-life vignettes show, social workers in every domain of the field—geriatrics, child welfare, substance abuse counseling, and so on—are connecting with the criminal justice system on a regular basis. Additionally, many social workers are hired directly by probation departments, correctional institutions, and juvenile services. Largely because of the war on drugs, with the arrests and sentencing of so many drug users, much treatment undoubtedly will continue to be provided under the auspices of department of correction.

The National Association of Social Workers (NASW, 2011) gives recognition to criminal justice as a major area of social work practice in their popular brochure, *Choices: Careers in Social Work*. The section on justice/corrections describes this burgeoning field as follows.

Case Example

Justice/Corrections

Joan, a woman in her mid-20s, has a history of drug addiction and writing bad checks. During a 4-year stay in prison, social work services including therapy and workshops on drug abuse and depression help her handle her addiction and make significant progress. But her children are in foster care, and she has lost touch with her mother and sisters.

As the time for her release approaches, Joan needs a job, housing, a continuing addiction recovery program, and reunification with her family. She meets with a prison social worker who arranges for placement in a halfway house and helps her find a job and transportation. After 8 months drug-free and holding her job, the halfway house social worker helps Joan find an apartment, arranges for the return of her children, locates her family, and helps her reunite with them.

In courts, rape crisis centers, police departments, and correctional facilities, you'll find social workers. In correctional facilities, the focus is on rehabilitation. Social workers may plan and provide drug and alcohol addiction treatment, life skills and basic competency training, and therapy to help offenders function once released into the community.

Social workers can be probation and parole officers, arranging for services after an offender is released, as in Joan's case, finding a group home residence, remedial classes, job training, addiction treatment, counseling, child care, and transportation. These activities generally help raise a client's independence and self-esteem.

Social workers may also be involved in restitution programs, or victim assistance services. They may serve the court as expert witnesses or work in partnership with attorneys. In police departments, social workers may help with domestic disputes or provide trauma and critical incident services to enforcement officers.

Social work activities in corrections are diverse, as are the clients, affording the chance to develop and use a broad range of skills. Corrections and justice is a field where a social worker can focus on rehabilitation and the constructive use of authority:

Related Areas

- Corrections
- Probation
- Forensics
- Youth services
- Parole

Employers

- Prisons
- Courts
- Police departments
- Victim services programs (NASW, 2011, Part I, Justice/Corrections, p. 6)

What the Statistics Show

According to the Bureau of Justice Statistics (BJS, 2010a), at the end of 2009, more than 7.2 million adult offenders were under some form of correctional supervision, including adult correctional institutions, juvenile correctional facilities, jails, detention centers, probation and parole agencies, or community diversion programs. The largest group, comprising more than 5 million persons, was under the supervision of probation or parole agencies.

More than 700,000 people are released from prison in the United States each year (Tahmincioglu, 2010). Recidivism rates are a major concern; these rates are high due to difficulty getting jobs, lack of support systems, and histories of mental illness and substance abuse. At least one-third of incarcerated women have mental disorders, and most have backgrounds of personal trauma (van Wormer, 2010).

Due to drug convictions and conspiracy sentencing laws, the number of women sent to prison is increasing at a rapid pace. The percentage of inmates who were women went from 4% in 1980 to 7% in 2009 (BJS, 2010b). About 70% of these women leave children behind; many of these children will become known to social workers in one capacity or another, and many require child welfare services (Gumz, 2004; van Wormer, 2010).

Victim assistance is another area in which counseling of victims plays a major role. According to the federal Office for Victims of Crime (OVC, 2011), in 2009 there were 20 million youths and adults ages 12 and over who were victims of crimes. However, there are only slightly over 16 million services that are provided through federal- and state-funded victim service and victim-witness assistance agencies, and 40% of these victims were domestic violence victims.

Census data from the 2009 Annual Survey of Social Work Programs (CSWE, 2009) of Council on Social Work Education accredited social work programs show that forensic practice field placements are commonplace. Of the 428 BSW and MSW programs, BSW students and MSW students were commonly in field placements that were primarily forensic practice settings or served forensic populations.

Of the approximately 15,000 BSW students, one out of three (5,000) were placed in forensic practice or related field placements. These placements included child welfare (15%), corrections/criminal justice (7%), domestic violence or crisis intervention (6%), and alcohol, drug, and substance abuse (4%) settings. However, it is important to note that BSW students in other field placements, such as mental health or community mental health, (6%), family services (10%) school social work (8%), and aging/gerontological social work (8%), may have provided services to individuals with histories of victimization or criminal charges.

Of 30,000 MSW students, approximately one out of four were in forensic practice field placements. These settings included child welfare (12%), corrections/criminal justice (4%), domestic violence or crisis intervention (3%), and alcohol, drug, and substance abuse (5%) settings. Similar the BSW programs, other field placements, such as mental health or community mental health (20%), family services (11%), and school social work (11%), may have provided services to individuals with histories of victimization or criminal charges.

If we conceptualized and reframed social work in corrections and probation, forensic mental health, substance abuse, family and criminal courts, domestic violence and child abuse/neglect, juvenile justice, crime victims including the elderly, and police social work, it would become clear that many in our profession are engaged in forensic social work. In fact, there is much more going on than is revealed in the mere statistics. Consider what is happening at Austin Peay University Social Work Department. In collaboration with the Clarksville, Tennessee Public Defender's Office, this social work department directly prepares social work students for work in the criminal justice or related field. This model program is described by member Stephanie Hicks (in private correspondence with van Wormer of July 31, 2011):

> Field practicum students in the bachelor's program have been able to complete their 400-hour field practicum for the past several semesters working at the Clarksville Public Defender's office. Under proper supervision they have been able to attend court sessions, perform jail site visits, locate and negotiate rehabilitative services for clients and act as a liaison between with the judges and lawyers for their clients. The students have had great opportunities to learn about the local, state, and federal level of the legal system as well as mental health and chemical dependency services for clients who would otherwise spend many days in the county jail.

> While it may seem unusual to envision a social worker employed in a lawyer's office, what the local lawyers have found is that a vast majority of the clients they have been working with have both chemical dependency and mental health

issues. It is the chemical dependency and mental health issues which often lead to criminal offenses. Historically, the judicial system takes a more punitive role rather than rehabilitative role in dealing with offenders, but the current economic crisis (not to mention the drug and alcohol crises) have forced the legal system to re-evaluate how they deal with offenders with chemical dependency and/or mental health issues. In doing so, they have started to employ more social workers on staff to work with these issues as social workers are usually very holistic in their approach to working with clients. However, our local Public Defender's office does not have the budget to hire enough social workers, thus they have affiliated their office with the APSU Social Work Department in order to fill the need. For the students this is a win/win situation as they are able to get incredible exposure to networking opportunities in our small community, and it has also exposed them to a complete different perspective of the legal system.

I should add that we've also had students placed in private law offices doing similar tasks. I've had a few students in the probation and parole system, the Nashville Public Defenders office and one student serving as a Legislative Intern at the State capital, all in the last year. Furthermore, I teach a Social Work and Law course as part of our undergrad program that assists in peaking [sic] the students interest in law as a possible field.

History of Social Work and Corrections

A brief historical overview of social welfare and social work demonstrates how much professional social work was identified with corrections and what we now define as forensic social work from its inception. For this overview, the authors use a modified version of the existing historical framework developed by Day (2008). Roberts and Brownell (1999) and Killian and Maschi (2009) offer more extensive overviews of the evolution of forensic social work in American social welfare history for those with special interest in this topic.

Post-Civil War and Recovery, and Progressive Era (1865 to 1925)

During colonial times and up to the first part of the 1800s, youths labeled as rowdy and out-of-control were either sent home for a court-observed whipping, assigned tasks as farmer's helpers, or placed in deplorable rat-infested prisons with hardened adult offenders. The turning point, in 1825, was the opening of a separate institution for juvenile offenders in New York City — "the New York House of Refuge . . . Similar juvenile facilities opened in 1826 and 1828 in Boston, and Philadelphia respectively" (Roberts, 2004b, pp. 130–131). By the mid-1800s, social work had become identified with corrections and other forms of social welfare institutions, including the "child-saving movement" whereby juvenile institutions and making juvenile delinquents indentured servants and apprentices for farmers and shop owners, also referred to as "parent surrogates," took place (Roberts, 2004b). By the late 1800s, many social reformers were involved with prisons, juvenile delinquency, and reformatories (Gibelman, 1995; Gumz,

2004; Killian & Maschi, 2009). Before social work became a profession, it was identified with corrections to the extent that the National Conference of Charities and Corrections was founded in 1879. Jane Addams, founder of Hull House, served as its first woman president (Solomon, 1994).

In 1898, the first social work training school was established as an annual summer course for agency workers by the New York Charity Organization Society (Killian & Maschi, 2009). Social workers of that time, whether associated with the charity organization movement or the settlement house movement, were viewed as social reformers whose primary concerns were with serving the poor, beggars and disadvantaged, and social outcasts.

While social Darwinism was embraced as the dominant social ethos of the charity organization movement, other social trends—including the settlement house movement—promoted progressive change (Day, 2008). The first juvenile court in the United States started in 1899 in Illinois as part of the circuit court of Chicago, through efforts initiated by the Chicago Women's Club (Popple & Leighninger, 2011). The Juvenile Psychopathic Institute was founded by William Healy, through the advocacy efforts of Hull House resident Julia Lathrop, to diagnose offenders brought before the Juvenile Court. The Institute began the practice of delinquency research and psychosocial assessment of children by a professional team (Popple & Leighninger, 2011).

Between 1915 and 1920, Women's Bureaus within police departments were established. All of the policewomen served in social work advocacy roles (particularly with juveniles). By 1919, Chicago had 29 police social workers; by 1920, there were police social workers in all the major urban areas (Roberts, 1997a).

Great Depression and Social Security for Americans (1925 to 1949)

While the 1929 stock market crash did not bring immediate and widespread devastation to the American economy, it damaged public confidence and brought to the surface a concern about the role of government in ensuring the social welfare of citizens (Day, 2008). While the charity organization and settlement house workers had successfully advocated for widow's pensions and old age assistance at the state and county levels, the federal government was not seen as responsible for social insurance and assistance. Private charity and local government were seen as the primary means of addressing poverty and deprivation until the widespread economic dislocations of the 1930s brought a realization that systems and not individual failings can cause poverty on a wide scale.

The Great Depression and the New Deal brought an influx of social workers into public life and government work. Harry Hopkins, a prominent New York social worker associated with the Charity Organization Movement, was appointed first by President Hoover and then by President F. D. Roosevelt to implement a program of emergency assistance and public works programs, including the WPA Youth Forestry Camps and the Civilian Conservation Corps, forerunners of modern day youth delinquency prevention programs. One of the earliest wilderness programs for juvenile offenders was established in the early 1930s in the Los Angeles County Forestry Department (Roberts, 2004b).

According to Roberts (2004b), "by the 1930s and 1940s, large numbers of psychiatric social workers had been hired to work in teams with psychiatrists to treat emotionally disturbed children, predelinquents and delinquents" (p. 131). This represented the beginning of interagency collaboration between the juvenile courts and child guidance clinics management. In addition, individualized treatment programs were started in Corrections. Casework with offenders, especially youthful offenders, drew social workers into forensic work as treatment specialists.

Civil and Welfare Rights in the New Reform Era (1945 to 1970)

The emerging critical need for social workers to work in the field of corrections was underscored by University of Pennsylvania social work dean Kenneth Pray (1945). Police social work expanded as interest in juvenile delinquency increased due to the widespread proliferation of youth gangs. By the late 1950s, the number of child guidance clinics had grown to more than 600 nationally: these included social workers who served as court liaisons (Roberts, 1998b).

In 1959, a set of 13 volumes on the social work curriculum was published by the Council on Social Work Education (CSWE). Among them was *Volume V: Curriculum for Teaching Correctional Social Work* by Studt (1959). This led to the development of correctional social work courses at major schools of social work.

During the 1940s, 1950s, and early 1960s, great strides were made in developing community-based councils and programs for delinquency prevention. Model programs such as NYC Mobilization for Youth, developed by social work professor Richard Cloward, the Midcity Program (Boston), and youth service bureaus proliferated (Roberts, 1998a). The continued concern about juvenile delinquency spurred innovative program initiatives, such as juvenile diversion, youth service bureaus, detached street workers (social workers doing group work and community organizing). President Johnson's Task Force Report on Juvenile Delinquency and Youth Crime in 1967 recommended dramatic policy innovations, such as decriminalization of status offenders and the diversion of juveniles from official court processing (McNeece & Jackson, 2004). In 1967, the *In re Gault* decision by the U.S. Supreme Court ruled that due process must be observed in juvenile delinquency proceedings. This landmark legal decision solidified due process protection for juveniles at the adjudication stage (Alexander, 1995).

The role of social workers in probation increased dramatically by the mid-1960s. Probation departments were established in all 50 states and more than 2,300 counties nationwide. Social worker Milton Rector, executive director of the National Council on Crime and Delinquency (NCCD), directed a national study of probation and recommended that all new probation officers and supervisors should be required to have an MSW and two years of casework experience (Roberts, 2004a).

Retreat From the Welfare State and the New Federalism (1970 to 1992)

Social welfare programs shrank during the 1970s and 1980s, as the country experienced a conservative retrenchment, especially during the Reagan era (Day, 2008). However, there continued to be advancements in services and programs for juvenile offenders as well as victim services. In 1972, community-based alternatives (e.g., a network of group homes) and education programs for juvenile delinquents were established by the Massachusetts Youth Services Department after it closed several juvenile reformatories (Alexander, 1995). By 1980, the closing of juvenile correctional institutions and the expansion of community-based group homes had extended to other states, such as Pennsylvania, Illinois, and Utah.

The Juvenile Justice and Delinquency Prevention Act of 1974 was the first major policy legislation with a major funding appropriation that resulted in a new federal office—the Office of Juvenile Justice and Delinquency Prevention (OJJDP). The first director of OJJDP was social worker Ira Schwartz (now provost, Temple University in Philadelphia). Schwartz and his staff implemented the far-reaching legislation that provided federal funding to many states to deinstitutionalize status offenders, remove juveniles from adult jails and lock-ups, establish runaway youth shelters and counseling programs, and improve delinquency prevention programs. Social workers, through their respective state governors' juvenile justice commissions and/or state criminal justice planning agencies, were able to advocate for important system changes, particularly the deinstitutionalizing of runaways, truants, and incorrigible youths.

The Child Abuse Prevention and Treatment Act of 1974 provided funding for demonstration programs to test prevention, intervention, and treatment strategies for child abuse and neglect, and resulted in the establishment of the National Center on Child Abuse and Neglect (Alexander, 1995). In 1978, the Act was extended and funded new adoption initiatives. This child abuse federal funding initiative resulted in the development of interdisciplinary hospital-based child abuse assessment and treatment teams, usually with medical social workers as the coordinators or team leaders.

To this point, the social work profession had made significant advances since what could be defined as the beginning of forensic social work—the opening of the first juvenile court in 1899 in Cook County, Illinois—and the first organization to assist abused women—the Chicago Protective Agency (for women and children) established in 1885 (Day, 2008). Jane Addams and Julia Lathrop, founders of the settlement movement and strong advocates for the legislation that led to the first juvenile court, were leaders among the Progressive era reformers who built a foundation for the significant reforms in juvenile justice, domestic violence, and victim assistance programs and services during the past 106 years (Ashford, 2009).

But there have also been setbacks. During these years and the key historical periods they represent, there were both declines and flourishing periods for major policy shifts in social workers' involvement and responsiveness to both criminal offenders and their innocent victims.

In the mid-1970s, a crushing indictment of all correctional treatment programs appeared in the form of a review of 231 studies of rehabilitative programs in existence at that time. Robert Martinson (1974) conducted the review. His conclusion that "nothing works" has been bandied about ever since. For conservative politicians and cynical liberals alike, Martinson's denunciation was an answer to their prayers. So even when Martinson later refuted his own findings, acknowledging that he had disregarded the positive outcomes in many of the reports, the damage could not be undone (van Wormer, 2010). Rehabilitation essentially was dead. Social workers and other counselors exited the field or were driven out by lack of funding. At the same time, as social work values clashed with the conservative ideology espoused by the American corrections system, social work simply abandoned the field (Gumz, 2004). This abandonment, by a profession that put clients first, no doubt further accelerated the increasing punitive nature of corrections and the lack of forceful advocacy to reverse this trend.

The women's movement focused attention on domestic violence and victims' rights issues and programs. The Law Enforcement Assistance Act (LEAA), which was passed in 1974, provided state block grants for local funding of police social work, as well as domestic violence and victim assistance programs. Model demonstration projects included the first shelter for battered women, which opened in St. Paul, Minnesota, and the first two police-based victim assistance programs, which were in Ft. Lauderdale and Indianapolis (Roberts, 1996). The civil rights movement and concerns about links between racism and imprisonment gave rise to a renewed focus on prison conditions and reform. In 1976, in a class action suit, the U.S. District Court of Alabama ruled that conditions of confinement in the Alabama penal system constituted cruel and unusual punishment when they bore "no reasonable relationship to legitimate institutional goals" (Alexander, 1995, p. 2644).

By the mid-1980s, a major policy shift resulted in provision of woefully needed social services and crisis intervention for crime victims and less rehabilitation programs for convicted felons. The crime victims' movement was bolstered significantly with the passage of the landmark Victims of Crime Act (VOCA) of 1984, in which the many millions of dollars in funding came from federal criminal penalties and fines.

Decade of The 1990s to Today

Victim assistance programming, including domestic violence advocacy, and community corrections are two major areas of expansion for social work practice. Between 1984 and 1997, $2 billion was allocated throughout the nation to aid domestic violence, rape, child sexual assault, and other violent crime victims. This helped finance thousands of victim/witness assistance, victim service, domestic violence, and sexual assault treatment programs nationwide. These programs have a total average staff of seven full-time workers, which includes many professional social workers (Roberts, 1997b). The growth phase for forensic social workers that began in the 1990s in victim assistance and domestic violence programs was much enhanced as a result of the $3.3 billion of funds through Violence against Women Act II.

One project of note conducted in collaboration with NASW/Texas and funded by the U.S. Department of Justice was led by social work educator Fran Davis as the principal investigator. This was the *Crime Victims: A Social Work Response, Building Skills to Strengthen Survivors* project. From this project, a CD-ROM has been produced by Davis (2006) that offers a comprehensive training kit for social work practitioners to provide information about the impact of violent crime and the services and legal rights available to adult crime victims.

As the prison census maintains its present high level, social work in community corrections continues to expand. Many social workers are moving into community corrections work today, and not only in work with victims of crime. The form that community corrections are taking today is largely through reentry programs, drug courts, and mental health courts. These exciting developments exist for the purpose of keeping people in trouble with the law in the community. Intensive therapy, addictions treatment, and correctional supervision are provided. Because federal funding is increasingly placed here in the form of grants to the states and counties, social workers are becoming actively involved in offering services (see Huddleston, 2011). The specialized domestic violence courts that started to emerge in 1999 and 2000 in major cities throughout the United States also bode well for the growing number of social workers working with domestic violence victims, batterers, and probationers (Keilitz, 2002).

Alternatives to incarceration programs for misdemeanor level crimes, as well as nonviolent felony level crimes related to IV drug use—highly associated with contemporary public health crises such as HIV, AIDS and hepatitis C—include social workers as case managers, addiction treatment specialists, crisis counselors, and family service specialists.

Today, fortunately, due to swings in the political pendulum, a public that wants offenders to change and believes they can, and evidence-based research proving the effectiveness of community-based programming such as drug courts and addiction treatment in general, rehabilitation is back.

A Rich Tradition in the Social Work Correctional Literature

According to Reamer (2004), "Relatively little serious scholarship on criminal justice issues is authored by social workers" (p. 213). We beg to differ with that assessment; we state our case in this section with a plethora of references provided from a sample of the voluminous body of research conducted by social work scholars. First, we will describe some basic textbooks that summarize empirical work done relevant to crime and delinquency; then we will consider some of the empirical research itself.

The late Professor Margaret Gibelman was one of a group of social work scholars who understood the need for greater attention by the profession to providing an active presence in the fields of crime and justice. Gibelman (1995) devoted an entire chapter to social work and the criminal justice system in the first edition of *What Social Workers Do,* published by NASW Press. H. Wayne Johnson (1998), similarly, emphasized practice in the criminal justice field in a widely used social services textbook that saw five editions. In *Social Work Almanac* (Ginsberg, 1995), substantial space is given to a discussion of corrections and juvenile delinquency. Among the social issues of increasing concern in the United States, noted by Ginsberg, "are crime and delinquency and the societal approaches for dealing with them" (p. 90). Van Wormer's (2006) introductory text, *Introduction to Social Welfare and Social Work: The U.S. in Global Perspective* contains an extensive chapter on human rights and criminal justice issues. Similarly, editors DiNitto and McNeece have included in their text *Social Work: Issues and Opportunities in a Challenging Profession* a chapter written by Diane Young (2008) on social work practice in the justice system.

Popple and Leighninger's (2011) *Social Work, Social Welfare, and American Society* also contains a chapter devoted to crime and criminal justice. Consider also Oxford's *Social Workers Desk Reference* (Roberts, 2009), which contains eight original chapters in the forensic social work section.

In recent years, four comprehensive volumes were published in which the latest social policies, social services, and social work practice roles with crime victims and offenders are documented. These books include original chapters by the leading forensic social workers in the United States. They are:

Substance Abuse Treatment for Criminal Offenders: An Evidence-Based Guide for Practitioners (Springer, McNeece, & Arnold, 2003)

Social Work in Juvenile and Criminal Justice Settings (Roberts & Springer, 2007)

Handbook of Forensic Mental Health with Victims and Offenders: Assessment, Treatment, and Research (Springer & Roberts, 2007)

Forensic Social Work: Psychosocial and Legal Issues in Diverse Practice Settings (Maschi, Bradley, & Ward, 2009)

Domestic Violence: Intersectionality and Culturally Competent Practice (Davis & Lockhart, 2010)

There are many other contributions on more specialized topics made by social work, including:

Criminal Lessons: Case Studies and Commentary on Crime and Justice (Reamer, 2003)

Social Work and Human Rights: A Foundation for Policy and Practice (Reichert, 2003)

Confronting Oppression, Restoring Justice: From Policy Analysis for Restorative Justice (van Wormer, 2004)

Women and the Criminal Justice System (van Wormer & Bartollas, 2010)

Battered Women and Their Families: Intervention Strategies and Treatment Programs (Roberts, Ed., 2007a)

Correctional Counseling and Treatment (Roberts, Ed., 2007b)

Human Rights and Social Justice in a Global Perspective: An Introduction to International Social Work (Mapp, 2008)

Death by Domestic Violence: Preventing the Murders and the Murder-Suicides (van Wormer, 2009)

Restorative Justice Dialogue: An Essential Guide for Research and Practice (Umbreit & Armour, 2010)

Social Work and Restorative Justice: Skills for Dialogue, Peacemaking, and Reconciliation (Beck, Kropf, & Leonard, 2011)

The profession can take pride in the appointment of two social work professionals as editors of criminal justice journals. The late Albert Roberts was the founding editor of the international journal, *Victims & Offenders: Journal of Evidence-Based Policies and Practices,* which began publication in 2006. Creasie Hairston, dean of the Jane Addams School of Social Work, was appointed as editor of the interdisciplinary *Journal of Offender Rehabilitation* beginning in 2007 and continues in this role. In January 2011, the inaugural issue of the *Journal of Forensic Social Work* was launched, which is the official journal of the National Organization of Forensic Social Workers. The journal is devoted to improving the specialty of forensic social work. It does so by publishing research and conceptual articles and research articles that promote evidence-based practices and the improvement of the service provision of victims and offenders of crime.

In July 2011, we conducted a comprehensive survey of the social work literature of articles published in *Social Work* from 2006 to 2010. In *Social Work* during this period, we found 13 articles that are germane to the field of forensic social work. Topics covered included, but were not limited to: domestic violence, the death penalty, expert testimony, male and female delinquency, restorative justice, and elderly inmates. Applying our definition of forensic social work, Roberts and Springer identified 29 articles in the prestigious *Research on Social Work Practice* during the six-year period (1999 to 2005). Of these articles, there were several that coalesced around social work with troubled youth and juvenile delinquents, including school violence, antisocial behavior in a runaway shelter, reintegration services for adjudicated delinquents, mental health and substance abuse problems for detained youth, risk prediction among juvenile offenders, short-term outcomes for runaway youth, and delinquency prevention programs.

Other related topics represented in this social work research journal were victim–offender mediation and reoffense, posttraumatic stress disorder among inmates, batterer intervention programs, child abuse issues, and sexual offender risk.

Under the able leadership of Editors in Chief Terry Mizrahi and Larry Davis, the latest edition of the *Encyclopedia of Social Work* (2008) was significantly expanded to include many articles related to forensic social work with victims and offenders. The 20th edition of the *Encyclopedia of Social Work* included dozens of articles on a number of forensic-related topics, specifically courts, criminality, forensic social work, incarceration, domestic violence, correctional counseling, and for the first time, harm reduction and restorative justice. The entry on forensic social work by Sunny Rome (2008) discusses social worker roles in providing courtroom testimony related to child abuse and working in death penalty cases to conduct background research in the interests of sentence mitigation. These roles are in addition to the more obvious ones of counseling juvenile and adults in the correctional system.

It is certainly evident based on this content analysis of *Social Work* and other publications that the National Association of Social Workers (NASW) recognizes the importance of social work involvement with forensic-related issues. This is in spite of the acknowledgment that forensic social work has not yet received the attention it deserves within the profession.

Promising Trends in Education

There has been a slow but steady growth in the number of forensic social work courses and continuing education workshops. The focus and content areas of these workshops and courses include the following:

- Child custody evaluations and assessments to determine whether parental rights of persons who are mentally ill, convicted felons, and/or abusive parents should be terminated
- Risk assessments of offenders who are mentally ill and substance-abusing (i.e., MICA [mentally ill, chemically addicted], also known as dual disorders), with special attention to their risk of future violence and repeat criminality
- Assessment and treatment of juvenile and adult mentally ill offenders in the criminal justice system and forensic mental health units to help in treatment planning as well as planning for a safe discharge or parole date
- Preparation of presentence reports for juvenile court and criminal court judges
- Assessment of dangerousness and likelihood of recidivism among convicted sex offenders
- Crisis assessment, crisis intervention, and trauma treatment protocols and strategies with victims of violent crimes
- Domestic violence policies and intervention strategies with battered women and their children

- Batterers' psychoeducational and group treatment protocols and intervention strategies
- Assessment and treatment with suicide-prone juvenile and adult offenders
- Motivational interviewing and other strengths-based treatment strategies with substance abusers
- Restorative justice policies and practices
- Treatment engagement and retention among substance-abusing offenders
- Applying the stages-of-change and transtheoretical models to clinical treatment with criminal offenders

Evidence-Based Research

A major challenge facing the future of forensic social workers is treatment engagement and retention of juvenile and criminal offenders receiving clinical treatment. Concern regarding challenges in attracting and retaining substance-abusing clients in treatment, for example, has led researchers to focus on motivation as a construct that may contribute to an enhanced understanding of treatment engagement and retention (Battjes, Gordon, O'Grady, Kinlock, & Carswell, 2003; van Wormer & Davis, in press). A growing body of research suggests that drug courts are effective in retaining a significant number of clients in substance abuse treatment and in reducing criminality thereby (Mueser, Noordsy, Drake, & Fox, 2003). The primary research in the field of the effectiveness of victim offender conferencing is conducted at the University of Minnesota School of Social Work, Center for Restorative Justice and Peacemaking, under director Mark Umbreit. Battjes and colleagues (2003) investigated factors that predict motivation among youth admitted to an adolescent outpatient substance abuse treatment program; findings revealed that factors involving various negative consequences of substance use emerged as important predictors of motivation, whereas severity of substance use did not.

Despite these advances, new research is needed to identify factors that impact retention and therapeutic engagement, with the need especially for research that examines the relationship between patient outcomes and elements of the therapeutic process—namely, the treatment environment, patient needs, and delivery of services. Additional concepts, such as those representing a client's stage of change and motivation (Miller, Forcehimes, & Zweben, 2011) should also be integrated into a more comprehensive analytic model. Increasingly, the role of social workers is expanding in the addictions treatment field, and more attention is being paid to evidence-based forms of treatment. The importance of motivation and retention is underscored by randomized trials that have shown the benefit of this approach to the retention of clients in treatment for substance use problems (Yeager, 2009). One theoretical framework relevant to motivation for engagement and retention in substance abuse treatment is the transtheoretical model (TTM). This model grew in response to dissatisfaction with simple behavioral models and the search for a more comprehensive approach to describe complex processes of human behavior change. Since its development, this model has been used extensively with practitioners, clinicians and researchers in the field of addictions and drug use. The stages-of-change model is the most frequently applied construct of the TTM model, and it offers the most research concerning the validity of TTM constructs (see Miller, Forcehimes, & Zweben, 2011; Prochaska, Norcross, Fowler, Follick, & Abrams, 1992; Prochaska et al., 1994; van Wormer & Davis, in press).

This model conceptualizes five stages-of-change that integrate processes and principles of change from a number of major theories (Prochaska & Norcross, 1999). The first stage is *precontemplation*, in which there is no intention or motivation to change. People in this stage generally have no awareness of the problem or have greatly underestimated the seriousness of the problem. The second stage is *contemplation*, in which there is awareness of a problem and a desire to overcome it, but no commitment to take the actions necessary to accomplish change. The third stage, *preparation*, involves a decision to take action sometime in the near future, but a specific plan for accomplishing this goal is not present or has not yet been implemented. The fourth stage is *action*, in which the individual makes changes in behavior and/or lifestyle and sustains those from one day to six months. The final stage, *maintenance*, involves those activities necessary to maintain change and avoid relapse.

Progression through these stages is not expected to be linear, and reversion to earlier stages is expected. Most clients move through the stages of change in a spiral pattern. Indeed, in one study (Prochaska & DiClemente, 1984), approximately 15% of smokers who relapsed went back to the precontemplation stage, and 85% went back to the pre-contemplation or contemplation stage. Preliminary data suggest that this framework is useful in providing services to minority clients (Longshore, Grills, & Annon, 1999), preventing alcohol-exposed pregnancy after a jail term (Mullen, Velasquez, von Sternberg, Cummins, & Green, 2005), and guiding treatment with substance-abusing juvenile offenders (Springer, Rivaux, Bohman, & Yeung, 2006), to name just a few.

A major challenge is the successful treatment and retention of persons with co-occurring disorders (persons with both a mental disorder and substance-related problems). Programs that are tailored to individuals' readiness for change and that do not force clients to abstain from all drug use but that engage clients in a collaborative effort to reduce the harm to themselves are more successful than other approaches with this population. In their review of the literature on treatment effectiveness with dually and multiply diagnosed populations, Mueser and colleagues (2003) found that the best outcomes were with integrated, long-term dual diagnosis treatment geared toward the client's level of motivation.

Springer and colleagues (2006) examined factors that predict, and interventions that maximize, substance abuse treatment retention in three modalities among high-risk Anglo, Mexican American, and African American juvenile offenders. The study sample includes youth ($N = 211$) who were discharged from probation supervision and who received substance abuse services through a CSAT-funded federal demonstration project. Among the juveniles in this sample, 56 (18%) were female and 255 (82%) were male. Approximately half ($n = 163$, 52.4%) were Mexican American, one-quarter ($n = 88$, 28.3%) were African American, and the remainder were Caucasian ($n = 50$, 28.3%). The key predictors examined included the stage of change (i.e., precontemplation, contemplation, preparation) in which a juvenile fell, various dimensions captured by the Comprehensive Addiction Severity Index for Adolescents, and other intervention status (probation, case management, and mental health treatment). The research questions were addressed using survival analysis statistical models that treated time from entry into substance abuse treatment to exit from substance abuse treatment as the outcomes. Among key findings were that females were 73% more likely to leave day treatment relative to males; for each additional family problem ever experienced, Mexican American adolescents were 15% more likely to leave residential treatment compared to African American adolescents; and African American and Mexican American adolescents in the contemplation stage of change were 50% less likely to leave day treatment compared to Caucasian adolescents.

The results from Springer and colleagues (2006) study suggest that continued research is needed to explore the extent to which various treatment components—such as family therapy or motivational interviewing—contribute to substance abuse treatment engagement and retention among African American and Mexican American clients across the stages-of-change continuum.

A Strengths Perspective

In social work, the idea of building on people's strengths has become an overriding theme associated with an emphasis on empowerment. There is nothing very new about this theoretical concept; the parallels with the self-fulfilling prophecy concept, labeling theory, and "the-power-of-positive-thinking" conceptualizations are obvious. As a framework for treatment intervention, the strengths approach can offer a mental map, as Norman Polansky (1986) eloquently suggested several decades ago. Such a mental map can operate as a reminder when we as therapists get off course (get too caught up in the use of formal diagnosis, for example). Within the correctional system, viewing clients solely through the lens of the crimes they have committed can obscure our vision and impede treatment progress.

More recently, the strengths perspective has been catapulted to prominence by such writers as Dennis Saleebey and others of the University of Kansas School of Social Work. Saleebey (2009) describes the essence of this approach in these words: "Practicing from a strengths orientation means this—*everything* you do as a social worker will be predicated, in some way, on helping to discover and embellish, explore and exploit clients' strengths and resources in the service of assisting them to achieve their goals, realize their dreams, and shed the irons of their own inhibitions and misgivings, and society's domination" (p. 1). The title of Saleebey's introductory chapter is "Power in the People." Within the justice context, the challenge consists of promoting personal power in people whose lives have become circumscribed to varying degrees and whose very existence has been devalued and even criminalized.

More than any other population, correctional clients are the failures of the failures. Not only have they publicly been labeled through some kind of court action, but their encounter with professional counselors usually relates to some kind of punishment. Work in the correctional realm, then, with all the negatives stacked against it, is an excellent testing ground for a framework of strengths. In contrast to a diagnostic, pathology-based therapy, direct practice from this multidimensional framework looks beyond a client's diagnosis or offense—for example, borderline personality or drug possession—to positive attributes that can serve as an important resource even in the most desperate of circumstances.

A second major challenge to correctional social work is the challenge of viewing causality reciprocally. With criminal behavior, the locus of the problem is not the individual alone but the individual and society in interaction. To study the person-in-the-environment is not enough; one also needs to study the environment-in-the-person. If we conceive of the environment as the prison, we can view the new recruits as bringing into this milieu all of what Irwin (1980) calls the "cultural baggage" from their social background. And then we can view aspects of prison life—the social control, the convict norms—as internalized within the prison inmate. Both the person and the environment can be seen to be in continuous and dynamic interaction in this way. If we come to frame the inmates' confinement in a political sense, then we have moved toward a linking of the personal and political levels of existence.

As we hear from correctional social worker Michael Clark:

Embracing a strengths perspective in a criminal justice world has been fraught with frustration. Criminal justice is a field that is unbalanced as it entertains only problems, failures, and flaws. Compliance is king while behavior change is often left wanting—viewed as something best left to others ("treatment"). I began to find inroads for using a strengths-based approach with my probation caseload and soon published articles detailing the application within juvenile delinquency. . . . I found a small group of like-minded practitioners and increased my skills. After a full year of advocacy, I was able to convince our court management to change a deficit-based family history from to one that was balanced between both problems and strengths.

The old form was so bad; I often have groups review the old deficits form in my trainings as a good example of "what not to do." To gain more experience,

I moved into a child welfare position and spent 5 years performing abuse and neglect casework. I was eventually appointed a Senior Juvenile Court Officer, which included the duties of Judicial Referee (Magistrate), holding preliminary hearings for our judges in both delinquency and child welfare cases. My publications led to conducting workshops and that spiraled into a complete career change. . . . I left the court and formed the Center for Strength-Based Strategies, a research and technical assistance organization that seeks to import strength-based and outcome-informed practices for work with mandated clients. Our Center champions direct practice and is actively engaged in training staffing groups in the "how to's" for one-on-one efforts with challenging clients.

Clark goes on to explain how reading Miller and Rollnick's *Motivational Interviewing* further enhanced his strengths approach:

I found formal training in this approach and then moved my practice to another level, completing a train-the-trainer session to be named a "MINT" member (Motivational Interviewing Network of Trainers). I now am engaged in training probation officers in motivational interviewing across the country. Several states are engaged in training all (!) of their supervising probation and parole officers in motivational approaches. (As cited in Roberts & Springer, 2007, pp. 9–10)

Initiatives such as these lend an enthusiasm to forensic social work that becomes altogether contagious.

Current Status of Forensic Social Work

According to Diane Young, who was quoted as an expert on prison reentry by *NASW News* reporter Stoesen (2006), more departments of social work should offer a concentration in criminal justice: "The need is really great for social work involvement" (p. 4). Her recommendation is that social work get more actively involved in reentry work, where the need is so urgent. As Jeffrey Draine, also interviewed in the article, observed, "People who might have been interested in going into social work went into criminal justice, which has a different set of professional standards. . . . Social workers need to reclaim this. We need to take initiative, propose innovation, (move beyond) the principle of surveillance and control as the primary organizing concept" (p. 4). Ashford (2009) decries the fact that so few schools of social work offer a concentration in this area. However, he knows personally of a few schools that have established postgraduate certifications in recent years.

Correctional social workers ideally are trained in knowledge and skills on diagnostic and risk assessments, the nature of human development and behavioral dysfunctions, juvenile and adult laws, juvenile and criminal court procedures and structure, crisis intervention and trauma treatment protocols, the strengths perspective and solution-focused therapy, and mental health treatments for criminal offenders as well as violent crime victims.

Opportunities exist for professional social workers at the Legal Aid Society and in family courts with abused and neglected children, as well as with juvenile offenders who have mental health and addictions problems. Victim service programs for crime victims and domestic violence survivors employ professional social workers to work with victims as well as perpetrators of family crimes.

The emergence of specialized courts, such as drug courts and domestic violence courts, has resulted in an increasing presence of social workers in the courts. Schools of social work have developed interdisciplinary programs with law schools, as well as joint degree programs in social work and the law.

The increase of women in prison due to some states' "get-tough" drug laws and the increased recognition of the plight of the forensic mentally ill require the services of professional social workers for counseling and to serve as the link between child welfare, substance abuse, and health and mental health systems on one hand, and the correctional system on the other (van Wormer, 2010). Other social and public health problems with which forensic social workers are engaged include the alarming surge of hepatitis C, HIV and AIDS, cancer, cardiovascular diseases, diabetes, and tuberculosis among the county and city jail and state prison populations, and the increasing recognition of a forensic MICA and developmentally disabled inmate population.

Contrasting Values: Criminal Justice and Social Work

Contrast the terminology of criminal justice—punishment, zero tolerance, criminal personality—with that of social work—empowerment, strengths perspective, social justice, cultural competence—and the fields come across as worlds apart. For these two fields to come together would take a paradigm shift.

Social workers in the criminal justice field will note that the empirically based cognitive approach is the dominant approach to counseling sessions. Counselors trained from this perspective focus on taking a very directive role in exposing the client's irrational thoughts, the "musts" and "shoulds" and the tendency to catastrophize in a crisis (model borrowed from Ellis, 2001). Social workers often use this model to help clients reframe their negative, self-defeating thoughts into positive statements. Correctional workers (and addictions counselors), however, typically draw on a format that is anything but positive. They utilize exercises derived from the theoretical framework of criminal psychologist Stanton Samenow (1984), which focuses on his understanding of "the criminal personality." Samenow's theory and techniques, which are geared to criminal thinking and manipulation, are commonly used in correctional addictions programming with both male and female offenders. His best-selling book, *Inside the Criminal Mind,* was based on work with psychopathic males in confinement at St. Elizabeth's Hospital for the "criminally insane" in Washington, DC. In programming that Samenow developed and teaches through nationwide workshops, offenders are required to focus on their wrongdoings, with the goal of instilling "self-disgust" and a desire to reform their errant ways (van Wormer, 2010).

This is emphatically not the method used in the strengths perspective. Many offenders, more victimized than victimizers, suffer from low self-esteem and shame due to their troubles with the law, pain inflicted on their families, and so on; a focus on the errors of their ways is counter-productive.

A competing philosophy that is now coming into its own within the criminal justice system is a cognitively based formulation that focuses on client motivation. *Motivational Interviewing*, developed by Miller and Rollnick (1996), combines aspects of a laid-back, client-centered approach with a focus on reinforcement of positive, self-motivational statements. Collaboration and choice are guiding precepts. Instead of confrontation, counselors are advised to "roll with resistance." Instead of telling clients what is wrong with their lives or thinking, therapists are taught to focus on the positive and elicit statements of intended change efforts from the clients themselves, then to reinforce such statements. A theme of this approach is a focus on the client's self-efficacy, similar to the strengths perspective tapping into the client's own inner resources. Motivational interviewing is evidence-based; every precept of this model is derived from proven findings from social psychology concerning how people change (for a breakdown of these statements, see van Wormer & Davis, in press). Motivational enhancement strategies are of demonstrated effectiveness with clients who are mandated to treatment and who are inclined to be angry (Miller et al., 2011; Wallace, 2005).

Correctional practice is very rarely social justice as endorsed in the social work code. "Strategies must be found for promoting social work values within the environmental contexts of offenders' lives," as Young and LoMonaco (2001, p. 479) note. Within total institutions and without, individuals need help in negotiating the system, however dehumanizing, so that ultimately they can be free from the shackles of the correctional system and maybe even reclaim their lives.

Social work, as a profession, is steeped in a history of advocacy for social justice and prevention work, especially with juveniles. Experience in family counseling and interdisciplinary teamwork are further relevant attributes of the profession that lend themselves to success in this work with people in trouble with the law. Significant numbers of social workers earn their living, as Reamer (2004) acknowledges, as probation and parole officers, caseworkers in public defender offices, counselors in correctional institutions and halfway houses, and so on. But as a profession, he indicates, social work no longer has a major presence in the criminal justice field. Social work, we might add, no longer has a major role in shaping legislation pertain to juvenile justice and adult corrections.

At the policy level, advocacy to change the system is vital. In order to curb crime and victimization, drug addiction must be viewed as a health problem, a disease that can be treated, rather than as a criminal justice problem. As social workers and students of social work visit their state legislators, as on lobby day, or testify at state legislative forums, the opportunity is provided to show legislators how they can be progressive and save the state money at the same time. A focus on the cost-effectiveness of prevention programming and diversionary programs such as drug courts that keep people with addiction problems in the community and out of the prison revolving door can be especially persuasive in times of budget tightening. Money saved in prison construction can be spent on treatment and prevention, and in the child welfare system, instead.

Rehabilitation, happily, is no longer a dirty word. The general public and politicians alike are speaking of the importance of offender treatment and rehabilitation. One sign that such a shift may be occurring is the proliferation of programming associated with a seemingly new movement that actually harks back to ancient times. This movement is known in its present reincarnation as restorative justice.

Restorative Justice: A Bridge Between Criminal Justice and Social Work

The adversary system will not be replaced; prisons will not be razed and correctional officers won't be throwing away their uniforms just yet, but, according to the National Institute of Corrections, "a revolution is occurring in criminal justice" (Barajas, 1995). Since he wrote those words, many of the states have incorporated restorative strategies into their correctional systems. As we learn from Pavelka (2008), who conducted a national survey of the progress the states have made since this time, virtually every state is implementing restorative justice at various levels (e.g., state, regional, or local, in program and policy). The majority of the states that have revised their statutes or codes to reflect restorative justice principles have done so in the past two decades. The states she singled out for their model juvenile justice programs are Pennsylvania, Alaska, and South Carolina.

Rarely noted until recently in the social work literature in the United States (but widely emphasized in the social work literature of Canada, Britain, and New Zealand), restorative justice involves a reorientation of how we think about crime and justice. As a set of values, restorative justice offers great promise in regard to promoting healing and strengthening community bonds by addressing the criminal harm done to victims and communities.

Restorative justice is a collective term that loosely refers to a number of initiatives that hold offenders directly accountable to victims and the community. Although the term restorative justice has become popular only since the 1990s, this form of dispensing justice is rooted in the rituals of indigenous populations, as tribal members settled disputes in sentencing circles. Its modern beginnings are in Canada in the 1970s. Canadian Mennonites, noted for their emphasis on pacifism and communal decision making, began to experiment with meetings between victims and offenders to establish restitution. From these simple beginnings, the victim–offender reconciliation movement was born; it continued to be used widely in Canada and came to the United States (Zehr, 2000). Feminist-inspired victim rights activists played a role in raising consciousness regarding the need for victims to be heard in the criminal justice process.

Restorative justice is the growing movement that aims to change the direction of criminal law by focusing it on the needs of victims and on repairing communities. Unlike retributive justice, which focuses on punishment of the guilty offender, restorative justice takes a more caring approach. Proponents of this nonadversarial model adopt a different lens for viewing crime and rectifying the harm done by the crime. Restorative justice entails active involvement by members of the community operating with official sanction of the local court. Just as calls for retribution often bring out the baser instincts in people, a focus on restoration and empowerment also tends to bring out the best in human nature.

Victim–offender conferencing is probably the most common restorative justice program in the United States; restitution and community service are widely used sanctions. There are now thousands of victim–offender programs in the United States (Orzech, 2006), and many more are operating around the world. New Zealand and Canada make extensive use of family group conferencing and healing circles for work with juveniles.

This focus is relevant to the field of social work first and foremost because social workers may have caseloads containing persons who have been victimized by crime or who are court-ordered into treatment because of offending behavior. Such clients may or may not be entangled with the criminal justice system. Social workers may be directly or indirectly involved in court proceedings; they may even be in a position to influence legislation pertaining to correctional treatment.

To learn how the process works, consider the Canadian healing circle facilitated by social worker Angel Yuen, as reported in the *Toronto Star* (Healing circle shows offenders their human toll, 2001). "All the people touched by an offense have an opportunity to speak about how they were affected," according to the article. "That means an offender sees and hears, firsthand, the human impact of his or her actions. It means the victim hears why the offense occurred. And it means the offender hears his or her own voice, often apologizing through tears, offering to make amends. At the close, a contract is drawn up detailing what took place and how the offender will repair the harm" (p. NE04). The impact of such a community encounter can be positive, eliciting sincere apologies, reconciling neighbors who may then lose their fear of each other. In contrast to court adjudication, the conferencing encourages truth-telling and creative ways of making amends.

In 1991, Vermont decided to overhaul its system, setting up reparative boards statewide to focus on repairing the damage to the victim and community (van Wormer, 2004). Composed of volunteers, the reparative group is charged with ensuring that low-risk, nonviolent offenders are made aware of the impact of their behavior on members of the community. Vermont, in fact, is the first state to implement such conferencing on a statewide basis and the first to institutionalize the restorative justice model. Minnesota followed and instituted restorative initiatives throughout the criminal justice system. Hawaii, as well, has made major strides in adopting this approach, a variety adapted from Native Hawaiian rituals that precede colonization.

The mission of social work is rooted in a set of core values. According to the NASW *Code of Ethics,* the core values of social work are as follows: social justice, dignity and worth of the person, importance of human relationships, integrity, and competence (1996). The priority given to humanity by both social work and restorative justice makes this model of handling wrongdoing especially appealing to social workers, who are uniquely trained to use a humanistic model of engagement (Umbreit & Armour, 2010).

Restorative justice relates closely to *social justice* or fairness in that the victims and offenders each have their interests represented in the proceedings. Social justice is provided to the victim in that effort is made to restore what the victim has lost, while at the same time requiring the offender to face the consequences of his or her acts and the personal pain caused to the victim, the victim's family, the offender's family, and the community. These strategies can be combined with those of community-based corrections to create multifaceted programs of benefit to all involved. Rehabilitation, rather than retribution, is the thrust of this approach.

Through embracing members of the extended family, restorative justice also has been found to be highly effective in minority communities. These minority communities—including Native American, African American, and Latino traditions—are collectively, rather than individually, focused. The Circle Sentencing approach, as used in the Yukon of Canada, utilizes traditional justice processes of tribal communities to view crime holistically. Tapping into the strengths of community resources, the process develops sanctions based on consensus of community members. Often a strong spiritual component is part of such sentencing and healing circles.

On a global scale, the most amazing example of truth-telling and catharsis for crime has taken place in South Africa before the Truth and Reconciliation Commission. In intensely emotional sessions, former officials of the apartheid regime were brought face-to-face with their victims, many of whom they had tortured. Healing was centered on the communication process itself rather than on retribution for the pain that was inflicted.

Dignity and worth of the person is the second core value of social work. Through restorative justice, the dignity of both the offender and victim are maintained through a process that is the opposite of customary criminal justice proceedings—the orange suit, publicity attached to the arrest and trial, the indignities and accusations heaped on witnesses by lawyers on the opposing side. The focus of restorative justice is on the offender's whole personality, not only on the acts that have caused the harm.

Importance of human relationships is another theme of the restorative justice movement. Through community service projects and psychologically through the contrition and remorse shown toward persons who are injured by the wrongdoing, offenders help compensate for what they have done.

The core social work value of *integrity* is evidenced in a format built on truth and frank disclosure. In contrast to conventional forms of justice, in which the accused remains silent while his or her lawyer fights against disclosures of guilt being admitted into evidence and challenges the integrity of prosecution witnesses, restorative justice encourages open sharing of information among involved parties.

As far as competence is concerned, we can look to the empirical evidence. What does research say about the effectiveness of victim offender conferencing, for example? Follow-up surveys show that victims consistently rate the process positively, according to Umbreit and Armour (2010), director of the Center for Restorative Justice and Peacemaking, School of Social Work, University of Minnesota, St. Paul. The most extensive research to date shows that while the possibility of receiving restitution appeared to motivate victims to enter the mediation process, they reported that meeting the offender and being able to talk about what happened was more satisfying than receiving restitution (Umbreit, Vos, Coates, & Brown, 2003). In closely monitored meetings between inmates and former victims in British Columbia, victims reported they could see the offender as a person rather than a monster. This view helped them feel less fear and more peace. Offenders, in turn, felt more empathy for their victims' feelings and provided evidence of increasing self-awareness.

Restorative justice principles very neatly bridge the gap between the formality of conventional criminal justice processes and the social work ethos. In its incorporation of activities related to personal and community empowerment, spirituality, conflict resolution, healing of relationships through dialogue, and learning techniques of decision making inspired by indigenous people's traditions, restorative justice effectively links practice with policy. Because restorative justice is about uniting rather than dividing people on opposite sides of the law, and whole communities, it also offers common ground between theoretically diverse disciplines, one of which, in the simplest terms, seeks to protect the individual from the society, and the other which serves to protect society from the individual (at least, certain individuals). The field of criminal justice deserves credit for the leadership it has provided in bringing much needed innovations that have taken place in prisons and courtrooms and churches across the land. References to restorative justice are ubiquitous in the criminal justice literature. If you type in restorative justice on the *Criminal Justice Abstracts* search engine, for example (as of August 2011), you will find more than 1,400 listings, compared to a mere 18 at *Social Work Abstracts*. Interestingly, the social work listings are all fairly recent, reflecting the fact that this model, at last, has gained some recognition within the profession.

Challenges for the Future

Schooled in strength-based interventions, social workers, at the present time, are striving to shift from a deficit, pathology-based model to one that builds on the untapped resources of people and communities. Criminal justice initiatives at the state and local levels are steadily moving in a more humanistic and pragmatic direction as well. The realization that massive numbers of released prisoners will be returning to in their communities is the impetus for serious concern about the need for expanded social services at all government levels (Orzech, 2006; Stoesen, 2006).

There has been a growing concern also in recent years regarding the increasing number of offenders and victims in urgent need of mental health treatment and social services, some of whom are at high risk of future violence if they do not receive the evidence-based interventions they urgently need. Our vision for the future is that all vulnerable and at-risk clients will have the opportunity to be helped by especially trained social work advocates, clinicians, and policymakers. Forensic work is complex and involves an understanding of systems: intrapsychic, interpersonal, familial, and societal. Case management is an important model with the highly vulnerable offender populations, one of the many services in which social workers excel. The primary functions of case management include intake assessment, formulating personal objectives and service goals, treatment planning, linking with informal and formal support groups, resource identification, matching clients to agencies and concrete services, monitoring, outcome evaluation, and termination. Forensic social workers often focus on providing the full range and continuum of concrete services and clinical interventions to their clients.

One of the major opportunities for forensic social workers and educators is to orient and inform legislators, juvenile and adult correctional administrators, corrections professionals, and students about the latest model offender treatment and prevention programs as well as the latest research documenting the effectiveness of these programs in reducing recidivism (Roberts, 2004b). At the present time, too many legislators, correctional administrators, and practitioners are unaware of the latest research documenting the most effective interventions. As indicated by McNeece and Jackson (2004), the current emphasis in a number of states on punitive treatment and contracting out to private correctional companies who care only about making money by providing the lowest cost services are unjust, ineffective, and inhumane. A number of promising, humane, and effective rehabilitation programs are available in different parts of the United States.

Roberts (2004b) and Springer (2004) documented more than 10 different evidence-based offender treatment models that are effective based on longitudinal research. These evidence-based interventions include: probation monitored restitution and work placement; establishing offender treatment goals and targets for change; motivational interviewing and solution-focused treatment; structured wilderness education programs;

occupational trades training and job placement; multisystemic therapy; problem-solving skills training; brief strategic family therapy; cognitive-behavioral approaches such as anger management and behavioral contracting; community day treatment and aftercare by case managers; and graduated community-based sanctions.

The tension between social control and social support is an ongoing and necessary one with which the profession must continue to struggle. Issues of poverty, gender, race, ethnicity, disabilities, domestic violence, mental illness, and pregnant and parenting substance abusers intersect with forensic social work. For decades there has been a debate among social workers as to whether we should help involuntary clients. A growing group of dedicated forensic social workers have navigated, advocated for, and overcome obstacles for their clients in the criminal justice system. Social workers in forensic settings do their best to adjust to the constraints of courts and correctional settings, while advocating for offenders and victims to realize their full potential.

The social work profession, with its long history of advocating for community-based treatment, believing that most human beings are redeemable, and stressing interdisciplinary teamwork, can expect to play an increasingly active role in facilitating such nonadversarial forms of justice as restorative justice. The challenge to members of social work, "the policy based profession" (Popple & Leighninger, 2010), is to discover ways of making correctional strategies more consistent with the ethic of social justice and to participate in the planning and implementation of restorative community justice and other progressive initiatives. Several trends in criminal justice complement social workers' values and perspectives (Reamer, 2004). Chief among these, as Reamer indicates, is the growth of interest in mediation and restorative programming. Alexander (2008), in his entry in the *Encyclopedia of Social Work*, discusses the importance of social work to the growing restorative justice movement. Effective strategies for restorative justice advocacy are as follows: to embark on cost-effective analyses of ongoing programs; engage in special outreach efforts to victim/witness assistance groups to dispel any initial skepticism; unite with progressives in the field of criminal justice as well as natural allies at the grassroots level for educational efforts; lobby legislators for funding of state and local pilot projects for certain designated categories of offenders; and, finally, build community support with outreach to minority groups, especially native populations, to promote a restorative framework. If we can begin to repair the harm that has been done to the offender while helping the offender take responsibility for his or her actions, the offender will begin to repair the harm he or she has done to the community. At the same time, paying attention to the victim's emotional and physical needs can promote recovery of personal losses and a sense of satisfaction through active involvement in the resolution and reconciliation process.

To learn more about restorative justice and ways this model can be integrated into various realms of social work practice—in the school system, child welfare, corrections, and victim assistance programs—we refer readers to two landmark contributions to the field. The first is *Social Work and Restorative Justice: Skills for Dialogue, Peacemaking, and Reconciliation* (edited by Beck, Kropf, and Leonard, 2011), which examines the ways in which social work and restorative justice intersect. The second title, *Restorative Justice Dialogue: An Essential Guide for Research and Practice* (Umbreit and Armour, 2010) is equally indispensible, social work–focused, and beautifully written. Together, these publications should help galvanize the field of forensic social work to move forward and in new directions consistent with social work values.

Toward 21st-Century Global Practice

Twentieth-first century practice has extended to a global practice setting with social problems that have no defined borders. National and international statistics reveal the disproportionate criminal justice involvement or poverty levels of people and the persistence of political torture, prison abuse, and genocide with minimal intervention to stop it (United Nations, 2010). The continued violation of civil and legal rights leaves women and children vulnerable to human trafficking, undocumented workers without access to services or civil liberties, and lesbians and gays without fundamental civil rights (Jou & Lazzarro, 2009; Maschi, Bradley, & Ward, 2009). In the early decades of the 21st century, social work had the opportunity to rejuvenate its reformer past to more actively combat structural violence and oppression underlying these global catastrophes.

Forensic Social Work: Social Justice and Human Rights-Based Practice

The era of competency-based education, including advancing human rights and social justice (CSWE, 2008), has elevated the specialized skills that forensic social workers commonly use, including advocacy and policy reform efforts, to help oppressed populations, such as women, children, people of color, and offenders. Forensic social work as a unified field of practice in both local and global settings is promising.

Social Justice

Social justice pursuits, such as transforming the criminal and juvenile justice systems to end unfair practices (e.g., the disproportionate criminal justice involvement of minorities and the global oppression of women) are another emerging trend where social workers can renew their efforts. If social justice is defined as an ideal condition in which every person is granted equal rights, protections, social benefits, and opportunities (Maschi, Baer, & Turner, 2011), there is surely more work to be done in the local and global arenas. As illustrated by the examples below, the ''justice'' system remains replete with social injustices in which institutional structures and everyday practices sustain oppression, such as racial biases in sentencing and the unfair court treatment of female rape victims and individuals with mental health histories or prior social service use (Schwalbe, Smith-Hatcher, & Maschi, 2009). Interpersonal, institutional and systemic inequities serve to advance the interests of dominant groups (e.g., whites and men) at the expense of others (e.g., people of color and women), including their rights, civil protections, and opportunities to actualize their full human potential (Maschi et al., 2011).

The Promise of Family Justice

An emerging trend that impacts forensic practice is the shift from a juvenile justice and criminal justice (or individual focus) to a family-focused approach to criminal justice or *family justice* model. A family justice model adopts a broad definition of family (e.g., immediate and extended family). It uses a multidisciplinary approach that includes fields such as public health, mental health, education, child welfare, housing, and law-enforcement agencies. It emphasizes a strengths-based approach (in a traditionally punitive system) to assess the strengths and assets of an individual and family. This model is applied throughout the different stages of the justice system, from arrest, to sentencing, to incarceration, to reentry into the community (Vera Institute of Justice, 2011). A family justice model is a very promising because it now involves families in offender rehabilitation and in cross-systems communication and continuity of care for individuals who have been victimized or who were charged of criminal offenses and who also may be involved in other systems, such as medical, mental health, social service, or substance abuse services.

Human Rights

Another emerging trend in forensic practice is its close alignment with the growing human rights movement in both social work and the world. In consonance with social work values, human rights are those "universal rights" that are inherent in our nature, "belong to every person," and honor the inherent "dignity and worth" of all persons. Since the future of forensic practice includes system reform efforts, human rights provide an internationally recognized mechanism and set of principles and laws to help guide the reform process. Social workers can help the oppressed populations, commonly by using empowerment strategies that help to foster equity in civil and political, economic, social, cultural rights, and collective rights (Wronka, 2008).

Human rights–based practice includes being aware of major international agreements that can be used to advocate for the attainment of human rights, such as children, refugees, and political asylees. Becoming familiar with the Universal Declaration of Human Rights (UDHR; United Nations, 1948) is an important first step. Ratified by the United Nations in 1948, the UDHR is a universally accepted legal document mandated by most world governments to fulfill human rights; it has been referred to as an "International Magna Carta" for all nations. Other important international human rights agreements that were adopted by many countries also can be used to guide practice. In 1976, these documents included the International Covenant on Civil and Political Rights. Today the UDHR along with these covenants comprise the International Bill of Rights (Wronka, 2008).

Despite progress in human rights over the past 60 years, as a collective, forensic practitioners can advocate to advance these rights within the United States. Despite being the "land of the free," the United States continues to lag behind in support for human rights. Since the signing of the UDHR, the United States has only signed and ratified major parts of the International Covenant on Civil and Political Rights (1966), which recognizes civil and political human rights (e.g., the right to life and liberty and rights to freedom of expression). In 1978, President Carter also signed the International Covenant on Economic, Social, and Cultural Rights (1966) that recognizes economic, social, and cultural rights (e.g., the rights to food, clothing, housing, and health care; Reichert, 2003). Additionally, as of 2010, the United States has made some strides, such as the election of the first African American president and the consideration of a bill proposing universal health care for all Americans, although, the U.S. government has not yet ratified this covenant (Wronka, 2008). In fact, the United States has ratified only a small number of other human rights international documents and lags far behind many other nations in its legal commitment to human rights.

Moreover, the few documents ratified by the United States include the Convention on the Prevention and Punishment of the Crime of Genocide (1948), International Convention on the Elimination of Racial Discrimination (1965), and the Convention against Torture and Other Cruel, Inhuman, or Degrading Treatment or Punishment (1984). Other important international treaties and documents remain unsigned or unratified by the United States. For example, the United States and Somalia are the only world nations who have not yet ratified the Convention on the Rights of the Child (1989). The United States also has not ratified the Convention to Eliminate Discrimination against Women (1979), which guarantees the equality of women to men, although U.S. grassroots support for it is growing (Reichert, 2003).

Therefore, emerging trends in forensic practice are research and practice strategies that advance human rights and social justice. This includes systems reform in juvenile justice, criminal justice, health care, immigration, mental health, victims' rights, civil rights for women, and for racial-ethnic and homosexual minorities, who are often victims of crimes, including hate crimes. For example, forensic practice efforts could be focused on juvenile and criminal justice human rights reform. This includes advocating for the rights of offenders of all ages detained in penal institutions, the rights of minorities disproportionately involved in the criminal justice system, the rights of criminal offenders to rehabilitation and training, the rights of children born to women prisoners, the rights of juvenile prisoners, the rights of political prisoners, the rights of probationers and the rights of those sentenced to capital punishment.

There also is the potential to greatly improve the dehumanizing aspects of prison, including improving prison conditions themselves, and to improve community conditions, such as living in poverty and crime-ridden neighborhoods, that place people at risk of engaging in criminal offenses. Some relevant United Nations documents with direct implications for 21st-century forensic social work for juvenile and criminal justice reform (listed in chronological order) include the Universal Declaration of Human Rights (1948); the Standard Minimum Rules for the Treatment of Prisoners (1955); the International Covenants on Economic, Social and Cultural Rights (1966); the Convention against Torture and Other Cruel, Inhuman, or Degrading Treatment or Punishment (1984); the Safeguards guaranteeing protection of the rights of those facing the death penalty (1984); the United Nations Standard Minimum Rules for the Administration of Juvenile Justice (1985); the Basic Principles on the Independence of the Judiciary (1985); and the Convention on the Rights of the Child (1989). Forensic social workers can familiarize themselves with the documents and the United Nations committees designated to address the issues that are most relevant to their practice issue and/or population (UN, 1994).

Forensic practice strategies could include the United Nations' (1994) 11 recommended intervention strategies to help advance human rights, which forensic social workers can adapt. These intervention strategies include: (1) work with local, regional, and national organizations to promote, develop, and implement needed changes in policy, planning, and programming on human rights issues, (2) recognize and adapt existing services to maximize effectiveness, (3) develop and involve appropriate and qualified leaders from the community to identify, plan, and implement needed services and advocacy efforts, (4) develop self-capacities of those disadvantaged in their human rights, (5) organize previously unorganized disadvantaged groups for self-help, (6) form alliances with like-minded social and political movements, (7) develop mechanisms to enhance local and global awareness, including the use of mass media, (8) fundraise for the cause, (9) assess the impact of actions undertaken in collaboration with persons and groups affected and associated groups and organizations, (10) document and disseminate information on human rights abuses, and (11) promote legislation that benefits disadvantaged groups (UN, 1994).

If forensic social workers individually and collectively engage in one or more of these strategies in their local communities, these incremental efforts can make a significant difference, as illustrated by our history. As we look forward with a human rights and social justice perspective, there is an opportunity to learn from our past to foster the new century of possibilities. Forensic social work history suggests the most effective efforts were when individual and social level action converged. In the 21st century, advancing the mission of forensic social work involves equipping practitioners with an awareness of human rights and social justice as well as the knowledge and skills to effectively navigate the legal system. This set of knowledge, values, and skills has potential for the next century of forensic social workers to achieve a memorable history of their own.

Conclusion

We wrote this chapter in recognition of the social work profession's past century of dedication to serving oppressed, vulnerable, at-risk, and devalued groups. During this time, the most neglected and devalued groups have been victims of violent crimes and criminal offenders. In the past two decades, professional social workers have made significant progress in advocating for and obtaining critically needed social services for juvenile offenders, adult offenders and victims of violent crimes and in placing student in the correctional field. We look to the support of our professional organizations—Society of Social Work and Research (SSWR), the National Association of Forensic Social Work (NAFSW), the Council on Social Work Education (CSWE), the National Association of Social Workers (NASW)—in recognizing the far-reaching potential of forensic social work.

In this chapter, we viewed how strategies built on a strengths perspective, stages of change, and motivational enhancement at the micro level, and principles of restorative justice at the macro level can do much to reduce the punitive ethos of the present system and move the system forward toward a focus on rehabilitation rather than retribution.

Our expectation is that the profession of social work will provide critically needed leadership in the correctional field and will reconnect with and reclaim, as a profession, the critically important domains of juvenile and criminal justice. This chapter is dedicated to that end.

Key Terms

Forensic social work	Motivational interviewing	Stages of change
Human rights	Restorative justice	Victim–offender conferencing

Review Questions for Critical Thinking

1. If you had an opportunity to work in the criminal justice field, how do you think your social work background would help you thrive in this field? What would be the challenges related to social work values?

2. In what way or ways is restorative justice considered a revolutionary model?

3. Consider the concept of social justice. How does the U.S. criminal justice system diverge from the teachings of a social justice model?

Online Resources

National Organization of Forensic Social Work: www.nofsw.org

Journal of Forensic Social Work: www.tandf.co.uk/journals/ WFOR

University of Minnesota Center for Restorative Justice and Peacemaking: http://rjp.umn.edu/index.html

Restorative Justice online: www.restorativejustice.org

References

Alexander, C. (1995). Distinctive dates in social welfare history. In R. Edwards & G. J. Hopps (Eds.), *Encyclopedia of social work* (19th ed., pp. 2631–2647). Washington, DC: National Association of Social Workers Press.

Alexander, R. (2002). *Understanding legal concepts that influence social welfare policy and practice*. Belmont, CA: Wadsworth.

Alexander, R. (2008). Criminal justice. In National Association of Social Work, *Encyclopedia of Social Work* (20th ed., Vol. 1; pp. 470–476). Washington, DC: NASW Press.

Ashford, J. (2009). Overview of forensic social work. In A. Roberts (Ed.), *Social workers' desk reference*. (pp. 1055–1060). New York, NY: Oxford University Press.

Barajas, E., Jr. (1995). *Moving toward community justice. Topics in community corrections*. Washington, DC: U.S. Department of Justice.

Barker, R. L. (2003). *The social work dictionary* (5th ed.). Washington, DC: National Association of Social Workers Press.

Barsky, A. (2010). *Ethics and values in social work: An integrated approach for a comprehensive curriculum*. New York, NY: Oxford University Press.

Battjes, R. J., Gordon, M. S., O'Grady, K. E., Kinlock, T. W., & Carswell, M. A. (2003). Factors that predict adolescent motivation for substance abuse treatment. *Journal of Substance Abuse Treatment, 24*(3), 221–232.

Beck, E., Kropf, N., & Leonard, P. (Eds.) (2011). *Social work and restorative justice: Skills for dialogue, peacemaking, and reconciliation*. New York, NY: Oxford University Press.

Bureau of Justice Statistics (2010a, December). *Correctional populations in the United States, 2009*. Washington, DC: U.S. Department of Justice.

Bureau of Justice Statistics (2010b, December). *Prisoners in 2009*. Washington, DC: U.S. Department of Justice.

Bureau of Justice Statistics. (2010c, October). *Criminal Victimization, 2009* (NCJ 231327). Washington, DC: U.S. Department of Justice.

Convetion against Torture and other Cruel, Unhuman, or Degrading Treatment or Punishment (1984). Retrieved from http://untreaty.un.org/cod/avl/ha/catcidtp/catcidtp.html

Convention to Eliminate Discrimination against Women (1979). Retrieved from http://www.un.org/womenwatch/daw/cedaw/

Convention on the Prevention and Punishment of the Crime of Genocide (1948). Retrieved from http://www.hrweb.org/legal/genocide.html

Convention on the Rights of the Child (1989). Retrieved from http://www2.ohchr.org/english/law/crc.htm

Council on Social Work Education (2008) *2008 Educational Policy and Accreditation Standards* [online]. Retrieved May 1, 2008, at: www.cswe .org/accreditation/EPAS/EPAS_start.htm

Council on Social Work Education (2009). *Statistics on social work education in the United States.* Alexandria, VA: CSWE. Retrieved October 15, 2011 from www.cswe.org/CentersInitiatives/ DataStatistics/ProgramData/47673/47683.aspx

Davis, F. S. (2006). *Victims of crime: A social work response, building skills to strengthen survivors.* Rockville, MD: U.S. Department of Justice: Office of Justice Programs.

Davis, F. S., & Lockhart, L. (2010). *Domestic violence: Intersectionality and culturally competent practice.* New York, NY: Columbia University Press.

Day, P. J. (2008). *A new history of social welfare* (8th ed.). Boston, MA: Allyn & Bacon.

de Zerega, M., & Verdone, M. (2011). *Setting an agenda for family-focused justice reform.* Vera Institute of Justice. Retrieved March 29, 2011 from http://www .vera.org/files/FJP-advisory-board-report-v6

Encyclopedia of social work (19th ed.). Washington, DC: National Association of Social Workers Press.

Ellis, A. (2001). *Overcoming destructive beliefs, feelings, and behaviors: New directions for national emotive behavior therapy.* Essex, UK: Prometheus Book.

Encyclopedia of social work (20th ed.). National Association of Social Work. Washington, DC: NASW Press.

Gibelman, M. (1995). *What social workers do.* Washington, DC: National Association of Social Workers Press.

Ginsberg, L. (1995). *The social work almanac.* Washington, DC: National Association of Social Workers Press.

Gumz, E. (2004). American social work, corrections, and restorative justice: An appraisal. *International Journal of Offender Therapy and Comparative Criminology, 48,* 449–460.

Healing circle shows offenders their human toll. (2001). *Toronto Star*, p. NE04.

Hicks, S. 2011

Hubbard, R. L., Cavanaugh, E. R., Craddock, S. G., & Rachel, J. V. (1985). Characteristics, behaviors, and outcomes for youth in the TOPS. In G. M. Beschner & A. S Friedman (Eds.), *Treatment services for adolescent substance abusers* (Treatment Research Monograph Series, DHHS Publication No. ADM 84–1286). Rockville, MD: National Institute on Drug Abuse.

Huddleston, C. W. (2011, May 24). "All rise!" National drug court month demonstrates that drug courts are a proven budget solution. The Partnership at drugfree.org. Retrieved May 24, 2011 from http://drugfree.org/jointogether

International Covenant on Civil & Political Rights (1966).

International Covenant on Human Rights (1966).

International Covenant on the Elimination of Racial Discrimination (1965).

Irwin, J. (1980). *Prisons in turmoil.* New York, NY: Little, Brown.

Johnson, H. W. (1998). *The social services: An introduction* (5th ed.). Belmont, CA: Wadsworth.

Jou, M. K., & Lazarro, L. (2009). Collaborative forensic social work with immigrants and refugees. In T. Maschi, C. Bradley, & K. Ward (Eds.), *Forensic social work: Psychosocial and legal issues across diverse practice settings* (pp. 374–394). New York, NY: Springer.

Keilitz, S. (2002). Specialized domestic violence courts. In A. R. Roberts (Ed.), *Handbook of domestic violence intervention strategies* (pp. 147–172). New York, NY: Oxford University Press.

Killian, M. L., & Maschi, T. (2009). A history of forensic social work in the United States. In T. Maschi, C. Bradley, and K. Ward (Eds.), *Forensic social work: Psychosocial and legal issues in diverse practice settings.* (pp. 11–20). New York, NY: Springer.

Longshore, D., Grills, C., & Annon, K. (1999). Effects of a culturally congruent intervention on cognitive factors related to drug-use recovery. *Substance Use and Misuse, 34*(9), 1223–1241.

Mapp, S. C. (2008). *Human rights and social justice in a global perspective: An introduction to international social work.* New York, NY: Oxford University Press.

Martinson, R. (1974). What works? Questions and answers about prison reform. *Public Interest, 35,* 22–54.

Maschi, T., Bradley, C., & Ward, K. (Eds). (2009). *Forensic social work: Psychosocial and legal issues in diverse practice settings.* New York, NY: Springer.

Maschi, T., Baer, J., & Turner, S. (2011). The psychological goods on clinical social work: a content analysis of the clinical social work and social justice literature. *Journal of Social Work Practice, 25*(2), 233–253.

McNeece, C. A., & Jackson, S. (2004). Juvenile justice policy: Current trends and 21st century issues. In A. R. Roberts (Ed.), *Juvenile justice sourcebook: Past, present, and future* (pp. 41–68). New York, NY: Oxford University Press.

Miller, W. R., Forcehimes, A., & Zweben, A. (2011). *Treating addiction: A guide for professionals.* New York, NY: Guilford Press.

Miller, W., & Rollnick, S. (1996). *Motivational interviewing: Preparing people to change addictive behavior.* New York, NY: Guilford Press.

Mizrahi & Davis (Eds.) *Encyclopedia of Social Work.*

Mueser, K., Noordsy, D., Drake, R., & Fox, L. (2003). *Integrated treatment for dual disorders: A guide to effective practice.* New York, NY: Guilford Press.

Mullen, P. D., Velasquez, M. M., von Sternberg, K., Cummins, A. G., & Green, C. (2005, April). Efficacy of a dual behavior focus, transtheoretical model-based motivational intervention with transition assistance to present an alcohol-exposed pregnancy (AEP) after a jail term. Poster presented at the 26th annual meeting and Scientific Sessions for the Society of Behavioral Medicine, Boston, MA.

National Association of Social Workers. (1996). *Code of ethics.* Washington, DC: Author.

National Association of Social Workers (2011). *Choices: Careers in social work.* Washington, DC: NASW Press. Retrieved October 15, 2011 from http://www.socialworkers.org/pubs/choices/choices1.asp#Justice

Office for Victims of Crime. (2011). *Report to the Nation 2011.* Washington, DC.

Orzech, D. (2006). Criminal justice social work—New models, new opportunities. *Social Work Today, 6*(6), 34–37.

Pavelka, S. (2008). Restorative justice legislation and policy: A national assessment. International *Journal of Restorative Justice, 14*(2), 100–118.

Polansky, N. (1986). There is nothing so practical as a good theory. *Child Welfare, 65*(1), 3–15.

Popple, P. R., & Leighninger, L. L. (2010). *The policy based profession: An introduction to social welfare policy analysis* (5th ed.). Boston, MA: Allyn & Bacon.

Popple, P. R., & Leighninger, L. L. (2011). *Social work, social welfare, and American society* (8th ed). Boston, MA: Allyn & Bacon.

Pray, K. (1945). The place of social casework in the treatment of delinquency. *Social Service Review, 19*, 244.

Prochaska, J. O., & DiClemente, C. C. (1984). *The transtheoretical approach: Crossing the traditional boundaries of therapy.* Homewood, IL: Dow Jones-Irwin.

Prochaska, J. O., & Norcross, J. C. (1999). *Systems of psychotherapy: A transtheoretical analysis* (4th ed.). Pacific Grove, CA: Brooks/Cole.

Prochaska, J. O., Norcross, J. C., Fowler, J. L., Follick, M. J., & Abrams, D. B. (1992). Attendance and outcome in a work site weight control program: Processes and stages of change as process and predictor variables. *Addictive Behaviors, 17*(1), 35–45.

Prochaska, J. O., Velicer, W. F., Rossi, J. S., Goldstein, M. G., Marcus, B. H., Rakowski, W., et al. (1994). Stages of change and decisional balance for twelve problem behaviors. *Health Psychology, 13*, 39–46.

Reamer, F. G. (2003). *Criminal lessons: Case studies and commentary on crime and justice.* New York, NY: Columbia University Press.

Reamer, F. G. (2004). Social work and criminal justice: The uneasy alliance. In E. Judah & M. Bryant (Eds.), *Criminal justice: Retribution vs. Restoration* (pp. 213–231). Binghamton, NY: Haworth.

Reichert, E. (2003). *Social work and human rights: A foundation for policy and practice.* New York, NY: Columbia University Press.

Roberts, A. R. (1996). *Helping battered women: New perspectives and remedies.* New York, NY: Oxford University Press.

Roberts, A. R. (1997a). The history and role of social work in law enforcement. In A. R. Roberts (Ed.), *Social work in juvenile and criminal justice settings* (2nd ed., pp. 105–115). Springfield, IL: Charles C Thomas.

Roberts, A. R. (1997b). The role of the social worker in victims/witness assistance programs. In A. R. Roberts (Ed.), *Social work in juvenile and criminal justice settings* (2nd ed., pp. 150–159). Springfield, IL: Charles C Thomas.

Roberts, A. R. (1998a). Community strategies with juvenile offenders. In A. R. Roberts (Ed.), *Juvenile justice: Policies, programs, and services* (2nd ed., pp. 126–134). Chicago, IL: Nelson-Hall.

Roberts, A. R. (1998b). *Juvenile justice: Policies, programs, and services* (2nd ed.). Chicago, IL: Nelson-Hall.

Roberts, A. R. (2004a). The emergence of the juvenile court and probation services. In A. R. Roberts (Ed.), *Juvenile justice sourcebook: Past, present and future* (pp. 163–182). New York, NY: Oxford University Press.

Roberts, A. R. (Ed.). (2004b). *Juvenile justice sourcebook: Past, present, and future.* New York, NY: Oxford University Press.

Roberts (2007). Battered Women & Their Families.

Roberts, A. R. (Ed.). (2007). *Correctional counseling and treatment.* Upper Saddle River, NJ: Prentice-Hall.

Roberts, A. R., & Brownell, P. (1999). A century of forensic social work. *Social Work, 44*(4), 359–369.

Roberts, A. R., & Springer, D. W. (2007). *Social work in juvenile and criminal justice settings.* Springfield, IL: Charles C. Thomas.

Roberts, A. R., Springer, D. W., & Brownell, P. (2007). The emergence and current developments in forensic social work. In A. R. Roberts & D. W. Springer (Eds.),

Social work in juvenile and criminal justice settings (pp. 5–24). Springfield, IL: Charles C Thomas.

Roberts, A. R. (2009) (Ed.). *Social workers' desk reference* (2nd ed.). New York, NY: Oxford University Press.

Rome, S. H. (2008). Forensic social work. In *Encyclopedia of social work* (20th ed.) (Vol. 3, pp. 221–223). National Association of Social Work. Washington, DC: NASW Press.

Saleebey, D. (2009). Power in the people: Introduction. In D. Saleebey (Ed.), *The strengths perspective in social work practice* (5th ed., pp. 1–23). Boston, MA: Allyn & Bacon.

Samenow, S. (1984). *Inside the criminal mind*. New York, NY: Times Books.

Schwalbe, C., Smith-Hatcher, S., & Maschi, T. (2009). The effects of treatment needs and prior social services utilization on juvenile court decision making. *Social Work Research, 33,* 31–40.

Seymour, C. B., & Hairston, C. F. (2001). *Children with parents in prison: Child welfare policy, program, and practice issues.* Piscataway, NJ: Transaction.

Solomon, B. (1994). *The empowerment tradition in American social work: A history.* New York, NY: Columbia University Press.

Springer, D. W. (2004). Evidence-based treatment of juvenile delinquents with externalizing disorders. In A. R. Roberts. (Ed.), *Juvenile justice sourcebook: Past, present and future* (pp. 365–380). New York, NY: Oxford University Press.

Springer, D. W., McNeece, C. A., & Arnold, E. M. (2003). *Substance abuse treatment for criminal offenders: An evidence-based guide for practitioners.* Washington, DC: American Psychological Association.

Springer, D. W., Rivaux, S. L., Bohman, T., & Yeung, A. (2006). Predicting retention in three substance abuse treatment modalities among Anglo, African American and Mexican American juvenile offenders. *Journal of Social Service Research, 32*(4), 135–155.

Springer, D. W., & Roberts, A. R. (Eds.). (2007). *Handbook of forensic mental health with victims and offenders: Assessment, treatment, and research.* New York, NY: Springer.

Stoesen, L. (2006). Prisoner reentry: Reclaiming the challenge: Professionals often have criminal justice backgrounds. *NASW News,* p. 4.

Studt, E. (Ed.). (1959). *Education for social workers in the correctional field: Social work education study* (Vol. 5). New York, NY: Council on Social Work Education.

Tahmincioglu, E. (2010, February, 17). Unable to get jobs, freed inmates return to jail. MSNBC News. Retrieved October 15, 2011 from www.msnbc .msn.com/id/35263313/ns/business-personal_finance/t/unable-get-jobs-freed-inmates-return-jail/

Umbreit, M., Vos, B., Coates, R. B., & Brown, K. A. (2003). *Facing violence: The path of restorative justice and dialogue.* Monsey, NY: Criminal Justice Press.

Umbreit, M., & Armour, M.P. (2010). *Restorative justice dialogue: An essential guide for research and practice.* New York, NY: Springer.

United Nations. (1948). Universal declaration of human rights. New York, NY: Author. Retrieved June 1, 2006, from http://www.un.org/en/documents/udhr

United Nations. (1994). Human rights and social work: A manual for schools of social work and the social work profession. Geneva, Switzerland: United Nations Centre for Human Rights.

United Nations. (2010). Programme of work: United Nations Statistical Division. Retrieved January 5, 2010, from http://unstats.un.org/unsd/default.htm

van Wormer, K. (2004). *Confronting oppression, restoring justice: From policy analysis for restorative justice.* Alexandria, VA: Council on Social Work Education Press.

van Wormer, K. (2006). *Introduction to social welfare and social work: The U.S. in global perspective.* Belmont, CA: Thomson.

van Wormer, K. (2009). *Death by Domestic Violence.*

van Wormer, K. (2010). *Working with female offenders: A gender-sensitive approach.* Hoboken, NJ: John Wiley & Sons.

van Wormer, K., & Bartollas, C. (2010). *Women and the criminal justice system* (3rd ed.). Boston, MA: Pearson.

van Wormer, K., & Davis, D. R. (in press). *Addiction treatment: A strengths perspective* (3rd ed.). Belmont, CA: Brooks/Cole.

Vera Intstitute of Justice, 2011.

Wronka, J. (2008). Human rights. In T. Mizrahi & L. E. Davis (Eds.), *Encyclopedia of social work* (20th ed., pp. 425–429). Washington, DC: National Association of Social Workers.

Wallace, B. C. (2005). *Making mandated addiction treatment work.* Lanham, MD: Aronson. In A. Roberts (Ed.), *Social workers' desk reference* (pp. 1055–1060). New York, NY: Oxford University Press.

Yeager, K. R. (2009). Overview of alcohol and drug dependence. In A. Roberts (Ed.), *Social workers' desk reference* (pp. 833–842). New York, NY: Oxford University Press.

Young, D. S. (2008). Social work practice in the justice system. In D. M. DiNitto and C. A. McNeece (Eds.), *Social work: Issues and opportunities in a challenging profession* (3rd ed.) (pp. 311–332). Chicago, IL: Lyceum Books.

Young, D. S., & LoMonaco, S. W. (2001). Incorporating content on offenders and corrections into social work curricula. *Journal of Social Work Education, 37*(3), 475–489.

Zehr, H. (2000). *The little book of restorative justice.* Intercourse, PA: Good Books.

Chapter 9
Veterinary Social Work Practice

Elizabeth Strand, Bethanie A. Poe, Sarina Lyall,
Jan Yorke, Janelle Nimer, Erin Allen,
Geneva Brown, and Teresa Nolen-Pratt

> Is it ethical to attend to animals in social work practice?

Social workers have attended to human–animal issues in practice for more than 30 years. The first known peer-reviewed account acknowledging the presence of animals in the social environment of clients was a case summary published in *Social Work* (Bikales, 1975). Gerda Bikales wrote about a medical social worker and a canine "case management client." The social worker recounted the case of an elderly woman and her only companion, "Lacey the mutt," with social work colleagues, and her "...sad ruminations brought forth a chorus of instant recognition and the somewhat stunned realization that they had discovered a sleeper in casework practice" (p. 150). This case summary, however, begs the question: is the canine the social work client, and if so, is that an ethical social work practice that should actually be taught in social work education and embraced by the social work profession?

Risley-Curtiss, Holley, and Wolf (2006) writes about the social work profession, "To give companion animals short shrift means we are missing a potentially vital connection and are paying only lip service to our claims of an ecological approach" (p. 267). Since 1975, social work literature has addressed issues of pet loss (Margolies, 1993) animal-assisted therapy (Reichert, 1998), companion animals and well-being (Sable, 1995), the importance of pets for the elderly (Netting & Wilson, 1987), the link between interpersonal violence and animal abuse (Strand & Faver, 2005), social work implications of animal hoarding (Arluke, Frost, Steketee, et al., 2002), the human–animal bond and diversity (Risley-Curtiss, 2006), and even social work in veterinary clinic settings (Netting, Wilson, & New, 1987).

Increasingly, colleges and schools of social work are incorporating content about human–animal relationships in social work education. This has taken the forms of classes providing a general overview of human–animal issues in peoples' social environments, online courses to provide certification in the treatment of animal abuse, certification in animal-assisted interventions, as well as field work in animal-related settings. However the underpinnings that support providing this type of education are not yet on solid ground but founded on debate. Is it appropriate for social work to provide educational credit for learning how to intervene with animal "case management clients," as Bikales defines it?

In 2000, Wolf called on the social work profession to include animal rights as part of the ethical responsibility of social workers. Although Wolf (2000) acknowledged that the NASW Code of Ethics specifies that social work provides help and support to "human beings," he argues that animals must still be included because (a) social workers must attend to the environmental issues plaguing human welfare across the world and animals fall into these "environmental issues," and (b) animals are an "oppressed population" and, like women and people of color whose rights have benefited from social work advocacy, animals also deserve to enjoy this advocacy. Wolf argues that to extend advocacy only to humans and not to animals is "speciesism" and a violation of the NASW Code of Ethics to advocate for oppressed populations.

In 2003, in response to Wolf's call, O'Brien (2003) writes that social workers engaging in animal rights advocacy put social work clients at risk. A major philosophical argument in animal rights is the argument for marginal cases (AMC), which states that there is no justifiable reason why a human being with lowered cognitive abilities should have rights that a nonhuman animal with the same level of cognitive abilities should not also have. O'Brien warns that, "by comparing marginal humans to animals, the AMC may unwittingly dehumanize people with cognitive disabilities and be yet another way our society justifies maltreatment of its most vulnerable members," (p. 331). This debate continues in a recent book by Thomas Ryan (2011) entitled, *Animals and Social Work: A Moral Introduction* in which Ryan rewrites social work codes of ethics to include consideration of animals within the ethical scope of social work practice.

Given social work's attention toward animals and the ensuing debates regarding that attention, it is necessary to have a paradigm for addressing these inevitable issues in the practice, education, and research of social work intervention in a cogent and clear manner. Special knowledge about human–animal relationships and the implications this knowledge has for social work practice are warranted.

The Development of Veterinary Social Work

The development of *veterinary social work* as a specialized area of social work practice is the answer to social work's professional quandary of what to do about animals. It not only adheres to the ethics, practice, and paradigm of social work, but also relies on the expertise of the veterinary medical profession for attending to the needs of animals within the wide-ranging oath that all veterinarians take. The ethical requirement to practice only within areas of competence makes partnering with the profession most knowledgeable about animals essential. Moreover, the breadth of practice veterinary medicine covers is only matched by how diverse a degree in social work can be. Therefore, veterinary social work is much broader than offering social work in a small animal veterinary practice, but includes vast areas of public health practice.

Human–animal studies is a very rich academic endeavor that is intensely multidisciplinary in nature. The development of veterinary social work not only follows social work's history of developing highly specialized knowledge in specific populations, but also takes the interdisciplinary history of human–animal studies and explores the result by "marrying" two professions to create an interdisciplinary partnership—creating highly specific approaches for dealing with human–animal relationships in a pragmatic, concrete day-to-day way in the lives of people and animals. In any good marriage, both partners are changed for the better through the union. Therefore the mission of veterinary social work is to support, inform, and enhance both professions in an interdisciplinary manner.

The Human–Animal Relationship

The remainder of this chapter reviews salient literature on the human–animal relationship and the four areas of veterinary social work: (1) the link between human and animal violence, (2) animal-assisted interactions, (3) grief and bereavement, and (4) compassion fatigue management. Then attention is directed toward veterinary social work as an ethical sub-specialty of social work practice. Lastly, future directions of veterinary social work are addressed.

Human beings value their relationships with companion animals as evidenced by the number of animals they own. Recent studies suggest that companion animals live in approximately 60% of American households including 60 million dogs, 70 million cats, 10 million birds, 5 million horses, and a variety of other small rodents, reptiles, and exotic pets (American Veterinary Medical Association [AVMA, 2007). Animals are often considered family members, playing an important role in child development, buffering loss and loneliness for children and the elderly, as well as contributing to health and wellness in a number of ways (Cohen, 2002; McNicholas et al., 2005; Melson, 2003)

North American culture portrays animals in the media dichotomously as human replicas, as well as consumer items. Animals are embedded in children's lives from the time they are born in toys, nursery rhymes, fairytales, books, and clothing (Franklin, 1999; Melson & Fine, 2006; Myers, 1988). Cultural edits include folklore (black cats, smothered babies) and cultural stereotypes (dogs as man's best friend) that socially construct animals, shaping our attitudes and our actions toward them. Animal welfare concerns and the important role that animal products play in our diets, economy, and national security all contribute to the impact of human–animal relationships.

Some of the early research in this field points to human–animal relationships as prophylactic with respect to risks in cardiac patients, such as contributing to the lowering of blood pressure and enhancing the quality of life for seniors, the disabled, the homeless, those with HIV/AIDS, and those who are lonely or isolated (Friedmann, Thomas, & Eddy, 2000). Companion animals intersect with important events and rituals in human-to-human relationships, connecting humans to the passage of life stages as well as significant benchmarks in their lives (Turner, 2005). Animals also become surrogate partners, children's friends, and companions in humans' lives, and are often bred and trained to act and look like humans. Serpell (2002) calls this the "cute" factor—fashioning animals in breeding to appear attractive and baby-like in their features, celebrating their birthdays, dressing them in clothes, and generally encouraging anthropomorphic attitudes toward them.

Human–animal relationships are enduring, and the attachments that are formed have been described in the literature as the human–animal bond. The American Veterinary Medical Association describes this relationship in the following way:

> The human–animal bond is a mutually beneficial and dynamic relationship between people and animals that is influenced by behaviors that are essential to the health and well-being of both. This includes, but is not limited to, emotional, psychological, and physical interactions of people, animals, and the environment. The veterinarian's role in the human–animal bond is to maximize the potentials of this relationship between people and animals.

> The AVMA officially recognizes: (1) the existence of the human–animal bond and its importance to client and community health, (2) that the human–animal bond has existed for thousands of years, and (3) that the human–animal bond has major significance for veterinary medicine, because, as veterinary medicine serves society, it fulfills both human and animal needs. (AVMA, retrieved October 4, 2011, http://www.avma.org/issues/human_animal_bond/default.asp)

This description speaks to the complexity and uniqueness of each human–animal partnership, as well as the obligation veterinarians have toward these relationships.

Measuring the extent and nature of the human–animal relationship has become more succinct but in many ways is still elusive. There are factors that appear to predict the nature of these relationships; for example, rescued animals are often animals with which humans have strong attachments (Lagoni, Butler, & Hetts, 1994). On the other hand, it is difficult to predict why a farmer or a breeder becomes attached to a particular cow or horse, given all of the animals they interact with, or what makes that relationship different or more intense than any other that they have.

Human–animal relationships exist across a continuum that Milani (1995) described broadly as "utilitarian" or "needs dependent." Utilitarian relationships include chattel orientations, research, food/production, or working animals where emotional ties to so many animals can overwhelm the individual (for example, bomb dogs in police work). Extremes on this end of the continuum can be exploitive and perhaps even abusive. Utilitarian relationships can also depict animals as objects or commodities (puppies with bows as gifts, pocket pets, ornaments), losing their value and owner's interest over time (Milani, 1995). On the other end of the continuum are need–dependency relationships that most resemble human-to-human relationships. These animals are siblings, children, companions, and partners to the human, fulfilling needs not otherwise met, and generating predictable feelings of grief and loss when they depart. The extreme on this end of the continuum may appear as enmeshed attachments that can result in hoarding, excessive rescuing, or even Munchausen's by proxy (clients who intentionally injure their animals to procure an ongoing relationship with veterinarians). Actualizing relationships, in the middle range of the spectrum, are reciprocal interactions that appear to be appreciated by both the human and the animal and not driven by utility or emotional support.

Whatever circumstance provides an avenue for a particular human–animal relationship, it can be argued that an effect will occur for both parties, for better or worse. Social work has a role in supporting, utilizing, and intervening in these important relationships to access help for at least the human beings that they serve. This help may, and hopefully will, have beneficial effects for animals as well. This could mean providing grief support at times of loss; resource support should a herd have to be culled, putting a family at financial risk; and even recognizing an abusive behavior toward an animal as a sign of potential psychopathology.

The Link Between Human and Animal Violence

Animal abuse is often defined in human and animal violence research as: "Socially unacceptable behavior that intentionally causes unnecessary pain, suffering, or distress to and/or death of an animal" (Ascione, 1993, p. 282). Within the past 20 years, researchers have investigated the relationships between animal cruelty and family violence (Adams, 1995; Arluke, Levin, Luke, & Ascione, 1999; Ascione, 1998; Faver & Strand, 2003, Felthous, 1980; Flynn 2000a, 2000b; Strand & Faver, 2005), including effects on children (Arluke, 2002; Ascione, 1993; Ascione, 2001; Ascione, Thompson, & Black, 1997; Duncan & Miller, 2002; Flynn, 1999; Hayden & Scarpa, 2005; Hensley & Tallichet, 2005; Kellert & Felthous, 1985; C. Miller, 2001; K. Miller & Knutson, 1997; Quinn, 2000; Wright & Hensley, 2003), and the elderly (Lockwood, 2002; Rosen, 1995).

Battering is a pattern of behavior used to establish power and control over another person within an intimate relationship using fear and intimidation, and often including the threat or use of violence (National Coalition Against Domestic Violence [NCADV], 2005). Adams (1995) identified three categories of reasons why batterers are cruel to animals: the enhancement of the batterer's dominance, the promotion of victim helplessness, and the maintenance of exclusivity within the abusive relationship. Research around the United States has found that companion animals are routinely threatened, harmed, and killed in domestic violence situations (Ascione,

1998; Ascione et al., 1997; Farer & Strand, 2003; Flynn, 1999; Flynn, 2000b; Strand & Faver, 2005). Concern for the safety of their pets can also influence women to delay leaving their violent situations; 12 independent surveys found that between 18% and 48% of battered women have delayed leaving, or have returned to their batterer, out of fear for the welfare of their pets or livestock (Ascione, 2007).

Childhood animal cruelty is one of the earliest signs of conduct disorder and best predictors of future aggression (Ascione, 1993; Kellert & Felthous, 1985; C. Miller, 2001; Quinn, 2000). The true prevalence and societal impact of pathological animal abuse are difficult to determine, because animal cruelty is often conducted in secret, only known by the perpetrator(s), therefore limiting the validity of adult caretaker reporting (Ascione, 2001; C. Miller, 2001). Additionally, most of the available reports are retrospective accounts by adults who abused animals as children (Hayden & Scarpa, 2005). However, it is estimated that approximately half of children are exposed to some type of animal cruelty (Flynn, 2000a; K. Miller & Knutson, 1997) with approximately 20% of those reporting that they have perpetrated animal abuse (Flynn, 2000a). Male children are much more likely than females to be exposed to animal abuse as well as to perpetrate animal abuse (Arluke, 2002; Ascione, Friedrich, Heath, & Hayashi, 2003; Flynn, 1999; Flynn, 2000a; Hayden & Scarpa, 2005). Childhood animal cruelty has been linked to exposure to domestic violence, sexual abuse, paternal use of corporal punishment, paternal neglect, and drug and/or alcohol abuse (Ascione, 2001; Ascione, 2007; Flynn, 2000a)

As demonstrated, there is a growing body of literature illustrating the correlations between the presence of child abuse and animal abuse in the home. This body of evidence has prompted 14 states to enact some form of a cross-reporting law (Arkow, 2011; Nolen, 2001). Cross-reporting laws stipulate that while working in an official capacity, child welfare and animal welfare professionals who observe or have suspicions of abuse or neglect of children or animals, respectively, are obligated to report their observations to the appropriate agencies. Therefore, that means that when child welfare professionals and animal welfare professionals are doing their jobs, they also look for signs of the other types of abuse. Child-welfare workers should be aware of the condition of the animals in clients' homes and be willing and capable of asking questions if they have suspicions that something abusive or neglectful is happening; conversely, animal welfare workers should also be looking for signs that children may be in danger when working animal cruelty cases. As of October 1, 2011, 14 states have passed some form of a law or combination of laws that permit or require child welfare and animal welfare organizations to cross-report (Arkow, 2011). Three states—Maine, California, and Oregon—have permissive cross-reporting laws that give the professionals the option of cross-reporting. Connecticut, Illinois, West Virginia, Louisiana, California, Massachusetts, Colorado, Nebraska, Ohio, Tennessee, and Virginia all have mandated reporting laws that require that the agencies cross-report to one another.

Based upon the literature citing the co-occurrence of child abuse and animal abuse in the same households, cross-training of child protection professionals and animal welfare professionals is recommended. In doing so, both professions would be better able to identify warning signs of abuse or crisis in children and in animals. If these signs are detected, there is greater potential that children will receive the services they need and animals be removed from dangerous situations when professionals report to one another. However, while what literature there is about cross-reporting agrees that it would be beneficial (D. Long, Long, & Kulkarni, 2007; Montminy-Danna, 2007; L. Zilney & Zilney, 2005), there is no literature showing that child welfare and animal welfare are routinely looking for the signs of abuse in the other group, or that they know what to do if they do notice warning signs, nor is there literature at present showing that making cross-reporting a law has improved cross-reporting rates.

Elder abuse also has a co-occurrence with violence to animals. It has been estimated that only 7% of all cases of elder abuse co-occurring with violence to animals reported (Pillemer & Finkelhor, 1988). In 2001, the Humane Society of the United States (HSUS) and the National Center on Elder Abuse (NCEA) surveyed 200 adult protective service (APS) workers from 40 different states and found that 35% of APS workers reported their clients talking about pets being threatened, injured, killed, or denied care by a caregiver. Forty-five percent of APS workers reported finding evidence of intentional caregiver neglect or abuse of pets when visiting clients. About 75% of APS workers noted that clients' concern for pet welfare affected decisions, such as whether to go to a hospital or nursing home. Lastly, 92% of the APS workers noted that animal neglect and self-neglect were coexisting, indicating that animal neglect may be a warning sign of the elderly person's inability to care for him or herself (NCEA, 2001; Pillemer & Finkelhor, 1988).

Another form of animal cruelty that has been linked to the elderly population is animal hoarding, or keeping an excessive number of animals without being able to provide adequate food, shelter, sanitation, or veterinary care. While it is believed that hoarders do not start out with the intention of amassing large quantities of animals, things get out of control and they lose perspective quickly. Animal hoarders generally have an overwhelming belief that they are providing good care for the animals, despite contrary evidence. They may also see themselves as the only one who cares about the animals, and believe that the animal shelter will only euthanize the animals. Animal hoarders live in a state of denial that can prevent them from truly seeing the conditions in which they and the animals are living (Patronek, 1999, 2006; Patronek & Nathanson, 2009).

Throughout each of the areas of the link between human and animal violence, it is clear that the circumstances people are experiencing influence the treatment of their animals. Social workers need to be knowledgeable about the link between human and animal violence and to be able to use that knowledge in order to better serve their client populations, whether that means helping a woman find a safe place for her pet so that she can leave an abusive partner, evaluating a child and the childs' family after learning about a child's abuse of a family pet, or connecting an elderly person to services after noticing that he or she is not taking care of his/her pet.

Animal-Assisted Interactions

Animal-Assisted Interactions (AAI) is the all-encompassing term that includes animal-assisted interventions and human–animal interactions. This can mean the intentional use of animals such as a dog or horse to attain some identified therapeutic goal, such as in animal-assisted therapy. It can also reference the relationship between a person and their companion animal, whatever that animal is: a bird, a cat, a ferret, a lama, or a pot-bellied pig. As indicated earlier, there are observed health and mental health benefits to these human–animal relationships. Additional animal-assisted interactions can include the interactions between a farmer and his or her herd, the relationship between the worker in a slaughterhouse and the animal "going to market" (Coleman, McGregor, Hemsworth, Boyce, & Dowling, 2003) and even the relationships between classroom pets and the children who interact with them. Given the breadth of "animal-assisted interactions" in veterinary social work, attention will be limited to animal-assisted interventions, including those utilizing horses. The first recorded therapeutic use of animals was in 1792 at the York Retreat in York, England, for people deemed to be insane. It was believed that the animals were of therapeutic value, and a program involving animals was implemented to help patients gain a sense of self-control and responsibility (Bustad & Hines, 1982). This humane approach valued kindness and understanding over the typical rigorous and harsh treatment delivered to the mentally ill. Reflecting on the advantages arising from the patient–pet relationship, an 18th-century belief about the human–animal relationship indicated that in addition to affording the patients pleasure, the interaction with animals sometimes tended to awaken social and benevolent feelings (Brickel, 1981; Levinson, 1969).

Some benefits of animal-assisted interventions have included decreased depression (Salmon, 1981), improved mental health (Kawamura, Niiyama, & Niiyama, 2007; Lutwack-Bloom, Wijewickrama, & Smith, 2005; Salmon, 1981), increased social interactions (Bernstein, Friedmann, & Malaspina, 2000; Haughie, Milne, & Elliot, 1992; Richeson, 2003; Zisselman, Rovner, Shmuely, & Ferric, 1996), reduced loneliness (M. Banks & Banks, 2002, 2005), reduced psychosis (Furstenberg, Rhodes, Powell, & Dunlop, 1984), and decreased blood pressure (Harris, Rinehart, & Gertsman, 1993).

Ways animals can help increase mental health in humans can vary according to the human and animal interaction and therapist. Maggitti (1987) defined AAI as a working theory grounded in the notion that animals can often help people when other people cannot. Currently, the literature on AAI has not agreed upon an overall term regarding the use of animals as an adjunct to traditional therapeutic interventions. Therefore, following Kruger and Serpell's (2006) recommendations, we define *animal-assisted interventions* as the deliberate inclusion of an animal in the therapeutic process, which includes the term that most people are familiar with, *animal-assisted therapy*. Animal-assisted interventions require a licensed therapist (e.g., physical therapist, recreational therapist, social worker), treatment goals that need to be accomplished, and the complete documentation of the goals and results of the individual who is participating in the animal-assisted intervention. Additionally, the inclusion of an animal is necessary to accomplish outcomes believed to be difficult to achieve without the animal (Nimer & Lundahl, 2007). Animals used in AAIs are trained to be touched, grabbed, hugged, and so forth without notice.

A professional should go through five specific steps to develop appropriate AAIs. The first step is to complete an assessment. This assessment needs to be done on the client as well as the animal to decide if they would be therapeutically compatible with one another. The second step is to review the client's diagnoses, as some diagnoses may be better to suited to AAIs than others, or certain animals may be more appropriate than others. The third step is to review the client's symptoms. Animals should not be placed in dangerous situations, and therefore clients displaying violent behaviors may not be appropriate for AAIs. The fourth step for the therapist is to review the client's treatment goals to decide whether an animal could help the client reach his/her goals. The final step is to develop an animal-assisted intervention that could help a client reach his/her treatment goals (Howie, 2000).

Animal-assisted interactions that do not use specific therapeutic interventions with a licensed professional include animal-assisted activities, service animals, and all other animals with which an individual might come in contact. Animal-assisted activities (AAA) are when animals and their owners volunteer to visit public locations (e.g., long-term care facilities, hospitals, schools) (Chandler, 2005). Service animals are trained to be medical assistants to the disabled and are legally permitted to accompany their owner into any facility (Chandler, 2005; Lane, McNicholas, & Collis, 1998). These animal interactions may bring feelings of confidence, support, and happiness to an individual.

Companion animals can also be used as a therapeutic intervention. When this happens, companion animals are placed with individuals on a permanent basis to therapeutically benefit the individual as a part of the treatment plan. Some benefits of using companion animals as therapeutic interventions include increased quality of life (Hart, 2006), decreased depression (Garrity, Stallones, Marx, & Johnson, 1989), increased positive behaviors (Hendy, 1984), increased social behaviors (D. Miller, Staats, & Partlo, 1992; Raina, Waltner-Toews, Bonnett, Woodward, & Abernathy, 1999), increased exercise (Roger, 2001), and decreased blood pressure (Riddick, 1985). However, if a companion animal cannot be properly cared for, it can have a negative impact on the animal owner, so extreme caution and a thorough assessment about capacity for responsible animal ownership is needed when introducing animal ownership.

The bonds formed between people and animals in animal-assisted interactions can be strong. Because of the generally shorter life span of animals, many people who bond to animals—clients receiving animal-assisted interventions, stewards whose herd has been in the family for generations, or handlers of therapy or service animals—experience grief and bereavement when they die. This is another area of practice for veterinary social work.

Grief and Bereavement

Any time a valued relationship is severed, a sense of loss and grieving might be expected. This is the case when human beings lose the valued relationships they have with their animal companions when the animal dies. Since people are likely to enjoy a longer lifespan than do animals, death of a companion animal can be anticipated for most pet owners. Over the past two decades, a number of authors have addressed this issue (Carmack, 1985; Cowles, 1985; Morley & Fook, 2005; Sable, 1995; Stallones, 1994). Some have analyzed the effects on individuals and families caused by the loss of a pet (Lagoni, Butler & Hetts, 1994) while others have addressed methods of supporting those grieving the loss of a pet (Milani, 1998; Toray, 2004; Turner, 2003). The broader body of literature related to death and loss (Becvar, 2003; Boss, 2006; Grollman, 1995; James & Friedman, 1998; Jarrat, 1994, York, 2000) also has application to pet loss.

It would appear useful that social workers providing service to people experiencing the loss of companion animals address two broad areas. The first area relates to the need to understand the reactions that may be expected from those whose animals have died or are terminally ill and, in addition, to know what circumstances and factors may influence these grief reactions. The second area requires that the program have a clear sense of what support and interventions are desirable and effective in assisting people in their loss of their animals and to provide these interventions in a compassionate and timely manner.

In our culture, typical reactions to the death of a loved one include confusion, crying, despair, forgetfulness, sleep disturbances, and various physical symptoms (Becvar, 2003). The same reactions observed in the loss of a human friend or family member is seen in the loss of a pet (Carmack, 1985; Lagoni, Butler, & Hetts, 1994; Quackenbush & Glickman, 1983). While many people are uncomfortable around grieving people and may hold many expectations and myths about what grieving people need (James & Friedman, 1998), this stance is even more extreme when it comes to the loss of animals.

The particular experience and severity of the grief reaction varies from person to person. The person's perception of the severity of their loss, their prior coping skills, their particular personality characteristics and their social support system all come into play (Becvar, 2003). A strong grief reaction to the loss of a companion animal has sometimes been seen as a pathological response, one unmerited by the magnitude of the loss (Sable, 1995). There is now greater support for viewing the particular loss in context and treating each situation accordingly (Morley & Fook, 2005). The kind of bond the person had with the animal, the emotional and monetary investment her or she had made regarding the animal, the amount of responsibility that is felt in the death of the animal—including the decision to euthanize—may have relevance to the grief reaction, as may the owner's psychological stability and emotionality. Whether or not a person has social support from others is also related to how well he or she copes. All of these issues point to the necessity to determine the particular needs of people who have lost their animals and to provide particular services to meet these needs.

The death of an animal is often *disenfranchised*, or discounted as being a loss worthy of grieving. Those who lose their animals often get the message, either directly or indirectly of, "It was only a dog" or "You can get another cat" (Morley & Fook, 2005). Indeed, Morley and Fook (2005) contend that grief over animal loss has often been pathologized, even by mental health professionals. These societal reactions may leave the grieving person feeling isolated with no one to understand the pain he or she is experiencing. Grief is particularly difficult when little social support is given (Becvar, 2003) and this may be the case when a person grieves the loss of an animal.

There are, of course, ways other than death for a person to lose an animal. Animals may get lost or may have to be given away for a variety of reasons, or an animal may be physically present but, due to illness, injury, or disability, has changed to such a degree that the owner has difficulty reconciling the changes that have taken place and integrating them into his or her former view of their animal. Conflicting feelings of hope, fear, and despair may be held simultaneously, and coming to a place of acceptance of the loss is very difficult. Pauline Boss (2006) calls this experience *ambiguous loss* and identifies it as a kind of "frozen grief," where, of course, closure is impossible.

Anticipatory grief may precede the death of an animal, as owners realize that their companions are aging or as they become seriously ill (Milani, 1998). Thoughts and feelings during this time vary from sadness at the forthcoming loss, to anxiety and exhaustion during the care and treatment of a sick animal, to wishing for death to release the animal from pain and suffering. The question of euthanasia may arise during this time as people attempt to determine what their responsibility is in ending the pain and suffering their animal may come to experience. These experiences and feelings are often accompanied by guilt, despair, and by a sense of being overwhelmed.

Effective support can be categorized in three general areas (Turner, 2003). The first is that people need to have their grief respected and normalized and to realize that their reaction is normal in light of their loss. An animal-related grief support group is one place this can happen for people, where they can be with others who understand their grief. People need, also, the opportunity to talk about their animal, to tell stories and construct meaning about what the animal has meant to them, and how it has changed their lives. A third thing they may need is help in problem solving and decision making. Decisions around treatment options and about euthanasia may need to be made. There may also be decisions about who to tell about the animal's death and how to do this, especially when children are involved; whether to cremate or bury the body; and how to honor and memorialize their animal. In addition to these services, some people may need a referral to a therapist or long-term grief counselor who understands the importance of the human–animal relationship. Also, more and more attention is being given to palliative and hospice care in veterinary medicine. These new developments include the incorporation of counselors as part of the health care team (Johnson, Patterson-Kane, Lamison, & Noyes, 2011).

Since animals can provide emotional support, engender a sense of responsibility, help reduce feelings of loneliness and isolation, and are often considered to be family members, confidants, and friends (K. Kaufman & Kaufman, 2006; Sable, 1995; Toray, 2004), the loss of animals can elicit feelings of grief similar to, or in some cases greater than, the loss of a human life (Dunn, Mehler, & Greenberg, 2005; Sharkin & Knox, 2003; Toray, 2004). Individuals who lack aforementioned support to help them cope with the loss may feel overwhelmed and isolated; therefore, it is not uncommon to hear individuals make suicidal statements after experiencing the loss of their animals (Lagoni, Butler, & Hetts, 1994). Having a client express suicidal thoughts can be disturbing to a veterinary team. Veterinary social workers are in a position to assist veterinary teams by, first and foremost, providing education to the team that the major loss of a relationship or family member can be a risk factor for suicidal ideation (Cheng, Chen, Chen, & Jenkins, 2000; Conwell, Duberstein, & Caine, 2002). Education about some of the risk factors or warning signs of suicide is perhaps the most important part of the social worker's role with the veterinary team. Social workers can help create a protocol for the team to follow if a client makes a suicidal statement. This may include a list of questions the veterinarian should ask the client; statements the veterinarian can make to assure the client that the veterinarian cares and the client is being taken seriously; and a list of resources, such as phone numbers for local mental health professionals and suicide hotlines, that the veterinarian can use if they feel the client is at high risk of committing suicide. Social workers can, also, provide a safe space for veterinary teams to discuss their thoughts and feelings about hearing a client make suicidal statements. There is compelling evidence that this form of support is very important for the health and well being in the veterinary environment. Without it, veterinary teams are at risk of developing compassion fatigue, the final area of veterinary social work.

Compassion Fatigue Management

Animal-related professionals include veterinarians, veterinary technicians, animal rescue workers, animal control officers, animal shelter workers, zookeepers, animal laboratory researchers, animal advocacy workers, and the students or trainees training in each of these areas. These professionals experience difficulties related to their work environment, one of the most prevalent of which is compassion fatigue.

Compassion fatigue, or secondary traumatic stress, is a form of burnout that manifests itself as physical, emotional, and spiritual exhaustion (Huggard 2003; Pfifferling & Gilley 2000). Another way of describing compassion fatigue is that it is *the result of working very hard, and caring very much, while not recognizing and caring for one's own personal needs.*

There are a wide variety of symptoms of compassion fatigue, including PTSD; abusing drugs, alcohol, or food; anger; blaming; depression; a diminished sense of personal accomplishment; physical and/or emotional exhaustion; headaches; gastrointestinal complaints; hopelessness; sleep disturbances; inability to maintain a balance between empathy and objectivity; less ability to feel joy; and workaholism. Persistent stress causes people to typically react by either attempting to conserve energy or by remaining overactive (Cohen, 2007). People on the energy-saving end of the spectrum tend to dissociate from stressors, functioning on autopilot (Cohen, 2007). For those who respond to persistent stress by remaining overcharged, compassion fatigue may present itself as hypervigilance and anxiety (Cohen, 2007).

Many risk factors for compassion fatigue are present in animal-related professions, including performing and/or witnessing euthanasia; treating animal cruelty cases; limited financial resources on the part of the organization or animal owner; volume of distressed clients and animals; the constant stream of unwanted and sick animals; and conflict within the workplace.

For veterinarians specifically, there is evidence that problems with stress, anxiety, and depression begin during educational training and continue on into professional life. Not only do veterinary students experience stress, but they also experience anxiety and depression (Hafen, Reisbig, White, & Rush, 2006). In fact, recent research indicates veterinary medical students are more prone to experience depressive symptomology than either human medical students (Hafen, Reisbig, White, & Rush, 2008) or the general population (Strand, Zaparanick, & Brace, 2005). Alarmingly, between 32–68% of veterinary medical student samples at three midwestern universities reported clinical levels of depression symptoms during their first year of study (Hafen et al., 2008).

The mental health difficulties reported by practicing veterinarians suggest that mental health concerns continue beyond veterinary medical school (Tremayne, 2010). Potential outcomes of poor mental health within the practice of veterinary medicine include burnout (L. Miller, 2004), substance abuse (Fishbain, 1986; Kogan & McConnell, 2001), depression

(Shouksmith & Hesketh, 1986; Strand et al., 2005), relationship distress (Bartram, Sinclair, & Baldwin, 2010) and suicide (Fishbain, 1986; Mellanby, 2005). Research from the United Kingdom indicates veterinarians are at a high risk of suicide, at rates approximately four times higher than the general population and twice the rate of other health care professionals (Bartram & Baldwin, 2008; Bartram, Sinclair, & Baldwin, 2010; Mellanby, 2005). While there is not current comparative data for the United States, this international research is attracting increasing attention from the American Veterinary Medical Association (Tremayne, 2010).

Giving bad news (Bragard, Etienne, Merckaert, Libert, & Razavi, 2010), managing adverse events (West, Tan, Haberman, Swan, & Shanafelt, 2009), interacting with difficult clients (Morrisey & Voiland, 2007), and working effectively in teams (Gilling & Parkinson, 2009) create stress for veterinary medical professionals. However, handling these communication-related challenges effectively is extremely important, not only for client satisfaction and patient health, but also for the health and well-being of veterinarians.

New veterinarians report that communication interactions with clients and within veterinary teams are a stressful part of their new role (Riggs, Routly, & Taylor, 2001). Additionally, new veterinarians experience significant stress and associated negative emotions when they make medical mistakes (Mellanby & Herrtage, 2004). A study assessing the psychosocial stress of Australian veterinarians found that higher levels of psychosocial stress (which included dealing with difficult customers and inability to balance work and private life) were associated with higher levels of demoralization and increased substance abuse (Harling, Strehmel, Schablon, & Nienhaus, 2009). Certainly impairment due to substance abuse could be the result of coping with the stress in the veterinary medical environment, much of which is communication related, as well as the cause of medical errors themselves (Fishbain, 1986; Knecht, 1992).

Although communication skills training does provide important skills for veterinarians, providing this training without a component that teaches the communication-related stress management techniques may not produce results needed for excellence in practice and reduction in negative outcomes for patients, clients, and veterinarians. Programs that address both communication skills and stress management techniques are beginning to show positive results (Cohen et al., 2005). In fact, a recent study found that a combination of communication skills training and stress management skills not only improved medical residents' feelings of self-confidence in medical interviews, but also reduced their stress and increased their willingness to communicate with clients about difficult topics such as giving poor diagnoses or poor outcomes. This is the first study to confirm this relationship between communication skills and stress management skills on communication outcomes (Bragard et al., 2010).

Being willing to have tough conversations with clients and colleagues is very important in handling complex ethical and interpersonal challenges in veterinary medicine. In fact, a breakdown in communication in these situations is often cited as one of the factors that prompts clients to pursue malpractice claims (Panting, 2004). However, even if communication skills training has been provided, veterinary professionals still may experience a high level of emotional and physical distress communicating in these complex and often emotionally charged situations. This level of emotional and physical dysregulation can negatively impact the communication skills needed for ensuring the highest level of ethical and compassionate care. Therefore, providing skills that address both communication and physical and emotional stress management skills are important as a risk management strategy in veterinary medical practice. Social workers have the skill-set necessary to help veterinarians and other animal-related professionals to recognize, as well as develop methods of addressing, factors that contribute to compassion fatigue on both micro and macro levels.

Veterinary Social Work and the Ethics of Practice

Because animals themselves have varying levels of importance and use in the eyes of people and the law, those professionals who care for animals often find themselves in disagreement with others' ideas and beliefs about "what is right" regarding care and stewardship of animals. There is intense conflict in the field regarding this subject. Social workers with mediation skills and a capacity to maintain a neutral position on issues of animal care and stewardship can create the space for conflict around these issues to be resolved. Therefore, the veterinary social worker is trained to contribute stress management, communication skills training, and mediation skills in managing the effects of compassion fatigue.

According to Risley-Curtiss (2010), it appears that social work practitioners have a basic working knowledge about the positive and negative aspects of human–animal relationships, yet only a small percentage of social workers are inquiring about animals in their assessments or utilizing animals in their interventions. When we consider that approximately 60% of American households have companion animals, social work is overlooking a crucial part of the ecological system by failing to acknowledge human–animal relationships (Risley-Curtiss, 2010).

Social work specialties are always emerging as the profession advances and meets the needs of an ever-changing society. Currently, social workers can specialize in hospital social work, school social work, organizational social work, gerontological social work, and even forensic social work. Given the knowledge base as well as the present debate regarding human–animal relationships, and given social work's commitment to practicing within an ecologically sensitive social context, the next essential step is the development of specialized social work knowledge and practice dedicated to human–animal relationships.

In veterinary social work, the practice is to look to animals as both a reflection of human functioning and as a method of enhancing that functioning. This is accomplished by viewing the human–animal relationship from both macro and micro perspectives. The four areas of veterinary social

Figure 9.1

Examples of practice areas at micro and macro levels of veterinary social work.

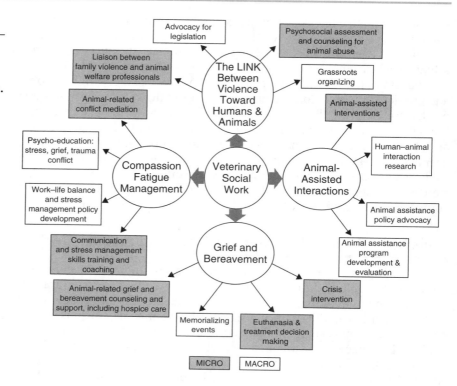

work — the link between human and animal violence, animal-assisted interactions, grief and bereavement, and compassion fatigue management — are all viewed and applied within the micro and macro social work paradigm.

The term we use for this specialized practice is "veterinary social work." This terminology is in keeping with other subspecialties that have social workers in hosted settings, such as school social work or hospital social work. Other terms have arisen for animal-sensitive social work practice such as *animal-assisted social work* or *human–animal bond specialist*; however, we argue that these terms neglect to give proper credit to the profession that has expertise in the knowledge and stewardship of animals and their welfare. These terms may also come perilously close to inviting social workers to operate outside their areas of competence, focusing more on animal-related issues of health and welfare than they are trained to do.

We all know that veterinarians are the people who take care of sick animals. However, veterinarians practice within very diverse populations and settings. They can be found in medical practice, in government regulatory roles, research, public health, academia, and industry, to name just a few. The veterinarian oath reads:

> Being admitted to the profession of veterinary medicine, I solemnly swear to use my scientific knowledge and skills for the benefit of society through the

protection of animal health and welfare, the prevention and relief of animal suffering, the conservation of animal resources, the promotion of public health, and the advancement of medical knowledge.

I will practice my profession conscientiously, with dignity, and in keeping with the principles of veterinary medical ethics.

I accept as a lifelong obligation the continual improvement of my professional knowledge and competence.

In this veterinary oath, there are similarities with the National Association of Social Workers Code of Ethics. Phrases such as "benefit society," "welfare," "prevention and relief of...suffering," "promotion of public health," "dignity," "knowledge and competence," are readily found in the ethical guidelines that govern social work practice as well. Like social workers, veterinarians are dedicated to the improvement of society through competent, ethical practice in a wide variety of settings. The name *veterinary social work* sets clear boundaries, including adherence to the social work code of ethics and practicing within the scope of human–animal interactions found in the social work literature, as well as within a sound partnership with the veterinary profession, which focuses its expertise on animal welfare and health.

As shown by the description of the four areas of veterinary social work, there are broad client populations and practice settings in which to conduct this work. However, the question still remains: Is attending to human–animal relationships truly a part of social work practice? At first glance, it may seem counterintuitive to say that the NASW Code of Ethics implies the need to attend to human–animal relationships, as social workers are human service professionals, not animal welfare professionals. However, many of the ethical principles and standards imply the need for social workers to attend to human–animal relationships when appropriate.

For instance, NASW Code of Ethics calls for social workers to respect the "dignity and worth of the person," meaning that we have to respect individual differences and beliefs, including those about animals. We are instructed to recognize the importance of human relationships, but we must also recognize that for some clients, human–animal relationships may be influencing or replacing human relationships. We argue that the directive to be culturally competent in our social work practice includes being aware of cultural differences in attitudes and beliefs about animals. When faced with human–animal relationship issues or when choosing to utilize an animal in practice, social workers must be competent in their work. Under the NASW Code of Ethics, social workers have an obligation to research and evaluate their practice, and while the field of human–animal relationships has been developing for more than 30 years, there are still gaps in the knowledge base to be filled. Lastly, social workers are often a part of a multidisciplinary team to assist clients. That team must consist of veterinarians, veterinary technicians, and other animal-related professionals when helping a client cope with an animal issue.

Ryan (2011), in his book *Social Work and Animals: A Moral Introduction*, has rewritten a social work code of ethics to be inclusive of nonhuman animals in social work practice. In fact, in this version of social work ethical guidelines, human and nonhuman animals share equally in moral consideration and social work intervention. It will be very interesting to observe how this debate continues. Veterinary social work's purpose is to specialize in all things relating to the "nonhuman animal," but within the ethical practice of addressing the human factors that affect both human and nonhuman factors. Special effort is always directed toward respecting the expertise of our fellow animal-related professionals when it comes to issues of animal care and welfare.

Current and Future Directions

As in any new field, growing pains are part of the development process. However, veterinary social work is off to a promising start. Currently, there are at least 16 veterinary schools that have a social worker on staff. Pet-loss support groups can be found all around the United States. Social workers who are interested in animal-assisted therapy can receive training from organizations such as the Delta Society or the Equine Assisted Growth and Learning Association (EAGALA) and even specialized courses in social work education. There are also conferences worldwide that address human–animal bond issues, including the 2nd Annual Veterinary Social Work Summit, which occurred in April 2010. Most recently, the University of Tennessee has started offering a veterinary social work certificate program to current master's of social work students at the university, which will be expanded to include post-master's students as well.

Veterinary social work, while off to a good start, has great potential for growth. In addition to programs like the UT veterinary social work certificate program, human–animal relationship topics can be brought into the general curricula of social work education. While individual veterinary practices may not be able to afford to have a social worker on staff full-time to assist clients with pet-loss issues and staff with compassion fatigue management, perhaps several in a community could afford to share a veterinary social worker's time. Recently, the UT veterinary social work program partnered with the American Animal Hospital Association (AAHA) to develop a set of Human Social Support Guidelines for small animal veterinary practices in the United States. These guidelines are the beginning of educating the veterinary profession about human support professionals and how they can extend the mission and practice of the veterinary oath in small animal medicine. Social workers trained in veterinary social work would have the immediate expertise to fill the role of human support in veterinary medicine. Animal shelters and facilities that use lab animals could benefit from having social work services on a regular basis to address compassion fatigue as well, and therefore potentially decrease employee turnover. Animal shelter veterinary social workers can also address animal abuse issues in a community by providing one-on-one counseling to animal abusers, as well as developing programs for care of the animals of domestic violence victims. Lastly, veterinary social work, like school, geriatric, and forensic social work before it, can become a recognized subspecialty of social work practice, endorsed by NASW, so that standards of practice can be developed and enforced.

Conclusion

Human and animal relationships are present in almost all of the settings in which social workers practice, whether it is supporting someone through the grieving process after the death of a beloved animal or speaking to legislators about allowing domestic violence victims to include their companion animals on their Orders of Protection and even in the domestic violence shelter itself. There are also opportunities to expand social work practice into veterinary schools and practices, animal shelters, and other animal-related settings. However, to practice competently in any of the areas of human–animal relationships, proper education and training is necessary. This can be difficult given the debate that surrounds the issue on animals in social work practice. As a recognized subspecialty of social work practice, however, veterinary social work can develop standards of practice, curriculum, and certification that will help to guarantee clients are receiving appropriate and competent care from their social worker, even when the debate ensues. Veterinary social work is not interested in proving the "right or wrong" of including animals in social work practice, but simply to respond to the needs of people who depend on animals in all the ways that people do.

Key Terms

Animal-assisted therapy	Compassion fatigue	Human–animal relationship
Animal cruelty	Ethics	Pet loss

Review Questions for Critical Thinking

1. How can social workers respond to animal issues most ethically in social work practice?

2. What are the four areas of veterinary social work? Give one micro and one macro example of each area of veterinary social work.

3. You are a social worker who is providing services to a family who has been investigated for child abuse. Your job is to provide in-home counseling to help teach parenting skills so that the children (ages 7 and 12) can remain in the home. On your visits, you notice a dog in the yard that is chained and does not always have ready access to water. What would you do?

4. You are in charge of developing an animal-assisted therapy program for a residential treatment center that treats at-risk youth. How would you go about this?

5. You are a social worker serving an elderly client who needs to go into assisted living and possibly a nursing home. She has a failing 17-year-old poodle and will not euthanize it or give consent for anyone to take care of it. What do you do as her social worker? What ethical guidelines are included in your decision making? How do you feel about the situation?

Online Resources

Veterinary Social Work: www.vet.utk.edu/socialwork

Pet-Abuse.Com: www.pet-abuse.com

International Association of Animal Hospice and Palliative Care: www.iaahpc.org

Delta Society: www.deltasociety.org

Compassion Fatigue Awareness Project: www.compassionfatigue.org

American Veterinary Medical Association: www.avma.org

American Animal Hospital Association: www.aahanet.org

American Humane Association: www.americanhumane.org

ASPCA: www.aspca.org

Association of Veterinary Family Practice: www.avfp.org

American Association of Human–Animal Bond Veterinarians: aahabv.org

References

Adams, C. J. (1995). Woman battering and harm to animals. In *Animals and women: Feminist theoretical explorations* (pp. 55–84). Durham, NC: Duke University Press.

Animal Law Coalition. (2009, August 14). Illinois joins states requiring cross-reporting of child and animal cruelty. Retrieved September 30, 2011 from www.animallawcoalition.com/animal-cruelty/article/1015

American Veterinary Medical Association (AVMA). (2007). *U.S. Pet Ownership & Demographics Sourcebook*. Schaumburg, IL: AVMA.

Arkow, P. (2011, July). *The link letter* [Web newsletter]. Retrieved September 30, 2011 from www.nationallinkcoalition.org

Arluke, A. (2002). Animal abuse as dirty play. *Symbolic Interaction*, 25(4), 405–430.

Arluke, A., Frost, R., Luke, C., & Messner, E. (2002). Health implications of animal hoarding. *Health and Social Work*, 27(2), 125–136.

Arluke, A., Frost, R., Steketee, G., Patronek, G., Luke, C., Messner, E., Nathanson, J., & Papazian, M. (2002). Press reports of animal hoarding. *Society & Animals* 10, 1–23.

Arluke, A., Levin, J., Luke, C., & Ascione, F. (1999). The relationship of animal abuse to violence and other forms of antisocial behavior. *Journal of Interpersonal Violence, 14*(9), 963–975.

Ascione, F. R. (1993). Children who are cruel to animals: A review of research and implications for developmental psychopathology. *Anthrozoos, 6*, 226–247.

Ascione, F. R. (1998). Battered women's reports of their partners' and their children's cruelty to animals. *Journal of Emotional Abuse, 1*(1), 119–133.

Ascione, F. R. (2001). *Animal abuse and youth violence.* Washington, DC: Office of Juvenile Justice and Delinquency Prevention.

Ascione, F. R. (2007). Emerging research on animal abuse as a risk factor for intimate partner violence. In K. Kendall-Tackett & S. Giacomoni (Eds.), *Intimate partner violence* (pp. 3.1–3.17). Kingston, NJ: Civic Research Institute.

Ascione, F., Friedrich, W., Heath, J., & Hayashi, K. (2003). Cruelty to animals in normative, sexually abused, and outpatient psychiatric samples of 6- to 12-year-old children: Relations to maltreatment and exposure to domestic violence. *Anthrozoos, 16*(3), 194–212.

Ascione, F. R., Thompson, T. M., & Black, T. (1997). Childhood cruelty to animals: Assessing cruelty dimensions and motivations. *Anthrozoos, 10*(4), 170–197.

Banks, M. R., & Banks, W. A. (2002). The effects of animal-assisted therapy on loneliness in an elderly population in long-term care facilities. *Journal of Gerontology: Medical Sciences, 57A*(7), M428–M432.

Banks, M. R., & Banks, W. A. (2005). The effects of group and individual animal-assisted therapy on loneliness in residents of long-term care facilities. *Anthrozoos, 18*(4), 396–408.

Bartram, D., & Baldwin, D. (2008). Mental health and wellbeing survey. *Veterinary Record, 162*, 868.

Bartram, D. J., Sinclair, J. M., & Baldwin, D. S. (2010). Interventions with potential to improve the mental health and wellbeing of UK veterinary surgeons. *Veterinary Record, 166*(17), 518–523.

Becvar, D. (2003). *In the presence of grief.* New York, NY: Guilford Press.

Bernstein, P. L., Friedmann, E., & Malaspina, A. (2000). Animal-assisted therapy enhances resident social interaction and initiation in long-term care facilities. *Anthrozoos, 13*(4), 213–224.

Bikales, G. (1975, March). The dog as "significant other." *Social Work*, 150–152.

Boss, P. (2006). *Loss, trauma, and resilience: Therapeutic work with ambiguous loss.* New York, NY: W.W. Norton & Company.

Bragard, I., Etienne, A. M., Merckaert, I., Libert, Y., & Razavi, D. (2010). Efficacy of a communication and stress management training on medical residents' self-efficacy, stress to communicate, and burnout: A randomized controlled study. *Journal of Health Psychology, 15*(7), 1075–1081.

Brickel, C. M. (1981). A review of the roles of pet animals in psychotherapy and with the elderly. *International Journal of Aging & Human Development, 12*(2), 119–128.

Bustad, L. K., & Hines, L. M. (1982). People and pets: A positive partnership. In proceedings, 3rd symposium, *Pets in society: The social importance of pets in an aging society.* Toronto, Canada, April.

Carmack, B. J. (1985). The effects on family members and functioning after the death of a pet. In M. B. Sussman (Ed.), *Pets and the family* (pp. 149–161). New York, NY: Haworth Press.

Chandler, C. K. (2005). *Animal-assisted therapy in counseling.* New York, NY: Taylor and Francis Group.

Cheng, A. T., Chen, T. H., Chen, C. C., & Jenkins, R. (2000). Psychosocial and psychiatric risk factors for suicide: Case-control psychological autopsy study. *British Journal of Psychiatry, 177,* 360–365. Retrieved from http://bjp.rcpsych.org/cgi/reprint/177/4/360

Cohen, D., Rollnick, S., Smail, S., Kinnersley, P., Houston, H., & Edwards, K. (2005). Communication, stress and distress: Evolution of an individual support programme for medical students and doctors. *Medical Education, 39*(5), 476–481.

Cohen, S. P., (2002). Can pets function as family members? *Western Journal of Nursing Research, 24*(6), 621–6.

Cohen, S. P. (2007). Compassion fatigue and the veterinary health team. *Veterinary Clinics of North America: Small Animal Practice, 37*(1), 123–134

Coleman, G., McGregor, M., Hemsworth, P., Boyce, J., & Dowling, S. (2003). The relationship between beliefs, attitudes, and observed behaviours of abattoir personnel in the pig industry. *Applied Animal Behaviour Science, 82*(3), 189–200

Conwell, Y., Duberstein, P. R., & Caine, E. D. (2002). Risk factors for suicide in later life. *Society of Biological Psychiatry, 52,* 193–204. Retrieved from www.public-health.uiowa.edu/ICMHA/outreach/documents/Risk-FactorsforSuicideinLaterLife.pdf

Cowles, K. V. (1985). The death of a pet: Human responses to the breaking of the bond. In M. B. Sussman (Ed.), *Pets and the family* (pp. 135–148). New York, NY: Haworth Press.

Duncan, A., & Miller, C. (2002). The impact of an abusive family context on childhood animal cruelty and adult violence. *Aggression and Violent Behavior, 7,* 365–383.

Dunn, K. L., Mehler, S. J., & Greenberg, H. S. (2005). Social work with a pet loss support group in a university veterinary hospital. *Social Work in Health Care, 4*(2), 59–70. Retrieved from www.haworthpress.com/web/SWHC

Faver, C. A., & Strand, E. B. (2003). To leave or to stay? Battered women's concern for vulnerable pets. *Journal of Interpersonal Violence, 18*(12), 1367–1377.

Felthous, A. R. (1980). Aggression against cats, dogs, and people. *Child Psychiatry and Human Development. 10*(3), 169–177.

Fishbain, D. A. (1986). Veterinarians with psychiatric impairment—a comparison with impaired physicians. *Journal of the National Medical Association, 78*(2), 133–137.

Flynn, C. P. (1999). Exploring the link between corporal punishment and children's cruelty to animals. *Journal of Marriage and the Family, 61*(4), 971–981.

Flynn, C. P. (2000a). Why family professionals can no longer ignore violence toward animals. *Family Relations, 49,* 87–95.

Flynn, C. P. (2000b). Women's best friend: Pet abuse and the role of companion animals in the lives of battered women. *Violence Against Women, 6,* 162–177.

Franklin, A. (1999). *Animals and modern cultures: A sociology of human-animal relations in modernity.* London, UK: Sage.

Friedmann, E., Thomas, S. A., & Eddy, T. J., (2000). Companion animals and human health: Physical and cardiovascular influences. In A. L. Podberscek & J. A. Serpell (Eds.), *Companion animals and us: Exploring the relationships between people and pets,* (pp. 125–142). Cambridge, UK: Cambridge University Press.

Furstenberg, F. F., Rhodes, P. S., Powell, S. K., & Dunlop, T. (1984). The effectiveness of pet therapy on nursing home patients suffering with dementia. *Gerontologist*, *24*, 240–245.

Garrity, T. F., Stallones, L., Marx, M. B., & Johnson, T. P. (1989). Pet ownership and attachment as supportive factors in the health of older adults. *Anthrozoos*, *3*(1), 35–44.

Gilling, M. L., & Parkinson, T. J. (2009). The transition from veterinary student to practitioner: a "make or break" period. *Journal of Veterinary Medical Education*, *36*(2), 209–215.

Grollman, E. (1995). *Bereaved children: A support guide for parents and professionals*. Boston, MA: Beacon Press.

Hafen, M., Reisbig, A. M., White, M. B., & Rush, B. R. (2006). Predictors of depression and anxiety in first-year veterinary students: A preliminary report. *Journal of Veterinary Medical Education*, *33*(3), 432–440.

Hafen, M., Reisbig, A. M., White, M. B., & Rush, B. R. (2008). The first-year veterinary student and mental health: The role of common stressors. *Journal of Veterinary Medical Education*, *35*(1), 102–109.

Harling, M., Strehmel, P., Schablon, A., & Nienhaus, A. (2009). Psychosocial stress, demoralization, and the consumption of tobacco, alcohol, and medical drugs by veterinarians. *Journal of Occupational Medicine and Toxicology*, *4*, 4.

Harris, M. D., Rinehart, J. M., & Gertsman, J. (1993). Animal assisted therapy for the homebound elderly. *Holistic Nursing Practice*, *8*(1), 27–37.

Hart, L. A. (2006). Community context and psychosocial benefits of animal companionship. In A. H. Fine (Ed.). *Handbook on animal-assisted therapy: Theoretical foundations and guidelines for practice* (pp. 73–94). San Diego, CA: Academic Press.

Haughie, E., Milne, D., & Elliott, V. (1992). An evaluation of companion pets with elderly psychiatric patients. *Behavioral Psychotherapy*, *20*, 367–372.

Hayden, S. C., & Scarpa, A. (2005). Childhood animal cruelty: A review of research, assessment, and therapeutic issues. *The Forensic Examiner*, *14*(2), 23–33.

Hendy, H. M. (1984). Effects of pets on the sociability and health activities of nursing home residents. In R. K. Anderson, B. L. Hart, & L. A. Hart (Eds.), *The pet connection: Its influence on our health and quality of life* (pp. 430–437). Minneapolis, MN: University of Minnesota Press, The Center to Study Human-Animal Relationship and Environments.

Hensley, C., & Tallichet, S. E. (2005). Learning to be cruel? Exploring the onset and frequency of animal cruelty. *International Journal of Offender Therapy and Comparative Criminology*, *49*(1), 37–47.

Howie, A. R. (2000). *Team training course manual* (5th ed.). Renton, WA: Delta Society.

Huggard, P. (2003, February). Compassion fatigue: How much can I give? *Medical Education*, *37*(2), 163–164.

Jarrat, C. J. (1994). *Helping children cope with separation and loss*. Boston, MA: Harvard Common Press.

James, J. W., & Friedman, R. (1998). *Grief recovery handbook*. New York, NY: HarperPerennial.

Johnson, C. L., Patterson-Kane, E., Lamison, A., & Noyes, H. L. (2011). Elements of and factors important in veterinary hospice. *Journal of the American Veterinary Medical Association*, *238*(2), 148–150.

Kaufman, K. R., & Kaufman, N. D. (2006). And then the dog died. *Death Studies*, *30*, 61–76. DOI:10.1080/07481180500348811.

Kawamura, N., Niiyama, M., & Niiyama, H. (2007). Long-term evaluation of animal-assisted therapy for institutionalized elderly people: A preliminary result. *Psychogeriatrics*, *7*(1), 8–13.

Kellert, S. R., & Felthous, A. R. (1985). Childhood cruelty toward animals among criminals and noncriminals. *Human Relations*, *38*, 1113–1129.

Knecht, C. D. (1992). Impaired veterinarians need and deserve our help and understanding. *Journal of the American Veterinary Medical Association*, *201*, 1138.

Kogan, L. R., & McConnell, S. L. (2001). Veterinary students and psychological services. *Journal of the American Veterinary Medical Association*, *218*(6), 873–875.

Kruger, K. A., & Serpell, J. A. (2006). Animal-assisted interventions in mental health: Definitions and theoretical foundations. In A. H. Fine (Ed.), *Handbook on animal-assisted therapy: Theoretical foundations and guidelines for practice* (2nd ed., pp. 21–38). London, UK: Elsevier.

Lagoni, L., Butler, C., & Hetts, S. (1994). *The human–animal bond and grief*. Philadelphia, PA: W. B. Saunders.

Lane, D. R., McNicholas, J., & Collis, G. M. (1998). Dogs for the disabled: Benefits to recipients and welfare of the dog. *Applied Animal Behaviour Science*, *59*, 49–60.

Levinson, B. M. (1969). Household pets in residential schools. *Mental Hygiene*, *52*, 1759–1766.

Lockwood, R. (2002). Making the connection between animal cruelty and abuse and neglect of vulnerable adults. *The Latham Letter*, *XXIII*(1), 10–13. Retrieved from www.latham.org/Issues/LLWI02.pdf

Long, D. D., Long, J. H., & Kulkarni, S. J. (2007). Interpersonal violence and animals: Mandated cross-sector reporting. *Journal of Sociology & Social Welfare*, *34*(3), 147–164.

Lutwack-Bloom, P., Wijewickrama, R., & Smith, B. (2005). Effects of pets versus people visits with nursing home residents. *Journal of Gerontological Social Work*, *44*(3–4), 137–159.

Margolies, L. (1999). The long good-bye: Women, companion animals, and maternal loss. *Clinical Social Work Journal*, *27*(3), 289–304.

Maggitti, P. (1987). Prisoners of war: The abuse of animals in military research. *The Animals Agenda*, *14*(3), 20–26.

McNicholas, J., Gibey, A., Rennie, A., Ahmedzai, S., Dono, J., & Omerod, E. (2005). Pet ownership and human health: A brief review of evidence and issues. *British Medical Journal*, *331*, 1252–1254.

Mellanby, R. J. (2005). Incidence of suicide in the veterinary profession in England and Wales. *Veterinary Record*, *157*(14), 415–417.

Mellanby, R. J., & Herrtage, M. E. (2004). Survey of mistakes made by recent veterinary graduates. *Veterinary Record*, *155*(24), 761–765.

Melson, G.F., (2003). Child development and the human-companion animal bond. *American Behavioral Scientist*, *47*, 31–39.

Melson, G. F. & Fine, A. (2006). Animals in the lives of children. In *Handbook on animal-assisted therapy: Theoretical foundations and guidelines for practice* (pp. 207–226). San Diego, CA: Elsevier.

Milani, M. (1995). The *art of veterinary practice: A guide to client communication*. Philadelphia, PA: University of Pennsylvania Press.

Milani, M. (1998). *Preparing for the loss of your pet*. Rocklin, CA: Prima Publishing.

Miller, C. (2001). Childhood animal cruelty and interpersonal violence. *Clinical Psychology Review. 21*, 735–749.

Miller, D., Staats, S. R., & Partlo, C. (1992). Discriminating positive and negative aspects of pet interaction: Sex differences in the older population. *Social Indicators Research, 27*(4), 363–374.

Miller, K. S., & Knutson, J. F. (1997). Reports of severe physical punishment and exposure to animal cruelty by inmates convicted of felonies and by university students. *Child Abuse and Neglect, 21*, 59–82.

Miller, L. (2004) Managing stress and avoiding burnout. A self-care primer for overly compassionate and overworked veterinarians. *Journal of the American Veterinary Medical Association, 225*, 492–493

Montminy-Danna, M. (2007). Child welfare and animal cruelty: A survey of child welfare workers. *Journal of Emotional Abuse, 7*(3), 83–96.

Morley, C., & Fook, J. (2005). The importance of pet loss and some implications for services. *Mortality, 10*(2), 127–142.

Morrisey, J. K., & Voiland, B. (2007). Difficult interactions with veterinary clients: Working in the challenge zone. *Veterinary Clinics of North America: Small Animal Practice, 37*(1), 65–77.

Myers, O. E. (1998). *Children and animals*. Boulder, CO: Westview Press.

National Coalition Against Domestic Violence. (2005). The problem. Retrieved May 15, 2007, from The Problem—The National Coalition Against Domestic Violence website: www.ncadv.org/learn/TheProblem_100.html

National Policy Summit on Elder Abuse. (2001, Dec. 4–6). National Center on Elder Abuse. Trends in elder abuse in domestic settings. *Elder Abuse Information Series No. 2.*

Netting, F. E., & Wilson, C. C. (1987). Restrictive leasing: Issues confronting the elderly and their companion animals. *Journal of Gerontological Social Work, 11*(3–4), 181–189.

Netting, F. E., Wilson, C. C., & New, J. C. (1987). The human–animal bond: Implications for practice. *Social Work, 32*(1), 60–64.

Nimer, J., & Lundahl, B. (2007). Animal-assisted therapy: A meta-analysis. *Anthrozoos, 20*(3), 225–238.

Nolen, R. S. (2001, March 1). Reporting laws suggest need for abuse standards. *Journal of the American Veterinary Association*. Retrieved December 12, 2008, from www.avma.org/onlnews/javma/mar01/s030101b.asp

O'Brien, G. V. (2003). People with cognitive disabilities: The argument from marginal cases and social work ethics. *Social Work, 48*(3), 331–337.

Panting, G. (2004). How to avoid being sued in clinical practice. *Postgraduate Medical Journal, 80*(941), 165–168.

Pfifferling J. H., & Gilley, K. (1999). Putting ''life'' back into your professional life. *Family Practice Management, 6*(6): 36–42.

Patronek, G. J. (1999). Hoarding of animals: An under-recognized public health problem in a difficult-to-study population. *Public Health Report 114*(1): 81–87.

Patronek, G. J. (2006). Animal hoarding: Its roots and recognition. *Veterinary Medicine, 101*(8), 520.

Patronek, G. J., & Nathanson, J. N. (2009). A theoretical perspective to inform assessment and treatment strategies for animal hoarders. *Clinical Psychology Review, 29*(3), 274–281.

Pillemer, K., and Finkelhor, D. (1988). The prevalence of elder abuse: A random sample survey. *The Gerontologist, 28*, 51–57.

Quackenbush, J., & Glickman, L. (1983). Social work services for bereaved pet owners: A retrospective case study in a veterinary teaching hospital. In A. Katcher & A. B. (Eds.), *New perspectives on our lives with companion animals* (pp. 377–389). Philadelphia, PA: University of Pennsylvania Press.

Quinn, K. M. (2000). Violent behavior: Animal abuse at early age linked to interpersonal violence. *The Brown University Child and Adolescent Behavior Letter*, *16*(3), Retrieved April 6, 2007, from www.childresearch.net/RESOURCE/NEWS/2000/200003.htm

Raina, P., Waltner-Toews, D., Bonnett, B., Woodward, C., & Abernathy, T. (1999). Influence of companion animals on the physical and psychological health of older people: An analysis of a one-year longitudinal study. *Journal of the American Geriatrics Society*, *47*(3), 323–329.

Reichert, E. (1998). Individual counseling for sexually abused children: A role for animals and storytelling. *Child and Adolescent Social Work Journal*, *15*(3), 177–183.

Richeson, N. E. (2003). Effects of animal-assisted therapy on agitated behaviors and social interactions of older adults with dementia. *American Journal of Alzheimer's Disease and Other Dementias*, *18*(6), 353–358.

Riddick, C. C. (1985). Health, aquariums, and the noninstitutionalized elderly. *Marriage and Family Review*, *8*(3–4), 163–173.

Riggs, E. A., Routly, J. E., & Taylor, I. R. (2001). Support needs of veterinary surgeons in the first few years of practice: A survey of recent and experienced graduates. *Veterinary Record*, *149*, 743–745.

Risley-Curtiss, C. (2010). Social work practitioners and the human-companion animal bond: A national study. *Social Work*, *55*(1), 38–46.

Risley-Curtiss, C., Holley, L., & Wolf, S. (2006). The human–animal bond and ethnic diversity. *Social Work*, *51*(3), 257–268.

Rogers, J., Hart, L. A., & Boltz, R. (2001). The role of pet dogs in casual conversations of elderly adults. *The Journal of Social Psychology*, *133*(3), 265–277.

Rosen, B. (1995, July). Watch for pet abuse—it might save your client's life. *Shepard's ElderCare Law Newsletter*, *5*. Thomson Legal Publishing.

Ryan, T. (2011). *Animals and social work: A moral introduction*. New York, NY: Palgrave McMillan.

Sable, P. (1995). Pets, attachment, and well-being across the life cycle. *Social Work*, *40*(3), 334–341.

Salmon, P. (1981). Who owns who? Psychological research into the human-pet bond in Australia. In abstracts of research papers, International Conference on the Human/Companion Animal Bond, Philadelphia, PA, Oct 5–7.

Seaman, S. C., Davidson, H. P. B., & Waran, N. K., (2002), *Applied Behavioural Sciences*, *78*, 175–191.

Serpell, J. A. (2002). Anthropomorphism and anthropomorphic selection beyond the "cute response." *Animals & Society*, *10*(4), 432–454.

Sharkin, B. S., & Knox, D. (2003). Pet loss: Issues and implications for the psychologist. *Professional Psychology: Research and Practice*, *34*(4), 414–421.

Shouksmith, G., & Hesketh, B. (1986). Changing horses in mid-stream: Job and life satisfactions for veterinarians. *N Z Vet J*, *34*(9), 141–144.

Siegel, A. (1962). Reaching the severely withdrawn through pet therapy. *American Journal of Psychiatry*, *118*, 1045–1046.

Stallones, L. (1994). Pet loss and mental health. *Anthrozoos*, *7*(1), 43–54.

Strand, E. B., & Faver, C. A. (2005). Battered women's concern for their pets: A closer look. *Journal of Family Social Work*. *9*(4), 39–58.

Strand, E. B., Zaparanick, T. L., & Brace, J. J. (2005). Quality of life and stress factors for veterinary medical students. *Journal of Veterinary Medical Education*, *32*(2), 182–192.

Toray, T. (2004). The human–animal bond and loss: Providing support for grieving clients. *Journal of Mental Health Counseling*, *26*(3), 244–259.

Tremayne, J. (2010) U.K. suicide study prompts call to act. *Veterinary Practice News*, *22*(1), 12–14.

Turner, W. G. (2003). Bereavement counseling: Using a social work model for pet loss. *Journal of Family Social Work*, *7*(1), 69–81.

Turner, W., (2005). The role of companion animals throughout the family life cycle, *Journal of Family Social Work*, *9*(4), 11–21.

West, C. P., Tan, A. D., Habermann, T. M , Sloan, J.A. & Shanafelt, T. D. (2009). Association of resident fatigue and distress with perceived medical errors. *JAMA*, *302*, 1294–300. DOI:3 [pii] 10.1001/jama.2009.1389

Wolf, D. B. (2000). Social work and speciesism. *Social Work*, *45*(1), 88–93.

Wright, J., & Hensley, C. (2003). From animal cruelty to serial murder: Applying the graduation hypothesis. *International Journal of Offender Therapy and Comparative Criminology*, *47*(1), 71–88.

York, S. (2000). *Remembering well: Rituals for celebrating life and mourning death.* San Francisco, CA: Jossey-Bass.

Zilney, L. A., & Zilney, M. (2005). Reunification of child and animal welfare agencies: Cross-reporting of abuse in Wellington County, Ontario. *Child Welfare. LXXXIV* (1), 47–66.

Zisselman, M., Rovner, B. W., Shmuely, Y., & Ferrie, P. (1996, January). A pet therapy intervention with geriatric psychiatry inpatients. *The America Journal of Occupational Therapy*, *50*(1), 47–51.

Chapter 10
Social Work Practice With the Military

Anthony M. Hassan and Marilyn Flynn

> How can the profession of social work contribute to a public–private partnership to care for and provide services to service members, veterans, and their families?

The purpose of this chapter is to describe the importance of military social work; describe distinguishing experiences of individuals, families, and communities impacted by connection to the military; identify the range of practice options; and provide an overview of the current service system.

War in Afghanistan and Iraq was launched at the beginning of the 21st century and has subsequently proved to be the longest-running conflict in the history of the United States. Although more than 2.2 million men and women in American military service were deployed to fight, this represented only about 1% of the nation's population. Military and civilian worlds rarely intersected except in the media. In the darkness of that disconnect, service members were repeatedly deployed to the Middle East to fight under unprecedented conditions of battle. A new generation then came home to their families, friends, jobs, and communities, some with physical and psychological scars that have drawn little notice from others in everyday life.

Survivors of 20th century combat have gradually disappeared. The last veterans of World War I have died; those from World War II and the Korean War have reached old age; and only Vietnam veterans haunt the streets to remind us of the costs of societal neglect. The first homeless veterans from the Afghanistan and Iraq wars are just making their appearance on Skid Row in Los Angeles and shelters on the East Coast, but more are to come (U.S. Interagency Council on Homelessness, 2010). It is estimated that as many as 300,000 of the 2.2 million men and women returning from Iraq and Afghanistan will bring with them both visible and invisible wounds of war (Tanielian & Jaycox, 2008; Institute of Medicine, 2010).

Unfortunately, it appears that there is no end in sight to ongoing stressors for military personnel and their families. Persistent instabilities in the Middle East, Europe, and Asia are likely to keep United States forces engaged in combat operations for many years to come. The need for military social workers is finally becoming recognized as an essential component of a just and compassionate social response to the impacts of war (Flynn & Hassan, 2010).

The strength and viability of an all-volunteer force is undermined when the health and well-being of its members and veterans is so precarious. Given the daunting issues facing our military, their families, and our communities, it is essential that the U.S. government can draw upon an emerging network of nongovernmental organizations and professionals to form a model of public–private partnerships that will greatly enhance the care and services provided to those who have served the nation.

History of Military Social Work

Military social work is not a new field of practice. The Smith School of Social Work was founded in 1921 to address the needs of returning World War I veterans, for example. The military employed social workers during World War II to act as "psychological technicians," and in 1944 finally adopted the formal classification of "social worker." The Red Cross and other international relief organizations in the nonprofit sector have employed social workers to offer emergency aid to help veterans cope with reintegration issues. Throughout the 1950s, a wave of new social work schools were founded across the nation, many with the responsibility of providing educational opportunity to returning veterans. By the early 1960s, with the return of Korean War veterans, established relationships with Veteran's Administration hospitals for social work internships were increasingly widespread, and social workers participated extensively in discharge planning, community reintegration, and provision of psychotherapy.

The relationship of social work to the military was profoundly affected by the Vietnam War, in which the majority of the social work profession was heavily aligned with the antiwar movement. Opposition to the war bled over into repudiation of men and women drafted into the service and almost complete societal failure to recognize the degree of their exposure to trauma. While estimates vary, perhaps as many as one-third of the 2.7 million persons sent to fight in Vietnam returned with persistent, untreated psychological damage, addictions, and ravaged personal relationships. Interest in military social work virtually disappeared from the academic landscape, and the number of social workers employed in the armed services gradually declined, with their functions assumed by psychologists, occupational therapists, nurses, chaplains, and other allied professions (Daley, 1999). The connection of social work to the Department of Veterans Affairs and the veteran's hospital system remained relatively robust, but practice experience in those settings was more related to medical social work, gerontology, and work with the homeless, and it generally lacked orientation to military culture.

With the advent of Operation Enduring Freedom (OEF) in Afghanistan and Operation Iraqi Freedom (OIF), society and the academic community were more sensitive to the distinction between military policy and the people who are asked to implement those policies. More sophisticated understanding of trauma had gradually emerged as a result of research in neurology, chemistry, cognitive psychology, and related disciplines. By 2005, there was a readiness to rebuild, expand, and redefine the contribution of military social work as a field of practice. Consequently, the University of Southern California launched the first military social work graduate subconcentration in 2008, initiating a military social work movement across the profession.

Importance of Social Work Practice With the Military

Only 1% of the United States population has served in the military, and the majority of military bases are concentrated in just five states (U.S. Census Bureau, 2010; U.S. Department of Interior, 2011). As a consequence, with the exception of media coverage, most people have little direct experience with the life of a soldier, sailor, Air Force member, or Marine. The presence of an all-volunteer military accentuates this social distance, since the responsibility for service is not broadly shared by all eligible citizens.

Today, the U.S. Department of Defense is annually recruiting 1.2 million men and women, while retaining only approximately 300,000 from each cohort. This means that 900,000 individuals "wash out" or are rejected at various points in the induction process, returning to civilian life with an adverse impression of their encounter with the armed services (K. Seaman, personal communication, November 4, 2011). Although Reservists and National Guard members live in their local communities, they are rarely visible in uniform and not typically viewed as a community responsibility. As a result, service members and their families encounter civilian environments ill-prepared to appropriately accommodate them with mental health care, employment readjustment, training support, education, financial guidance, and other vitally needed services.

At a clinical level, it has been estimated that between 15% and 30% of veterans returning from Iraq and Afghanistan are likely to demonstrate mental health problems, typically depression or posttraumatic stress disorder (PTSD) (Hoge, Auchterlonie, & Milliken, 2006; Tanielian & Jaycox, 2008). Moreover, the prevalence of problems appears to rise steadily over time following release from service (Schell & Marshall, 2008).

Rising suicide rates in the Army and Marine Corps have been alarming (Braswell & Kushner, 2010; Fulginiti & Rice, 2011). Suicide is now the second leading cause of death in the military (Ritchie, Keppler, & Rothberg, 2003; U.S. Department of Defense, 2007, in Bryan & Cukrowicz, 2011) and rates have consistently increased across all branches since 2006 (Carden, 2010, in Braswell & Kushner, 2010). Today, the Army suicide rate is at its highest in 16 years, affecting soldiers during predeployment, deployment, and postdeployment. (Braswell & Kushner, 2010; Fulginiti & Rice, 2011). It is not clear what forces are at work and whether these rates are a product of combat-related assignments, a changed pool of recruits in an all-volunteer army, inexperienced leadership by officers, or other factors.

It does seem to be true that women veterans, who comprise 14% of those serving in Iraq and Afghanistan, may be even more susceptible to combat stress and might encounter unique—and yet unrecognized— pressures in carrying out their assignments (Vogt, Pless, King, & King, 2005). Sexual assault and harassment appear to be more extensive than originally expected; as many as one-third of all females report encounters of this kind (Bastian, Lancaster, & Reyst, 1996; Fontana & Rosenheck, 1998; Kang, Dalager, Mahan, & Ishii, 2005). And since many of these women serve dual roles as wives and mothers, they have a compounded risk factor with divorce rates as high as 2.5 times the national average and high suicide rates (Karney & Crown, 2006; McFarland, Kaplan, & Huguet, 2010; Street, Vogt, & Dutra, 2009).

The impact of military service on children and families has been increasingly documented (Atuel, Esqueda, & Jacobson, 2011; Figley, 1998; Flake, Davis, Johnson, & Middleton, 2009; Lester et al., 2010; U.S. Department of Defense, 2010). The return of a service member with symptoms of posttraumatic stress, such as sleeplessness, lack of concentration, irritability, depression, and hypervigilance, can throw family members into disarray. Clinicians now describe these reactions as "secondary posttraumatic stress disorder," requiring professional treatment (Nissly & Turner, 2011). The phenomenon of secondary posttraumatic stress was first identified by an Israeli scholar, Zahava Solomon (1993), and has subsequently been closely studied by scholars in the United States. Research now confirms that children's response to deployment can include long-term depression, bullying, withdrawal, poor scholarship, and a variety of anxiety disorders (Atuel, Esqueda, & Jacobson, 2011). These are particularly prevalent among children who are living off-base; those living on base often fare better than their civilian counterparts. The extent of these problems is now perhaps more thoroughly recognized than in previous decades, when all men were supposed to be "heroes" and their families, admiring.

Perhaps the most vulnerable group are Reservists and National Guard members, who comprised 26% of all those with OIF/OEF deployments and are more likely than active duty personnel to meet diagnostic screening criteria for mental health problems (Schell & Tanielian, 2011; Tanielian & Jaycox, 2008). Their exposure to psychological risk is greater perhaps because they lack the protective social environment a full-time military base offers, have little appropriate transitional support from combat duty back to life in a civilian community, and were less prepared for combat experience. They have been subject to frequent deployments, often do not fight with their own unit, and have more family and job responsibilities. (Riviere, Kendall-Robbins, McGurk, Castro, & Hoge, 2011).

The problem of unemployment among OEF/OIF veterans has begun to command public attention. Between 20% and 40% of service members have remained without a job for more than 3 months following their discharge into a dispirited economy. Some military specialized occupational classifications do not translate directly into civilian positions; the civilian workplace produces culture shock among service members accustomed to military regimentation; communities do not "own" the problem of veteran unemployment and fail to give it priority. Veterans with physical injuries encounter additional barriers. Poor employment prospects combine with low incomes, inadequate veteran's benefits, and shortages of affordable housing to worsen the reintegration scene (Little & Alenkin, 2011).

Warfare of the future will wreak greater individual and societal pain than previous hostilities for many reasons. There will be no "fronts," few conventional enemies as targets, limited victories, no rallying by the entire country around the troops, moral ambiguity, vagueness in mission, and uncertain leadership. Both those who follow and those who lead will be highly vulnerable. Military social work has never been more important in promoting positive relationships, improved social policies, and improved well-being among those who serve our country and those impacted by military presence.

Definition of Military Social Work

"Military social work" may be described in many ways. The most recent formal definition was developed by a military social work steering committee lead by Dr. Anthony Hassan for the National Council on Social Work Education and is marked by conceptual inclusiveness (CSWE, 2010). It includes all branches of the United States Armed Forces (Army, Navy Marine Corps, Coast Guard, State Guards, and National Reserves), together with veterans of all eras and conflicts served by the Department of Veterans Affairs. Civilian populations affected by war and other disasters, families of service members, and communities impacted in other ways by the presence of the military constitute an important population group that is not always as explicitly addressed in policy and practice but which also falls within the purview of the military social work field.

Military social workers themselves may be uniformed or not, veteran or not, government or nonprofit sector employees, private contractors or private practitioners. Noncombatant uniformed service men and women employed by the Department of Homeland Security, commissioned members of the United States Public Health Service Corps, and the National Oceanic and Atmospheric Administration staff also fall within this purview.

Military social work is distinguished from other fields of practice by three primary features. The first is the explicit connection to war and violence. The professional military force in the United States is the only societal institution sanctioned to kill. In the modern armed forces, new expectations have been added, such as peacekeeping, nation-building, natural disaster management, and other restorative or quasi-diplomatic responsibilities. For example, service members have been called to support nation-building in East African countries, assist with earthquake relief in Haiti, and fight terrorism in distant jungles of the Philippines. Nonetheless, the fundamental commitment of service members is to destroy a target and, if required, surrender their own lives in the process. This ultimate sacrifice and the related threat of loss are especially pronounced for war fighters in direct combat, but this touches everyone at all levels in time of war. It should be noted that in some other societies, the right to kill is not reserved to the military alone, but is acceptable when carried out by other groups such as the family. "Honor killings" are one example, in which communities acknowledge the right of a family member to exact vengeance on another family; another example is female infanticide in some areas of the world. These practices may occur in the United States but are not permissible legally or even morally in our country. The socially sanctioned right to defend and, within certain rules, take life, has been present in all societies and at all periods in human history. It is sometimes associated with aggression, but equally often with protection. The human consequences for war fighters, families, and civilian populations are both institutional and personal. Military social workers learn how to build and rebuild community, evaluate and mitigate trauma, organize support networks, and promote well-being in this context.

Second, military social work is strongly shaped by a workplace perspective. The United States military and associated veteran's programs represent large organized employment structures with values, purposes, hierarchies and work classifications, allocations of power, decision structures, and productivity goals. Individuals, groups, and communities interacting with the military as a workplace are subject to all of the adjustment challenges, motivational incentives, and output expectations common to any formal organization. Work within and supportive services to the military can be interpreted in the same way that any pattern of careers and interorganizational networks can be seen. Military social workers therefore scrutinize the effects of personnel policies as they affect service members and veterans; contribute to orientation, plan for separation or discharge, and leadership training; work to bridge gaps in the administration of benefits and services; help to reduce workplace discrimination; and carry out standard workplace functions.

The third distinguishing feature of military social work is a focus on the sociological, political, and psychological consequences of transition. Perhaps there is no other profession in which individuals and families are required to make such frequent changes, not only in the form of transfers to other localities, but between statuses. To clarify, veterans and retirees have usually served in approximately seven geographic locations/assignments before discharge, bringing families with them. In the case of war fighters, they have shifted between combat zones and return to home, with family roles and responsibilities altering in the process; for some this shift has occurred in excess of five times in OIF/OEF. Service members also move from military to civilian life, crossing over a cultural chasm larger than they ever anticipated. Communities adjacent to military installations experience these transitions on a macro level, with new commanders moving into local bases on a regular basis, rotating populations in local schools, and repeated disruption of patterns in communication between community and base service providers.

Consequently, identification and understanding of separation, transition, and reconnection are critical to military social work. While the field has explored these issues extensively in relation to child welfare and foster care, the field of military social work also presents a specialty area for similar theory development and evidence-based practice.

Military Culture

Military culture is a shared system of values, rituals, customary patterns of social relationships, and the use of symbols that guides and reinforces group behavior. As one of society's oldest institutions, military culture has traditions and associated meanings that are very rich and inspiring. For example, the revered tradition of the salute between an officer and enlisted service member is an enduring sign of respect that can be traced back hundreds of years. Core military values that honor unit cohesion, teamwork, duty, integrity, service before self, loyalty, respect, personal courage, and self-sacrifice have been deeply imparted through the generations.

In one familiar and often-repeated joke, a private asks for a new pair of boots.

The supply clerk asks, "What size?"

The private looks surprised, and then responds, "Why, size 10—just like everyone else."

Group identity is essential in combat; survival may depend upon it. Military social workers will also recognize the personal tensions that may emerge from exacting pressure for conformity For example, it may be more psychologically damaging for a service member to retreat from the theater of battle than to stay injured with unit comrades. The power of unit identity outweighs the self-preservation instinct.

Military culture is dynamic and includes many subgroups and subcultures within the active duty and veteran communities. For example, one Army soldier may hold the job of infantryman while another serves in an intelligence unit. They both belong to the Army and live together, but they work apart in very different environments. Military social workers must carefully learn the power and authority structure within the military from both a workplace and cultural perspective and appreciate the impact this command and communication structure can have on the lives of service members and their families. Military hierarchy and rank are more strictly delineated than in civilian society and impinge heavily on the way in which informal and formal communications are carried out. For example, in civilian society an employee might interrupt her boss in a moment of intense discussion; this would be much less acceptable between a military officer and an enlisted service member.

When racial status, gender, service cultures, "family" composition, sexual orientation, age, life stage, ethnicity, citizenship status, and other factors interact with command structure and military culture, this intersectionality can—and does—produce tensions and inequities. Women, minorities, gays and lesbians, and persons with amputations or other permanent physical limitations have been accepted for service or allowed to reenlist. Women have been appointed as generals in command of active theaters of war, as have members of racial minorities. Within the rigidities of custom and culture, there is a dynamic underlying process that has sometimes meant that the military is more socially progressive than society as a whole, but with the purpose of maintaining a vigorous fighting force.

Each branch of service proudly owns its distinctive history and conventions. Perhaps elements of the Marine Corps culture may be the most widely recognized outside the military, but all the forces have their own occupational titles, unit structures, and other distinguishing cultures. For example, in the Navy and Air Force a senior noncommissioned officer (E-7) is called *Chief*, in the Marine Corps *Gunnery Sergeant*, and in the Army *Sergeant First Class*. Military social workers will, as with any approach to cultural competence, attempt to treat these variations with respect and to identify symbols within each branch that have exceptional significance. This may include badges, colors, uniform styles, past victories, or other icons.

Military culture has traditionally disdained weakness and, by inference, help-seeking for emotional, marital, or other personal problems. A deep stigma remains, despite new policies and a public relations campaign adopted by the armed forces to normalize counseling. Procedural barriers remain. Service members continue to expect negative career consequences, although discharge from service for mental health reasons is rare. On the contrary, service members who attend to their mental health needs perform better and are often promoted above those who fail to seek help. Behavioral problems that affect a service member's work performance and career, such as driving intoxicated, domestic violence, child maltreatment, or insubordination toward supervisors, are highly amenable to social work intervention and, if unaddressed, often result in discharge or punishment in a military court.

Roles of Military Social Workers

Today there is very little written about the specific roles and associated skills of military social work beyond social work position descriptions in the U.S. Department of Defense and the Veteran's Administration. The only published document that addresses this area is the CSWE *Guidebook for Military Social Work* (2010).

Military social workers conduct practice at all levels, from intervention with individual services members and their families to group and community work, advocacy, program design, policy development, research, and education. Like the practice of social work as a whole, the purpose of military social work is to enhance human well-being and empower individuals, families, communities, and societies to achieve their best potential for development. Social workers do not endorse war or aggression, but do extend meaningful help to those who have been most affected by military presence. Social workers working with the military, veterans, and/or family members are more than likely not wearing a military uniform. They are social workers working within community children and family service agencies, county health and mental health centers, housing departments, legislative offices, nonprofit community veteran service organizations, student affairs offices, and the like.

Clinical Social Work

Recent reports by the U.S. Department of Defense (2009) and the Institute of Medicine (IOM) (2010) reveal a pressing need for more social work practitioners who are able to extend clinical and vocational counseling to service members now returning from Afghanistan and Iraq. The IOM report underscores the importance of a complete bio-psycho-social-spiritual assessment, given the complexity of multiphase treatment plans. Specialized education and training in work with military clients was strongly encouraged and is gradually beginning to emerge across the nation.

At the individual level, military social workers are interested in building resilience and reducing risk of psychological harm resulting from military-related experiences. They offer treatment to individuals and families in order to restore interpersonal functioning, evaluate the outcomes of intervention, and deliver ongoing support in many forms for those with severe and persistent illness. Social workers are concerned with the successful adaptation by service members to the military as a workplace, to issues of employment and re-employment of veterans in community settings, and with the management of disabilities that may produce workplace exclusion. Military social workers understand military culture and the adjustment difficulties that individuals may experience as a consequence of their own belief systems, identity, status in the service, or other factors associated with diversity. Problem-solving around these characteristics and values will differ from solutions in civilian society to some extent.

There is a close correlation between traditional medical social work and military social work, both because of the physical injuries that warriors suffer but also in relation to services for aging veterans. Research on the biochemical processes associated with aging and disability now suggests that persons exposed to sustained high stress may age prematurely and manifest breakdown in physical functioning early (Epel et al., 2004). With the polytraumatic wounds of blindness, deafness, spinal cord injury, and loss of limbs from the OIF/OEF warfare, the connection between health and military social work has grown even more pronounced.

Military social workers are expected to apply a range of skills from case management to clinical modalities for individual, couples, family, and group therapy. A behavioral health focus that combines knowledge in primary health care, substance abuse, and mental health is required, because problems are so frequently co-occurring in nature. Following the field of social work in general, a high value is now being placed on evidence-based interventions, although the pace of adoption has been slow. As in all domains of practice, military social workers approach their clients with a relationally based, culturally responsive, and theoretically-informed perspective.

Treatment goals in military social work may, in the case of veterans, look very similar to those of any clinical population—to facilitate independence, promote healthy behaviors, and build competence in problem-solving. For the active duty population, on the other hand, the focus of the helping process is to minimize the consequences of psychological and physical harm, strengthen resiliency, raise morale, and return the soldier to duty. Social workers can be highly influential in helping combatants and their families face the risks, threats, and consequences of warfare in a way that preserves psychological well-being and human relationships. This is critically important for the military unit, the individual, and the family.

Community Organization, Policy, and Administration

At a community and societal level, military social workers are valued for their ability to assist base commanders and other leaders to develop more responsive policies. Social workers make a powerful contribution to moving service members and their families through transitions, from induction to separation to re-integration into civilian life. Leadership training, creation of orientation and reintegration programs, development of new networks for communication between military and civilian organizations, direction of veteran's service organizations, and participation on multidisciplinary research teams in military settings are all familiar roles. Attention to policies and other environmental forces that generate problems in living for military client systems are fundamental to a military social work perspective.

It should be noted that assistance to civilian populations in war-torn countries, negotiations with tribal and religious leaders, promotion of cultural competence in foreign lands, and community redevelopment have sometimes fallen within the purview of military social work. To date, these roles have been limited by the relatively few numbers of trained social workers available for this work and lack of recognition by military and foreign service professionals of the contribution social workers might make.

In summary, as with any field of practice, social work with the military involves mastery of content relating to social policies, understanding of specialized service structures and mechanisms for service delivery, targeted clinical, organizing, and administrative practice skills, and knowledge of population characteristics.

Military Structures and Services Systems in the United States

The demographic profile of the military community was composed of 2,527,229 service members in 2009 (U.S. Department of Defense, 2009). There were 1,447,602 active duty and 1,079,627 reserve/guard service members. These forces served within one of the seven branches of service—Army, Navy, Air Force, Marines, Coast Guard, Reserves, or National Guard. The total force was comprised of approximately 86% male and 14% female, with over 55% married. The formal education of the armed forces was at a higher level than that of the general civilian population, with 86% of the officers holding a minimum of a bachelor's degree and 96% of the enlisted ranks having a minimum of a high school diploma, compared to the civilian population with 29% and 86% respectively. The cultures of these service branches vary significantly. The Army represents the largest division with the youngest fighting force (U.S. Department of Defense, 2009); the Air Force members, by contrast, are more educated and closer in culture to civilian society.

As of May 2010, 43% of the active-duty and reserve service members had children, with about 142,000 active-duty/Guard/Reserve parents who were single custodians of minor children. An additional 40,000 active-duty families had dual-military parents. An estimated 220,000 children have a parent who is currently deployed; 75,000 have parents who have been deployed multiple times (West, 2011).

Service Systems

The U.S. Department of Defense (DoD) is responsible for all personnel actively engaged in defense-related activities for the United States. The DoD constructs and maintains 662 military bases throughout the world, each of which provides sophisticated support services for the men and women living there. Schools, psychological and social work counseling, medical care, chaplain services, family counseling, legal aid, housing and benefits and are available at most military locations. Uniformed social workers typically are assigned to a position within the hospital, mental health, family advocacy, or substance abuse centers and eventually go on to provide leadership within these same organizations. In addition, uniformed social workers are afforded the opportunity to work in various staff, teaching, and career-broadening positions. Each branch of service has a senior social worker who serves as a consultant to the service's Surgeon General and to all subordinate social workers within that service. To receive social work or psychological counseling, a service member is required to seek assistance initially from the on-base clinic, unless permission is given by the on-base clinic commander or command policy allowing the individual to visit with a civilian provider off-base. A service member does not have to inform his/her direct leader about the decision to seek mental health services, but merely needs to state that a "medical appointment" has been made. Confidentiality does not apply, however, when a service member is deemed potentially harmful to self or others, or when the individual's behavior is counter to their occupational specialty and the sensitivities required for that position, such as the role of military police, pilot, aircraft mechanic, or intelligence officer.

The armed services have been working intensively to reduce these barriers to help-seeking, and have increased their outreach education campaigns with "buddy to buddy" training, senior leader mental health messages, chaplain support, and expanded counseling options through civilian channels such as Military OneSource, Military Family Life Counselors, FOCUS, and other local installation initiatives. Nonetheless, many military families turn to professionals in the local nearby community, when possible, where greater anonymity and availability of family services is thought to exist. Community-dwelling service members not living on base also face the challenge of an environment where military culture is not well understood. Children in these families, especially those with deployed or injured parents, must contend with public school environments that often have little understanding of their stress in the face of parental deployment, frequent geographic relocation, and problems accompanying parental reintegration following deployment (Atuel, Esqueda, & Jackson, 2011).

The Department of Veterans Affairs (VA) is responsible for addressing service-related needs and benefits of individuals once they have separated from service. The Department has two major divisions: The first is dedicated to administration of benefits such as pensions, disability allowances, and educational stipends; and the second is a health division, responsible for inpatient, outpatient, and community-based care such as nursing homes, group homes, mental health care, and residential facilities for homeless veterans. Veterans' hospitals also conduct research on medical and psychological interventions, function as training and educational centers for social work and almost all health disciplines, and collaborate with public and private community groups to ensure increased access to service by veterans from all wars. Programs through the health division of the VA are most familiar to social workers, since the VA is the largest employer of social workers in the United States, with approximately 9,000 employed in 2011.

In an attempt to reach veterans more effectively, the VA has also organized Veterans Centers throughout the United States. Staffed by veterans and dedicated to creating an atmosphere of respect and support for those who seek help, the Vets Centers have grown relatively popular in preference to the large and more impersonal setting of the VA Hospitals. At the present time, there are approximately 300 Vet Centers and 50 mobile vet centers serving more than 191,000 men and women through individual counseling, group therapy, and other forms of family support conducted by graduate level social workers.

An important but much more decentralized source of service for both active military and veterans are the not-for-profit Veteran's Service Organizations (VSOs), which are not government entities. These groups range from wives who have lost their husbands in war to veterans of previous wars and private groups seeking to assist disabled veterans in finding employment. VSOs play an important role in advocacy for the rights of soldiers and veterans, in the organization of community events that welcome and attempt to reintegrate returning troops, in local service provision to help fill specific gaps such as need for specialized medical equipment, and in volunteering to augment VA or DoD services. Examples of VSOs include the Veterans of Foreign Wars, United Service Organization (USO), the Marine Corps Scholarship Foundation, the U.S. Vets Program, Gary Sinise Foundation, Iraq and Afghanistan Veterans of America (IAVA), Women Veterans of America, and hundreds of others. In addition, community colleges, legal aid societies, universities, private corporations' labor unions, chambers of commerce, United Ways, and other charitable groups have given thousands of hours of volunteer assistance, mentoring, hiring options, and other forms of grassroots aid. Unfortunately, these programs have been little evaluated, tend to be episodic, and do not appear to have cumulative or sustained effect.

The Future of Military Social Work

The number of social work positions allocated to each branch of the uniformed services has been growing since 2005 with approximately 430+ social workers in the Army, Air Force, and Navy. Specifically, the Army and Air Force employ approximately 200 and the Navy 34 uniformed social workers. All three services are expanding the uniformed social worker ranks, especially the Navy, with generous recruitment incentives, advanced education opportunities, and reenlistment bonuses. The Army developed an internal military social work degree program in 2008 called the Army–Fayetteville State University Master of Social Work Program in conjunction with the Army Medical Department Center and School, which is in essence their succession planning strategy for sustaining their Army uniformed social worker force. They have reached within the Army ranks to recruit 30 individuals each year to enter their MSW program and, upon graduation, return those graduates to the Army as uniformed social work officers. In addition to uniformed social workers, the DoD employs nonuniformed social workers to fill critical social work positions on bases throughout the world and within TRICARE, the healthcare program that serves uniformed service members, veterans, and their families worldwide with more than 49,000 mental health providers, including social workers, within its network of care to the military.

Interest in certification and specialization in military social work is also more widespread, both within universities and among practicing professionals. The needs of veterans from Vietnam and the OEF/OIF conflicts are likely to extend for the next 40 years, according to military experts, creating demand for social work services well into the next generation. At the same time, nursing and other forms of medical practice have expanded even more rapidly in the military. To remain part of the team and a voice in the dialogue on services for those affected by military presence, military social work requires much more intensive attention by professional educators and employers.

Despite recent efforts to increase access to appropriate care for veterans, many difficulties remain. These include veterans' access to care, their reluctance to seek care, insufficient workforce capacity, low levels of competency in evidence-based treatments, and inadequate community-based systems of support. Clinical social workers who can implement the best evidence-based practices in settings across the entire community constitute one vital resource in attacking these issues.

However, it is unlikely that the health of veterans and their families, the quality and access to care, or the lack of qualified providers will be adequately addressed unless local, state, and federal agencies join forces. Because of their knowledge of community networks, social workers are uniquely qualified to bring diverse resources together, identify new opportunities across public and private sectors, and lay the foundation for a coordinated approach to supporting and engaging veterans and their families for many years to come. Approaches orchestrated by social workers that play to the strengths of communities—small, scalable clusters of stakeholders who have the resources and relationships in place to work well together—will be most successful. These types of initiatives can help guide community practitioners, build community networks, inform policymakers, and identify broadly applicable and scalable translational research with promising real-world prevention interventions. The overall goal is for social workers to build new "policy bridges" that permit more effective and fiscally sound programs for the reintegration of veterans into our civilian communities across the United States. Ultimately, social work is the safety net for a civil society that is committed to supporting the brave men and women who wear the uniform in combat.

Key Terms

Military	PTSD	Service members
Military families	Reintegration	Social work veterans

Review Questions for Critical Thinking

1. Do you believe there are parallels between working with veteran populations and other types of populations? What are the similarities? What are some differences?

2. After reading this chapter, how have your thoughts, feelings, assumptions, beliefs, values, or attitudes changed toward working with the veteran and military family populations? If they have not changed, explain why.

3. What were the strengths and limitations about the material covered in this chapter? What are the implications for you in your practice?

Online Resources

Social Work in the U.S. Army: www.armymedicine.army.mil/prr/social_work.html

Social Work: Clinical Care Providers: Health Care: Careers—Navy: www.navy.com/careers/healthcare/clinical-care/social-work.html

Veterans Affairs | Helpstartshere.org: www.helpstartshere.org/veterans-affairs

Air Force Social Workers | AirForce.com: www.airforce.com

References

Atuel, H., Esqueda, M., & Jacobson, L. (2011). *The military child within the public school education system.* Los Angeles, CA: USC Center for Innovation and Research on Veterans & Military Families.

Bastian, L., Lancaster, A., & Reyst, H. (1996). U.S. Department of Defense 1995 Sexual Harrassment Survey. U.S. Department of Defense. Retrieved November 20, 2011 from www.dtic.mil/dtfs/doc_research/p18_11.pdf

Braswell, H., & Kushner, H. I. (2010). Suicide, social integration, and masculinity in the U.S. military. *Social Science and Medicine.* DOI:10.1016/j.socscimed.2010.07.031

Bryan, C. J., & Cukrowicz, K. C. (2011). Associations between types of combat violence and the acquired capability for suicide. *Suicide and Life-Threatening Behavior, 41,* 126–136.

Council on Social Work Education. (2010). *Advanced Social Work Practice in Military Social Work.* Retrieved November 20, 2011 from www.cswe.org/File.aspx?id=42466

Daley, J. G. (Ed). (1999). *Social work practice in the military.* Binghamton, NY: Hawthorne Press.

Epel, E., Blackburn, E. H., Lin, J., Dhabhar, F., Adler, N., Morrow, J. D., & Cathow, R. M. (2004). Accelerated telomere shortening in response to life stress. *Proceedings of the National Academy of Sciences, 101,* 17312–17315.

Figley, C. (1998). Burnout in families: The penultimate fatigue of family relationships. *The Family Digest, 10,* 1–6.

Flake, E., Davis, B. E., Johnson, P., & Middleton, L. (2009). The psychosocial effects of deployment on military children. *Journal of Developmental and Behavioral Pediatrics, 30,* 271–278.

Flynn, M., & Hassan, A. M. (2010). Unique challenges of war in Iraq and Afghanistan. *Journal of Social Work Education, 46,* 169–173.

Fontana, A., & Rosenheck, R. (1998). Duty-related and sexual stress in the etiology of PTSD among women veterans who seek treatment. *Psychiatric Services, 49,* 658–662.

Fulginiti, A., & Rice, E. (2011). Together we stand: Divided we fall: Connectedness, suicide, and social media in the military. *Policy Brief addendum.* Los Angeles, CA: USC Center for Innovation and Research on Veterans and Military Families.

Kang, H., Dalager, N., Mahan, C., & Ishii, E. (2005). The role of sexual assault on the risk of PTSD among Gulf War veterans. *Annals of Epidemiology, 15,* 191–195.

Karney, B., & Crown, J. (2006). *Families under stress: An assessment of data, theory, and research on marriage and divorce in the military.* Santa Monica, CA: Rand Corporation.

Hoge, C. W., Auchterlonie, J. L., & Milliken, C. S. (2006). Mental health problems, use of mental health services and attrition from military service after returning from deployment to Iraq or Afghanistan. *Journal of the American Medical Association, 295,* 1023–1032.

Institute of Medicine. (2010). *Returning home from Iraq and Afghanistan: Preliminary assessment of readjustment needs of veterans, service members, and their families.* Washington, D.C.: The National Academies Press.

Lester, P., Peterson, K., Knauss, L., Glover, D., Mogil, C., Saltzman, W., Pynoos, R., Wilt, K., & Beardslee, W. (2010). The long war and parental combat deployment: Effects on military children and at-home spouses. *Journal of the American Academy of Child & Adolescent Psychiatry, 49,* 310–320.

Little, R., & Alenkin, N. (2011). *Overcoming barriers to employment for veterans: Current trends and practical approaches.* Los Angeles, CA: USC Center for Innovation and Research on Veterans & Military Families.

McFarland, B. H., Kaplan, M. S., & Huguet, N. (2010). Self-inflicted deaths among women with U.S. military service: A hidden epidemic? *Psychiatric Services, 61,* 1177.

Nissly, J. A., & Turner, K. L. (2011). *Ensuring behavioral healthcare capacity and quality for servicemembers, veterans, and military families.* Los Angeles: USC Center for Innovation and Research on Veterans and Military Families (CIR).

Rice, E., & Fulginits, A. (2011). CIR policy brief addendum: ''Togethr we stand, divided we fall: Connectedness, suicide, and social media in the Military.'' USC Center for Innovation and Research on Veterans & Military Families (CIR). Retrieved March 28, 2012 from http://cir.usc.edu

Ritchie, E., Keppler, W., & Rothberg, J. (2003). Suicidal admissions in the United States military. *Military Medicine, 168,* 177–181.

Riviere, L. Kendall-Robbins, A. McGurk, D., Castro, C., & Hoge, C. (2011). Coming home may hurt: Risk factors for mental ill health in U.S. reservists after deployment in Iraq. *The British Journal of Psychiatry, 198,* 136–142.

Schell, T. L., & Marshall, G. N. (2008). Survey of individuals previously deployed for OEF/OIF. In T. Tanielian & L. H. Jaycox (Eds.), *Invisible wounds of war: Psychological and cognitive injuries, their consequences, and services to assist recovery.* Retrieved November 20, 2011 from www.rand.org/pubs/monographs/2008/RAND_MG720.pdf

Schell, T., & Tanielian, T. (Eds.). (2011). *A needs assessment of New York State veterans. A final report to the New York State health foundation.* Retrieved November 2, 2011 from www.rand.org/pubs/technical_reports/TR920.html

Solomon, Z. (1993). *Combat stress reaction: The enduring toll of war.* New York, NY: Plenum Press.

Street, A. E., Vogt, D., & Dutra, L. (2009). A new generation of women veterans: Stressors faced by women deployed to Iraq and Afghanistan. *Clinical Psychology Review, 29,* 685–694.

Tanielian, T., & Jaycox, L. (2008). *Invisible wounds of war: Psychological and cognitive injuries, their consequences, and services to assist recovery.* Arlington, VA: Rand Corporation.

U.S. Census Bureau. (2010). *American community survey: Veterans*. Retrieved November 8, 2011, from http://factfinder2.census.gov/faces/tableservices/jsf/pages/productview.xhtml?pid=ACS_10_1YR_S2101&prodType=table

U.S. Department of the Interior. (2011). [Graph illustration of military basis 1993] Military basis in the contiguous United States. Retrieved December 1, 2011 from www.nps.gov/nagpra/documents/basesmilitarymap.htm

U.S. Department of Defense. (2009). *Demographic report*. Washington, DC: Department of Defense.

U.S. Department of Defense. (2010). *Report on the impact of deployment of members of the armed forces on their dependent children*. Washington, DC: Department of Defense.

U.S. Interagency Council on Homelessness. (2010). Opening doors: Federal strategic plan to prevent and end homelessness. Retrieved December 1, 2011 from www.usich.gov/opening_doors

West, K. M. (2011). *The courts and military families: Urgent action needed*. Los Angeles, CA: USC Center for Innovation and Research on Veterans and Military Families.

Vogt, D. S., Pless, A. P., King, L. A., & King, D. W. (2005). Deployment stressors, gender, and mental health outcomes among Gulf War I veterans. *Journal of Traumatic Stress, 18*, 272–284.

Chapter 11
International Social Work Practice

Doreen Elliott and Uma A. Segal

Should international social work be considered in a textbook on fields of social work practice? How is it relevant to practitioners who do not plan on practicing outside the United States?

In discussing the term *international social work,* we can consider three groups of professional social worker responses. For ease of recognition we may call them (a) the *cynics,* (b) the *pragmatic converts,* and (c) the *progressive idealist* internationalists. For many social workers in the first group, *the cynics,* international social work raises a number of questions, such as: What is international social work? Is international social work inevitably oppressive of indigenous cultures? How can social work be international when it is socially constructed—that is, when it is so dependent on local culture, values, laws, norms, and service delivery systems? Why should we bother with social work practice in other countries when the need is so great at home? How is international social work relevant to my practice at home? These questions are legitimate and need to be considered.

For a second group of social workers, *the pragmatic converts,* the term *international social work* involves recognition that after 9/11, world perspectives are irrevocably changed, and professional perspectives, like their broader political, economic and cultural counterparts, acknowledge that the profession must address more thoroughly the consequences of economic and cultural globalization, human migration, disaster, human rights abuses, poverty, HIV/AIDS, and so forth. Increasing globalization, with heightened international communication, commerce, migration, and a variety of cross-national exchanges, they argue, must influence the social work profession in the United States, extending its understanding of the implications of international interdependence across and beyond U.S. borders. Increasingly, schools of social work are calling on their students to recognize that international issues touch the practice of all social workers, and it is essential that they be cognizant of, and responsive to, the effects of globalization.

The third group, the *progressive idealist* internationalist social workers, believe that in the Westernized postindustrial nations we may learn from other countries, including learning from the so-called developing nations, and that international exchange should be a truly reciprocal exercise in which both parties give and receive benefits. Hockenstad and Midgley (2004) in their book *Lessons from Abroad* include chapters that explore, among other topics, what we might learn from social security reform in Chile, Singapore, and Britain, as well as from child welfare initiatives and mental health programs around the world. Because early international social work initiatives were set against the backdrop of colonialism, the interaction inevitably was patriarchal and unidirectional, with ideas being exported from Western nations. Midgley (1990) gives examples from the developing world of community cooperatives in working with disabled people, of disaster preparedness and responses, and of working with people in poverty as areas where the developed nations have much to learn. Toors (1992) makes similar arguments for reciprocity in international professional relations. Elliott & Mayadas (1997), in discussing the history of social work, present four phases, the last phase being an ideal situation in which there are multiple learning networks and professional information exchange across the globe. This last phase is in contrast to earlier phases marked by the unidirectional export of professional ideas from the Western world and later the reaction of the developing world against this unidirectional approach. Elliott and Mayadas (2000) offer a social development model of social work practice that encompasses an international approach. In their compendium of models of international collaboration in social work, Healy, Asamoah, and Hockenstad (2003) state that "mutuality is a cornerstone of collaboration" (p. 20). They selected the models for publication using mutuality as one of the main criteria for acceptance. Ferguson (2005) reviews the limitations of four existing models of social work exchange, and posits an alternative model of technology transfer demonstrating "global dissemination of initiatives originating in developing countries that are successfully applied in the developed world." Cox and Pawar (2006) also reiterate the importance of the developed world's needs to learn from innovations in the developing world. Thus the *progressive idealists* represent a strong element in current international social work thinking and practice.

However, a caveat should be noted about the categories presented here: In reality, these three categories are not necessarily discrete; progressive idealists may at times be cynics, and all of us may be pragmatists to some extent. The division of social workers into these categories is more of a literary device to illustrate these three significant trends in current social work thinking about international issues. An example of this is that the radical idealists also have their feet on the ground: Healy (2003) concludes an introduction to the models of international collaboration compendium by recognizing that given the history of unequal exchange, the profession needs to work hard to ensure that all international collaborations are based on mutuality. We should further note that knowledge of the history of internationalism in social work becomes important in ensuring that this goal of mutuality and equality in international exchange is carried out, lest ignorant but well-meaning interventions take us back to the colonial past. For this reason, a later section of this chapter is given to history of international social work.

This chapter is focused on the concerns of the cynics, the position of the pragmatists, and the optimism of the progressive idealists. The concerns of the *cynics* will be addressed through discussion of definitions of international social work, the pros and cons of international social work, and the relevance of a global dimension in local practice. The position of the *pragmatists* will be more fully explored by considering the implications for the profession of globalization and the international political context of social work practice. The optimism of the *progressive idealists* will be further examined and evaluated through consideration of history and of examples where we can and have already learned from the developing world. In doing so, we believe that we have contributed some new dimensions to discussions on international social work: a new definition of international social work is offered, and Table 11.1 offers a new

Table 11.1 Defining International Social Work: Examples of Activities.

Students	• Study abroad • Student exchange programs • International field placements • Comparative research, projects, theses, dissertations • Peace Corps and other international volunteer agency work
Social work educators	• Faculty exchanges to foreign universities • Hosting overseas faculty at home university • Government and NGO consultancies • Conducting comparative social research • Disseminating knowledge through writing and teaching
United Nations and associated agencies	• Disseminating information • Disaster response • Providing direct services, e.g., UNICEF, UNHCR. • Research and inquiry, e.g., UNDP Research Unit • Developing measures for intervention effectiveness: e.g., human development index, gender development index
Service delivery in International NGOs: "Social work across borders"	• Developmental work with communities • Programs targeted on specific problems: e.g., AIDS; poverty; hunger; health; child labor and, child sexual exploitation, e.g.,. Oxfam, Save the Children; World Vision; Amnesty International; Human Rights Watch • www.un.org/esa/socdev/iyop/iyopac04.htm#INPEA
International professional organizations	• Disseminate knowledge and research through conferences and journals • Facilitate international professional networking • International policy and practice advocacy • e.g., IFSW; IASSW; ICSD; ICSW
International practice at home: "Global is local; local is global"	• Working with refugees • International adoptions • Social work on American military bases overseas

representation of activities. A new discussion of professional imperialism is presented in a recent context in social work education, and this is summarized in figure three. The discussion of a previously presented model of international social work history has been significantly expanded and a summary of the most recent debate on indigenization and universalism is discussed. This chapter presents no easy solutions to some of the dilemmas presented: it would be reductionist to do so. We do signal ways forward for further discussion and development and trust that readers will find both motivation and resources within this introductory chapter to pursue these issues in greater detail.

Definitions

In reviewing the literature for definitions of international social work, it was noted that surprisingly, the 19th *Encyclopedia of Social Work* (Edwards & Hopps, 1995) has no entry on international social work. It does have related entries on international and comparative social welfare; international social welfare organizations and activities; and international social work education. This may accurately reflect the fact that international social work, though not new, is still a growing field, while there is much more information, literature, and studies on international social policy and social welfare. It also reflects a pre-9/11 world where there was less emphasis on the need for global understanding and where a small minority of social workers and social work educators in the United States and abroad were interested in international social work, for reasons that will become clearer in the section of this chapter that reviews a historical perspective on international social work. It was only later, with the publication of the Educational Policy and Accreditation Standards (EPAS) in 2001, that the Council on Social Work Education recommended, but did not require, inclusion of a global perspective. Implementation of the recommendation was patchy at best, given the many other curriculum requirements to consider. After 9/11, the pattern changed considerably but not completely. There are many more presentations at professional meetings with international content, and new active international committees were formed in the Baccalaureate Program Directors' Group (BPD) and the National Association of Deans and Directors of Social Work (NADD). The Directors of Field Education established a group to recommend standards for international field placements; CSWE replaced the International Commission with two councils and a Global Commission, as well as establishing the Katherine A. Kendall Institute for International Social Work Education. On the other hand, a key shortcoming is that the current CSWE accreditation standards no longer mention the global perspective in social work education. Thus, from a curriculum perspective there are no expectations of programs to provide an international context to social policy teaching, for example. However, while the accrediting body may have reverted to being more isolationist, many individual programs run study abroad courses, international field placements, and student and faculty exchange programs, so in practice social work education maintains its global context. Thus there is some evidence of revived interest and activity in international social work, and this is a good time to review current views and definitions of international social work.

Watts (1997) reviews a number of definitions of international social work, including that of Barker (1999) in the *Dictionary of Social Work*, who defines international social work as follows:

> *A term loosely applied to (1) international organizations using social work methods or personnel, (2) social work cooperation between countries, and (3) transfer between countries of methods or knowledge about social work. (p. 250)*

Another definition offered by Healy (2008) focuses on four social work practice areas: domestic policy advocacy and practice where there is a distinct global context; professional exchange of ideas; practice in relief and development situations; and global policy advocacy.

This definition makes a useful distinction between international practice, which some commentators have called *social work across borders*, and the use of global knowledge to aid practice locally, which has elsewhere been called *think globally, act locally,* or *the global is local.* This notion of the local is global in international social work represents increasing recognition of the importance of global knowledge in multicultural practice and with migrant populations. Dominelli's (2005) definition emphasizes this view: "... to consider international social work as a form of practice that localizes the global and globalizes the local."

Healy's definition also includes the importance of social workers' potential in using global knowledge to assist in domestic policy developments. Both Barker's and Healy's definitions separate professional intervention (action) and knowledge transfer.

Cox and Pawar (2006) develop the definition further, demonstrating how thinking is constantly developing in the field of international social work:

> *International social work is the promotion of social work education and practice globally and locally, with the purpose of building a truly integrated international profession that reflects social work's capacity to respond appropriately and effectively, in education and practice terms, to the various global challenges that are having a significant impact on the well-being of large sections of the world's population. This global and local promotion of social work education and practice is based on an integrated perspectives approach that synthesizes global, human rights, ecological, and social development perspectives of international situations and responses to them. (p. 20).*

Cox and Pawar's definition gives significance to the idea of a global profession, and separates out the functions of social work education and social work practice as well as focuses on a conceptual framework for international practice that they call an integrated perspectives approach. This definition includes a much-needed theoretical and conceptual perspective.

Healy and Link (2012) present an expanded definition of international social work as having underpinned their planning of the *Handbook of International Social Work*. While it builds on Healy's 2008 definition, it adds a values context in recognizing the importance of human rights and the need for global change. It also adds the importance of a global worldview and the need to understand the global profession of social work.

Because international social work is so varied and is still developing, more than one definition is inevitable and healthy. Hence, the present authors expand the debate by offering a new definition on the basis that multiple definitions give a broader range of perspectives:

> *International social work is concerned with the development, administration, implementation, research, and evaluation, in and through global social institutions and organizations, of policies and programs that promote human rights, human diversity, the well-being and empowerment of people worldwide, and global and social and economic justice. In the postmodern era, international social work values difference and diversity in human experience and seeks to engage with and to learn and adapt from people creating indigenous solutions to socioeconomic problems around the world. International social work subscribes to ideologies, value systems, and theoretical approaches that support these directions.*

In this definition, we have included research of international problems and issues and evaluation of international programs and practice. International social work, just like other parts of the profession, has lacked a research and evaluation base, and it is essential to develop this if practice is to be demonstrated as effective. We have specified a range of practice methods, including administration and development; with the use of the word *promote* we imply advocacy, and in this way have offered a more specific definition than previous ones. Perhaps the most significant addition in this definition is the recognition of the indigenization movements around the world and the need for Western social workers and social work educators to work cooperatively and learn from these efforts. Thus the reciprocal nature of international social work is emphasized in this new definition. We do not claim that this definition covers all issues, and we hope and trust that there will be continuing debate and development.

Table 11.1 further explicates the authors' definition by outlining examples of the activities that can be considered to be international social work. As can be seen, it is a broad field, and the table gives examples in each category, but is not a comprehensive survey of all that may be considered to be international social work.

In clarification, while considering definitions of international social work, we should consider briefly here a definition that sometimes has been quoted as a definition of international social work, that of the joint International Association of Schools of Social Work and the International Federation of Social Workers (IASSW/IFSW), agreed upon in Copenhagen in 2001. The definition quoted below from the IASSW website is, in fact, an international definition of social work, not a definition of international social work. This means that the definition is the consequence of extended discussions and an agreement reached by IASSW and IFSW representatives in 2001.

> The social work profession promotes social change, problem solving in human relationships and the empowerment and liberation of people to enhance well-being. Utilising1theories of human behaviour and social systems, social work intervenes at the points where people interact with their environments. Principles of human rights and social justice are fundamental to social work. (IASSW/IFSW, 2001)

This definition represents an attempt to identify the universals in the profession of social work worldwide. Human rights, empowerment, social change, and problem-solving are central. In a later section of this chapter we discuss further some of the problems associated with attempting to find universals in a profession that is socially constructed. The danger is that such a definition, or in fact in any of the above definitions of international social work, may be said to represent a Western neoliberal perspective on professional social work, and not represent the many indigenous approaches that may also place less emphasis on the organized and professional aspects of the profession. The following section, giving a brief history of international social work, explains further the development of indigenous approaches.

History

Internationalism has been a part of social work since the beginnings of the profession in the 19th century. In this section, we review the role and nature of internationalism in the history of the social work profession in four phases first proposed by Mayadas and Elliott (1997). Table 11.2 summarizes these phases: the first column shows the dates of the four phases, the second column indicates the direction of the exchange, the third column shows the predominant professional values of the period, and the fourth column shows model of service delivery.

Phase One: Early Pioneers, 1880s–1930s

Two organizations, the Settlement Movement and the Charity Organization Society (COS), are generally considered to be the beginnings of the profession in establishing the major modes of service delivery: casework, individual and family solutions to social problems, and community practice and social reform.

Both the COS (1869) and the Settlement Movement (1884) began in England, and the models were exported to the United States. There is well-documented evidence of much interaction and comings and goings across the Atlantic after the establishment of Toynbee Hall Settlement House in the East End of London in 1884 (Reinders, 1982; Kendall, 2000;

Table 11.2 [2]Phases in International Social Work Exchange.

Time Period	Predominant Direction of Exchange	Values	Model of Services
Phase I: 1880s–1930s Early Pioneers The COS, Settlement Movement The influence of Freud The influence of the Fabian Movement	Mostly Europe to America Largely unidirectional America builds the basis of professional hegemony in social work	Paternalistic Ethnocentric	Social Control Charity Philanthropy
Phase II: 1930s–1970s Professional Imperialism	America to rest of world Centrifugal	Paternalistic Ethnocentric Colonialism Universalism	Remedial Medical Crisis-Oriented
Phase III: 1970s–1990s Reconceptualization and Indigenization	Within regions Worldwide Centripetal	Regionalization Polarization Separation Localization	Developmental in Developing Countries Remedial in Western Industrial Nations
Phase IV: 21st-century International Social Development	International Networking	Globalization Transcultural/ Multicultural Democratic, Social, Cultural, and Ethnic Interchange	Developmental in Rural and Urban Areas Worldwide

Estes, 1997). It is interesting to note that at a time when transportation across the Atlantic was much slower and more difficult, there seemed to be much more international cooperation and exchange in terms of practice and service delivery than it may be said that we have now. The COS was established in London in 1869, and its influence spread quickly to the United States, where Charles Gordon Ames, who was said to be impressed with the London organization, founded the Philadelphia COS in 1873 (Rauch, 1976). The COS organizations spread quickly across the United States, and the Reverend Stephen Gurteen founded the Boston COS in 1877.

The beginning of the American Settlement Movement had similar transatlantic influences: visitors from the United States to Toynbee Hall included Jane Addams and Stanton Coit. The establishment of Hull House in Chicago in 1889 was influenced by these visits and the friendship between Jane Addams and Henrietta Barnett, wife of Canon Samuel Barnett, founder of Toynbee Hall. Jane Addams was inspired by Toynbee Hall and The People's Palace on her visit there in 1888, and the Barnetts subsequently had much admiration for Jane Addams and her work at Hull House (Besant, 1887; Kendall, 2000). Stanton Coit founded the neighborhood guild in New York in 1886, which later became known as the University Settlement (Trattner, 1994). This period of the export of an idea from one country, followed by the rapid expansion of COS organizations and Settlement Houses across the United States, is probably an unparalleled period of internationalism in the history of the profession. Books were translated into other languages, and there were regular conferences and meetings, such as the International Congress of Charities, Corrections, and Philanthropy in 1893. Beatrice and Sidney Webb, leaders in the British Fabian movement, influenced Edith Abbott and the School of Social Service Administration in Chicago. The ideas of Charles Booth, founder of the Salvation Army and social reformer, were also influential across the Atlantic (R. Pumphrey & Pumphrey, 1967; Kendall, 2000).

Kendall (2000) documents that additionally at this time, both Britain and America were influenced by the Elberfeld movement in Germany, where a volunteer system based on districts dispensed social welfare assistance without the questions and terms associated with the more social control model of the COS. Another influence from Europe around this time that shaped social work in the years to come was the ideas of Sigmund Freud and others in the psychoanalytic movement (Freud, 1914). An area where the European influence was also strong was in the founding of schools of social work, for education and training in the social services. Following the establishment of the first school in Amsterdam in 1899 and the London School of Sociology in 1903, schools were established in quick succession in New York (1904), Boston (1904), Chicago (1904), and in South America in Santiago, Chile, in 1925 (Kendall, 2000).

Hence, this first phase is characterized by a transmission of knowledge and service delivery methods from Western Europe to the Americas. The traditional charity/philanthropy approach and its accompanying social control function dating back to the Poor Laws was the focal point of services. It can be argued that the Settlement Movement was founded as much as an antidote to concerns and fears of a beginning labor movement and to address social unrest in the crowded and violent urban industrial areas as it was to promote idealistic altruism for the poor. It was during this period, however, that American knowledge and practice of social services and social work was consolidated, strengthened, and developed to position America to become a world leader in the next phase.

Phase Two: Professional Imperialism, 1930s–1970s

This phase represents America's role in global leadership in social work and social services. During the previous period, the emphasis in the United States was on training (especially on a scientific approach to training), on the location of social work education in the university, and on the building of the major models of service delivery for the new profession: Casework, group work, and community work all contributed to America's position as leader in the profession. Schools of social work or social work training courses were established in Bombay (Mumbai) in 1936; Sao Paulo, Brazil, 1936; Cairo, 1936; Uruguay, 1937; Sydney, 1940; Costa Rica, 1942;

Delhi, 1946; Hong Kong, 1950; Lahore, 1954; University of Ghana, 1956; Indonesia, 1957; Tehran, Iran, 1958; Makere, Uganda, 1960; Ethiopia, 1961; Philippines, 1965; Khartoum, 1969 (Midgley, 1981; Abo El Nasr, 1997; Cornely & Bruno, 1997; Ife, 1997). These independent schools, or programs conducted within a department of social administration or sociology, were funded from a variety of public and private sources and staffed largely by Westerners, British, French, and Americans, in the colonial style. Curricula were based on Western models of social work practice, and libraries and reading lists built from Western, predominantly American social work literature became the primary source of knowledge (Guzetta, 1996). Indigenous literature was sparse and little used, consistent with colonial practices. The United Nations sent teams of advisors to assist in setting up schools in many regions, and also conducted a study on the status of social work training around the world in 1950.

While this statement seems to us as rather self-serving, Stein, lamenting the difficulties of obtaining sufficient faculty and of selecting good faculty for service abroad, also points out the beginnings of questioning the export model of social work. He quotes Professor Livingstone of Liverpool University as saying that the West has had an undesirable influence on the development of social work training overseas and in developing countries in particular. Livingstone "deprecates the use of the individual premise in social work, the influence of Freud and Western social policy as having any relevance for developing countries across the globe" (Stein, 1964, p. 240). During this phase, values remained predominantly paternalistic, and social work was seen in the Western tradition as being individually based with the medical and remedial model of service delivery. This involved more focus on reaction to social problems than prevention and offering as little help as possible for as short a time as possible. This was despite the fact that societies in developing countries were more family group–oriented and that large-scale prevention programs were needed in areas such as health care.

In reviewing the colonial period of social work history, some interpreters have deemed "inflammatory" Midgley's coining of the term *Professional Imperialism*; yet others have depicted, with rose-tinted hindsight, that the technology transfer was not colonialist, but a gift relationship in the Titmus sense (Healy, Asamoah, & Hockenstad, 2003; Titmus, 1971; Wagner, 1992). Still others have taken a more pragmatic view, recognizing that this transfer will be a one-way street, at least at times, and Billups and Julià (1996) have suggested that given the inevitability of the one-way street, it is essential that we implement mechanisms for a more careful review of the materials for transfer to ensure they are appropriate. For the present authors, it is hard to see this period, given the political, socioeconomic context and our present-day analysis and understanding of the effects of the colonial period, as anything other than colonial. We may compare the analysis in hindsight of the missionary movement in religion, and of course many schools of social work as well as social work and social welfare service delivery systems were influenced by missionary movements. This view is not to denigrate the work of individuals who, like all of us, are a product of socialization, and who thought that it was a "good thing" to share the "superior knowledge" of the West with developing countries so they could become more like the West. Many were inspired by noble individual motives, did good work, and contributed to the building of institutions. Many, at the same time as providing the services, were the first to raise questions about their efficacy. In the larger scheme of things, Midgley's (1981) critique was timely: He was reared and schooled under the colonial system, and his experience as a student in an oppressive apartheid regime gave his message a clarity that many in the developed world could not see so clearly at the time. This message has more recent relevance, also. After the fall of the Soviet Union, social work educators from Europe and America went to the newly independent states at their invitation to advise on the setting up of social services. To date, many social work programs in the United States and European countries have set up links with universities in developing countries to deliver their programs with little if any consideration of indigenous knowledge. Many of these transactions are not recorded, but the question is raised, Have we really learned the message of professional imperialism, or was it repeated again in the 1990s and to this day, largely through ignorance of the profession's international history? A debate in the Council on Social Work Education Board also reflects this history: the question of whether the CSWE should offer an international accreditation was raised. A working party appointed by the Executive Director to write a background report for the board, chaired by the Chair of the International Commission, reported strong differences of opinion in the working group in relation to an overseas request for CSWE accreditation. Arguments for and against are summarized in Table 11.3, where the shadows of this phase of American dominance in social work education and indeed also of the third phase, reconceptualization and indigenization, can be seen.

Phase Three: Reconceptualization and Indigenization, 1970s–1990s

The lack of goodness of fit of the exported model of Western social work led to a questioning of the appropriateness of importing technology on the part of developing countries. Also, newly independent states free from colonial ties, especially in Africa, wanted to divest themselves of systems that reflected a colonial and oppressive past. The reconceptulization movement in South America and the indigenization movements in Africa, the Middle East and India all had the goals of shaking off the dependence on American and European models of social work and fostering a more culturally appropriate model for each country. This period is thus marked by a retreat to regionalism and separatism.

In South America the strong influences were liberation theology, social development, and the ideas of Paulo Freire, such as "conscientization," which made people more aware of their dependency on developed nations. Quiero-Tajalli (1988) reports Alayón's (1988) model of the four stages of social work development in Argentina: the first stage was marked

Table 11.3 International Accreditation of Social Work Education Programs: Pros And Cons.

Against	For
• **Social work is socially constructed** and reflects the linguistic, social, legal, economic, cultural, health, and educational perspective of a particular country. It is a sufficiently complex task as it is for the commission on accreditation to be fully aware and sensitive to all the diversity within the United States.	• **A strength of the current accreditation standards** as represented by EPAS is that they are nonprescriptive and flexible and therefore lend themselves to enabling site teams to judge whether a program is fulfilling its own standards on its own terms. This would apply equally to overseas programs.
• **Ethnocentricity:** The assumption that social work educators are qualified to judge foreign programs for accreditation is based on an ethnocentric view of the world.	• **Competence of site visitors:** The qualifications of existing site visitors are sufficient guarantees of competence. In fact it is predicted that there will be no shortage of volunteers for international site visitors.
• **Role of the international organizations**: It was noted that IASSW had reviewed and decided against international accreditation and had settled for producing some international guidelines for social work. It was felt that even these draft guidelines were sufficiently controversial, albeit having been made with international input.	• **International Association of School of Social Work:** There is nothing in the IASSW guidelines that conflicts with the CSWE accreditation standards. The CSWE possesses the world's largest quality accreditation system for social work, there is little reason for IASSW to object, as they are not seeking to accredit. Why should not overseas programs seek voluntary accreditation if this will attract students and faculty?
• **Representation in the accreditation process**: It was argued that while US educators would be represented on various commissions and boards of the CSWE, there is no current provision for extending this representation to overseas educators. Even if that were to be the case, how to represent the many countries involved? Therefore overseas participation in the process for international accreditation would be severely limited.	• **Deans, directors, and faculty of accredited programs** are eligible for election and nomination to various Boards and committees. This would apply to overseas accredited programs, also.
• **Influence of American foreign policy**: This proposal was considered in 2003, and there was heightened awareness of the post 9/11 treatment of foreigners and the beginning of the war in Iraq. There was heightened awareness of American socioeconomic and political hegemony. For the social work profession to ignore the broader political context was not acceptable to many of the respondents to the working parties' inquiries.	• **American hegemony**: If this were a serious concern, then CSWE would not give equivalent status to Canadian social-work education programs.

Table 11.3 (Continued)

Against	For
• **Cost-benefit analysis**: The argument that international accreditation would be a new source of income for CSWE would perpetuate the historic economic exploitation of the global south. Additionally, accreditation is already costly and labor intensive and the costs would seem to outweigh the benefits.	• **Costs:** If the accreditation process imposes a burden on an overseas program, this would be similar to the situation in the United States. The overseas program has the choice to participate or not. This is not an imposed requirement. Furthermore, some overseas programs would be located in some affluent areas without concurrency conversion problems. CSWE might gain financially because more people would enroll for the APM.
	• **Impact of CSWE accreditation on non-accredited programs:** This situation exists currently in the United States, where nonaccredited programs exist side by side with accredited programs. If the impact of accreditation is to raise standards, all programs will seek accreditation eventually.
	• **CHEA accreditation of CSWE:** CSWE itself is accredited by the Council for Higher Education Accreditation (CHEA). There would have to be special arrangements made or this criterion would have to be wanted as irrelevant to foreign programs.
	• **"Brain drain"**: It would be easier for both foreign and U.S. faculty to work in each other's programs. It would encourage more faculty and student exchange, and would support the trend for portability of qualifications in the international job arena.

From a figure first published in "Lessons from International Social Work: Policies and Practices" (p. 176), by N. S. Mayadas and D. Elliott, in *Social Work in the 21st Century*, M. Reisch and E. Gambrill (Eds.), 1997, Thousand Oaks, CA: Pine Forge Press. Adapted with permission.

by *asistencialismo* (assistance) and corresponded to the charity model that perpetuated rather than solved the poverty problem. The second stage was *cientificismo* (scientificism). This focused on community development and was not adequately resourced. The third stage was *reconcepualización* (reconceptualization or transformation). This stage was different in each Latin American country, but it began at a conference held at the Federal University of Rio Grande do Sul in Porto Alegre, Brazil, in 1965, and its aim was to change the methodological influences of the exported American and European models of social work to a more indigenous model. Political participation was encouraged in social workers with the goal of eradicating oppressive social conditions, along with the mobilization and conscientization of the population (Cornely & Bruno, 1997). Many conferences were held under the auspices of CELATS (The Latin American Center of Social Work) and ALEATS (Latin American Schools of Social Work) towards the development of an indigenous progressive radical model of social work. Quiero-Tajalli (1988) reports that the last and fourth phase of Alayón's model is *post-reconceptualization*, beginning in the early 1980s. This phase involved reconciling what could be salvaged from the more progressive period after the neo-conservative military regime placed stringent limits on social work. Privatization and the move from universal benefits to targeted benefits all affected the profession and those they served.

In Africa, the Middle East, and India, there was more focus on a developmental approach to social problems and especially to poverty and survival. Nanavatty (1997) argues that in India, casework, usually carried out by trained social workers, predominated in the urban areas, and a more developmental, community-based approach in the rural areas was not carried out by trained social workers but by local volunteers, teachers, and community workers. In Africa, it was inevitable that there was a search for a local model of social work, since the origin of almost all schools of social work in Africa was from overseas. A focus for the indigenization movement in Africa was a meeting of ministers of social welfare in 1968, where a developmental orientation was proposed to counteract the remedial model of existing services (Asamoah, 1997). This was followed by subsequent meetings and the creation of ministries of social development so that this approach became well-established in countries such as South Africa and Zimbabwe. As well as the developmental perspective, and the challenge of merging the remedial and developmental models, Asamoah also argues (p. 314) that the indigenization of social work in Africa, was influenced by three main theoretical strains: *agology*, a Dutch model meaning the "science of guiding or leading"; the German model of *social pedagogy*, an educational approach to social work; and *conscientization*, the South American empowerment model which raises consciousness of the masses in order to create social change from the grass roots. With respect to indigenization, it was encouraged in Egypt by a United Nations' international survey of social work training in 1971, in which the term *indigenization* was used. Abo El Nasr (1997) suggests a distinction between *indigenization*, as the process by which a country accommodates the Western model of social work to local conditions, and *authenticization*, which is the creation of a model originating from local philosophy, culture, norms, and practices. There are few truly authentic models existent around the world, but this is an important distinction to remember when the term *indigenization* is so freely used.

This phase is clearly still not finished and merges with the fourth phase discussed below. Many areas of the world, including most notably South Africa and China, are still searching for or developing an indigenized or truly authentic model of social work practice at the present time

(Midgley, 2001; Yuen-Tsang & Wang, 2002; Gray, 2006). Miu and Kwok (2006) discuss the political implications of this process and the professional power struggles involved in bringing about "recontextualization." Recognizing the importance of this search for indigenization or recontextualization, Western authors have raised the question as to whether the idea of international social work is inevitably oppressive and whether it is possible to identify any kind of true universalism within the profession because of the social constructionist nature of the profession (Ahmadi, 2003; Dominelli, 2005; Gray, 2005; Gray & Fook, 2004; Nagy & Falk, 2000). This debate is discussed more fully after the fourth phase.

Phase Four: International Social Development, 21st Century

Where developing countries have succeeded in making a paradigm shift from a Western-based service delivery model to an indigenous and, most often, social development model of social work, this has the potential to move from a reactivist, remedial model of social work and social welfare to a new kind of international cooperation where there is equality, mutuality, reciprocal benefits, and a true exchange of ideas around the globe. International networking is the key to this phase, as opposed to binational relations. The values of social development are consistent with those of social work: Social justice, cooperation, planning, prevention, participation, democracy, human dignity and worth, institutional change and empowerment are all values common to both social development and social work (Midgley, 1995). Social development emphasizes a multicausal view of both assessment and intervention in social problems, and thus moves away from the individual pathology perspective of the medical model. Social development sees diversity as a central principle because the context of practice is multicultural (Mayadas & Elliott, 1997). Social development is not inconsistent with clinical practice, but rather adds a new dimension to clinical practice. Elliott and Mayadas (1996) report how considering the economics of clinical practice according to social development principles, for example, increases the awareness in clinical practice of the multibillion health insurance industry behind the DSM. Another example of the social development approach that has had worldwide applications from its beginnings in Bangladesh in 1974 is the name "Grameen Bank," meaning "village bank" (Elliott & Mayadas, 1996). An organization founded by a professor of economics, Muhammud Yunus, today the Grameen Bank has worldwide applications of microcredit in 58 countries and lends to more than 5 million people, of whom 96% are women, for the purpose of investing in small entrepreneurial projects (Yunus, 2003). The Grameen Bank pioneered an approach to poverty reduction based on microcredit. This emphasizes the use of social capital in repaying the loans and in the development of centers and groups through which the loans are organized; it has the highest loan repayment rate of any banking system (Yunus, 2011). The Grameen Foundation supports initiatives in 36 countries, including the United States. The opening of the New York City branch of the bank in 2011 was reported by the *Wall Street Journal* and TV's *Morning Joe*. Examples of successful U.S. projects are illustrated on the Grameen America website: Maria Sanchez runs a fruit drink cart in Manhattan. Her Grameen loan helped her diversify her stock and increase business, and she now plans to borrow an even larger loan to expand her business to a storefront location. Nicole Gates took out a $1,500 loan to purchase barbeque and tables and chairs for her Soul Quisine business. Lisette, a hairdresser in Upper Manhattan, had no access to credit to purchase supplies and operate her own home-based hairdressing business instead of working in a salon. She took out two loans with Grameen to make her business successful (Grameen America, 2011). "Give us Credit" by Counts (1996) is another account of how the Grameen Bank microcredit idea was adapted in the United States, in Chicago's South Side.

The activities of the Grameen Bank epitomize the characteristics of the fourth phase under discussion here, and those that most clearly meet the goals of the progressive idealist group of internationalists mentioned earlier in this chapter. International networking; transculturalism; globalization; democracy; and social, cultural, and ethnic interchanges, all irrespective of where in the world the idea originates and, as indicated in phase four of the model represented in Table 11.2, are all represented in this successful worldwide project. Imagine if this degree of success could be applied to address universal health care; day-care provision; nursing homes; disaster readiness, response, and recovery; and other pressing social problems in the United States through a genuine exploration of worldwide ideas and best practices—then this fourth phase would have become a reality.

There is no doubt that among Western social work educators with experience in international programs and research, there is a large measure of agreement that the way forward for international social work has to be one of mutual respect, equality, and reciprocity in exchange, similar to the conditions described in phase four of the model discussed above. Healy, Asamoah, and Hockenstad (2003) in their *Models of International Collaboration in Social Work Education*, make very clear that criteria for a successful collaboration are sustainability, mutuality, and the synergy that develops when an institution, rather than just individuals, becomes involved in an international collaboration.

The Search for Global Standards for Social Work Education and a Global Definition of Social Work: Universalism Versus Indigenization?

However, there have been views expressed that suggest that even this fourth phase may now become outdated: Dominelli (2005) quotes the view of IASSW President Tassé Abye of Ethiopia that powerful elites in the globalized mega-cities of the world are already internationalized and quite probably trained in the West: internationalizing or globalizing social work is therefore, he argues, a Western preoccupation, while the developing world is much more concerned with indigenization and developing new models of practice. Nevertheless, while recognizing some of the shortcomings of an approach that searches for a universal definition and global standards, the joint IASSW/IFSW task force secured the remarkable achievement of getting broad agreement on the global definition quoted earlier in this chapter and also in 2004 on a document setting out global standards for social work education worldwide. This represented a historic achievement for social work and a step toward its recognition as a global profession. The global standards for education and training in the social work profession identify 13 core purposes for the profession from which one may distill several principles: (a) working to include and protect "marginalized, excluded, dispossessed, vulnerable, and at-risk" populations; (b) working towards politico-socio-economic structural change to enhance people's life situations; and (c) encourage advocacy at all levels—global, national, regional, organizational, and interpersonal. A significant area of discussion is the principle that "promotes respect for traditions, cultures, ideologies, beliefs, and religions among different ethnic groups and societies, *insofar as these do not conflict with the fundamental human rights of people.*" The italicized phrase raises the question of who defines the fundamental human rights of people. Is this standard based on a Western notion of human rights? Are Western democracy and its concomitant values the only acceptable political solution for human rights? Clearly the debate will continue, but the global standards have carried forward this debate significantly. The document also sets out standards for program objectives and outcomes as well as field and core curricula, and also identifies eight paradigms that are really value sets, which, it is argued are the basis of the social work profession worldwide. In fact, in setting global standards for social work education, inevitably, the standards have moved forward the concept of a universal, global definition of social work.

The preparation, numerous consultations, discussion forums, and publication in 2004 of the final agreed-upon *Global Standards for Social Work Practice Around the World* prompted a discussion in the literature about the nature of international social work (Ahmadi, 2003; Dominelli 2005; Gray, 2005; Gray and Fook, 2004; Nagy & Falk, 2000). Gray (2005) has argued, in summarizing the arguments of other authors on the topic, that social work is struggling with the contradictory and competing issues of universalism, indigenization against a background of imperialism. The challenge that is raised is how can social work be authentic and socially constructed, yet also seek global commonalities? In the view of the present authors, these are not mutually exclusive. However, international social work must recognize postmodern developments and the adverse effects as well as the advantages of globalization, and support directions that strengthen indigenous approaches as we included in our definition.

The Rationale for International Social Work

Globalization as an economic and social phenomenon is an accepted fact in the early 21st century. This can be seen in the following ways: multinational corporations with transnational employees, the globalization of food: restaurants around the world serve food from foreign countries; the Internet has facilitated international communications from the personal to governmental levels; popular culture and the media, including music, movies, and television, have all contributed to or are a result of globalization. Globalization has brought with it increasing recognition of the interdependence of nations and inevitably, at the same time, that of their social and economic problems. The boundaries between nations have become porous and in some cases in the European community have become nonexistent. The profession of social work cannot be unaffected by this context. Here are the views of one commentator on the impact of globalization on social work:

> *International migration makes poverty, political and religious oppression, and the lack of civil rights in one society the concern of other societies. Woman trafficking and sex tourism make the sexual exploitation of women and children in one part of the world the moral, legal, and public health concern of other parts. Low wages, harsh work conditions, and the exploitation of underage work force in one country affect national employment policies and labour markets in other countries. (Ahmadi, 2003 p. 15)*

We may add other areas of practice that bring global problems into domestic practice. Dominelli (2005) has used the term "globalize the local and localize the global" for this process of internationalizing in social work practice. International adoptions, child abductions across national boundaries, social work with asylees, migrant workers, immigrant populations, and undocumented immigrants are increasingly common in the caseload of social workers in the United States. A newer group of individuals are transnationals who, unlike traditional immigrants, may be professionals who work for a global corporation or other institution or may be unskilled workers who come across the Mexico–United States border daily or for a few months at a time for seasonal work. The impact of changing demographics affects social workers' caseloads in all major U.S. cities.

The 2009 American Community Survey reports that the foreign-born population has grown from 9.6 million, or 4.7% of the total population in 1970, to 38.5 million foreign-born residents, representing 12.5% of the total population (U.S. Census Bureau, 2010). Segments of the foreign-born population are disproportionately affected by the recession: The Pew Hispanic Center (2011) reports that 6.1 million Hispanic children were in poverty in 2010. Of these children, more than two-thirds were the children of immigrants. This is the first year since these records have been kept that the majority of children living in poverty were not white children.

Social workers' caseloads in all settings, schools, hospitals, and child welfare agencies are therefore increasing in diversity, not only with domestic diverse populations but also with populations that are foreign born. This requires a new kind of knowledge of international social issues, as they are likely to be met in domestic practice to be incorporated into the curriculum for the training and education of social workers.

After the fall of the Soviet Union, and the dropping of political barriers in the European community, many more social workers train in one country and practice in another. In these circumstances, to have a developed and commonly accepted sense of international standards, values, knowledge, and skills that make up the social work profession would greatly enhance the portability and prestige of the profession.

A global perspective in social work offers "multiple dimensions of analysis and provides new ways of analyzing problems from a multicultural and pluralistic viewpoint" (Elliott & Mayadas, 1999, p. 53). It offers a new perspective on social problems, because they may be "writ large" or experienced at a more intense level than in the United States. For example, the study of poverty in different countries gives new insights into the experience of poverty at home. A comparative study such as the World Bank ethnographic study, "Voices of the Poor," gives an insight into the universality of the problems associated with poverty and a better understanding of poverty at home (Narayan, Chambers, Shah, & Petesch, 2000). Similarly, a study of social justice in which the dynamics of injustice and oppression are understood from an international perspective can enhance appreciation at home of social justice and oppression. Use of international materials such as the United Nations Declaration of Human Rights, the United Nations Convention on the Rights of the Child, the United Nations Declaration on the Elimination of All Forms of Racial Discrimination, or the Convention on the Elimination of Discrimination against Women can also enhance an appreciation of social justice at home (United Nations, 1963; 2006; van Wormer, 2004, 2006).

Elliott and Mayadas (1996, 1999, 2000) have proposed that strengthening the international connections of social work and thus incorporating a stronger worldwide perspective and a greater shared identity into the profession can enhance the somewhat uncertain and fragile identity of the profession at home.

Broadening the perspective of social work practice with an international appreciation of the human condition challenges ethnocentrism and paternalism in social work practice. Overseas experiences such as study abroad can help social workers recognize that different is not necessarily "weird" and thus improve their responses to diverse populations at home. Ultimately, relationships formed, knowledge gained, and attitudes changed in an experience such as study abroad, which students often refer to as "life changing," can assist in international understanding and contribute ultimately to world peace.

A comparative perspective is needed to increase knowledge about social issues and problems. It is recognized that no one country can have all the answers or all the best services for every social problem; surely there must be something to be learned from global practice, with a possible view to adoption at home, but maybe also rejection with efforts to seek further alternatives. We need more comparative studies in all areas of social problems to consider what is most effective across the globe, as well as research and comparative analysis of social policies. The comparative studies we have already provide a good insight for those who care to read them. We need more, and we need them to be mainstreamed in social work education for maximum future benefit.

So far, the rationales mentioned consider the majority of social workers working within the United States and the benefits bestowed by an international perspective and experience for domestic practice. The focus of an international perspective is in making service at home more effective, especially when involving international populations or bringing new ideas for more effective service delivery from overseas. There are a minority of social workers who wish to work across borders in international agencies, such as Save the Children, Oxfam, or agencies of the United Nations such as UNICEF, UNHCR, and UNDP. These require a different kind of training and perspective, and there is little evidence that present training is effective (Hockenstad & Kendall, 1995). The focus in this kind of specialized training for international service should be on the knowledge and skill needed to function effectively across borders. Knowledge and skills in social development practice, as well as comparative social research and comparative policy analysis, are required.

Barriers to Success in International Social Work

A major barrier can be seen in the difference in models of practice in different countries. Many countries have adopted a community development or social development model of practice in international social work, with less emphasis on individual work. In social work at home, the medical model on the whole still prevails, with the addition of new approaches such as strengths perspective and empowerment. It is difficult for individually trained practitioners to grasp a more group-oriented community approach, as in international social work (Elliott & Mayadas, 1996; Mayadas & Elliott, 1995). Another barrier is seen in the difference in service delivery systems: The privatization of welfare services, the role of government, and the functions of NGOs (sometimes called voluntary agencies and sometimes nonprofit agencies) differ to a great extent around the world (Elliott, 1997; Mayadas, Watts, & Elliott, 1997).

With regard to social work education, the established curriculum is already crowded with requirements for accreditation both at the professional level and at the university level. Many programs are reluctant to add more content and more hours to the program. Resources in social work education are limited, and international social work requires funding of exchanges for students and faculty. Outside funding is limited and is often difficult for nonresearch-based smaller schools and departments to obtain. Additionally, the difficulty in determining where multicultural social work ends and where international social work begins acts as a barrier to implementation of curricula and practice. Is working with immigrant populations in the United States multicultural social work, or is it international social work?

The general modus operandi in the United States is that of protectionism and isolationism as a principle of foreign policy. This is a large obstacle to overcome in social work schools and departments. Local TV news has little international content, and it is difficult to generate interest or for students and practitioners to identify the relevance of international social work. An example is the reaction within the United States to Hurricane Katrina: The media focused intensely on the problem for many days. Individual stories of hardship were told, and public sympathy was aroused. On the other hand, the devastating monsoon floods in Bangladesh or the Calcutta Basin may be reported sparsely if at all, and with little or no inclusion of personal stories to make the problem more understandable or arouse social concern, as the similar situation of Katrina did for social work agencies.

On the other side of the coin, perhaps international social work has not sufficiently defined what it is and why it is relevant. An example of this is that the majority of social work textbooks do not generally include an international perspective. It is hard, therefore, for some programs where faculty have no international experience or links to implement the recommendations of the Council on Social Work Education in its Educational Policy and Accreditation Standards (EPAS).

Another problem is that practical obstacles are sometimes difficult to overcome: language differences, value differences, commitment to a nationalistic identity, and absence of universally accepted arrangements for equivalency determination of social work qualifications (Harris, 1997; Midgely, 1997). While practitioners and social work students may have idealism in adherence to the ideas of social justice, oppression, and human rights, these have not been sufficiently operationalized at the concrete practice level (Elliott & Mayadas, 1999).

International Social Welfare Organizations

There are numerous international organizations, and those organizations involved in social work, social welfare, and social policy may be categorized into governmental, nongovernmental (NGO), and professional organizations (Elliott, 2008).

The United Nations, created by charter in 1945, is the largest service provider of international social welfare services, as well as having policy-making, educational, and research functions.

The social welfare–related services of the UN are carried out in agencies reporting both to the General Assembly and to the Economic and Social Council. Agencies such as the Office of the United Nations High Commissioner for Refugees (UNHCR), the United Nations Development Program (UNDP), the World Food Program, and the World Bank address major world problems such as forced migration, hunger, poverty, and development.

The policy-making functions of the United Nations are carried out through conventions (international treaties) and declarations that have been previously discussed at length by many interested parties in conferences, seminars, and summits. An example of these policies is the

Millennium Development Goals, often referred to as MDGs. By the year 2015, the MDGs aim to have made significant inroads into world poverty, gender rights, child mortality, maternal health, AIDS, and HIV. The human rights agenda of the United Nations is also an important policy function and has led to declarations and conventions affecting many vulnerable groups such as children, women, the disabled, and also the Convention on the elimination of all forms of discrimination. The Convention on the Rights of the Child is the most broadly ratified UN Convention to date (Elliott, 2008).

The research functions of the United Nations provide free access to valuable materials and data sets for scholars on health, demographics, and poverty and to indicators such as the Human Development Indices.

U.S. governmental agencies, in addition to being involved in UN programs, often participate in international collaborations and multilateral relationships, many that address social work issues. The U.S. Department of Health and Human Services,[3] the primary governmental social welfare agency in the United States, has several components with significant international emphases, including, for example, programs for children, women, and families in an international context (Healy, 1999). The Centers for Disease Control tackle both national and international health concerns, including prevention, mental health intervention, and services for trauma and violence. The Office of Global Health Affairs[4] connects with other nations around healthcare policy and programs. The U.S. Social Security Administration,[5] in addition to conducting research on social security programs worldwide, is engaged as the U.S. link with the International Social Security Association (Healy, 1999). The U.S. Department of Homeland Security, which now houses U.S. Citizenship and Immigration and Services,[6] is responsible for immigration flows into the country as well as refugee resettlement. Other programs, such as the Peace Corps, which was established in 1961 and contributes to social and economic development in several countries, and U.S. AID,[7] which among other goals supports global health, conflict prevention, and humanitarian assistance, involve numerous international efforts in delivering social welfare services.

The second category of organization engaged in international social welfare is that of the nongovernmental organizations (NGOs), also known as private voluntary organizations (PVOs) or just voluntary organizations. Their functions may be viewed as coordinating, advocacy, service, and faith-based organizations. An example of a coordinating NGO is the International Federation of Red Cross and Red Crescent Societies, which coordinates disaster response functions globally. An example of an advocacy NGO is Amnesty International, advocating worldwide for human rights. Service-oriented NGOs are organizations such as Acción (microeconomic projects), Save the Children (poverty and children's rights), and the YMCA and the YWCA, serving families and communities globally. Faith-based NGOs such as World Vision International and Catholic Relief Services offer significant social welfare services across the globe (Elliott, 2008).

A third group of international organizations relevant to social work and social welfare are professional organizations. Global interdependence has been recognized by segments of the social work profession in several nations, and professional organizations in social welfare have been in existence for several decades. The International Association of Schools of Social Work (IASSW)[8] was founded in 1928 with 51 schools; it was based primarily in Europe, but now has members in all regions of the world. The IASSW promotes the development of social work education and standards to enhance its quality; it encourages and provides forums for international exchanges and engages in advocacy activities. In addition, it has a consultative role and participates as an NGO with the UN. The International Federation of Social Workers (IFSW)[9] is a global organization committed to the improvement of the human condition through the development of social work and international cooperation between professionals. The International Council on Social Welfare (ICSW)[10] and the International Consortium for Social Development (ICSD),[11] both committed to social development and the empowerment of individuals and groups, serve as consultants to the UN, the World Bank, and other international organizations.

Although less known, the National Association of Social Workers (NASW) and the Council on Social Work Education (CSWE) have also long been internationally involved respectively through the International Activities Committee and the International Commission. In 2004, CSWE, in increasing recognition of the need to globalize social work education, established the Katherine Kendall Institute for Social Work Education.[12] This new initiative, inspired by the life work of Katherine A. Kendall, a legendary, inspirational, and longtime leader in international social work, has the mission of fostering the mainstreaming of international social work in social work education curricula in the United States, and also of facilitating the development of resources to support educators and practitioners in achieving this goal. Also in 2004, CSWE restructured the International Commission, which became known as the Global Commission; consistent with other changes within the organization, two councils of the Global Commission were established: the Council on Global Research and Practice and the Council on External Relations. The Global Commission is charged by the CSWE Board with furthering the global agenda of CSWE; supporting the growth and development of the Katherine A. Kendall International Institute; encouraging the integration of global social work in the social work curriculum; providing leadership in research on global social work issues; and collaborating with international organizations to aid in these efforts. These efforts strengthened the role of international social work in the social work education agenda of the United States.

With increasing globalization, including in communication, trade, and migration, international social welfare organizations may be called upon with growing regularity. The field of international social welfare has long been cognizant of international interdependence, as is reflected by the numerous organizations engaged in international social welfare activities, and it is time that the mainstream profession integrate it into its normal structure.

2011: The Global Dimension in Local Practice: Local Is Global and Global Is Local

An increasingly important aspect of International Social Work is the recognition that international issues and information are no longer a separate part of social work, but influence the everyday interactions of social workers with their clients. In this section we present information to illustrate this point. The first example relates to immigration from a direct practice perspective and shows how work with immigrant individuals and their families within the United States can be influenced by knowledge of human migration and knowledge about the prior experiences and culture of immigrants in their own countries. The second example relates to family violence around the world and how a global perspective can influence the way in which we understand the problem at home.

Global Awareness in Social Work With Immigrants

Individuals and families from around the globe form a continuous stream of immigrants to the United States. The backlog of new visa applications and waiting lists to enter the United States stretches for several years. Undocumented immigrants,[13] both those who enter without legal papers and those who overstay their visits, abound. Refugees and asylees continue to enter in record numbers from countries in political turmoil. Disproportionately large numbers of entrants into the United States in recent years have been people of color from Asia, Africa, and Central and South America, and despite encountering a series of barriers, immigrants' adaptation in a new country reflects the interplay of the reasons for departure from the homeland, the experience of migration, their tangible and intangible resources for functioning in unfamiliar environments, and the effects of the receptiveness of the host country (both politically and socially) to their presence (Segal, 2011). Furthermore, regardless of the length of time immigrants are in the U.S., they are invariably faced with a duality of cultures and must learn to function within norms and expectations that frequently conflict.

The U.S. Bureau of the Census indicates that in 2010, of the approximately 307 million residents of the country, 37.6.5 million (12.4%) were foreign born and another 34.1 million (11.2%) were children of those who had migrated from other countries (Table 11.4). These two groups, taken together, have been termed the "New Americans" and constitute 23.6% of the U.S. population. Table 11.5 presents census data on immigrants in 1990, 2000, and 2010 by region of birth, while Table 11.6 identifies the region of birth of those refugees who became permanent residents (immigrants) between 1991 and 2010 (U.S. Census Bureau, 2010; Office of Immigration Statistics, 2010).

Table 11.4 U.S. Population by Sex, Age, and Generation in 2010 (in thousands.)

	Total		Generation[14]					
			First		*Second*		*Third-and-Higher*	
Gender and Age	**Number**	**Percent**	**Number**	**Percent**	**Number**	**Percent**	**Number**	**Percent**
Total Male and Female	304,280	100	37,606	100	34,115	100	232,559	100
Under 16 years	66,185	21.8	2,198	5.8	13,921	40.8	50,066	21.5
16–65 years	199,482	65.5	30,819	82	15,722	46.1	152,941	65.8
65 years and over	38,613	12.7	4,589	12.2	4,472	13.1	29,552	12.7
MEDIAN AGE (years)	36.7	(X)	41.3	(X)	21	(X)	37.5	(X)
Total Male	149,485	100	18,757	100	17,192	100	113,536	100
Under 16 years	33,833	22.6	1,091	5.8	7,124	41.4	25,618	22.6
16–65 years	98,859	66.2	15,761	84	8,142	47.4	74,956	66
65 years and over	16,793	11.2	1,905	10.2	1,926	11.2	12,962	11.4
.MEDIAN AGE (years)	35.5	(X)	40.2	(X)	20.3	(X)	36.3	(X)
Total Female	154,795	100	18,848	100	16,923	100	119,023	100
Under 16 years	32,352	20.9	1,107	5.9	6,797	40.2	24,449	20.5
16–65 years	100,623	65	15,058	79.9	7,579	44.8	77,985	65.6
65 years and over	21,820	14.1	2,684	14.2	2,547	15	16,590	13.9
.MEDIAN AGE (years)	37.9	(X)	42.4	(X)	21.8	(X)	38.7	(X)

(X) = Not Applicable

Source: U.S. Census Bureau, Current Population Survey, Annual Social and Economic Supplement, 2010 www.census.gov/population/foreign/data/cps2010.html

With increasing globalization and the ease of transnational migration, U.S. social workers are increasingly recognizing that "international" social work now occurs within the country. Immigrants bring with them their range of cultures and experiences, many of which may be useful in adapting to the U.S. society, environment, and economy, while many may conflict with dominant values (Segal, 2004). As immigrants learn to negotiate the U.S. system, they may struggle to understand the laws, programs, services, and opportunities and may turn to social workers in the process. Some may find adaptation relatively easy, if they arrive with the requisite skills and language capabilities, but may learn later that their children have difficulty reconciling their own bicultural identities. Refugees, who arrive in the country after fleeing horrific experiences in their own homelands and being divested of all that is familiar to them, can suffer a number of serious psychosocial difficulties that require extensive social work intervention, both immediately upon arrival and after they have established themselves. Social workers need to be cognizant of immigrants' and refugees' experiences prior to entering the country in order to better understand the problems

Table 11.5   Immigrants by Region of Birth: 1990 to 2010.

Region of Birth	1990 Total	2000 Total	2010 Total
All countries	7,338.10	9,095.40	37,606.00
Europe	705.6	1,311.40	4,509
Asia	2,817.40	2,892.20	10,126
Africa	192.3	383	
Oceania	(NA)	48	
North America	**3,125.00**	**3,917.40**	
Canada	119.2	137.6	
Mexico	1,653.30	2,251.40	11,580
Caribbean	892.7	996.1	3,649
Central America	458.7	531.8	2,820
South America	455.9	539.9	2,370
Other areas**			2,551

(Number in Thousands)

* Includes Mexico

** Other areas: Includes Africa, Oceania, North America, and born at sea.

Source: U.S. Department of Homeland Security, Office of Immigration Statistics, 2004 Yearbook of Immigration Statistics. U.S. Census Bureau, Current Population Survey, "Annual Social and Economic Supplement". See also: www.cenus.gov/population/www/socdemo/foreign/datatbls.htm

Table 11.6   Immigrants Admitted as Permanent Residents Under Refugee Acts, by Region of Birth: 1991 to 2010.

Region and Country of Birth	1991 to 2000 Total	2001 to 2002 Total	2004	2005	2010
Total	**1,021,266**	**234,590**	**71,230**	**142,962**	**136,291**
Europe	426,565	118,736	24,854	46,588	4770
Asia	351,347	41,406	14,335	32,009	68,587
Africa	51,649	20,360	12,443	25,143	22,634
Oceania	291	52	28	55	52
North America	185,333	51,503	18,323	35,709	34,657
Cuba	144,612	47,580	16,678	32,555	29,804
Haiti	9,364	1,504	536	1118	2817
El Salvador	4,073	382	263	D	D
Guatemala	2,033	809	387	D	
Nicaragua	22,486	631	137	208	121
South America	5,857	2,158	1,150	3,312	5,362

See also: www.dhs.gov/files/statistics/publications/yearbook.shtm.

Source: U.S. Department of Homeland Security, Office of Immigration Statistics, 2010 Yearbook of Immigration Statistics.

they present to social services on entry and after (Mayadas & Lasan, 1984; Pine & Drachman, 2005; Segal, Mayadas, & Elliott, 2006; Sherraden & Martin, 1994). Undocumented workers may come to the attention of the social services, and social workers must balance their ethical responsibilities to those in need with their responsibility to the nation and its laws.

Relatively little attention in the literature is devoted to temporary migrants (on short-term work visas) to the United States and business people and their families. While many are not eligible for social services, they may require social work intervention if they are hospitalized, their children have difficulties in school, there are domestic violence or substance abuse issues, and so forth.

Example One: Mail-Order Brides

A little-recognized group of entrants into the United States, who may well arrive legally as immigrants but who often suffer from culture shock and isolation, are mail-order brides. Many have difficulty adapting to the new lifestyle they encounter, have no knowledge of the men they will marry, and usually leave their families of origin permanently. Nevertheless, this business is a booming one that has yet to be regulated by the United States. A Google search of the term *mail-order brides* yields over 10 million websites in less than 10 seconds, attesting to (1) the popularity of getting a wife and (2) the desire of women who may not otherwise qualify to enter the United States to immigrate. Furthermore, the last decade has brought increasing awareness to the issue of human trafficking, and the persistent social and economic servitude experienced by individuals brought into the country, either against their will or through false promises. Potocky (2011) indicates that although the government has no mechanism to systematically collect data, more than 15,000 victims of human trafficking enter the United States annually. Human trafficking may include the trafficking of either minors or adults across borders, primarily for domestic service or sex trade (Agustin, 2007). Social workers in the United States are gradually learning of new and unanticipated issues. Shier, Engstrom, and Graham (2011) in their review of the literature on international migration and social work indicate that between 1985 and 2005, they have identified at least four major themes that emerge and that may influence social work practice with migrant populations: (1) demographic and sociological/psychological experiences, (2) service delivery, (3) physical and mental health, and (4) macrostructure and its impact on migration.

Clearly, social workers may engage in international social work without ever having left the United States. They must draw on their diversity training, their knowledge of multiculturalism, and their openness to new worldviews in order to adequately work with the increasingly international group of clients they are likely to encounter (Segal & Mayadas, 2005; U. Segal, Segal, & Diwakaran, 2006). It is essential that, in the process of being culturally sensitive and competent, social workers be mindful of extreme cultural relativism and carefully evaluate varying cultural norms that may conflict with fundamental social work values.

Example Two: Global Awareness in Working With Family Violence

A second example shows how viewing family violence internationally from a human behavior perspective deepens our understanding of the issue at home. Awareness of family violence in the United States, coupled with less awareness and less openness about this issue in other countries, has often led people to assume that maltreatment in the family is more common in the United States than elsewhere. This may merely be because many other nations continue to view relationships within families as private matters. Focus in many developing countries, such as those of Africa, Asia, and South America, has traditionally been on the health, education, and welfare needs of families, or on the societal (institutionalized) or extrafamilial abuse of individuals. The family has been sacrosanct and has been protected from inspection of its internal relations by outsiders, and all the while, the society has claimed that no intrafamilial violence exists.

Although still in its infancy, awareness of family violence is beginning to burgeon in other countries. In 1983, as recently as three decades ago, Gelles and Cornell reported that literature claimed that child abuse in countries such as India and Japan was low. Yet, in 1988, India held its First National Seminar on Child Abuse and Neglect. In 1996, Japan established the Japan Society for the Prevention of Child Abuse and Neglect (JaSPCAN) and, in 2000, the Japan Diet passed the Child Abuse Prevention Act. In 1983, Kumagai and Strauss (1983) published findings that conjugal violence was low in India and Japan, with discussion suggesting that these are pacifist nations. However, Koithara (1996) indicated that violence against women in India is widespread, but not discussed, and Yoshihama and Sorenson (1994) found that 58.7% of 796 women who responded to a nation survey in Japan indicated that they were victims of marital violence. Clearly, family violence may well be as much a problem in those countries that do not acknowledge or study it as it is in those that do. In fact, even if the legal system recognizes family violence as a problem, the general public may be unaware of it. In 2001, the Japanese Diet passed the nation's domestic violence law, but as recently as April 15, 2006, *The Mainichi Daily News* reported that a nationwide survey conducted by the Japanese Cabinet revealed that of the 2,888 (64.2%) respondents, 66.2% were unaware of the contents of the law and 13.3% were even unaware of its existence, but in 2005, the reported cases of domestic violence jumped by 17.5% to 16,888 occurrences (Mainichi, 2006). The United Nations reports that violence against women is chronic and persistent, with statistics suggesting that 60% of all women experience some form of physical and/or sexual violence at some time (www.unifem.org/gender_issues/violence_against_women/).

The 2006 *In-Depth Study on All Forms of Violence against Women* by the UN Secretary General indicated that at least 89 countries have developed some form of legislation regarding domestic violence (www.un.org/ga/search/view_doc.asp?symbol=A/61/122/Add.1, retrieved October 31, 2011). The International Network for the Prevention of Elder Abuse

(INPEA), established in 1997, launched World Elder Abuse Prevention Day on June 15, 2006, and this is marked annually on June 15 (www.inpea.net/, retrieved October 31, 2011). Societies are torn between cultural norms that protect families from inspection and increasing recognition of the need for society to intervene to protect human rights violations. Increasingly, resources are being established around the world, and information about them is readily accessible to service users and providers through a variety of Internet search engines. Andrew Vachss, an attorney well-known for his work with child abuse and neglect, maintains a Web site called "The Zero" that includes a list of international resources that address family violence (www.vachss.com/help_text/domestic_violence_intl.html, retrieved October 31, 2011), and the Hot Peaches Pages is a global inventory of hotlines, shelters, refuges, crisis centers, and women's organizations; this can be searched by country and in more than 70 languages (www.hotpeachpages .net/, retrieved October 31, 2011).

Violence may be defined as any act of commission or omission that results in physical, sexual, or emotional injury to another. Although there are a number of theories of family violence, many of which focus on individual psychological problems of perpetrators, victim characteristics, and environmental circumstances, another set of theories suggest that the cause of family violence lies in the structure of society (Connors, 1989) which is both a product and a reinforcement of the unequal distribution of power between men and women, between adult and child, and between provider and dependent. Patriarchal values support female inferiority and are transmitted to younger generations with family violence tolerated as a male right to control those who are dependent (Carrillo, 1992; Heise, Pitanguy, & Germain, 1994). Most theories on the structure of family violence tend to agree that when society tolerates physical violence as a mechanism for conflict resolution, and when it accepts male authority and superiority in decision making within the home, it provides the ideal blueprint for family violence (Connors, 1989; Kantor, 1996).

In 2002, the World Health Organization (WHO) released its *World Report on Violence and Health* (Krug, Dahlberg, Mercy, Zwi, & Lozano, 2002), still the most up-to-date publication of its kind, and prominent in the amount of information given on child abuse, intimate partner violence, and elder abuse. The report assumes an ecological model for the understanding of violence, suggesting that a variety of factors influence violence including the biological, social, economic, political, and cultural. The report identifies a relatively universal definition of child abuse that was developed in 1999 through a review of definitions from 58 countries and with the cooperation of the International Society for the Prevention of Child Abuse and Neglect (Krug et al., 2002). A 48-country population-based study from around the world revealed high levels of intimate partner violence (Krug et al., 2002). In industrialized nations, violence appeared to result from either high levels of possessiveness on the part of the (usually) male partner or chronic frustration and anger that erupted into violence, while in more traditional societies, wife-beating was considered the right of the male to elicit obedience and was considered acceptable to the women, who felt that much of the punishment was justified. Interestingly, however, in both industrialized and developing countries, the triggers for intimate partner violence appear to be similar, with most revolving around the female not attending to the perceived rights of the male. The WHO report further indicates that elder abuse is prevalent in all nations of the world, and that since the 1975 "granny battering" described by British scientific journals, industrialized as well as developing countries have reported the prevalence of elder maltreatment (Krug et al., 2002).

While it appears that most societies recognize that there are both psychosocial and structural components to family violence, prevention and intervention programs seem to indicate that cultures differ in the extent to which they credit one component over another. It appears, further, that cultures and communities that are more allocentric (those with a group orientation) tend to focus on societal and environmental interventions, and those that are idiocentric (more individual-focused) are more likely to take the psychosocial and family intervention models. Three articles in Volume 49 of the journal *International Social Work* reported studies of domestic violence in Medan, Indonesia (Rowe, FakihSutan, & Dulka, 2006), an Australian indigenous community (Cheers et al., 2006), and Chinese families (Chan, 2006) and appear to provide explanation of domestic violence in cultural and structural terms. In Medan, the professional women's general tolerance of marital violence reflects acceptance of patriarchal values; in the Australian Aboriginal community, a new perspective of family violence places it " . . . in the historical context of colonization, oppression, dispossession, disempowerment, dislocation, and poverty" (p. 51), and in China, the higher the level of "face-saving" concerns of males, the greater the likelihood of violence against a significant female. A review of articles in journals such as the *Journal of Child Abuse and Neglect*, the *Journal of Elder Abuse*, and several journals on family studies indicates that studies in many Western, industrialized countries tend to focus more on perpetrator/victim characteristics and experiences to provide explanations of behavior, and tend to suggest interventions that are focused on altering individuals' behavior. Based on cultural perceptions of the cause, or correlates, of violent behavior, recommendations for intervention target either the perpetrator/victim or public awareness and societal education. The focus in idiocentric (Hofstede, 1980) cultures appears to be on dealing with the psychosocial health of victims, while in allocentric (Hofstede, 1980) countries, focus is on community development (i.e., Cheers et al., 2006) or on helping women develop independent economic stability. In either case, one underlying aim is to provide victims with the resources, both psychological and practical, to strengthen coping abilities. In reviewing family violence from this global perspective, we see U.S. social work practice as falling into the idiocentric category of responses worldwide. By reviewing new developments around the world new programs and policies can be considered for more structural approaches to the problem.

Theoretical Frameworks and International Social Work Research

A review of the international social work literature shows that there is limited discussion and no consensus relating to practice models or theoretical frameworks: the IASSW/IFSW global standards discussed earlier are largely atheoretical. Theoretical approaches so far are very much at the beginning stages of formulation and much more debate and interaction is needed to develop fully fledged theoretical and evidence based knowledge to take international social work into the next phase. Asamoah, Healy, and Mayadas (1997) review some theoretical approaches: In discussing unifying frameworks, they consider social work as a human rights profession; social work as social development; and "cross-cultural competence as a core social work skill and focus" (p. 397). Healy (2003) discusses "globally relevant conceptual frameworks including: social development; human rights, multiculturalism, social exclusion/inclusion; security and sustainability." Guzetta (1998) addresses finding unity in diversity and argues that all religions require their followers to practice some form of assisting those in need. He proposes that distributive mechanisms, personal obligation, state responsibility, and family organization may be components of a unifying theme. Link (1999) discussed the role of international professional ethics and values and the IFSW International Code of Ethics, and Ramanathan & Link (1999) propose two frameworks: one to assess engagement in global and social work learning, and the second, seven steps to global orientation. Van Wormer's (1997, 2004, 2006) approach to international social work includes a consideration of values, economic oppression, social oppression, and human rights and restorative justice. Midgley (1997), Billups (1990, 1994), Estes (1995, 1997), Elliott (1993), Mayadas and Elliott (1997), and Elliott and Mayadas (2000) all see potential in the social development framework for international social work practice. The social development approach offers a framework that encompasses many of the approaches mentioned above: empowerment, institution building, prevention and development, sustainability and ecological issues, investment in human and social capital, human rights and social justice, diversity, multisystem and interdisciplinary focused universal programs and optimal benefits for the fulfillment of human potential. Elliott (1993, 2010) and Elliott and Mayadas (2000), offer practice models that include both domestic and transnational social work practice with social development as a common factor. Cox and Pawar (2006) propose an Integrated Perspectives Approach to international social work and incorporate this into their definition of international social work quoted earlier. This approach includes the following "guiding perspectives" (p. 45): globalization; ecological; human rights; and social development. This approach provides a very clear framework for their text on international social work and represents significant progress in the direction of a theoretical framework for international social work. Midgley and Conley's (2010) model offers the most comprehensive social work practice model to date from a social development perspective. Inspired by international social work practice, this book applies social development to social work in the United States offering a new model of social work practice based on assets, strengths, and capabilities. Like the Grameen Bank, it is a good example of technology transfer from the developing to the developed world, and has much potential as a model of international social work practice.

Tripodi and Potocky-Tripodi (2007) advance a much-needed model for international social work research. While there has been consistent comparative research over the years in the field of social welfare, theoretical frameworks for international social work research have been largely neglected in the literature. Tripodi and Potocky-Tripodi have made a significant development in extending the definition of international social work research, which they define as follows: *"international social work research can be considered social work research that is relevant to international social work"* (p. 18). They also offer a typology on international social work research, which includes supranational, intranational, and transnational research. According to the definitions proposed by Tripodi and Potocky-Tripodi, *supranational social work research* or research beyond borders includes research with native-born populations within one country, research where the research problem and the implications drawn are framed from the literature of more than one country. *Intranational social work research* or research within borders includes research with international migrants within a country, and literature from both countries is used. *Transnational social work* research or research across borders is comparative research. In this way, the remit of international social work research is extended and it is argued that through the Internet research tools it is possible for a scholar to do international research while sitting at home. Through this definition and typology, Tripodi and Potock-Tripodi hope that more people will be encouraged to undertake international social work research.

Conclusion

In this chapter we have offered a new definition, considered history, identified some of the main issues in international social work, and addressed applications. We are only too aware of the many issues left unconsidered. To conclude, we offer a way forward to strengthen the position of international or global social work.

In order to build an effective body of knowledge for international social work, we propose that the following three steps are needed

- Agreement on common values, practices, skills, and models. This has been largely achieved by the IASSW/IFSW Global Standards document. However, dissenting voices and conflicting issues around oppression and indigenous models need to be understood and incorporated.

- Applying what Cox and Pawar (2006) have called guiding perspectives, we have extended these to include recognition of:
  - The worldwide social construction of social work
  - All human rights
  - Global social work professional ethics and values
  - The centrality of respect for and knowledge of human diversity and Indigenous approaches
  - The role of economics in the global and local and personal economies
  - The importance of social and economic justice, including issues of restoration, power, and politics
  - The need to build a verifiable and testable knowledge base in a postmodern intellectual climate, including both quantitative and qualitative international social work research
  - Approaches to facilitating the empowerment of individuals, communities, and peoples
  - Incorporating technology such as Internet use into international practice
  - Research- and evidence-informed approaches to social work practice
  - Application of "globalcentric" paradigms and way of thinking
  - The need for many approaches to advance thinking and practice
- The development of practice-based models to guide international practice at a more detailed and tested level.

Each of these stages has been addressed to some extent by the international scholars quoted above and by many others whose ideas space precludes the opportunity to discuss here. The enormous task before us as social workers and social work educators is to build on this base and extend and frame the context for international social work.

We still, indeed, have "miles to go."

NOTES

1. In some of the quotations included in this chapter the non-American spelling is evident, for example, "behaviour," "utilising," "indigenisation," and "moulding." These have been included as originally published where there are direct quotes from non-American authors. Otherwise American English spelling conventions are followed.

2. Table 11.2 is adapted from a figure first published by N. S. Mayadas and D. Elliott (1997), Lessons From International Social Work: Policies and Practices. In M. Reisch & E. Gambrill (Eds.), *Social Work in the 21st Century* (pp. 175–185). Thousand Oaks, CA: Pine Forge Press.

3. See www.hhs.gov

4. See www.hhs.gov/ogha/europeaffairsdhhs.shtml

5. See www.ssa.gov

6. See www.uscis.gov/graphics/index.htm
7. See www.usaid.gov/about_usaid
8. See www.iassw-aiets.org
9. See www.ifsw.org/home
10. See www.icsw.org
11. See http://socialdevelopment.net/about.htm
12. See www.cswe.org/about/kakinstitute.htm
13. The terms "illegal," "undocumented," and "unauthorized" are used interchangeably in referring to immigrants who do not have the requisite legal papers to be in the United States.
14. *First generation* refers to those who are foreign born; *second generation* refers to those with at least one foreign-born parent; *third-and-higher generation* includes those with two U.S. native parents. *Source:* US Bureaus of the Census. Characteristics of the foreign born by generation. www.census.gov/population/foreign/data/cps2010.html

Key Terms

Comparative social policy

Developing countries

Global exchange

Indigenization of social work

International collaboration

International social work

Social development

Review Questions for Critical Thinking

1. How can social workers collaborate to ensure global human rights?
2. In what ways are individual social workers in the United States and other developed countries affected in their practice by globalization?
3. What can developing countries learn from developed nations and vice versa?
4. How transferable are social work skills across national borders?
5. Is international social work possible in a profession such as social work that is socially constructed?

Online Resources

Professional Organizations

International Federation of Social Workers: www.ifsw.org/f38000041.html

International Association of Schools of Social Work: www.iassw-aiets.org

ICSW: International Council on Social Welfare: www.icsw.org

ICSD: International Consortium on Social Development: www.iucisd .org

United Nations Links

United Nations: http://www.un.org/en/

United Nations Development Program: www.beta.undp.org/undp/en/ home.html

International Social Work Journal: isw.sagepub.com

United Nations Women: Addresses issues relating to women worldwide: www.unwomen.org

HDI Human Development Indices: Measuring social progress across the world: http://hdr.undp.org/en/statistics

UNICEF: State of the World's Children annual reports: www.unicef.org/ sowc/index.html

UN World Food Program: Fighting hunger and working for food security worldwide: www.wfp.org

UNHCR: The Office of The United Nations High Commissioner on Refugees: www.unhcr.org/cgi-bin/texis/vtx/home

International Advocacy Organizations

Human Rights Watch: Monitoring and preventing human rights abuses globally: www.hrw.org

Amnesty International: Protecting human rights globally: www.amnesty .org/

CRIN: Child Rights International Network: www.crin.org/about/index .asp

Service-Providing NGOs

OXFAM International: www.oxfam.org/

Catholic Relief Services: International social welfare/social work branch of the Catholic Church): http://crs.org

World Vision International: Provides advocacy, disaster relief, and development programs worldwide: www.wvi.org/wvi/wviweb.nsf

International Red Cross: www.icrc.org/eng

Save the Children: www.savethechildren.org/site/c.8rKLIXMGIpI4E/b .6115947/k.8D6E/Official_Site.htm

WHO: World Health Organization: www.who.int/en

IMF: The International Monetary Fund: Fighting global poverty: www .imf.org/external/np/exr/facts/sia.htm

Further resources containing a wealth of links

CSWE Katherine Kendall International Institute: Has many links to jobs and study abroad funding: www.cswe.org/CentersInitiatives/KAKI/KAKIResources/25104.aspx

PRAXIS: The home page of Dr. Richard Estes, University of Pennsylvania, with many links and resources related to international social work and social development: www.sp2.upenn.edu/restes/praxis.html

References

Abo El Nasr, M. M. (1997). Egypt. In N. S. Mayadas, T. D. Watts, & D. Elliott (Eds.), *International handbook on social work theory and practice* (chap. 13). Westport, CT: Greenwood Press.

Agustín, L. M. (2007). *Sex at the margins: Migration, labour markets and the rescue industry.* London, UK: Zed Books.

Ahmadi, N. (2003). Globalisation of consciousness and new challenges for international social work. *International Journal of Social Welfare, 12,* 14–23.

Alfe, J. (1997). Australia. In N. S. Mayadas, T. D. Watts, & D. Elliott (Eds.), *International handbook on social work theory and practice* (chap. 22). Westport, CT: Greenwood Press.

Alayón, N. (1988). *Perspectivas del Trabajo Social* (2nd ed.). Buenos Aires Argentina: Editorial Humanitas. Quoted in Quiero-Tajalli, I. (1997). Argentina. In N. S. Mayadas, T. D. Watts, & D. Elliott (Eds.), *International handbook on social work theory and practice* (chap. 6). Westport, CT: Greenwood Press

Asamoah, Y. (1997). Africa. In N. S. Mayadas, T. D. Watts, & D. Elliott (Eds.), *International handbook on social work theory and practice* (chap. 18). Westport, CT: Greenwood Press.

Asamoah, Y. (2003) International collaboration in social work education: Overview. In L. Healy, Y. Asamoah, & M. C. Hockenstad. (Eds.) *Models of international collaboration in social work* (chap. 1). Alexandria, VA: Council on Social Work Education.

Asamoah, Y., Healy, L. M., & Mayadas, N. S. (1997). Ending the international domestic dichotomy: New approaches to a global curriculum for the millennium. *Journal of Social Work Education, 33*(2), 389–401.

Barker, R. L. (1999). *Dictionary of social work.* Washington, DC: NASW Press.

Besant, W. (1887). The people's palace. *Contemporary Review, 51,* 226–233. Available at http://tigger.uic.edu/htbin/cgiwrap/bin/urbanexp/main.cgi?file=new/show_doc.ptt&doc=462&chap=6; (Hull House Museum, Historical Narrative.).

Billups, J. O. (1990). Towards social development as an organizing concept for social work and related social professions and movements. *Social Development Issues, 12*(3), 14–26.

Billups, J. O. (1994). The social development model as an organizing framework for social work practice. In R. G. Meinert, J. T. Pardeck, & W. P. Sullivan (Eds.), *Issues in social work: A critical analysis.* Westport, CT: Auburn House.

Billups, J. O., & Julià, M. C. (1996). Technology transfer and integrated social development: International issues and possibilities for social work. *Journal of Sociology and Social Welfare, 23,* 175–188.

Carrillo, R. (1992). *Battered dreams*. New York: NY: UNIFEM.

Chan, K. L. (2006). The Chinese concept of face and violence against women. *International Social Work, 49*, 65–73.

Cheers, B., Binell, M., Coleman, H., Gentle, I., Miller, G., Taylor, J., & Weetra, C. (2006). Family violence: An Australian indigenous community tells its story. *International Social Work, 49*, 51–63.

Connors, J. F. (1989). *Violence against women in the family*. New York, NY: United Nations.

Cornely, S. A., & Bruno, D. (1997). Brazil. In N. S. Mayadas, T. D. Watts, & D. Elliott (Eds.), *International handbook on social work theory and practice* (chap. 7). Westport, CT: Greenwood Press.

Counts, A. (1996). *Give us credit*. New York, NY: Crown.

Cox, D., & Pawar, M. (2006). *International social work: Issues strategies and programs*. Thousand Oaks, CA: Sage.

Dominelli, L. (2005). International social work: Themes and issues for the 21st century. *International Social Work, 48*(4), 504–507.

Edwards, R., & Hopps, G. J. (Eds.) (1995). *Encyclopedia of social work*. (19th ed.). Washington, DC: NASW.

Elliott, D. (1993). Social work and social development: Towards an integrative model for social work practice. *International Social Work, 36*, 21–36.

Elliott, D. (1997). Conclusion. In N. S. Mayadas, T. D. Watts, & D. Elliott (Eds.), *International handbook on social work practice and theory* (pp. 441–449). Westport, CT: Greenwood Press.

Elliott, D. (2008). International social work organizations. In *20th encyclopedia of social work* (pp. 480–482). New York, NY: Oxford/NASW Press.

Elliott, D. (2010). A social development model for infusing disaster in the social work curriculum. In D. Gillespie & K. Danso (Eds.), *Disaster concepts and issues: A guide for social work education and practice* (chap. 5). Alexandria, VA: Council on Social Work Education Press.

Elliott, D., & Mayadas, N. S. (1996). Social development and clinical practice in social work. *Journal of Applied Social Sciences, 21*(1), 61–68.

Elliott, D., & Mayadas, N. S. (1999). Infusing global perspectives into social work practice. In C. S. Ramanatham & R. Link (Eds.), *All our futures: Principles and resources for social work practice in a global era* (pp. 52–68). Belmont, CA: Wadsworth.

Elliott, D., & Mayadas, N. S. (2000). International perspectives on social work practice. In P. A. Meares & C. Garvin (Eds.), *The handbook of social work direct practice* (pp. 519–535). Thousand Oaks, CA: Sage.

Estes, R. (1995). Education for social development: Curricular issues and models. *Social Development Issues, 16*(3), 68–90.

Estes, R. (1997). Social work, social development and community welfare centers in international perspective. *International Social Work, 40*, 43–55.

Ferguson, K. M. (2005). Beyond indigenization and reconceptualization: Towards a global multidirectional model of technology transfer. *International Social Work, 48*(5), 519–535.

Freud, S. (1914). The history of the psychoanalytic movement. German original first published in the *Jahrbuch der Psychoanalyse, 4*. Translation first published in the Nervous and Mental Disease Monograph Series (No. 25). New York: Nervous and Mental Disease Pub. Co. Reproduced in C. D. Green (2006), *Classics in the history of psychology*. York University, Ontario, Canada. Retrieved from http://psychclassics.yorku.ca/Freud/History

Gelles, R. J., & Cornell, C. P. (1983). Introduction: An international perspective on family violence. In R. J. Gelles & C. P. Cornell (Eds.), *International perspectives on family violence* (pp. 1–22). Lexington, MA: D.C. Heath & Co.

Grameen Bank (2006). Retrieved May 14, 2006, from www.grameen-info.org/

Grameen America. (2011). Success stories. Available at www.grameenamerica.com/our-borrowers/success-stories/success-stories.html

Grameen Foundation. (2011). Available at www.grameenfoundation.org

Gray, M. (2005). Dilemmas of international social work: Paradoxical processes in indigenization, universalism, and imperialism. *International Journal of Social Welfare, 14*, 231–238

Gray, M. (2006). The progress of social development in South Africa. *International Journal of Social Welfare, 15* (suppl. 1), S53-S64.

Gray, M., & Fook, J. (2004). The quest for a universal social work: Some issues and implications. *Social Work Education, 23*(5), 652–644.

Guzetta, C. (1996). The decline of the North American model of social work education. *International Social Work, 39*, 301–315.

Guzetta, C. (1998). Our economy's global: Can our social work education be global? *Journal of International and Comparative Social Welfare, XIV*, 23–33.

Harris, R. (1997). Internationalizing social work: Some themes and issues. In N. S. Mayadas, T. D. Watts, & D. Elliott (Eds.), *International handbook on social work theory and practice* (chap. 24). Westport, CT: Greenwood Press.

Healy, L. M. (1999). International social welfare: Organizations and activities. In R. Edwards & G. J. Hopps (Eds.). *Encyclopedia of social work* (19th ed., pp. 1499–1510). New York, NY: Oxford/NASW Press.

Healy, L. M. (2003). A theory of international collaboration: Lessons for social work education. In L. Healy, Y. Asamoah, & M. C. Hockenstad. *Models of international collaboration in social work* (chap. 2). Alexandria, VA: Council on Social Work Education.

Healy, L. M. (2008). *International social work: Professional action in an interdependent world* (2nd ed.). New York, NY: Oxford University Press.

Healy, L. M., Asamoah, Y., & Hockenstad, M. C. (2003) *Models of international collaboration in social work*. Alexandria, VA: Council on Social Work Education.

Healy, L. M., & Link, R. J. (2012). *Handbook of international social work, human rights, development, and the global profession*. New York, NY: Oxford University Press.

Heise, L., Pitanguy, J., & Germain, A. (1994). *Violence against women: The hidden health burden* (World Bank Discussion Paper 255). Washington, DC: World Bank.

Hockenstad, M. C., & Kendall, K. A. (1995). International social work education. In R. Edwards & G. J. Hopps (Eds.), *19th encyclopedia of social work*. Washington, DC: NASW Press.

Hockenstad, M. C., & Midgley, J. (2004). *Lessons from abroad: Adapting international social welfare innovations*. Washington, DC: NASW Press.

Hofstede, G. (1980). *Culture's consequences*. Beverly Hills, CA: Sage.

IASSW/IFSW. (2001). International definition of social work. Retrieved August 18, 2006, from www.iassw-aiets.org

IASSW/IFSW. (2004). Global standards for the education and training of the social work profession. Final document adopted at the general assemblies of IASSW and IFSW, Adelaide, Australia in 2004. Vishanthie Sewpaul (IASSW Chair) and David Jones (IFSW Co-Chair). Available at www.iassw-aiets.org

Kantor, P. (1996). *Domestic violence against women: A global issue.* Unpublished manuscript, University of North Carolina at Chapel Hill, Department of City and Regional Planning.

Kendall, K. A. (2000). *Social work education: Its origins in Europe.* Washington, DC: CSWE.

Koithara, I. (Director). (1996, February 6). *Social workers and the challenge of violence worldwide.* Chapel Hill, NC: Closed circuit national telecast.

Kumagai, F., & Strauss, M. (1983). Conflict resolution tactics in Japan, India, and the USA. *Journal of Comparative Family Studies, 14,* 377–387.

Krug, E. G., Dahlberg, L. L., Mercy, J. A., Zwi, A. B., & Lozano, R. (2002). *World report on violence and health.* Geneva, Switzerland: World Health Organization. Retrieved May 14, 2006, from www.who.int/violence_injury_prevention/violence/world_report/en/full_en.pdf

Link, R. (1999). Infusing global perspectives into social work values and ethics. In C. S. Ramanathan & R. J. Link (Eds.), *All our futures: Principles and resources for social work practice in a global era* (chap. 5). Belmont, CA: Brooks/Cole.

Link, R. J., & Healy, L. M. (2005). Introduction to the collection. In R. J. Link & L. M. Healy (Eds.), *Teaching international content: Curriculum resources for social work education.* Alexandria, VA: Council on Social Work Education.

Mainichi Daily News (2006, April 15). Most Japanese unaware of domestic violence law, counseling facilities. Available at http://mdn.mainichimsn.co.jp/national/news/20060415p2a00m0na023000c.html

Mayadas, N. S., & Lasan, D. B. (1984). Integrating refugees into alien cultures. In C. Guzzetta, A. J. Katz, & R. A. English (Eds.), *Education for social work practice: Selected international models.* New York, NY: IASSW/CSWE.

Mayadas, N. S., Watts, T. D., & Elliott, D. (Eds.). (1997). *International handbook on social work practice and theory* (pp. 441–449). Westport, CT: Greenwood Press.

Mayadas, N. S., & Elliott, D. (1995). Developing professional identity through social group work: A social development model for education. In M. D. Feit, J. H. Ramey, J. S. Wodarski, & A. R. Mann (Eds.), *Capturing the power of diversity* (pp. 89–107). New York, NY: Haworth.

Mayadas, N. S., & Elliott, D. (1997). Lessons from international social work: Policies and practices. In M. Reisch & E. Gambrill (Eds.), *Social work in the 21st century* (pp. 175–185). Thousand Oaks, CA: Pine Forge Press.

Midgley, J. (1981). *Professional imperialism.* London: Heinemann Educational Books.

Midgley, J. (1990). International social work: Learning from the third world. *Social Work. 35*(4), 295–301.

Midgley, J. (1995). *Social development: the developmental perspective in social welfare.* Thousand Oaks, CA: Sage.

Midgley, J. (1997). *Social welfare in global context.* Thousand Oaks, CA: Sage.

Midgely, J. (2001). South Africa: the challenge of social development. *International Journal of Social Welfare, 10,* 267–275.

Midgley, J., & Conley, A. (2010). *Social work and social development: Theories and skills for developmental social work.* New York, NY: Oxford University Press.

Midgley, J., & Livermore, M. (1997). The developmental perspective in social work: Educational implications for a new century. *Journal of Social Work Education, 33*(3), 573–586.

Miu, C. Y., & Kwok, W. C. (2006). Politics of indigenization: A case study of development of social work in China. *Journal of Society & Social Welfare, 63,* 33.

Nagy, G., & Falk, D. (2000). Dilemmas in international and cross-cultural education. *International Social Work, 43*(1), 49–60.

Nanavatty, M. (1997). India. In N. S. Mayadas, T. D. Watts, & D. Elliott (Eds.), *International handbook on social work theory and practice* (chap. 15). Westport, CT: Greenwood Press.

Narayan, D., Chambers, R., Shah, M. K., & Petesch, P. (2000). *Voices of the poor: Crying out for change.* New York, NY: Oxford University Press.

Office of Immigration Statistics. (2006). *2004 yearbook of immigration statistics.* Washington, DC: Office of Homeland Security.

Pew Hispanic Center. (2011). The toll of the great recession. Available at www.cenus.gov/population/www/socdemo/foreign/datatbls.htm

Pine, B. A., & Drachman, D. (2005). Effective child welfare practice with immigrant and refugee children and their families. *Child Welfare, LXXXIV*(5), 537–562.

Potocky, M. (2011). Human trafficking training and identification of international victims in the United States. *Journal of Immigrant & Refugee Studies, 19*(2), 196–200.

Pumphrey, R. E., & Pumphrey, M. W. (1967). *The heritage of American social work: Readings in its philosophical and institutional development.* New York, NY: Columbia University Press.

Quiero-Tajalli, I. (1997). Argentina. In N. S. Mayadas, T. D. Watts, & D. Elliott (Eds.), *International handbook on social work theory and practice* (chap. 6). Westport, CT: Greenwood Press.

Ramanathan, C. S., & Link, R. J. (1999). Future visions for global studies in social work. In C. S. Ramanathan & R. J. Link (Eds.), *All our futures: Principles and resources for social work practice in a global era* (chap. 13). Belmont, CA: Brooks/Cole.

Rauch, J. (1976). The charity organization movement in Philadelphia. *Social Work, 21*(1), 55–62.

Reinders, R. (1982). Toynbee Hall and the American settlement movement. *Social Service Review, 56,* 39–54.

Rowe, W. S., FakihSutan, N., & Dulka, I. M. (2006). A study of domestic violence against academic working wives in Medan. *International Social Work, 49,* 41–50.

Segal, U. A. (2004). Practicing with immigrants and refugees. In D. Lum (Ed.), *Cultural competence, practice stages, and client systems* (pp. 230–286). Belmont, CA: Brooks/Cole.

Segal, U. A. (2011). Work with immigrants and refugees. In L. N. Healy & R. J. Link (Eds.), *Handbook of international social work* (pp. 73–80). New York, NY: Oxford University Press.

Segal, U. A., & Ashtekar, A. (1994). Evidence of parental child abuse among children admitted to a Children's Observation Home in India. *Child Abuse and Neglect. 18*(11), 957–967.

Segal, U. A., & Mayadas, N. S. (2005). Assessment of issues facing refugee and immigrant families. *Child Welfare, 84*(5), 563–584.

Segal, U. A., Mayadas, N. S., & Elliott, D. (2006). A framework for immigration. *Journal of Immigrant and Refugee Studies, 4*(1), 3–24.

Segal, U. A., Segal, Zubin N., & Diwakaran, Anu R. (2006). Immigrant children in poverty. In B. A. Arrighi & D. J. Maume (Eds.), *Child poverty in America today: Children and the state.* New York, NY: Praeger.

Sherraden, M. S., & Martin, J. J. (1994). Social work with immigrants: International issues in service delivery. *International Social Work, 37*, 369–384.

Shier, M. L., Engstrom, S. & Graham, J. R. (2011). International migration and social work: A review of the literature. *Journal of Immigrant & Refugee Studies, 9*(1), 38–56.

Stein, H. (1964). *International responsibilities of U.S. social work education.* in N. L. Aronoff (2003) *Challenge and change in social work education; toward a world view. Selected papers by Herman D. Stein.* Alexandria, VA. Council on Social Work Education.

Taylor, Z. (1999). Values, theories, and methods in social work education: A culturally transferable core? *International Social Work, 42*(3), 309–318.

Titmus, R. M. (1971). *The gift relationship.* London: Allen & Unwin.

Toors, M. (1992). Is international social work a one-way transfer of ideas and practice methods from the United States to other countries? No. In E. D. Gambrill & R. H. Pruger (Eds.), *Controversial issues in social work* (pp. 98–104). Needham Heights, MA. Allyn & Bacon.

Trattner, W. I. (1994). *From poor law to welfare state: A history of social welfare in America.* New York, NY: The Free Press.

Tripodi, T., & Potocky-Tripodi, M., (2007 International social work research: issues and prosepcts. New York, NY., Oxford University Press.

University of Washington. (2006). *What is international social work and why is it important?* Seattle, WA: School of Social Work. Available at http://depts.washington.edu/sswweb/isw/

United Nations. (1963). United Nations Declaration on the Elimination of All Forms of Racial Discrimination. Available at www.unhchr.ch/html/menu3/b/9.htm

United Nations. (2006). A summary of United Nations agreements on human rights. Available at www.hrweb.org/legal/undocs.html#UDHR

U.S. Census Bureau. (2004). Current population survey, *Annual Social and Economic Supplement.*

U.S. Census Bureau. (2006). Statistical abstract of the United States: 2006. *The National Data Book* (125th edition). Washington, DC: U.S. Department of Commerce, Economics, and Statistics Administration.

U.S. Census Bureau. (2010) Place of Birth of the foreign-born population 2009 American community. Survey Briefs retrieved November 1, 2011, from http://www.census.gov/prod/2010pubs/acsbr09--15.pdf

U.S. Department of Homeland Security (2004) Office of Immigration Statistics. *2004 yearbook of immigration statistics.* Washington, DC.

van Wormer, K. S. (1997). *Social welfare: A world view.* Chicago, IL: Nelson-Hall.

van Wormer, K. S. (2004) *Confronting oppression, restoring justice: From policy analysis to social action.* Alexandria, VA: Council on Social Work Education.

van Wormer, K. (2006) *Introduction to social welfare and social work: The U.S. in global perspective.* Belmont, CA: Thomson Brooks/Cole.

Wagner, A. (1992). Social work education in an integrated Europe: Plea for a global perspective. *Journal of Teaching in Social Work, 6*(2), 115–130.

Watts, T. D. (1997). An introduction to the world of social work. In N. S. Mayadas, T. D. Watts, & D. Elliott (Eds.), *International handbook on social work theory and practice* (chap. 1). Westport, CT: Greenwood Press.

Yoshihama, M., & Sorenson, S. B. (1994). Physical, sexual, and emotional abuse by male intimates: Experiences of women in Japan. *Violence and Victims, 9*(1), 63–78.

Yuen-Tsang, A. W. K., & Wang, S. (2002). Tensions confronting the development of social work education in China: challenges and opportunities. *International Social Work. 45*(3), 375–388.

Yunus, M. (2003). *Banker to the poor: Micro-lending and the battle against world poverty*. New York, NY: Public Affairs.

Yunus, M. (2011) What is micro credit? Available at www.grameen-info.org/bank/WhatisMicrocredit.htm

Zohlberg, A. R. (2006). *A nation by design: Immigration policy in the fashioning of America*. Cambridge, MA: Harvard University Press.

Chapter 12
Immigrant and Indigenous Populations

Special Populations in Social Work

Jon Matsuoka and Hamilton I. McCubbin

Can indigenous knowledge offer new theories for social work practice?

Special populations have been defined as select clusters of individuals, families, or communities who were designated by a majority of members in society or the community to become the focus of stigmatization, prejudice, and discrimination. For whatever reason, such as skin color, ancestry, behaviors, or socially defined labels, these special populations are identified as unique—that is, distinguishable in contrast to the majority adopted and imposed social norms, values, and expectations. Consequently, they are ostracized and treated as subordinate, if not less than human, in the eyes of the majority. Thus, they are scorned and treated with disrespect and humiliation.

These special populations emerge in the course of history, much as lepers, immigrants, and slaves, and have become constant reference points for ridicule and, at times, inhuman subordination. At another extreme, but also stigmatized, are subpopulations who fail to possess the expected characteristics of the time, such as beauty, physical health, fitness, slimness, and glamour. Clearly, the subject of special populations can be so broad as to defy meaningful analysis, particularly in the context of the social work profession. Consequently, the sifting and winnowing process of focusing this chapter has been both a challenge and an opportunity. The invitation to address the complex and vast subject of special populations became an opportunity to frame a social work issue that is ancient and at the same time emergent and pressing as a current issue. The focus of choice in this chapter begins with immersion in the struggles of special immigrant and indigenous populations, largely created through the historic processes of immigrations as well as colonization, but whose voices as a collective whole are coming to the foreground of social work concerns accompanied by frontal challenges to social work theory, research, and practice (Kim & Berry, 1993).

Special Populations: Roots of Diversity and Tension

What makes a special population special is that they reveal the importance of diversity in society and thus also in the social work profession. The value of diversity varies according to social sector. There are large sectors of society that frown on diversity and hold firm to the beliefs that immigration and colonized groups have a responsibility to suppress, subordinate, or eliminate their cultural heritage, inclusive of language and traditions, and assimilate into the mainstream of the majority population and its way of life. However, those groups that represent the diversity and culture tend to hold fast to their unique identities and properties while striving toward a bicultural and multicultural existence. Consequently, these diverse and special populations have established a solid foundation in American society upon which to build a future.

This chapter introduces the often overlooked but evolving populations endowed with indigenous histories and cultures as well as traumatic life experiences. Given their indigenous origins and immigration experiences, they present important challenges for the social work profession both in the present and the future. The challenges include the need to minimize our historic dependence on stereotypes and to be proactive to seek understanding of the roots of special populations, their belief systems and values, traditions and practices, their assimilation, and their adaptation to the host or majority culture. The profession has a compelling need to develop theories and research methodologies, as well as intervention strategies, based upon knowledge of their unique histories, which reveal their vulnerabilities, strengths, and resilience. The social work profession has a commitment to serve these populations guided by competencies based on research, evidence-based practice, and policies.

The authors of this chapter have chosen to focus on the core issues surrounding indigenous and immigration populations in order that a conceptual framework may be presented to guide the profession as it engages these special populations. The overview of core issues, inclusive of special intelligence, historical trauma, ancestral memory, family system, resilience, diversity, collectivity and culture, research strategies, and the transformation of communities, is intended to emphasize the key concepts for social work understanding of special populations as well as gaps in knowledge. This overview is intended to serve as the stimulus as well as opportunity for the social work profession to take a leadership role in improving upon our knowledge base, research methodology, theories, and intervention to better serve these populations based upon best practice.

This emphasis is not intended to minimize the proliferation of extant ethnocentric writings describing the numerous indigenous populations (e.g., Hawaiians, American Indians and Native Alaskans, Samoans, Maoris, etc.) and immigrant populations (e.g., Chinese, Japanese, Filipino, Portuguese, Vietnamese, Koreans, etc.) whose contributions to the United States have enriched the American way of life. Writings include ethnicity-focused professional journals such as *Hulili*, a multidisciplinary journal on research on Hawaiian well-being (www.ksbe.edu/spi/Hilili.php); *Ethnicity & Health*, an international academic journal designed to meet the worldwide interest in the health of ethnic groups (www.tandf.co.uk/journals/carfax/13557858.html); *Urban Review* (www.springer.com/education+%26+language/journal/22256); *American Indian Culture and Research Journal* (aisc.metapress.com/content/120819); *Journal of American Indian Education* (www.jaie.asu.edu); Asian American Journal of Psychology (www.apa.org), dedicated to research, practice, advocacy, education, and policy within Asian American psychology; and the *Journal of Indigenous Social Development* (www.hawaii.edu/sswork jisd). The following analysis of special populations is built upon these foundational publications and the knowledge gleaned from these varied sources.

Indigenous People: Culture and Ancestry

As a society becomes increasingly diverse, competing forces ultimately determine the form and ideology underlying institutional design (Freire, 2002). Under a dominant design, all subsequent cultural entries are subjugated and modified. In American society, whose multicultural formation is driven by economics, the cultural base has been primarily Euro-American. Thus, as new cultures enter society with immigrants seeking economic opportunities, the bases of imported cultures eventually erode and are replaced by Euro-American values. Immigrants are a self-selected population comprised of cohorts who leave their homelands in search of more promising economic or political opportunities to benefit their families. After generations of acculturation and miscegenation, ancestral traits have become disenfranchised.

This social process stands in stark contrast to indigenous people and groups who were involuntarily marginalized and subordinated in their ancestral homelands. American Indians, Alaskan Natives, Native Hawaiians, and other Pacific Islanders have a qualitatively different cultural contract experience than that of immigrants from other countries. First Nations people of North America, Native Hawaiians, and other Pacific Islanders had developed thriving and sovereign societies when Europeans and Euro-Americans arrived on the scene. The subsequent subjugation and genocide of these indigenous populations is well documented (Benham & Heck, 1998; Stannard, 1992). Resistance to the imposing forces of the West, especially when protecting their valued resources, accelerated the decline of the indigenous people.

Indigenous experiences of imposition and genocide, and their resulting worldviews and behaviors, diverge from that of immigrants. This is not to minimize the overt racism and struggles faced by immigrant groups, however, especially the first generations who came from abroad. The mentality of immigrants reflects a ''push-pull'' dynamic that includes a decision to move to what is conceived of as a better place with new and better opportunities, and choices made in relation to acculturation as a means to improve socioeconomic standing. This worldview is in sharp contrast with that of indigenous people, whose identities, strengths, resources, beliefs, and values were trivialized or eliminated, leaving them with a loss of self-governance accompanied by diminished hopes and aspirations.

Thus, the experiences and social outcomes of immigrants and indigenous peoples depend in large part on where they find themselves on the continuum of assimilation and acculturation. Those who willfully immigrate are predisposed to acculturate to American cultural norms. Those who were invaded or taken against their will may be less motivated, if not outright resistant, to adopt what they perceive to be an invasive and hostile culture. Ethnic minorities who resist American culture are chastised for being unpatriotic or ungrateful. These notions turn into a collective sentiment of "blaming the victim." Perhaps this sentiment is most prominently directed toward immigrants who came to this country seeking a better life and entered into open competition with the majority stakeholders for resources and status.

Disparities in educational achievement and socioeconomic mobility are reflected in differential group histories. Asian Americans have been deemed the "model minority" and are often compared to other minority groups who have struggled to "make it" in American society. Attributions for differential success include higher intelligence, strong work ethic, and cultural affinity. Pervasive notions exist that Asians are predisposed to success because they possess inherent qualities of discipline and aspirations. In contrast, indigenous populations (such as the case of Native Hawaiians) are characterized as being unmotivated and with minimal aspirations. Thus, they are overrepresented in vocational and special education programs (Benham & Heck, 1998; Kamehameha Schools/Bishop Estate, 1983). These contrasting depictions of immigrants and indigenous people should not detract from the salience of their strengths and capabilities, which are often masked by stereotypes and overgeneralizations. Equally important is the emergent voices of these special populations that render clarity as to how they see themselves, their culture, and their futures. The remainder of this chapter is dedicated to their unique characteristics, and delineating their expectations of themselves and of the social work profession in aiding them to survive, develop, and thrive.

Special Intelligence

Special populations in America are often confined to living within segregated communities that are removed from society's socioeconomic mainstream. Within these enclaves, people are socialized according to unique behavioral and cognitive norms. Insular and often materially deprived environs can serve to repress healthy human development, but such circumstances can also breed creativity and innovation. A unique intelligence emerges that reflects a blend of cultural elements and oppressive circumstances. Innovations in terms of music and the arts, fashion, and idiomatic language have emerged from ethnic subcultures and crossed over into mainstream popular culture. Trends emerging from Native Hawaiian and American Indian youth culture have become the cultural standard in our society.

Intelligence is very much determined by situation and context. In resource-deprived environments, intelligence is measured by people's ability to survive by developing skill sets that enable them to function while tending to constant and immediate threats from their surroundings. Those living in safe environments are not required to expend energies to guard against such threats and can focus on personal educational and career goals, as well as family needs. In other words, attending to personal safety issues and basic survival needs is not a primary issue of concern for privileged sectors of society; however, these issues can be major detractors from the achievements of the less advantaged.

Although there are great variations in social environs and associated intelligences within society, in society's effort to promote homogeneity, notions of intelligence are narrowly defined by standardized measures. Such measures are the means to assess whether persons have the requisite intellectual capacity to warrant opportunities to further advance their education and careers.

Special populations raised in insulated environs that choose to venture out to pursue new opportunities are required to adopt broader behavioral, cognitive, and linguistic sets in order to function effectively. Except in rare circumstances, Euro-Americans are not required to venture out in the same way and acquire new cultural skill sets. "Making it" occurs within a cultural context with which they are familiar. Special groups who succeed in the larger society are required to be multicultural by the very nature of such success. That is, they must possess a repertoire of behaviors that allows them to move readily between sociocultural spheres and manage parallel and sometimes contradictory realities. Thus, in the process of becoming multicultural, special populations must develop a high level of social intelligence. This type of intelligence is manifested in the following examples:

- The acquisition of dual and sometimes conflicting behavioral and cognitive sets
- Highly refined observational and sensory skills in order to accurately read and respond effectively to cues across sociocultural spheres
- Mastery over the sociopolitics of culture and race while pursuing educational and career interests
- Negotiating value conflicts shaped by ancestry and cultural differences
- Balancing demands, social expectations, and priorities of different groups
- Recalibration of competing priorities to fulfill cultural and achievement goals

Historical Trauma and Ancestral Memory

Notions of posttraumatic stress disorder as defined in the DSM-IV suggest that symptoms associated with this disorder occur as a direct result of discrete and relatively recent life events. It is surmised that exposure to violent events such as military combat or rape predisposes individuals to exhibit uncontrolled rage, nightmares, and isolationism. Etiological conceptions generally do not consider the cumulative effects of historical trauma and a long-term process of reconciling pain that extends across generations. Trauma alters human behavior and associated thinking.

Populations subjected to collective trauma have modified their strategies of socialization and survival as a way to protect themselves from external threats. Immigrants to the United States settled into ethnic enclaves not only as a way to recreate a familiar sociocultural environment with higher levels of predictability, but also as a way to guard against a vigilant majority who blamed them for their economic woes. Native people in America experienced holocausts that culminated in their near extermination.

The first Western voyagers to Hawaii estimated a native population of approximately 400,000. Subsequent estimates based on more scientific data place the number of Hawaiians at the point of Western contact closer to 800,000 to 1 million. Hawaii is one of the most isolated landmasses in the world. It lies in the middle of the world's largest body of water. Because of its remoteness, anthropologists theorize that Hawaii was one of the last places on earth to be inhabited by humans, and that occurred about 1,000 A.D. The first Europeans, led by British sea captain James Cook, arrived in Hawaii in 1778. Missionaries arrived from New England in 1820. By 1831, through a mixture of both choice by the Hawaiian people and the pressing influence of missionaries, the indigenous spiritual and cultural system had been abolished and 1,000 Christian schools had been built. The second generation of missionaries abandoned their religious pursuits and embraced self-serving opportunities for wealth once they realized the vast economic opportunities in Hawaii.

In 1848, businessmen were the major force behind changing the traditional system of land ownership. The Mahele, as it is referred to in the Hawaiian language, allowed nonnative people to own Hawaiian land for the first time. From that point on, Americans hoarded lands through purchase, quit title, and adverse possession. By the turn of the century, a mere 50 years later, Whites owned four acres of land for every own acre owned by a Hawaiian. They used their vast land holdings to cultivate sugar and pineapple. Once firmly situated in the Hawaiian economic and political system, a group of American sugar barons, whose lineage could be tied directly to the original missionaries, staged an overthrow, with the backing of the U.S. Marines, that ousted the last reigning monarch of Hawaii, Queen Lili'uokalani in 1893.

By this time, the native Hawaiian population was vastly reduced. Captain Cook's maiden voyage to Hawaii brought sexually transmitted diseases.

Missionaries, whalers, and other foreigners brought a host of other diseases that Hawaiians had no immunity to. By some estimates, the Hawaiian population diminished by 90% of its original pre-Western contact level. Hawaiians today continue to suffer severe health and social problems.

Native Hawaiians have some of the highest per capita rates of heart disease and cancer, diabetes, severe problems related to drug and alcohol abuse and consequent domestic violence problems, disproportionately high levels of mental health problems and suicide, the lowest educational achievement and employment levels, the highest number of teen pregnancies, and the highest rates of criminal convictions and incarceration (Office of Hawaiian Affairs, 2002).

In Hawaii, there is the highest number of residents in public housing and the highest percentage of homeless in the United States. Demographers predict that the population of pure Native Hawaiians will be extinct by the year 2040. The contemporary status of Hawaiians is obviously the result of their history of culture contact and dispossession. This storyline of overthrow and colonization has been played out multiple times throughout North America and the Pacific region, and the social consequences are strikingly similar. Trauma is incurred from the loss of culture, traditional lands and resources, family members, and leaders; violent encounters and witnessing the physical and emotional suffering of your people; being rendered a minority in one's own homeland; being required to live by the strictures of an alien society; and a deep inner sense of social injustice.

On a collective scale, symptoms of posttraumatic stress disorder are manifested in various ways, including anger turned outward into violence or inward in the form of substance abuse and helplessness; refusal to conform to Western strictures, or an obsessive adherence to tradition; high rates of fertility and teenage pregnancies; and political radicalism. Not all of these manifestations are negative if placed in a certain context. Being steadfast in protecting traditions is critical in perpetuating culture. High fertility can be viewed as a form of sociobiological compensation for reduced populations, and political activism is a healthy expression of social discontent.

The attitudes and dispositions of oppressed and traumatized populations do not necessarily follow a predictable schema but are a part of a larger and highly complex intaglio. As mentioned, strategies to avoid conflict and violence served to alter settlement and socialization patterns. Interpretations of direct experience and oral knowledge handed down by predecessors are mixed into a cognitive brew that influences political orientation and behavioral expression.

In cases where traditions and associated behaviors have been severed, efforts to restore culture have been met with competing notions of originality and authenticity. While such efforts are noble in the sense that entities are committed to cultural revival, they also serve to fracture cultural and political movements. In short, attitudes and behaviors that are borne out of collective trauma are not always decipherable, and the unaccountability is especially perplexing to those not living the experience. Historical legacies can be used to understand posttraumatic reactions that extend well beyond our current conceptions. Two hundred years of oppression and trauma are not remedied through job opportunities and new economies. Ancestral memory leads special populations to not trust or conform, especially when conformity means buying into a system that eradicated their stabilizing foundation through colonization.

Family System as a Superorganic Structure

Families are generally conceptualized as nuclear systems comprised of one or two parents and children. More progressive notions of family include single-parent households and gay and lesbian parents raising natural or adopted children. In the many cultures that exist in the United States, the concept of family extends well beyond the notion of nuclear or even extended family systems. Those who pay homage to their ancestors through rituals or other practices view themselves as one segment in a highly protracted genealogical order. They are members of a family system that is connected to a superorganic structure existing across past, present, and future generations.

The families of today are current manifestations, linking ancestors to future generations. In cultures with oral traditions, knowledge of family progeny is passed between generations through stories, chants, and other customary practices. Often, these processes of passing information between generations have been interrupted by migration, language replacement, and genocide. Thus, families have lost their connection to their genealogical past. Stories and tales of ancestors' (whether accurate or exaggerated) character and virtues, roles and statuses, deeds and misfortunes, have ceased to exist. The displacement and diaspora of peoples have rendered meaningless the skill sets and technological knowledge that once defined the social status of ancestors.

Next, two personal family stories from each of the authors are shared with the intention of giving voice to immigration and indigenous oral family histories passed on across generations and to give meaning to the concept of the superorganic family.

Case Study: The Matsuoka Family

My grandfather brought to America the katana or sword of the famous samurai Saigo Takamori. Saigo Takamori was the figure portrayed in the story of the Last Samurai. One day before the turn of the 19th century, my great-grandfather was walking in his village in southern Japan when a dog began to follow him. This dog followed him all the way home. Once he arrived home, his neighbor informed him that that was the favorite dog of Saigo Takamori. Feeling an obligation to return the pet to its esteemed owner, my great-grandfather took the dog to the temple where Saigo Takamori resided. On seeing his favorite dog, Saigo Takamori was extremely grateful and presented my great-grandfather with his sword as a gift in return.

On the eve that my grandfather left Japan, his father presented him with the precious samurai sword. He wished him well and told him to never forget his homeland. When my father was growing up, the sword sat prominently on the mantle in the family home until the war broke out. Fearing that the FBI would confiscate the sword after the Japanese bombed Pearl Harbor, the family buried the sword underneath their house. Soon thereafter they were forced to leave their home and possessions and were relocated away from the West Coast. After the war was over, they returned to their house in Los Angeles' Little Tokyo area and found that the house had been razed and converted into a parking lot. According to my uncle who shared this story, the most painful part about losing the family house was losing the sword. The sword had symbolized a connection to family genealogy and the legacy of a revered figure who held fast to cultural tradition in the face of modernity and Westernization. The sword was a conduit for conveying stories with embedded cultural values regarding character, honorable behavior, and continuity across time and place. The loss of the sword and the war experience as a whole changed the mentality surrounding my father's family's approach to living in the United States. For survival purposes, they made a concerted effort to detach themselves from their homeland and blend in behaviorally to American society. Now all that remains is the story of the sword itself.

Case Study: The McCubbin Family

This family, it is told, had two members who were diagnosed with leprosy or Hansen's disease, which at that time was a diagnosis of isolation and death. The diagnosis was confirmed when my uncles were in their early teens and they were transported to Kalaupapa, Molokai, the Hawaiian leper colony. Being unaware of this family history, I joined a team of mental-health specialists who spent a week on Kalaupapa to gain first-hand knowledge and experience in working and talking with the residents of this highly stigmatized and isolated community. On arrival, a resident greeted me as I left the aircraft. His arms were wide open, inviting a physical hug and personal greeting. In spite of our host's fingers being lost all the way to the knuckles and a face with a missing nose, the embrace was warm, genuine, and reciprocated. I felt at home. Following the exchange of names, my host shouted: "McCubbin? Mmmmm ... Did you have relatives here?" Taken back by the surprising inquiry, I paused to think, then responded, "I don't think so." He replied, "Your last name is unusual ... I wonder. There were two McCubbins here, you know. Follow me to the graveyard, then to the records office, where anyone who resided here can be identified. I do recall that Hamilton, the youngest, died here and Willy, well, he is buried on Oahu. See we keep track of everyone who ever lived here." The burial site was confirmed and the records revealed my past, my history, and my genealogy.

My mother anticipated this discovery and anxiously awaited my return from Kalaupapa. The matriarch, my mother, carried family secrets and told the story of my uncles with care, respect, and appreciation. Leprosy and Kalaupapa were not spoken of in public for fear of social stigma. In the family, however, although I was too young at the time to remember, both subjects were discussed openly and passed on from one generation to another. The story was not about the trials and tribulations, but about the family's commitment to care for their own no matter where they lived and under no matter what conditions. On relocation, the McCubbin family worked together to find ways to keep the family intact and together, with weekly trips to Molokai to do what they could so Hammy and Willy could see them. My mother, a nurse, was able to connect with them directly. My father served as cook when he visited. This story was told over and over as a reminder of this organic family unity, united spiritually but torn apart physically. It was the strength of the family that became folklore in storytelling. Importantly, the family history gave meaning to a dismal situation but one graced with respect, pride, and appreciation for my uncles. The story kept us connected, spiritually and emotionally. Leprosy, the scourge and bane of our existence, became part of our past, a meaningful past, as well as a part of genealogy, identity, and future.

All too often, support is defined as the exchange of tangible goods and interpersonal contact. The oral histories of the Matsuoka and McCubbin families reveal the strength of symbols, the sword and the isolated island, and the meaning attached to them, which unifies family and hope. Through storytelling, people are able to pass on a rich past, the meaning of adversity, and the value of cultural symbols, and in doing so, they capture and reaffirm the spiritual strength or mana underlying the story.

The loss of family history parallels the loss of culture. Where once there were thriving indigenous systems of knowledge transmission and continuity tied inherently to economic survival, there now exists a post-modern colonial system that is generally intolerant of cultural separation and distinctiveness within its national boundaries. The sociopolitical processes that have systematically and effectively severed people from their past have deposed many to a state of confused cultural identity.

Families who have studied their genealogy are able to connect themselves to ancestors who lived hundreds or even thousands of years ago. In the process of exploring genealogy, knowledge emerges that reunites extended families that evolved along different lines. Knowledge also provides information regarding the community role or specialization of ancestors and mends the fractured cultural identity by connecting people to their histories.

A strong sense of familial connectedness and obligation takes on a different meaning when we subscribe to a superorganic family conception. Many ethnic minority and indigenous people have been instilled with the responsibility of maintaining the beliefs and practices tied to their lineage. They have been assigned to be the proprietors of traditions.

Faculty of the School of Social Work at the University of Hawaii were contacted by the U.S. Department of Energy to conduct an ethnographic study of the sociocultural impacts of geothermal development of Hawaii's Kilauea volcano. Native Hawaiian subsistence practitioners living around the perimeter of the volcano were interviewed in depth. Economic change and infiltration had bypassed those residing in the remote corridor between the great mountain and the sea. Many residents shared their belief in and worship of Pele, the Hawaiian goddess of fire. She was believed to be the animate manifestation of the volcano.

Pele and her progeny are the core of an ancient religious system that was essentially eradicated by the introduction of Christianity to Hawaii. Over the centuries, a thin stream of practitioners managed to promulgate religious practices associated with Pele. To these practitioners, Kilauea volcano was not merely a geologic anomaly, it was a living deity not to be desecrated by tapping it for energy. They felt an absolute commitment to protecting the volcano from energy exploitation and honoring their ancestral beliefs. Drawing energy from the volcano was construed as a threat to the spiritual vitality of Pele. The goddess and all she represents would not die on their generation's watch. A political action group was formed called the Pele Defense Fund, and they succeeded in staving off the geothermal development.

Collectivity and Culture

Collective cultures, or those oriented toward group behaviors, exist because group members rely heavily on each other for livelihood and survival. Many cultures that originated from agricultural and subsistence-based economies continue to espouse collective values emphasizing social cohesiveness. Collective people through their socialization are inherently sensitive to their social ecology—its dynamic forces and the ramifications of change within a social milieu. A critical objective is to maintain balance and harmony in the social economy in their milieu.

Collective peoples have developed highly sophisticated social economies that are essentially safety nets for families and communities. Extended family and communal networks are relied on for support in raising children and caring for the aged, assisting in times of crisis, organizing special events, and engaging in work projects that benefit the community at large. With the exception of the aged and infirmed, participation in providing support is requisite. Prescriptive and proscriptive norms guide a stringent system of reciprocity that provides order and assigns roles to the group.

For both immigrant and indigenous people in the United States, settlement patterns and the formation of enclaves served to further affirm cultural values related to collectivity. A collective orientation was the basis for the development of community-based practices leading to economic self-reliance. Cultural and political associations, rotating loan and banking systems, and other informal services that aided the socioeconomic mobility of fellow ethnics emanated from community-based institutions that offered greater reliability and trust to the communities they served.

Resistance to change could be attributed to self-protective mechanisms. Cultural conservatism is reinforced by undesirable changes individuals observe in other domains. Through this orientation, they have created novel ways to protect their esteem and mental health.

Early research indicated that culturally divergent child-rearing practices resulted in differential personality traits in people. In some cultures, attachment and emotional bonding with parent and child, especially mothers, was observed through continuous physical attachment and tactile stimulation. The outcome of these behaviors, along with brevity of speech and verbal exchange, was developing children who were less verbally expressive. Children were also observed to be more attentive to other people and to their environment.

What emerges from differential child-rearing practices is an intelligence that is influenced by cultural values. In the West, intelligence is often equated to the ability to express ideas in words and through articulation of thought. In the Eastern and Pacific regions, intelligence is often equated to an ability to read social situations and to act in accordance with socially prescribed roles and protocols. A heightened sensitivity to social situations, as well as a self-consciousness regarding how people engage others socially, has also been explained as a basis for highly developed appraisal skills and social intelligence. This heightened sensitivity is also an explanation for the development of neurotic behavior when it goes awry. A strong collective sense is inversely related to individualism. Those who possess a collective identity generally consider the sentiment of the group before taking action.

Research on Special Populations

Current theoretical formats and paradigms are remiss when it comes to understanding phenomenology of special populations (Kahakalau, 2004). Traditional approaches relying on inferential statistics can only remotely capture the everyday social realms of those societies. Unfortunately, alternative methods, including grounded theoretical approaches that serve to provide holistic impressions of phenomenon, are deemed "soft" and lacking in credibility (Denzin & Lincoln, 1998). The tension generated from conflicting perspectives has stretched the boundaries of traditional research and led to new sensibilities that emphasize multimethod research approaches.

Bolland and Atherton (2000) described a heuristic paradigm that accepts all research methodologies, not privileging any ontology, epistemology, or method. They propose a relativistic approach that suggests there are no universal standards of right or wrong and that all knowledge is dependent on the subjective knower. The acceptance of broader conceptualizations of scientific inquiry leads to the evolution of paradigms and techniques that enable social scientists and policy makers to hold a clearer and deeper understanding of alternative life ways and issues.

The traditional period of positivism and associated methods and paradigms has done much to damage the reputation of social science in communities. This period has also challenged subsequent generations of researchers, both nonindigenous and indigenous, to erase the perceptions of anthropologists, sociologists, and others who exploited their trust and goodwill. Moreover, it has been difficult to convince indigenous leaders of the utility of empirical data in terms of protecting their rights, resources, and traditional and customary practices. As Smith (1999) stated, indigenous people are on an important quest to recover their languages and epistemological foundations. Research is a critical means to reclaim their histories.

Gaining Trust

Many communities, especially indigenous ones, have an inherent mistrust of government and university researchers. Overcoming the barrier of mistrust is the first major challenge in conducting community-based research. The mistrust is drawn from a history of exploitation from outsiders and a general community impression that study results unilaterally benefit the academic careers of researchers. Communities have acquired a political sensitivity and savvy that requires researchers to explain how the study will benefit residents. A researcher may possess an immense amount of technical and methodological knowledge and have the right motives for engaging in community-based research, yet still be denied entry into a community. Those bent on preserving their cultures and communities are not impressed by credentials and technical know-how.

In locales where communities are tightly linked through cultural or political affiliation, there is a high level of exchange between civic leaders. Researchers acquire reputations based on whom they typically are contracted by (state, private developer, community), the rigor of their work, quality of the product, applications of the study results, sensitivity to community protocol, and the extent to which they make long-term commitments to a community. In many situations, the reputation of the researcher precedes him or her, and this determines his/her level of acceptance. For example, research consultants in Hawaii who are frequently contracted by developers for environmental impact assessments have at times been systematically locked out of communities opposed to development projects. However, research consultants who traditionally work in communities and have applied a participatory action approach leading to tangible benefits are often sought after and embraced by communities. Level of compensation can be considered a determinant of motivation. Some residents may question the motivations and commitment to community well-being by high-paid research consultants, while consultants working on a pro bono basis will not be accused of having ulterior motives.

Access and Protocol

There is an array of culturally based protocols that must be applied when initiating a research project. Contacting and gaining endorsements from the "right" persons, who are often respected elders or *kupuna*, will determine the degree to which a researcher is able to access other critical informants. Indigenous communities are fraught with dynamics related to family affiliation and length of stay, history of personal contact, political orientation, socioeconomic status, and race/ethnic relations. It is requisite for researchers, through a reconnaissance, to explore and gain an awareness of these dynamics. Negotiating ties with one sector, however, may inadvertently close the door with competing sectors in the community and obviate a cross-sectional analysis.

Engaging a community in research requires many of the same strategies as community organizing, including exhibiting culturally appropriate mannerisms and a nonintrusive style. In communities, maintaining objectivity through social distance is counterintuitive to gaining the trust of residents through a process of social immersion.

Social distancing does not permit a researcher to embrace the culture and its intricacies and subtleties, let alone gain access to residents who are inherently suspicious of strangers. Abiding by cultural protocol, such as asking permission rather than imposing oneself, sensitivity to nonverbal situations, sharing family background and genealogies (especially if they are tied to the geographic area), speaking the dialect and using idiomatic language, and generally building a base of commonality are all means of establishing rapport and trust.

Thrusting uninvited researchers onto the community scene with a research agenda is a form of "carpetbagging." This seemingly standard approach in earlier years has generated widespread skepticism in communities and subsequently created barriers for well-intentioned researchers who are committed to gathering critically needed data. Under such conditions, researchers must lay the groundwork for research by convincing community leaders that qualitative and quantitative data can be vital ammunition for promoting policies and planning decisions aimed at community preservation and social development.

In Pacific cultures, social reciprocity is a critical aspect of interpersonal relations. From an indigenous perspective, the economy of speech between negotiating parties is a good predictor of balance and parity in a working relationship. The role of the researcher is to listen, acknowledge the intelligence and wisdom of the residents, incorporate indigenous perspectives into the research methodology, and involve a working team of residents at every phase of the research process. "Politically enlightened" communities strive to develop true partnerships with researchers by providing critical information that guides the research process.

In many Pacific societies, strangers greet each other by reciting their family genealogy. This protocol is significant in that it serves to inform each party of the other's lineage and pays homage to each person's ancestors. Though there are varying degrees of this practice, from the highly ritualized to a less formal and indirect inquiry into one's family background, the practice remains strong. In Hawaii, for example, the typical first questions of a stranger are "What high school did you attend?" and "Are you related to so and so?" (with the same surname). These questions tie a person to a community or island and gather important information on their family background. Such contextualization is a means to appraise the person. Researchers are not immune to this practice. Despite having credentials that reflect academic qualification, indigenous residents are keen to learn more about the researcher's values and motives that are often linked to place and family of origin. For many indigenous people, credibility is derived from the integrity of the individual and less so from academic degrees.

Trust and social bonding are contingent on the extent to which people share common features. Behaviorally disparate parties must overcome huge obstacles in order to know enough about the other to trust them. Establishing trust is facilitated by behavioral and semantic concurrence. Fluency in the native language, when it is the first language of residents, removes major logistical problems related to translation and conceptual equivalence and breeds trust.

Striving for Authenticity

Researchers working in indigenous communities must recognize that society is indoctrinated with a colonial version of historicity whose rendition serves to justify colonial mastery. Much of the accepted narratives on indigenous people are really the narratives of colonialists and cultural hegemons (Touraine, 2001). In the Pacific, indigenous claimants have emerged to assert contending visions of the cultural past. There is a revitalized struggle occurring globally among indigenous people to manage, define, and promulgate their own histories and cultural realities.

This legacy, and subsequent movements to alter previous conceptions, has politicized the research process. Indigenous communities are becoming aware of the power of research and its utility and are assuming greater control over who is involved, how the research is conducted, and how data are interpreted and used. Past attempts to document the life ways of indigenous people were fraught with cultural biases, misinterpretations, and even deliberate efforts to deceive foreign observers as a form of mockery. Communities are taking corrective action by supporting research that promotes authenticity and sets an important standard for future investigations.

Authenticity has many different attributes. It is about peoples' interpretations of and reactions to phenomena drawn from deeply imbedded values and culturally constructed notions of reality. Researchers bent on finding "truth" must reconsider *mythology, lore*, and *superstition* as terms used to describe and denigrate indigenous beliefs. That is, a phenomenon that is not easily demystified and apprehended through measurement is often deemed to be imaginary.

In many Pacific cultures, spirituality and metaphysics are essential elements in an ecology that supports human well-being. Western social science does not have available methodologies capable of apprehending indigenous spirituality and other empirically elusive phenomenon. Authenticity is brought to bear through methods that are adapted to capturing the inherent qualities of spirituality and other phenomena.

While objectivity may be viewed as critical in any research venture, maintaining personal distance impedes the comprehension of authentic culture. Even researchers who manifest excellent rapport and behavioral sensitivity must spend volunteer time with subjects of inquiry in order to observe a spectrum of behaviors. Behavior is situational and multidimensional. Immersion in a context provides researchers with an opportunity to understand the social interactions. Relying on multiple data sources enables researchers to coalesce empirical themes and draw whole and more complete impressions.

Appropriate Research Methods

The positivism that emerged during the modern era is gradually being replaced with heuristic paradigms promoting notions of data discovery and triangulation (Bolland & Atherton, 2000). This multimethod approach is well suited for securing rich descriptions of indigenous life conditions. Statistics drawn from multivariate analysis are useful in determining broad relational patterns between factors. Statistical results represent the tip of the phenomena and should be placed amid other forms of data as a way to cross-validate impressions.

Some researchers who subscribe to a multimethod research approach use survey results as the central force that drives the acquisition and interpretation of qualitative data. This is problematic if measures are unreliable across cultures, data processing is prone to systematic error, samples are unrepresentative of indigenous populations, and so on. Methods used in data gathering should not be staged as an incremental process with one method taking precedence over another. Rather, they should be "stand-alone" activities contributing to a broad, multidimensional dataset that is triangulated or woven together into mosaic-like community profiles. After all, communities are nested, layered, and multidimensional systems, and single data source profiling is reductionist.

Other than the typical quantitative survey and qualitative key informant methods, there are highly viable research methods used with indigenous communities (Turner, Beeghley, & Powers, 2002). One of these methods is Geographic Information Systems (GIS) mapping, which we have used to chart behavioral patterns related to traditional and customary practices, subsistence patterns and resource areas, sacred sites, and population changes (Minerbi, McGregor, & Matsuoka, 2003). In other studies, GIS has been used to demarcate land ownership boundaries and jurisdictions, zone designations, service locations, and catchment areas. Data acquired in this manner is transformed into GIS maps and used to assist social planners and decision makers in determining the location and extent of cultural impacts related to proposed development projects. The technique resonates with indigenous informants because it is used to collect data that is "place based."

A major challenge in indigenous research is settling on a time frame that satisfies the expectations of funders/contractors and addresses community issues related to the time-consuming process of building trust and rapport (Morrow, 1994). Researchers must find a pace that moves the study process forward to meet contractual agreements and is sensitive to participant involvement. For indigenous participants not used to being subjects of scientific inquiry, it may require more time and persuading to garner a sample large enough to validate results. Westernized cohorts who understand the utility and power of empirical data are generally less resistant, and thus time requirements are easier to meet. Although research plans are posed at the outset of a study, it is critical to maintain a degree of flexibility. If a methodological approach is not resonating well with participants, then alternatives must be considered. In some cases, even pretesting instruments do not always provide investigators with enough predictive information regarding their applicability.

On multiple occasions, everyone has been a part of a larger communal research process that involved civic and indigenous leaders, heads of government agencies, and business leaders from the geographic areas of interest. The study or task group served to develop a conceptual framework, reviewed questionnaires for language and content, publicized the study, organized community involvement, assisted in interpreting study results, and helped develop an empirically based action plan. From beginning to end, indigenous leadership was enmeshed in the research process. The depth of their involvement encouraged communities to assume ownership of the data and to realize the significance of research in terms of policy development and social planning.

The joint involvement of multiple stakeholders ensures objectivity and a government-facilitated planning and action process. Constituents sitting at the table create a context for multiperspectivism, mutuality, and buy-in, and ultimately, the validation of indigenous issues and practices.

Emergent Methodologies

The transformation of communities, and particularly the people of indigenous communities, to achieve a stronger alignment with their own culture, beliefs, and values, is a formidable challenge. Of Smith's (1999) 25 identified projects to advance this transformation, six are mentioned in this chapter as central to the theme of generating knowledge and research to improve the well-being and health of special populations.

Claiming and Reclaiming

Guided by tribunals and international courts, indigenous people are called on to conduct systematic research resulting in the documentation of national, tribal, and familial histories. The purpose of this line of research is to establish the legitimacy of claims to land, resources, identity, language, and culture.

Storytelling and Testimonies

Scholarly work must capture the essence and identity of cultures that have depended on oral histories and life experience as the basis for the transformation and transfer of knowledge across generations. Testimonies provide the basis for claims by articulating the truth. Testimonies are also the process and means by which a person is afforded protection and space for expression.

Storytelling is a process for gaining the perspectives of native people, particularly the elders and women whose voices were silenced in the colonizing process. For many indigenous writers, storytelling is the means of passing down the beliefs and values of a culture with the expectation that future generations will find meaning and a sense of place and identity. The storyteller is able to connect the past with the future. Storytelling is also a fundamental process of facilitating dialogue and conversations among indigenous people as people of the culture and the land. As suggested, research on storytelling indicates that it is a culturally appropriate tool "of representing the 'diversities of truth' within which the storyteller rather than the researcher maintains control" (Bishop, 1996, p. 24). Storytelling is a process through which "the indigenous community becomes a story that is a collection of individual stories ever unfolding through the lives of the people who share the life of that community" (Bishop, 1996, p. 169).

Celebrating Survival

Scientific inquiry into indigenous communities has emphasized the demise and cultural assimilation of the people. Often these individuals' life experiences have been characterized as fragile in the wake of the historical trauma that resulted from the colonizing process. This trauma includes aspects of genocide, lost of identity, culture, language, and land. Survival is key process of indigenous nations, characterized by "the degree to which indigenous peoples have retained cultural and spiritual values and authenticity" (Smith, 1999, p. 145). Celebration may take the form of dancing, music, athletic events, a collective experience intended to create a sense of life of shared history, meaning, and identity. Critical to this process is the contemporary concept of resilience. This requires indigenous people, both as individuals and collectively, to acknowledge their strengths, capabilities, and commitment to the preservation and meaning of their history and past.

Intervening

Under the rubric of action research, intervening is a process of becoming involved and proactive in an effort to improve on current conditions, rectifying wrongs, and shaping policies and conditions for the benefit of indigenous people. Of greatest importance, intervening is characterized as a community process that invites an intervening process into the community and sets the parameters for the intervention. Intervening from this perspective is directed at changing institutions, policies, programs, educational experiences, and training of staff. This program is not about changing indigenous people, but rather the transformation of institutions that serve the people.

Revitalizing

Crisis-oriented and problem-focused professions and related programs set their parameters and targets directed at the immediate issues that lead to resolution, reconciliation, and improved well-being. *Revitalizing* focuses on a crisis of lost, if not diminished, existence of culture and elements of culture that are vital to the survival of special populations who have historically embraced these elements. Revitalizing calls for the expanded worldview of professionals and their approach to special populations. It also requires them to be inclusive of cultural preservation and revitalization as critical elements to the well-being and development of special populations. Language and its revitalization have been, and will continue to be, critical elements in the preservation of many special populations. Strategies to support or cultivate policies directed at language revival, to promote exchanges among native speakers, and to promote the publication of information in native languages are critical parts of the revitalization process.

Discovering

This is a process of central importance to both Western and indigenous populations. Science has been an integral part of indigenous ways of knowing. Western science, however, has been neither sensitive to nor respectful of indigenous ways of knowing. The knowledge base of indigenous people, an untapped and underdeveloped resource of scientific information, has been relegated to being inconsequential and thus an antithesis to the advancement of knowledge, particularly in the social, behavioral, biological, and medical sciences. Despite this, discovering remains a priority in both worlds. The bridging concepts of ethnoscience are among many ideas that can serve to foster the advancement of knowledge to better serve these special populations.

Sharing

The dissemination of knowledge among special populations about knowledge gained from and with special populations is vital to the continuous improvement in the well-being of the people being served. Professional disciplines have emphasized the dissemination of knowledge among professionals and specialized audiences, thus leaving the populations being served outside of the loop of information sharing. The current emphasis on community-based research and the invitation of scientists to communities as a basic right of entrance will shape the future of research on special populations, but the preparation of professions to involve the community before, during, and after the conduct of inquiries must be given a higher priority in the training process. Dissemination, in the indigenous community, is more than the transmission of knowledge gained. It is also a process of "demystifying knowledge and information" and presenting it in plain terms. "Oral presentations must conform to community protocols and expectations" (Smith, 1999, p. 161).

Diverse Identities in Special Populations

Indigenous and immigrant populations change as a result of assimilation, adaptation, and preservation. The evidence is clear that these special populations are called upon to make some degree of accommodation by engaging the processes of assimilation and adaptation in order that they may establish themselves in the foreign and sometimes resistant host populations. To achieve a sense of "fit," the special population is called upon to find meaning, purpose, and a way of life in the face of a dominant culture. Even in the face of colonization or oppression, the special populations are called upon to subordinate their identity, culture, language, and traditions in order to survive (Dubos, 1974). On the other hand, it is equally true that families do preserve their cultures inclusive of language, beliefs, and values while adapting to a new and demanding social context (Wright, Mendel, Thaan, & Habenstein, 2011). The transformation of special populations reveals the diversity in the adaptation process, which is of particular importance to the social work professional in search of understanding and best practices to serve these populations. The diversity in transformation may be summarized.

Science has treated ethnicity and ethnic identity as a categorical variable, one used to classify special populations and to trace the genealogical origins of the special population. The Hawaiian family, Japanese family, Chinese family, Korean family, Vietnamese family, Italian family, Jewish family, to name a few, all come to mind. Simply put, ethnicity may be viewed as a social classification grounded in our knowledge of the ethnic origins of the family unit. From this classification may flow a list of ethnically related factors or processes that best describe and predict family adjustment and adaptation, resilience, and well-being.

Unfortunately, this simple but useful system for indigenous and immigrant classification has prominent limitations that deserve consideration in our efforts to understand these special populations. Clearly, ethnic origins and identity emerge by virtue of assumptions made about one's cultural legacy, which is taught and transferred from parents and kin and is transferred across generations from their ancestors. When viewed from this perspective, descent may be genetic and/or social (Keyes, 1981), and one comes to realize that family systems may have multiple ethnic ancestries. This family condition may emerge as a result of different processes, inclusive of interethnic marriages, local adoptions and international adoptions, blended family systems, and a family system created by artificial insemination. This complexity is exacerbated by the simple fact that there is no invariable pattern to which cultural differences will be used as emblematic of their ethnic difference. Language is often identified as a universal distinguishing feature, but not all ethnic groups/families have a distinctive language.

Even cultural characteristics emblematic of ethnic identity depend upon the interpretation of the experience and actions of ancestors or forebears. These interpretations are often presented in the form of myths or legends in which historical events are accorded symbolic significance (Eliade, 1959). Ethnic origins and identity may be founding cultural traditions related to crises in the life cycle, such as coming of age, marriage, illness, and death (Braun, Pietsch, & Blancette, 2000). It is particularly in rites of passage that one finds highly emotional symbolic reinforcement of ethnic patterns.

Ethnic identity and classification may involve choices by the individual, family, community, and the professional.

- In adopting a Hawaiian-American genealogy, for example, an individual, family, community, and professional may stress the successes of previous generation of leaders who have gained the respect and admiration of the people. King Kamehameha I and Bernice Pauahi Bishop come to mind as ethnic leaders worthy of emulation.

- Another individual, family, community, and professional may underscore the vulnerability and historically traumatized past of colonization and the loss of land, culture, and sovereignty.

- Still another individual, family, community, and professional may embrace the Hawaiian-American identity of the emphasis through a Western perspective, with emphases on achievement and material goods, as well as individual success.

- Still another individual, family, community, and professional may adopt the social activist identity, with a commitment to reclaim land, independence, and sovereignty.

- Another individual, family, community, or professional may adopt the perspective that they are Citizens of the Indigenous Kingdom. The Indigenous Kingdom is not a state of the United States, but an independent national under United States occupation.

- Another type of ethnic grouping selected by the individual, family, community, or profession is the Pan-Ethnic identity movement (Pan-Indian, Pan-Polynesian, and Pan-Asian). This process emerges when ethnic groups who perceive themselves as too small in number and power decide to form a collective identity to engage the dominant population's search for common ground and access to power and influence. The mobilized groups work together to form and create an identity that encompasses several ethnic groups, with the purpose of confronting the agencies of the state and federal government and seek to establish autonomy and control over their lives.

- Finally, the individual, family, community, and professional may adopt an exclusive "I am an American" identity and seek to dismiss their ethnic origins and descent (Keyes, 1981).

In all cases the individual, family, community, and professional seek to differentiate their own special population from others and to find membership in or belonging to other interpersonal or social units who share this same worldview.

With these options and choices, we are now in a position to clarify two myths. First, assimilation does not mean the indigenous or immigrant minority ethnic group disappears into the dominant society and loses its ethnic distinctiveness. We argue that this "total assimilation" does not occur. Assimilation as part of resilience is best viewed as the "reduction of cultural distance between specific groups with respect to particular aspects of behavior" (Banton, 1981, p. 37). Adaptation from our perspective depends on a minority group retaining the distinctive identity or what Light (1981) called *ethnic consciousness*. Secondly, we need to recognize that special populations are in engaged in a transformation process, the outcome of which is shaped by self identification, family identification, group identification, and professional identification. Where the individual, family, community or the profession exercises its choice among the options noted above has significant bearing upon our understanding and prediction of the behavior and the professional strategy for intervention.

Developing Theories: Resilience and Relational Well-Being

Witkin and Iversen (2008, p. 479) addresses the profession's struggles and emerging issues in social work. Of importance to special populations, these authors point to the role of science and particularly the development of theory needed to advance research as well as to guide evidence-based practice. The study of indigenous and immigrant populations reveals the underlying theories of culture-based behavior worthy of consideration as a basis for the advancement of the social work profession. While it is beyond the scope of this chapter to present the various frameworks that have viability for the profession and particularly its work with special populations, it is instructive to introduce one framework to demonstrate the potential of social work contribution to the theory development, practice, and policy.

A relational worldview and measure of well-being (L. McCubbin, McCubbin, Kehl, Strom, & Zhang, 2011) emerged from the community-based studies of McGregor, Morelli, Matsuoka, and Minerbi (2003) and the therapy-oriented transactional systems theory of Spiegel (1971) and Papajohn and Spiegel (1975). McGregor and colleagues' (2003) investigation of rural indigenous communities cultivated a worldview of relational well-being, a conceptualization based on cultural history and systems theory. Central to their conceptualization are the interdependence between the indigenous people and nature, the beliefs in the sacredness of the animate and inanimate world, the collective gathering and sharing, and the organic family system. To focus their central thesis: "Well-being is synonymous with people-environment kinship and the organic relationship that bonds humans to the land" (McGregor et al., 2003, p. 109). When this relationship is enhanced or disrupted, the well-being of the people is impacted.

These theorists point to a core belief in the indigenous worldview that the land lives as do the spirits of family ancestors who care for the ancestral land. The land, a living entity, has and will continue to provide for generations. Drawing from the ecological conceptualizations of Bronfenbrenner and Ceci (1994), McGregor and colleagues (2003) also created a relational–ecological model that reflects this interdependence but adds land as a sense of place and source of nurturance and energy, well-being, and the health of the nation, community, family, and individual. Stewardship of the land is central to the creation of well-being which itself is rooted in spirituality and all that the ancestors have passed on to future generations. In return, the future generations gain knowledge of the life of the land, understand the fundamentals of cultural resource management and land use, and embrace the natural elements of land, air, water, and ocean as interconnected and interdependent parts of their family and individual lives. In this worldview, water is wealth and ultimately the use of cultural resources for conservation as an investment and giving back to future generations.

Community well-being, an integral dimension of relational well-being, is viewed as part and parcel of residing in a location thus resulting in a sense of place. From this perspective, longevity in partnership with a sense of place ensures continuity and the sharing of beliefs and values across generations. It is this context in which community leadership is cultivated, economic development is nurtured, and cultural and spiritual practices give roots to their sense of security, predictability, and the meaning of life. The community cultivates spiritual energy and an environment for learning and practicing values and beliefs as well as the transmission of knowledge. Of importance, the community is defined by a system of rules, expectations, and norms related to roles, responsibilities, and behaviors.

Ancestors and ancestral history are fundamental elements of an indigenous worldview, and thus multigenerational relationships are integral to fabric of the indigenous theory. McGregor and Collegaues (2003, p. 121) state, "The deep sense of relatedness is at the core of indigenous values, beliefs, interactions, processes, and traditions that form the foundation of harmonious family life." In this framework, the family is connected to the past, present, and future. The family system's identity or schema (L. McCubbin & McCubbin, 2005) is defined by its ethnic origins, values, beliefs, expectations, and traditions.

The application of systems or ecological conceptualizations to indigenous theory brings the relational worldview into a sharper focus. While we have described the key elements of well-being (land, nation, community, family, and individual) to render clarity to the dimensions, it is the relational worldview, described in the writings by Cross (1998) and McGregor and colleagues, (2003) and at the family level by L. McCubbin and H. McCubbin (2005). This portrayal of well-being as a holistic interconnectedness (relational worldview) between humans, nature, Earth, and universe, and the social processes of nations, communities, families, and individuals guides our efforts to conceptualize and measure well-being at a systems level.

Conclusions

For indigenous populations, also classified as special populations, the future is today. The metaphor of a dormant volcano coming to life is appropriate, for it depicts the once silent or muted voices of colonized people throughout the Pacific and in the continental United States inclusive of Alaska, seething, seeking an outlet and expression, and claiming what was once theirs. The Western stereotypes and analytical categories we have come to depend on to explain the behavior of immigrant and indigenous people are being challenged. The Western and European grounded theories used to guide our predictions, explanations, and interventions are being confronted and questioned, and the tried-and-true research methodologies are being reframed in the context of culture, beliefs, respect, and values.

This chapter has been about groups of special people whose eligibility was shaped by a history of immigration and colonization and exploitation that marginalized and nearly destroyed a community of people enriched by a past, language, traditions, values, beliefs, and expectations, and that have come to life. Their demands are reasonable and serve as reference points, as a GIS if you will, to guide the profession of social work in its efforts to search for deeper understanding of immigrant and indigenous people. The profession expects to give rise to relevant theories and propositions and to conduct research based on protocol and respect for the cultures that they expect to be partnered with in the scientific process. In this sea of change, the profession has aligned itself with best practices and has given new meaning to the idea of being culturally competent. The chapter highlights and introduces the elements of an indigenous strategy for understanding, explaining, predicting, and studying special populations in a culturally sensitive and respectful manner. While provocative in its confrontation of current practices, the indigenous strategy is inviting and calling for the profession to engage the population in its own quest for understanding and to search for ways to enhance its spiritual, social, emotional, and economic well-being.

Key Terms

Culturally relevant   Diversity   Indigenous

Review Questions for Critical Thinking

1. What are special populations?
2. Why are indigenous and immigrant populations important?
3. In what ways is historical trauma importance?
4. What is a superorganic family?

5. Why are ancestors important in our work with individuals and families?

6. How can "land" be important to the well-being of people and families?

7. What are theories and research methods for these populations?

8. What are the implications for social work training?

Online Resources

Indigenous Peoples Issues and Resources: www.indigenouspeoplesissues.com/

The leading source for news, information, videos, and more on indigenous peoples from around the world.

The Rights of Indigenous Peoples: www1.umn.edu/humanrts/edumat/studyguides/indigenous.html

Declaration on the Rights of *Indigenous Peoples*—United Nations: www.un.org/esa/socdev/unpfii/en/declaration.html

References

Banton, M. (1977). *Relational choice: A theory of racial and ethnic relations*. London, UK: Tavistock.

Banton, M. (1981). The direction and speed of ethnic change. In C. Keyes (Ed.), *Ethnic change* (pp. 32–52). Seattle, WA University of Washington Press.

Benham, K. P. M., & Heck, R. H. (1998). *Culture and educational policy in Hawaii: Silencing of native voices*. Hillsdale, NJ: Lawrence Erlbaum.

Bishop, R. (1996). *Collaborative research stories: Whatawhanaungatanga*. Palmerton North, NZ: Dunmore Press.

Bolland, K., & Atherton, C. (2000). Heuristics versus logical positivism: Solving the wrong problem. *Families in Society*, *83*(1), 7–13.

Bronfenbrenner, U., & Ceci, S. (1994). Nature-nurture reconceptualized in developmental perspective: A biological model. *Psychological Review*, *101*(4), 568–586.

Braun, K., Pietsch, J., & Blanchette, P. (Eds.) (2000). *Cultural issues in end-of-life decision making*. Thousand Oaks: CA. Sage.

Cross, T. (1998). Understanding family resilience from a relational worldview. In H. I. McCubbin, E. A. Thompson, A. I. Thompson, & J. E. Fromer (Eds.), *Resiliency in ethnic minority families: Native and immigrant American minority families* (Vol. 1, pp. 143–157). Thousand Oaks, CA: Sage.

Denzin, N. K., & Lincoln, Y. S. (Eds.). (1998). *The landscape of qualitative research: Theories and issues*. Thousand Oaks, CA: Sage.

Dubos, R. (1974). *Of human diversity*. New York, NY: Clark University Press.

Eliade, M. (1950). *The sacred and the profane: The nature of religion*. W. Trask (Trans.). New York, NY: Harper and Row.

Kahakalau, K. (2004). Indigenous heuristic action research: Bridging Western and indigenous research methodologies. *Hulili: Multidisplinary Research on Hawaiian Well-Being*, *1*(1), 19–33.

Kamehameha Schools/Bishop Estate. (1983). *Native Hawaiian educational assessmenta*. Honolulu, HI: Kamehameha Press.

Keyes, C. (1981). The dialectics of ethnic change. In C. Keyes (Ed.), *Ethnic change* (pp. 3–30). Seattle, WA: University of Washington Press.

Kim, U., & Berry, J. W. (1993). *Indigenous psychologies: Research and experience in cultural context*. Newbury Park, CA: Sage.

Light, I. (1981). *Ethnic succession*. In C. Keyes (Ed.), *Ethnic change* (pp. 54–86). Seattle, WA: University of Washington Press.

Minerbi, L., McGregor, D., & Matsuoka, J. (2003). Using geographic information systems for cultural impact assessment. In H. A. Becker & F. Vanclay (Eds.), *The international handbook of social impact assessment* (p. 16). Camberley, UK: Elgar.

McCubbin, L., & McCubbin, H. (2005). Culture and ethnic identity in family resilience: Dynamic processes in trauma and transformation of indigenous people. In M. Unger (Ed.), *Handbook for working with children and youth: Pathways to resilience across cultures and contexts* (pp. 27–44). Thousand Oaks, CA: Sage.

McCubbin, L., McCubbin, H., Kehl, L., Strom, I., & Zhang, W. (In review). *Relational well-being and resilience: An indigenous family perspective and measure*.

McGregor, D., Morelli, P., Matsuoka, J., & Minerbi, L. (2003). An ecological model of well-being. In H. Becker & F. Vanclay (Eds.), *The international handbook of social impact assessment*. (pp. 108–128). Camberley, UK: Elgar.

Morrow, R. A. (1994). *Foundations of metatheory: Between subjectivism and objectivism, critical theory and methodology*. Thousand Oaks, CA: Sage.

Papajohn, J., & Spiegel, J. (1975). *Transactions: The interplay between individual, family, and society*. New York, NY: Science House.

Smith, L. T. (1999). *Decolonizing methodologies*. London, UK: Zed Books.

Stannard, D. (1992). *American holocaust*. London, UK: Oxford University Press.

Spiegel, J. (1971). Transactions inquiry: Descriptions of systems. In J. Papajohn & J. Spiegel(Ed.) *Transactions: The interplay between individual family and society*. New York, NY: Science.

Touraine, A. (2001). *Beyond neoliberalism*. Cambridge, UK: Polity Press.

Turner, J. H., Beeghley, L., & Powers, C. H. (2002). *The early masters and the prospects for scientific theory: The emergence of sociological theory* (5th ed.). Belmont, CA: Wadsworth.

Witkin, S., & Iversen, R. (2008). Issues in social work. In B. White, K. Sowers, & C. Dulmus (Eds.), *Comprehensive handbook of social work and social welfare* (Vol. 1, pp. 467–496). Hoboken, NJ: John Wiley & Sons.

Wright, R., Mindel, C., Thanh, V., & Habenstein, R. (2011). *Ethnic families in America: Patterns and variations* (5th ed.). New York, NY: Elsevier North-Holland.

Chapter 13
Diversity

Iris B. Carlton-LaNey and Sharon Warren Cook

> With the multiple layers of diversity in social work, why is a historical perspective critical to understanding diversity and to engaging in culturally competent practice?

The social work profession is an extremely diverse profession that has worked to embrace diversity throughout its existence. This has not always been an easy task, and social workers, like other Americans, have sometimes struggled to be responsive and celebratory toward diversity. The social work profession, like society in general, faces discrimination in the form of sexism, racism, ageism, ableism, heterosexism, and ethnocentrism. In an effort to counter these societal ills, the social work profession has embraced diversity and culturally competent practice. Diversity of populations served, diversity of skills and knowledge, and diversity of services and programs provided characterize the mission of the social work profession.

Diversity has become essential to the social work profession's fundamental mission, which is to serve people in need and simultaneously to make social institutions more responsive to people and their problems (Bent-Goodley & Fowler, 2006; Morales, Sheafor, & Scott, 2007). Social workers view diversity favorably and acknowledge the variation within the profession as an enriching quality. Essentially, the diversity within the profession enables social workers to respond more adequately to human needs that exist within a fluid and dynamic world. Several definitions of diversity have been presented throughout social work literature. *The Social Work Dictionary* (Barker, 2003, p. 126) defines diversity as:

> *Variety, or the opposite of homogeneity. In social organizations the term usually refers to the range of personnel who more accurately represent minority populations and people from varied backgrounds, cultures, ethnicities, and viewpoints. Environmentalists use the term to indicate a variety of plant and animal forms in the area rather than a system in which only one or a few species exist.*

Lum (2003, p. 36) says that diversity focuses on the differences that make a person distinct and unique from another person. It offers an opportunity for a person to name those distinctions and invites another person to discover those particular qualities about that particular individual. It is an inclusive term that encompasses groups distinguished by race, ethnicity, culture, class, gender, sexual orientation, religion, physical or intellectual ability, age, and national origin.

Others, like William W. Chace (1989), laced their definitions with admonitions for the reader to act in a socially just way in order to embrace differences:

> Generally understood and embraced, [diversity] is not casual liberal tolerance of anything and everything not yourself. It is not polite accommodation. Instead, diversity is the action, the sometimes painful awareness that other people, other races, other voices, other habits of mind, have as much integrity of being, as much claim upon the world, as you do. No one has an obligation greater than your own to change, or yield, or to assimilate into the mass. The irreconcilable is as much a part of social life as the congenial. Being strong in life is being strong amid difference while accepting the fact that your own self can be a considerable imposition upon everyone you meet. I urge you to consider your own oddity before you are troubled or offended by that of others. And I urge you amid all the differences present to the eye and mind to reach out and create the bonds that will sustain the common wealth that will protect us all. We are meant to be together. (Berg-Weger, 2005, p. 112)

As noted by these various definitions, diversity in fields of practice, diversity of clientele, diversity in knowledge and skills, diversity of services, and diversity in social and political policy perspectives characterize social work. Clearly, the social work profession has a long history of involvement with issues of human diversity, albeit not always adequate or effective. Some would argue that the United States' and social work's "ambivalence to human diversity has been greater than its acceptance" (Burwell, 1998, p. 388). Likewise, others acknowledge that social work's concern with persons of various racial, cultural, and ethnic identification tends to "ebb and flow" (Leigh, 1998, p. 3).

The 19th edition of the *Encyclopedia of Social Work* published in 1995 highlights the existence of a global view that has had a concomitant effect on sensitivity to and appreciation for diversity (Edwards, 1995). The interconnectedness of a global village has resulted from many factors, including an increase in mobility of the world's citizens along with an easy, rapid flow of information and ideas.

As the United States is becoming a more racially diverse country, it is simultaneously aging. The United States recently celebrated reaching a population milestone of 300 million. By the year 2050, more than 392 million people are expected to inhabit the United States, with 206 million Whites, 88 million Latinos, 56 million African Americans, 38 million Asians, and 3.7 million American Indians (Ozawa, 1997).

When data like these are presented, it is important for social workers to remember what Schriver (2001) calls "diversity within diversity" or recognizing that there are numerous diverse groups with diverse qualities within each group. First Nations People typify this concept of "diversity within diversity." The United States is home to more than 500 distinct Native American nations. Many of these nations are very small, with fewer than 100 enrollees, while others like the Cherokee and

Lakota/Dakota/Nakota have over 100,000 members (Weaver, 2003). Size is only one of many variables that contribute to the diversity among American Indians.

The Lumbee Indians of North Carolina "challenge almost every perception of what Indians should be" (Bordewich, 1996, p. 63). The Lumbee Indians range in appearance from African to Nordic, with blond hair and blue eyes. They do not have reserved lands, U.S. treaties, or medicine men. They are English-speaking Baptists who have "an unflagging conviction that they are simply and utterly Indian" (Bordewich, 1996, p. 63). They have state recognition but have for over 100 years sought, but failed, to receive, full federal recognition.

Other groups that typify "diversity within diversity" are the disabled. Scholars who engage in research with this population find themselves studying a diverse group of people and an equally diverse set of problems or issues, ranging from long-term care for or deinstitutionalization of people with intellectual or physical disabilities (Parish, 2005; Parish & Lutwick, 2005), to financial well-being of young children with disabilities and their families (Parish & Cloud, 2006), to health disparities of people of color and among women.

Further, diversity within all groups is anticipated as the population ages. The number of elders is expected to increase from 12.8% in 1995 to 20.7% in 2040. These elders will be more mobile than their predecessors and will relocate to new communities for various lifestyle opportunities. Social workers must understand that working with older people adds a special challenge to the diversity mix. They must understand family, local and community history, formal and informal resources, and the help-seeking patterns within each particular group. For example, the help-seeking journey that rural African Americans elders might follow begins with their personal resources, which include the nuclear family, fictive kin, extended family, friends, and neighbors. The second source of help, or the informal/communal resources, might include church family and related organizations, secret/fraternal orders, faith healers, and other groups unique to that particular environment. Social workers, doctors, and other healthcare providers are part of the formal/professional network and are generally the last group approached in this journey (Carlton-LaNey, 2006).

The elderly face a range of problems and issues, and their responses vary depending on available resources. Social workers must be knowledgeable and respectful of the history and methods of problem solving to which elders adhere.

The following vignette illustrates the type of issues that arise and the various problems to which social workers should respond with sensitivity, skill, and compassion as they work with these individuals. Since the population of elders is diverse, social workers must be diverse in their approaches. Advocacy for elders must be neither color- nor gender-blind. Instead, the unique lifestyles of various ethnic and racial groups require that their specific needs be acknowledged and served (Carlton-LaNey, 1997).

When Aunt Cullie Started to Wander

It was about 1:00 in the morning. It was late fall and starting to get cool outside. Mama and Daddy were asleep when someone knocked on the back door. People don't stop by this time of morning unless something real bad has happened. Giving each other that "wonder-who-that-could-be" look, Mama and Daddy got up together to answer the door.

It was Aunt Cullie. She had a still, blank look in her eyes and she was trying to find her daughter Bonita. But Bonita no longer lived in our neighborhood. She had been living in New York for over 35 years. Aunt Cullie said that she heard Bonita call for her, and she believed that her daughter was there.

It was a scary time, because we knew that Aunt Cullie was changing. When Mama called Aunt Cullie's husband, Uncle Bryant, to tell him that she was up at our house, he was alarmed and surprised because he hadn't heard her leave their house. He came up to take her back home. He said that he had seen some changes in her lately, but he knew this wandering was very dangerous. He paused, shaking his head and looking downward, as if searching for some answers in the cold, faded linoleum on the kitchen floor.

That next week, Aunt Cullie made another early morning visit to her niece's house further up the road. Aunt Cullie was still looking for her only child, Bonita.

Uncle Bryant telephoned Bonita.

About a month later, Bonita came home from New York and moved Aunt Cullie away. The following summer, Bonita brought Aunt Cullie home for a visit. We all walked down the road to see her. She looked good; her skin was beautiful and flawless. She seemed more like her old self, but we were told that her mind would come and go. That was the last time we saw our aunt.

We knew that Aunt Cullie was leaving our neighborhood for good, but that reality was too burdensome, so we smiled anyway and waved good-bye as we watched Bonita's station wagon head up the road taking Aunt Cullie to live out her days far away in New York (Carlton-LaNey, 2005, pp. 37–38).

As this vignette shows, many elderly have aged in place—staying in the same living situation for years as their personal competence has declined (Hooyman & Kiyak, 2005). They, in many instances, lack the resources of their counterparts who have been more mobile throughout their lives. Many of these individuals have few advocates since their children and often their siblings have long since migrated to urban centers seeking better opportunities.

We also note an increase in the elderly who relocate to the U.S. Sunbelt. Other states like North Carolina and Florida have also seen net gains in migrants over the years. As the elderly move to new communities for various amenities, they bring resources that are welcomed into the local economy. In North Carolina, those same resources create local housing booms, for example, that obstruct the mountain vistas in the Western part of the state or contribute to coastal erosion and compromise the delicate ecosystems in the East. Unfortunately, this increase in diversity adds to public expressions of ageism and other prejudices that contribute to discrimination.

Housing and independent living arrangements are critical issues for elders and their families. The vignette illustrates the circumstances that rural elders experience that, in turn, create crises for their families and communities. It is not uncommon for family members to provide informal care in such situations. Called *assistance migrants*, family members who have moved away but are forced to return to their place of birth to care for the ailing older relative find their lives altered. Or, as this case illustrates, the elder is relocated to the caregiver's home—removing him or her from familiar living arrangements and altering life for an entire family. This demands change from all involved and may lead to caregiver strain that sometimes causes resentment and bitterness among family members.

Essentially, the diversity that characterizes the United States has also created tensions. Opposing values, beliefs, and practices have vigorously interacted, causing differential treatment and unequal access to resources. While the democratic principles that support equality for all people exist in theory and law, these principles pale when sociopolitical and economic competition and the whims of powerful people prevail. Pinderhughes (1989) summarized the results cogently when she said, "Forces pressing for equality and for discrimination, for rights and privileges for all and for men only, for democracy and for slavery have interacted dynamically with the superior resources and power of the most influential—middle-class White Anglo-Saxon Protestants—often determining the outcome" (p. 2). Essentially, a perspective that views the center of power and superiority as being among "White, males, middle-class, heterosexual, able-bodied, mentally healthy, church-going Christians" (Anderson & Carter, 2003, p. 13) marginalizes all others.

Those individuals who embraced the values, behaviors, and customs of the most influential group were rewarded. Others who refused or were unable to acquiesce have felt the wrath of an unforgiving social system. The societal pressures to protect the status quo, to maintain an ordered society, and to promote an environment of sameness remained firmly intact well into the 1960s.

Diversity and Social Work Paternalism

Prior to the 1960s consciousness-raising, social justice meant a color-blind response to societal ills. Pinderhughes (1989) notes that the human service needs and problems along with targeted solutions were identified and promulgated by the White middle class. "The definition of problems, that is, what is pathological and deviant, the theoretical constructs that determine assessment and intervention methods, the strategies devised, the programming of services, and even the evaluation of outcomes had been developed in terms of what seemed appropriate for the White American middle class" (p. 3). These attitudes maintained and propagated a guiding ethic of paternalism. Social work's propensity toward paternalism has also helped to focus the profession on the imperative of diversity.

Embracing paternalism posed a problem that has taken the profession some time to overcome. As the profession emerged, the roots of paternalism served as the guiding principle for actions and sometimes inaction. Simon (1994) describes paternalism as a system of relations in which those in authority act on behalf of other people without their permission to do so, while maintaining a belief that their action was in the best interest of the person in need, regardless of that person's belief and wishes. The social work profession's history is replete with examples of such paternalism. Progressive Era responses to poverty and need included many organizations that adhered to expressions of paternalism. For example, the Charity Organization Society (COS), the settlement house movement, the National League on Urban Conditions among Negroes (renamed the National Urban League; NUL), and the National Association of Colored Women's Clubs (NACW) illustrate this point.

COS pioneers like Josephine Shaw Lowell and Mary Richmond targeted individual shortcomings and moral weaknesses in their casework practice. The avoidance of duplication of services was paramount and changing individual behavior was entrenched in the COS movement's work. The COS embraced several fundamental ideas, including inter-agency cooperation, individualization, adequacy of relief, preventative philanthropy, and personal service (Axinn & Stern, 2005), all of which were couched in paternalism. The White middle-class women who dominated the COS visited low-income neighborhoods to share their advice and wisdom on living wholesome lives (Berg-Weger, 2005). They role-modeled the wholesome living they espoused and liberally reprimanded women, and sometimes men, who strayed from their admonitions.

Settlement house leaders also embraced the notion of paternalism, albeit to a lesser extent. Less prone to directly reproach individuals for "inappropriate conduct," the settlement house leaders encouraged, cajoled, and massaged newcomers, both immigrants and migrants, to convince them of the merits of assimilation and acceptable public conduct. To become true Americans, immigrants were expected and often encouraged to give up old-country ways, change their names and time-honored customs, and learn to speak flawless English. Settlement houses provided classes and clubs such as English-speaking classes to facilitate this "Americanizing." Simon (1994) noted that some paternalism crept into the various clubs and programs of the settlement houses as leaders held themselves up as role models and stalwarts of the American dream. While settlement house leaders touted the notion that residing in communities demonstrated the idea that dependency of the classes on each other was reciprocal, their methods of direct practice reflected paternalism and role modeling for assimilation and protection of the middle and upper classes (Berg-Weger, 2005; Carlton-LaNey & Andrews, 1998).

National Urban League leaders viewed their work as a way to integrate African Americans into the mainstream of American life through social services and social programs. The NUL, founded in 1911, had become synonymous with social work in the African American community by 1916. The organization's goals included (a) demonstrating the advantages of cooperation to social welfare agencies, (b) securing and training social workers, (c) protecting women and children from deceitful persons, (d) fitting workers for/to work, (e) helping to secure boys' and girls' clubs and neighborhood unions, (f) working with delinquents, (g) maintaining a country home for convalescent women, and (h) investigating conditions of city life as a basis for practical work (Carlton-LaNey, 1996b; Parris & Brooks, 1971; Weiss, 1974).

Urban Leaguers, like Forrester B. Washington, for example, were described as "paternalistic" in their roles. Washington believed that African Americans who migrated to the city were "very vulnerable to bad influences because they were without the retaining influences of their families, friends, and those who knew them" (Barrow, 2001, p. 132). With this, Washington set out to shape the behaviors and attitudes of the new migrants so they could be acceptable to Whites and to the better classes of African American people. He printed and distributed guidance cards, called "Helpful Hints," which contained directives on acceptable behavior and dress (Barrow, 2001).

The NUL's methods, however, were not universally accepted as the best way to serve the African American community. A. Phillip Randolph and Chandler Owens used their socialist magazine, *The Messenger*, to criticize the NUL's work, calling it an organization of, for, and by capital (Reisch & Andrews, 2002). They condemned the NUL and other social work organizations, noting that they were "stifling" the promising young college men and women who work for the organization, while "thwarting [sic] their energies and sapping their judgment" (Invisible Government of Negro Social Work, 1920, p. 176).

The National Association of Colored Women's (NACW) clubs' motto of "Lifting as We Climb" reflects the clubwomen's bond with their lower-class sisters. It also reflected their elitist paternalism. The movement began in response to growing unmet social welfare needs in the African American communities, to the increased racial tension of the late 19th century, and to the need to build a social reform movement with African American women's leadership (Salem, 1993). The emphases on self-help and racial solidarity were prominent in the movement. In their zeal to make African American womanhood respectable, capable, and morally correct, the clubwomen did not hesitate to represent and speak for their lower-class sisters. In fact, a sense of class superiority and privilege permeated the club movement. In their efforts to teach social and cultural improvement and moral uplift, they also tried to teach African American women how to make their "homes bulwarks in the defense of black womanhood" (White, 1999, p. 69). Published guides of conduct included books like Charlotte Hawkins Brown's *The Correct Thing: To Do, To Say, To Wear* (1941). Essentially, the clubwomen's constant stream of advice ran the gamut from Brown's all-encompassing book to an array of specific admonitions such as "stop sitting on stoops and talking and laughing loudly in public," to choosing their husbands more carefully, all of which served to make clear the clubwomen's "feeling that the masses of black women did not measure up to middle-class standards" (White, 1999, p. 71).

This brief historical review of pioneering social welfare organizations demonstrates that social work began as a profession dominated by Whites and Protestants, laced with the values that they espoused. It is critical to also note that Jews, Catholics, and African Americans, regardless of religious orientation, have a rich and respected history of social welfare service delivery for the poor and needy. Further, their efforts have also been essential to the development of the profession and its acknowledgment of the vital need to embrace diversity. Moreover, diversity among social work pioneers and their approaches to problem solving have helped to augment the diversity that characterizes the profession.

Diversity and Social Work Pioneers

Social work pioneers have included well-known White pioneers such as Paul Kellogg, Jane Addams, and Grace and Edith Abbott. George Edmund Haynes, Eugene Kinkle Jones, Edna Jane Hunter, Ida Bell Wells-Barnett, and Janie Porter Barrett can be counted among prominent African American pioneers. These individuals' works included pioneering social work education and training, establishing housing for young, single African American men and women moving to cities, and establishing organizations like the NUL to serve African Americans moving from the agrarian South to cities in the North, South, and Midwest. Social settlements like Hull House and the Locust Street Settlement helped immigrants in large cities and migrants from small towns, respectively. Each of these agencies, organizations, services, and programs was designed to serve a diverse population of individuals with diverse needs and diverse circumstances (Carlton-LaNey, 1999).

These individuals' diversity of race, gender, age, sexual orientation, class, and so on is an enriching quality that has helped to create a dynamic profession capable of responding to human needs in a vibrant, changing society. While discrimination and exclusion certainly existed within the profession, reflecting societal norms, social workers have continuously acknowledged the need to serve diverse clients with diverse needs in diverse settings. Settlement house pioneer Lillian Wald, for example, wanted to provide health care to needy women and children in their homes and communities. Through the Henry Street Settlement, as well as through her involvement with the Lincoln House Settlement, which served African Americans, Wald helped to train visiting nurses, visiting teachers, and social workers to respond to community needs with respect and acceptance. While this was a time of strict segregation, Wald nonetheless identified ways to function within the accepted norms of the day and to simultaneously engage in policy practice. On one occasion, both African Americans and Whites were to gather at the Henry Street Settlement for a meeting. Racial etiquette presented a dilemma as to how to serve dinner to a mixed-race group. The solution was to forgo a sit-down meal and instead to serve a buffet, which would allow the races to "mix" while standing, a much more socially acceptable practice.

Intimately involved with a network of female pioneers throughout her career, Wald was among the group of women who advocated for gender equity within Progressive Era parameters. Part of these women's advocacy was to promote Frances Perkins's appointment as the Secretary of Labor under the Roosevelt administration. Perkins's appointment was a political "hot potato," since no woman had ever held a presidential Cabinet position. Even Perkins herself needed some persuading, which Wald and her brigade of lady leaders provided handily. Furthermore, Wald and other pioneers in social work adhered to the Cult of True Womanhood, which assigned women the roles of defenders of the moral order. This made it acceptable for them to work, whether as paid employees or volunteers, outside the home, since their compassion, nurturance, and morality made them suitable to tackle societal uncleanness and immorality (Day, 1997). These social work pioneer women's goals included the importance of women practicing and modeling integrative roles for other women.

Diversity and Contemporary Social Work Organizations

As the social work profession developed during the Progressive Era and beyond, its work toward embracing diversity continued. While the transition has not always been smooth and universally accepted, the National Association of Social Workers (NASW) and the Council on Social Work Education (CSWE) have both taken a stand supporting diversity, albeit not always with the desired fervor, rapidity, and zeal.

Today, the significance of diversity in social work is highlighted in the documents of both NASW and the CSWE—the largest individual member organization and the organization that shapes social work education curricula, respectively. NASW's 2006 to 2009 policy statements clearly demonstrate the profession's commitment to diversity and cultural competence. Policy statements supporting diversity include Affirmative Action; Civil Liberties and Justice; Cultural and Linguistic Competence in the Social Work Profession; Gender-, Ethnic-, and Race-Based Workplace Discrimination; Linguistic/Cultural Diversity in the United States; Racism, Transgender, and Gender Identity Issues; and Women's Issues. Several of these statements are summarized in Table 13.1.

The CSWE included a statement in its 2008 *Educational Policy Accreditation Standards* (EPAS) that mandates content on diversity in bachelor's and master's of social work programs. The impetus for this policy stems from a desire to produce students who understand the consequences of difference and are capable of competent and culturally respectful practice within a diverse society. The educational policies mandate that BSW and MSW social work programs have content that supports an understanding of the critical nature of diversity and ways that diversity helps to form identity and characterizes and shapes the human experience (CSWE, 2008). These educational programs are encouraged to add competencies consistent with their mission and goals and to develop their curriculum to reflect the diversity in their regions. For example, a social work program in eastern North Carolina might reflect content about the Lumbee Indians—the largest tribe

Table 13.1 NASW Policy Statements that Demonstrate a Commitment to Diversity.

Affirmative Action—NASW is committed to affirmative action and will pursue its development and implementation at all organizational levels (p. 18).

Civil Liberties and Justice—NASW calls on the social work profession to reaffirm its commitment to individual liberties, criminal justice reform, and equal protection under the law (pp. 43–51).

Cultural and Linguistic Competence—NASW promotes and supports the implementation of cultural and linguistic competence at the individual, institutional, and societal levels. Collaboration with consumers, families, and cultural communities is a precondition for the creation of culturally and linguistically competent services (p. 81).

Gender, Ethnic, and Race-Based Workplace Discrimination—NASW reaffirms its commitment to public/private sector affirmative action and supports principles and strategies for change in legislative, administrative, and educational areas (p. 176).

Racism—NASW supports an inclusive, multicultural society in which race, ethnicity, class, sexual orientation, age, physical and intellectual ability, religion and spirituality, gender and other cultural and social identities are valued and respected (p. 310).

Transgender and Gender Identity Issues—NASW asserts that discrimination and prejudice directed against any individuals are damaging to those persons' well-being and should be eliminated from both inside and outside the profession (p. 368).

Women's Issues—NASW is committed to advancing policies and practices to improve the well-being of all women. NASW believes that it is vital for social workers to develop a critical consciousness about gender or use a feminist policy analysis that enables the ramifications of gender to be made visible in policy and practice (p. 390).

Source: Social Work Speaks: National Association of Social Workers Policy Statements 2006–2009, 7th ed., by National Association of Social Workers. Washington, DC: National Association of Social Workers Press.

east of the Mississippi River. Because of the diversity within diversity, Lumbee Indians do not share the same history and response to oppression as their Plains Indians counterparts.

CSWE EPAS also requires that social work programs address the multiple dimensions of diversity and the intersectionality of diversity including race, color, age, disability, religion, gender, and other qualities. Mandated content on social and economic justice also require that social work programs prepare students to combat discrimination, oppression, and economic deprivation. The tremendous growth in the number of accredited social work programs may suggest that an effort is being made to design curriculum that produce culturally competent social workers (CSWE, 2008).

While the NASW *Code of Ethics* and the CSWE *Educational Policy Accreditation Standards* requirements are valuable instruments, the social work profession must also identify and present ''diverse policy perspectives and explore the inequity within the social policy'' if social and economic justice for a diverse society is genuinely desired (Davis, 2004). Essentially, social workers must also actively engage in policy practice. Davis and Bent-Goodley's book *The Color of Social Policy* (2004) is a significant contribution that provides content for sound policy practice and social justice. In an effort to ground the concept of social justice in social work education, Davis (2004) provides the following cogent definition of social justice:

> Social justice is a basic value and desired goal in democratic societies and includes equable and fair access to all social institutions, laws, resources, opportunities, rights, goods, and services for all groups and individuals within arbitrary limitations or barriers based on observations or interpretations of the value of differences in age, color, culture, physical or mental ability, education, income language, national origin, race, religion, or sexual orientation. (p. 236)

According to Davis, when this definition of social justice is used as the "operating framework...in the curriculum," it means that social work education is "committed to building and implementing the curriculum...around this basic value" (p. 236). Davis notes that it also means "that a school's faculty is also committing themselves to action" aimed at the concrete achievement of social justice.

Davis' treatise has been met with some resistance. The contemporary political climate has postulated what he calls a "divisive and unproductive philosophical debate" regarding social justice and the government's role (p. 235). Some of this rejection has found its way into conversations among social work educators (Gerdes, Segal, & Ressler, 2003). While the CSWE standards are clear and the mandate generally accepted, there remains "little agreement within the social work literature regarding how and where to teach this content and the form that it should take" (Gutierrez, Fredricksen, & Soifer, 1999, p. 410). The extent to which faculty are comfortable with diversity content is critical and challenging (Nagda et al., 1999). Gutierrez and her colleagues argue that social work faculty must be both comfortable with the content and competent in teaching it for useful educational preparation to take place. They further caution that the content on diversity may be altogether excluded or covered inadequately if there is no genuine commitment to its inclusion. Noted feminist scholar Peggy McIntosh (1988) drew similar conclusions when she examined the inclusion of content on women's issues. She indicated that men were willing to admit that this content was important and worthy of inclusion in courses, yet were simultaneously unwilling to acknowledge their privilege. This would likely present a biased perspective if the content were included at all. Essentially, opponents generally argue that there is no place to put additional content in an already overcrowded curriculum.

For content on diversity to be taught in social work education programs, junior faculty and members of oppressed groups must not be the only advocates for including the materials. Moreover, they should not be the only faculty called on to teach this content. Clearly, adhering to CSWE's standards presents a challenge for many social work educators. To rise to the challenge, it is necessary that social work faculty, especially those less inclined to be supportive of content on diversity, engage in greater honest dialogue about this issue (Fellin, 2000; Gutierrez et al., 1999).

Many scholars believe that multiculturalism is an overarching concept for the inclusion and study of content in social work education that deals with populations-at-risk and human diversity (Fellin, 2000). Understanding multiculturalism requires that you value and have knowledge of history. Group identity and ethnicity result from historical and social influences. Therefore, a knowledge and understanding of this history provides insights into a community's strengths (Gutierrez, 1997). Again, there is disagreement among social work scholars about the virtues of multiculturalism for achieving social justice and providing equal access to societal resources. It is critical that the dialogue on the merits of multiculturalism continue among social work educators. Fellin (2000) believes that multiculturalism provides a foundation for teaching about cultural groups in social work education. He has postulated four principles (Table 13.2) useful in human diversity curriculum development. Further, Fellin believes that to achieve multiculturalism in social work education, this organizing concept should guide the selection and generation of knowledge and information about diverse groups in the United States.

Other professional social work organizations reflect recognition of the importance of diversity. Two examples include the National Association of Black Social Workers (NABSW) and the North American Association of Christians in Social Work (NACSW), both of which operate within the social work value system and serve specific professionals. In the case of the NABSW, social workers focus on the importance of cultural competency in work with African American clients/consumers, while NACSW has a part of its mission the integration of the Christian faith and social work practice.

Table 13.2 Four Principles for Curriculum Development.

A multicultural perspective should be inclusive of all subcultural groups, viewed as distinct groups that are interdependent with mainstream U.S. culture.

A multicultural perspective should recognize that all people in the United States society identify with "multiple cultures," with varying degrees of affiliation and social involvement.

A multicultural perspective should recognize that all members of U.S. society engage in various types of relationships within their various cultures, and in relation to a mainstream U.S. culture. Biculturalism, acculturation, amalgamation, and assimilation, as forms of attachment and social relationships with these cultures, are proposed as options for members of U.S. society.

A multicultural perspective would recognize the changing nature of U.S. society, as it is continually influenced by all of its subcultures and by national demographic, social, and institutional trends.

Data from Phillip Fellin, "Revisiting Multiculturalism in Social Work," *Journal of Social Work Education,* 36(2) (Spring 2000), pp. 271–272.

Diversity of Theoretical Frameworks

In addition to a historical perspective, it is also important to consider diversity and work with different groups from a theoretical perspective. Several theories have been set forth regarding work with diverse populations. Theoretical frameworks that enhance social workers' understanding and intervention with consumers include the ecological perspective, the strengths perspective, and the Afrocentric perspective.

The ecological perspective views the client system within the context of the environment in which the client lives. The environment includes family, work, religion, culture, and life events. The social worker must consider every aspect of the client's life in the practice relationship. The ecological perspective also notes that the client's past and present life experiences have influenced his or her beliefs, behaviors, interactions, and emotions. With an emphasis on the environment, the ecological perspective dictates that the social worker maintain an awareness of the influence that cultural factors—including race, place of origin, ethnicity, age, social class, religion, gender, and sexual orientation—have on the client. Historical, political, and societal issues must also be taken into account in order to understand the client system and environment (Germain & Gitterman, 1995). If, for example, the client has experienced a history of racial oppression, it might help to explain the client's reluctance to develop an effective relationship with a worker who is from the majority group (Berg-Weger, 2005). Similarly, elderly individuals who have experienced an indifferent healthcare provider may be reluctant to continue to seek health care when needed. Likewise, First Nations People who have experienced the removal and placement of their children outside their tribe/nation may fail to report suspected child abuse or neglect. Levy (1995) believes that the ecological perspective, with its focus on the "goodness of fit" between a person and his or her environment, also shares a close alignment with the feminist principle that the "personal is political" (p. 289).

The strength perspective is deemed important for working with diverse groups. The strength perspective has been presented as a central, fundamental part of all social work practice with diverse populations. The strength perspective requires incorporating the consumers' culture into the social work strategy as a strength that is consistent with the social work value that touts respect for individual uniqueness. The strength perspective also focuses on solutions instead of problems and relies on strengths as the central organizing principles for practice (Saleebey, 1997). The strengths perspective requires that the social worker build a relationship around the experience and life of the client system. In so doing, the social worker demonstrates an understanding of, and respect for, the client's culture, lifestyle, and right to self-determination.

The strengths perspective requires that social workers understand how a history of oppression has influenced the survival and adaptive resources of many groups in America. The source of these strengths include family and community structures that develop self-esteem and a network of psychosocial and economic resources, survival determination and skills, and personal transformation qualities resulting from overcoming self-depreciating forces (Anderson & Carter, 2003; Billingsley, 1992; Chestang, 1982; Hopps, Pinderhughes, & Shankar, 1995).

The strength perspective embraces empowerment principles (Solomon, 1976) that say that people have a right to engage in actions that define their existence. Levy argues that the strengths perspective "reinforce[s] feminist practice principles of renaming, valuing process, and empowerment" (p. 290). In discussing practice implications for gay and lesbian elderly, Levy cites examples that note the multiple losses that this group incurs. The loss of life partners and friends often goes unnoticed because of societal secrecy regarding sexual orientation. These people are often hospitalized or placed in long-term care facilities where their sexual orientation is ignored and their relationships disrespected. Even when living wills and healthcare powers of attorney have been put into place, the urgency of the medical crises may render the documents meaningless. Ageism in the gay and lesbian community, and in society at large, can lower self-esteem and create a sense of powerlessness.

Social workers learn how to be more effective practitioners when they openly and honestly embrace the strength perspective, which creates a client–worker partnership. Principles in the strength perspective guide social workers to truly embrace the client's belief system, coping patterns, and behavioral styles. These principles tell us to place the clients in central positions emphasizing their gifts, talents, knowledge, experiences, and resilience. Social workers who work from a strengths perspective must avoid victimizing clients with labels and instead emphasis positive expectations with a genuine and supportive focus (Lum, 2003).

The Afrocentric paradigm has been presented as an alternative way to engage in social work practice, acknowledging and underscoring the connection between African Americans and traditional Africa. It is believed that African Americans' enslavement and subsequent racial segregation, along with a desire to maintain tradition, have helped to preserve African philosophies and traditions among members of this group (Franklin, 1980; Harvey, 2001; E. Martin & Martin, 1985).

Schiele (1996) provides three objectives of the Afrocentric paradigm: (1) promote an alternative social science paradigm more reflective of the cultural and political reality of African Americans; (2) dispel the negative distortions of people of African ancestry by legitimizing and disseminating a worldview that goes back thousands of years and that exists in the hearts and minds of many people of African descent today; and (3) promote a worldview that will facilitate human and societal transformation toward spiritual, moral, and humanistic ends and will persuade people of different cultural and ethnic groups that they share a mutual interest in this regard (p. 286). Essentially, Schiele contends, theorists who embrace the Afrocentric paradigm do not believe in "social science universalism—that one theory or paradigm can be used to explain social phenomena among all people in all cultures" (p. 285).

Table 13.3   Measures of the Afrocentric Paradigm.

1. People of African descent share a common experience, struggle, and origin.

2. Present in African culture is a nonmaterial element of resistance to the assault on traditional values caused by the intrusion of European legal procedures, medicines, political processes, and religions into African culture.

3. African culture takes the view that an Afrocentric modernization process would be based on three traditional values: harmony with nature, humanness, and rhythm.

4. Afrocentricity involves the development of a theory of an African way of knowing and interpreting the world.

5. Some form of communalism or socialism is an important component for the way wealth is produced, owned, and distributed.

Data from David Covin, ''Afrocentricity in O Movimento Negro Unificado,'' *Journal of Black Studies, 21*(2) (December 1990), p. 127–128.

Covin's (1990) five measures of the Afrocentric paradigm are outlined in Table 13.3.

Swigonski (1996) says that Afrocentric theory ''shows how developing knowledge of another culture from the perspective of that culture can transform social work practice'' (p. 156). Harvey and Coleman (1997) provide guidelines for an Afrocentric approach to service delivery for youth and their families who are in the juvenile justice system. They claim that, while no one single approach is the answer, the Afrocentric approach is ''a vehicle for helping to reestablish a sense of self-dignity self-worth, spirituality, and community among this youth population'' (p. 210). Chipungu, Everett, and Leashore (1991) in their book, *Child Welfare: An Afrocentric Perspective*, provide guidelines for incorporating the Afrocentric perspective into the assessment, planning, and delivery of services to African American children and their families. They initially use the Afrocentric perspective to frame the cultural and sociohistorical context of African Americans while describing the values and worldviews of African. Chipungu's and her colleagues' work can be reflected in recent practice approaches in child welfare, such as family group conferencing, in which family culture and cultural responsiveness are critical for best practice with abused or neglected children. In family group conferencing, family members are the cultural amplifiers and cultural guides for the child welfare professionals involved with the at-risk child(ren) (Waites, Macgowan, Pennell, Carlton-LaNey, & Weil, 2004).

Many social work scholars have embraced the Afrocentric perspective as a valuable approach to social work practice with various African American client groups. Bent-Goodley (2005, 2011) emphasizes the importance of culture and Afrocentricity around partner violence, and Harvey (2001) underscores cultural competence and the Afrocentric perspective in juvenile justice programming for African American youth. Yet others argue that this perspective may fall short in many ways. Anderson and Carter (2003), for example, contend that more conceptual work needs to be done for the

Afrocentric perspective to emerge as a "widespread alternative" paradigm for social work. They believe that two important conceptual problems exist that involve the centrality of race versus the centrality of other defining features and the issue of differential adherence to the Afrocentric world-view within the African American community. As social work continues to embrace diversity as an essential element of best practice, we will continue to explore the veracity of Afrocentricity and its role in social work practice. Regardless of whether or not this perspective is embraced as a "widespread alternative," it is important to acknowledge that various individuals and families do embrace Afrocentricity as strength without naming it as such.

We are more likely to see the Afrocentric perspective reflected in programs and services as social workers make concerted efforts to seek and design culturally sensitive programs and practice approaches. The Afrocentric perspective reflects a critical consciousness that is derived from the knowledge and appreciation of history. We generally recognize the importance of historical influences on policy development and implementation, but sadly we are not always clear in our articulation of how history influences contemporary practice. Our inability to connect history to contemporary practice can lead to cultural incompetence. Even as we discourse on the importance of culture, we often fail to understand that culture itself evolves within a historical context.

In an effort to acknowledge and understand the diversity of cultures and family systems, we utilize various mechanisms, including the cultural genogram. The cultural genogram, a highly valuable assessment and therapeutic tool, captures history within a cultural context that helps the family and the social worker to understand aspects of cultural heritage, including influences of family behavior, rituals, traditions and spiritual dimensions (McCullough-Chavis & Waites, 2004).

Case Study

While the history and theoretical frameworks related to diversity are checkered and varied, the social work profession continues to advocate that attention be given to issues of social justice since discrimination, inequalities, and oppression continue as significant social problems in the United States. The *Case of Trent* demonstrates that attention to diversity and culture is essential. Jo, a White female graduate student working toward her master's degree in social work, engaged in culturally competent school social work practice with a young boy named Trent. Jo typified school social workers, a group consisting primarily of White women who use clinical practice as their primary method of intervention (Shaffer, 2006).

Working with Trent reinforced for Jo the importance of cultural awareness, self-awareness, and respect for diversity. The following *Case of Trent* explains how Jo handled this challenge and demonstrates that her cultural competence helped to make a difference in a young boy's life.

The Case of Trent

Two weeks ago, Jo began her field placement at Cover Elementary School. She was excited about this opportunity, since she planned a career in school social work after completing her degree. She was also enthused about her new field instructor and wanted to learn his approach to working with children in a school setting. Jo was told she would be working closely with the school psychologist and a number of other professionals. The prospect of interdisciplinary collaboration also greatly appealed to her.

Because Jo had some beginning ideas about her role as a school social worker, part of her daily routine included a morning walk through the school to acquaint herself with the teachers and support staff, to learn children's names and have them recognize her, and to make herself available for referrals. As she was walking through the freshly painted and brightly decorated school halls, one morning, she noticed a small boy yelling and screaming loudly, begging for his mother. A somewhat frustrated-looking teacher's aide hovered over the boy, responding to him with similar yells and screams and trying to force his small rigid frame into a chair placed in an isolated section of the corridor used for time-out.

Initial Engagement

Jo approached the teacher's aide quizzically, hoping to find out the nature of the problem. Trent, a small, attractive, bright-eyed 5-year-old African American child looked relieved that someone was coming to his rescue. The teacher's aide told Jo that throughout the day Trent was totally disruptive, rowdy, and aggressive toward other children in the classroom. She explained that the usual method of time-out, sitting quietly in another teacher's room, did not work for Trent. Therefore, placing him in the hallway was her only option. Jo spoke briefly to Trent, informing him about the time-out process and asking him to cooperate with the teacher's aide. She explained that his time-out would begin only after he stopped crying and could sit quietly. Jo said, "By the time I count to five, you should be perfectly still and quiet. Then your time-out will begin." Trent responded appropriately, and Jo stayed with him for the two-minute time-out session.

The next morning, Jo spoke with Trent's teacher. She confirmed the aide's version of Trent's behavior. Both the teacher and the aide were certain the only option for Trent was to have him tested for behavioral and emotional handicapped (BEH) certification and evaluated for intensive services such as placement in a self-contained classroom.

Since school had been in session for only two weeks, Jo was both surprised and concerned that Trent's teacher had so quickly reached such a drastic conclusion about Trent's needs. She was also curious as to why such a young child was causing such uproar. Jo also found it difficult to understand how Trent could be described as "rowdy" and "aggressive," since his behavior seemed to her to be rather deliberate and slow. Jo wondered if Trent's teacher had tried any systematic interventions other than time-outs. Jo understood that African American children, especially boys, are often labeled very early in school and that these labels follow them throughout their education. She remembered that labels influence how teachers and other staff react to kids and could compromise the quality of education that children obtain.

Data Collection and Assessment

Jo's enthusiasm showed when her field instructor told her to pursue Trent's situation and see what she could do to help. She began by consulting the school psychologist. Together they decided that Jo should gather as much information as possible. This would help her test her idea that Trent was labeled in error. It was suggested that Jo try every possible alternative to get needed information before making a referral.

Further discussions with Trent's teacher revealed that she had not really tried other intervention strategies with Trent, nor had she talked with others at the school about ways to handle him. Jo was concerned that Trent's teacher, a White female, was operating with some preconceived ideas and stereotypes about African American male children. Since Trent was slow-moving, deliberate in his speech, and inattentive, Jo feared that his teacher had labeled him as a slow learner with behavior problems and was seeking confirmation for her assessment. Jo, who was also White, tried to be sensitive to her own role in working with an African American child. She expected that Trent's family would be more guarded in their interaction with her, and that the issue of race might need to be discussed with the family. She knew that it was important for her to develop an early positive relationship with them to understand the family dynamics and to help Trent. Jo was aware that for African American families there are often key decision makers and networks of support within the extended family. She concluded that it would be important to get to know the significant family members and include them in working with Trent.

Jo set her plans into action over the next 2 weeks. Her first actions included contracting a BEH specialist to observe Trent and determine whether he should be tested for exceptionality, gathering information from the school on family background as a preliminary step to conducting an in-depth social history, and scheduling one-on-one sessions with Trent to complete a developmental evaluation.

The BEH specialist saw Trent within the week, and she and Jo discussed Trent's behavior since the beginning of the school year. The BEH specialist observed that Trent appeared to be a very intelligent child who was very slow in his movements and mannerisms. She felt that the crowded and visually stimulating classroom was too much for Trent to process quickly and easily. The specialist and Jo agreed that a plan could be implemented to help Trent be successful in kindergarten.

Jo began investigating Trent's family situation by reading the school record and speaking by telephone with Trent's father. It was revealed that, until recently, Trent had been living with his mother. A few weeks ago, Trent's mother enrolled in graduate school and decided Trent should live with his father and stepmother while she completed graduate work. Trent's stepmother had two older daughters who lived in the home, so Trent was introduced to a new family living situation. Trent's father tried to make the transition easy for him, often spending Saturday alone with Trent. To avoid imposing Trent on his new wife, Trent's father took full responsibility for his care. Unfortunately, Trent's father treated him like a toddler instead of a five-year-old, requiring little responsibility from Trent. The stepmother did little for Trent and did not participate in his discipline.

Jo tried to complete a genogram to better understand the family dynamics. The genogram would allow her to collect and visualize data about several generations of family members, their significant life events, and other family patterns. As Jo suspected, the father and stepmother were responsive yet guarded during their first meeting at the school. The interview provided Jo with very little information and left her feeling frustrated and ineffective. Jo knew that African Americans sometimes feel alienated from formal systems, and she tried to convince her field instructor that this might explain some of the resistance to disclosing family information. The field instructor assured Jo that the school was the best place to schedule the second interview and cautioned her that a young White woman might not be safe doing an in-home interview in that neighborhood. Jo argued that because of the problems with the first interview, a home visit was the best strategy. Against her field instructor's judgment, Jo scheduled the second interview a week later in the father's home.

Jo arrived at the home a little late. The family greeted her warmly and appeared to be much more relaxed. Jo told the couple that she had gotten lost trying to locate their home, and she apologized for her tardiness. She also told them the route she had taken and admitted being a little scared. They empathized and said that they would have also been uncomfortable in that area and told Jo of a safer route to and from their home. Admitting that she was uncomfortable relieved Jo of much of her anxiety and simultaneously helped Trent's family see Jo as a sincere person genuinely concerned about Trent.

During the second interview, Jo explained the purpose of their meeting and discussed the genogram with them. The father and stepmother provided information. Jo knew a more complete picture was needed and later contacted Trent's mother for additional information. Upon completing her interviews, she was able to complete a genogram that revealed a stable and functioning extended family. It also showed a grandmother who played a significant role in Trent's life, providing child care while his mother worked. Jo remembered that grandmothers often play an intricate role in African American families and add major strengths to the family unit. Jo also found that prior to moving in with his father, other members of the extended family were routinely involved with Trent.

To complete Trent's developmental evaluation, Jo scheduled half-hour sessions with him twice each week. The sessions allowed Jo to further develop a helping relationship with him. During the meetings, Jo asked Trent to complete several activities that required him to use classification skills, to show evidence of understanding concepts of conversation, and to identify common symbols (e.g., letters of the alphabet, stop signs). Trent completed each task without difficulty. He was able to form patterns with various colored and shaped blocks, read simple words, and identify the letters of the alphabet in various contexts. Trent showed no developmental delays in physical ability and was able to run, hop, skip, and gallop when asked. He was skilled at catching, throwing, and kicking a large rubber ball, and his fine motor skills appeared appropriate for his age. Essentially, Jo found no evidence of cognitive or physical developmental delays.

Intervention

After several meetings with the school psychologist, the teacher, the teacher's aide, Trent, and his parents, an intervention plan was devised. Jo helped identify goals for Trent including being able to maintain appropriate behavior at school, and being able to act responsibly at home. Jo decided to follow Trent's progress at school by using a chart illustrating four behaviors: (1) obeys the teacher and classroom rules, (2) keeps hands and feet to himself, (3) uses good manners, and (4) walks in line/sits in seat correctly. Trent participated in making the chart; including decorating it and deciding the types of stickers he would like to use to reward appropriate behavior. With his interest in animals, Jo was not surprised that Trent selected brightly colored zoo animals for his stickers. Participating in the construction of the chart and selecting stickers helped invest Trent in the behavioral change process.

In addition to the behavior chart and task list, Jo suggested that Trent's care plan include a small social skills group. Five other boys from Trent's class were in need of some special attention in the area of social skills, and Trent was included in this group. The members of the group also functioned as a potential source of friends for Trent, since he had not made many friends since moving in with his father. The group also provided an opportunity for Trent to learn and practice socially appropriate behavior through group interaction in a safe setting.

Jo paired Trent with a seventh grader who would act as his "lunch pal." This student, an African American youngster, would have lunch with Trent three times during the week, serving as an older role model and reinforcing appropriate social skills. Although Jo felt Trent's father was an excellent caregiver and role model, she was concerned that there was a lack of understanding and appreciation of African American culture within the school setting. Jo felt that choosing an African American youngster as a lunch pal might minimize the negative effort of the school "culture" on Trent and enhance his school survival skills. Jo also assigned Trent a science tutor. The science tutor could nurture Trent's extraordinary interest in science and nature by spending time with him in the science center at the school. This allowed Trent to explore his interest in animal life and learn new responsibilities.

Evaluation

Jo maintained regular contact with Trent's mother and father, teacher, and the other support personnel. The parents cooperated by maintaining behavior charts at home, while Trent's teacher followed Trent's progress by charting his behavior in the classroom. The teacher and Trent's parents reported positive changes in Trent's behavior and maturity level. By Christmas break, Trent was interacting with his classmates with much more ease and confidence. The teacher and the aide were relieved that Trent spent time outside the classroom in regular sessions with Jo and with the science tutor. They identified fewer disruptive outbursts and were better able to manage the ones that did occur. Jo felt confident that she had been effective in her work with Trent. Her plan helped him to modify his behavior and to adjust to kindergarten.

Jo remained skeptical and concerned that Trent was at risk in the public school system because of the history of discrimination African American males have faced within that system. She decided, as a long-range career goal, to address this problem by researching the extent to which African American males are treated differently within the schools. She suspected that differential treatment would be found and that a wider change effort would be necessary to remedy this condition. She wondered how she could help the school to be more sensitive to African American males (Carlton-LaNey, 1996a, pp. 3–5). Jo's experience demonstrated that she engaged in ethnic-sensitive practice, acknowledging and respecting Trent and his family's racial/ethnic reality. According to Schlesinger and Devore (1995), the social worker must have multiple skills at the cognitive (knowledge of diversity history), affective (emotional), and behavioral (language and communication skills) levels in order to be culturally competent. Jo relied on her knowledge of African American culture and an honest, caring approach when working with Trent and his family. Her understanding and respect for diversity guided her intervention strategies.

Understanding diversity is essential when choosing to use a genogram for engaging in family exploration (McCullough-Chavis & Waites, 2004). Boyd-Franklin (1989) notes that information gathering, through mechanisms such as genograms, should come later in the treatment process when working with African American families. This is sometimes counter to the approach that many practitioners have been taught. Building trust must take place before families are receptive to this intensive information gathering. Jo's initial effort to construct the genogram was met with resistance. She recognized the resistance and delayed the information gathering until the family demonstrated a level of comfort with her and their environment. However, her initial problem-solving approach began before the completion of the genogram.

An understanding of, and respect for, diversity may not only dictate when the genogram is completed as Jo found, it may also need to be altered to become a culturally responsive instrument. Watts-Jones (1997) believes that expanding the concept of family when working with African Americans and other groups in which functional kinship relationships are important provides "a more accurate reflection of how 'family' is defined and functions in this population" (p. 6). Jo found that extended family was significant in Trent's life and that their rather abrupt departure from his everyday existence may have contributed to his acting-out behavior. It is important that social workers know that other groups, including Latinos and First Nations People, also embrace the notion of family broadly, relying much more on the functional concept of family.

With the *Case of Trent*, it was critical that the social worker be aware, as Jo seemed to have been, that African American students are disproportionately referred to school administrators for disciplinary action and are also more than twice as likely as their White counterparts to be referred for corporal punishment (Haynes, 2005). Furthermore, schools disproportionately suspend students of color and teachers and administrators use disciplinary practices as ways to express their racial and class biases (Cameron, 2006). School disciplinary action targets boys more than girls and impacts disabled students and students receiving special education services disproportionably. As a result, students with the most challenges are forced to experience even more challenges.

Conclusion

As demonstrated throughout this chapter, social work continues to struggle with the importance and inclusion of diversity in professional practice, research, and social work education. It is not unusual to find scholarship that completely ignores any discussion of diversity. Authors are aware that they can write manuscripts without including any content on diverse groups and have those manuscripts published in reputable social work journals and texts. Professionals continue to write about the dominant cultural group, including content on different racial and ethnic groups as a footnote, preferring to write about Asian Americans, Native Americans, or Latinos in separate articles, books, monographs, and so on. Furthermore, there is a propensity to discuss diverse groups in terms of pathology while ignoring the strengths that have sustained them in a country where racism, ageism, sexism, heterosexism, and ableism are institutionalized.

While practitioners continue to express our commitment to including diversity in every facet of the social work profession, a stronger emphasis on cultural competence is necessary. Further, that knowledge should be applied in practice, research, education, policy development, and policy implementation. Embracing diversity is laudable, and the continued commitment to foster the concept of diversity is a challenge that the profession is prepared to meet. To be effective, social workers must continuously and aggressively assess and evaluate their performance in this effort.

Key Terms

Afrocentric paradigm	Cultural competence	Empowerment
Cultural awareness	CSWE	Genogram
	Diversity	NASW
		Social justice

Review Questions for Critical Thinking

1. Identify and analyze some of the reasons that members of diverse groups are presented from a deficit or pathological perspective versus a strength perspective.

2. Discuss the importance of diversity in each case vignette and think of the lessons to be learned from these histories.

3. Compare and contrast the concept of paternalism and the role of government intervention in the provision of social welfare services from a historical and contemporary perspective.

4. Discuss ways in which the profession of social work promotes a commitment to individual liberties and social justice.

5. Discuss the tensions between a commitment to social justice and the inertia of social policies and systems that social workers must negotiate.

6. Discuss the necessity of understanding "diversity within diversity" and how this understanding promotes competency in practice.

Online Resources

National Association of Social Workers: www.naswdc.org

National Association of Social Workers—Diversity and Equity: www.naswdc.org/diversity/default.asp

Oxford Journals: http://bjsw.oxfordjournals.org.

Social Work Today—National newsmagazine committed to enhancing the entire social work profession by exploring its difficult issues, new challenges, and current successes: www.socialworktoday.com

The Office on Women's Health provides information, tools, calculators, and statistics on women's health topics as well as information for health professionals: www.womenshealth.gov

The Department of Health and Human Services offers comprehensive information for seniors including news, benefits and government programs: www.aoa.gov

The National Association of Black Social Workers: www.nabsw.org

Black Administrators in Child Welfare, Inc.—A non-profit organization dedicated to improving the lives of African American children in the nation's child welfare system: www.blackadministrators.org

Indian Health Service—U.S. Department of Health and Human Services agency providing healthcare to Native American and Alaskan Native peoples: www.ihs.gov

Culture, Language and Health Literacy—Health Resources and Services Administration (HRSA): www.hrsa.gov/culturalcompetence/index.html

The Office of Minority Health: http://minorityhealth.hhs.gov

Gender Education and Advocacy—The website of Gender Education and Advocacy, provides resources and activism for the transgender community: www.gender.org

Human Rights Campaign—Works for lesbian, gay, bisexual and transgender equal rights by lobbying the federal government and educating the public: www.hrc.org

References

Anderson, J., & Carter, R. (Eds.). (2003). *Diversity perspectives for social work practice.* Upper Saddle River, NJ: Pearson Education.

Axinn, J., & Stern, M. (2005). *Social welfare: A history of the American response to need.* Boston, MA: Allyn & Bacon.

Barker, R. (2003). *The social work dictionary.* Washington, DC: National Association of Social Workers Press.

Barrow, F. (2001). The social work career and contributions of Forrester Blanchard Washington, a life course analysis. Unpublished doctoral dissertation, Howard University, Washington, DC.

Bent-Goodley, T. (2005). Culture and domestic violence: Transforming knowledge development. *Journal of Interpersonal Violence, 20,* 195–203.

Bent-Goodley, T. (2011). *The ultimate betrayal: A renewed look at intimate partner violence.* Washington, DC: NASW Press.

Bent-Goodley, T., & Fowler, D. (2006). Spiritual and religious abuse: Expanding what is known about domestic violence. *Affilia Journal of Women and Social Work, 21,* 282–295.

Berg-Weger, M. (2005). *Social work and social welfare.* Boston, MA: McGraw-Hill.

Billingsley, A. (1992). *Climbing Jacob's ladder: The enduring legacy of African American families.* New York, NY: Simon & Schuster.

Bordewich, F. (1996). *Killing the white man's Indian: Reinventing Native Americans at the end of the twentieth century.* New York, NY: Doubleday.

Boyd-Franklin, N. (1989). *Black families in therapy: A multisystems approach.* New York, NY: Guilford Press.

Brown, C. H. (1941). *The correct thing: To do, to say, to wear.* Boston, MA: Christopher.

Burwell, Y. (1998). Human diversity and empowerment. In W. Johnson (Ed.), *The social services: An introduction* (pp. 385–398). Itasca, IL: Peacock.

Cameron, M. (2006). Managing school discipline and implications for school social workers: A review of the literature. *Children and Schools, 28,* 219–227.

Carlton-LaNey, I. (1996a). The case of Trent. In R. Rivas & G. Hull (Eds.), *Case studies in generalist practice* (pp. 1–7). Pacific Grove, CA: Brooks/Cole.

Carlton-LaNey, I. (1996b). George and Birdye Haynes' legacy to community practice. In I. Carlton-LaNey & N. Y. Burwell (Eds.), *African American community practice models: Historical and contemporary responses* (pp. 27–48). New York, NY: Haworth Press.

Carlton-LaNey, I. (1997). Social workers as advocates for elders. In M. Reisch & E. Gambrill (Eds.), *Social work in the 21st century* (pp. 285–295). Thousand Oaks, CA: Pine Forge Press.

Carlton-LaNey, I. (1999). African American social work pioneers' response to need. *Social Work, 42*, 573–583.

Carlton-LaNey, I. (Ed.). (2001). *African American leadership: An empowerment tradition in social welfare history.* Washington, DC: National Association of Social Workers Press.

Carlton-LaNey, I. (2005). *African Americans aging in the rural south: Stories of faith, family, and community.* Durham, NC: Sourwood Press.

Carlton-LaNey, I. (2006). Rural African American caregiving. In B. Berkman (Ed.), *Handbook of social work in health and aging* (pp. 381–390). New York, NY: Oxford University Press.

Carlton-LaNey, I., & Andrews, J. (1998). Direct practice addressing gender in practice from a multicultural feminist perspective. In J. Figueira-McDonough, E. Netting, & A. Nicholes-Casebolt (Eds.), *The role of gender in practice knowledge claiming half the human experience* (pp. 93–125). New York, NY: Garland.

Chace, W. (1989) The language of action. *Wesleyan, 62*, 32–43.

Chestang, L. (1982). *Character development in a hostile society.* Occasional paper. Chicago, IL: University of Chicago Press.

Chipungu, S., Everett, J., & Leashore, B. (Eds.). (1991). *Child welfare: An Afrocentric perspective.* New Brunswick, NJ: Rutgers University Press.

Council on Social Work Education. (2001). *Educational policy and accreditation standards.* Alexandria, VA: CSWE Press.

Covin, D. (1990). Afrocentricity in O Movimento Negro Unificade. *Journal of Black Studies, 21*, 126–145.

Davis, K. (2004). Social work's commitment to social justice and social policy. In K. Davis & T. Bent-Goodley (Eds.), *The color of social policy* (pp. 229–241). Alexandria, VA: Council on Social Work Education Press.

Day, P. (1997). *A new history of social welfare.* Englewood Cliffs, NJ: Prentice Hall.

Edwards, R. (1995). Introduction. In R. Edwards (Ed.), *Encyclopedia of social work* (19th ed., pp. 1–5). Washington, DC: National Association of Social Workers Press.

Fellin, P. (2000). Revisiting multiculturalism in social work. *Journal of Social Work Education, 36*, 261–278.

Franklin, J. (1980). *From slavery to freedom: A history of negro Americans* (5th ed.). New York, NY: Alfred A. Knopf.

Gerdes, K., Segal, E., & Ressler, L. (2003). Should faith-based social-work programs be required to comply with nondiscrimination standards if they violate the beliefs of these institutions? In H. Karger, J. Midgley, & C. Brown (Eds.), *Controversial issues in social policy* (pp. 263–282). Boston, MA: Allyn & Bacon.

Germain, C., & Gitterman, A. (1995). Ecological perspective. In R. Edwards (Ed.), *Encyclopedia of social work* (19th ed., pp. 816–823). Washington, DC: National Association of Social Workers Press.

Gutierrez, L. (1997). Multicultural community organizing. In M. Reisch & E. Gambrill (Eds.), *Social work in the 21st century* (pp. 249–250). Thousand Oak, CA: Pine Forge Press.

Gutierrez, L., Fredricksen, K., & Soifer, S. (1999). Perspectives of social work faculty on diversity and societal oppression content: Results from a national survey. *Journal of Social Work Education, 35*, 409–420.

Harvey, A. (2001). Individual and family intervention skills with African Americans: An Africentric approach. In F. Fong & S. Furuto (Eds.), *Culturally competent practice: Skills, interventions, and evaluation* (pp. 225–240). New York, NY: Harworth.

Harvey, A., & Coleman, A. (1997). An Afrocentric program for African American males in the juvenile justice system. *Child Welfare, 76,* 197–211.

Haynes, B. (2005). The paradox of the excluded child. *Educational Philosophy and Theory, 37,* 333–341.

Hooyman, N., & Kiyak, H. (2005). *Social gerontology: A multidisciplinary perspective.* Boston, MA: Allyn & Bacon.

Hopps, J., Pinderhughes, E., & Shankar, R. (1995). *The power of care: Clinical practice effectiveness with overwhelming clients.* New York, NY: Free Press.

Invisible Government of Negro Social Work. (1920). The National League on Urban Conditions Among Negroes. *Messenger, 2,* 174–177.

Leigh, J. (1998). *Communicating for cultural competence.* Prospect Heights, IL: Waveland Press.

Levy, E. (1995). Feminist social work practice with lesbian and gay clients. In N. Van Den Bergh (Ed.), *Feminist practice in the 21st century* (pp. 278–294). Washington, DC: National Association of Social Workers Press.

Lum, D. (Ed.). (2003). *Culturally competent practice: A framework for understanding diverse groups and justice issues.* Pacific Grove, CA: Brooks/Cole.

Martin, E., & Martin, J. (1985). *The helping tradition in the Black family and community.* Silver Spring, MD: National Association of Social Workers Press.

McCullough-Chavis, A., & Waites, C. (2004). Genograms with African American families: Considering cultural content. *Journal of Family Social Work, 8,* 1–19.

McIntosh, P. (1988). *White privilege and male privilege: A personal account of coming to see correspondences though work in women's studies* (Working Paper 189). Wellesley, MA: Wellesley College, Center for Research on Women.

Morales, A., Sheafor, B., & Scott, M. (2007). *Social work: A profession of many faces.* Boston, MA: Allyn & Beacon Press.

Nagda, B., Spearmon, M., Holley, L., Harding, S., Balassone, M., Moise-Swanson, D., et al. (1999). Intergroup dialogues: An innovative approach to teaching about diversity and justice in social work programs. *Journal of Social Work Education, 35,* 433–449.

National Association of Social Workers. (2006). *Social work speaks: National Association of Social Workers Policy Statements 2006--2009* (17th ed.). Washington, DC: National Association of Social Workers Press.

Ozawa, M. (1997). Demographic changes and their implications. In M. Riesch & E. Gambrill (Eds.), *Social work in the 21st century* (p. 8–27). Thousand Oaks, CA: Pine Forge Press.

Parish, S. (2005). Deinstitutionalization in two states: The impact of advocacy, policy, and other social forces on services for people with developmental disabilities. *Research and Practice for Persons with Severe Disabilities, 30,* 219–231.

Parish, S., & Cloud, J. (2006). Financial well-being of young children with disabilities and their families. *Social Work, 51,* 223–232.

Parish, S., & Lutwick, Z. (2005). A critical analysis of the emerging crisis in long-term care for people with developmental disabilities. *Social Work, 50,* 345–354.

Parris, G., & Brooks, L. (1971). *Blacks in the city.* Boston, MA: Little, Brown.

Pinderhughes, E. (1989). *Understanding race, ethnicity, and power.* New York, NY: Free Press.

Reisch, M., & Andrews, J. (2002). *The road not taken: A history of radical social work in the United States.* New York, NY: Brunner-Routledge.

Saleebey, D. (Ed.). (1997). *The strengths perspective in social work practice* (2nd ed.). New York, NY: Longman.

Salem, D. (1993). National Association of Colored Women. In D. C. Hine (Ed.), *Black women in America: An historical encyclopedia* (p. 842–851). Bloomington, IN: Indiana University Press.

Schiele, J. (1996). Afrocenricity: An emerging paradigm in social work practice. *Social Work, 41,* 284–294.

Schlesinger, E., & Devore, W. (1995). Ethnic-sensitive practice. In R. Edwards (Ed.), *Encyclopedia of Social Work* (p. 902–908). Washington, DC: National Association of Social Workers Press.

Schriver, J. (2001). *Human behavior and the social environment: Shifting paradigms in essential knowledge for social work practice.* Boston, MA: Allyn & Bacon.

Shaffer, G. (2006). Promising school social work practices of the 1920s: Reflections for today. *Children and Schools, 28,* 243–251.

Simon, B. (1994). *The empowerment tradition in American social work: A history.* New York, NY: Columbia University Press.

Social work speaks: National Association of Social Workers Policy Statement 2006--2009 (7th ed.). (2006). Washington, DC: NASW Press.

Solomon, B. (1976). *Black empowerment: Social work in oppressed communities.* New York, NY: Columbia University Press.

Swigonski, M. (1996). Challenging privilege through Africentric social work practice. *Social Work, 141,* 153–161.

Waites, C., Macgowan, M., Pennell, J., Carlton-LaNey, I., & Weil, M. (2004). Increasing the cultural responsiveness of family group conferencing. *Social Work, 40,* 291–300.

Watts-Jones, D. (1997). Toward an African American genogram. *Family Process, 36,* 1–7.

Weaver, H. (2003). Cultural competency with first nations peoples. In D. Lum (Ed.), *Culturally competent practice* (p. 197–216). Pacific Grove, CA: Brooks/Cole.

Weiss, N. (1974). *National Urban League 1900--1940.* New York, NY: Oxford University Press.

White, D. (1999). *Too heavy a load.* New York, NY: Norton.

Author Index

Subject Index